Mastering Student Success

Strategies for College and Lifelong Learning

Santa Monica College

1st Editoin

Dave Ellis | Skip Downing | Dianna L. Van Blerkom

CENGAGE
Learning·

Australia • Brazil • Japan • Korea • Mexico • Singapore • Spain • United Kingdom • United States

Printed in the United
1 2 3 4 5 6 7 8 9 10 16

Mastering Student Success: Strategies for College and Lifelong Learning, Santa Monica College, 1st Edition

Becoming a Master Student, Fourteenth Edition
Dave Ellis

© 2013, 2011, 2009 Cengage Learning. All rights reserved.

On Course: Strategies for Creating Success
in College and in Life, Second Edition
Study Skills Plus Edition
Skip Downing

© 2014, 2011 Cengage Learning. All rights reserved.

Orientation to College Learning, Seventh Edition
Dianna L. Van Blerkom

© 2013, 2010, 2007 Cengage Learning. All rights reserved.
.

Senior Project Development Manager:
 Linda deStefano

Market Development Manager:
 Heather Kramer

Senior Production/Manufacturing Manager:
 Donna M. Brown

Production Editorial Manager:
 Kim Fry

Sr. Rights Acquisition Account Manager:
 Todd Osborne

For product information and technology assistance, contact us at
Cengage Learning Customer & Sales Support, 1-800-354-9706

For permission to use material from this text or product,
submit all requests online at **cengage.com/permissions**
Further permissions questions can be emailed to
permissionrequest@cengage.com

This book contains select works from existing Cengage Learning resources and
was produced by Cengage Learning Custom Solutions for collegiate use. As such,
those adopting and/or contributing to this work are responsible for editorial
content accuracy, continuity and completeness.

Compilation © 2013 Cengage Learning
ISBN-13: 978-1-285-88431-8

ISBN-10: 1-285-88431-0
Cengage Learning
5191 Natorp Boulevard
Mason, Ohio 45040
USA

Cengage Learning is a leading provider of customized learning solutions with
office locations around the globe, including Singapore, the United Kingdom,
Australia, Mexico, Brazil, and Japan. Locate your local office at:
international.cengage.com/region.
Cengage Learning products are represented in Canada by Nelson Education, Ltd.
For your lifelong learning solutions, visit **www.cengage.com/custom.**
Visit our corporate website at **www.cengage.com.**

States of America
15 14 13

Creating a custom textbook for Counseling 20 was quite an undertaking—much more so than any of us could imagine when we first began. However, because we believe in the course and the potential and capability of each of our students, we took the task seriously and wanted the text to encompass many pieces— more than any individual text that we could find.

This textbook is a culmination of a process where we examined many chapters of many books, contemplated and debated many versions and revisions, and which had us editing and proofing with a fine-toothed comb. Given that, we agree that this is a work in progress, which means several things: we will have future editions, since, like our students, we will learn and adjust; and even with our best efforts, you still may find errors—references to incorrect pages or non-existent websites, for example.

This book was a true collaboration, and we would like to acknowledge and thank our contacts at Cengage Learning. Julie Underwood, our energetic Learning Consultant, was a dream, accommodating all of our requests, returning emails at all hours of the day and night, helping us to negotiate a fair price, problem-solving with our bookstore, and just being an all-around wonderful person and collaborator. And thanks and a salute to Kathleen Benjey, our Custom Project Manager, for her patience with helping us access proofs, keeping us on task and on time patiently, and her tremendous skill and patience with helping us pull this final product together.

Lastly, special thanks to Jim Serikawa and Charles Mark-Walker for their cover photographs, which helped to capture SMC and Counseling 20 in images.

The Counseling 20 Textbook Committee
Spring, 2013

Acknowledgements

The content of this text has been adapted from the following product(s):

Source Title: Becoming a Master Student
Authors: Ellis
ISBN10: 1111827532
ISBN13: 9781111827533

Source Title: On Course
Authors: Downing
ISBN10: 1133309747
ISBN13: 9781133309741

Source Title: Orientation to College Learning
Authors: Van Blerkom
ISBN10: 1111833648
ISBN13: 9781111833640

Brief Contents

Images: Oliver Cleve/Getty Images

INTRODUCTION	The Master Student	1
CHAPTER 1	First Steps	31
CHAPTER 2	Time	63
CHAPTER 3	Memory	101
CHAPTER 4	Reading	125
CHAPTER 5	Notes	151
CHAPTER 6	Tests	177
CHAPTER 7	Thinking	203
CHAPTER 8	Communicating	235
CHAPTER 9	Diversity	271
CHAPTER 10	Money	295
CHAPTER 11	Health	321
CHAPTER 12	What's Next?	351
CHAPTER 13	Getting On Course to Your Success	385
CHAPTER 14	Accepting Personal Responsibility	423
CHAPTER 15	Goal Setting	453
CHAPTER 16	Improving Concentration	477

Contents

INTRODUCTION The Master Student **1**

Master Student Map   1

Exercise 1: *Textbook reconnaissance*   1

power process DISCOVER WHAT YOU WANT   2

Master student qualities   3

Exercise 2: *The master student in you*   6

This book is worthless—if you just read it   7

Exercise 3: *Commitment*   8

Master Students in Action   8

Get the most out of this book   9

The Discovery and Intention Journal Entry system   11

Discovery and Intention Statement Guidelines   13

Journal Entry 1 *Declare what you want*   13

The value of higher education   14

Making the transition to higher education   16

Rewrite this book   18

Succeeding in school—at any age   19

Enroll your instructor in your success   21

Meeting with your instructor   22

Motivation—I'm just not in the mood   23

Attitudes, affirmations, and visualizations   25

Attitude replacements   25

Exercise 4: *Reprogram your attitude*   27

Ways to change a habit   28

Classroom civility—what's in it for you   30

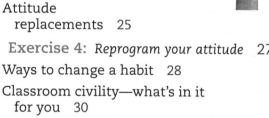

Oliver Cleve/Getty Images

CHAPTER 1 First Steps **31**

Master Student Map   31

Journal Entry 2 *Create value from this chapter*   31

power process IDEAS ARE TOOLS   32

First Step: Truth is a key to mastery   33

Exercise 5: *Taking the First Step*   35

Exercise 6: *The Discovery Wheel*   36

Skills Snapshot   40

Learning Styles: Discovering how you learn   41

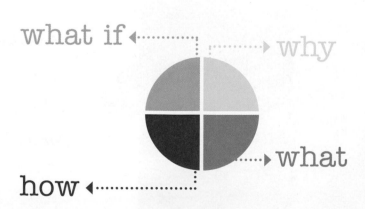

Journal Entry 3 *Prepare for the Learning Style Inventory (LSI)* 42

Directions for completing the Learning Style Inventory 42

Learning Style Inventory LSI-1

Taking the next steps LSI-2

Scoring your Inventory LSI-3

Learning Style Graph LSI-5

Interpreting your Learning Style Graph LSI-6

Developing all four modes of learning LSI-7

Balancing your preferences LSI-8

Using your Learning Style Profile to succeed 43

Claim your multiple intelligences 47

Exercise 7: *Develop your multiple intelligences* 47

Learning by seeing, hearing, and moving: The VAK system 50

Master Students in Action 52

Journal Entry 4 *Choosing your purpose* 53

Connect to resources 54

Extracurricular activities: Reap the benefits 55

Make the career connection 56

You don't need this course—but you might want it 57

Practicing Critical Thinking 1 58

Master Student Profile Lalita Booth 59

Put This Chapter To Work 60

Chapter 1 Quiz 61

Skills Snapshot 62

CHAPTER 2 Time **63**

Master Student Map 63

Journal Entry 5 *Create value from this chapter* 63

power process BE HERE NOW 64

You've got the time 65

Exercise 8: *The Time Monitor* 66

Setting and achieving goals 71

Exercise 9: *Create a lifeline* 72

Exercise 10: *Get real with your goals* 73

The ABC daily to-do list 74

Make choices about multitasking 76

More strategies for planning 77

Exercise 11: *Master monthly calendar* 79

Break it down, get it done: Using a long-term planner 82

Mastering technology: Use Web-based tools to save time 85

Stop procrastination now 86

The 7-day antiprocrastination plan 87

Practicing Critical Thinking 2 88

25 ways to get the most out of now 89

Setting limits on screen time 91

Master Students in Action 93

Beyond time management: Stay focused on what matters 94

Forget time management—just get things done 96

Master Student Profile Al Gore 97

Put This Chapter To Work 98

Chapter 2 Quiz 99

Skills Snapshot 100

CHAPTER 3 Memory **101**

©Istockphoto.com/Tatiana Popova

Master Student Map 101

Journal Entry 6
Create value from this chapter 101

power process LOVE YOUR PROBLEMS (AND EXPERIENCE YOUR BARRIERS) 102

Take your memory out of the closet 103

The memory jungle 104

Master Students in Action 105

20 memory techniques 106

Use your computer to enhance memory 110

Your mind, online 111

Exercise 12: *Use Q-Cards to reinforce memory* 112

Set a trap for your memory 113

Exercise 13: *Remembering your car keys—or anything else* 113

Your brain—its care and feeding 114

Mnemonic devices 116

Exercise 14: *Get creative* 117

Notable failures 117

Practicing Critical Thinking 3 118

Exercise 15: *Move from problems to solutions* 119

Journal Entry 7 *Revisit your memory skills* 119

Remembering names 120

Master Student Profile Pablo Alvarado 121

Put This Chapter To Work 122

Chapter 3 Quiz 123

Skills Snapshot 124

CHAPTER 4 Reading **125**

© Chris Pancewicz/Alamy

Master Student Map 125

Journal Entry 8 *Declare what you want from this chapter* 125

power process NOTICE YOUR PICTURES AND LET THEM GO 126

Muscle Reading 127

How Muscle Reading works 128

Phase 1: *Before you read* 129

Phase 2: *While you read* 130

Five smart ways to highlight a text 130

Phase 3: *After you read* 132

Muscle Reading—a leaner approach 132

Journal Entry 9 *Experimenting with Muscle Reading* 133

When reading is tough 134

Getting past roadblocks to reading 135

Reading faster 137

Master Students in Action 138

Exercise 16: *Relax* 138

Word power—expanding your vocabulary   139
Mastering the English language   140
Developing information literacy   142
Practicing Critical Thinking 4   146

Master Student Profile Matias Manzano   147
Put This Chapter To Work   148
Chapter 4 Quiz   149
Skills Snapshot   150

CHAPTER 5 Notes **151**

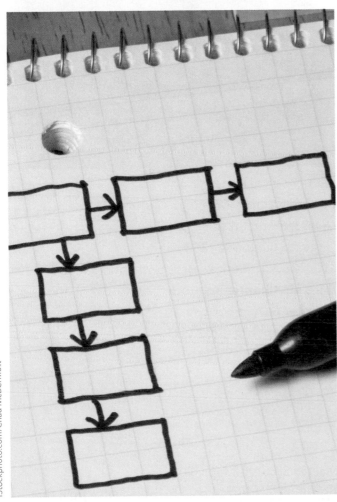

The note-taking process flows   153
OBSERVE The note-taking process flows   154
What to do when you miss a class   155
Journal Entry 11 Create more value from lectures   156
RECORD The note-taking process flows   157
REVIEW The note-taking process flows   162
Journal Entry 12 Reflect on your review habits   163
Turn PowerPoints into powerful notes   164
When your instructor talks quickly   165
Exercise 17: Taking notes under pressure   165
Taking notes while reading   166
Note this information about your sources   167
Get to the bones of your book with concept maps   169
Taking effective notes for online coursework   170
Practicing Critical Thinking 5   172
Master Student Profile Harvey Milk   173
Put This Chapter To Work   174
Chapter 5 Quiz   175
Skills Snapshot   176

Master Student Map   151
Journal Entry 10 Get what you want from this chapter   151
power process I CREATE IT ALL   152

CHAPTER 6 Tests **177**

Master Student Map   177

Journal Entry 13 *Use this chapter to transform your experience with tests*   177

power process DETACH   178

Disarm tests   179

Practicing Critical Thinking 6   179

Journal Entry 14 *Explore your feelings about tests*   180

Journal Entry 15 *Notice your excuses and let them go*   180

What to do before the test   181

How to cram (even though you "shouldn't")   182

Ways to predict test questions   183

Cooperative learning: Studying in groups   184

Master Students in Action   185

What to do during the test   186

Words to watch for in essay questions   188

The test isn't over until . . .   189

The high costs of cheating   190

Perils of high-tech cheating   190

Let go of test anxiety   191

Have some fun!   191

Exercise 18: *Twenty things I like to do*   192

Getting ready for math tests   193

Exercise 19: *Use learning styles for math success*   196

iStockphoto.com/DNY59

Studying across the curriculum   197

Celebrate mistakes   198

"F" is for feedback   198

Master Student Profile Bert and John Jacobs   199

Put This Chapter To Work   200

Chapter 6 Quiz   201

Skills Snapshot   202

CHAPTER 7 Thinking **203**

Steve Cole/Getty Images

Master Student Map   203

Journal Entry 16 *Choose to create value from this chapter*   203

power process FIND A BIGGER PROBLEM   204

Critical thinking: a survival skill   205

Becoming a critical thinker   207

Finding "aha!"—creativity fuels critical thinking   211

Tangram   211

Ways to create ideas   212

Create on your feet   213

Exercise 20: *Explore emotional reactions*   215

Don't fool yourself: Fifteen common mistakes in logic   216

Master Students in Action   218

Uncovering assumptions   219

Think critically about information on the Internet   220

Gaining skill at decision making   221

Four ways to solve problems   222

Asking questions—learning through inquiry   223

15 questions to try on for size   224

Thinking about your major   225

Journal Entry 17 *Reflect on choosing a major*   227

Service-learning: The art of learning by contributing   228

Exercise 21: *Translating goals into action*   227

Practicing Critical Thinking 7   230

Master Student Profile Twyla Tharp   231

Put This Chapter To Work   232

Chapter 7 Quiz   233

Skills Snapshot   234

CHAPTER 8 Communicating **235**

Master Student Map   235

Journal Entry 18 *Commit to create value from this chapter*   235

power process EMPLOY YOUR WORD   236

Communicating creates our world   237

Communication— keeping the channels open   238

iStockphoto.com/Clayton Hansen

Exercise 22: *Practice sending or receiving*   238

Choosing to listen   239

Choosing to speak   241

Five ways to say "I"   242

Exercise 23: *Write an "I" message*   243

Master Students in Action   243

Journal Entry 19 *Discover communication styles*   244

Developing emotional intelligence   245

Collaborating for success   246

Managing conflict   247

Resolve conflicts with roommates   248

Journal Entry 20 *Recreate a relationship*   249

Five ways to say no . . . respectfully   250

You deserve compliments   250

Exercise 24: *VIPs (Very Important Persons)*   251

Five steps to effective complaints   252

Criticism is constructive   252

Mastering social networks   253

Text message etiquette—five key points   254

Three phases of effective writing   255

Academic integrity: Avoid plagiarism   260

Mastering public speaking   262

Making the grade in group presentations   265

Practicing Critical Thinking 8   266

Master Student Profile Mark Zuckerberg   267

Put This Chapter To Work   268

Chapter 8 Quiz   269

Skills Snapshot   270

CHAPTER 9 Diversity **271**

Jeff Hunter/Getty Images

Master Student Map   271

Journal Entry 21 Commit to create value from this chapter   271

power process CHOOSE YOUR CONVERSATIONS AND YOUR COMMUNITY   272

Waking up to diversity   273

Journal Entry 22 Reflect on the quality of a recent conversation   273

Diversity is real—and valuable   274

Exercise 25: Explore the influence of stereotypes   275

Building relationships across cultures   276

Master Students in Action   279

Exercise 26: Becoming a culture learner   280

Overcome stereotypes with critical thinking   281

Students with disabilities: Know your rights   282

Dealing with sexism and sexual harassment   284

Seven strategies for nonsexist communication   285

Leadership in a diverse world   286

Journal Entry 23 Removing barriers to communication   289

Practicing Critical Thinking 9   290

Master Student Profile Sampson Davis   291

Put This Chapter To Work   292

Chapter 9 Quiz   293

Skills Snapshot   294

CHAPTER 10 Money **295**

Master Student Map   295

Journal Entry 24 Commit to a new experience of money   295

power process RISK BEING A FOOL   296

The end of money worries   297

This book is worth $1,000   297

Exercise 27: The Money Monitor/ Money Plan   298

No budgeting required   299

Journal Entry 25 Reflect on your Money Monitor/Money Plan   303

Make more money   304

Master Students in Action   304

Spend less money   305

iStockphoto.com/Laurent davoust

Exercise 28: Show me the money   306

Managing money during tough times   307

Take charge of your credit   309

Common credit terms 310

Exercise 29: *Start setting money goals* 312

If you're in trouble . . . 312

Education is worth it— and you can pay for it 313

Exercise 30: *Education by the hour* 313

Your learning styles and your money 314
Your money and your values 315
Free fun 315
Practicing Critical Thinking 10 316
Master Student Profile Lisa Price 317
Put This Chapter To Work 318
Chapter 10 Quiz 319
Skills Snapshot 320

CHAPTER 11 Health **321**

Master Student Map 321

Journal Entry 26 *Take a First Step about your health* 321

power process SURRENDER 322

Wake up to health 323

Choose your fuel 324

Prevent and treat eating disorders 324

Choose to exercise 325

Choose emotional health 326

Choose to rest 327

Master Students in Action 328
Developing a strong self-image 329
Asking for help 331
Suicide is no solution 332
Choose to stay safe 333
Observe thyself 333
Choose sexual health: Prevent infection 334
Choose sexual health: Prevent unwanted pregnancy 335
Alcohol, tobacco, and drugs: The Truth 339

Exercise 31: *Addiction: How do I know?* 340

Some facts . . . 341
From dependence to recovery 342
Succeed in quitting smoking 343
Warning: Advertising can be dangerous to your health 344

Journal Entry 27 *Advertisements and your health* 344

Practicing Critical Thinking 11 345
Master Student Profile Randy Pausch 347
Put This Chapter To Work 348
Chapter 11 Quiz 349
Skills Snapshot 350

CHAPTER 12 What's Next 351

iStockphoto.com/esolla

Master Student Map 351

Journal Entry 28 *Revisiting what you want and how you intend to get it* 351

power process BE IT 352

Define your values; align your actions 353

Jumpstart your education with transferable skills 354

65 transferable skills 355

Exercise 32: *Recognize your skills* 357

Create your career now 358

Sample career plans 361

Exercise 33: *Create your career plan—now* 362

Exercise 34: *Make a trial choice of major* 363

Exercise 35: *Create your academic plan* 363

Transferring to a new school 364

Master Students in Action 365

Build an irresistible résumé 366

Fine tune your cover letter 368

Use job interviews to "hire" an employer 369

Exercise 36: *The Discovery Wheel—coming full circle* 372

Skills Snapshot 376

Now that you're done—BEGIN 377

"Use the following suggestions to continue . . ." 378

Exercise 37: *This book shouts, "Use me!"* 379

Practicing Critical Thinking 12 380

Exercise 38: *Do something you can't* 380

Master Student Profile Lisa Ling 381

Put This Chapter To Work 382

Chapter 12 Quiz 383

Skills Snapshot 384

CHAPTER 13 Getting On Course to Your Success 385

Taking the First Step 386

Journal Entry 1: 396

One Student's Story: Jalayna Onaga 397

Understanding the Culture of Higher Education 397

Journal Entry 2: 403

Becoming an Active Learner 405

How the human brain learns 405

Three principles of deep and lasting learning 406

The core learning system 409

Journal Entry 3: 411

One Student's Story: Kase Cormier 412

On Course Principles at Work 413

Develop Self-Acceptance 415

Self-esteem and core beliefs 415

Know and accept yourself 416

Journal Entry 4: 417

Wise Choices in College 418

CHAPTER 14: Accepting Personal Responsibility 423

Case Study in Critical Thinking:
The late paper   424

Adopting a Creator Mindset   425

Victim and creator mindsets   426

Responsibility and culture   427

Responsibility and choice   428

Journal Entry 5:   430

One Student's Story: Brian Moore   431

Mastering Creator Language   431

Self-talk   432

The language of responsibility   435

Journal Entry 6:   437

One Student's Story: Alexsandr
Kanevskiy   438

Making Wise Decisions   439

Journal Entry 7:   443

One Student's Story: Freddie Davila   444

Personal Responsibility at Work   445

Change Your Inner Conversation   447

The curse of stinkin' thinkin'   447

Disputing irrational beliefs   449

Stereotype threat   450

Journal Entry 8:   451

One Student's Story: Dominic Grasseth   452

CHAPTER 15: Goal Setting 453

Where Are You Now?   454

What are Goals?   455

Set Goals for the New Semester   459

Ten Tips to Get Off to the Right Start
This Semester   464

Write Effective Goal Statements   466

Explore Career Goals   470

Summary   474

Activities   474

Chapter Review   475

CHAPTER 16: Improving Concentration 477

Where are You Now?   478

What is Concentration?   479

Causes of Poor Concentration   484

Strategies for Improving Concentration   487

Ten Tips for Setting Up a Good Study
Environment   490

Benefits of Improved Concentration   495

Summary   495

Activities   496

Chapter Review   497

ACKNOWLEDGMENTS

ADVISORY BOARD

Faculty Advisor: Dean Mancina, Golden West College

Annette McCreedy, Nashville State Community College

Paula Wimbish, Hinds Community College

Leigh Smith, Lamar Institute of Technology

Charlene Aldrich, Trident Technical College

Krista Clay-Lieffring, Neosho County Community College

FACULTY REVIEWERS

Johanna Bacik, Cuyahoga Community College

Frank Baker, Golden West College

Marla Barbee, South Plains College

Victoria Basnett, St. Johns River State College

Laura Bazan, Central Piedmont Community College

Donald Becker, Delaware State University

Mark Binkley, South Dakota State University

Barbara Braid, Bakersfield College

Paula Calahan, Middle Tennessee State University

Carole Comarcho, Broward College

Dennis Congos, University of Central Florida

Tim Cook, Clark College

Dana Dildine, Eastern New Mexico University, Ruidoso Branch

Marnice Emerson, Sierra College

Shirley Flor, San Diego Mesa College

Joseph Fly, South Plains College, Reese Campus

Beth Giroir, Arkansas Tech University

Dale S. Haralson, Hinds Community College

Sellestine Hunt, Angelina College

Judith Isonhood, Hinds Community College

Jon Jones, Shasta Community College

Leila A. Llewelyn Rowe, Delaware State University

Rajone Lyman, Houston Community College, NE

Judy Lynch, Kansas State University

Angel Moore, Mesa Community College

Maria Parnell, Brevard Community College

Karey Pharris, Pikes Peak Community College

Terry Lee Rafter Carles, Valencia Community College

Anthony Reuss, San Diego Mesa College

Star Rivera, San Diego Mesa College

Margaret Seymour, South Plains College

Dawn Shaffer, Central Piedmont Community College

Patricia Sheriff-Taylor, Jackson State University

Londell Smith, James A. Rhodes State College

Jane Speer, Alpena Community College

Deborah Warfield, Seminole State College of Florida

STUDENT REVIEWERS

NyKailia Bailey, Hinds Community College, Rankin Campus

Jonathan M. Brown, Hinds Community College, Rankin Campus

Scott Bruning, Alpena Community College

Alissa Bullock, Hinds Community College, Rankin Campus

Morgan Callahan, Hinds Community College, Rankin Campus

Bennie Carey, Hinds Community College

Brianna Creson, Nashville State Community College

Jack Daniel Stewart, Hinds Community College, Rankin Campus

Carson Drennan, South Plains College

Micah Elliott, Nashville State Community College

Shelby Ellis, Hinds Community College

Kendale Enoch, Hinds Community College, Rankin Campus

Adrian Flores, South Plains College

Katie Garrett, Hinds Community College

Taylor Gehrer, Neosho County Community College

Lorri Haddix Fetty, Alpena Community College

Randall Hicks, South Plains College

Asisah Johnson, Hinds Community College

Esmi Lee, South Plains College

Alex Logan, Hinds Community College

Kelly Martin Lalair, Nashville State Community College

Jacob McCord, Nashville State Community College

Amanda Mink, Alpena Community College

Tracey Mitchell, Hinds Community College, Rankin Campus

Jean M. Mixon, Hinds Community College

Walter Moore, Hinds Community College

Sanyonette Myles, Hinds Community College

Eric Newman, Hinds Community College, Rankin Campus

Kim Nguyen, Golden West College

Percy Nichols, Hinds Community College, Rankin Campus

Lauren Plagens, South Plains College

Deidra Powell, Hinds Community College

Christina Rodgers, Hinds Community College, Rankin Campus

Akeem Ruhman Hall, Nashville State Community College

Joseph Schlink, Hinds Community College

Shelby Self, Hinds Community College, Rankin Campus

Jonathan Steinke, Mesa Community College

Kamesha Stokes, Hinds Community College

Betty Vittitoe, Hinds Community College, Rankin Campus

Emily Watkins, Hinds Community College

Learning Style Inventory

Complete items 1–12 below. Use the following example as a guide:

A. When I learn: _2_ I am happy.　_3_ I am fast.　_4_ I am logical.　_1_ I am careful.

Remember:　**4** = Most like you　**3** = Second most like you　**2** = Third most like you　**1** = Least like you

Do not leave any endings blank. Use each number only once for each question. Before completing the items, remove the sheet of paper following this page. While writing, press firmly.

1. When I learn:	_____ I like to deal with my feelings.	_____ I like to think about ideas.	_____ I like to be doing things.	_____ I like to watch and listen.
2. I learn best when:	_____ I listen and watch carefully.	_____ I rely on logical thinking.	_____ I trust my hunches and feelings.	_____ I work hard to get things done.
3. When I am learning:	_____ I tend to reason things out.	_____ I am responsible about things.	_____ I am quiet and reserved.	_____ I have strong feelings and reactions.
4. I learn by:	_____ feeling.	_____ doing.	_____ watching.	_____ thinking.
5. When I learn:	_____ I am open to new experiences.	_____ I look at all sides of issues.	_____ I like to analyze things, break them down into their parts.	_____ I like to try things out.
6. When I am learning:	_____ I am an observing person.	_____ I am an active person.	_____ I am an intuitive person.	_____ I am a logical person.
7. I learn best from:	_____ observation.	_____ personal relationships.	_____ rational theories.	_____ a chance to try out and practice.
8. When I learn:	_____ I like to see results from my work.	_____ I like ideas and theories.	_____ I take my time before acting.	_____ I feel personally involved in things.
9. I learn best when:	_____ I rely on my observations.	_____ I rely on my feelings.	_____ I can try things out for myself.	_____ I rely on my ideas.
10. When I am learning:	_____ I am a reserved person.	_____ I am an accepting person.	_____ I am a responsible person.	_____ I am a rational person.
11. When I learn:	_____ I get involved.	_____ I like to observe.	_____ I evaluate things.	_____ I like to be active.
12. I learn best when:	_____ I analyze ideas.	_____ I am receptive and open-minded.	_____ I am careful.	_____ I am practical.

Taking the next steps

Now that you've finished taking the Learning Style Inventory, you probably have some questions about what it means. You're about to discover some answers! In the following pages, you will find instructions for:

- Scoring your inventory (page LSI–3)
- Plotting your scores on to a Learning Style Graph that literally gives a "big picture" of your learning style (page LSI–5)
- Interpreting your Learning Style Graph by seeing how it relates to four distinct modes, or styles, of learning (page LSI–6)
- Developing all four modes of learning (page LSI–7)
- Balancing your learning preferences (page LSI–8)

Take your time to absorb all this material. Be willing to read through it several times and ask questions.

Your efforts will be rewarded. In addition to discovering more details about *how* you learn, you'll gain a set of strategies for applying this knowledge to your courses. With these strategies, you can use your knowledge of learning styles to actively promote your success in school.

Above all, aim to recover your natural gift for learning—the defining quality of a master student. Rediscover a world where the boundaries between learning and fun, between work and play, all disappear. While immersing yourself in new experiences, blend the sophistication of an adult with the wonder of a child. This path is one that you can travel for the rest of your life.

Remove this sheet before completing the Learning Style Inventory.

This page is inserted to ensure that the other writing you do in this book doesn't show through on page LSI–3.

Remove this sheet before completing the Learning Style Inventory.

This page is inserted to ensure that the other writing you do in this book doesn't show through on page LSI–3.

Scoring your Inventory

Now that you have taken the Learning Style Inventory, it's time to fill out the Learning Style Graph (page LSI–5) and interpret your results. To do this, follow these steps.

STEP 1 First, add up all of the numbers you gave to the items marked with brown F letters. Then write down that total in the box to the right, next to **"Brown F."** Next, add up all of the numbers for **"Teal W,"** **"Purple T,"** and **"Orange D,"** and also write down those totals in the box to the right.

STEP 2 Add the four totals to arrive at a GRAND TOTAL, and write down that figure in the box to the right. (**Note:** The grand total should equal 120. If you have a different amount, go back and re-add the colored letters; it was probably just an addition error.) Now remove this page and continue with Step 3 on page LSI–5.

F	T	D	W
W	T	F	D
T	D	W	F
F	D	W	T
F	W	T	D
W	D	F	T
W	F	T	D
D	T	W	F
W	F	D	T
W	F	D	T
F	W	T	D
T	F	W	D

Remove this page after you have completed
Steps 1 and 2 on page LSI-3.
Then continue with Step 3 on page LSI-5.

Learning Style Graph

STEP 3 Remove the sheet of paper that follows this page. Then transfer your totals from Step 2 on page LSI–3 to the lines on the Learning Style Graph below. On the brown (F) line, find the number that corresponds to your "Brown F" total from page LSI–3. Then write an X on this number. Do the same for your "Teal W," "Purple T," and "Orange D" totals. The graph on this page is for you to keep. The graph on page LSI–7 is for you to turn in to your instructor if required to do so.

STEP 4 Now, pressing firmly, draw four straight lines to connect the four X's, and shade in the area to form a "kite." This is your learning style profile. (For an example, see the illustration to the right.) Each X that you placed on these lines indicates your preference for a different aspect of learning:

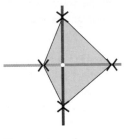

F "Feeling" (Concrete Experience) The number where you put your X on this line indicates your preference for learning things that have personal meaning. The higher your score on this

line, the more you like to learn things that you feel are important and relevant to yourself.

W "Watching" (Reflective Observation) Your number on this line indicates how important it is for you to reflect on the things you are learning. If your score is high on this line, you probably find it important to watch others as they learn about an assignment and then report on it to the class. You probably like to plan things out and take the time to make sure that you fully understand a topic.

T "Thinking" (Abstract Conceptualization) Your number on this line indicates your preference for learning ideas, facts, and figures. If your score is high on this line, you probably like to absorb many concepts and gather lots of information on a new topic.

D "Doing" (Active Experimentation) Your number on this line indicates your preference for applying ideas, using trial and error, and practicing what you learn. If your score is high on this line, you probably enjoy hands-on activities that allow you to test out ideas to see what works.

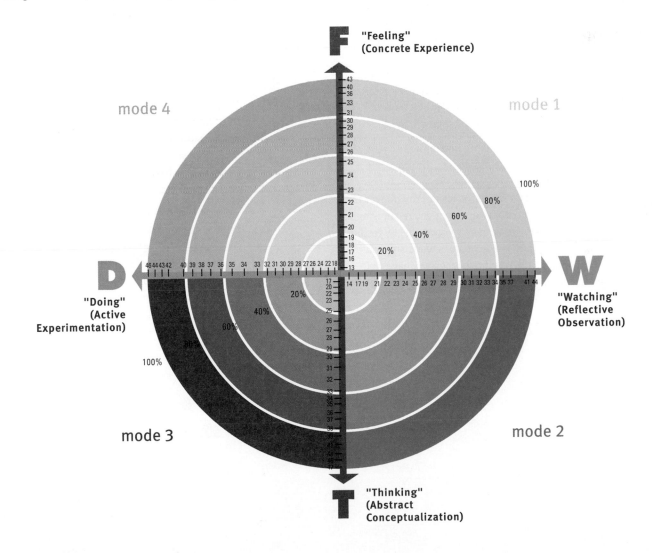

© 2013 Cengage Learning. All Rights Reserved. May not be scanned, copied or duplicated, or posted to a publicly accessible website, in whole or in part.

LSI-5

Interpreting your Learning Style Graph

When you examine your completed Learning Style Graph on page LSI–5, you will notice that your learning style profile (the "kite" that you drew) might be located primarily in one part of the graph. This will give you an idea of your preferred **mode** of learning—the kind of behaviors that feel most comfortable and familiar to you when you are learning something.

Using the descriptions below and the sample graphs, identify your preferred learning mode.

 Mode 1 blends feeling and watching. If the majority of your learning style profile is in the upper right-hand corner of the Learning Style Graph, you probably prefer Mode 1 learning. You seek a purpose for new information and a personal connection with the content. You want to know why a course matters and how it challenges or fits in with what they already know. You embrace new ideas that relate directly to their current interests and goals.

 Mode 2 blends watching and thinking. If your learning style profile is mostly in the lower right-hand corner of the Learning Style Graph, you probably prefer Mode 2 learning. You are interested in knowing what ideas or techniques are important. You seek a theory to explain events and are interested in what experts have to say. You enjoy learning lots of facts and then arranging these facts in a logical and concise manner. You break a subject down into its key elements or steps and master each one in a systematic way.

 Mode 3 blends thinking and doing. If most of your learning style profile is in the lower left-hand corner of the Learning Style Graph, you probably prefer Mode 3 learning. You hunger for an opportunity to try out what you're studying. You get involved with new knowledge by testing it out. You investigate how ideas and techniques work, and you put into practice what you learn. You thrive when you have well-defined tasks, guided practice, and frequent feedback.

 Mode 4 blends doing and feeling. If most of your learning style profile is in the upper left-hand corner of the Learning Style Graph, you probably prefer Mode 4 learning. You get excited about going beyond classroom assignments. You like to take what you have practiced and find other uses for it. You seek ways to apply this newly gained skill or information at your workplace or in your personal relationships.

It might be easier for you to remember the modes if you summarize each one as a single question:

- Mode 1 means asking, *Why* learn this?
- Mode 2 means asking, *What* is this about?
- Mode 3 means asking, *How* does this work?
- Mode 4 means asking, *What if* I tried this in a different setting?

 Combinations. Some learning style profiles combine all four modes. The profile to the left reflects a learner who is focused primarily on gathering information—*lots* of information! People with this profile tend to ask for additional facts from an instructor, or they want to know where they can go to discover more about a subject.

 The profile to the left applies to learners who focus more on understanding what they learn and less on gathering lots of information. People with this profile prefer smaller chunks of data with plenty of time to process it. Long lectures can be difficult for these learners.

 The profile to the left indicates a learner whose preferences are fairly well balanced. People with this profile can be highly adaptable and tend to excel no matter what the instructor does in the classroom. ■

Remove this sheet before completing the Learning Style Graph.

This page is inserted to ensure that the other writing you do in this book does not show through on page LSI–7.

Remove this sheet before completing the Learning Style Graph.

This page is inserted to ensure that the other writing you do in this book does not show through on page LSI–7.

Developing all four modes of learning

Each mode of learning represents a unique blend of feeling, watching, thinking, and doing. No matter which of these you've tended to prefer, you can develop the ability to use all four modes:

- **To develop Mode 1,** ask questions that help you understand *why* it is important for you to learn about a specific topic. You might also want to form a study group.
- **To develop Mode 2,** ask questions that help you understand *what* the main points and key facts are. Also, learn a new subject in stages. For example, divide a large reading assignment into sections and then read each section carefully before moving on to the next one.
- **To develop Mode 3,** ask questions about *how* a theory relates to daily life. Also allow time to practice what you learn. You can do experiments, conduct interviews, create presentations, find a relevant work or internship experience, or even write a song that summarizes key concepts. Learn through hands-on practice.
- **To develop Mode 4,** ask *what-if* questions about ways to use what you have just learned in several different situations. Also,

seek opportunities to demonstrate your understanding. You could coach a classmate about what you have learned, present findings from your research, explain how your project works, or perform your song.

Developing all four modes offers many potential benefits. For example, you can excel in many types of courses and find more opportunities to learn outside the classroom. You can expand your options for declaring a major and choosing a career. You can also work more effectively with people who learn differently from you.

In addition, you'll be able to learn from instructors no matter how they teach. Let go of statements such as "My teachers don't get me" and "The instructor doesn't teach to my learning style." Replace those excuses with attitudes such as "I am responsible for what I learn" and "I will master this subject by using several modes of learning."

The graph on this page is here for you to turn in to your instructor if required to do so.

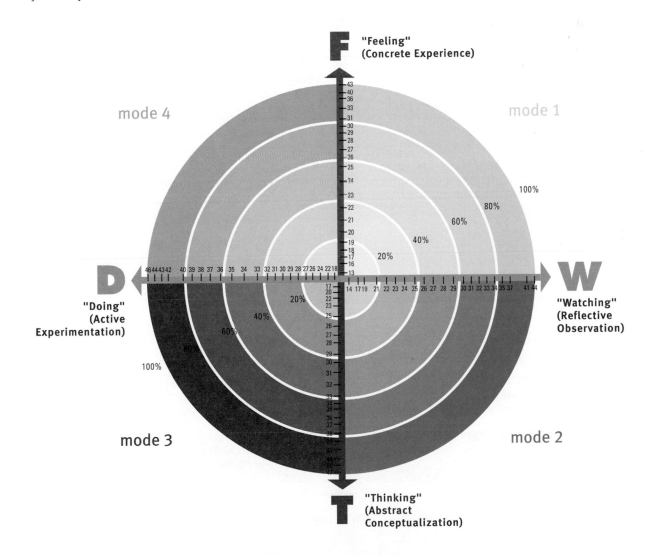

Balancing your preferences

The chart below identifies some of the natural talents people have, as well as challenges for people who have a strong preference for any one mode of learning. For example, if most of your "kite" is in Mode 2 of the Learning Style Graph, then look at the lower right-hand corner of the following chart to see whether it gives an accurate description of you.

After reviewing the description of your preferred learning mode, read all of the sections that start with the words "People with other preferred modes." These sections explain what actions you can take to become a more balanced learner.

Feeling

mode 4

Strengths:
- Getting things done
- Leadership
- Risk taking

Too much of this mode can lead to:
- Trivial improvements
- Meaningless activity

Too little of this mode can lead to:
- Work not completed on time
- Impractical plans
- Lack of motivation to achieve goals

People with other preferred modes can develop Mode 4 by:
- Making a commitment to objectives
- Seeking new opportunities
- Influencing and leading others
- Being personally involved
- Dealing with people

mode 1

Strengths:
- Imaginative ability
- Understanding people
- Recognizing problems
- Brainstorming

Too much of this mode can lead to:
- Feeling paralyzed by alternatives
- Inability to make decisions

Too little of this mode can lead to:
- Lack of ideas
- Not recognizing problems and opportunities

People with other preferred modes can develop Mode 1 by:
- Being aware of other people's feelings
- Being sensitive to values
- Listening with an open mind
- Gathering information
- Imagining the implications of ambiguous situations

Doing ← → **Watching**

mode 3

Strengths:
- Problem solving
- Decision making
- Deductive reasoning
- Defining problems

Too much of this mode can lead to:
- Solving the wrong problem
- Hasty decision making

Too little of this mode can lead to:
- Lack of focus
- Reluctance to consider alternatives
- Scattered thoughts

People with other preferred modes can develop Mode 3 by:
- Creating new ways of thinking and doing
- Experimenting with fresh ideas
- Choosing the best solution
- Setting goals
- Making decisions

mode 2

Strengths:
- Planning
- Creating models
- Defining problems
- Developing theories

Too much of this mode can lead to:
- Vague ideals ("castles in the air")
- Lack of practical application

Too little of this mode can lead to:
- Inability to learn from mistakes
- No sound basis for work
- No systematic approach

People with other preferred modes can develop Mode 2 by:
- Organizing information
- Building conceptual models
- Testing theories and ideas
- Designing experiments
- Analyzing quantitative data

Thinking

The Master Student

Use this **Master Student Map** to ask yourself,

WHY THE INTRODUCTION MATTERS . . .

- You can ease your transition to higher education and set up a lifelong pattern of success by starting with some key strategies.

WHAT IS INCLUDED . . .

- Power Process: Discover what you want   2
- Master student qualities   3
- This book is worthless—if you just read it   7
- Get the most out of this book   9
- The Discovery and Intention Journal Entry system   11
- Discovery and Intention Statement guidelines   13
- The value of higher education   14
- Making the transition to higher education   16
- Succeeding in school—at any age   19
- Enroll your instructor in your success   21
- Motivation—I'm just not in the mood   23
- Attitudes, affirmations, and visualizations   25
- Ways to change a habit   29
- Classroom civility—what's in it for you   30

HOW CAN I USE THIS INTRODUCTION . . .

- Connect with the natural learner within you.
- Discover a way to interact with books that multiplies their value.
- Use a journal to translate personal discoveries into powerful new behaviors.

WHAT IF . . .

- I could use the ideas in this book to more consistently get what I want in my life?

✔ EXERCISE 1

Textbook reconnaissance

Start becoming a master student this moment by doing a 15-minute "textbook reconnaissance." First, read this book's Table of Contents. Do it in 3 minutes or less. Next, look at every page in the book. Move quickly. Scan headlines. Look at pictures. Notice forms, charts, and diagrams.

Look especially for ideas you can use. When you find one, write the page number and a short description of the idea here. You also can use sticky notes to flag pages that look useful. (If you're reading *Becoming a Master Student* as an ebook, you can flag pages electronically.)

_____

_____

_____

_____

_____

_____

_____

_____

_____

_____

_____

Discover what you want

Imagine a person who walks up to a counter at the airport to buy a plane ticket for his next vacation. "Just give me a ticket," he says to the reservation agent. "Anywhere will do."

The agent stares back at him in disbelief. "I'm sorry, sir," she replies. "I'll need some more details. Just minor things—such as the name of your destination city and your arrival and departure dates."

"Oh, I'm not fussy," says the would-be vacationer. "I just want to get away. You choose for me."

Compare this person to another traveler who walks up to the counter and says, "I'd like a ticket to Ixtapa, Mexico, departing on Saturday, March 23, and returning Sunday, April 7. Please give me a window seat, first class, with vegetarian meals."

Now, ask yourself which traveler is more likely to end up with a vacation that he'll enjoy.

The same principle applies in any area of life. Knowing where we want to go increases the probability that we will arrive at our destination. Discovering what we want makes it more likely that we'll attain it.

Okay, so the example about the traveler with no destination is far-fetched. Before you dismiss it, though, do an informal experiment: Ask three other students what they want to get out of their education. Be prepared for hemming and hawing, vague generalities, and maybe even a helping of pie in the sky à la mode.

This is amazing, considering the stakes involved. Students routinely invest years of their lives and thousands of dollars, with only a hazy idea of their destination in life.

Now suppose that you asked someone what she wanted from her education and you got this answer: "I plan to get a degree in journalism with double minors in earth science and Portuguese so that I can work as a reporter covering the environment in Brazil." The details of a person's vision offer clues to their skills and sense of purpose.

Another clue is the presence of "stretch goals"—those that are big *and* achievable. A 40-year-old might spend years talking about his desire to be a professional athlete some day. Chances are, that's no longer achievable. However, setting a goal to lose 10 pounds by playing basketball at the gym 3 days a week is another matter. That's a stretch—a challenge. It's also doable.

Discovering what you want helps you succeed in higher education. Many students quit school simply because they are unsure about what they want from it. With well-defined goals in mind, you can look for connections between what you want and what you study. The more connections, the more likely you'll stay in school—and get what you want in every area of life.[1]

You're One Click Away...
from accessing Power Process media online and finding out more about "Discovering what you want."

Master student
qualities

This book is about something that cannot be taught. It's about becoming a master student.

Mastery means attaining a level of skill that goes beyond technique. For a master, work is effortless; struggle evaporates. The master carpenter is so familiar with her tools that they are part of her. To a master chef, utensils are old friends. Because these masters don't have to think about the details of the process, they bring more of themselves to their work.

Mastery can lead to flashy results: an incredible painting, for example, or a gem of a short story. In basketball, mastery might

result in an unbelievable shot at the buzzer. For a musician, it might be the performance of a lifetime, the moment when everything comes together. You could describe the experience as "flow" or being "in the zone."

Often, the result of mastery is a sense of profound satisfaction, well-being, and timelessness. Distractions fade. Time stops. Work becomes play. After hours of patient practice, after setting clear goals and getting precise feedback, the master has learned to be fully in control.

At the same time, he lets go of control. Results happen without effort, struggle, or worry. Work seems self-propelled. The master is in control by being out of control. He lets go and allows the creative process to take over. That's why after a spectacular performance by an athlete or performer, observers often say, "He played full out—and made it look like he wasn't even trying."

Likewise, the master student is one who makes learning look easy. She works hard without seeming to make any effort. She's relaxed *and* alert, disciplined *and* spontaneous, focused *and* fun-loving.

You might say that those statements don't make sense. Actually, mastery does *not* make sense. It cannot be captured with words. It defies analysis. Mastery cannot be taught. It can only be learned and experienced.

By design, you are a learning machine. As an infant, you learned to walk. As a toddler, you learned to talk. By the time you reached age 5, you'd mastered many skills needed to thrive in the world. And you learned all these things without formal instruction, without lectures, without books, without conscious effort, and without fear.

Shortly after we start school, however, something happens to us. Somehow we start forgetting about the master student inside us. Even under the best teachers, we experience the discomfort that sometimes accompanies learning. We start avoiding situations that might lead to embarrassment. We turn away from experiences that could lead to mistakes. We accumulate a growing list of ideas to defend, a catalog of familiar experiences that discourages us from learning anything new. Slowly, we restrict our possibilities and potentials.

However, the story doesn't end there. You can open a new chapter in your life, starting today. You can rediscover the natural learner within you. Each chapter of this book is about a step you can take on this path.

Master students share certain qualities. These are attitudes and core values. Though they imply various strategies for learning,

Oliver Cleve/Getty Images

they ultimately go beyond what you do. Master student qualities are ways of *being* exceptional.

Following is a list of master student qualities. Remember that the list is not complete. It merely points in a direction.

As you read the following list, look to yourself. Put a check mark next to each quality that you've already demonstrated. Put another mark, say an exclamation point, next to each quality you want to actively work on possessing. This is not a test. It is simply a chance to celebrate what you've accomplished so far—and start thinking about what's possible for your future.

☐ **Inquisitive.** The master student is curious about everything. By posing questions, she can generate interest in the most mundane, humdrum situations. When she is bored during a biology lecture, she thinks to herself, "I always get bored when I listen to this instructor. Why is that? Maybe it's because he reminds me of my boring Uncle Ralph, who always tells those endless fishing stories. He even looks like Uncle Ralph. Amazing! Boredom is certainly interesting." Then she asks herself, "What can I do to get value out of this lecture, even though it seems boring?" And she finds an answer.

☐ **Able to focus attention.** Watch a 2-year-old at play. Pay attention to his eyes. The wide-eyed look reveals an energy and a capacity for amazement that keep his attention absolutely focused in the here and now. The master student's focused attention has a childlike quality. The world, to a child, is always new. Because the master student can focus attention, to him the world is always new too.

☐ **Willing to change.** The unknown does not frighten the master student. In fact, she welcomes it—even the unknown in herself. We all have pictures of who we think we are, and these pictures can be useful. But they also can prevent learning and growth. The master student is open to changes in her environment and in herself.

☐ **Able to organize and sort.** The master student can take a large body of information and sift through it to discover relationships. He can play with information, organizing data by size, color, function, timeliness, and hundreds of other categories. He has the guts to set big goals—and the precision to plan carefully so that those goals can be achieved.

☐ **Competent.** Mastery of skills is important to the master student. When she learns mathematical formulas, she studies them until they become second nature. She practices until she knows them cold, then puts in a few extra minutes. She also is able to apply what she learns to new and different situations.

☐ **Joyful.** More often than not, the master student is seen with a smile on his face—sometimes a smile at nothing in particular other than amazement at the world and his experience of it.

> For example, if a master student takes a required class that most students consider boring, she chooses to take responsibility for her interest level. She looks for ways to link the class to one of her goals. She sees the class as an opportunity to experiment with new study techniques that will enhance her performance in any course.

☐ **Able to suspend judgment.** The master student has opinions and positions, and she is able to let go of them when appropriate. She realizes she is more than her thoughts. She can quiet her internal dialogue and listen to an opposing viewpoint. She doesn't let judgment get in the way of learning. Rather than approaching discussions with a "Prove it to me, and then I'll believe it" attitude, she asks herself, "What if this is true?" and explores possibilities.

☐ **Energetic.** Notice the student with a spring in his step, the one who is enthusiastic and involved in class. When he reads, he often sits on the very edge of his chair, and he plays with the same intensity. He is determined and persistent. He is a master student.

☐ **Well.** Health is important to the master student, though not necessarily in the sense of being free of illness. Rather, she values her body and treats it with respect. She tends to her emotional and spiritual health as well as her physical health.

☐ **Self-aware.** The master student is willing to evaluate himself and his behavior. He regularly tells the truth about his strengths and those aspects that could be improved.

☐ **Responsible.** There is a difference between responsibility and blame, and the master student knows it well. She is willing to take responsibility for everything in her life—even for events that most people would blame on others. For example, if a master student takes a required class that most students consider boring, she chooses to take responsibility for her interest level. She looks for ways to link the class to one of her goals. She sees the class as an opportunity to experiment with new study techniques that will enhance her performance in any course. She remembers that by choosing her thoughts and behaviors, she can create interesting classes, enjoyable relationships, fulfilling work experiences, or just about anything else she wants.

☐ **Willing to take risks.** The master student often takes on projects with no guarantee of success. He participates in class dialogues at the risk of looking foolish. He tackles difficult subjects in term papers. He welcomes the risk of a challenging course.

☐ **Willing to participate.** Don't look for the master student on the sidelines. She's in the game. She is a team player who can be counted on. She is engaged at school, at work, and with friends and family. She is willing to make a commitment and to follow through on it.

☐ **A generalist.** The master student is interested in everything around him. In the classroom, he is fully present. Outside the classroom, he actively seeks out ways to deepen his learning—through study groups, campus events, student organizations, and team-based projects. Through such experiences, he develops a broad base of knowledge in many fields that can apply to his specialties.

☐ **Willing to accept paradox.** The word *paradox* comes from two Greek words, *para* ("beyond") and *doxen* ("opinion"). A paradox is something that is beyond opinion or, more accurately, something that might seem contradictory or absurd yet might actually have meaning. For example, the master student can be committed to managing money and reaching her financial goals. At the same time, she can be totally detached from money, knowing that her real worth is independent of how much money she has. The master student recognizes the limitations of the mind and is at home with paradox. She can accept that ambiguity.

☐ **Courageous.** The master student admits his fear and fully experiences it. For example, he will approach a tough exam as an opportunity to explore feelings of anxiety and tension related to the pressure to perform. He does not deny fear; he embraces it. If he doesn't understand something or if he makes a mistake, he admits it. When he faces a challenge and bumps into his limits, he asks for help. And he's just as willing to give help as to receive it.

☐ **Self-directed.** Rewards or punishments provided by others do not motivate the master student. Her desire to learn comes from within, and her goals come from herself. She competes like a star athlete—not to defeat other people, but to push herself to the next level of excellence.

☐ **Spontaneous.** The master student is truly in the here and now. He is able to respond to the moment in fresh, surprising, and unplanned ways.

☐ **Relaxed about grades.** Grades make the master student neither depressed nor euphoric. She recognizes that sometimes grades are important. At the same time, grades are not the only reason she studies. She does not measure her worth as a human being by the grades she receives.

☐ **"Tech" savvy.** A master student defines "technology" as any tool that's used to achieve a human purpose. From this point of view, computers become tools for deeper learning, higher productivity, and greater success in the workplace. When faced with a task to accomplish, the master student chooses effectively from the latest options in hardware and software. He searches for information efficiently, thinks critically about data, and uses technology to create online communities. If he isn't familiar with a type of technology, he doesn't get overwhelmed. Instead, he embraces learning about the new technology and finding ways to use the technology to help him succeed at the given task. He also knows when to go "offline" and fully engage with his personal community of friends, family members, classmates, instructors, and coworkers.

☐ **Intuitive.** The master student has an inner sense that cannot be explained by logic alone. She trusts her "gut instincts" as well as her mind.

☐ **Creative.** Where others see dull details and trivia, the master student sees opportunities to create. He can gather pieces of knowledge from a wide range of subjects and put them together in new ways. The master student is creative in every aspect of his life.

☐ **Willing to be uncomfortable.** The master student does not place comfort first. When discomfort is necessary to reach a goal, she is willing to experience it. She can endure personal hardships and can look at unpleasant things with detachment.

☐ **Optimistic.** The master student sees setbacks as temporary and isolated, knowing that he can choose his response to any circumstance.

☐ **Willing to laugh.** The master student might laugh at any moment, and her sense of humor includes the ability to laugh at herself. While going to school is a big investment, with high stakes, you don't have to enroll in the deferred-fun program. A master student celebrates learning, and one of the best ways of doing that is to laugh now and then.

Hungry. Human beings begin life with a natural appetite for knowledge. In some people, it soon gets dulled. The master student has tapped that hunger, and it gives him a desire to learn for the sake of learning.

Willing to work. Once inspired, the master student is willing to follow through with sweat. She knows that genius and creativity are the result of persistence and work. When in high gear, the master student works with the intensity of a child at play.

Caring. A master student cares about knowledge and has a passion for ideas. He also cares about people and appreciates learning from others. He collaborates on projects and thrives on teams. He flourishes in a community that values win-win outcomes, cooperation, and love. ■

✓ EXERCISE 2

The master student in you

The purpose of this exercise is to demonstrate to yourself that you truly are a master student. Start by remembering a time in your life when you learned something well or demonstrated mastery. This experience does not have to relate to school. It might be a time when you aced a test, played a flawless soccer game, created a work of art that won recognition, or burst forth with a blazing guitar solo. It might be a time when you spoke from your heart in a way that moved someone else. Or it might be a time when you listened deeply to another person who was in pain, comforted him, and connected with him at a level beyond words.

Describe the details of such an experience in your life. Include the place, time, and people involved. Describe what happened and how you felt about it.

_____

_____

_____

_____

_____

_____

_____

_____

Now, review the article "Master student qualities" and take a look at the master student qualities that you checked off. These are the qualities that apply to you.

Give a brief example of how you demonstrated at least one of those qualities.

_____

_____

_____

_____

_____

_____

_____

_____

_____

Now think of other qualities of a master student—characteristics that were not mentioned in the article. List those qualities here, along with a one-sentence description of each.

_____

_____

_____

_____

_____

_____

_____

_____

_____

_____

This book is worthless—
if you just read it

The first edition of this book began with the sentence *This book is worthless.* Many students thought beginning this way was a trick to get their attention. It wasn't. Others thought it was reverse psychology. It wasn't that either. Still others thought it meant that the book was worthless if they didn't read it. It meant more than that.

This book is worthless *even if you read it*—if reading it is all you do. What was true of that first edition is true of this one as well. Until you take action and use the ideas in it, *Becoming a Master Student* really is worthless.

The purpose of this book is to help you make a successful transition to higher education by setting up a pattern of success that will last the rest of your life. You probably won't take action and use the ideas in this book until you are convinced that you have something to gain. That's the reason for this introduction—to persuade you to use this book actively.

Before you stiffen up and resist this sales pitch, remember that you have already bought the book. Now you can get something for your money by committing yourself to take action—in other words, by committing yourself to becoming a master student. Here's what's in it for you.

Pitch #1: You can save money now and make more money later. Start with money. Your college education is one of the most expensive things you will ever buy. You might find yourself paying $100 an hour to sit in class. (See Exercise 30: "Education by the hour," on page 313, to come up with a specific figure that applies to your own education.)

As a master student, you control the value you get out of your education, and that value can be considerable. The joy of learning aside, higher levels of education relate to higher lifetime income and more consistent employment.[2] It pays to be a master student.

Pitch #2: You can rediscover the natural learner in you. Joy is important too. As you become a master student, you will learn to gain knowledge in the most effective way possible—by discovering the joyful, natural learner within you.

Children are great natural students. They quickly master complex skills, such as language, and they have fun doing it. For young children, learning is a high-energy process involving experimentation, discovery, and sometimes broken dishes. Then comes school. For some students, drill and drudgery replace discovery and dish breaking. Learning can become a drag. You can use this book to reverse that process and rediscover what you knew as a child—that laughter and learning go hand in hand.

Sometimes—and especially in college—learning does take effort. As you become a master student, you will learn many ways to get the most out of that effort.

Pitch #3: You can choose from hundreds of techniques. *Becoming a Master Student* is packed with hundreds of practical, nuts-and-bolts techniques. And you can begin using them immediately. For example, during the "Textbook reconnaissance," on page 1, you might find three powerful learning techniques in one exercise. Even if you doze in lectures, drift off during tests, or dawdle on term papers, you'll find ideas in this book that you can use to become a more effective student.

Not all of these ideas will work for you. That's why there are so many of them in *Becoming a Master Student.* You should experiment with the techniques. As you discover what works, you will develop a unique style of learning that you can use for the rest of your life.

Pitch #4: You get the best suggestions from thousands of students. The concepts and techniques in this book are here not just because learning theorists, educators, and psychologists say they work, but because tens of thousands of students from all kinds of backgrounds have tried them and agree that they work. These are students who dreaded giving speeches, couldn't read their own notes, and fell behind in their course work. Then they figured out how to solve those problems. Now you can use their ideas.

Pitch #5: You can learn about yourself. The process of self-discovery is an important theme in *Becoming a Master Student*. Throughout the book, you can use Journal Entries for everything from organizing your desk to choosing long-term goals. Studying for an organic chemistry quiz is a lot easier with a clean desk and a clear idea of the course's importance to you.

Pitch #6: You can use a proven product. The previous editions of this book have proved successful for hundreds of thousands of students. Student feedback has been positive. In particular, students with successful histories have praised the techniques in this book.

Pitch #7: You can learn the secret of student success. If this sales pitch still hasn't persuaded you to use this book actively, maybe it's time to reveal the secret of student success.

(Provide your own drum roll here.)

The secret is . . . there are no secrets. The ultimate formula is to give up formulas, keep experimenting, and find strategies that actually help you meet your goals.

The strategies that successful students use are well-known. You have hundreds of them at your fingertips right now, in this book. Use them. Modify them. Invent new ones. You're the authority on what works for you.

However, what makes any technique work is commitment—and action. Without them, the pages of *Becoming a Master Student* are just 2.1 pounds of expensive mulch.

Add your participation to the mulch, and these pages become priceless. ■

Master Students IN ACTION

"Use all of the resources on campus. Get to know your instructors and professors, attend every class, accept all new challenges, get a support group, have outside hobbies and passions, believe in yourself."

—Timothy Allen,
American River College

 You're One Click Away...
from watching a video about Master Students in Action online.

Photo courtesy of Timothy Alley/American River College

✓ EXERCISE 3

Commitment

This book is worthless unless you actively participate in its activities and exercises. One powerful way to begin taking action is to make a commitment. Conversely, if you don't make a commitment, then sustained action is unlikely. The result is a worthless book. Therefore, in the interest of saving your valuable time and energy, this exercise gives you a chance to declare your level of involvement up front. From the options below, choose the sentence that best reflects your commitment to using this book. Write the number of the sentence in the space provided at the end of the list.

1. "Well, I'm reading this book right now, aren't I?"
2. "I will skim the book and read the interesting parts."
3. "I will read the book, think about it, and do the exercises that look interesting."
4. "I will read the book, do some exercises, and complete some of the Journal Entries."
5. "I will read the book, do some exercises and Journal Entries, and use some of the techniques."
6. "I will read the book, do most of the exercises and Journal Entries, and use some of the techniques."
7. "I will study this book, do most of the exercises and Journal Entries, and use some of the techniques."
8. "I will study this book, do most of the exercises and Journal Entries, and experiment with many of the techniques in order to discover what works best for me."
9. "I promise myself that I will create value from this course by studying this book, doing all the exercises and Journal Entries, and experimenting with most of the techniques."
10. "I will use this book as if the quality of my education depended on it—doing all the exercises and Journal Entries, experimenting with most of the techniques, inventing techniques of my own, and planning to reread this book in the future."

Write the sentence number that best describes your commitment level and today's date here:

Commitment level _____ Date _____

If you selected commitment level 1 or 2, you probably won't create a lot of value in this class, and you might consider passing this book on to a friend. If your commitment level is 9 or 10, you are on your way to terrific success in school. If your level is somewhere in between, experiment with the techniques and learning strategies in this book. If you find that they work, consider returning to this exercise and raising your level of commitment.

Get the most out of this book

Get used to a new look and tone. This book looks different from traditional textbooks. *Becoming a Master Student* presents major ideas in magazine-style articles. There are lots of lists, blurbs, one-liners, pictures, charts, graphs, illustrations, and even a joke or two.

Rip 'em out. The pages of *Becoming a Master Student* are perforated because some of the information here is too important to leave in the book. You can rip out pages, then reinsert them later by sticking them into the spine of the book. A piece of tape will hold them in place.

Skip around. Feel free to use this book in several different ways. Read it straight through. Or pick it up, turn to any page, and find an idea you can use right now.

You might find that this book presents similar ideas in several places. This repetition is intentional. Repetition reinforces key points. A technique that works in one area of your life might work in others as well.

If it works, use it. If it doesn't, lose it. If there are sections of this book that don't apply to you at all, skip them—unless, of course, they are assigned. In that case, see whether you can gain value from those sections anyway. When you commit to get value from this book, even an idea that seems irrelevant or ineffective at first can turn out to be a powerful tool in the future.

Listen to your peers. Throughout this book, you will find features titled Master Students in Action. These are short quotations from students who used this text. As you dig into the following chapters, think about what you would say if you could add your voice to theirs.

Own this book. Determine what you want to get out of school, and create a record of how you intend to get it by completing the Journal Entries throughout this book. Every time your pen touches a page, you move closer to mastery.

Do the exercises. Action makes this book work. To get the most out of this book, do most of the exercises. (It's never too late to go back and do the ones you skipped.) Exercises invite you to write, touch, feel, move, see, search, ponder, speak, listen, recall, choose, commit, and create. You might even sing and dance. Learning often works best when it involves action.

Practice critical thinking. Practicing Critical Thinking activities appear throughout this book. Other elements of this text, including Chapter 7: Thinking, the exercises, and Journal Entries, also promote critical thinking.

Learn about learning styles. Check out the Learning Styles Inventory and related articles in Chapter 1. This material can help you discover your preferred learning styles and allow you to explore new styles. Then, throughout the rest of this book, you'll find suggestions for applying your knowledge of learning styles. The modes of learning can be accessed by asking four basic questions: *Why? What? How?* and *What if?*

PRACTICING critical thinking 2

Psychologist Benjamin Bloom described six kinds of thinking... even writing a song—then discuss this with your instructor.

Level 1: Remembering—recalling an idea.

Level 2: Understanding—explaining an idea in your own words and giving examples from your own experience.

Level 3: Applying—using an idea to produced a desired result.

Level 4: Analyzing—dividing an idea into parts or steps.

Level 5: Evaluating—rating the truth, usefulness, or quality of an idea—and giving reasons for your rating.

Level 6: Creating—inventing something new based on an idea.

You can recall any suggestion from this book (Level 1: Remembering) and take that idea to a higher level of thinking.

For example, recall the suggestion to "take it apart" from the "The 7-day antiprocrastination plan" on page 87. Think about how you could use this suggestion to write a paper. Write notes on your calendar to:

* Choose a topic for the paper by October 1.
* Finish the first draft by October 15.
* Finish the final draft by October 28 (2 days before the paper is due).

Creating a step-by-step plan like this one is an example of Level 3: Applying. Thinking at this level often means answering questions such as: How can I actually use this idea? What is the very next action I would take? When? Where? Who else might be involved?

Now it's your turn. Choose another suggestion from this chapter (Level 1: Remembering) and think about it at Level 3: Applying. In the space provided here, state the suggestion and write a brief paragraph that summarizes your higher-level thinking. If you'd like to demonstrate your thinking in another way—such as by making a drawing, building a model, or...

For more information on the six kinds of thinking, see "Becoming a critical thinker" in Chapter 7.

---

what if ← · · · · · · · · · · · → why

how ← · · · · · · · · · · · → what

Navigate through learning experiences with the Master Student Map. You can orient yourself for maximum learning every time you open this book by asking those same four questions: *Why? What? How?* and *What if?* That's the idea behind the Master Student Map included on the first page of each chapter, which includes sample answers to those questions. Remember that you can use the four-part structure of this map to effectively learn anything.

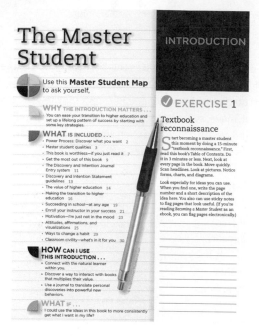

Experience the power of the Power Processes. A Power Process is a suggestion to shift your perspective or try on a new behavior. Look for this feature on the second page of each chapter. Users of *Becoming a Master Student* often refer to these articles as their favorite part of the book. Approach them with a sense of play and possibility. Start with an open mind, experiment with the ideas, and see what works.

Link to the Web. Throughout this book, you'll notice reminders to visit the College Success Coursemate for *Becoming a Master Student.* There you'll discover ways to take your involvement with this book to a deeper level. For example, access the Web site to do an online version of the Discovery Wheel exercise. Also look for videos, additional exercises, articles, practice tests, and forms. Scan this code with your smartphone to go directly to CengageBrain.com and login to CourseMate.

 You're One Click Away...

To get access, visit CengageBrain.com

Read the sidebars. Look for sidebars—short bursts of words placed between longer articles—throughout this book. These short pieces might offer insights that transform your experience of higher education.

Making the grade in group presentations

When preparing group presentations, you can use three strategies for making a memorable impression.

Get organized. As soon as you get the assignment, select a group leader and exchange contact information. Schedule specific times and places for planning, researching, writing, and practicing your presentation.

At your first meeting, write a to-do list that includes all of the tasks involved in completing the assignment. Distribute tasks fairly, paying attention to the strengths of individuals in your group. For example, some people excel at brainstorming, whereas others prefer researching.

One powerful way to get started is to define clearly the topic and thesis, or main point, of your presentation. Then support your thesis by looking for the most powerful facts, quotations, and anecdotes you can find.

As you get organized, remember how your presentation will be evaluated. If the instructor doesn't give grading criteria, create your own.

Take this book to work. With a little tweaking, in some cases, you can apply nearly all of the techniques in this book to your career. For more details, see the Put This Chapter to Work articles in each chapter. Use these articles to make a seamless transition from success in school to success on the job. ■

PUT THIS CHAPTER TO WORK

To get more value from *Becoming a Master Student*, make the career connection. Think about how you can use strategies from this chapter to find a job you want and do the work you love. Following are ways to get started.

REMEMBER LEARNING STYLES DURING JOB INTERVIEWS. You probably feel more comfortable with a person when you feel that you have something in common. That feeling is called *rapport.*

When meeting with a job interviewer, look for clues to that person's learning style. Then see whether you can establish rapport by matching that person's style in a small, significant way.

For example, mirror the interviewer's word choice. Some people like to process information *visually.* You might hear them say, "I'll look into that" or "Give me the big picture first." Those who like to solve problems *verbally* might say, "Let's talk through this problem" or "I hear you!" And some interviewers express *kinesthetic* preferences by referring to body sensations ("This product feels great") or action ("Let's run with this idea and see what happens").

Kinesthetic preferences are also expressed in posture. Notice whether the job interviewer is sitting with arms and legs crossed or open. If you can mirror that posture in a natural way, then do so.

As you look for ways to establish rapport, be subtle. The goal is not to manipulate—it's to find common ground.

DISCOVER YOUR COWORKERS' LEARNING STYLES. Once

• A supervisor might write goals and detailed plans before taking action. This person has a preference for *thinking.*

• The worker who's continually on the move might prefer concrete experience over memos or meetings. She likes to learn by *doing.*

NOW CREATE A CAREER CONNECTION OF YOUR OWN. Spend five minutes reviewing this chapter. Look for a suggestion that you will commit to use while you're working or looking for a job. In a sentence or two, describe your new behavior and the benefit you want to gain from it. For example: "I will speak about *differences in styles* rather than *deficiencies* in my coworkers. This can help me prevent and resolve conflict at work."

Describe your planned behavior and desired benefit here:

_____

_____

_____

_____

_____

The **Discovery** and Intention Journal Entry **system**

One way to become a better student is to grit your teeth and try harder. There is a better way: The Discovery and Intention Journal Entry system. This system can increase your effectiveness by showing you how to focus your energy.

Using the Discovery and Intention Journal Entry system is a little like flying a plane. Airplanes are seldom exactly on course. Human

and automatic pilots are always checking an airplane's positions and making corrections. The resulting flight path looks like a zigzag. The plane is almost always flying in the wrong direction, but because of constant observation and course correction, it arrives at the right destination.

As a student, you can use a similar approach. Journal Entries throughout this book are labeled as Discovery Statements, Intention Statements, or Discovery/Intention Statements. Each Journal Entry contains a short set of suggestions that involve writing.

Through Discovery Statements, you gain **awareness** of "where you are." These statements are a record of what you are learning about yourself as a student—both your strengths and your weaknesses. **Discovery Statements can also be declarations of your goals, descriptions of your attitudes, statements of your feelings, transcripts of your thoughts, and chronicles of your behavior.**

Sometimes Discovery Statements chronicle an "aha!" moment—a flash of insight that results when you connect a new idea with your prior experiences, preferred styles of learning, or both. Perhaps a solution to a long-standing problem suddenly occurs to you. Or a life-changing insight wells up from the deepest recesses of your mind. Don't let such moments disappear. Capture them in Discovery Statements.

Intention Statements can be used to alter your course. These statements are about your **commitment** to take action based on increased awareness. An intention arises out of your choice to direct your energy toward a specific task and to aim at a particular goal. The processes of discovery and intention reinforce each other.

Even simple changes in behavior can produce results. If you feel like procrastinating, then tackle just one small, specific task related to your intention. Find something you can complete in 5 minutes or less, and do it *now*. For example, access just one Web site related to the topic of your next assigned paper. Spend just 3 minutes previewing a reading assignment. Taking "baby steps" like these can move you into action with grace and ease.

· ·

That's the system in a nutshell. Discovery leads to awareness. Intention leads to commitment, which naturally leads to focused action.

· ·

The purpose of this system is not to get you pumped up and excited to go out there and try harder. In fact, Discovery and Intention Statements are intended to help you work smarter rather than harder.

The process of discovery, intention, and action creates a dynamic and efficient cycle. First, you write Discovery Statements about where you are now. Next, you write Intention Statements about where you want to be and the specific steps you will take to get there. Finally, you follow up with action—the sooner, the better.

Then you start the cycle again. Write Discovery Statements about whether or how you act on your Intention Statements—and what you learn in the process. Follow up with more Intention Statements about what you will do differently in the future. Then move into action and describe what happens next.

This process never ends. Each time you repeat the cycle, you get new results. It's all about getting what you want and becoming more effective in everything you do. This is the path of mastery—a path that you can travel for the rest of your life.

Sometimes a Discovery or Intention Statement will be long and detailed. Usually, it will be short—maybe just a line or two. With practice, the cycle will become automatic.

Don't panic when you fail to complete an intended task. Straying off course is normal. Simply make the necessary corrections. Consider the first word in the title of this book—*becoming*. This word implies that mastery is not an end state or final goal. Rather, mastery is a process that never ends.

Miraculous progress might not come immediately. Do not be concerned. Stay with the cycle. Give it time. Use Discovery Statements to get a clear view of your world. Then use Intention Statements to direct your actions. Whenever you notice progress, record it.

The following statement might strike you as improbable, but it is true: It can take the same amount of energy to get what you *don't* want in school as it takes to get what you *do* want. Sometimes getting what you don't want takes even more effort. An airplane burns the same amount of fuel flying away from its destination as it does flying toward it. It pays to stay on course.

You can use the Discovery and Intention Journal Entry system to stay on your own course and get what you want out of school. Start with the Journal Entries included in the text. Then go beyond them. Write Discovery and Intention Statements of your own at any time, for any purpose. Create new strategies whenever you need them, based on your current situation.

Once you get the hang of it, you might discover you can fly. ■

Discovery and Intention Statement Guidelines

Writing Journal Entries helps you to develop self-awareness, self-direction, and other master student qualities. Use the following guidelines as a checklist. Consider removing this page from the book and posting it in a prominent place where you'll typically be writing your responses to the Journal Entries.

DISCOVERY STATEMENTS

☐ **Record the specifics about your thoughts, feelings, and behavior.** Notice your thoughts, observe your actions, and record them accurately. Get the facts. If you spent 90 minutes chatting online with a favorite cousin instead of reading your anatomy text, write about it. Include details.

☐ **Use discomfort as a signal.** When you approach a daunting task, such as a difficult math problem, notice your physical sensations. Feeling uncomfortable, bored, or tired might be a signal that you're about to do valuable work. Stick with it. Write about it. Tell yourself you can handle the discomfort just a little bit longer. You will be rewarded with a new insight.

☐ **Suspend judgment.** When you are discovering yourself, be gentle. Suspend self-judgment. If you continually judge your behaviors as "bad" or "stupid," your mind will quit making discoveries. For your own benefit, be kind to yourself.

☐ **Tell the truth.** Suspending judgment helps you tell the truth about yourself. "The truth will set you free" is a saying that endures for a reason. The closer you get to the truth, the more powerful your Discovery Statements. If you notice that you are avoiding the truth, don't blame yourself. Just tell the truth about it.

INTENTION STATEMENTS

☐ **Make intentions positive.** The purpose of writing Intention Statements is to focus on what you want rather than what you don't want. Instead of writing "I will not fall asleep while studying chemistry," write, "I intend to stay awake when studying chemistry." Also avoid the word *try*. Trying is not doing. When we hedge our bets with *try,* we can always tell ourselves, "Well, I *tried* to stay awake."

☐ **Make intentions observable.** Rather than writing "I intend to work harder on my history assignments," write, "I intend to review my class notes, and I intend to make summary sheets of my reading."

☐ **Make intentions small and achievable.** Break large goals into small, specific tasks that can be accomplished quickly. Small and simple changes in behavior—when practiced consistently over time—can have large and lasting effects.

When setting your goals, anticipate self-sabotage. Be aware of what you might do, consciously or unconsciously, to undermine your best intentions. Also, be careful with intentions that depend on other people. If you intend for your study group to complete an assignment by Monday, then your success depends on the students in the group. Likewise, you can support your group's success by following through on your stated intentions.

☐ **Set time lines.** For example, if you are assigned a paper to write, break the assignment into small tasks and set a precise due date for each one: "I intend to select a topic for my paper by 9:00 A.M. Wednesday."

☐ **Move from intention to action.** Intention Statements are of little use until you act on them. If you want new results in your life, then take action. Life responds to what you *do.* ∎

JOURNAL ENTRY 1
Discovery Statement

Declare what you want

Review the Power Process: "Discover what you want" on page 2. Then, writing on separate paper, brainstorm possible ways to complete the following sentence. When you're done, choose the ending that feels best to you and write it below.

I discovered that what I want most from my education is . . .

_____

_____

_____

_____

_____

_____

_____

The value of higher education

When you're waist-deep in reading assignments, writing papers, and studying for tests, you might well ask yourself, "Is all this effort going to pay off someday?"

That's a fair question. And it addresses a core issue—the value of getting an education beyond high school. Be reassured. The potential benefits of higher education and lifetime learning are enormous. To begin with, there are economic benefits. Over their lifetime, college graduates on average earn more than high school graduates. That's just one potential payoff. Consider the others explained below.

GAIN A BROAD VISION

It's been said that a large corporation is a collection of departments connected only by a plumbing system. This quip makes a point: As workers in different fields become more specialized, they run the risk of forgetting how to talk to one another.

Higher education can change that. One benefit of studying the liberal arts is the chance to gain a broad vision. People with a liberal arts background are aware of the various kinds of problems tackled in psychology and theology, philosophy and physics, literature and mathematics. They understand how people in all of these fields arrive at conclusions and how these fields relate.

MASTER THE LIBERAL ARTS

According to one traditional model, education means mastering two essential tasks: the use of language and the use of numbers. To acquire these skills, students once immersed themselves in seven subjects: grammar, rhetoric, logic, arithmetic, geometry, music, and astronomy. These subjects were called the liberal arts. They complemented the fine arts, such as poetry, and the practical arts, such as farming.

This model of liberal arts education still has something to offer. Today we master the use of language through the basic processes of communication: reading, writing, speaking, and listening. In addition, courses in mathematics and science help us understand the world in quantitative terms. The abilities to communicate and calculate are essential to almost every profession. Excellence at these skills has long been considered an essential characteristic of an educated person.

The word *liberal* comes from the Latin verb *libero,* which means "to free." Liberal arts are those that promote critical thinking. Studying them can free us from irrational ideas, half-truths, racism, and prejudice. The liberal arts grant us freedom to explore alternatives and create a system of personal values. These benefits are priceless—the very basis of personal fulfillment and political freedom.

DISCOVER YOUR VALUES

We do not spend all of our waking hours at our jobs. This leaves us with a decision that affects the quality of our lives: how to spend leisure time. By cultivating our interest in the arts and community affairs, the liberal arts provide us with many options for activities outside work. These studies add a dimension to life that goes beyond having a job and paying the bills.

Our values are practical. They determine the ways that we commit our time and spend our money. Higher education offers the opportunity to question, discover, and refine our values.

DISCOVER NEW INTERESTS

Taking a broad range of courses has the potential to change your direction in life. A student previously committed to a career in science might try out a drawing class and eventually switch to a degree in studio arts. Or a person who swears that she has no aptitude for technical subjects might change her major to computer science after taking an introductory computer course.

To make effective choices about your long-term goals, base those choices on a variety of academic and personal experiences. Even if you don't change majors or switch career directions, you could discover an important avocation or gain a complementary skill. For example, science majors who will eventually write for professional journals can benefit from taking English courses.

Higher education can also introduce you to people with a variety of backgrounds. Besides learning to appreciate diversity, you can develop new friends and discover new interests.

HANG OUT WITH THE GREATS

Today we enjoy a huge legacy from our ancestors. The creative minds of our species have given us great works of art, systems of science, and technological advances that defy the imagination. Through higher education, we can gain firsthand knowledge of humanity's greatest creations.

The poet Ezra Pound defined literature as "news that stays news."[3] Most of the writing in newspapers and magazines becomes dated quickly. In contrast, many of the books you read in higher education have passed the hardest test of all—time. Such works have created value for people for decades, sometimes for centuries. These creations are inexhaustible. We can return to them time after time and gain new insights. These are the works we can justifiably deem great. Hanging out with them transforms us. Getting to know them exercises our minds, just as running exercises our bodies.

By studying the greatest works in many fields, we raise our standards. We learn ways to distinguish what is superficial and fleeting from what is lasting and profound.

The criteria for a great novel, poem, painting, or piece of music or dance might vary among individuals. Differences in taste reflect the differences in our backgrounds. The point is to discover those works that have enduring value—and enjoy them for a lifetime.

LEARN SKILLS THAT APPLY ACROSS CAREERS

Jobs that involve responsibility, prestige, and higher incomes depend on self-management skills. These skills include knowing ways to manage time, resolve conflicts, set goals, learn new skills, and relate to people of diverse cultures. Higher education is a place to learn and practice such skills.

Judging by recent trends, most of us will have multiple careers in our lifetimes. In this environment of constant change, we benefit by gaining skills that apply across careers.

As many studies reveal, this is true even if you work in technical fields. For example, the College of Science and Engineering at the University of Minnesota surveyed managers in technical firms, asking them about the qualities they valued in employees. The most important were the ability to write and speak well, intellectual honesty, willingness to take risks and learn from mistakes, self-confidence, perseverance, and the ability to work with people of diverse backgrounds.[4] All of these are potential benefits of higher education.

> ## Some of the most important qualities managers valued in employees were communicating well, taking risks and learning from mistakes, and working with people of diverse backgrounds.

JOIN THE CONVERSATION

Long ago, before the advent of printing presses, televisions, and computers, people educated themselves by conversing with one another. Students in ancient Athens were often called *peripatetic* (a word that means "walking around") because they were frequently seen strolling around the city, engaged in heated philosophical debate.

Since then, the debate has deepened and broadened. The world's finest scientists and artists have joined voices in a conversation that spans centuries and crosses cultures. This conversation is about the nature of truth and beauty, knowledge and compassion, good and evil—ideas that form the very basis of society.

Robert Hutchins, former president of the University of Chicago, called this exchange the "great conversation."[5] Our greatest thinkers have left behind tangible records. You'll find them in libraries, concert halls, museums, and scientific laboratories across the world. Through higher education, you gain a front-row seat for the great conversation—and an opportunity to add your own voice. ∎

Andresr/Shutterstock.com

MAKING THE TRANSITION TO higher education

You share one thing in common with other students at your vocational school, college, or university: Entering higher education represents a major change in your life. You've joined a new culture with its own set of rules, both spoken and unspoken.

Whether you've just graduated from high school or have been out of the classroom for decades, you'll discover many differences between secondary and post-secondary education. The sooner you understand such differences, the sooner you can deal with them. Some examples of what you might face include the following:

- **New academic standards.** Once you enter higher education, you'll probably find yourself working harder in school than ever before. Instructors will often present more material at a faster pace. There probably will be fewer tests in higher education than in high school, and the grading might be tougher. Compared to high school, you'll have more to read, more to write, more problems to solve, and more to remember.

- **A new level of independence.** College instructors typically give less guidance about how or when to study. You may not get reminders about when assignments are due or when quizzes and tests will take place. You probably won't get

study sheets before a test. And anything that's said in class or included in assigned readings might appear on an exam. Overall, you might receive less consistent feedback about how well you are doing in each of your courses. Don't let this tempt you into putting off work until the last minute. You will still be held accountable for all course work. And anything that's said in class or included in assigned readings might appear on an exam.

- **Differences in teaching styles.** Instructors at colleges, universities, and vocational schools are often steeped in their subject matter. Many did not take courses on how to teach and might not be as interesting as some of your high school teachers. And some professors might seem more focused on research than on teaching.

- **A larger playing field.** The institution you've just joined might seem immense, impersonal, and even frightening. The sheer size of the campus, the variety of courses offered, the large number of departments—all of these opportunities can add up to a confusing array of options.

- **More students and more diversity.** The school you're attending right now might enroll hundreds or thousands more students than your high school. And the range of diversity among these students might surprise you.

In summary, you are now responsible for structuring your time and creating new relationships. Perhaps more than ever before, you'll find that your life is your own creation. You are free to set different goals, explore alternative ways of thinking, change habits, and expand your circle of friends. All this can add up to a new identity—a new way of being in the world.

At first, this world of choices might seem overwhelming or even frightening. You might feel that you're just going through the motions of being a student or playing a role that you've never rehearsed.

That feeling is understandable. Use it to your advantage. Consider that you *are* assuming a new role in life—that of being a student in higher education. And just as actors enter the minds of the characters that they portray, you can take on the character of a master student.

When you're willing to take responsibility for the quality of your education, you can create the future of your dreams. Keep the following strategies in mind.

Decrease the unknowns. To reduce surprise, anticipate changes. Before classes begin, get a map of the school property and walk through your first day's schedule, perhaps with a classmate or friend. Visit your instructors in their offices and introduce yourself. Anything you can do to get familiar with the new routine will help. In addition, consider buying your textbooks before class begins. Scan them to get a preview of your courses.

Admit your feelings—whatever they are. School can be an intimidating experience for new students. People of diverse cultures, adult learners, commuters, and people with disabilities may feel excluded. Anyone can feel anxious, isolated, homesick, or worried.

Those emotions are common among new students, and there's nothing wrong with them. Simply admitting the truth about how you feel—to yourself and to someone else—can help you cope. And you can almost always do something constructive in the present moment, no matter how you feel.

If your feelings about this transition make it hard for you to carry out the activities of daily life—going to class, working, studying, and relating to people—then get professional help. Start with a counselor at the student health service on your campus. The mere act of seeking help can make a difference.

Allow time for transition. You don't have to master the transition to higher education right away. Give it some time. Also, plan your academic schedule with your needs for transition in mind. Balance time-intensive courses with others that don't make as many demands.

Find resources. A supercharger increases the air supply to an internal combustion engine. The resulting difference in power can be dramatic. You can make just as powerful a difference in your education if you supercharge it by using all of the resources available to students. In this case, your "air supply" includes people, campus clubs and organizations, and school and community services.

Of all resources, people are the most important. You can isolate yourself, study hard, and get a good education. However, doing this is not the most powerful use of your tuition money. When you establish relationships with teachers, staff members, fellow students, and employers, you can get a *great* education. Build a network of people who will personally support your success in school.

Accessing resources is especially important if you are the first person in your family to enter higher education. As a first-generation student, you are having experiences that people in your family may not understand. Talk to your relatives about your activities at school. If they ask how they can help you, give specific answers. Also, ask your instructors about programs for first-generation students on your campus.

Meet with your academic advisor. One person in particular—your academic advisor—can help you access resources and make the transition to higher education. Meet with this person regularly. Advisors generally know about course requirements, options for declaring majors, and the resources available at your school. Peer advisors might also be available.

When you work with an advisor, remember that you're a paying customer and have a right to be satisfied with the service you get. Don't be afraid to change advisors when that seems appropriate.

Learn the language of higher education. Terms such as *grade point average* (GPA), *prerequisite, accreditation, matriculation, tenure,* and *syllabus* might be new to you. Ease your transition to higher education by checking your school catalog or school Web site for definitions of these words and others that you don't understand. Also ask your academic advisor for clarification.

Show up for class. In higher education, teachers generally don't take attendance. Yet you'll find that attending class is essential to your success. The amount that you pay in tuition and fees makes a powerful argument for going to classes regularly and getting your money's worth. In large part, the material that you're tested on comes from events that take place in class.

Showing up for class occurs on two levels. The most visible level is being physically present in the classroom. Even more important, though, is showing up mentally. This kind of attendance includes taking detailed notes, asking questions, and contributing to class discussions.

Research on college freshmen indicates a link between regular class attendance and academic success.[6] Succeeding in school can help you get almost anything you want, including the career, income, and relationships you desire. Attending class is an investment in yourself.

Manage out-of-class time. For students in higher education, time management takes on a new meaning. What you do *outside* class matters as much as—or even more than—what you do in class. Instructors give you the raw materials for understanding a subject while a class meets. You then take those materials, combine them, and *teach yourself* outside of class.

To allow for this process, schedule two hours of study time for each hour that you spend in class. Also, get a calendar that covers the entire academic year. With the syllabus for each of your courses in hand, note key events for the entire term—dates for tests, papers, and other projects. Getting a big picture of your course load makes it easier to get assignments done on time and prevent all-night study sessions.

Experiment with new ways to study. You can cope with increased workloads and higher academic expectations by putting all of your study habits on the table and evaluating them. Don't assume that the learning strategies you used in the past—in high school or the workplace—will automatically transfer to your new role in higher education. Keep the habits that serve you, drop those that hold you back, and adopt new ones to promote your success. On every page of this book, you'll find helpful suggestions.

Take the initiative in meeting new people. Introduce yourself to classmates and instructors. Just before or after class is a good time. Realize that most of the people in this new world of higher education are waiting to be welcomed. You can help them and help yourself at the same time.

Perhaps you imagined that higher education would be a hotbed of social activity—and now find yourself feeling lonely and disconnected. Your feelings are common. Remember that plugging into the social networks at any school takes time. And it's worth the effort. Connecting to school socially as well as academically promotes your success and your enjoyment.

Become a self-regulated learner. Reflect on your transition to higher education. Think about what's working well, what you'd like to change, and ways to make those changes. Psychologists use the term *self-regulation* to describe this kind of thinking.[7] Self-regulated learners set goals, monitor their progress toward those goals, and change their behavior based on the results they get.

Becoming a Master Student promotes self-regulation through the ongoing cycle of discovery, intention, and action. Write Discovery Statements to monitor your behavior and evaluate the results you're currently creating in any area of your life. Write about your level of commitment to school, your satisfaction with your classes and grades, your social life, and your family's support for your education.

Based on your discoveries, write Intention Statements about your goals for this term, this year, next year, and the rest of your college career. Describe exactly what you will do to create new

Rewrite
this book

Some books should be preserved in pristine condition. This book isn't one of them.

Something happens when you interact with your book by writing in it. *Becoming a Master Student* is about learning, and learning results when you are active. When you make notes in the margin, you can hear yourself talking with the author. When you doodle and underline, you see the author's ideas taking shape. You can even argue with the author and come up with your own theories and explanations. In all of these ways, you can become a coauthor of this book. Rewrite it to make it yours.

While you're at it, you can create symbols or codes that will help you when reviewing the text later on. You might insert a "Q" where you have questions or put exclamation points or stars next to important ideas. You could also circle words to look up in a dictionary.

Remember, if any idea in this book doesn't work for you, you can rewrite it. Change the exercises to fit your needs. Create a new technique by combining several others. Create a technique out of thin air!

Find something you agree or disagree with on this page, and write a short note in the margin about it. Or draw a diagram. Better yet, do both. Let creativity be your guide. Have fun.

Begin rewriting now.

results in each of these time frames. Then follow through with action. In this way, you take charge of your transition to higher education, starting now. ◼

You're One Click Away...
from finding more strategies for mastering the art of transition online.

Succeeding in school—
at any age

David Buffington/Getty Images

David Buffington/Blend Images/Getty Images

Being an adult learner puts you on a strong footing. With a rich store of life experiences, you can ask meaningful questions and make connections between course work and daily life. Any abilities that you've developed to work on teams, manage projects, meet deadlines, and solve problems are assets. Many instructors will especially enjoy working with you.

Following are some suggestions for adult learners who want to ease their transition to higher education. If you're a younger student, commuting student, or community college student, look for useful ideas here as well.

Acknowledge your concerns. Adult learners might express any of the following fears:

- *I'll be the oldest person in all my classes.*
- *I've been out of the classroom too long.*
- *I'm concerned about my math, reading, and writing skills.*

- *I'm worried about making tuition payments.*
- *How will I ever make the time to study, on top of everything else I'm doing?*
- *I won't be able to keep up with all the new technology.*

Those concerns are understandable. Now consider some facts:

- College classrooms are more diverse than ever before. According to the U.S. Census Bureau, 37 percent of students in the nation's colleges are age 25 and older. The majority of these older students attend school part-time.[8]
- Adult learners can take advantage of evening classes, weekend classes, summer classes, distance learning, and online courses. Also look for classes in off-campus locations, closer to where you work or live.
- Colleges offer financial aid for students of all ages, including scholarships, grants, and low-interest loans.

- You can meet other students and make new friends by taking part in orientation programs. Look for programs that are targeted to adult learners.
- You are now enrolled in a course that can help boost your skills at math, reading, writing, note taking, time management, and other key skills.

Ease into it. If you're new to higher education, consider easing into it. You can choose to attend school part-time before making a full-time commitment. If you've taken college-level classes in the past, find out if any of those credits will transfer into your current program.

Plan ahead. By planning a week or month at a time, you get a bigger picture of your multiple roles as a student, an employee, and a family member. With that awareness, you can make conscious adjustments in the number of hours you devote to each domain of activity in your life. For example:

- If your responsibilities at work or home will be heavy in the near future, then register for fewer classes next term.
- Choose recreational activities carefully, focusing on those that relax you and recharge you the most.
- Don't load your schedule with classes that require unusually heavy amounts of reading or writing.

For related suggestions, see Chapter 2: Time.

Delegate tasks. If you have children, delegate some of the household chores to them. Or start a meal co-op in your neighborhood. Cook dinner for yourself and someone else one night each week. In return, ask that person to furnish you with a meal on another night. A similar strategy can apply to child care and other household tasks.

Get to know other returning students. Introduce yourself to other adult learners. Being in the same classroom gives you an immediate bond. You can exchange work, home, or cell phone numbers and build a network of mutual support. Some students adopt a buddy system, pairing up with another student in each class to complete assignments and prepare for tests.

In addition, learn about student services and organizations. Many schools have a learning assistance center with workshops geared to adult learners. Sign up and attend. Meet people on campus. Personal connections are key to your success.

Find common ground with traditional students. Traditional and nontraditional students have many things in common. They seek to gain knowledge and skills for their chosen careers. They desire financial stability and personal fulfillment. And, like their older peers, many younger students are concerned about whether they have the skills to succeed in higher education.

Consider pooling resources with younger students. Share notes, edit one another's papers, and form study groups. Look for ways to build on one another's strengths. If you want help with using a computer for assignments, you might ask a younger student for help. In group projects and case studies, you can expand the discussion by sharing insights from your experiences.

Enlist your employer's support. Let your employer in on your educational plans. Point out how the skills you gain in the classroom will help you meet work objectives. Offer informal seminars at work to share what you're learning in school. You might find that your company reimburses its employees for some tuition costs or even grants time off to attend classes.

Get extra mileage out of your current tasks. Look for ways to relate your schoolwork to your job. For example, when you're assigned a research paper, choose a topic that relates to your current job tasks. Some schools even offer academic credit for work and life experience.

Review your subjects before you start classes. Say that you've registered for trigonometry and you haven't taken a math class since high school. Consider brushing up on the subject before classes begin. Also, talk with future instructors about ways to prepare for their classes.

"Publish" your schedule. After you plan your study and class sessions for the week, write up your schedule and post it in a place where others who live with you will see it. If you use an online calendar, print out copies to put in your school binder or on your refrigerator door, bathroom mirror, or kitchen cupboard.

Enroll family and friends in your success. School can cut into your social life. Prepare friends and family members by discussing this issue ahead of time. See Chapter 8: Communicating for ways to prevent and resolve conflict.

You can also involve your spouse, partner, children, or close friends in your schooling. Offer to give them a tour of the campus, introduce them to your instructors and classmates, and encourage them to attend social events at school with you. Share ideas from this book, and from your other courses.

Take this process a step further, and ask the key people in your life for help. Share your reason for getting a degree, and talk about what your whole family has to gain from this change in your life. Ask them to think of ways that they can support your success in school and to commit to those actions. Make your own education a joint mission that benefits everyone. ■

You're One Click Away...
from finding more strategies for adult learners online.

Enroll your instructor
in your SUCCESS

Faced with an instructor you don't like, you have two basic choices. One is to label the instructor a "dud." When you make this choice, you endure class and complain to other students. This choice gives your instructor sole responsibility for the quality of your education and the value of your tuition payments.

There is another option. Don't give away your power. Instead, take responsibility for your education.

The word *enroll* in this headline is a play on words. Usually we think of students as the people who enroll in school. Turn this idea on its head. See whether you can enlist instructors as partners in getting what you want from higher education.

Research the instructor. When deciding what classes to take, you can look for formal and informal sources of information about instructors. One source is the school catalog. Alumni magazines or newsletters or the school newspaper might run articles on teachers. At some schools, students post informal evaluations of instructors on Web sites. Also talk to students who have taken courses from the instructor you're researching.

Or introduce yourself to the instructor. Set up a visit during office hours, and ask about the course. This conversation can help you get the flavor of a class and the instructor's teaching style. Other clues to an instructor's style include the *types* of material he presents (ranging from theory or fact) and the *ways* that the material is presented (ranging from lectures to discussion and other in-class activity).

Show interest in class. Students give teachers moment-by-moment feedback in class. That feedback comes through posture, eye contact, responses to questions, and participation in class discussions. If you find a class boring, recreate the instructor through a massive display of interest. Ask lots of questions. Sit up straight, make eye contact, take detailed notes. Your enthusiasm might enliven your instructor. If not, you are still creating a more enjoyable class for yourself.

Release judgments. Maybe your instructor reminds you of someone you don't like—your annoying Aunt Edna or a rude store clerk. Your attitudes are in your own head and beyond the instructor's control. Likewise, an instructor's beliefs about politics, religion, or feminism are not related to teaching ability. Being aware of such things can help you let go of negative judgments.

Instructors are a lot like you. They have opinions about politics, sports, and music. They worry about their health, finances, and career path. They're sometimes in a good mood and sometimes sad or angry. What distinguishes them is a lifelong passion for the subject that they teach.

Thinkstock/Getty

Get to know the instructor. Meet with your instructor during office hours. Teachers who seem boring in class can be fascinating in person. Prepare to notice your pictures and let them go. An instructor that someone told you to avoid might become one of your favorite teachers. You might hear conflicting reports about teachers from other students. The same instructor could be described by two different students as a riveting speaker and as completely lacking in charisma. Decide for yourself what descriptions are accurate.

Students who do well in higher education often get to know at least one instructor outside of class. In some cases, these instructors become mentors and informal advisors.

Open up to diversity. Sometimes students can create their instructors by letting go of pictures about different races and ethnic groups. According to one picture, a Hispanic person cannot teach English literature. According to other pictures, a white teacher cannot have anything valid to say about African music, and a teacher in a wheelchair cannot command the attention of a hundred people in a lecture hall. All of those pictures can clash with reality. Releasing them can open up new opportunities for understanding and appreciation.

Separate liking from learning. You don't have to like an instructor to learn from her. See whether you can focus on content instead of form. *Form* is the way something is organized or presented. If you are irritated at the sound of an instructor's voice, you're focusing on form. When you put aside your concern about her voice and turn your attention to the points she's making, you're focusing on *content*.

Seek alternatives. You might feel more comfortable with another teacher's style or method of organizing course materials. Consider changing teachers, asking another teacher for help outside class, or attending an additional section taught by a different instructor.

If you cannot change instructors, then take charge of your learning. Actively use the suggestions in this article. You can also learn from other students, courses, tutors, study groups, books, and DVDs. Be a master student, no matter who teaches your classes. Your education is your own creation.

Avoid excuses. Instructors know them all. Most teachers can see a snow job coming before the first flake hits the ground. Accept responsibility for your own mistakes, and avoid thinking that you can fool the teacher.

Submit professional work. Prepare papers and projects as if you were submitting them to an employer. Imagine that your work will determine whether you get a promotion and raise. Instructors often grade hundreds of papers during a term. Your neat, orderly, well-organized paper can stand out and lift a teacher's spirits.

Accept criticism. Learn from your teachers' comments about your work. It is a teacher's job to give feedback. Don't take it personally.

Use course evaluations. In many classes, you'll have an opportunity to evaluate the instructor. Respond honestly. Write about the aspects of the class that did not work well for you. Offer specific ideas for improvement. Also note what *did* work well.

Communicate effectively by phone and e-mail. Ask your instructors how they prefer to be contacted. If they take phone calls, leave a voice mail message that includes your first and last name, course name, section, and phone number.

If your instructor encourages contact via e-mail, then craft your messages with care. Start by including your name, course title, and section number in the subject line. Keep the body of your message brief and get to the point immediately.

Remember that the recipient of online communication is a human being whose culture, language, and humor may have different points of reference from your own. Write clearly, and keep the tone positive. Do not type in FULL CAPS, which is equivalent to shouting.

If there's a problem to solve, focus on solutions rather than blame. For example, avoid: "Why do you grade so unfairly?" Instead, write, "I'd like to understand your criteria for grading our assignments so that I can raise my scores."

Also proofread your message carefully and fix any errors. Write with full words and complete sentences. Avoid the abbreviations that you might use in a text message.

Finally, remember that instructors are busy people with personal lives. Don't expect them to be online at the same time as you.

Take further steps, if appropriate. Sometimes severe conflict develops between students and instructors. In such cases, you might decide to file a complaint or ask for help from an administrator.

Be prepared to document your case in writing. Describe specific actions that created problems. Stick to the facts—events that other class members can verify. Your school has grievance procedures to use in these cases. Use them. You are a consumer of education and have a right to fair treatment. ■

You're One Click Away...
from discovering more ways to create positive relationships with instructors online.

Meeting with
YOUR INSTRUCTOR

Meeting with an instructor outside class can save hours of study time and help boost your grade. Instead of trying to resolve a conflict with an instructor in the few minutes before or after class, schedule a time during office hours. During this meeting, state your concerns in a respectful way. Then focus on finding solutions. To get the most from these meetings, consider doing the following:

- Schedule a meeting time during the instructor's office hours. These are often listed in the course syllabus and on the instructor's office door.

- If you need to cancel or reschedule an appointment, let your instructor know well in advance.

- During the meeting, relax. This activity is not graded.

- Come prepared with a list of questions and any materials you'll need. During the meeting, take notes on the instructor's suggestions.

- Show the instructor your class notes to see whether you're capturing essential material.

- Get feedback on outlines that you've created for papers.

- Go over items you missed on exams.

- Get overall feedback on your progress.

- Ask about ways to prepare for upcoming exams.

- If the course is in a subject area that interests you, ask about the possibilities of declaring a major in that area and the possible careers associated with that major.

- Avoid questions that might offend your instructor—for example, "I missed class on Monday. Did we do anything important?"

- Ask whether your instructor is willing to answer occasional short questions via e-mail or a phone call.

- When the meeting is over, thank your instructor for making time for you.

- Remember that meeting during office hours is something that you do in addition to attending class regularly.

MOTIVATION—
I'm just not in the mood

In large part, this chapter is about your motivation to succeed in school. There are at least two ways to think about motivation. One is that the terms *self-discipline, willpower,* and *motivation* describe something missing in ourselves. We use these words to explain another person's success—or our own shortcomings: "If I were more motivated, I'd get more involved in school." "Of course she got an 'A.' She has self-discipline." "If I had more willpower, I'd lose weight." It seems that certain people are born with lots of motivation, whereas others miss out on it.

A second approach to thinking about motivation is to stop assuming that motivation is mysterious, determined at birth, or hard to come by. Perhaps there's nothing missing in you. What we call motivation could be something that you already possess—the ability to do a task even when you don't feel like it. This is a habit that you can develop with practice. The following suggestions offer ways to do that.

Promise it. Motivation can come simply from being clear about your goals and acting on them. Say that you want to start a study group. You can commit yourself to inviting people and setting a time and place to meet. Promise your classmates that you'll do this, and ask them to hold you accountable. Self-discipline, willpower, motivation—none of these mysterious characteristics has to get in your way. Just make a promise and keep your word.

Befriend your discomfort. Sometimes keeping your word means doing a task you'd rather put off. The mere thought of doing laundry, reading a chapter in a statistics book, or proofreading a term paper can lead to discomfort. In the face of such discomfort, you can procrastinate. Or you can use this barrier as a means to getting the job done.

Begin by investigating the discomfort. Notice the thoughts running through your head, and speak them out loud: "I'd rather walk on a bed of coals than do this." "This is the last thing I want to do right now."

Also observe what's happening with your body. For example, are you breathing faster or slower than usual? Is your breathing shallow or deep? Are your shoulders tight? Do you feel any tension in your stomach?

Once you're in contact with your mind and body, stay with the discomfort a few minutes longer. Don't judge it as good or bad. Accepting the thoughts and body sensations robs them of power. They might still be there, but in time they can stop being a barrier for you.

Discomfort can be a gift—an opportunity to do valuable work on yourself. On the other side of discomfort lies mastery.

Change your mind—and your body. You can also get past discomfort by planting new thoughts in your mind or changing your physical stance. For example, instead of slumping in a chair, sit up straight or stand up. You can also get physically active by taking a short walk. Notice what happens to your discomfort.

Work with your thoughts also. Replace "I can't stand this" with "I'll feel great when this is done" or "Doing this will help me get something I want."

Sweeten the task. Sometimes it's just one aspect of a task that holds you back. You can stop procrastinating merely by changing that aspect. If distaste for your physical environment keeps you from studying, you can change that environment. Reading about social psychology might seem like a yawner when you're alone in a dark corner of the house. Moving to a cheery, well-lit library can sweeten the task.

Galina Barskaya/Shutterstock.com

When you're done with an important task, reward yourself for a job well done. The simplest rewards—such as a walk, a hot bath, or a favorite snack—can be the most effective.

Talk about how bad it is. One way to get past negative attitudes is to take them to an extreme. When faced with an unpleasant task, launch into a no-holds-barred gripe session. Pull out all the stops: "There's no way I can start my income taxes now. This is terrible beyond words—an absolute disaster. This is a catastrophe of global proportions!" Griping taken this far can restore perspective. It shows how self-talk can turn inconveniences into crises.

Turn up the pressure. Sometimes motivation is a luxury. Pretend that the due date for your project has been moved up 1 month, 1 week, or 1 day. Raising the stress level slightly can spur you into action. Then the issue of motivation seems beside the point, and meeting the due date moves to the forefront.

Turn down the pressure. The mere thought of starting a huge task can induce anxiety. To get past this feeling, turn down the pressure by taking "baby steps." Divide a large project into small tasks. In 30 minutes or less, you could preview a book, create a rough outline for a paper, or solve two or three math problems. Careful planning can help you discover many such steps to make a big job doable.

Ask for support. Other people can become your allies in overcoming procrastination. For example, form a support group and declare what you intend to accomplish before each meeting. Then ask members to hold you accountable. If you want to begin exercising regularly, ask another person to walk with you three times weekly. People in support groups ranging from Alcoholics Anonymous to Weight Watchers know the power of this strategy.

Adopt a model. One strategy for succeeding at any task is to hang around the masters. Find someone you consider successful, and spend time with her. Observe this person and use her as a model for your own behavior. You can "try on" this person's actions and attitudes. Look for tools that feel right for you. This person can become a mentor for you.

Compare the payoffs to the costs. All behaviors have payoffs and costs. Even unwanted behaviors such as cramming for exams or neglecting exercise have payoffs. Cramming might give you more time that's free of commitments. Neglecting exercise can give you more time to sleep.

One way to let go of such unwanted behaviors is first to celebrate them—even embrace them. We can openly acknowledge the payoffs.

Celebration can be especially powerful when you follow it up with the next step—determining the costs. For example, skipping a reading assignment can give you time to go to the movies. However, you might be unprepared for class and have twice as much to read the following week.

Maybe there is another way to get the payoff (going to the movies) without paying the cost (skipping the reading assignment). With some thoughtful weekly planning, you might choose to give up a few hours of television and end up with enough time to read the assignment *and* go to the movies.

Comparing the costs and benefits of any behavior can fuel our motivation. We can choose new behaviors because they align with what we want most.

Do it later. At times, it's effective to save a task for later. For example, writing a résumé can wait until you've taken the time to analyze your job skills and map out your career goals. Putting it off does not show a lack of motivation—it shows planning.

When you do choose to do a task later, turn this decision into a promise. Estimate how long the task will take, and schedule a specific date and time for it on your calendar.

Heed the message. Sometimes lack of motivation carries a message that's worth heeding. An example is the student who majors in accounting but seizes every chance to be with children. His chronic reluctance to read accounting textbooks might not be a problem. Instead, it might reveal his desire to major in elementary education. His original career choice might have come from the belief that "real men don't teach kindergarten." In such cases, an apparent lack of motivation signals a deeper wisdom trying to get through. ■

ATTITUDES, AFFIRMATIONS, and VISUALIZATIONS

"I have a bad attitude." Some of us say this as if we were talking about having the flu. An attitude is certainly as strong as the flu, but it isn't something we have to live with forever anymore than the flu is.

Attitudes are judgments—enduring, deeply rooted views about what we like and what we dislike. Attitudes are also powerful. They mold behavior. If your attitude is that you're not interesting at a party, then your behavior will probably match your attitude. If your attitude is that you are fun at a party, then your behavior is more likely to be playful.

Visible measures of success—such as top grades and résumés filled with accomplishments—start with invisible assets called attitudes. Some attitudes will help you benefit from all the money and time you invest in higher education, for example: "Every course is worthwhile." "I learn something from any instructor." "The most important factors in the quality of my education are my own choices."

Other attitudes will render your investment worthless, for instance: "This required class is a total waste of time." "You can't learn anything from some instructors." "Success depends on luck more than anything else." "I've never been good at school."

Changing attitudes starts with detecting them. One clue to the presence of a negative attitude is sadness, anger, or fear. Our

I am willing to change!

Be inquisitive, intuitive, optimistic.

Attitude
REPLACEMENTS

You can use affirmations to replace a negative attitude with a positive one. There are no limitations, other than your imagination and your willingness to practice. Here are some sample affirmations. Modify them to suit your individual hopes and dreams, and then practice them.

I, _____, have abundant energy and vitality throughout the day.

I, _____, exercise regularly.

I, _____, work effectively with many different kinds of people.

I, _____, eat wisely.

I, _____, plan my days and use time wisely.

I, _____, have a powerful memory.

I, _____, take tests calmly and confidently.

I, _____, fall asleep quickly and sleep soundly.

I, _____, have relationships that are mutually satisfying.

I, _____, contribute to other people through my job.

I, _____, know ways to play and have fun.

I, _____, focus my attention easily.

I, _____, like myself.

I, _____, have an income that far exceeds my expenses.

I, _____, live my life in positive ways for the highest good of all people.

For more ideas, review "Master student qualities," on page 3. You can turn any of those qualities into an affirmation.

You're One Click Away... *from finding an online version of these affirmations.*

attitudes and emotions are closely connected. If you feel a negative emotion, then there's probably a negative attitude hiding behind it. Chances are also good that those attitudes lean heavily on words such as *must, should,* and *have to*: "Other people must always behave the way I want them to." "Things should always turn out well." "I have to be in control at all times."

One way to change such attitudes is to change your language. Practice dropping *must, should,* and *have to*. Also stop behaving on the basis of those thoughts. Over time and with repeated practice, your attitudes will change.

You can also change your attitudes through regular practice with affirmations and visualizations.

Affirm it. An affirmation is a statement describing what you want. The most effective affirmations are personal, positive, and written in the present tense.

To use affirmations, first determine what you want, then describe yourself as if you already have it. To get what you want from your education, you could write, "I, Malika Jones, am a master student. I take full responsibility for my education. I learn with joy, and I use my experiences in each course to create the life that I want."

If you decide that you want a wonderful job, you might write, "I, Peter Webster, have a wonderful job. I respect and love my colleagues, and they feel the same way about me. I look forward to going to work each day."

Effective affirmations include detail. Use brand names, people's names, and your own name. Involve all of your senses—sight, sound, smell, taste, touch. Take a positive approach. Instead of saying, "I am not fat," say, "I am slender."

Once you have written an affirmation, repeat it. Practice saying it out loud several times a day. Do this at a regular time, such as just before you go to sleep or just after you wake up. Sit in a chair in a relaxed position. Take a few deep and relaxing breaths, and then repeat your affirmation with emotion. It's also effective to look in a mirror while saying the affirmation. Keep looking and repeating until you are saying your affirmation with conviction.

Visualize it. You can improve your golf swing, tennis serve, or batting average while lying in bed. You can become a better driver, speaker, or cook while sitting silently in a chair. In line at the grocery store, you can improve your ability to type or to take tests. This is all possible through visualization—the technique of seeing yourself being successful.

Here's one way to begin. Choose what you want to improve. Then describe in writing what it would look like, sound like, and feel like to have that improvement in your life. If you are learning to play the piano, write down briefly what you would see,

I am responsible!

hear, and feel if you were playing skillfully. If you want to improve your relationships with your children, write down what you would see, hear, and feel if you were communicating with them successfully.

Once you have a sketch of what it would be like to be successful, practice it in your imagination. Then wait for the results to unfold in your life. Whenever you toss the basketball, it swishes through the net. Every time you invite someone out on a date, the person says "yes." Each test the teacher hands back to you is graded an "A." Practice at least once a day. Then wait for the results to unfold in your life.

You can also use visualizations to replay errors. When you make a mistake, replay it in your imagination. After a bad golf shot, stop and imagine yourself making that same shot again, this time very successfully. If you just had a discussion with your roommate that turned into a fight, replay it successfully.

Visualizations and affirmations can alter your attitudes and behaviors. Reinforce them by writing them down and posting them in prominent places, such as your refrigerator and bathroom mirror. Also surround yourself with positive people—those who support and demonstrate your values and goals.

Be clear about what you want, and then practice it. ■

Visualizations and affirmations can alter your attitudes and behaviors. Reinforce them by writing them down and posting them in prominent places, such as your refrigerator and bathroom mirror. Also surround yourself with positive people— those who support and demonstrate your values and goals.

✔ EXERCISE 4

Reprogram your attitude

Use this exercise to change your approach to any situation.

Step 1

Pick something in your life that you would like to change. It can be related to anything—relationships, work, money, or personal skills. Write a brief description here of what you choose to change.

_____

_____

_____

_____

Step 2

Add more details about the change you described in Step 1. Write down how you would like the change to come about. Be outlandish. Imagine that you are about to ask your fairy godmother for a wish that you know she will grant. Be detailed in your description of your wish.

_____

_____

_____

_____

_____

_____

Step 3

Use affirmations and visualizations to start yourself on the path to creating exactly what you wrote about in Step 2. Write down here at least two affirmations

that describe your dream wish. Also, briefly outline a visualization that you can use to picture your wish. Be specific, detailed, and positive.

_____

_____

_____

_____

_____

_____

_____

Step 4

Put your new attitudes to work. Set up a schedule to practice them. Let the first time you practice be right now. Then set up at least five other times and places where you intend to practice your affirmations and visualizations.

I intend to relax and practice my affirmations and visualizations for at least 5 minutes on the following dates and at the time(s) and location(s) given.

	Date	Time	Location
1.			
2.			
3.			
4.			
5.			

You're One Click Away...
from completing this exercise online under Exercises.

Jason Stitt/Shutterstock.com

Ways to change a habit

Consider a new way to think about the word *habit*. Imagine for a moment that many of our most troublesome problems and even our most basic traits are just habits.

The expanding waistline that your friend is blaming on her spouse's cooking—maybe that's just a habit called overeating.

The fit of rage that a student blames on a teacher—maybe that's just the student's habit of closing the door to new ideas.

Procrastination, stress, and money shortages might just be names that we give to collections of habits—scores of simple, small, repeated behaviors that combine to create a huge result. The same goes for health, wealth, love, and many of the other things that we want from life.

One way of thinking about success or failure is to focus on habits. Behaviors such as failing to complete reading assignments or skipping class might be habits leading to outcomes that "could not" be avoided, including dropping out of school. In the same way, behaviors such as completing assignments and attending class might lead to the outcome of getting an "A."

When you confront a behavior that undermines your goals or creates a circumstance that you don't want, consider a new attitude: That behavior is just a habit. And it can be changed.

Thinking about ourselves as creatures of habit actually gives us power. Then we are not faced with the monumental task of changing our very nature. Rather, we can take on the doable job of changing our habits. One change in behavior that seems insignificant at first can have effects that ripple throughout your life.

After interviewing hundreds of people, psychologists James Prochaska, John Norcross, and Carlo DiClemente identified stages that people typically go through when adopting a new behavior.[9] These stages take people from *contemplating* a change and making a clear *determination* to change, to taking *action* and *maintaining* the new behavior. Following are ways to help yourself move successfully through each stage as you attempt to change a habit.

TELL THE TRUTH

Telling the truth about any habit—from chewing our fingernails to cheating on tests—frees us. Without taking this step, our efforts to change might be as ineffective as rearranging the deck chairs on the *Titanic*. Telling the truth allows us to see what's actually sinking the ship.

When we admit what's really going on in our lives, our defenses are down. We're open to accepting help from others. The support we need to change a habit has an opportunity to make an impact.

CHOOSE AND COMMIT TO A NEW BEHAVIOR

It often helps to choose a new habit to replace an old one. First, make a commitment to practice the new habit. Tell key people in your life about your decision to change. Set up a plan for when and how. Answer questions such as these: When will I apply the new habit? Where will I be? Who will be with me? What will I be seeing, hearing, touching, saying, or doing? Exactly how will I think, speak, or act differently?

For example, consider the student who always snacks when he studies. Each time he sits down to read, he positions a bag of potato chips within easy reach. For him, opening a book is a cue to start chewing. Snacking is especially easy, given the place he chooses to study: the kitchen. He decides to change this habit by studying at a desk in his bedroom instead of at the kitchen table. And every time he feels the urge to bite into a potato chip, he drinks from a glass of water instead.

Richard Malott, a psychologist who specializes in helping people overcome procrastination, lists three key steps in committing to a new behavior.[10] First, *specify* your goal in numerical terms whenever possible. For example, commit to reading 30 pages per day, Monday through Friday. Second, *observe* your behavior and record the results—in this case, the number of pages that you actually read every day. Finally, set up a small *consequence* for failing to keep your commitment. For instance, pay a friend one quarter for each day that you read less than 30 pages.

AFFIRM YOUR INTENTION

You can pave the way for a new behavior by clearing a mental path for it. Before you apply the new behavior, rehearse it in your mind. Mentally picture what actions you will take and in what order.

Say that you plan to improve your handwriting when taking notes. Imagine yourself in class with a blank notebook poised before you. See yourself taking up a finely crafted pen. Notice how comfortable it feels in your hand. See yourself writing clearly and legibly. You can even picture how you will make individual letters: the *e*'s, *i*'s, and *r*'s. Then, when class is over, see yourself reviewing your notes and taking pleasure in how easy they are to read.

START WITH A SMALL CHANGE

You can sometimes rearrange a whole pattern of behaviors by changing one small habit. If you have a habit of always being late for classes, then be on time for one class. As soon as you change the old pattern by getting ready and going on time to one class, you might find yourself arriving at all of your classes on time. You might even start arriving everywhere else on time too.

The joy of this process is watching one small change of habit ripple through your whole life.

GET FEEDBACK AND SUPPORT

Getting feedback and support is a crucial step in adopting a new behavior. It is also a point at which many plans for change break down. It's easy to practice your new behavior with great enthusiasm for a few days. After the initial rush of excitement, though, things can get a little tougher. You begin to find excuses for slipping back into old habits: "One more cigarette won't hurt." "I can get back to my paper tomorrow." "It's been a tough day. I deserve to skip the rest of my classes."

One way to get feedback is to bring other people into the picture. Ask others to remind you that you are changing your habit if they see you backsliding. If you want to stop an old behavior, such as cramming for tests, then tell everyone about your goal. When you want to start a new behavior, though, consider telling only a few people—those who truly support your efforts.

Starting new habits might call for the more focused, long-lasting support that close friends or family members can give. Support from others can be as simple as a quick phone call: "Hi. Have you started that outline for your research paper yet?" Or it can be as formal as a support group that meets once a week to review everyone's goals and action plans.

One effective source of feedback is yourself. You know yourself better than anyone else does and can design a system to monitor your behavior. Create your own charts to track your behavior,

or write about your progress in your journal. Figure out a way to monitor your progress.

Jerry Seinfeld told one aspiring comedian that "the way to be a better comic was to create better jokes, and the way to create better jokes was to write every day."[11] Seinfeld also revealed his own system for creating a writing habit: He bought a big wall calendar that displayed the whole year on one page. On each day that he wrote jokes, Seinfeld marked a big red "X" on the appropriate day on the wall calendar. He knew that he'd established a new habit when he looked at the calendar and saw an unbroken chain of "X's." You can use the same strategy to take a series of small steps that add up to a big change.

PRACTICE, PRACTICE, PRACTICE— WITHOUT SELF-JUDGMENT

Psychologists such as B. F. Skinner define learning as a stable change in behavior that comes as a result of practice.[12] This widely accepted idea is key to changing habits. Act on your intention over and over again. If you fail or forget, let go of any self-judgment. Just keep practicing the new habit. Allow whatever time it takes to make a change.

Accept the feelings of discomfort that might come with a new habit. Keep practicing the new behavior, even if it feels unnatural. Trust the process. Grow into the new behavior. However, if this new habit doesn't work, simply note what happened (without guilt or blame), select a new behavior, and begin this cycle of steps over again.

Making mistakes as you practice doesn't mean that you've failed. Even when you don't get the results you want from a new behavior, you learn something valuable in the process. Once you understand ways to change one habit, you understand ways to change almost any habit. ■

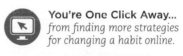

You're One Click Away...
from finding more strategies for changing a habit online.

CLASSROOM CIVILITY—
what's in it for you

This topic might seem like common sense, yet some students forget that simple behaviors create a sense of safety, mutual respect, and community.

Consider an example: A student arrives 15 minutes late to a lecture and lets the door slam behind her. She pulls a fast-food burger out of a crackling paper bag. Then her cell phone rings at full volume—and she answers it. Behaviors like these send a message to everyone in the room: "I'm ignoring you."

Without civility, you lose. Even a small problem with classroom civility can create a barrier for everyone. Learning gets interrupted. Trust breaks down. Your tuition dollars go down the drain. You deserve to enter classrooms that are free of discipline problems and bullies. Many schools have formal policies about classroom civility. Find out what policies apply to you. The consequences for violating them can be serious and may include dismissal or legal action.

With civility, you win. When you treat instructors with respect, you're more likely to be treated that way in return. A respectful relationship with an instructor could turn into a favorable reference letter, a mentorship, a job referral, or a friendship that lasts for years after you graduate. Politeness pays.

Classroom civility does not mean that you have to be passive or insincere. You can present your opinions with passion and even disagree with an instructor in a way that leaves everyone enriched rather than threatened.

Lack of civility boils down to a group of habits. Like any other habits, these can be changed. The following suggestions reflect common sense, and they make an uncommon difference.

Attend classes regularly and on time. If you know that you're going to miss a class or be late, let your instructor know. Take the initiative to ask your instructor or another student about what you missed.

If you arrive late, do not disrupt class. Close the door quietly and take a seat. When you know that you will have to leave class early, tell your instructor before class begins, and sit near an exit. If you leave class to use the restroom or handle an emergency, do so quietly.

During class, participate fully. Take notes and join in discussions. Turn off your cell phone or any other electronic device that you don't need for class. Remember that sleeping, texting, or doing work for another class is a waste of your time and money. Instructors notice distracting activities and take them as a sign of your lack of interest and commitment. So do employers.

Before packing up your notebooks and other materials, wait until class has been dismissed. Instructors often give assignments or make a key point at the end of a class period. Be there when it happens.

Communicate respect. When you speak in class, begin by addressing your instructor as *Ms., Mrs., Mr., Dr., Professor,* or whatever the teacher prefers.

Discussions gain value when everyone gets a chance to speak. Show respect for others by not monopolizing class discussions. Refrain from side conversations and profanity. When presenting viewpoints that conflict with those of classmates or your instructor, combine the passion for your opinion with respect for the opinions of others. Similarly, if you disagree with a class requirement or grade you received, then talk to your instructor about it after class in a respectful way. In a private setting, your ideas will get more attention.

Respect gets communicated in small details. Don't make distracting noises. Cover your mouth if you yawn or cough. Avoid wearing inappropriate clothing. And even if you meet your future spouse in class, refrain from public displays of affection.

Embrace diversity. Master students—and teachers—come in endless variety. They are old and young, male and female. They come from every culture, race, and ethnic group. Part of civility is staying open to the value that other people have to offer. For more ideas, see Chapter 9.

See civility as a contribution. Every class you enter has the potential to become a community of people who talk openly, listen fully, share laughter, and arrive at life-changing insights. These are master student qualities. Every time you demonstrate them, you make a contribution to your community. ■

First Steps

 Use this **Master Student Map** to ask yourself,

 WHY THIS CHAPTER MATTERS . . .

- Success starts with telling the truth about what *is* working—and what *isn't*—in our lives right now.

WHAT IS INCLUDED . . .

- Power Process: Ideas are tools   32
- First Step: Truth is a key to mastery   33
- The Discovery Wheel   36
- Learning styles: Discovering how you learn   41
- Learning Style Inventory   LSI-1
- Using your learning style profile to succeed   43
- Claim your multiple intelligences   47
- Learning by seeing, hearing, and moving: The VAK system   50
- Connect to resources   54
- Extracurricular activities: Reap the benefits   55
- Make the career connection   56
- Master Student Profile: Lalita Booth   59

 HOW CAN I USE THIS CHAPTER . . .

- Experience the power of telling the truth about your current skills.
- Discover your preferred learning styles and develop new ones.
- Choose learning strategies that promote your success.

 WHAT IF . . .

- I could start to create new outcomes in my life by accepting the way I am right now?

JOURNAL ENTRY 2
Intention Statement

Create value from this chapter

Skim this chapter for three techniques that you'd like to use in school or in your personal life during the upcoming week. List each technique and a related page number here.

I intend to use . . .

_____

_____

_____

_____

_____

_____

_____

_____

_____

_____

_____

_____

© Ruslan Ivantsov/Shutterstock.com

POWER process

Ideas are tools

There are many ideas in this book. When you first encounter them, don't believe any of them. Instead, think of the ideas as tools.

For example, you use a hammer for a purpose—to drive a nail. You don't try to figure out whether the hammer is "right." You just use it. If it works, you use it again. If it doesn't work, you get a different hammer.

People have plenty of room in their lives for different kinds of hammers, but they tend to limit their openness to different kinds of ideas. A new idea, at some level, is a threat to their very being—unlike a new hammer, which is simply a new hammer.

Most of us have a built-in desire to be right. Our ideas, we often think, represent ourselves.

Some ideas are worth dying for. But please note: This book does not contain any of those ideas. The ideas on these pages are strictly "hammers."

Imagine someone defending a hammer. Picture this person holding up a hammer and declaring, "I hold this hammer to be self-evident. Give me this hammer or give me death. Those other hammers are flawed. There are only two kinds of people in this world: people who believe in this hammer and people who don't."

That ridiculous picture makes a point. This book is not a manifesto. It's a toolbox, and tools are meant to be used.

If you read about a tool in this book that doesn't sound "right" or one that sounds a little goofy, remember that the ideas here are for using, not necessarily for believing. Suspend your judgment. Test the idea for yourself. If it works, use it. If it doesn't, don't use it.

Any tool—whether it's a hammer, a computer program, or a study technique based on your knowledge of learning styles—is designed to do a specific job. A master mechanic carries a variety of tools, because no single tool works for all jobs. If you throw a tool away because it doesn't work in one situation, you won't be able to pull it out later when it's just what you need. So if an idea doesn't work for you and you are satisfied that you gave it a fair chance, don't throw it away. File it away instead. The idea might come in handy soon.

And remember, this book is not about figuring out the "right" way. Even the "ideas are tools" approach is not "right."

It's a hammer . . . (or maybe a saw).

You're One Click Away...
from accessing the Power Process Media online and finding out more about how "ideas are tools."

First Step: Truth is a
key to mastery

The First Step technique is simple: Tell the truth about who you are and what you want.

End of discussion. Now, proceed to Chapter 2.

Well . . . it's not *quite* that simple.

The First Step is one of the most valuable tools in this book. It magnifies the power of all the other techniques. It is a key to becoming a master student.

To succeed in school, tell the truth about what kind of student you are and what kind of student you want to become. Success starts with telling the truth about what *is* working—and what is *not* working—in our lives right now. When we acknowledge our strengths, we gain an accurate picture of what we can accomplish. When we admit that we have a problem, we are free to find a solution. Ignoring the truth, on the other hand, can lead to problems that stick around for decades.

FIRST STEPS ARE UNIVERSAL

An article about telling the truth might sound like pie-in-the-sky moralizing. However, there is nothing pie-in-the-sky or moralizing about a First Step. It is a practical, down-to-earth principle to use whenever we want to change our behavior.

When you see a doctor, the First Step is to tell the truth about your current symptoms. That way you can get an accurate diagnosis and effective treatment plan. This principle is universal. It works for just about any problem in any area of life.

First Steps are used by millions of people who want to turn their lives around. No technique in this book has been field-tested more often or more successfully—or under tougher circumstances.

For example, members of Alcoholics Anonymous start by telling the truth about their drinking. Their First Step is to admit that they are powerless over alcohol. That's when their lives start to change.

When people join Weight Watchers, their First Step is telling the truth about how much they currently weigh.

When people go for credit counseling, their First Step is telling the truth about how much money they earn, how much they spend, and how much they owe.

People dealing with a variety of other challenges—including troubled relationships with food, drugs, sex, and work—also start by telling the truth. They use First Steps to change their behavior, and they do it for a reason: First Steps work.

FIRST STEPS ARE CHALLENGING—AND REWARDING

Let's be truthful: It's not easy to tell the truth about ourselves.

It's not fun to admit our weaknesses. Many of us approach a frank evaluation of ourselves about as enthusiastically as we'd greet a phone call from the bank about an overdrawn account. We might end up admitting that we're afraid of algebra, that we don't complete term papers on time, or that coming up with the money to pay for tuition is a constant challenge.

There is another way to think about self-evaluations. If we could see them as opportunities to solve problems and take charge of our lives, we might welcome them. Believe it or not, we can begin working with our list of weaknesses by celebrating them.

Consider the most accomplished, "together" people you know. If they were totally candid with you, they would talk about their mistakes and regrets as well as their rewards and recognition. The most successful people tend to be the most willing to look at their flaws.

It may seem natural to judge our own shortcomings and feel bad about them. Some people believe that such feelings are necessary to correct their errors. Others think that a healthy dose of shame can prevent the moral decay of our society.

Think again. In fact, consider the opposite idea: We can gain skill without feeling rotten about the past. We can change the way things *are* without having to criticize the way things *have been*. We can learn to see shame or blame as excess baggage and just set them aside.

If the whole idea of telling the truth about yourself puts a knot in your stomach, that's good. Notice the knot. It is your friend. It is a reminder that First Steps call for courage and compassion. These are qualities of a master student.

FIRST STEPS FREE US TO CHANGE

Master students get the most value from a First Step by turning their perceived shortcomings into goals. "I don't exercise enough" turns into "I will walk briskly for 30 minutes at least three times per week."

"I don't take clear notes" turns into "I will review my notes within 24 hours after class and rewrite them for clarity."

"I am in conflict with my parents" turns into "When my parents call, I will take time to understand their point of view before disagreeing with them."

"I get so nervous during the night before a big test that I find it hard to sleep" turns into "I will find ways to reduce stress during the 24 hours before a test so that I sleep better."

Another quality of master students is that they refuse to let their First Steps turn into excuses. These students avoid using the phrase "I can't" and its endless variations.

The key is to state First Steps in a way that allows for new possibilities in the future. Use language in a way that reinforces your freedom to change.

For example, "I can't succeed in math" is better stated like this: "During math courses, I tend to get confused early in the term and find it hard to ask questions. I could be more assertive in asking for help right away."

"I can't say no to my underage friends who like to drink until they get drunk" is better stated as: "I have friends who drink illegally and drink too much. I want to be alcohol-free and still be friends with them."

Telling the truth about what we don't want gives us more clarity about what we *do* want. By taking a First Step, we can free up all the energy that it takes to deny our problems and avoid change. We can redirect that energy and use it to take actions that align with our values.

FIRST STEPS INCLUDE STRENGTHS

For some of us, it's even harder to recognize our strengths than to recognize our weaknesses. Maybe we don't want to brag. Maybe we're attached to a poor self-image.

The reasons don't matter. The point is that using the First Step technique in *Becoming a Master Student* means telling the truth about our positive qualities, too.

Remember that weaknesses are often strengths taken to an extreme. The student who carefully revises her writing can make significant improvements in a term paper. If she revises too much and hands in the paper late, though, her grade might suffer. Any success strategy carried too far can backfire.

FIRST STEPS ARE SPECIFIC

Whether written or verbal, the ways that we express our First Steps are more powerful when they are specific.

For example, if you want to improve your note-taking skills, you might write, "I am an awful note taker"; but it would be more effective to write, "I can't read 80 percent of the notes I took in Introduction to Psychology last week, and I have no idea what was important in that class."

Be just as specific about what you plan to achieve. You might declare, "I want to take legible notes that help me predict what questions will be on the final exam."

The exercises and Journal Entries in this chapter are all about getting specific. They can help you tap resources you never knew you had. For example, do the Discovery Wheel to get a big-picture view of your personal effectiveness. And use the Learning Styles Inventory, along with the articles about multiple intelligences and the VAK system, to tell the truth about how you perceive and process information.

As you use these elements of *Becoming a Master Student*, you might feel surprised at what you discover. You might even disagree with the results of an exercise. That's fine. Just tell the truth about it. Use your disagreement as a tool for further discussion and self-discovery.

This book is full of First Steps. It's just that simple. The truth has power. ■

✓ EXERCISE 5

Taking the First Step

The purpose of this exercise is to give you a chance to discover and acknowledge your own strengths, as well as areas for improvement. For many students, this exercise is the most difficult one in the book. To make the exercise worthwhile, do it with courage.

Some people suggest that looking at areas for improvement means focusing on personal weaknesses. They view it as a negative approach that runs counter to positive thinking. Well, perhaps. Positive thinking is a great technique. So is telling the truth, especially when we see the whole picture—the negative aspects as well as the positive ones.

If you admit that you can't add or subtract and that's the truth, then you have taken a strong, positive First Step toward learning basic math. On the other hand, if you say that you are a terrible math student and that's not the truth, then you are programming yourself to accept unnecessary failure.

The point is to tell the truth. This exercise is similar to the Discovery Statements that appear throughout the chapters. The difference is that, in this case, for reasons of confidentiality, you won't write down your discoveries in the book.

You are likely to disclose some things about yourself that you wouldn't want others to read. You might even write down some truths that could get you into trouble. Do this exercise on separate sheets of paper; then hide or destroy them. Protect your privacy. To make this exercise work, follow these suggestions.

Be specific. It is not effective to write, "I can improve my communication skills." Of course you can. Instead, write down precisely what you can *do* to improve your communication skills—for example, "I can spend more time really listening while the other person is talking, instead of thinking about what I'm going to say next."

Be self-aware. Look beyond the classroom. What goes on outside school often has the greatest impact on your ability to be an effective student. Consider your strengths and weaknesses that you may think have nothing to do with school.

Be courageous. This exercise calls for an important master student quality—courage. It is a waste of time if this exercise is done half-heartedly. Be willing to take risks. You might open a door that reveals a part of yourself that you didn't want to admit was there. The power of this technique is that once you know what is there, you can do something about it.

Part 1

Time yourself, and for 10 minutes write as fast as you can, completing each of the following sentences at least 10 times with anything that comes to mind. If you get stuck, don't stop. Just write something—even if it seems crazy.

> I never succeed when I . . .
>
> I'm not very good at . . .
>
> Something I'd like to change about myself is . . .

Part 2

When you have completed the first part of the exercise, review what you have written, crossing off things that don't make any sense. The sentences that remain suggest possible goals for becoming a master student.

Part 3

Here's the tough part. Time yourself, and for 10 minutes write as fast as you can, completing the following sentences with anything that comes to mind. As in Part 1, complete each sentence at least 10 times. Just keep writing, even if it sounds silly.

> I always succeed when I . . .
>
> I am very good at . . .
>
> Something I like about myself is . . .

Part 4

Review what you have written, and circle the things that you can fully celebrate. This list is a good thing to keep for those times when you question your own value and worth.

You're One Click Away...
from completing this exercise online under Exercises.

✓ EXERCISE 6
THE DISCOVERY WHEEL

The Discovery Wheel is another opportunity to tell the truth about the kind of student you are and the kind of student you want to become. Like many other students, you might find the Discovery Wheel to be the most valuable exercise in the book.

This is not a test. There are no trick questions, and the answers will have meaning only for yourself.

Here are two suggestions to make this exercise more effective. First, think of it as the beginning of an opportunity to change. There is another Discovery Wheel at the end of this book. You will have a chance to measure your progress there, so be honest about where you are now. Second, lighten up. A little laughter can make self-evaluations a lot more effective.

Here's how the Discovery Wheel works. By the end of this exercise, you will have filled in a circle similar to the one on this page. The Discovery Wheel circle is a picture of how you see yourself as a student. The closer the shading comes to the outer edge of the circle, the higher the evaluation of a specific skill. In the example below, the student has rated her reading skills low and her note-taking skills high.

The terms *high* and *low* are not meant to reflect judgment. The Discovery Wheel is not a permanent picture of who you are. It is a picture of how you view your strengths and weaknesses as a student today. To begin this exercise, read the statements beginning on the next page and award yourself points for each one, using the point system described below. Then add up your point total for each section, and shade the Discovery Wheel on page 39 to the appropriate level.

5 points: This statement is always or almost always true of me.

4 points: This statement is often true of me.

3 points: This statement is true of me about half the time.

2 points: This statement is seldom true of me.

1 point: This statement is never or almost never true of me.

1. _____ I enjoy learning.

2. _____ I understand and apply the concept of multiple intelligences.

3. _____ I connect my courses to my purpose for being in school.

4. _____ I make a habit of assessing my personal strengths and areas for improvement.

5. _____ I am satisfied with how I am progressing toward achieving my goals.

6. _____ I use my knowledge of learning styles to support my success in school.

7. _____ I am willing to consider any idea that can help me succeed in school—even if I initially disagree with that idea.

8. _____ I regularly remind myself of the benefits I intend to get from my education.

_____ **Total score (1) Attitude**

1. _____ I set long-term goals and periodically review them.

2. _____ I set short-term goals to support my long-term goals.

3. _____ I write a plan for each day and each week.

4. _____ I assign priorities to what I choose to do each day.

5. _____ I plan review time so I don't have to cram before tests.

6. _____ I plan regular recreation time.

7. _____ I adjust my study time to meet the demands of individual courses.

8. _____ I have adequate time each day to accomplish what I plan.

_____ **Total score (2) Time**

1. _____ I am confident of my ability to remember.

2. _____ I can remember people's names.

3. _____ At the end of a lecture, I can summarize what was presented.

4. _____ I apply techniques that enhance my memory skills.

5. _____ I can recall information when I'm under pressure.

6. _____ I remember important information clearly and easily.

7. _____ I can jog my memory when I have difficulty recalling.

8. _____ I can relate new information to what I've already learned.

_____ **Total score (3) Memory**

1. _____ I preview and review reading assignments.

2. _____ When reading, I ask myself questions about the material.

3. _____ I underline or highlight important passages when reading.

4. _____ When I read textbooks, I am alert and awake.

5. _____ I relate what I read to my life.

6. _____ I select a reading strategy to fit the type of material I'm reading.

7. _____ I take effective notes when I read.

8. _____ When I don't understand what I'm reading, I note my questions and find answers.

_____ **Total score (4) Reading**

1. _____ When I am in class, I focus my attention.

2. _____ I take notes in class.

3. _____ I am aware of various methods for taking notes and choose those that work best for me.

4. _____ I distinguish important material and note key phrases in a lecture.

5. _____ I copy down material that the instructor writes on the board or overhead display.

6. _____ I can put important concepts into my own words.

7. _____ My notes are valuable for review.

8. _____ I review class notes within 24 hours.

_____ **Total score (5) Notes**

1. _____ I use techniques to manage stress related to exams.

2. _____ I manage my time during exams and am able to complete them.

3. _____ I am able to predict test questions.

4. _____ I adapt my test-taking strategy to the kind of test I'm taking.

5. _____ I understand what essay questions ask and can answer them completely and accurately.

6. _____ I start reviewing for tests at the beginning of the term.

7. _____ I continue reviewing for tests throughout the term.

8. _____ My sense of personal worth is independent of my test scores.

_____ **Total score (6) Tests**

1. _____ I have flashes of insight and think of solutions to problems at unusual times.

2. _____ I use brainstorming to generate solutions to a variety of problems.

3. _____ When I get stuck on a creative project, I use specific methods to get unstuck.

4. _____ I learn by thinking about ways to contribute to the lives of other people.

5. _____ I am willing to consider different points of view and alternative solutions.

6. _____ I can detect common errors in logic.

7. _____ I construct viewpoints by drawing on information and ideas from many sources.

8. _____ As I share my viewpoints with others, I am open to their feedback.

_____ **Total score (7) Thinking**

1. _____ I am honest with others about who I am, what I feel, and what I want.

2. _____ Other people tell me that I am a good listener.

3. _____ I can communicate my upset and anger without blaming others.

4. _____ I can make friends and create valuable relationships in a new setting.

5. _____ I am open to being with people I don't especially like in order to learn from them.

6. _____ I can effectively plan and research a large writing assignment.

7. _____ I create first drafts without criticizing my writing, then edit later for clarity, accuracy, and coherence.

8. _____ I know ways to prepare and deliver effective speeches.

_____ **Total score (8) Communicating**

1. _____ I build rewarding relationships with people from diverse backgrounds.

2. _____ I use critical thinking to overcome stereotypes.

3. _____ I point out examples of discrimination and sexual harassment and effectively respond to them.

4. _____ I am constantly learning ways to thrive with diversity.

5. _____ I can effectively resolve conflict with people from other cultures.

6. _____ My writing and speaking are free of sexist expressions.

7. _____ I take diversity into account when assuming a leadership role.

8. _____ I respond effectively to changing demographics in my country and community.

_____ **Total score (9) Diversity**

1. _____ I am in control of my personal finances.

2. _____ I can access a variety of resources to finance my education.

3. _____ I am confident that I will have enough money to complete my education.

4. _____ I take on debts carefully and repay them on time.

5. _____ I have long-range financial goals and a plan to meet them.

6. _____ I make regular deposits to a savings account.

7. _____ I pay off the balance on credit card accounts each month.

8. _____ I can have fun without spending money.

_____ **Total score (10) Money**

1. _____ I have enough energy to study and work—and still enjoy other areas of my life.

2. _____ If the situation calls for it, I have enough reserve energy to put in a long day.

3. _____ The way I eat supports my long-term health.

4. _____ The way I eat is independent of my feelings of self-worth.

5. _____ I exercise regularly to maintain a healthful weight.

6. _____ My emotional health supports my ability to learn.

7. _____ I notice changes in my physical condition and respond effectively.

8. _____ I am in control of any alcohol or other drugs I put into my body.

_____ **Total score (11) Health**

1. _____ I see learning as a lifelong process.

2. _____ I relate school to what I plan to do for the rest of my life.

3. _____ I see problems and tough choices as opportunities for learning and personal growth.

4. _____ I have a written career plan and update it regularly.

5. _____ I am gaining skills to support my success in the workplace.

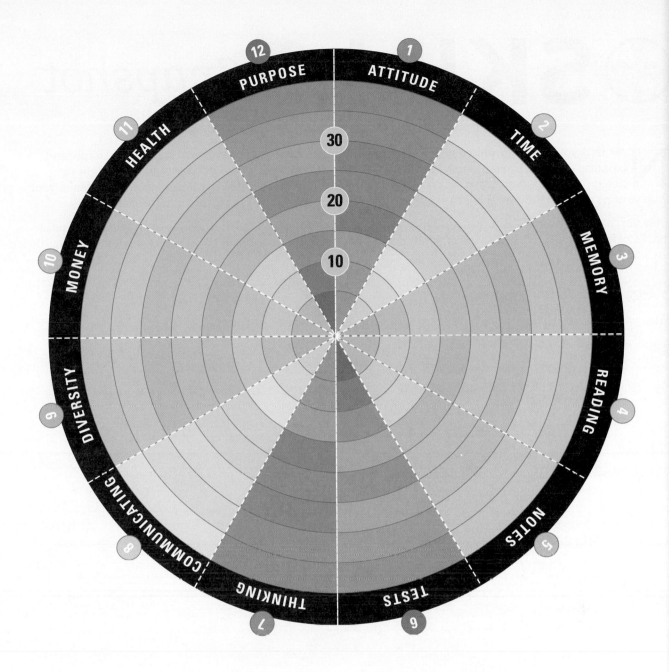

The Discovery Wheel, with the following labeled sections around the perimeter (numbered 1–12):

- 1 ATTITUDE
- 2 TIME
- 3 MEMORY
- 4 READING
- 5 NOTES
- 6 TESTS
- 7 THINKING
- 8 COMMUNICATING
- 9 DIVERSITY
- 10 MONEY
- 11 HEALTH
- 12 PURPOSE

Concentric rings labeled: 10, 20, 30

6. _____ I take responsibility for the quality of my education—and my life.

7. _____ I live by a set of values that translates into daily actions.

8. _____ I am willing to accept challenges even when I'm not sure how to meet them.

_____ **Total score (12) Purpose**

FILLING IN YOUR DISCOVERY WHEEL

Using the total score from each category, shade in each section of the Discovery Wheel. Use different colors, if you want. For example, you could use green to denote areas you want to work on. When you have finished, complete the Skills Snapshot on the next page. ■

You're One Click Away...
from having your Discovery Wheel scores calculated automatically for you online.

⊗SKILLS *Snapshot*

Now that you have completed your Discovery Wheel, it's time to get a sense of its weight, shape, and balance. Can you imagine running your hands around it? If you could lift it, would it feel light or heavy? How would it sound if it rolled down a hill? Would it roll very far? Would it wobble? Make your observations without judging the wheel as good or bad. Simply be with the picture you have created.

After you have spent a few minutes studying your Discovery Wheel, complete the following sentences in the spaces below them. Don't worry about what to write. Just put down whatever comes to mind. Remember, this is not a test.

OVERVIEW

This wheel is an accurate picture of my ability as a student because . . .

My self-evaluation surprises me because . . .

STRENGTHS

One area where I show strong skills is . . .

Another area of strength is . . .

GOALS

The area in which I most want to improve is . . .

It is also important for me to get better at . . .

I want to concentrate on improving these areas because . . .

To meet my goals for improvement, I intend to . . .

Note: You'll get an opportunity to reflect on your progress when you do the Discovery Wheel exercise again in Chapter 12.

LEARNING STYLES
Discovering how you learn

Right now, you are investing substantial amounts of time, money, and energy in your education. What you get in return for this investment depends on how well you understand the process of learning and use it to your advantage.

If you don't understand learning, you might feel bored or confused in class. After getting a low grade, you might have no idea how to respond. Over time, frustration can mount to the point where you question the value of being in school.

Some students answer that question by dropping out of school. These students lose a chance to create the life they want, and society loses the contributions of educated workers.

You can prevent that outcome. Gain strategies for going beyond boredom and confusion. Discover new options for achieving goals, solving problems, listening more fully, speaking more persuasively, and resolving conflicts between people. Start by understanding the different ways that people create meaning from their experience and change their behavior. In other words, learn about *how* we learn.

WE LEARN BY PERCEIVING AND PROCESSING

When we learn well, says psychologist David Kolb, two things happen.[1] First, we *perceive*. That is, we notice events and "take in" new experiences.

Second, we *process*. We "deal with" experiences in a way that helps us make sense of them.

Some people especially prefer to perceive through *feeling* (also called *concrete experience*). They like to absorb information through their five senses. They learn by getting directly involved in new experiences. When solving problems, they rely on intuition as much as intellect. These people typically function well in unstructured classes that allow them to take initiative.

Some people prefer to process by *watching* (also called *reflective observation*). They prefer to stand back, watch what is going on, and think about it. They consider several points of view as they attempt to make sense of things and generate many ideas about how something happens. They value patience, good judgment, and a thorough approach to learning.

Other people like to perceive by *thinking* (also called *abstract conceptualization*). They take in information best when they can think about it as a subject separate from themselves. They analyze, intellectualize, and create theories. Often these people take a scientific approach to problem solving and excel in traditional classrooms.

Other people like to process by *doing* (also called *active experimentation*). They prefer to jump in and start doing things immediately. These people do not mind taking risks as they attempt to make sense of things; this helps them learn. They are results oriented and look for practical ways to apply what they have learned.

PERCEIVING AND PROCESSING—AN EXAMPLE

Suppose that you get a new cell phone. It has more features than any phone you've used before. You have many options for learning how to use it. For example:

- Just get your hands on the phone right away, press some buttons, and see whether you can dial a number or send a text message.

- Recall experiences you've had with phones in the past and what you've learned by watching other people use their cell phones.

- Read the instruction manual and view help screens on the phone before you try to make a call.

- Ask a friend who owns the same type of phone to coach you as you experiment with making calls and sending messages.

These actions illustrate the different approaches to learning:

- Getting your hands on the phone right away and seeing whether you can make it work is an example of learning through *feeling* (or *concrete experience*).

- Recalling what you've experienced in the past is an example of learning through *watching* (or *reflective observation*).

- Reading the manual and help screens before you use the phone is an example of learning through *thinking* (or *abstract conceptualization*).

- Asking a friend to coach you through a "hands-on" activity with the phone is an example of learning through *doing* (or *active experimentation*).

In summary, your learning style is the unique way that you blend feeling, thinking, watching, and doing. You tend to use this approach in learning anything—from cell phones to English composition to calculus. Reading the next few pages and doing the recommended activities will help you explore your learning style in more detail. ■

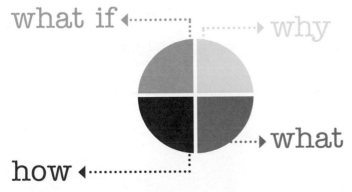

Prepare for the Learning Style Inventory (LSI)

As a "warm-up" for the Learning Style Inventory that follows, think about times when you felt successful at learning. Underline or highlight any of the following statements that describe those situations.

- I was in a structured setting, with a lot of directions about what to do.
- I was free to learn at my own pace and in my own way.
- I learned as part of a small group.
- I learned mainly by working alone in a quiet place.
- I learned in a place where there was a lot of activity going on.
- I formed pictures in my mind.
- I learned by *doing* something—moving around, touching something, or trying out a process for myself.
- I learned by talking to myself or explaining ideas to other people.
- I got the "big picture" before I tried to understand the details.
- I listened to a lecture and then thought about it after class.
- I read a book or article and then thought about it afterward.
- I used a variety of media—such as videos, films, audio recordings, or computers—to assist my learning.
- I was considering where to attend school and had to actually set foot on each campus before choosing.
- I was shopping for a car and paid more attention to how I felt about test-driving each one than to the sticker prices or mileage estimates.
- I was thinking about going to a movie and carefully read the reviews before choosing one.

Reviewing this list, do you see any patterns in the way you prefer to learn? If so, briefly describe them.

Directions for completing the Learning Style Inventory

To help you become more aware of learning styles, a psychologist named David Kolb developed the Learning Style Inventory (LSI). This inventory is included on the next page. Responding to the items in the LSI can help you discover a lot about the ways you learn. Following the LSI are suggestions for using your results to promote your success.

The LSI is not a test. There are no right or wrong answers. Your goal is simply to develop a profile of your current learning style. So, take the LSI quickly. You might find it useful to recall a recent time when you learned something new at school, home, or work. However, do not agonize over your responses.

Note that the LSI consists of 12 sentences, each with four different endings. You will read each sentence, and then write a "4" next to the ending that best describes the way you currently learn. Then you will continue ranking the other endings with a "3," "2," or "1," representing the ending that least describes you. This is a forced-choice inventory, so you must rank each ending. Do not leave any endings blank. Use each number only once for each question.

Following are more specific directions:

1. Before you write on page LSI–1, remove the sheet of paper following page LSI–2.
2. Read the instructions at the top of page LSI–1. When you understand example A, you are ready to begin.
3. While writing on page LSI–1, *press firmly* so that your answers will show up on page LSI–3.

Using your
LEARNING STYLE PROFILE
to succeed

DEVELOP ALL FOUR MODES OF LEARNING

Each mode of learning highlighted in the Learning Style Inventory represents a unique blend of concrete experience ("feeling"), reflective observation ("watching"), abstract conceptualization ("thinking"), and active experimentation ("doing"). You can explore new learning styles simply by adopting new habits related to each of these activities. Consider the following suggestions as places to start. Also remember that any idea about learning styles will make a difference in your life only when it leads to changes in your behavior.

- Conduct an informational interview with someone in your chosen career or "shadow" that person for a day on the job.
- Look for a part-time job, internship, or volunteer experience that complements what you do in class.
- Deepen your understanding of another culture and extend your foreign language skills by studying abroad.

To become more reflective:
- Keep a personal journal, and write about connections among your courses.

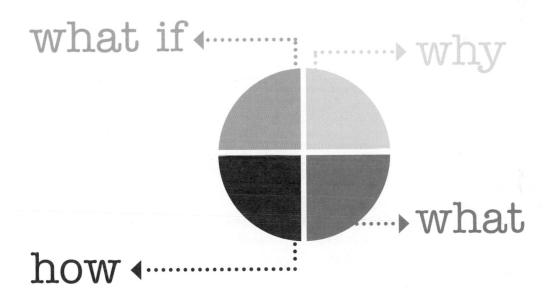

To gain concrete experiences:
- See a live demonstration or performance related to your course content.
- Engage your emotions by reading a novel or seeing a video related to your course.
- Interview an expert in the subject you're learning or a master practitioner of a skill you want to gain.
- Conduct role-plays, exercises, or games based on your courses.

- Form a study group to discuss and debate topics related to your courses.
- Set up a Web site, blog, e-mail listserv, or online chat room related to your major.
- Create analogies to make sense of concepts; for instance, see whether you can find similarities between career planning and putting together a puzzle.
- Visit your course instructor during office hours to ask questions.

- During social events with friends and relatives, briefly explain what your courses are about.

To develop abstract thinking:

- Take notes on your reading in outline form; consider using word-processing software with an outlining feature.

- Supplement assigned texts with other books, magazine and newspaper articles, and related Web sites.

- Attend lectures given by your current instructors and others who teach the same subjects.

- Take ideas presented in text or lectures and translate them into visual form—tables, charts, diagrams, and maps (see Chapter 5: Notes).

- Create visuals and use computer software to recreate them with more complex graphics and animation.

To become more active:

- Conduct laboratory experiments or field observations.

- Go to settings where theories are being applied or tested.

- Make predictions based on theories you learn, and then see whether events in your daily life confirm your predictions.

- Try out a new behavior described in a lecture or reading, and observe its consequences in your life.

LOOK FOR EXAMPLES OF THE MODES IN ACTION

To understand the modes of learning, notice when they occur in your daily life. You are a natural learner, and this means that the modes are often at work. You use them when you solve problems, make choices, and experiment with new ideas.

Suppose that your family asks about your career plans. You've just enrolled for your first semester of classes, and you think it's too early to think about careers. Yet you choose to brainstorm some career options anyway. If nothing else, it might be fun, and you'll have some answers for when people ask you what you're going to do after college. This is an example of Mode 1. You asked, "Why learn about career planning?" and came up with an answer.

During the next meeting of your psychology class, your instructor mentions the career planning center on campus. You visit the center's Web site and discover its list of services. While you're online, you also register for one of the center's workshops because you want more information about writing a career plan. This illustrates Mode 2: You asked, "What career planning options are available?" and discovered several answers.

In this workshop, you learn about the role that internships and extracurricular activities play in career planning. All of these are ways to test an early career choice and discover whether it appeals to you. You enjoy being with children, so you

choose to volunteer at a campus-based child care center. You want to discover how this service learning experience might help you choose a career. This is Mode 3: You asked, "How can I use what I learned in the workshop?" This led you to working with children.

Your experience at the center leads to a work-study assignment there. On the basis of this new experience, you choose to declare a major in early childhood education. This is an example of Mode 4: You asked, "What if this assignment points to a new direction for my future?" The answer led to a new commitment.

USE THE MODES WHILE CHOOSING COURSES

Remember your learning style profile when you're thinking about which classes to take and how to study for each class. Look for a fit between your preferred mode of learning and your course work.

If you prefer Mode 1, for example, then look for courses that sound interesting and seem worthwhile to you. If you prefer Mode 2, then consider classes that center on lectures, reading, and discussion. If you prefer Mode 3, then choose courses that include demonstrations, lab sessions, role-playing, and others ways to take action. And if you prefer Mode 4, then look for courses that could apply to many situations in your life—at work, at home, and in your relationships.

You won't always be able to match your courses to your learning styles. View those situations as opportunities to practice becoming a flexible learner. By developing your skills in all four modes, you can excel in many types of courses.

USE THE MODES TO EXPLORE YOUR MAJOR

If you enjoy learning in Mode 1, you probably value creativity and human relationships. When choosing a major, consider the arts, English, psychology, or political science.

If Mode 2 is your preference, then you enjoy gathering information and building theories. A major related to math or science might be ideal for you.

If Mode 3 is your favorite, then you like to diagnose problems, arrive at solutions, and use technology. A major related to health care, engineering, or economics is a logical choice for you.

And if your preference is Mode 4, you probably enjoy taking the initiative, implementing decisions, teaching, managing projects, and moving quickly from planning into action. Consider a major in business or education.

As you prepare to declare a major, remain flexible. Use your knowledge of learning styles to open up possibilities rather than restrict them. Remember that regardless of your mode, you can excel at any job or major; it just may mean developing new skills in other modes.

USE THE MODES OF LEARNING TO EXPLORE YOUR CAREER

Knowing about learning styles becomes especially useful when planning your career.

People who excel at Mode 1 are often skilled at tuning in to the feelings of clients and coworkers. These people can listen with an open mind, tolerate confusion, be sensitive to people's feelings, open up to problems that are difficult to define, and brainstorm a variety of solutions. If you like Mode 1, you may be drawn to a career in counseling, social services, the ministry, or another field that centers on human relationships. You might also enjoy a career in the performing arts.

People who prefer Mode 2 like to do research and work with ideas. They are skilled at gathering data, interpreting information, and summarizing—arriving at the big picture. They may excel at careers that center on science, math, technical communications, or planning. Mode 2 learners may also work as college teachers, lawyers, technical writers, or journalists.

People who like Mode 3 are drawn to solving problems, making decisions, and checking on progress toward goals. Careers in medicine, engineering, information technology, or another applied science are often ideal for them.

People who enjoy Mode 4 like to influence and lead others. These people are often described as "doers" and "risk takers." They like to take action and complete projects. Mode 4 learners often excel at managing, negotiating, selling, training, and teaching. They might also work for a government agency.

Keep in mind that there is no strict match between certain learning styles and certain careers. Learning is essential to success in all careers. Also, any career can attract people with a variety of learning styles. For instance, the health care field is large enough to include people who prefer Mode 3 and become family physicians—*and* people who prefer Mode 2 and become medical researchers.

> # Keep in mind that there is no strict match between certain learning styles and certain careers. Learning is essential to success in all careers.

EXPECT TO ENCOUNTER DIFFERENT STYLES

As higher education and the workplace become more diverse and technology creates a global marketplace, you'll meet people who differ from you in profound ways. Your fellow students and co-workers will behave in ways that express a variety of preferences for perceiving information, processing ideas, and acting on what they learn. Consider these examples:

- A roommate who's continually moving while studying—reciting facts out loud, pacing, and gesturing—probably prefers concrete experience and learning by taking action.

- A coworker who talks continually on the phone about a project may prefer to learn by listening, talking, and forging key relationships.

- A supervisor who excels at abstract conceptualization may want to see detailed project plans and budgets submitted in writing well before a project swings into high gear.

- A study group member who always takes the initiative, manages the discussion, delegates any work involved, and follows up with everyone probably prefers active experimentation.

Differences in learning style can be a stumbling block—or an opportunity. When differences intersect, there is the potential for conflict as well as for creativity. Succeeding with peers often means seeing the classroom and workplace as a laboratory for learning from experience. Resolving conflict and learning from mistakes are all part of the learning cycle.

LOOK FOR SPECIFIC CLUES TO ANOTHER PERSON'S STYLE

You can learn a lot about other people's styles of learning simply by observing them during the work day. Look for clues such as these:

Approaches to a task that requires learning. Some people process new information and ideas by sitting quietly and reading or writing. When learning to use a piece of equipment, such as a new computer, they'll read the instruction manual first. Others will skip the manual, unpack all the boxes, and start setting up equipment. And others might ask a more experienced colleague to guide them in person, step by step.

Word choice. Some people like to process information visually. You might hear them say, "I'll look into that" or "Give me the big picture first." Others like to solve problems verbally: "Let's talk through this problem" or "I hear you!" In contrast, some people focus on body sensations ("This product feels great") or action ("Let's run with this idea and see what happens").

Body language. Notice how often coworkers or classmates make eye contact with you and how close they sit or stand next to you. Observe their gestures, as well as the volume and tone of their voice.

Content preferences. Notice what subjects coworkers or classmates openly discuss and which topics that they avoid. Some people talk freely about their feelings, their families, and even their personal finances. Others choose to remain silent on such topics and stick to work-related matters.

Process preferences. Look for patterns in the way that your coworkers and classmates meet goals. When attending meetings, for example, some of them might stick closely to the agenda and keep an eye on the clock. Other people might prefer to go with the flow, even if it means working an extra hour or scrapping the agenda.

ACCOMMODATE DIFFERING STYLES

Once you've discovered differences in styles, look for ways to accommodate them. As you collaborate on projects with other students or coworkers, keep the following suggestions in mind:

Remember that some people want to reflect on the big picture first. When introducing a project plan, you might say, "This process has four major steps." Before explaining the plan in detail, talk about the purpose of the project and the benefits of completing each step.

Allow time for active experimentation and concrete experience. Offer people a chance to try out a new product or process for themselves—to literally get the feel of it.

Allow for abstract conceptualization. When leading a study group or conducting a training session, provide handouts that include plenty of visuals and step-by-step instructions. Visual learners and people who like to think abstractly will appreciate it. Also schedule periods for questions and answers.

When planning a project, encourage people to answer key questions. Remember the four essential questions that guide learning. Answering *Why?* means defining the purpose and desired outcomes of the project. Answering *What?* means assigning major tasks, setting due dates for each task, and generating commitment to action. Answering *How?* means carrying out assigned tasks and meeting regularly to discuss things that are working well and ways to improve the project. And answering *What if?* means discussing what the team has learned from the project and ways to apply that learning to the whole class or larger organization.

When working on teams, look for ways that members can complement one another's strengths. If you're skilled at planning, find someone who excels at doing. Also seek people who can reflect on and interpret the team's experience. Pooling different styles allows you to draw on everyone's strengths.

RESOLVE CONFLICT WITH RESPECT FOR STYLES

When people's styles clash in educational or work settings, you have several options. One is to throw up your hands and resign yourself to personality conflicts. Another option is to recognize differences, accept them, and respect them as complementary ways to meet common goals. Taking that perspective allows you to act constructively. You might do one of the following:

Resolve conflict within yourself. You might have mental pictures of classrooms and workplaces as places where people are all supposed to have the same style. Notice if you have those pictures and gently let them go. If you *expect* to find differences in styles, you can more easily respect those differences.

Introduce a conversation about learning styles. Attend a workshop on learning styles. Then bring such training directly to your classroom or office.

Let people take on tasks that fit their learning styles. People gravitate toward the kinds of tasks they've succeeded at in the past, and that's fine. Remember, though, that learning styles are both stable and dynamic. People can also broaden their styles by tackling new tasks to reinforce different modes of learning.

Rephrase complaints as requests. "This class is a waste of my time" can be recast as "Please tell me what I'll gain if I participate actively in class." "The instructor talks too fast" can become "What strategies can I use for taking notes when the instructor covers the material rapidly?"

ACCEPT CHANGE—AND OCCASIONAL DISCOMFORT

Seek out chances to develop new modes of learning. If your instructor asks you to form a group to complete an assignment, avoid joining a group where everyone shares your learning style. Work on project teams with people who learn differently than you. Get together with people who both complement and challenge you.

Also look for situations where you can safely practice new skills. If you enjoy reading, for example, look for ways to express what you learn by speaking, such as leading a study group on a textbook chapter.

Discomfort is a natural part of the learning process. Allow yourself to notice any struggle with a task or lack of interest in completing it. Remember that such feelings are temporary and that you are balancing your learning preferences. By choosing to move through discomfort, you consciously expand your ability to learn in new ways. ■

Claim your
multiple INTELLIGENCES

People often think that being smart means the same thing as having a high IQ, and that having a high IQ automatically leads to success. However, psychologists are finding that IQ scores do not always foretell which students will do well in academic settings—or after they graduate.[2]

Howard Gardner of Harvard University believes that no single measure of intelligence can tell us how smart we are. Instead, Gardner defines intelligence in a flexible way as "the ability to solve problems, or to create products, that are valued within one or more cultural settings." He also identifies several types of intelligence, as described here.[3]

People using **verbal/linguistic intelligence** are adept at language skills and learn best by speaking, writing, reading, and listening. They are likely to enjoy activities such as telling stories and doing crossword puzzles.

People who use **mathematical/logical intelligence** are good with numbers, logic, problem solving, patterns, relationships, and categories. They are generally precise and methodical, and are likely to enjoy science.

When people learn visually and by organizing things spatially, they display **visual/spatial intelligence**. They think in images and pictures, and understand best by seeing the subject. They enjoy charts, graphs, maps, mazes, tables, illustrations, art, models, puzzles, and costumes.

People using **bodily/kinesthetic intelligence** prefer physical activity. They enjoy activities such as building things, woodworking, dancing, skiing, sewing, and crafts. They generally are coordinated and athletic, and they would rather participate in games than just watch.

Individuals using **musical/rhythmic intelligence** enjoy musical expression through songs, rhythms, and musical instruments. They are responsive to various kinds of sounds; remember melodies easily; and might enjoy drumming, humming, and whistling.

People using **intrapersonal intelligence** are exceptionally aware of their own feelings and values. They are generally reserved, self-motivated, and intuitive.

Outgoing people show evidence of **interpersonal intelligence.** They do well with cooperative learning and are sensitive to the feelings, intentions, and motivations of others. They often make good leaders.

People using **naturalist intelligence** love the outdoors and recognize details in plants, animals, rocks, clouds, and other natural formations. These people excel in observing fine distinctions among similar items.

Each of us has all of these intelligences to some degree. And each of us can learn to enhance them. Experiment with learning in ways that draw on a variety of intelligences—including those that might be less familiar. When we acknowledge all of our intelligences, we can constantly explore new ways of being smart. ■

✔ EXERCISE 7

Develop your multiple intelligences

Gardner's theory of multiple intelligences complements the discussion of different learning styles in this chapter. The main point is that there are many ways to gain knowledge and acquire new behaviors. You can use Gardner's concepts to explore a range of options for achieving success in school, work, and relationships.

The chart on the next page summarizes the content of "Claim your multiple intelligences" and suggests ways to apply the main ideas. Instead of merely glancing through this chart, get active. Place a check mark next to any of the "Possible characteristics" that describe you. Also check off the "Possible learning strategies" that you intend to use. Finally, underline or highlight any of the "Possible careers" that spark your interest.

Remember that the chart is not an exhaustive list or a formal inventory. Take what you find merely as points of departure. You can invent strategies of your own to cultivate different intelligences.

Type of intelligence	Possible characteristics	Possible learning strategies	Possible careers
Verbal/linguistic	❏ You enjoy writing letters, stories, and papers. ❏ You prefer to write directions rather than draw maps. ❏ You take excellent notes from textbooks and lectures. ❏ You enjoy reading, telling stories, and listening to them.	❏ Highlight, underline, and write notes in your textbooks. ❏ Recite new ideas in your own words. ❏ Rewrite and edit your class notes. ❏ Talk to other people often about what you're studying.	Librarian, lawyer, editor, journalist, English teacher, radio or television announcer
Mathematical/logical	❏ You enjoy solving puzzles. ❏ You prefer math or science class over English class. ❏ You want to know how and why things work. ❏ You make careful, step-by-step plans.	❏ Analyze tasks so you can order them in a sequence of steps. ❏ Group concepts into categories, and look for underlying patterns. ❏ Convert text into tables, charts, and graphs. ❏ Look for ways to quantify ideas—to express them in numerical terms.	Accountant, auditor, tax preparer, mathematician, computer programmer, actuary, economist, math or science teacher
Visual/spatial	❏ You draw pictures to give an example or clarify an explanation. ❏ You understand maps and illustrations more readily than text. ❏ You assemble things from illustrated instructions. ❏ You especially enjoy books that have a lot of illustrations.	❏ When taking notes, create concept maps, mind maps, and other visuals (see Chapter 5: Notes). ❏ Code your notes by using different colors to highlight main topics, major points, and key details. ❏ When your attention wanders, focus it by sketching or drawing. ❏ Before you try a new task, visualize yourself doing it well.	Architect, commercial artist, fine artist, graphic designer, photographer, interior decorator, engineer, cartographer
Bodily/kinesthetic	❏ You enjoy physical exercise. ❏ You tend not to sit still for long periods of time. ❏ You enjoy working with your hands. ❏ You use a lot of gestures when talking.	❏ Be active in ways that support concentration; for example, pace as you recite, read while standing up, and create flash cards. ❏ Carry materials with you, and practice studying in several different locations. ❏ Create hands-on activities related to key concepts; for example, create a game based on course content. ❏ Notice the sensations involved with learning something well.	Physical education teacher, athlete, athletic coach, physical therapist, chiropractor, massage therapist, yoga teacher, dancer, choreographer, actor

Type of intelligence	Possible characteristics	Possible learning strategies	Possible careers
Musical/rhythmic	❏ You often sing in the car or shower. ❏ You easily tap your foot to the beat of a song. ❏ You play a musical instrument. ❏ You feel most engaged and productive when music is playing.	❏ During a study break, play music or dance to restore energy. ❏ Put on background music that enhances your concentration while studying. ❏ Relate key concepts to songs you know. ❏ Write your own songs based on course content.	Professional musician, music teacher, music therapist, choral director, musical instrument sales representative, musical instrument maker, piano tuner
Intrapersonal	❏ You enjoy writing in a journal and being alone with your thoughts. ❏ You think a lot about what you want in the future. ❏ You prefer to work on individual projects over group projects. ❏ You take time to think things through before talking or taking action.	❏ Connect course content to your personal values and goals. ❏ Study a topic alone before attending a study group. ❏ Connect readings and lectures to a strong feeling or significant past experience. ❏ Keep a journal that relates your course work to events in your daily life.	Minister, priest, rabbi, professor of philosophy or religion, counseling psychologist, creator of a home-based or small business
Interpersonal	❏ You enjoy group work over working alone. ❏ You have plenty of friends and regularly spend time with them. ❏ You prefer talking and listening over reading or writing. ❏ You thrive in positions of leadership.	❏ Form and conduct study groups early in the term. ❏ Create flash cards, and use them to quiz study partners. ❏ Volunteer to give a speech or lead group presentations on course topics. ❏ Teach the topic you're studying to someone else.	Manager, school administrator, salesperson, teacher, counseling psychologist, arbitrator, police officer, nurse, travel agent, public relations specialist, creator of a midsize to large business
Naturalist	❏ As a child, you enjoyed collecting insects, leaves, or other natural objects. ❏ You enjoy being outdoors. ❏ You find that important insights occur during times you spend in nature. ❏ You read books and magazines on nature-related topics.	❏ During study breaks, take walks outside. ❏ Post pictures of outdoor scenes where you study, and play recordings of outdoor sounds while you read. ❏ Invite classmates to discuss course work while taking a hike or going on a camping trip. ❏ Focus on careers that hold the potential for working outdoors.	Environmental activist, park ranger, recreation supervisor, historian, museum curator, biologist, criminologist, mechanic, woodworker, construction worker, construction contractor or estimator

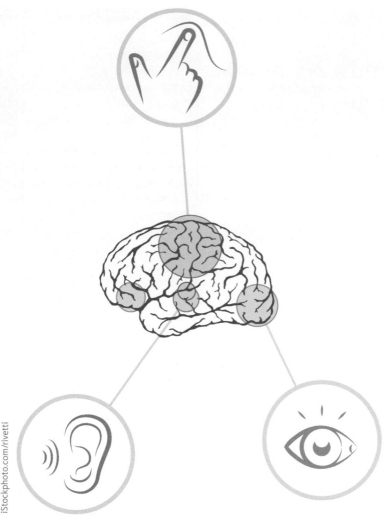

LEARNING
BY SEEING, HEARING, AND MOVING:
the VAK system

Alternatively, you can approach the topic of learning styles with a simple and powerful system—one that focuses on just three ways of perceiving through your senses:

• Seeing, or visual learning

• Hearing, or auditory learning

• Movement, or kinesthetic learning

To recall this system, remember the letters **VAK**, which stand for **visual**, **auditory**, and **kinesthetic**. The theory is that each of us prefers to learn through one of these senses. And we can enrich our learning with activities that draw on the other channels.

To reflect on your VAK preferences, answer the following questions. Each question has three possible answers. Circle the answer that best describes how you would respond in the stated situation. This is not a formal inventory—just a way to prompt some self-discovery.

When you have problems spelling a word, you prefer to:
1. Look it up in the dictionary.
2. Say the word out loud several times before you write it down.
3. Write out the word with several different spellings and then choose one.

You enjoy courses the most when you get to:
1. View slides, overhead displays, videos, and readings with plenty of charts, tables, and illustrations.
2. Ask questions, engage in small-group discussions, and listen to guest speakers.
3. Take field trips, participate in lab sessions, or apply the course content while working as a volunteer or intern.

When giving someone directions on how to drive to a destination, you prefer to:
1. Pull out a piece of paper and sketch a map.
2. Give verbal instructions.
3. Say, "I'm driving to a place near there, so just follow me."

When planning an extended vacation to a new destination, you prefer to:
1. Read colorful, illustrated brochures or articles about that place.
2. Talk directly to someone who's been there.
3. Spend a day or two at that destination on a work-related trip before taking a vacation there.

You've made a commitment to learn to play the guitar. The first thing you do is:
1. Go to a library or music store and find an instruction book with plenty of diagrams and chord charts.
2. Pull out your favorite CDs, listen closely to the guitar solos, and see whether you can play along with them.
3. Buy or borrow a guitar, pluck the strings, and ask someone to show you how to play a few chords.

You've saved up enough money to lease a car. When choosing from among several new models, the most important factor in your decision is:
1. Reading information about the car from sources like *Consumer Reports*.
2. The information you get by talking to people who own the cars you're considering.
3. The overall impression you get by taking each car on a test drive.

You've just bought a new computer system. When setting up the system, the first thing you do is:
1. Skim through the printed instructions that come with the equipment.
2. Call someone with a similar system and ask her for directions.
3. Assemble the components as best as you can, see whether everything works, and consult the instructions only as a last resort.

You get a scholarship to study abroad next semester, which starts in just three months. You will travel to a country where French is the most widely spoken language. To learn as much French as you can before you depart, you:
1. Buy a video-based language course that's recorded on a DVD.
2. Set up tutoring sessions with a friend who's fluent in French.
3. Sign up for a short immersion course in an environment in which you speak only French, starting with the first class.

Now take a few minutes to reflect on the meaning of your responses. All of the answers numbered "1" are examples of visual learning. The "2's" refer to auditory learning, and the "3's" illustrate kinesthetic learning. Finding a consistent pattern in your answers indicates that you prefer learning through one sense channel more than the others. Or you might find that your preferences are fairly balanced.

Listed here are suggestions for learning through each sense channel. Experiment with these examples, and create more techniques of your own. Use the suggestions to build on your current preferences and develop new options for learning.

TO ENHANCE VISUAL LEARNING:

- Preview reading assignments by looking for elements that are highlighted visually—bold headlines, charts, graphs, illustrations, and photographs.
- When taking notes in class, leave plenty of room to add your own charts, diagrams, tables, and other visuals later.
- Whenever an instructor writes information on a blackboard or overhead display, copy it exactly in your notes.
- Transfer your handwritten notes to your computer. Use word-processing software that allows you to format your notes in lists, add headings in different fonts, and create visuals in color.
- Before you begin an exam, quickly sketch a diagram on scratch paper. Use this diagram to summarize the key formulas or facts you want to remember.
- During tests, see whether you can visualize pages from your handwritten notes or images from your computer-based notes.

TO ENHANCE AUDITORY LEARNING:

- Reinforce memory of your notes and readings by talking about them. When studying, stop often to recite key points and examples in your own words.

1

- After reciting several summaries of key points and examples, record your favorite version or write it out.

- Read difficult passages in your textbooks slowly and out loud.

- Join study groups, and create short presentations about course topics.

- Visit your instructors during office hours to ask questions.

TO ENHANCE KINESTHETIC LEARNING:

- Look for ways to translate course content into three-dimensional models that you can build. While studying biology, for example, create a model of a human cell using different colors of clay.

- Supplement lectures with trips to museums, field observations, lab sessions, tutorials, and other hands-on activities.

- Recite key concepts from your courses while you walk or exercise.

- Intentionally set up situations in which you can learn by trial and error.

- Create a practice test, and write out the answers in the room where you will actually take the exam.

One variation of the VAK system has been called VARK.[4] The *R* describes a preference for learning by reading and writing. People with this preference might benefit from translating charts and diagrams into statements, taking notes in lists, and converting those lists into possible items on a multiple-choice test. ■

Master Students
IN ACTION

You're One Click Away...
from a video about Master Students in Action.

"*At the beginning of the term, I would have said that I learned best by doing (hands-on). But now that I have grown and expanded the boundaries of my mind's learning capabilities, I learn best with a mixture of all three (watching, listening, and doing). This is because I have come to realize that all three types of learning are connected through a balance; leading one to discover the "perfect" method of learning.*"

—Deondré Lucas, Valencia Community College

Courtesy of DeonDré Lucas

Choosing your purpose

Success is a choice—your choice. To *get* what you want, it helps to *know* what you want. That is the purpose of this two-part Journal Entry. You can begin choosing success by completing this Journal Entry right now. If you choose to do it later, then plan a date, time, and place and then block out the time on your calendar.

Date: _____   Time: _____   Place: _____

Part 1

Select a time and place when you know you will not be disturbed for at least 20 minutes. (The library is a good place to do this exercise.) Relax for two or three minutes, clearing your mind. Next, complete the following sentences—and then keep writing. When you run out of things to write, stick with it just a bit longer. Be willing to experience a little discomfort. Keep writing. What you discover might be well worth the extra effort.

What I want from my education is . . . _____

_____

When I complete my education, I want to be able to . . . _____

_____

I also want . . . _____

_____

_____

_____

Part 2

After completing Part 1, take a short break. Reward yourself by doing something that you enjoy. Then come back to this Journal Entry.

Now, review the list you just created of things that you want from your education. See whether you can summarize them in one sentence. Start this sentence with "My purpose for being in school is. . . ." Allow yourself to write many drafts of this mission statement, and review it periodically as you continue your education. With each draft, see whether you can capture the essence of what you want from higher education and from your life. State it in a vivid way—in a short sentence that you can easily memorize, one that sparks your enthusiasm and makes you want to get up in the morning.

You might find it difficult to express your purpose statement in one sentence. If so, write a paragraph or more. Then look for the sentence that seems most charged with energy for you. Following are some sample purpose statements:

• My purpose for being in school is to gain skills that I can use to contribute to others.

• My purpose for being in school is to live an abundant life that is filled with happiness, health, love, and wealth.

• My purpose for being in school is to enjoy myself by making lasting friendships and following the lead of my interests.

Write at least one draft of your purpose statement here:

_____

_____

_____

_____

Connect to
RESOURCES

As a student in higher education, you can access a world of student services and community resources. Any of them can help you succeed in school. Many of them are free.

EDHAR/Shutterstock.com

Name a problem that you're facing right now or that you anticipate facing in the future: finding money to pay for classes, resolving conflicts with a teacher, lining up a job after graduation. Chances are that a school or community resource can help you. The ability to access resources is a skill that will serve you long after you stop being a student. In addition, taking advantage of services and getting involved with organizations can lead you to new experiences that expand your learning styles.

Resources often go unused. Following are examples of what you can find. Check your school and city Web sites for more options. Remember that you can connect with many of them online as well as in person.

Academic advisors/counselors can help you select courses, choose a major, plan your career, and adjust in general to the culture of higher education.

Arts organizations connect you to local museums, concert venues, clubs, and stadiums.

Athletic centers often open weight rooms, swimming pools, indoor tracks, basketball courts, and racquetball and tennis courts to all students.

Child care is sometimes made available to students at a reasonable cost through the early childhood education department on campus or community agencies.

Churches, synagogues, mosques, and temples have members who are happy to welcome fellow worshippers who are away from home.

Computer labs on campus are places where students can go to work on projects and access the Internet. Computer access is often available off-campus as well. Check public libraries for this service. Some students get permission to use computers at their workplace after hours.

Consumer credit counseling can help even if you've really blown your budget. And it's usually free. Do your research, and choose a reputable and not-for-profit consumer credit counselor.

Counseling centers in the community can assist you with a problem when you can't get help at school. Look for career-planning services, rehabilitation offices, outreach programs for veterans, and mental health clinics.

The **financial aid office** assists students with loans, scholarships, work-study, and grants.

Governments (city, county, state, and federal) often have programs for students. Check the government listings in your local telephone directory.

Hotlines offer a way to get emergency care, personal counseling, and other kinds of help via a phone call. Do an Internet search on *phone hotlines* in your area that assist with the specific kind of help you're looking for, and check your school catalog for more resources.

Job placement offices can help you find part-time employment while you are in school and a full-time job after you graduate.

Legal aid services provide free or inexpensive assistance to low-income people.

Libraries are a treasure on campus and in any community. They employ people who are happy to help you locate information.

Newspapers published on campus and in the local community list events and services that are free or inexpensive.

The **school catalog** lists course descriptions, and tuition fees, requirements for graduation, and information on everything from the school's history to its grading practices.

School security agencies can tell you what's safe and what's not. They can also provide information about parking, bicycle regulations, and traffic rules.

Special needs and disability services assist college students who have learning disabilities or other disabilities.

Student health clinics often provide free or inexpensive counseling and other medical treatment.

Student organizations present opportunities for extracurricular activities. Explore student government, fraternities, sororities, service clubs, religious groups, sports clubs, and political groups. Find women's centers; multicultural student centers; and organizations for international students, disabled students with disabilities, and gay, lesbian, bisexual, and transgender (GLBT) students.

Support groups exist for people with almost any problem, from drug addiction to cancer. You can find people with problems who meet every week to share suggestions, information, and concerns about problems they share.

Tutoring is usually free and is available through academic departments or counseling centers and is often free or low cost. ■

EXTRACURRICULAR ACTIVITIES
reap the benefits

As you enter higher education, you may find that you are busier than you've ever been before. Often that's due to the variety of extracurricular activities available to you: athletics, fraternities, sororities, student newspapers, debate teams, study groups, service learning projects, internships, student government, and political action groups, to name just a few. Your school might also offer conferences, films, concerts, museums, art galleries, and speakers—all for free or reduced prices. Student organizations help to make these activities possible, and you can join any of them.

People who participate in extracurricular activities gain many benefits. They bridge the worlds inside and outside the classroom. They expand their learning styles by testing theories in action and gaining concrete experiences. Through student organizations, they explore possible careers, make contacts for jobs, and build a lifelong habit of giving back to their communities. They make new friends among both students and faculty and work on teams with people from other cultures.

Getting involved in such organizations also comes with some risks. When students don't balance extracurricular activities with class work, their success in school can suffer. They can also compromise their health by losing sleep, neglecting exercise, skipping meals, or relying on fast food. These costs are easier to avoid if you keep a few suggestions in mind:

- **Make conscious choices** about how to divide your time between schoolwork and extracurricular activities. Decide up front how many hours each week or month you can devote to a student organization. Leave room in your schedule for relaxing and for unplanned events. For more ideas, see Chapter 2: "Time."

- **Look to the future** when making commitments. Write down three or four of the most important goals you'd like to achieve in your lifetime. Then choose extracurricular activities that directly support those goals.

- **Create a career plan** that includes a list of skills needed for your next job. Then choose extracurricular activities to develop those skills. If you're unsure of your career choice, then get involved in campus organizations to explore your options.

- **Whenever possible, develop leadership experience** by holding an office in an organization. If that's too much of a commitment, then volunteer to lead a committee or plan a special event.

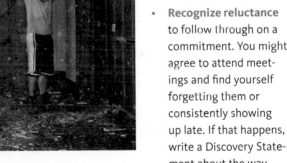

- **Get involved** in a variety of extracurricular activities. Varying your activities demonstrates to future employers that you can work with a variety of people in a range of settings.

- **Recognize reluctance** to follow through on a commitment. You might agree to attend meetings and find yourself forgetting them or consistently showing up late. If that happens, write a Discovery Statement about the way you're using time. Follow that with an Intention Statement about ways to keep your agreements—or consider renegotiating those agreements.

- **Say no** to activities that fail to create value for you. Avoid joining groups only because you feel guilty or obligated to do so.

- **Check out the rules** before joining any student organization. Ask about dues and attendance requirements. ∎

MAKE THE CAREER
connection

One theory of education separates life into two distinct domains: work and school. One domain is the "real" world. The other is the place where you attend classes to prepare for the real world. Consider another point of view: Success in higher education promotes success on the job.

When you graduate from school, you don't leave your capacity for mastery locked inside a classroom. Excellence in one setting paves the way for excellence in other settings. For example, a student who knows how to show up for class on time is ready to show up for work on time. A student who knows how to focus attention during a lecture is ready to focus attention during a training session at work. And a student who's worked cooperatively in a study group brings skills to the table when joining a project team at work.

Staying current in the job market means continually expanding your knowledge and skills. You will probably change careers and start new jobs at several points during your working life. This calls for continuous learning. As a master student, you can make those transitions with ease. You'll also gain favor with employers by quickly getting up to speed quickly on new projects.

Starting now, read this book with a mental filter in place. Ask yourself, "How can I use this idea to meet my career goals? How can I apply this technique to my current job or the next job I see for myself?" The answers can help you thrive in any job, whether you work full time or part time.

To stimulate your thinking, look for the Put This Chapter to Work articles located near the end of each chapter. In addition, invent techniques of your own based on what you read, and test them at work. There's no limit to the possibilities.

For example, use the Discovery and Intention Journal Entry system while you're in the work force. Write Discovery Statements to note your current job skills, as well as areas for improvement. Also use Discovery Statements to describe what you want from your career.

Follow up with Intention Statements that detail specifically what you want to be doing 1 year, 5 years, and 10 years or more from today. Write additional Intention Statements about specific actions you can take to meet those career goals.

Here is a textbook reconnaissance that lists articles in this book with workplace applications. These are just a few examples. As you read, look for more.

The techniques presented in *Setting and achieving goals* (page 71) can help you plan and complete projects on time. Supplement these ideas with suggestions from *The ABC daily to-do list* (page 74), *More strategies for planning* (page 77), and *Stop procrastination now* (page 86). The article *25 ways to get the most out of now* (page 89) is packed with ideas you can transfer to the workplace. For example, tackle difficult tasks first thing in the day, or at any other time when your energy peaks. Also find 5-minute tasks that you can complete while waiting for a meeting to start. The article *20 memory techniques* (page 106) will come in handy as you learn the policies and procedures for a new job.

Techniques presented in *Remembering names* (page 120) can help as you meet people during your job search and as you are being introduced to new coworkers.

Use *How Muscle Reading works* (page 128) to keep up with journals and books in your field. This set of techniques can also help you scan Web sites for the information you want and keep up with ever-increasing volumes of e-mail.

The article *Record* (page 157) explains different formats for taking notes—mind maps, concept maps, the Cornell format, and more. You can use these tools to document what happens at work-related meetings.

Adapt the ideas mentioned in *Cooperative learning—Studying in groups* (page 184) in order to cooperate more effectively with members of a project team.

Let go of test anxiety (page 191) is full of strategies that can help you manage stress in any situation. Use them when you're under deadline pressure or dealing with a difficult customer.

Use the thinking skills presented in *Gaining skill at decision making* (page 221) when it comes time to choose a career, weigh job offers, or make work-related decisions.

Robert Reich, former U.S. secretary of labor, said that jobs of the future will call for the abilities to "define problems, quickly assimilate relevant data, conceptualize and reorganize the information, make deductive and inductive leaps with it, ask hard questions about it, discuss findings with colleagues, work collaboratively to find solutions and then convince others."[5] See *Ways to create ideas* (page 212), *Becoming a critical thinker* (page 207), and *Four ways to solve problems* (page 222) for strategies related to each skill that Reich describes.

According to a survey of managers in government and business settings, workers who lack writing skills will struggle to advance in their careers.[6] Your own career path may require you to produce e-mails, reports, memos, articles, abstracts, proposals, job descriptions, and other business documents. *Three phases of effective writing* (page 255) offers a core process for completing all these assignments.

The U.S. Department of Labor issued an influential report on key skills needed by members of the workforce in the twenty-first century.[7] That report described the need for people with public speaking skills, including making group presentations, targeting messages to specific audiences, and responding to listener feedback. Take the next step in developing these skills with *Mastering public speaking* (page 262). Ideas from *Managing conflict* (page 247) can help you defuse tensions among coworkers.

The suggestions in *Building relationships across cultures* (page 276) can assist you in adapting to the culture of a new job. Each company, large or small, develops its own culture—a set of shared values and basic assumptions. Even if you are self-employed, you can benefit by discovering and adapting to a client's corporate culture.

Return to *Create your career now* (page 358) at any time in the future when you're redefining the kind of work that you want to do. Then hone your job-hunting skills with *Build an irresistible résumé* (page 366) and *Use job interviews to "hire" an employer* (page 369).

The only job security available today is the ability to transfer skills from one position to another. *Now that you're done—begin* (page 377) opens up pathways to lifelong learning. Use these suggestions to continually update your job skills and explore new areas for personal development. ■

YOU DON'T *NEED*
this course—but you might *want* it

Some students don't believe they need a student success course. They might be right. These students may tell you that many schools don't even offer such a class. That's true.

Consider the benefits of taking this course anyway.

Start with a single question: What's one new thing that you could do on a regular basis to make a significant, positive difference in your life? This question might be the most important thing you ask yourself this term. The answer does not have to involve a huge behavior change. Over weeks and months, even a small shift in the way you take notes, read a textbook, or interact with instructors can make a major difference in how well you do in school.

Students who open up to this idea experience benefits. These comments from a recent student success course evaluation are typical:

I didn't expect to get anything out of this course except

an easy "A." Boy, was I ever wrong. This course has changed my life.

I entered college with no confidence. Now that I have taken this class, I feel like I can succeed in any class.

This course has truly showed that I have the power to change any situation for the better.

I am now ready for the rest of my college years.

A student success course gives you dozens of strategies for creating the life of your dreams.

It's possible that you might arrive at these strategies on your own, given enough time. Why wait, however? Approach this book and your course as if the quality of your education depended on them. Then watch the benefits start to unfold.

Psychologist Benjamin Bloom described six kinds of thinking:

Level 1: Remembering—recalling an idea.

Level 2: Understanding—explaining an idea in your own words and giving examples from your own experience.

Level 3: Applying—using an idea to produced a desired result.

Level 4: Analyzing—dividing an idea into parts or steps.

Level 5: Evaluating—rating the truth, usefulness, or quality of an idea—and giving reasons for your rating.

Level 6: Creating—inventing something new based on an idea.

You can recall any suggestion from this book (**Level 1: Remembering**) and take that idea to a higher level of thinking. For example, the article "Extracurricular activities—reap the benefits," on page 55, includes this suggestion: "Get involved in a variety of extracurricular activities." You could take this suggestion to **Level 2: Understanding** by adding personal examples:

Extracurricular activities are worthwhile things to do while I'm in school. These activities go beyond the assignments in my classes and help me develop skills that I can use in my career after I graduate. At my school, for example, I could do volunteer fund raising for the campus radio station. I could also join an intramural volleyball team or run for student senate.

Now it's your turn. Choose another suggestion from this chapter (**Level 1: Remembering**) and think about it at **Level 2: Understanding**. In the space below, state the suggestion and write a brief paragraph that summarizes your higher-level thinking.

_____

_____

_____

_____

_____

_____

Note: If you'd like to demonstrate your thinking in another way—such as by making a drawing, building a model, or even writing a song—then discuss this with your instructor.

For more information on the six levels of thinking, see "Becoming a critical thinker" in Chapter 7.

MASTER STUDENT
profiles

In each chapter of this text there is an example of a person who embodies one or more of the master student qualities mentioned in the Introduction to this book. As you read about these people and others like them, ask yourself: "How can I apply this?" Look for the timeless qualities in the people you read about. Many of the strategies used by master students from another time or place are tools that you can use today.

The master students in this book demonstrated unusual and effective ways to learn. Remember that these are just 12 examples of master students (one for each chapter). You can read more about them in the Master Student Hall of Fame on the Web site.

As you read the Master Student Profiles, ask questions based on each mode of learning: Why is this person considered a master student? What attitudes or behaviors helped to create her mastery? How can I develop those qualities? What if I could use his example to create positive new results in my own life?

Also reflect on other master students you've read about or know personally. Focus on people who excel at learning. The master student is not a vague or remote ideal. Rather, master students move freely among us.

In fact, there's one living inside your skin.

masterstudentprofile

Lalita Booth

Once homeless, and now a student at the University of Central Florida (UCF), and accepted to Harvard University Business School.

Sitting in front of a classroom of LEAD Scholars, Lalita Booth looks like any other junior. The brown-eyed, freckle-faced student blends in with her peers in the University of Central Florida (UCF) leadership development program in every way.

That is, until she opens her mouth.

"You're looking at the face of a child abuse survivor, a perpetual runaway, a high school dropout," she says, as idle chitchat turns to complete silence.

"I was a teenage mother, a homeless parent, and a former welfare recipient."

Lalita's parents divorced when she was young; by age 12 she was a runaway pro—asking for permission to go somewhere and then simply not returning for a few days or a few weeks. . . .

She became proficient in "couch surfing" at friends' homes. When there was no couch to crash on, the teen would take her nightly refuge behind the closest dumpster and rest in the park during the day.

Furthering her quest to be a grownup, at 17 she married her long-time buddy and fellow high-school-dropout, Quinn. Three months later, she found out she was pregnant with her son, Kieren. What normally would be a joyful time was instead a stressful one while the new couple struggled in a prison of deep poverty. The miserable situation began to take its toll, and after just 2½ years of marriage, Quinn was ready to call it quits.

With her new boyfriend, Carl, and her most precious cargo, Kieren, in tow, Booth fled to Boulder, Colorado. Kieren lived with his paternal grandparents for 7 months while Lalita and Carl attempted to get back on their feet.

Being in Colorado proved to be fruitful for the 21-year-old Lalita. It started with an interesting job opportunity as an enrolled agent—an expert in U.S. taxation who can represent taxpayers before the Internal Revenue Service. Lalita could acquire the license without further schooling. Better yet, it would boost her income to

$32,000. She buckled down and read all 4,000 pages of the study guide, and, thanks to her nearly photographic memory, she aced the test.

But once again, she was in the wrong place at the wrong time. Carl's brother in Orlando was very ill, and he needed to move to Florida.

The only way to insure her independence was to do something that frightened her to the very core—go back to school. . . .

And soon after, she enrolled at Seminole Community College. . . .

In May 2005, Lalita was selected to attend the Salzburg Global Seminar, where she brainstormed ways to solve global problems with a group of international students. The thought-provoking trip led to her mission: to help others escape the choke hold of poverty.

Back in the states, Booth's world became even more dream-like when she won the Jack Kent Cooke Foundation Scholarship.

Lalita Booth strongly believes, and for good reason, that "things that are worth achieving are absolutely unreasonable." She advises, "Set unreasonable goals, and chase them unreasonably."

LALITA BOOTH . . . is willing to work.

YOU . . . can work effectively by starting with a First Step.

Adapted from Sarah Sekula, "Escape Artist," *Pegasus*, July/August 2008, *UCF Alumni Life*, 20–26. Reprinted with permission.

You're One Click Away...
from learning more about Lalita Booth online at the Master Student Profiles. You can also visit the Master Student Hall of Fame to learn about other master students.

© Istockphoto.com/pagadesign

PUT THIS CHAPTER TO WORK

To get more value from *Becoming a Master Student*, make the career connection. Think about how you can use strategies from this chapter to find a job you want and do the work you love. Following are ways to get started.

REMEMBER LEARNING STYLES DURING JOB INTERVIEWS. You probably feel more comfortable with a person when you feel that you have something in common. That feeling is called *rapport*.

When meeting with a job interviewer, look for clues to that person's learning style. Then see whether you can establish rapport by matching that person's style in a small, significant way.

For example, mirror the interviewer's word choice. Some people like to process information *visually*. You might hear them say, "I'll look into that" or "Give me the big picture first." Those who like to solve problems *verbally* might say, "Let's talk through this problem" or "I hear you!" And some interviewers express *kinesthetic* preferences by referring to body sensations ("This product feels great") or action ("Let's run with this idea and see what happens").

Kinesthetic preferences are also expressed in posture. Notice whether the job interviewer is sitting with arms and legs crossed or open. If you can mirror that posture in a natural way, then do so.

As you look for ways to establish rapport, be subtle. The goal is not to manipulate—it's to find common ground.

DISCOVER YOUR COWORKERS' LEARNING STYLES. Once you're at work, remember that people constantly express their preferences for learning. Look for clues such as these:

- A person who's often on the phone with customers or clients makes it a priority to build relationships. She learns by *feeling*.
- During a training session, one of your coworkers might do a lot of observation before practicing a new skill. She prefers to learn by *watching*.

- A supervisor might write goals and detailed plans before taking action. This person has a preference for *thinking*.
- The worker who's continually on the move might prefer concrete experience over memos or meetings. She likes to learn by *doing*.

NOW CREATE A CAREER CONNECTION OF YOUR OWN. Spend five minutes reviewing this chapter. Look for a suggestion that you will commit to use while you're working or looking for a job. In a sentence or two, describe your new behavior and the benefit you want to gain from it. For example: "I will speak about *differences in styles* rather than *deficiencies* in my coworkers. This can help me prevent and resolve conflict at work."

Describe your planned behavior and desired benefit here:

_____

_____

_____

_____

_____

_____

_____

_____

_____

_____

_____

_____

_____

CHAPTER 1 QUIZ

Name _____

Date _____

1

1. The Power Process: "Ideas are tools" states that if you want to *use* an idea, you must *believe* in it. True or false? Explain your answer.

2. The First Step technique refers only to telling the truth about your areas for improvement. True or false? Explain your answer.

3. The four modes of learning are associated with certain questions. Give the appropriate question for each mode.

4. List the types of intelligence defined by Howard Gardner.

5. Describe three learning strategies related to one type of intelligence that you listed.

6. What does the word *kinesthetic* refer to?
   (a) Moving
   (b) Hearing
   (c) Seeing
   (d) Listening

7. List three strategies for getting the most from extracurricular activities.

8. Find an article in this book with suggestions that you could use in the workplace. List the title of that article and summarize at least two of those suggestions here.

9. To get the most value from this course, the text suggests that you ask:
   (a) What's one new thing that you could do on a regular basis to make a significant, positive difference in your life?
   (b) How can you make a big change in your behavior within the next week?
   (c) How can you make several big changes in your behavior during this term?
   (d) None of the above.

10. List the six levels of thinking described by psychologist Benjamin Bloom.

SKILLS Snapshot

You'll find a Skills Snapshot at the end of each chapter in this book. Use these exercises to stay aware of your changing attitudes and behaviors—including your progress in developing the qualities of a master student.

The Discovery Wheel in this chapter includes a section labeled *Attitude*. For the next 10 to 15 minutes, go beyond your initial responses to that exercise. Take a snapshot of your skills as they exist today, after reading and completing the exercises in this chapter. Begin by reflecting on some recent experiences. Then take another step toward mastery by choosing to follow up on your reflections with a specific action.

DISCOVERY

My score on the Attitude section of the Discovery Wheel on page 37 was . . .

Three things I do well as a student are . . .

Three ways that I'd like to improve as a student are . . .

If asked to describe my learning style in one sentence, I would say that I am . . .

To become a more flexible learner, I could . . .

When I disagree with what someone else says, my first response is usually to . . .

INTENTION

When disagreements occur, I could be more effective by . . .

I'll know that I've adopted new attitudes to support my success when I'm able to say . . .

NEXT ACTION

To make the change I just described, the most important thing I can do is to . . .

At the end of this course, I would like my Attitude score on the Discovery Wheel to be . . .

Time

Use this **Master Student Map** to ask yourself,

WHY THIS CHAPTER MATTERS . . .

- Procrastination and lack of planning can quickly undermine your success in school.

WHAT IS INCLUDED . . .

- Power Process: Be here now   64
- You've got the time   65
- Setting and achieving goals   71
- The ABC daily to-do list   74
- Make choices about multitasking   76
- More strategies for planning   77
- Break it down, get it done: Using a long-term planner   82
- Mastering technology: Use Web-based tools to save time   85
- Stop procrastination NOW   86
- 25 ways to get the most out of now   89
- Beyond time management: Stay focused on what matters   94
- Master Student Profile: Al Gore   97

HOW CAN I USE THIS CHAPTER . . .

- Discover the details about how you currently use time.
- Set goals that make a difference in the quality of your life.
- Know exactly what to do today, this week, and this month to achieve your goals.
- Eliminate procrastination.

WHAT IF . . .

- I could meet my goals with time to spare?

JOURNAL ENTRY 5
Intention Statement

Create value from this chapter

Take a few minutes to skim this chapter. Find at least three techniques that you intend to use. List them below, along with their associated page numbers.

Strategy	Page number
_____	_____
_____	_____
_____	_____
_____	_____
_____	_____
_____	_____
_____	_____
_____	_____
_____	_____
_____	_____
_____	_____
_____	_____
_____	_____
_____	_____
_____	_____
_____	_____

© Ruslan Ivantsov/Shutterstock.com

POWER process
Be here now

Being right here, right now is such a simple idea. It seems obvious. Where else can you be but where you are? When else can you be there but when you are there?

The answer is that you can be somewhere else at any time—in your head. It's common for our thoughts to distract us from where we've chosen to be. When we let this happen, we lose the benefits of focusing our attention on what's important to us in the present moment.

To "be here now" means to do what you're doing when you're doing it. It means to be where you are when you're there. Students consistently report that focusing attention on the here and now is one of the most powerful tools in this book.

We all have a voice in our head that hardly ever shuts up. If you don't believe it, conduct this experiment: Close your eyes for 10 seconds, and pay attention to what is going on in your head. Please do this right now.

Notice something? Perhaps a voice in your head was saying, "Forget it. I'm in a hurry." Another might have said, "I wonder when 10 seconds is up?" Another could have been saying, "What little voice? I don't hear any little voice."

That's the voice.

This voice can take you anywhere at any time—especially when you are studying. When the voice takes you away, you might appear to be studying, but your brain is somewhere else.

All of us have experienced this voice, as well as the absence of it. When our inner voices are silent, time no longer seems to exist. We forget worries, aches, pains, reasons, excuses, and justifications. We fully experience the here and now. Life is magic.

Do not expect to be rid of the voice entirely. That is neither possible nor desirable. Inner voices serve a purpose. They enable us to analyze, predict, classify, and understand events out there in the "real" world. The trick is to consciously choose when to be with your inner voice and when to let it go.

Instead of trying to force a stray thought out of your head, simply notice it. Accept it. Tell yourself, "There's that thought again." Then gently return your attention to the task at hand. That thought, or another, will come back. Your mind will drift. Simply notice again where your thoughts take you, and gently bring yourself back to the here and now.

Also remember that planning supports this Power Process. Goals are tools that we create to guide our action in the present. Time management techniques—calendars, lists, and all the rest—have only one purpose. They reveal what's most important for you to focus on right *now*.

The idea behind this Power Process is simple. When you listen to a lecture, listen to a lecture. When you read this book, read this book. And when you choose to daydream, daydream. Do what you're doing when you're doing it. Be where you are when you're there.

Be here now . . . and now . . . and now.

You're One Click Away...
from accessing Power Process Media online and finding out more about how to "be here now."

YOU'VE GOT
the time

The words *time management* may call forth images of restriction and control. You might visualize a prune-faced Scrooge hunched over your shoulder, stopwatch in hand, telling you what to do every minute. Bad news.

Good news: You do have enough time for the things you want to do. All it takes is thinking about the possibilities and making conscious choices.

• •

Time is an equal opportunity resource. All of us, regardless of gender, race, creed, or national origin, have exactly the same number of hours in a week. No matter how famous we are, no matter how rich or poor, we get 168 hours to spend each week—no more, no less.

• •

Time is also an unusual commodity. It cannot be saved. You can't stockpile time like wood for the stove or food for the winter. It can't be seen, heard, touched, tasted, or smelled. You can't sense time directly. Even scientists and philosophers find it hard to describe. Because time is so elusive, it is easy to ignore. That doesn't bother time at all. Time is perfectly content to remain hidden until you are nearly out of it. And when you are out of it, you are out of it.

Time is a nonrenewable resource. If you're out of wood, you can chop some more. If you're out of money, you can earn a little extra. If you're out of love, there is still hope. If you're out of health, it can often be restored. But when you're out of time, that's it. When this minute is gone, it's gone.

Time seems to pass at varying speeds. Sometimes it crawls, and sometimes it's faster than a speeding bullet. On Friday afternoons, classroom clocks can creep. After you've worked a 10-hour day, reading the last few pages of an economics assignment can turn minutes into hours. A year in school can stretch out to an eternity.

At the other end of the spectrum, time flies. There are moments when you are so absorbed in what you're doing that hours disappear like magic.

Sometimes it seems that your friends control your time; your boss controls your time; your teachers or your parents or your kids or somebody else controls your time. Maybe that is not true, though.

Approach time as if you were in control. When you say you don't have enough time, you might really be saying that you are not spending the time you *do* have in the way that you want. This chapter is about ways to solve that problem.

Everything written about time management can be reduced to three main ideas:

1. **Know exactly *what* you want.** State your wants as clear, specific goals. And put them in writing.

2. **Know *how* to get what you want.** Take action to meet your goals. Determine what you'll do *today* to get what you want in the future. Put those actions in writing as well.

3. **Go for balance.** When our lives lack this quality, we spend most of our time responding to interruptions, last-minute projects, and emergencies. Life feels like a scramble to just survive. We're so busy achieving someone else's goals that we forget about getting what *we* want.

According to Stephen R. Covey, the purpose of planning is to carve out space in your life for things that are not urgent but are truly important.[1] Examples are exercising regularly, reading, praying or meditating, spending quality time alone or with family members and friends, traveling, and cooking nutritious meals. Each of these contributes directly to our personal goals for the future and to the overall quality of our lives in the present.

Yet when schedules get tight, we often drop important activities. We postpone them for that elusive day when we'll finally "have more time."

Don't wait for that time to come. *Make* the time. Use the exercises in this chapter to empower yourself. Spend your most valuable resource in the way you choose. ■

# EXERCISE 8

The Time Monitor

The purpose of this exercise is to transform time into a knowable and predictable resource. To do this, monitor your time in 15-minute intervals, 24 hours a day, for 7 days. Record how much time you spend sleeping, eating, studying, attending lectures, traveling to and from class, working, watching television, listening to music, taking care of the kids, running errands—everything.

If this sounds crazy, hang on for a minute. This exercise is not about keeping track of the rest of your life in 15-minute intervals. It is an opportunity to become conscious of how you spend your time—your life. Use the Time Monitor only for as long as it helps you do that.

When you know exactly how you spend your time, you can make choices with open eyes. You can plan to spend more time on the things that are most important to you and less time on the unimportant. Monitoring your time puts you in control of your life.

To do this exercise, complete the following steps:

1. **Look at Figure 2.1, a sample Time Monitor, on page 67.** On Monday, the student in this sample got up at 6:45 A.M., showered, and got dressed. He finished this activity and began breakfast at 7:15. He put this new activity in at the time he began, and drew a line just above it. He ate from 7:15 to 7:45. It took him 15 minutes to walk to class (7:45 to 8:00), and he attended classes from 8:00 to 11:00.

   You will list your activities in the same way. When you begin an activity, write it down next to the time you begin. Round off to the nearest 15 minutes. If, for example, you begin eating at 8:06, enter your starting time as 8:00.

2. **Fill out your Time Monitor.** Now it's your turn. Make copies of the blank Time Monitor (Figure 2.2 on page 68), or plan to do this exercise online. With your instructor, choose a day to begin monitoring your time. On that day, start filling out your Time Monitor. Keep it with you all day and use it for one full week. Take a few moments every couple of hours to record what you've done. Or, enter a note each time that you change activities.

3. **After you've monitored your time for one week, group your activities together into categories.** List them in the "Category" column in Figure 2.3 on

page 70. This chart already includes the categories "sleep," "class," "study," and "meals." Think of other categories to add. "Grooming" might include showering, putting on makeup, brushing teeth, and getting dressed. "Travel" could include walking, driving, taking the bus, and riding your bike. Other categories might be "exercise," "entertainment," "work," "television," "domestic," and "children." Write in the categories that work for you.

4. **List your *estimated* hours for each category of activity.** Guess how many hours you *think* you spent on each category of activity. List these hours in the "Estimated" column in Figure 2.3.

5. **List your *actual* hours for each category of activity.** Now, add up the figures from your Time Monitor. List these hours in the "Actual" column in Figure 2.3. Make sure that the grand total of all categories is 168 hours.

6. **Reflect on the results of this exercise.** Compare the "Estimated" and "Actual" columns. Take a few minutes and let these numbers sink in. Notice your reactions. You might feel disappointed or even angry about where your time goes. Use those feelings as motivation to make different choices. Complete the following sentences:

   I was surprised at the amount of time I spent on . . .

   _____

   I want to spend more time on . . .

   _____

   I want to spend less time on . . .

   _____

7. **Repeat this exercise.** Do this exercise as many times as you want. The benefit is developing a constant awareness of your activities. With that awareness, you can make informed choices about how to spend the time of your life.

You're One Click Away...
from doing this exercise online under Exercises.

MONDAY _9_ / _12_	
	Get up
	Shower
7:00	
7:15	Breakfast
7:30	
7:45	Walk to class
8:00	Econ 1
8:15	
8:30	
8:45	
9:00	
9:15	
9:30	
9:45	
10:00	Bio 1
10:15	
10:30	
10:45	
11:00	
11:15	Study
11:30	
11:45	
12:00	
12:15	Lunch
12:30	
12:45	
1:00	
1:15	Eng. Lit
1:30	
1:45	
2:00	
2:15	Coffeehouse
2:30	
2:45	
3:00	
3:15	
3:30	
3:45	
4:00	
4:15	Study
4:30	
4:45	
5:00	
5:15	Dinner
5:30	
5:45	
6:00	
6:15	
6:30	Babysit
6:45	
7:00	

TUESDAY _9_ / _13_	
	Sleep
7:00	
7:15	
7:30	
7:45	Shower
8:00	Dress
8:15	Eat
8:30	
8:45	
9:00	Art
9:15	Apprec.
9:30	Project
9:45	
10:00	
10:15	
10:30	
10:45	
11:00	Data
11:15	process
11:30	
11:45	
12:00	
12:15	
12:30	
12:45	
1:00	
1:15	Lunch
1:30	
1:45	
2:00	Work
2:15	on book
2:30	report
2:45	
3:00	Art
3:15	Apprec.
3:30	
3:45	
4:00	
4:15	
4:30	
4:45	
5:00	Dinner
5:15	
5:30	
5:45	
6:00	Letter to
6:15	Uncle Jim
6:30	
6:45	
7:00	

Figure 2.1 Sample Time Monitor

2

MONDAY ___ / ___ / ___ /	TUESDAY ___ / ___ / ___ /	WEDNESDAY ___ / ___ / ___ /	THURSDAY ___ / ___ / ___ /
7:00	7:00	7:00	7:00
7:15	7:15	7:15	7:15
7:30	7:30	7:30	7:30
7:45	7:45	7:45	7:45
8:00	8:00	8:00	8:00
8:15	8:15	8:15	8:15
8:30	8:30	8:30	8:30
8:45	8:45	8:45	8:45
9:00	9:00	9:00	9:00
9:15	9:15	9:15	9:15
9:30	9:30	9:30	9:30
9:45	9:45	9:45	9:45
10:00	10:00	10:00	10:00
10:15	10:15	10:15	10:15
10:30	10:30	10:30	10:30
10:45	10:45	10:45	10:45
11:00	11:00	11:00	11:00
11:15	11:15	11:15	11:15
11:30	11:30	11:30	11:30
11:45	11:45	11:45	11:45
12:00	12:00	12:00	12:00
12:15	12:15	12:15	12:15
12:30	12:30	12:30	12:30
12:45	12:45	12:45	12:45
1:00	1:00	1:00	1:00
1:15	1:15	1:15	1:15
1:30	1:30	1:30	1:30
1:45	1:45	1:45	1:45
2:00	2:00	2:00	2:00
2:15	2:15	2:15	2:15
2:30	2:30	2:30	2:30
2:45	2:45	2:45	2:45
3:00	3:00	3:00	3:00
3:15	3:15	3:15	3:15
3:30	3:30	3:30	3:30
3:45	3:45	3:45	3:45
4:00	4:00	4:00	4:00
4:15	4:15	4:15	4:15
4:30	4:30	4:30	4:30
4:45	4:45	4:45	4:45
5:00	5:00	5:00	5:00
5:15	5:15	5:15	5:15
5:30	5:30	5:30	5:30
5:45	5:45	5:45	5:45
6:00	6:00	6:00	6:00
6:15	6:15	6:15	6:15
6:30	6:30	6:30	6:30
6:45	6:45	6:45	6:45
7:00	7:00	7:00	7:00
7:15	7:15	7:15	7:15
7:30	7:30	7:30	7:30
7:45	7:45	7:45	7:45
8:00	8:00	8:00	8:00
8:15	8:15	8:15	8:15
8:30	8:30	8:30	8:30
8:45	8:45	8:45	8:45
9:00	9:00	9:00	9:00
9:15	9:15	9:15	9:15
9:30	9:30	9:30	9:30
9:45	9:45	9:45	9:45
10:00	10:00	10:00	10:00
10:15	10:15	10:15	10:15
10:30	10:30	10:30	10:30
10:45	10:45	10:45	10:45
11:00	11:00	11:00	11:00
11:15	11:15	11:15	11:15
11:30	11:30	11:30	11:30
11:45	11:45	11:45	11:45
12:00	12:00	12:00	12:00

Figure 2.2 Your Time Monitor

FRIDAY ___ / ___ / ___ /	SATURDAY ___ / ___ / ___ /	SUNDAY ___ / ___ / ___ /
7:00	7:00	7:00
7:15	7:15	7:15
7:30	7:30	7:30
7:45	7:45	7:45
8:00	8:00	8:00
8:15	8:15	8:15
8:30	8:30	8:30
8:45	8:45	8:45
9:00	9:00	9:00
9:15	9:15	9:15
9:30	9:30	9:30
9:45	9:45	9:45
10:00	10:00	10:00
10:15	10:15	10:15
10:30	10:30	10:30
10:45	10:45	10:45
11:00	11:00	11:00
11:15	11:15	11:15
11:30	11:30	11:30
11:45	11:45	11:45
12:00	12:00	12:00
12:15	12:15	12:15
12:30	12:30	12:30
12:45	12:45	12:45
1:00	1:00	1:00
1:15	1:15	1:15
1:30	1:30	1:30
1:45	1:45	1:45
2:00	2:00	2:00
2:15	2:15	2:15
2:30	2:30	2:30
2:45	2:45	2:45
3:00	3:00	3:00
3:15	3:15	3:15
3:30	3:30	3:30
3:45	3:45	3:45
4:00	4:00	4:00
4:15	4:15	4:15
4:30	4:30	4:30
4:45	4:45	4:45
5:00	5:00	5:00
5:15	5:15	5:15
5:30	5:30	5:30
5:45	5:45	5:45
6:00	6:00	6:00
6:15	6:15	6:15
6:30	6:30	6:30
6:45	6:45	6:45
7:00	7:00	7:00
7:15	7:15	7:15
7:30	7:30	7:30
7:45	7:45	7:45
8:00	8:00	8:00
8:15	8:15	8:15
8:30	8:30	8:30
8:45	8:45	8:45
9:00	9:00	9:00
9:15	9:15	9:15
9:30	9:30	9:30
9:45	9:45	9:45
10:00	10:00	10:00
10:15	10:15	10:15
10:30	10:30	10:30
10:45	10:45	10:45
11:00	11:00	11:00
11:15	11:15	11:15
11:30	11:30	11:30
11:45	11:45	11:45
12:00	12:00	12:00

2

WEEK OF ___ / ___ / ___ /		
Category	Estimated Hours	Actual Hours
Sleep		
Class		
Study		
Meals		

Figure 2.3 Your Estimated and Actual Hours

SETTING *and* ACHIEVING *goals*

Many people have no goals, or have only vague, idealized notions of what they want. These notions float among the clouds in their heads. They are wonderful, fuzzy, safe thoughts such as "I want to be a good person," "I want to be financially secure," or "I want to be happy."

Generalized outcomes have great potential as achievable goals. When we keep these goals in a nonspecific form, however, we may become confused about ways to actually achieve them.

Make your goal as real as a finely tuned engine. There is nothing vague or fuzzy about engines. You can see them, feel them, and hear them. You can take them apart and inspect the moving parts. Goals can be every bit as real and useful. If you really want to meet a goal, then take it apart. Inspect the moving parts—the physical actions that you will take to make the goal happen and fine-tune your life.

There are many useful methods for setting goals. You're about to learn one of them. This method is based on writing goals that relate to several time frames and areas of your life. Experiment, and modify as you see fit.

Write down your goals. Writing down your goals greatly increases your chances of meeting them. Writing exposes undefined terms, unrealistic time frames, and other symptoms of fuzzy thinking. If you've been completing Intention Statements as explained in the Introduction to this book, then you've already had experience writing goals. Both goals and Intention Statements address changes you want to make in your behavior, your values, your circumstances—or all of these.

To keep track of your goals, write each one on a separate 3 × 5 card, or type them all into a file on your computer. Update this file as your goals change, and back it up when you back up your other files. Consider storing this file on a flash drive so you can access it any time you are at a computer.

Write specific goals. State your goals in writing as observable actions or measurable results. Think in detail about how things will be different once your goals are attained. List the changes in what you'll see, feel, touch, taste, hear, be, do, or have.

Suppose that one of your goals is to become a better student by studying harder. You're headed in a powerful direction; now translate that goal into a concrete action, such as "I will study 2 hours for every hour I'm in class." Specific goals make clear what actions are needed or what results are expected.

Vague goal	Specific goal
Get a good education.	Graduate with B.S. degree in engineering, with honors, by 2012.
Get good grades.	Earn a 3.5 grade point average next semester.
Enhance my spiritual life.	Meditate for 15 minutes daily.
Improve my appearance.	Lose 6 pounds during the next 6 months
Get control of my money.	Transfer $100 to my savings account each month.

When stated specifically, a goal might look different to you. If you examine it closely, a goal you once thought you wanted might not be something you want after all. Or you might discover that you want to choose a new path to achieve a goal that you are sure you want.

Write goals in several time frames. To get a comprehensive vision of your future, write down the following:

- *Long-term goals.* Long-term goals represent major targets in your life. These goals can take 5 to 20 years to achieve. In some cases, they will take a lifetime. They can include goals in education, careers, personal relationships, travel, financial security—whatever is important to you. Consider the answers to the following questions as you create your long-term goals: What do you want to accomplish in your life? Do you want your life to make a statement? If so, what is that statement?

- *Midterm goals.* Midterm goals are objectives you can accomplish in 1 to 5 years. They include goals such as completing a course of education, paying off a car loan, or achieving a specific career level. These goals usually support your long-term goals.

- *Short-term goals.* Short-term goals are the ones you can accomplish in a year or less. These goals are specific achievements, such as completing a particular course, hiking the Appalachian Trail, or organizing a family reunion. A short-term financial goal would probably include a dollar amount. Whatever your short-term goals are, they require action now or in the near future.

Write goals in several areas of life. People who set goals in only one area of life—such as their career—may find that their personal growth becomes one-sided. They might experience success at work while neglecting their health or relationships with family members and friends.

To avoid this outcome, set goals in a variety of categories. Consider what you want to experience in these areas and add goals in other areas as they occur to you:

- Education
- Career
- Financial life
- Family life or relationships
- Social life
- Spiritual life
- Level of health

Reflect on your goals. Each week, take a few minutes to think about your goals. You can perform the following spot checks:

- *Check in with your feelings.* Think about how the process of setting your goals felt. Consider the satisfaction you'll gain in attaining your objectives. If you don't feel a significant emotional connection with a written goal, consider letting it go or filing it away to review later.
- *Check for alignment.* Look for connections among your goals. Do your short-term goals align with your midterm goals? Will your midterm goals help you achieve your long-term goals? Look for a fit between all of your goals and your purpose for taking part in higher education, as well as your overall purpose in life.
- *Check for obstacles.* All kinds of things can come between you and your goals, such as constraints on time and money. Anticipate obstacles, and start looking now for workable solutions.

Move into action immediately. To increase your odds of success, take immediate action. Decrease the gap between stating a goal and starting to achieve it. If you slip and forget about the goal, you can get back on track at any time by *doing* something about it. Here's a way to link goal setting to time management. Decide on a list of small, achievable steps you can take right away to accomplish each of your short-term goals. Write these small steps down on a daily to-do list. If you want to accomplish some of these steps by a certain date, enter them in a calendar that you consult daily. Then, over the coming weeks, review your to-do list and calendar. Take note of your progress and celebrate your successes.

One of the most effective actions you can take is to share your goals with people who will assist you to achieve them. Tap into the the power of a supportive community.

Reward yourself with care. When you meet your goal on time, reward yourself. Remember that there are two types of rewards. The first type includes rewards that follow naturally from achieving a goal. For example, your reward for earning a degree might be getting the job you've always wanted.

The second type of reward is something that you design. After turning in a paper, you might reward yourself with a nap or an afternoon in the park. A reward like this works best when you're willing to withhold it. If you plan to take a nap on Sunday afternoon, whether you've finished your chemistry assignment or not, then the nap is not an effective reward.

Another way to reward yourself after you achieve a goal is to just sit quietly and savor the feeling. One reason why success breeds success is that it feels good.

Get back to benefits. Achieving a long-term goal, such as graduating from school, poses a special challenge. You might go through periods when you lose enthusiasm. The payoff in the future seems so distant. And the work in the present seems so hard.

See whether you can close that gap in time. Take the future rewards of your goals and make them as vivid as possible in the present. Post visible reminders of the benefits you'll gain. If you want to graduate, then post photographs of people wearing caps and gowns at a ceremony. If you want to stop smoking, then post a list of the benefits that you'll gain from quitting.

Some presentations about goal setting make the whole process seem like a dry, dusty exercise in self-discipline. Don't believe it. In the end, setting and achieving goals is about having the most fun over the long run. It's about getting what you want in the future and enjoying every step along the way. ∎

 EXERCISE 9

Create a lifeline

On a large sheet of paper, draw a horizontal line. This line will represent your lifetime. Now add key events in your life to this line, in chronological order. Examples are birth, first day at school, graduation from high school, and enrollment in higher education.

Now extend the lifeline into the future. Write down key events you would like to see occur 1 year, 5 years, and 10 or more years from now. Choose events that align with your core values. Work quickly in the spirit of a brainstorm, bearing in mind that this plan is not a final one.

Afterward, take a few minutes to review your lifeline. Select one key event for the future, and list any actions you could take in the next month to bring yourself closer to that goal. Do the same with the other key events on your lifeline. You now have the rudiments of a comprehensive plan for your life.

Finally, extend your lifeline another 50 years beyond the year when you would reach age 100. Describe in detail what changes in the world you'd like to see as a result of the goals you attained in your lifetime.

 You're One Click Away...
from doing this exercise online under Exercises.

✓ EXERCISE 10

Get real with your goals

One way to make goals effective is to examine them up close. That's what this exercise is about. Using a process of brainstorming and evaluation, you can break a long-term goal into smaller segments until you have taken it completely apart. When you analyze a goal to this level of detail, you're well on the way to meeting it.

For this exercise, you will use a pen, extra paper, and a watch with a second hand. (A digital watch with a built-in stopwatch feature is even better.) Timing is an important part of the brainstorming process, so follow the stated time limits. This entire exercise takes about an hour.

Part 1: Long-term goals

Brainstorm. Begin with an 8-minute brainstorm. Use a separate sheet of paper for this part of the exercise. For 8 minutes, write down everything you think you want in your life. Write as fast as you can, and write whatever comes into your head. Leave no thought out. Don't worry about accuracy. The object of a brainstorm is to generate as many ideas as possible.

Evaluate. After you have finished brainstorming, spend the next 6 minutes looking over your list. Analyze what you wrote. Read the list out loud. If something is missing, add it. Look for common themes or relationships among your goals. Then select three long-term goals that are important to you—goals that will take many years to achieve. Write these goals below in the space provided.

_____

_____

_____

Before you continue, take a minute to reflect on the process you've used so far. What criteria did you use to select your top three goals?

Part 2: Midterm goals

Brainstorm. Read out loud the three long-term goals you selected in Part 1. Choose one of them. Then brainstorm a list of goals you might achieve in the next 1 to 5 years that would lead to the accomplishment of that one long-term goal. These are midterm goals. Spend 8 minutes on this brainstorm. Go for quantity.

Evaluate. Analyze your brainstorm of midterm goals. Then select three that you determine to be important in meeting the long-term goal you picked. Allow yourself 6 minutes for this part of the exercise. Write your selections below in the space provided.

_____

_____

_____

Why do you see these three goals as more important than the other midterm goals you generated? On a separate sheet of paper, write about your reasons for selecting these three goals.

Part 3: Short-term goals

Brainstorm. Review your list of midterm goals and select one. In another 8-minute brainstorm, generate a list of short-term goals—those you can accomplish in a year or less that will lead to the attainment of that midterm goal. Write down everything that comes to mind. Do not evaluate or judge these ideas yet. For now, the more ideas you write down, the better.

Evaluate. Analyze your list of short-term goals. The most effective brainstorms are conducted by suspending judgment, so you might find some bizarre ideas on your list. That's fine. Now is the time to cross them out. Next, evaluate your remaining short-term goals, and select three that you are willing and able to accomplish. Allow yourself 6 minutes for this part of the exercise. Then write your selections below in the space provided.

_____

_____

_____

The more you practice, the more effective you can be at choosing goals that have meaning for you. You can repeat this exercise, employing the other long-term goals you generated or creating new ones.

 **You're One Click Away...**
from completing this exercise online under Exercises.

One of the most effective ways to stay on track and actually get things done is to use a daily to-do list. Although the Time Monitor gives you a general picture of the week, your daily to-do list itemizes specific tasks you want to complete within the next 24 hours.

The ABC
daily to-do list

One advantage of keeping a daily to-do list is that you don't have to remember what to do next. It's on the list. A typical day in the life of a student is full of separate, often unrelated tasks—reading, attending lectures, reviewing notes, working at a job, writing papers, researching special projects, running errands. It's easy to forget an important task on a busy day. When that task is written down, you don't have to rely on your memory.

The following steps present one method for creating and using to-do lists. This method involves ranking each item on your list according to three levels of importance—A, B, or C. Experiment with these steps, modify them as you see fit, and invent new techniques that work for you.

STEP 1 BRAINSTORM TASKS

To get started, list all of the tasks you want to get done tomorrow. Each task will become an item on a to-do list. Don't worry about putting the entries in order or scheduling them yet. Just list everything you want to accomplish on a sheet of paper or planning calendar, or in a special notebook. You can also use 3 × 5 cards, writing one task on each card. Cards work well because you

can slip them into your pocket or rearrange them, and you never have to copy to-do items from one list to another.

STEP 2 ESTIMATE TIME

For each task you wrote down in Step 1, estimate how long it will take you to complete it. This can be tricky. If you allow too little time, you end up feeling rushed. If you allow too much time, you become less productive. For now, give it your best guess. If you are unsure, overestimate rather than underestimate how long it will take for each task. Overestimating has two benefits: (1) It avoids a schedule that is too tight, missed deadlines, and the resulting feelings of frustration and failure; and (2) it allows time for the unexpected things that come up every day—the spontaneous to-dos. Now pull out your calendar or Time Monitor. You've probably scheduled some hours for activities such as classes or work. This leaves the unscheduled hours for tackling your to-do lists.

Add up the time needed to complete all your to-do items. Also add up the number of unscheduled hours in your day. Then compare the two totals. The power of this step is that you can spot overload in advance. If you have 8 hours' worth of to-do items but only 4 unscheduled hours, that's a potential problem. To solve it, proceed to Step 3.

Step 1: Brainstorm tasks
Step 2: Estimate time
Step 3: Rate each task by priority
Step 4: Cross off tasks
Step 5: Evaluate
Bonus Step: Tinker

STEP 3 RATE EACH TASK BY PRIORITY

To prevent overscheduling, decide which to-do items are the most important, given the time you have available. One suggestion for making this decision comes from the book *How to Get Control of Your Time and Your Life*, by Alan Lakein: Simply label each task A, B, or C.[2]

The A's on your list are those things that are the most critical. They include assignments that are coming due or jobs that need to be done immediately. Also included are activities that lead directly to your short-term goals.

The B's on your list are important, but less so than the A's. B's might someday become A's. For the present, these tasks are not as urgent as A's. They can be postponed, if necessary, for another day.

The C's do not require immediate attention. C priorities include activities such as "shop for a new blender" and "research genealogy on the Internet." C's are often small, easy jobs with no set time line. They too can be postponed.

Once you've labeled the items on your to-do list, schedule time for all of the A's. The B's and C's can be done randomly during the day when you are in between tasks and are not yet ready to start the next A. Even if you only get only one or two of your A's done, you'll still be moving toward your goals.

STEP 4 CROSS OFF TASKS

Keep your to-do list with you at all times. Cross off activities when you finish them, and add new ones when you think of them. If you're using 3 × 5 cards, you can toss away or recycle the cards with completed items. Crossing off tasks and releasing cards can be fun—a visible reward for your diligence. This step fosters a sense of accomplishment.

When using the ABC priority method, you might experience an ailment common to students: C fever. Symptoms include the uncontrollable urge to drop that A task and begin crossing C's off your to-do list. If your history paper is due tomorrow, you might feel compelled to vacuum the rug, call your third cousin in Tulsa, and make a trip to the store for shoelaces. The reason C fever

is so common is that A tasks are usually more difficult or time-consuming to achieve, with a higher risk of failure.

If you notice symptoms of C fever, ask yourself, "Does this job really need to be done now? Do I really need to alphabetize my DVD collection, or might I better use this time to study for tomorrow's data-processing exam?" Use your to-do list to keep yourself on task, working on your A's. But don't panic or berate yourself when you realize that in the last 6 hours, you have completed eleven C's and not a single A. Just calmly return to the A's.

STEP 5 EVALUATE

At the end of the day, evaluate your performance. Look for A priorities you didn't complete. Look for items that repeatedly turn up as B's or C's on your list and never seem to get done. Consider changing them to A's or dropping them altogether. Similarly, you might consider changing an A that didn't get done to a B or C priority.

Be willing to admit mistakes. You might at first rank some items as A's only to realize later that they are actually C's. And some of the C's that lurk at the bottom of your list day after day might really be A's. When you keep a daily to-do list, you can adjust these priorities *before* they become problems.

When you're done evaluating, start on tomorrow's to-do list. That way you can wake up and start getting things done right away.

BONUS STEP TINKER

When it comes to to-do lists, one size does not fit all. Feel free to experiment. Tweak the format of your list so that it works for you.

For example, the ABC system is not the only way to rank items on your to-do list. Some people prefer the 80-20 system. This method is based on the idea that 80 percent of the value of any to-do list comes from only 20 percent of the tasks on that list. So on a to-do list of 10 items, find the 2 that will contribute most to your life today. Complete those tasks without fail.

Another option is to rank items as "yes," "no," or "maybe." Do all of the tasks marked "yes." Delete those marked "no." And put all of the "maybes" on the shelf for later. You can come back to the "maybes" at a future point and rank them as "yes" or "no."

You might find that grouping items by categories such as "errands" and "calls" works best. Be creative.

In any case, use your to-do list in close connection with your calendar. On your calendar, note appointments, classes, and other events that take place on a specific date, a specific time, or both. Use your to-do list for items that you can complete between scheduled events. Keeping a separate to-do list means that you don't have to clutter up your calendar with all those reminders.

In addition, consider planning a whole week or even 2 weeks in advance. Planning in this way can make it easier to put activities in context and see how your daily goals relate to your long-term goals. Weekly planning can also free you from feeling that you have to polish off your whole to-do list in 1 day. Instead, you can spread tasks out over the whole week.

In any case, make starting your own to-do list an A priority. ∎

You're One Click Away...
from finding more strategies online for daily planning.

Make choices about
MULTITASKING

When we get busy, we get tempted to do several things at the same time. It seems like such a natural solution: Watch TV *and* read a textbook. Talk on the phone *and* outline a paper. Write an e-mail *and* listen to a lecture. These are examples of multitasking.

There's a problem with this strategy: Multitasking is much harder than it looks.

Despite the awe-inspiring complexity of the human brain, research reveals that we are basically wired to do one thing at a time.[3] One study found that people who interrupted work to check e-mail or surf the Internet took up to 25 minutes to get back to their original task.[4] In addition, people who use cell phones while driving have more accidents than anyone except drunk drivers.[5]

The solution is an old-fashioned one: Whenever possible, take life one task at a time. Develop a key quality of master students—focused attention. Start by reviewing and using the Power Process: "Be here now." Then add the following strategies to your toolbox.

UNPLUG FROM TECHNOLOGY

To reduce the temptation of multitasking, turn off distracting devices. Shut off your TV and cell phone. Disconnect from the Internet unless it's required for your planned task. Later, you can take a break to make calls, send texts, check e-mail, and browse the Web.

CAPTURE FAST-BREAKING IDEAS WITH MINIMAL INTERRUPTION

Your brain is an expert nagger. After you choose to focus on one task, it might issue urgent reminders about 10 more things you need to do. Keep 3 × 5 cards or paper and a pen handy to write down those reminders. You can take a break later and add them to your to-do list. Your mind can quiet down once it knows that a task has been captured in writing.

MONITOR THE MOMENT-TO-MOMENT SHIFTS IN YOUR ATTENTION

Whenever you're studying and notice that you're distracted by thoughts of doing something else, make a tally mark on a sheet of paper. Simply being aware of your tendency to multitask can help you reclaim your attention.

HANDLE INTERRUPTIONS WITH CARE

Some breaking events are so urgent that they call for your immediate attention. When this happens, note what you were doing when you were interrupted. For example, write down the number of the page you were reading, or the name of the computer file you were creating. When you return to the task, your notes can help you get up to speed again.

MULTITASK BY CONSCIOUS CHOICE

If multitasking seems inevitable, then do it with skill. Pair one activity that requires concentration with another activity that you can do almost automatically. For example, studying for your psychology exam while downloading music is a way to reduce the disadvantages of multitasking. Pretending to listen to your children while watching TV is not.

ALIGN YOUR ACTIVITIES WITH YOUR PASSIONS

Our attention naturally wanders when we find a task to be trivial, pointless, or irritating. At those times, switching attention to another activity becomes a way to reduce discomfort.

Handling routine tasks is a necessary part of daily life. But if you find that your attention frequently wanders throughout the day, ask yourself: Am I really doing what I want to do? Do my work and my classes connect to my interests?

If the answer is no, then the path beyond multitasking might call for a change in your academic and career plans. Determine what you want most in life. Then use the techniques in this chapter to set goals that inspire you. Whenever an activity aligns with your passion, the temptation to multitask loses power. ■

MORE strategies for planning

Planning sets you free. When you set goals and manage time, your life does not just happen by chance. You are on equal terms with the greatest sculptor, painter, or playwright. More than creating a work of art, you are designing a life.

Without planning, we fall prey to simply digging in—engaging in frantic activity with uncertain results. Planning replaces this behavior with clearly defined outcomes and action steps.

An effective plan is flexible, not carved in stone. You can change your plans frequently and still preserve the advantages of planning—choosing your overall direction and taking charge of your life. And even when other people set the goal, you can choose how to achieve it.

Planning is a self-creative venture that lasts for a lifetime. Following are nine ways to get the most from this process. The first four are suggestions about goal setting. The rest cover the details of scheduling activities based on your goals.

Back up to a bigger picture. When choosing activities for the day or week, take some time to lift your eyes to the horizon. Step back for a few minutes and consider your longer-range goals—what you want to accomplish in the next 6 months, the next year, the next 5 years, and beyond.

Ask whether the activities you're about to schedule actually contribute to those goals. If they do, great. If not, ask whether you can delete some items from your calendar or to-do list to make room for goal-related activities. See whether you can free up at least 1 hour each day for doing something you love instead of putting it off to a more "reasonable" or "convenient" time.

You can back up to a bigger picture even when your goals are not precisely defined. You might suddenly sense that now is the time in your life to start a new relationship, take a long trip, or move to a new apartment or house. Pay attention to these intuitions. Allow space in your daily and weekly schedule to explore and act on your dreams.

Look boldly for things to change. When creating your future, be bold. You can write goals related to money, marriage, relationships or anything else. Don't accept the idea that you have to put up with substandard results in a certain area of your life. Staying open-minded about what is possible to achieve can lead to a future you never dreamed was possible.

Look for what's missing—and what to maintain. Goals often arise from a sense of what's missing in our lives. Goal setting is fueled by problems that are not resolved, projects that are incomplete, relationships we want to develop, and careers we still want to pursue.

However, not all planning has to spring from a sense of need. You can set goals to maintain things that you already have, or to keep doing the effective things that you already do. If you exercise vigorously three times each week, you can set a goal to keep exercising. If you already have a loving relationship with your spouse, you can set a goal to nurture that relationship for the rest of your life.

Think even further into the future. To have fun and unleash your creativity, set goals as far in the future as you can. The specific length of time doesn't matter. For some people, long-range planning might mean 10, 20, or even 50 years from now. For others, imagining 3 years feels right. Do whatever works for you.

iStockphoto.com/parema

2

Becoming a Master Student **77**

Once you've stated your longest-range goals, work backward until you can define a next step to take. Suppose your 30-year goal is to retire and maintain your present standard of living. Ask yourself, "To do that, what financial goals do I need to achieve in 20 years? In 10 years? In 1 year? In 1 month? In 1 week?" Put the answers to these questions in writing.

Schedule fixed blocks of time first. When planning your week, start with class time and work time. These time periods are usually determined in advance, so other activities must be scheduled around them. Then schedule essential daily activities such as sleeping and eating. In addition, schedule some time each week for actions that lead directly to one of your written goals.

Set clear starting and stopping times. Tasks often expand to fill the time we allot to them. "It always takes me an hour just to settle into a reading assignment" might become a self-fulfilling prophecy.

As an alternative, schedule a certain amount of time for a reading assignment. Set a timer, and stick to it. Students often find that they can decrease study time by forcing themselves to read faster. They can usually do so without sacrificing comprehension.

A variation of this technique is called *time boxing*. Set aside a specific number of minutes or hours to spend on a certain task. Instead of working on that task until it's done, commit to work on it just for that specific amount of time. Then set a timer, and get to work. In effect, you are placing the task inside a definite "box"—a specific space on your daily calendar.

Time boxing is one way to overcome resistance to a task, focus your attention, and make a meaningful dent in large projects. The amount of time you choose can be relatively small—such as 10 minutes. Start with short periods, and gradually increase them.

Scheduling a fixed time can apply to other tasks. Some people find they can get up 15 minutes earlier in the morning and still feel alert throughout the day. Plan 45 minutes for a trip to the grocery store instead of an hour. Over the course of a year, those extra minutes can add up to hours.

Feeling rushed or sacrificing quality is not the goal here. The point is to push yourself a little and discover what your time requirements really are.

Schedule for flexibility and fun. Recognize that unexpected things will happen, and allow for them. Leave some holes in your schedule. Build in blocks of unplanned time. Consider setting aside time each week marked "flex time" or "open time." Use these hours for emergencies, spontaneous activities, catching up, or seizing new opportunities.

Include time for errands. The time we spend buying toothpaste, paying bills, and doing laundry is easy to overlook. These little errands can destroy a tight schedule and make us feel rushed and harried all week. Plan for them, and remember to allow for travel time between locations.

Also make room for fun. Fun is important. Brains that are constantly stimulated by new ideas and new challenges need time off

to digest them. Take time to browse aimlessly through the library, stroll with no destination, ride a bike, or do other things you enjoy. It's important to "waste" time once in a while.

To maintain flexibility and fun, be realistic. Don't set yourself up for failure by telling yourself you can do a 4-hour job in 2 hours. There are only 168 hours in a week. If you schedule 169 hours, you're sunk.

Plan for changes in your workload. You might find yourself with a lighter load of assignments to complete during the first few days or weeks of any course. This typically happens when instructors give an overview of the subject or take time to review material that you already know from another course.

Faced with this situation, some students are tempted to let early homework slide. They figure that they'll have plenty of time to catch up later. These students often get a rude surprise when the course shifts into warp speed. After reviewing the basics, instructors may cover new and more difficult material at a faster pace, piling on extra readings, writing assignments, and quizzes.

To stay on top of your workload over the entire term, plan for such a change of pace. Stay on top of your assignments right from the start. Whenever possible, work ahead. This tactic gives you an edge when the load for a course gets heavier or when big assignments for several courses are due during the same week.

Involve others when appropriate. Sometimes the activities you schedule depend on gaining information, assistance, or direct participation from other people. If you neglect to inform others of your plans or forget to ask for their cooperation at the outset—surprise! Your schedule can crash.

Statements such as these often follow the communications breakdown: "I just assumed you were going to pick up the kids from school on Tuesday." "I'm working overtime this week and hoped that you'd take over the cooking for a while."

When you schedule a task that depends on another person's involvement, let that person know—the sooner, the better.

Start the day with your Most Important Task. Review your to-do list and calendar first thing each morning. Then visualize the rest of your day as a succession of tasks. For an extra level of clarity, pretend that you have to condense your to-do list to only one top-priority item. This is the thing that you want to complete today *without fail*. Behold your Most Important Task (MIT). Do it as soon as possible. Also do your MIT impeccably, with total attention.

This technique offers two benefits. First, you get an immediate experience of focused attention. This sets a positive tone for the rest of the day. Second, you get an early experience of success.

On busy days, you might feel that several MITs are competing for first place. That's fine. Just begin with one of them. Then set aside specific times during the day to handle the others. ∎

EXERCISE 11

Master monthly calendar

This exercise will give you an opportunity to step back from the details of your daily schedule and get a bigger picture of your life. The more difficult it is for you to plan beyond the current day or week, the greater the benefit of this exercise.

Your basic tool is a 1-month calendar. Use it to block out specific times for upcoming events such as study group meetings, due dates for assignments, review periods before tests, and other time-sensitive tasks.

To get started, you might want to copy the blank monthly calendar on pages 80–81 onto both sides of a sheet of paper.

Or make several copies of these pages and tape them together so that you can see several months at a glance.

Be creative. Experiment with a variety of uses for your monthly calendar. For instance, you can note day-to-day changes in your health or moods, list the places you visit while you are on vacation, or circle each day that you practice a new habit. For examples of filled-in monthly calendars, see below.

You're One Click Away...
from finding printable copies of this monthly calendar online.

2

MONDAY	TUESDAY	WEDNESDAY	THURSDAY	FRIDAY	SATURDAY	SUNDAY

Name _____

Month _____

MONDAY	TUESDAY	WEDNESDAY	THURSDAY	FRIDAY	SATURDAY	SUNDAY

Name _____

Month _____

2

BREAK IT DOWN, GET IT DONE
Using a long-term planner

With a long-term planner, you can eliminate a lot of unpleasant surprises. Long-term planning allows you to avoid scheduling conflicts—the kind that obligate you to be in two places at the same time 3 weeks from now. You can also anticipate busy periods, such as finals week, and start preparing for them now. Good-bye, all-night cram sessions. Hello, serenity.

Find a long-term planner, or make your own. Many office supply stores carry academic planners in paper form that cover an entire school year. Computer software for time management offers the same features. You can also be creative and make your own long-term planner. A big roll of newsprint pinned to a bulletin board or taped to a wall will do nicely. You can also search the Internet for a computer application or smartphone app that's designed for planning.

Enter scheduled dates that extend into the future. Use your long-term planner to list commitments that extend beyond the current month. Enter test dates, lab sessions, days that classes will be canceled, and other events that will take place over this term and next term.

Create a master assignment list. Find the syllabus for each course you're currently taking. Then, in your long-term planner, enter the due dates for all of the assignments in all of your courses. This step can be a powerful reality check.

The purpose of this technique is to not to make you feel overwhelmed with all the things you have to do. Rather, its aim is to help you take a First Step toward recognizing the demands on your time. Armed with the truth about how you use your time, you can make more accurate plans.

Include nonacademic events. In addition to tracking academic commitments, you can use your long-term planner to mark significant events in your life outside school. Include birthdays, doctors' appointments, concert dates, credit card payment due dates, and car maintenance schedules.

> Planning a day, a week, or a month ahead is a powerful practice. Using a long-term planner—one that displays an entire quarter, semester, or year at a glance—can yield even more benefits.

Use your long-term planner to divide and conquer. For some people, academic life is a series of last-minute crises punctuated by periods of exhaustion. You can avoid that fate. The trick is to break down big assignments and projects into smaller assignments and subprojects, each with their own due date.

When planning to write a paper, for instance, enter the final due date in your long-term planner. Then set individual due dates for each milestone in the writing process—creating an outline, completing your research, finishing a first draft, editing the draft, and preparing the final copy. By meeting these interim due dates, you make steady progress on the assignment throughout the term. That sure beats trying to crank out all those pages at the last minute. ■

 You're One Click Away...
from finding printable copies of this long-term planner online.

Week of	Monday	Tuesday	Wednesday	Thursday	Friday	Saturday	Sunday
9 / 5							
9 / 12		English quiz					
9 / 19			English paper due		Speech #1		
9 / 26	Chemistry test					Skiing at the lake	
10 / 3		English quiz			Speech #2		
10 / 10				Geography project due			
10 / 17				--- No classes ---			

LONG-TERM PLANNER ___ / ___ / ___ to ___ / ___ / ___

Week of	Monday	Tuesday	Wednesday	Thursday	Friday	Saturday	Sunday
___ / ___							
___ / ___							
___ / ___							
___ / ___							
___ / ___							
___ / ___							
___ / ___							
___ / ___							
___ / ___							
___ / ___							
___ / ___							
___ / ___							
___ / ___							
___ / ___							
___ / ___							
___ / ___							
___ / ___							
___ / ___							
___ / ___							
___ / ___							
___ / ___							
___ / ___							
___ / ___							
___ / ___							
___ / ___							

Name _____

LONG-TERM PLANNER ___ / ___ / ___ to ___ / ___ / ___

Week of	Monday	Tuesday	Wednesday	Thursday	Friday	Saturday	Sunday
___ / ___							
___ / ___							
___ / ___							
___ / ___							
___ / ___							
___ / ___							
___ / ___							
___ / ___							
___ / ___							
___ / ___							
___ / ___							
___ / ___							
___ / ___							
___ / ___							
___ / ___							
___ / ___							
___ / ___							
___ / ___							
___ / ___							
___ / ___							
___ / ___							
___ / ___							
___ / ___							
___ / ___							
___ / ___							
___ / ___							
___ / ___							
___ / ___							
___ / ___							
___ / ___							
___ / ___							

Mastering**technology**
Use Web-based tools to save time

Time management tools generally fall into three major categories, no matter which system or set of techniques you use:

- **Lists** of goals and planned actions for meeting those goals (to-do items).
- **Calendars** for scheduling appointments and keeping track of due dates.
- **Contact managers**—sometimes called *personal relationship managers*—for keeping track of other people's addresses, phone numbers, e-mail addresses, and other contact information, along with notes from meetings with clients, customers, or coworkers.

Today you can choose from dozens of free online applications that fill these functions. Online applications can save you time because they're available from *any* computer that you can access, in any location—as long as it's connected to the Web. Smartphone applications are also available to help you organize your time. Using these applications saves you from keeping track of information scrawled on random pieces of paper. All the data you've entered from the digital devices that you've "synced" are at your fingertips, at any time.

Many Web-based applications are aimed directly at students. A few of the options are described below. To find more, do an Internet search using the key words *web*, *tools*, and *students*. ∎

Purpose	Application	Uses
Calendar	Google Calendar (www.google.com/calendar)	Keep track of scheduled events and share them with other people; coordinate your data with other Google online applications.
Calendar	30 Boxes (30boxes.com)	Keep track of scheduled events, and share them with other people.
Goal setting	43Things (www.43things.com)	List goals, and track your progress toward them as part of an online community.
Goal setting	myGoals.com (www.mygoals.com)	List goals, get automatic action reminders, and choose from a library of "GoalPlans" based on expert-recommended content.
Lists	Gubb (www.gubb.net)	Create and edit lists (including to-do lists), check off completed items, assign due dates to items, and send lists via e-mail or text messaging.
Lists	Remember the Milk (www.rememberthemilk.com)	Create and manage tasks online and offline, and send yourself reminders.
Multipurpose	Google Docs (docs.google.com)	Create and share documents, spreadsheets, presentations, and forms.
Multipurpose	Zoho (www.zoho.com)	Create and share documents, spreadsheets, presentations, and forms; create a wiki (a Web site that anyone can edit); send and receive e-mail; manage to-do lists; create a calendar; chat online; and clip content (audio, video, text, and images) from the Web.
Multipurpose	Yahoo (www.yahoo.com)	Send and receive e-mail, manage contact information, take notes, and create a calendar.
Multipurpose	OpenOffice (www.openoffice.org)	Create documents, spreadsheets, presentations, graphics, and databases.

You're One Click Away...
from finding an additional list of Web-based applications online.

Poleze/Shutterstock.com

STOP
Procrastination
Now

Consider a bold idea: The way to stop procrastinating is to stop procrastinating. Giving up procrastination is actually a simple choice. People just make it complicated. Sound crazy? Well, test this idea for yourself.

Think of something that you've been putting off. Choose a small, specific task—one that you can complete in 5 minutes or less. Then do that task today.

Tomorrow, choose another task and do it. Repeat this strategy each day for 1 week. Notice what happens to your habit of procrastination.

If the above suggestion just doesn't work for you, then experiment with any strategy from the 7-day antiprocrastination plan on page 87.

DISCOVER THE COSTS.
Find out whether procrastination keeps you from getting what you want. Clearly seeing the side effects of procrastination can help you kick the habit.

DISCOVER YOUR PROCRASTINATION STYLE.
Psychologist Linda Sapadin identifies different styles of procrastination.[6] For example, *dreamers* have big goals that they seldom translate into specific plans. *Worriers* focus on the worst-case scenario and are likely to talk more about problems than about solutions. *Defiers* resist new tasks or promise to do them and then don't follow through. *Overdoers* create extra work for themselves by refusing to delegate tasks and neglecting to set priorities. And *perfectionists* put off tasks for fear of making a mistake.

Awareness of your procrastination style is a key to changing your behavior. If you exhibit the characteristics of an overdoer, for example, then say no to new projects. Also ask for help in completing your current projects.

To discover your procrastination style, observe your behavior. Avoid judgments. Just be a scientist: Record the facts. Write Discovery Statements about specific ways you procrastinate. Follow up with Intention Statements about what to do differently.

TRICK YOURSELF INTO GETTING STARTED.
If you have a 50-page chapter to read, then grab the book and say to yourself, "I'm not really going to read this chapter right now. I'm just going to flip through the pages and scan the headings for 10 minutes." Tricks like these can get you started on a task you've been dreading.

LET FEELINGS FOLLOW ACTION.
If you put off exercising until you feel energetic, you might wait for months. Instead, get moving now. Then watch your feelings change. After 5 minutes of brisk walking, you might be in the mood for a 20-minute run. This principle—action generates motivation—can apply to any task that you've put on the back burner.

CHOOSE TO WORK UNDER PRESSURE. Sometimes people thrive under pressure. As one writer puts it, "I don't do my *best* work under deadline. I do my *only* work under deadline." Used selectively, this strategy might also work for you.

Put yourself in control. If you choose to work with a due date staring you right in the face, then schedule a big block of time during the preceding week. Until then, enjoy!

THINK AHEAD. Use the monthly calendar on page 80 or the long-term planner on page 83 to list due dates for assignments in all your courses. Using these tools, you can anticipate heavy demands on your time and take action to prevent last-minute crunches. Make *Becoming a Master Student* your home base—the first place to turn in taking control of your schedule.

CREATE GOALS THAT DRAW YOU FORWARD. A goal that grabs you by the heartstrings is an inspiration to act now. If you're procrastinating, then set some goals that excite you. Then you might wake up one day and discover that procrastination is part of your past. ■

You're One Click Away...
from finding more strategies online for ending procrastination.

THE 7-DAY
antiprocrastination plan

Listed here are seven strategies you can use to reduce or eliminate many sources of procrastination. The suggestions are tied to the days of the week to help you remember them. Use this list to remind yourself that each day of your life presents an opportunity to stop the cycle of procrastination.

MONDAY Make it Meaningful. What is important about the task you've been putting off? List all the benefits of completing that task. Look at it in relation to your short-, mid-, or long-term goals. Be specific about the rewards for getting it done, including how you will feel when the task is completed. To remember this strategy, keep in mind that it starts with the letter **M**, as in the word *Monday*.

TUESDAY Take it Apart. Break big jobs into a series of small ones you can do in 15 minutes or less. If a long reading assignment intimidates you, divide it into two- or three-page sections. Make a list of the sections, and cross them off as you complete them so you can see your progress. Even the biggest projects can be broken down into a series of small tasks. This strategy starts with the letter **T**, so mentally tie it to *Tuesday*.

WEDNESDAY Write an Intention Statement. If you can't get started on a term paper, you might write, "I intend to write a list of at least 10 possible topics by 9:00 p.m. I will reward myself with an hour of guilt-free recreational reading." Write your intention on a 3 × 5 card. Carry it with you or post it in your study area, where you can see it often. In your memory, file the first word in this strategy—*write*—with *Wednesday*.

THURSDAY Tell Everyone. Publicly announce your intention to get a task done. Tell a friend that you intend to learn 10 irregular French verbs by Saturday. Tell your spouse, roommate, parents, and children. Include anyone who will ask whether you've completed the assignment or who will suggest ways to get it done. Make the world your support group. Associate *tell* with *Thursday*.

FRIDAY Find a Reward. Construct rewards to yourself carefully. Be willing to withhold them if you do not complete the task. Don't pick a movie as a reward for studying biology if you plan to go to the movie anyway. And when you legitimately reap your reward, notice how it feels. Remember that *Friday* is a fine day to *find* a reward. (Of course, you can find a reward on any day of the week. Rhyming *Friday* with *fine* day is just a memory trick.)

SATURDAY Settle it Now. Do it now. The minute you notice yourself procrastinating, plunge into the task. Imagine yourself at a cold mountain lake, poised to dive. Gradual immersion would be slow torture. It's often less painful to leap. Then be sure to savor the feeling of having the task behind you. Link *settle* with *Saturday*.

SUNDAY Say No. When you keep pushing a task into a low-priority category, reexamine your purpose for doing that task at all. If you realize that you really don't intend to do something, quit telling yourself that you will. That's procrastinating. Just say no. Then you're not procrastinating. You don't have to carry around the baggage of an undone task. *Sunday*—the last day of this 7-day plan—is a great day to finally let go and just *say* no.

PRACTICING
critical thinking 2

Psychologist Benjamin Bloom described six kinds of thinking:

> **Level 1: Remembering**—recalling an idea.
>
> **Level 2: Understanding**—explaining an idea in your own words and giving examples from your own experience.
>
> **Level 3: Applying**—using an idea to produced a desired result.
>
> **Level 4: Analyzing**—dividing an idea into parts or steps.
>
> **Level 5: Evaluating**—rating the truth, usefulness, or quality of an idea—and giving reasons for your rating.
>
> **Level 6: Creating**—inventing something new based on an idea.

You can recall any suggestion from this book (**Level 1: Remembering**) and take that idea to a higher level of thinking.

For example, recall the suggestion to "take it apart" from the "The 7-day antiprocrastination plan" on page 87. Think about how you could use this suggestion to write a paper. Write notes on your calendar to:

- Choose a topic for the paper by October 1.

- Finish the first draft by October 15.

- Finish the final draft by October 28 (2 days before the paper is due).

Creating a step-by-step plan like this one is an example of **Level 3: Applying**. Thinking at this level often means answering questions such as: How can I actually use this idea? What is the very next action I would take? When? Where? Who else might be involved?

Now it's your turn. Choose another suggestion from this chapter (**Level 1: Remembering**) and think about it at **Level 3: Applying**. In the space provided here, state the suggestion and write a brief paragraph that summarizes your higher-level thinking. If you'd like to demonstrate your thinking in another way—such as by making a drawing, building a model, or even writing a song—then discuss this with your instructor.

_____
_____
_____
_____
_____
_____
_____
_____
_____
_____
_____
_____
_____
_____
_____
_____
_____
_____
_____
_____
_____
_____

For more information on the six levels of thinking, see "Becoming a critical thinker" in Chapter 7.

25 WAYS
TO GET
THE MOST
OUT OF
now

Ferenc Szelepcsenyi/Shutterstock.com

The following techniques are about getting the most from study time. They're listed in four categories:

- When to study
- Where to study
- Getting focused when you study
- Questions that keep you focused

Don't feel pressured to use all of the techniques or to tackle them in order. As you read, note the suggestions you think will be helpful. Pick one technique to use now. When it becomes a habit, come back to this article and select another one. Repeat this cycle, and enjoy the results as they unfold in your life.

WHEN TO STUDY

Study difficult (or boring) subjects first. If your chemistry problems put you to sleep, get to them first, while you are fresh. We tend to give top priority to what we enjoy studying, yet the courses that we find most difficult often require the most creative energy. Save your favorite subjects for later. If you find yourself avoiding a particular subject, get up an hour earlier to study it before breakfast. With that chore out of the way, the rest of the day can be a breeze.

Continually being late with course assignments indicates a trouble area. Further action is required. Clarify your intentions about the course by writing down your feelings in a journal, talking with an instructor, or asking for help from a friend or counselor. Consistently avoiding study tasks can also be a signal to reexamine your major or course program.

Be aware of your best time of day. Many people learn best in daylight hours. If this is true for you, schedule study time for your most difficult subjects or most difficult people before nightfall.

Unless you grew up on a farm, the idea of being conscious at 5:00 A.M. might seem ridiculous. Yet many successful business-people begin the day at 5:00 A.M. or earlier. Athletes and yoga practitioners use the early morning too. Some writers complete their best work before 9:00 A.M.

Others experience the same benefits by staying up late. They flourish after midnight. If you aren't convinced, then experiment. When you're in a time crunch, get up early or stay up late. You might even see a sunrise.

Use waiting time. Five minutes waiting for a subway, 20 minutes waiting for the dentist, 10 minutes in between classes—waiting time adds up fast. Have short study tasks ready to do during these periods, and keep your study materials handy. For example, carry 3 × 5 cards with facts, formulas, or definitions and pull them out anywhere. A mobile phone with an audio recording app can help you use commuting time to your advantage. Make a recording of yourself reading your notes. Play back the recording as you drive, or listen through headphones as you ride on the bus or subway.

Study 2 hours for every hour you're in class. Students in higher education are regularly advised to allow 2 hours of study time for every hour spent in class. If you are taking 15 credit hours, then plan to spend 30 hours a week studying. That adds up to 45 hours each week for school—more than a full-time job. The benefits of thinking in these terms will be apparent at exam time.

This guideline is just that—a guideline, not an absolute rule. Consider what's best for you. If you do the Time Monitor exercise in this chapter, note how many hours you actually spend studying for each hour of class. Then ask how your schedule is working. You might want to allow more study time for some subjects.

Keep in mind that the "2 hours for 1" rule doesn't distinguish between focused time and unfocused time. In one 4-hour block of study time, it's possible to use up 2 of those hours with phone calls, breaks, daydreaming, and doodling. With study time, quality counts as much as quantity.

Avoid marathon study sessions. With so many hours ahead of you, the temptation is to tell yourself, "Well, it's going to be a long day. No sense rushing into it. Better sharpen about a dozen of these pencils and change the light bulbs." Three 3-hour sessions are usually more productive than one 9-hour session.

If you must study in a large block of time, work on several subjects. Avoid studying similar topics one after the other.

Whenever you study, stop and rest for a few minutes every hour. Give your brain a chance to take a break. Simply moving to a new location might be enough to maintain your focus. When taking breaks fails to restore your energy, it's time to close the books and do something else for a while.

Monitor how much time you spend online. To get an accurate picture of your involvement in social networking and other online activities, use the Time Monitor process in this chapter. Then make conscious choices about how much time you want to spend on these activities. Staying connected is fine. Staying on constant alert for a new text, Twitter stream, or Facebook update distracts you from achieving your goals.

WHERE TO STUDY

Use a regular study area. Your body and your mind know where you are. Using the same place to study, day after day, helps train your responses. When you arrive at that particular place, you can focus your attention more quickly.

Study where you'll be alert. In bed, your body gets a signal. For most students, that signal is more likely to be "Time to sleep!" than "Time to study!" Just as you train your body to be alert at your desk, you also train it to slow down near your bed. For that reason, don't study where you sleep.

Easy chairs and sofas are also dangerous places to study. Learning requires energy. Give your body a message that energy is needed. Put yourself in a situation that supports this message. For example, some schools offer empty classrooms as places to study. If you want to avoid distractions, look for a room where friends are not likely to find you.

Use a library. Libraries are designed for learning. The lighting is perfect. The noise level is low. A wealth of material is available. Entering a library is a signal to focus the mind and get to work. Many students can get more done in a shorter time frame at the library than anywhere else. Experiment for yourself.

GETTING FOCUSED WHEN YOU STUDY

Pay attention to your attention. Breaks in concentration are often caused by internal interruptions. Your own thoughts jump in to divert you from your studies. When this happens, notice these thoughts and let them go. Perhaps the thought of getting something else done is distracting you. One option is to handle that other task now and study later. Or you can write yourself a note about it or schedule a specific time to do it.

Agree with living mates about study time. This agreement includes roommates, spouses, and children. Make the rules about study time clear, and be sure to follow them yourself. Explicit agreements—even written contracts—work well. One student always wears a colorful hat when he wants to study. When his wife and children see the hat, they respect his wish to be left alone.

Get off the phone. The phone is the ultimate interrupter. People who wouldn't think of distracting you in person might call or text you at the worst times because they can't see that you are studying. You don't have to be a victim of your cell phone. If a simple "I can't talk; I'm studying" doesn't work, use dead silence. It's a conversation killer. Or short-circuit the whole problem: Turn off your phone or silence it.

Learn to say no. Saying no is a time-saver and a valuable life skill for everyone. Some people feel it is rude to refuse a request. But you can say no effectively and courteously. Others want you to succeed as a student. When you tell them that you can't do what they ask because you are busy educating yourself, most people will understand.

Hang a "do not disturb" sign on your door. Many hotels will give you a free sign, for the advertising. Or you can create a

SETTING LIMITS ON screen time

Access to the Internet and wireless communication offers easy ways to procrastinate. We call it "surfing," "texting," "IMing,"—and sometimes "researching" or "working." In his book *Crazy Busy: Overstretched, Overbooked, and About to Snap*, Edward Hallowell coined a word to describe these activities when they're done too often—*screensucking*.

Digital devices create value. With a computer you can stream music, watch videos, listen to podcasts, scan newspapers, read books, check e-mail, and send instant messages. With a smartphone you consume online content while staying available to key people when it counts. And any of these activities can become a constant source of distraction.

Discover how much time you spend online. People who update their Twitter stream or Facebook page every hour may be sending an unintended message—that they have no life offline.

To get an accurate picture of your involvement in social networking and other online activity, use the Time Monitor exercise included earlier in this chapter. Then make conscious choices about how much time you want to spend online and on the phone. Don't let social

networking distract you from meeting personal and academic goals.

Go offline to send the message that other people matter. It's hard to pay attention to the person who is right in front of you when you're hammering out text messages or updating your Twitter stream. You can also tell when someone else is doing these things and only half-listening to you. How engaged in your conversation do you think that person is?

An alternative is to close up your devices and "be here now." When you're eating, stop answering the phone. Notice how the food tastes. When you're with a friend, close up your laptop. Hear every word he says. Rediscover where life actually takes place—in the present moment.

Developing emotional intelligence requires being with people and away from a computer or cell phone. People who break up with a partner through text messaging are not developing that intelligence. True friends know when to go offline and head across campus to resolve a conflict. They know when to go back home and support a family member in crisis. When it counts, your presence is your greatest present.

---

sign yourself. They work. Using signs can relieve you of making a decision about cutting off each interruption—a time-saver in itself.

Get ready the night before. Completing a few simple tasks just before you go to bed can help you get in gear the next day. If you need to make some phone calls first thing in the morning, look up those numbers, write them on 3 × 5 cards, and set them near the phone. If you need to drive to a new location, make a note of the address and put it next to your car keys. If you plan to spend the next afternoon writing a paper, get your materials together: dictionary, notes, outline, paper, pencil, flash drive, laptop—whatever you need. Pack your lunch or put gas in the car. Organize the baby's diaper bag and your briefcase or backpack.

Call ahead. We often think of talking on the telephone as a prime time-waster. Used wisely, though, the telephone can actually help manage time. Before you go shopping, call the store to see whether it carries the items you're looking for. A few seconds on the phone or computer can save hours in wasted trips and wrong turns.

Avoid noise distractions. To promote concentration, avoid studying in front of the television, and turn off the radio. Many students insist that they study better with background noise, and it might be true. Some students report good results with carefully selected and controlled music. For many others, silence is the best form of music to study by.

At times noise levels might be out of your control. A neighbor or roommate might decide to find out how far she can turn up her music before the walls crumble. Meanwhile, your ability to concentrate on the principles of sociology goes down the drain. To avoid this scenario, schedule study sessions during periods when your living environment is usually quiet. If you live in a residence hall, ask whether study rooms are available. Or go somewhere else where it's quiet, such as the library. Some students have even found refuge in quiet coffee shops, self-service laundries, and places of worship.

Manage interruptions. Notice how others misuse your time. Be aware of repeat offenders. Ask yourself whether there are certain friends or relatives who consistently interrupt your study time.

If avoiding the interrupter is impractical, send a clear message. Sometimes others don't realize that they are breaking your concentration. You can give them a gentle, yet firm, reminder: "What you're saying is important. Can we schedule a time to talk about it when I can give you my full attention?" If this strategy doesn't work, there are other ways to make your message more effective. For more ideas, see Chapter 8: Communicating.

See whether you can "firewall" yourself for selected study periods each week. Find a place where you can count on being alone and work without interruption.

Sometimes interruptions still happen, though. Create a system for dealing with them. One option is to take an index card and write a quick note about what you're doing the moment an interruption occurs. As soon as possible, return to the card and pick up the task where you left off.

QUESTIONS THAT KEEP YOU FOCUSED

Ask: "What is one task I can accomplish toward achieving my goal?" This technique is helpful when you face a big, imposing job. Pick out one small accomplishment, preferably one you can complete in about 5 minutes; then do it. The satisfaction of getting one thing done can spur you on to get one more thing done. Meanwhile, the job gets smaller.

Ask: "Am I being too hard on myself?" If you are feeling frustrated with a reading assignment, your attention wanders repeatedly, or you've fallen behind on math problems that are due tomorrow, take a minute to listen to the messages you are giving yourself. Are you scolding yourself too harshly? Lighten up. Allow yourself to feel a little foolish, and then get on with the task at hand. Don't add to the problem by berating yourself.

Worrying about the future is another way people beat themselves up: "How will I ever get all this done?" "What if every paper I'm assigned turns out to be this hard?" "If I can't do the simple calculations now, how will I ever pass the final?" Instead of promoting learning, such questions fuel anxiety and waste valuable time.

Labeling and generalizing weaknesses are other ways people are hard on themselves. Being objective and specific in the messages you send yourself will help eliminate this form of self-punishment and will likely generate new possibilities. An alternative to saying "I'm terrible in algebra" is to say, "I don't understand factoring equations." This rewording suggests a plan to improve.

You might be able to lighten the load by discovering how your learning styles affect your behavior. For example, you may have a bias toward concrete experience rather than abstract thinking. If so, after setting a goal, you might want to move directly into action.

In large part, the ability to learn through concrete experience is a valuable trait. After all, action is necessary to achieve goals. At the same time, you might find it helpful to allow extra time to plan. Careful planning can help you avoid unnecessary activity. Instead of using a planner that shows a day at a time, experiment with a calendar that displays a week or month at a glance. The expanded format can help you look further into the future and stay on track as you set out to meet long-term goals.

Ask: "Is this a piano?" Carpenters who construct rough frames for buildings have a saying they use when they bend a nail or accidentally hack a chunk out of a two-by-four: "Well, this ain't no piano." It means that perfection is not necessary. Ask yourself whether what you are doing needs to be perfect. Perhaps you don't have to apply the same standards of grammar to lecture notes that you would apply to a term paper. If you can complete a job 95 percent perfectly in 2 hours and 100 percent perfectly in 4 hours, ask yourself whether the additional 5 percent improvement is worth doubling the amount of time you spend.

Sometimes, though, it *is* a piano. A tiny miscalculation can ruin an entire lab experiment. A misstep in solving a complex math problem can negate hours of work. Computers are notorious for turning little errors into nightmares. Accept lower standards only when appropriate.

A related suggestion is to weed out low-priority tasks. The to-do list for a large project can include dozens of items, not all of which are equally important. Some can be done later, while others can be skipped altogether, if time is short.

Apply this idea when you study. In a long reading assignment, look for pages you can skim or skip. When it's appropriate, read chapter summaries or article abstracts. As you review your notes, look for material that might not be covered on a test, and decide whether you want to study it.

Ask: "Would I pay myself for what I'm doing right now?" If you were employed as a student, would you be earning your wages? Ask yourself this question when you notice that you've taken your third snack break in 30 minutes. Then remember that you are, in fact, employed as a student. You are investing in your own productivity and are paying a big price for the privilege of being a student. Doing a mediocre job now might result in fewer opportunities in the future.

Ask: "Can I do just one more thing?" Ask yourself this question at the end of a long day. Almost always you will have enough energy to do just one more short task. The overall increase in your productivity might surprise you.

Ask: "Can I delegate this?" Instead of slogging through complicated tasks alone, you can draw on the talents and energy of other people. Busy executives know the value of delegating tasks to coworkers. Without delegation, many projects would flounder or die.

You can apply the same principle in your life. Instead of doing all the housework or cooking by yourself, for example, you can assign some of the tasks to family members or roommates. Rather than making a trip to the library to look up a simple fact, you can call and ask a library assistant to research it for you. Instead of driving across town to deliver a package, you can hire a delivery service to do so. All of these tactics can free up extra hours for studying.

It's not practical to delegate certain study tasks, such as writing term papers or completing reading assignments. However, you can still draw on the ideas of others in completing such tasks. For instance, form a writing group to edit and critique papers, brainstorm topics or titles, and develop lists of sources.

If you're absent from a class, find a classmate to summarize the lecture, discussion, and any upcoming assignments. Presidents depend on briefings. You can use the same technique.

Ask: "How did I just waste time?" Notice when time passes and you haven't accomplished what you had planned to do. Take a minute to review your actions and note the specific ways you wasted time. We tend to operate by habit, wasting time in the same ways over and over again. When you are aware of things you do that drain your time, you are more likely to catch yourself in the act next time. Observing one small quirk might save you hours. But keep this in mind: Asking you to notice how you waste time is not intended to make you feel guilty. The point is to increase your skill by getting specific information about how you use time.

Ask: "Could I find the time if I really wanted to?" The way people speak often rules out the option of finding more time. An alternative is to speak about time with more possibility.

The next time you're tempted to say, "I just don't have time," pause for a minute. Question the truth of this statement. Could you find 4 more hours this week for studying? Suppose that someone offered to pay you $10,000 to find those 4 hours. Suppose too that you will get paid only if you don't lose sleep, call in sick for work, or sacrifice anything important to you. Could you find the time if vast sums of money were involved?

Remember that when it comes to school, vast sums of money *are* involved.

Ask: "Am I willing to promise it?" This time-management idea might be the most powerful of all: If you want to find time for a task, promise yourself—and others—that you'll get it done. Unleash one of the key qualities of master students and take responsibility for producing an outcome.

To make this technique work, do more than say that you'll try to keep a promise or that you'll give it your best shot. Take an oath, as you would in court. Give it your word.

One way to accomplish big things in life is to make big promises. There's little reward in promising what's safe or predictable. No athlete promises to place seventh in the Olympic games. Chances are that if you're not making big promises, you're not stretching yourself.

The point of making a promise is not to chain yourself to a rigid schedule or impossible expectations. You can promise to reach goals without unbearable stress. You can keep schedules flexible and carry out your plans with ease, joy, and satisfaction.

At times, though, you might go too far. Some promises may be truly beyond you, and you might break them. However, failing to keep a promise is just that—failing to keep a promise. A broken promise is not the end of the world.

Promises can work magic. When your word is on the line, it's possible to discover reserves of time and energy you didn't know existed. Promises can push you to exceed your expectations. ■

You're One Click Away...
from discovering even more ways online to get the most out of now.

Master Students
IN ACTION

You're One Click Away...
from a video about Master Students in Action.

“*I have found that it is essential to keep a constantly updated calendar and personal planner. Without my own planner, I would most likely draw a blank as to what I need to accomplish for the day, week, month, and beyond. I recommend that any student use both as a means of keeping organized.*”

—*Deeanna Mosher,*
Arizona State University

Beyond *time management*
Stay *focused* on what matters

Ask some people about managing time, and a dreaded image appears in their minds.

They see a person with a 100-item to-do list clutching a calendar chock full of appointments. They imagine a robot who values cold efficiency, compulsively accounts for every minute, and has no time for people.

These stereotypes about time management hold a kernel of truth. Sometimes people fixate so much on time management that they fail to appreciate what they are doing. Time management becomes a burden, a chore, a process that prevents them from actually enjoying the task at hand.

At other times, people who pride themselves on efficiency are merely keeping busy. In their rush to check items off a to-do list, they might be fussing over activities that create little value in the first place.

It might help you to think beyond time management to the larger concept of *planning*. The point of planning is not to load your schedule with obligations. Instead, planning is about getting the important things done and still having time to be human. An effective planner is productive and relaxed at the same time.

DISCOVER YOUR STYLE

Many time management techniques appeal to "left-brained" people—those who thrive on making lists, scheduling events, and handling details. Those suggestions might not work for people who like to see wholes and think visually.

Falko Matte/Shutterstock

Hill Street Studios/Getty Images

Remember that there are many styles of planning. Some people prefer a written action plan that carefully details each step leading to a long-range goal. If you prefer a Mode 2 or Mode 3 learning style as explained in Chapter 1, written action plans might appeal to you. Other people just keep a list of current projects and periodically assess their progress. Both approaches can work.

Give time management strategies a fair chance. Strategies that don't seem to your taste at first might be suitable with a few modifications. Instead of writing a conventional to-do list, for instance, you can plot your day on a mind map. (Mind maps are explained in Chapter 5: Notes.) Doing so might feel especially comfortable if you're blessed with a natural visual intelligence, as explained in the discussion of Howard Gardner's theory of multiple intelligences in Chapter 1.

Another approach might be to write to-do items, one per 3 × 5 card, in any order in which tasks occur to you. Later you can edit, sort, and rank the cards, choosing which items to do. This method will probably appeal to you if you learn best through active experimentation and using your kinesthetic intelligence, which involves movement and the sense of touch.

FOCUS ON VALUES

View your activities from the perspective of an entire lifetime. Given the finite space between birth and death, determine what matters most to you.

As a way to define your values, write your own obituary. Describe the ways you want to be remembered. List the contributions you intend to make during your lifetime and the kind of person you wish to become. If this exercise is too spooky, then complete the lifeline exercise on page 72 instead. Or simply write your life purpose—a sentence or short paragraph that describes what's most important to you.

Next, return to the Time Monitor process on page 66. Look at your completed Time Monitor, and place a check mark next to the activities that are directly aligned with your values. Write a Discovery Statement about how "on purpose" you were for the week. Follow it with an Intention Statement about any resulting changes in your plan for next week.

FOCUS ON OUTCOMES

You might feel guilty when you occasionally stray from your schedule and spend 2 hours napping or watching soap operas. But if you're regularly meeting your goals, there's probably no harm done.

Managing time and getting organized are not ends in themselves. It is possible to be efficient, organized, and miserable. Larger outcomes such as personal satisfaction and effectiveness count more than the means used to achieve them.

Visualizing a desired outcome can be as important as having a detailed action plan. Here's an experiment: Write a list of goals you plan to accomplish over the next 6 months. Next, create a vivid mental picture of yourself attaining those goals and enjoying the resulting benefits. Visualize this image several times in the next few weeks. Then file the list away, making a note on your calendar to review it in 6 months. When 6 months have passed, look over the list and note how many of your goals you have actually accomplished.

DO LESS

Planning is as much about dropping worthless activities as about adding new ones. See whether you can reduce or eliminate activities that contribute little to your values. When you add a new item to your calendar or to-do list, consider dropping a current one.

BUY LESS

Before you purchase an item, estimate how much time it will take to locate, assemble, use, repair, and maintain it. You might be able to free up hours by doing without. If the product comes with a 400-page manual or 20 hours of training, beware. Before rushing to the store to add another possession to your life, see whether you can reuse or adapt something you already own.

Janaka Dharmasena/Shutterstock.com

Hill Street Studios/Getty Images

SLOW DOWN

Sometimes it's useful to hurry, such as when you're late for a meeting or about to miss a plane. At other times, haste is a choice that serves no real purpose. If you're speeding through the day like a launched missile, consider what would happen if you got to your next destination a few minutes later than planned. Rushing might not be worth the added strain.

HANDLE IT NOW

A long to-do list can result from postponing decisions and procrastinating. An alternative is to handle a task or decision immediately. Answer that letter now. Make that phone call as soon as it occurs to you. Then you don't have to add the task to your calendar or to-do list.

The same idea applies when someone asks you to volunteer for a project and you realize immediately that you don't want to do it. Save time by graciously telling the truth up front. Saying "I'll think about it and get back to you" just postpones the conversation until later, when it might take more time.

REMEMBER PEOPLE

Few people on their deathbeds ever say, "I wish I'd spent more time at the office." They're more likely to say, "I wish I'd spent more time with my family and friends." The pace of daily life can lead us to neglect the people we cherish.

Efficiency is a concept that applies to things—not people. When it comes to maintaining and nurturing relationships, we can often benefit from loosening up our schedules. We can allow extra time for conflict management, spontaneous visits, and free-ranging conversations.

FORGET ABOUT TIME

Take time away from time. Schedule downtime—a space in your day where you ignore to-do lists, appointments, and accomplishments. This period is when you're accountable to no one else and have nothing to accomplish. Even a few minutes spent in this way can yield a sense of renewal. One way to manage time is periodically to forget about it.

Experiment with decreasing your overall awareness of time. Spend time in an area that's free of clocks. Notice how often you glance at the time, and make a conscious effort to do so less often.

If you still want some sense of time, use alternatives to the almighty, unforgiving clock. Measure certain activities with a sundial, hourglass, or egg timer. Or synchronize your activities with the rhythms of nature—for example, by rising at dawn.

You can also plan activities to harmonize with the rhythms of your body. Schedule your most demanding tasks for times when you're normally most alert. Eat when you're hungry, not according to the clock. Toss out schedules when it's appropriate. Sometimes the best-laid plans are best laid to rest.

Strictly speaking, time cannot be managed. The minutes, hours, days, and years simply march ahead. What we can do is manage *ourselves* with respect to time. A few basic principles can help us do that as well as a truckload of cold-blooded techniques. ■

Forget time management— just get things done

David Allen, author of *Getting Things Done: The Art of Stress-free Productivity*, says that a lack of time is not the real issue for the people he coaches in time management. Instead, the problem is "a lack of clarity and definition about what a project really is, and what the associated next-action steps required are."[7] Allen translates this idea into the following suggestions.

1. **Collect.** To begin, gather every unfinished project, incomplete task, misplaced object—or anything else that's nagging you—and dump it into a "bucket," or collection area. This area could be an actual bucket that's big enough to hold various objects, a file folder, a traditional in-basket, or all of these receptacles. If an item is too big to store in a bucket, write a reminder of it on a 3 × 5 card or a piece of paper—one item per card or sheet—so that it's easier to file later. Stick this reminder in one of your buckets.

2. **Process.** Now go to each of your buckets, one at a time. Take whatever item is at the top of the pile and ask, "Do I truly want to or need to do something about this?" If the answer is no, calmly dispose of the item. If the answer is yes, then choose immediately how to respond:

   • If you can take action on this item in 2 minutes or less, do so now.

   • If you're dealing with an item that can best be handled by someone else, delegate it to that person.

   • If you're dealing with an item that will take more than 2 minutes for you to do, write a reminder to do it later.

   Repeat the above procedure for each item in each of your buckets. The overall goal is to *empty* the buckets at least once each week.

3. **Organize.** Now group your reminders into appropriate lists by category. The categories are ultimately up to you, but Allen's recommendations include the following:

   • A calendar for listing actions to be completed on a specific date or at a specific time.

   • A list of current projects. A *project* is an outcome that requires two or more actions to produce.

   • A to-do list. Group the items on this list by the physical location where you will do them—for example, *at phone* or *at computer*.

4. **Review.** Every week, review your reminders and ask yourself, "What are all my current projects? And what is the *very next physical action* (such as a phone call or errand) that I can take to move each project forward?"

5. **Do.** Every day, review your calendar or lists. Based on this information and on your intuition, make moment-to-moment choices about how to spend your time.

masterstudentprofile

Al Gore

(1948–) Former vice president of the United States. Gore refocused his career on climate change, won a Nobel Peace Prize, and—in his film *An Inconvenient Truth*—invented a new type of documentary.

One hundred and nineteen years ago, a wealthy inventor read his own obituary, mistakenly published years before his death. Wrongly believing the inventor had just died, a newspaper printed a harsh judgment of his life's work, unfairly labeling him "The Merchant of Death" because of his invention—dynamite. Shaken by this condemnation, the inventor made a fateful choice to serve the cause of peace.

Seven years later, Alfred Nobel created this prize and the others that bear his name.

Seven years ago tomorrow, I read my own political obituary in a judgment that seemed to me harsh and mistaken—if not premature. But that unwelcome verdict also brought a precious if painful gift: an opportunity to search for fresh new ways to serve my purpose.

Unexpectedly, that quest has brought me here. Even though I fear my words cannot match this moment, I pray what I am feeling in my heart will be communicated clearly enough that those who hear me will say, "We must act." . . .

In the last few months, it has been harder and harder to misinterpret the signs that our world is spinning out of kilter. Major cities in North and South America, Asia, and Australia are nearly out of water due to massive droughts and melting glaciers. Desperate farmers are losing their livelihoods. Peoples in the frozen Arctic and on low-lying Pacific islands are planning evacuations of places they have long called home. Unprecedented wildfires have forced a half million people from their homes in one country and caused a national emergency that almost brought down the government in another. Climate refugees have migrated into areas already inhabited by people with different cultures, religions, and traditions, increasing the potential for conflict. Stronger storms in the Pacific and Atlantic have threatened whole cities. Millions have been displaced by massive flooding in South Asia, Mexico, and 18 countries in Africa. As temperature extremes have increased, tens of thousands have lost their lives. We are recklessly burning and clearing our forests and driving more and more species into extinction.

There is an African proverb that says, "If you want to go quickly, go alone. If you want to go far, go together." We need to go far, quickly. . . .

Fifteen years ago, I made that case at the "Earth Summit" in Rio de Janeiro. Ten years ago, I presented it in Kyoto. This week, I will urge the delegates in Bali to adopt a bold mandate for a treaty that establishes a universal global cap on emissions and uses the market in emissions trading to efficiently allocate resources to the most effective opportunities for speedy reductions.

This treaty should be ratified and brought into effect everywhere in the world by the beginning of 2010—2 years sooner than presently contemplated. The pace of our response must be accelerated to match the accelerating pace of the crisis itself. . . .

Make no mistake, the next generation will ask us one of two questions. Either they will ask: "What were you thinking; why didn't you act?"

Or they will ask instead: "How did you find the moral courage to rise and successfully resolve a crisis that so many said was impossible to solve?"

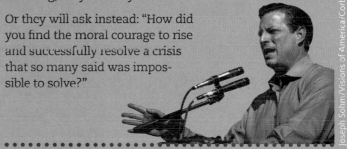

Joseph Sohm/Visions of America/Corbis

AL GORE . . . is optimistic.

YOU . . . can be more optimistic by focusing on your goals.

You're One Click Away...
from learning more about Al Gore online at the Master Student Profiles. You can also visit the Master Student Hall of Fame to learn about other master students.

© iStockphoto.com/pagadesign

PUT THIS CHAPTER TO WORK

Students experience extraordinary demands on their time, especially when juggling classes with job hunting and working. To get the most satisfaction from your 24 hours a day and 168 hours a week, consider the following suggestions.

TREAT LOOKING FOR A JOB AS A JOB IN ITSELF. The more hours you can devote to your job search, the better. Think of yourself as being employed as a job hunter, either part-time or full-time. Do this for as long as it takes to find your next job.

FOCUS ON THE MOST EFFECTIVE METHODS OF FINDING WORK. Remember that the purpose of creating a résumé, writing cover letters, and filling out applications is to get job interviews. Use the Time Monitor to track your job-hunting activities. See whether you can tell which activities yield the most interviews.

SCHEDULE FOLLOW-UP ACTIONS. After filling out a job application or finishing a job interview, ask when the next step in the hiring process will take place. Put that date on your calendar. Also ask whether there's anything you can do to follow up before that date, and put that task on your to-do list.

USE JOB INTERVIEW TIME EFFECTIVELY. Notice how much time you spend speaking during a job interview. This calls for a delicate balance. Remember that the interview has two purposes. One is for an employer to gather information about you. The other is for *you* to gather information about the employer. A reasonable goal to spend 50 percent of the interview time talking and 50 percent of your time listening.

CONNECT YOUR JOB TO YOUR GOALS. Any job can help you meet some of your long-term goals. Even if you work a part-time job at minimum wage, you can develop skills such as working on a team and demonstrating a work ethic (reliability and a positive attitude). These are *transferable skills*, meaning that you can use them in any job. For more information on skills, see Chapter 12.

USE A LONG-TERM PLANNER TO BALANCE SCHOOL, WORK, AND FAMILY COMMITMENTS. If you're working while going to school, use the long-term planner in this chapter to get a big picture of your commitments. Enter test dates and due dates for assignments. Also indicate the days you're scheduled to work. Look for potential conflicts now and think of ways to prevent them. For example, ask whether you can reduce work hours during finals week.

SEE TIME MANAGEMENT AS A WAY TO COMMUNICATE RESPECT. When you're looking for work, be on time for interviews. When you're employed, be punctual and work with full energy until you leave. This shows people that you value their time. It also demonstrates a work ethic that employers value. You can start developing this habit now.

NOW CREATE A CAREER CONNECTION OF YOUR OWN. Review this chapter and look for a suggestion that you will commit to use while working or looking for a job. In a sentence or two, describe exactly what you plan to do and the primary benefit you want to gain. For example: "I will estimate the number of hours needed to complete the A-priority tasks on my to-do list. This will help me create more realistic schedules."

State your strategy and desired benefit in the space below:

_____

_____

_____

_____

_____

_____

_____

_____

_____

Name _____

Date _____

2

1. The Power Process: "Be here now" rules out planning. True or false? Explain your answer.

2. According to the text, everything written about time management can be reduced to three main ideas. What are they?

3. Rewrite the statement "I want to study harder" so that it becomes a specific goal.

4. Define *C fever* as it applies to the ABC priority method.

5. You can rank your to-do list items with the ABC system. Explain an alternative to this system.

6. Define the term *multitasking* and explain one strategy for dealing with it.

7. Define the term *time boxing*.

8. The text suggests that you do your Most Important Task (MIT):
   (a) During the middle of the day.
   (b) As early in the day as possible.
   (c) Right before going to sleep.
   (d) At whatever time during the day that you can squeeze it in.

9. According to the text, overcoming procrastination is a complex process that can take months or even years. True or false? Explain your answer.

10. What are at least 3 of the 25 ways to get the most out of now?

2 SKILLS *Snapshot*

CHAPTER

Take a snapshot of your current skills at working with time. Also think about the next step you'll take to develop more mastery in this area of life.

DISCOVERY

My score on the Time section of the Discovery Wheel on page 37 was . . .

I would describe my ability to set specific goals as . . .

When setting priorities for what to do each day, the first thing I consider is . . .

I keep track of my daily to-do items by . . .

My strategies for overcoming procrastination currently include . . .

INTENTION

I'll know that I've reached a new level of mastery with time when . . .

In other words, my goal for making better use of time is . . .

ACTION

To achieve that goal, the most important thing I can do next is . . .

At the end of this course, I would like my Time score on the Discovery Wheel to be . . .

Memory

Use this **Master Student Map** to ask yourself,

WHY THIS CHAPTER MATTERS . . .

- Learning memory techniques can boost your skills at test taking, reading, note taking, and many other tasks.

WHAT IS INCLUDED . . .

- Power Process: Love your problems (and experience your barriers)   102
- Take your memory out of the closet   103
- The memory jungle   104
- 20 memory techniques   106
- Set a trap for your memory   113
- Your brain—its care and feeding   114
- Mnemonic devices   116
- Remembering names   120
- Master Student Profile: Pablo Alvarado   121

HOW CAN I USE THIS CHAPTER . . .

- Focus your attention.
- Make conscious choices about what to remember.
- Recall facts and ideas with more ease.

WHAT IF . . .

- I could use my memory to its full potential?

JOURNAL ENTRY 6
Intention Statement

Create value from this chapter

Think of a time when you struggled to remember something that was important. Perhaps you were trying to remember someone's name or recall some key information for a test. Then scan this chapter and find at least three strategies that you will use to prevent this problem in the future.

Strategy   Page number

_____   _____

_____   _____

_____   _____

_____

_____

_____

_____

_____

_____

_____

_____

_____

_____

_____

_____

© Ruslan Ivantsov/Shutterstock.com

POWER process

Love your problems
(and experience your barriers)

We all have problems and barriers that block our progress or prevent us from moving into new areas. Often, the way we respond to our problems places limitations on what we can be, do, and have.

Problems often work like barriers. When we bump up against one of our problems, we usually turn away and start walking along a different path. And all of a sudden—bump!—we've struck another barrier. And we turn away again.

As we continue to bump into problems and turn away from them, our lives stay inside the same old boundaries. Inside these boundaries, we are unlikely to have new adventures. We are unlikely to keep learning.

If we respond to problems by loving them instead of resisting them, we can expand the boundaries in which we live our lives.

The word *love* might sound like an overstatement. In this Power Process, the word means to unconditionally accept the fact that your problems exist. The more we deny or resist a problem, the stronger it seems to become. When we accept the fact that we have a problem, we can find effective ways to deal with it.

Suppose one of your barriers is speaking in front of a group. You fear that you'll forget everything you planned to say.

One option for dealing with this barrier is denial. You could get up in front of a group and pretend that you're not afraid. You could tell yourself, "I'm not going to be scared," and then try to keep your knees from knocking.

A more effective approach is to love your fear. Go to the front of the room, look out into the audience, and say to yourself, "I am scared. I notice that my knees are shaking and my mouth feels dry, and I'm having a rush of thoughts about what might happen if I say the wrong thing. Yup, I'm scared, and I'm not going to fight it. I'm going to give this speech anyway."

The beauty of this Power Process is that you continue to take action—giving your speech, for example—no matter what you feel. You walk right up to the barrier and then *through* it. You might even find that if you totally accept and experience a barrier, such as fear, it shrinks or disappears. When you relax, you reclaim your natural abilities. You can recall memories, learn something new, and even laugh a little. Even if this does not happen right away, you can still open up to a new experience.

Loving a problem does not need *liking* it. Instead, loving a problem means admitting the truth about it. This helps us take effective action—which can free us of the problem once and for all.

You're One Click Away...
from accessing Power Process Media online and finding out more ways to love your problems.

Take your memory
out of the closet

Once upon a time, people talked about human memory as if it were a closet. You stored individual memories there as you would old shirts and stray socks. Remembering something was a matter of rummaging through all that stuff. If you were lucky, you found what you wanted.

This view of memory creates some problems. For one thing, closets can get crowded. Things too easily disappear. Even with the biggest closet, you eventually run out of space. If you want to pack some new memories in there—well, too bad. There's no room.

Brain researchers shattered this image to bits. Memory is not a closet. It's not a place or a thing. Instead, memory is a *process*.

On a conscious level, memories appear as distinct and unconnected mental events: words, sensations, images. They can include details from the distant past—the smell of cookies baking in your grandmother's kitchen or the feel of sunlight warming your face through the window of your first-grade classroom.

On a biological level, each of those memories involves millions of brain cells, or neurons, firing chemical messages to one another. If you could observe these exchanges in real time, you'd see regions of cells all over the brain glowing with electrical charges at speeds that would put a computer to shame.

When a series of brain cells connects several times in a similar pattern, the result is a memory. Psychologist Donald Hebb explains it this way: "Neurons which fire together, wire together."[1] It means that memories are not really stored. Instead, remembering is a process in which you *encode* information as links between active neurons that fire together. You also *decode*, or reactivate, neurons that wired together in the past.

There are critical moments in this process. Say that you're enjoying a lecture in introduction to psychology. It really makes sense. In fact, it's so interesting that you choose to just sit and listen—without taking notes. Two days later, you're studying for a test and wish you'd made a different choice. You remember that the lecture was interesting, but you don't recall much else. In technical terms, your decision to skip note taking was an *encoding error*.

So, you decide to change your behavior and take extensive notes during the next psychology lecture. Your goal is to capture everything the instructor says. This too has mixed results—a case of writer's cramp and 10 pages of dense, confusing scribbles. Oops. Another encoding error.

Effective encoding is finding a middle ground between these two extremes. As you listen and read, you make

> **Memory is the probability that certain patterns of brain activity will occur again in the future. In effect, you recreate a memory each time you recall it. In more practical terms, a good memory is not something you *have*. It's something you *do*.**

moment-to-moment choices about what you want to remember. You distinguish between key points, transitions, and minor details. You predict what material is likely to appear on a test. You also stay alert for ideas you can actively apply. These are things you capture in your notes.

Signs of memory mastery are making choices about *what* to remember and *how* to remember it. This in turn makes it easier for you to decode, or recall, the material at a crucial point in the future—such as during a test.

Whenever you efficiently encode and decode something new, your brain changes physically. You grow more connections between neurons. The more you learn, the greater the number of connections. For all practical purposes, there's no limit to how many memories your brain can process.

There's a lot you can do to wire those neural connections into place. That's where the memory techniques described in this chapter come into play. Use them to step out of your crowded mental closet into a world of infinite possibilities. ■

The MEMORY JUNGLE

Think of your memory as a vast, overgrown jungle. This memory jungle is thick with wild plants, exotic shrubs, twisted trees, and creeping vines. It spreads over thousands of square miles—dense, tangled, forbidding.

Imagine that the jungle is encompassed on all sides by towering mountains. There is only one entrance to the jungle, a small meadow that is reached by a narrow pass through the mountains.

In the jungle there are animals, millions of them. The animals represent all of the information in your memory. Imagine that every thought, mental picture, or perception you ever had is represented by an animal in this jungle. Every single event ever perceived by any of your five senses—sight, touch, hearing, smell, or taste—is a thought animal that has also passed through the meadow and entered the jungle. Some of the thought animals, such as the color of your seventh-grade teacher's favorite sweater, are well hidden. Other thoughts, such as your cell phone number or the position of the reverse gear in your car, are easier to find.

The memory jungle has two rules: Each thought animal must pass through the meadow at the entrance to the jungle. And once an animal enters the jungle, it never leaves.

The meadow represents short-term memory. You use this kind of memory when you look up a telephone number and hold it in your memory long enough to make a call. Short-term memory appears to have a limited capacity (the meadow is small) and disappears fast (animals pass through the meadow quickly).

Tippawan Kunkeaw/Shutterstock.com

The jungle itself represents long-term memory. This kind of memory allows you to recall information from day to day, week to week, and year to year. Remember that thought animals never leave the long-term memory jungle. The following visualizations can help you recall useful concepts about memory.

VISUALIZATION #1: A WELL-WORN PATH

Imagine what happens as a thought—in this case, we'll call it an elephant—bounds across short-term memory and into the jungle. The elephant leaves a trail of broken twigs and hoof prints that you can follow.

Brain research suggests that thoughts can wear "paths" in the brain.[2] These paths consist of dendrites—string-like fibers that connect brain cells. The more these connections are activated, the easier it is to retrieve (recall) the thought. In other words, the more often the elephant retraces the path, the clearer the path becomes. The more often you recall information and the more often you put the same information into your memory, the easier it is to find.

When you buy a new car, for example, the first few times you try to find reverse, you have to think for a moment. After you have found reverse gear every day for a week, the path is worn into your memory. After a year, the path is so well-worn that when you dream about driving your car backward, you even dream the correct motion for putting the gear in reverse.

VISUALIZATION #2: A HERD OF THOUGHTS

The second picture you can use to your advantage in recalling concepts about memory is the picture of many animals gathering at a clearing—like thoughts gathering at a central location in memory. It is easier to retrieve thoughts that are grouped together, just as it is easier to find a herd of animals than it is to find a single elephant.

Pieces of information are easier to recall if you can associate them with similar information. For example, you can more readily remember a particular player's batting average if you can associate it with other baseball statistics.

VISUALIZATION #3: TURNING YOUR BACK

Imagine releasing the elephant into the jungle, turning your back, and counting to 10. When you turn around, the elephant is gone. This is exactly what happens to most of the information you receive.

Psychological research consistently shows that we start forgetting new material almost as soon as we learn it. The memory loss is steep, with most of it occurring within the first 24 hours.[3] This means that much of the material is not being encoded. It is wandering around, lost in the memory jungle.

The remedy is simple: Review quickly. Do not take your eyes off the thought animal as it crosses the short-term memory meadow. Look at it again (review it) soon after it enters the long-term memory jungle. Wear a path in your memory immediately.

VISUALIZATION #4: DIRECTING THE ANIMAL TRAFFIC

The fourth picture is one you are in. You are standing at the entrance to the short-term memory meadow, directing herds of thought animals as they file through the pass, across the meadow, and into your long-term memory. You are taking an active role in the learning process. You are paying attention. You are doing more than sitting on a rock and watching the animals file past into your brain. You have become part of the process, and in doing so, you have taken control of your memory. ■

You're One Click Away...
from finding guided visualizations based on the memory jungle online.

Master Students
IN ACTION

You're One Click Away...
from a video about Master Students in Action.

"Before I read the Memory chapter, I had trouble remembering what I had studied when taking a test or quiz. Visualization is by far the most useful technique I have come across in this book. While I'm taking the test, I visualize the book or paper that I studied from. It also helps with names. I visualize something funny to go along with someone's name."

—Tauni Aldinger,
Saddleback College

Photo courtesy of Tauni Aldinger

20 MEMORY *Techniques*

Experiment with these techniques to develop a flexible, custom-made memory system that fits your style of learning.

The 20 techniques discussed here are divided into four categories, each of which represents a general principle for improving memory:

Organize it. Organized information is easier to find.

Use your body. Learning is an active process; get all of your senses involved.

Use your brain. Work *with* your memory, not *against* it.

Recall it. Regularly retrieve and apply key information.

ORGANIZE IT

1 Be selective. There's a difference between gaining understanding and drowning in information. During your stay in higher education, you will be exposed to thousands of facts and ideas. No one expects you to memorize all of them. To a large degree, the art of memory is the art of selecting what to remember in the first place.

As you dig into your textbooks and notes, make choices about what is most important to learn. Imagine that you are going to create a test on the material, and consider the questions you would ask.

When reading, look for chapter previews, summaries, and review questions. Pay attention to anything printed in bold type. Also notice visual elements—tables, charts, graphs, and illustrations. They are all clues pointing to what's important. During lectures, notice what the instructor emphasizes. Anything that's presented visually—on the board, in overheads, or with slides—is probably key.

2 Make it meaningful. You remember things better if they have meaning for you. One way to create meaning is to learn from the general to the specific. Before you begin your next reading assignment, skim the passage to locate the main ideas. If you're ever lost, step back and look at the big picture. The details then might make more sense.

You can organize any list of items—even random items—in a meaningful way to make them easier to remember. Although there are probably an infinite number of facts, there are only a finite number of ways to organize them.

One option is to organize any group of items by *category*. You can apply this suggestion to long to-do lists. For example, write each item on a separate index card. Then create a pile of cards for calls to make, errands to run, and household chores to complete. These will become your working categories.

The same concept applies to the content of your courses. In chemistry, a common example of organizing by category is the periodic table of chemical elements. When reading a novel for a literature course, you can organize your notes in categories such as theme, setting, and plot. Then take any of these categories and divide them into subcategories such as major events and minor events in the story. Use index cards to describe each event.

Another option is to organize by *chronological order*. Any time that you create a numbered list of ideas, events, or steps, you are organizing by chronological order. To remember the events that led up to the stock market crash of 1929, for instance, create a time line. List the key events on index cards. Then arrange the cards by the date of each event.

A third option is to organize by *spatial order*. In plain English, this means making a map. When studying for a history exam, for example, you can create a rough map of the major locations where events take place.

Fourth, there's an old standby for organizing lists—putting a list of items in *alphabetical* order. It's simple, and it works.

3 Create associations. The data already encoded in your neural networks are arranged according to a scheme that makes sense to you. When you introduce new data, you can remember them more effectively if you associate them with similar or related data.

Think about your favorite courses. They probably relate to subjects that you already know something about. If you have been interested in politics over the last few years, you'll find it easier to remember the facts in a modern history course. Even when you're tackling a new subject, you can build a mental store of basic background information—the raw material for creating associations. Preview reading assignments, and complete those readings before you attend lectures. Before taking upper-level courses, master the prerequisites.

USE YOUR BODY

4 Learn actively. Action is a great memory enhancer. Test this theory by studying your assignments with the same energy that you bring to the dance floor or the basketball court.

You can use simple, direct methods to infuse your learning with action. When you sit at your desk, sit up straight. Sit on the edge of your chair as if you were about to spring out of it and sprint across the room.

Also experiment with standing up when you study. It's harder to fall asleep in this position. Some people insist that their brains work better when they stand. Pace back and forth and gesture as you recite material out loud. Use your hands. Get your body moving.

Don't forget to move your mouth. During a lecture, ask questions. Read key passages from textbooks out loud. Use a louder voice for the main points.

Active learning also involves a variety of learning styles. In Chapter 1, the article "Learning styles: Discovering how you learn" explains four aspects of learning: feeling, watching, thinking, and doing. Many courses in higher education lean heavily toward thinking—lectures, papers, and reading. These courses might not offer chances to actively experiment with ideas or test them by "feeling."

Create those opportunities yourself. For example, your introductory psychology book probably offers some theories about how people remember information. Choose one of those theories, and test it on yourself. See whether you can discover a new memory technique.

Your sociology class might include a discussion about how groups of people resolve conflict. See whether you can apply any of those ideas to resolving conflict in your own life. The point behind each of these examples is the same: To remember an idea, go beyond thinking about it. Make it personal. *Do* something with it.

5 Relax. When you're relaxed, you absorb new information quickly and recall it with greater ease and accuracy. Students who can't recall information under the stress of a final exam can often recite the same facts later when they are relaxed.

Relaxing might seem to contradict the idea of active learning as explained in technique #4, but it doesn't. Being relaxed is not the same as being drowsy, zoned out, or asleep. Relaxation is a state of alertness, free of tension, during which your mind can play with new information, roll it around, create associations with it, and apply many of the other memory techniques. You can be active *and* relaxed. See Exercise #16: "Relax," in Chapter 4, for some tips on how to relax.

6 Create pictures. Draw diagrams. Make cartoons. Use these images to connect facts and illustrate relationships. You can "see" and recall associations within and among abstract concepts more easily when you visualize both the concepts and the associations. The key is to use your imagination. Creating pictures reinforces visual and kinesthetic learning styles.

For example, Boyle's law states that at a constant temperature the volume of a confined ideal gas varies inversely with its pressure. Simply put, cutting the volume in half doubles the pressure. To remember this concept, you might picture someone "doubled over," using a bicycle pump. As she increases the pressure in the pump by decreasing the volume in the pump cylinder, she seems to be getting angrier. By the time she has doubled the pressure (and halved the volume), she is boiling ("Boyle-ing") mad.

Another reason to create pictures is that visual information is associated with a part of the brain that is different from the part that processes verbal information. When you create a picture of a concept, you are anchoring the information in a second part of your brain. Doing so increases your chances of recalling that information.

To visualize abstract relationships effectively, create an action-oriented image, such as the person using the pump. Make the picture vivid too. The person's face could be bright red. And involve all of your senses. Imagine how the cold metal of the pump would feel and how the person would grunt as she struggled with it.

You can also create pictures as you study by using *graphic organizers*. These preformatted charts prompt you to visualize relationships among facts and ideas.

One example is a *topic-point-details* chart. At the top of this chart, write the main topic of a lecture or reading assignment. In the left column, list the main points you want to remember. And in the right column, list key details related to each point. Figure 3.1 is the beginning of a chart based on this article.

Influx Productions/Getty Images

20 MEMORY TECHNIQUES

Point	Details
1. Be selective	Choose what not to remember. Look for clues to important material.
2. Make it meaningful	Organize by time, location, category, continuum, or alphabet.
3. Create associations	Link new facts with facts you already know.
4. Learn actively	Sit straight. Stand while studying. Recite while walking.
5. Relax	Release tension. Remain alert.

Figure 3.1 Topic-Point-Details Chart

STIMULATE THE ECONOMY WITH TAX CUTS?

Opinion	Support
Yes	Savings from tax cuts allow businesses to invest money in new equipment. Tax cuts encourage businesses to expand and hire new employees.
No	Years of tax cuts under the Bush administration failed to prevent the mortgage credit crisis. Tax cuts create budget deficits.
Maybe	Tax cuts might work in some economic conditions. Budget deficits might be only temporary.

Figure 3.2 Question-Opinion-Support Chart

You could use a similar chart to prompt critical thinking about an issue. Express that issue as a question, and write it at the top. In the left column, note the opinion about the issue. In the right column, list notable facts, expert opinions, reasons, and examples that support each opinion. Figure 3.2 is about tax cuts as a strategy for stimulating the economy.

Sometimes you'll want to remember the main actions in a story or historical event. Create a time line by drawing a straight line. Place points in order on that line to represent key events. Place earlier events toward the left end of the line and later events toward the right. Figure 3.3 shows the start of time line of events relating the U.S. war with Iraq.

When you want to compare or contrast two things, play with a Venn diagram. Represent each thing as a circle. Draw the circles

3/19/03	3/30/03	4/9/03	5/1/03	5/29/03
U.S. invades Iraq	Rumsfeld announces location of WMD	Soldiers topple statue of Saddam	Bush declares mission accomplished	Bush: We found WMD

Figure 3.3 Time Line

so that they overlap. In the overlapping area, list characteristics that the two things share. In the outer parts of each circle, list the unique characteristics of each thing. Figure 3.4 compares the two types of journal entries included in this book—Discovery Statements and Intention Statements.

The graphic organizers described here are just a few of the many kinds available. To find more examples, do an Internet search. Have fun, and invent graphic organizers of your own.

7 Recite and repeat. When you repeat something out loud, you anchor the concept in two different senses. First, you get the physical sensation in your throat, tongue, and lips when voicing the concept. Second, you hear it. The combined result is synergistic, just as it is when you create pictures. That is, the effect of using two different senses is greater than the sum of their individual effects.

The "out loud" part is important. Reciting silently in your head can be useful—in the library, for example—but it is not as effective as making noise. Your mind can trick itself into thinking it knows something when it doesn't. Your ears are harder to fool.

The repetition part is important too. Repetition is a common memory device because it works. Repetition blazes a trail through the pathways of your brain, making the information easier to find. Repeat a concept out loud until you know it; then say it five more times.

Recitation works best when you recite concepts in your own words. For example, if you want to remember that the acceleration of a falling body due to gravity at sea level equals 32 feet per second per second, you might say, "Gravity makes an object accelerate 32 feet per second faster for each second that it's in the air at sea level." Putting a concept into your own words forces you to think about it.

Have some fun with this technique. Recite by writing a song about what you're learning. Sing it in the shower. Use any style you want. (Country, jazz, rock, or rap—when you sing out loud, learning's a snap!)

Or imitate someone. Imagine your textbook being read by Will Ferrell, Madonna, or Clint Eastwood. ("Go ahead, punk. Make my density equal mass over volume.")

8 Write it down. The technique of writing things down is obvious, yet easy to forget. Writing a note to yourself helps you remember an idea, even if you never look at the note again. Writing notes in the margins of your textbooks can help you remember what you read.

You can extend this technique by writing down an idea not just once, but many times. Let go of the old image of being forced to write "I will not throw paper wads" a hundred times on the chalkboard after school. When you choose to remember something, repetitive writing is a powerful tool.

Writing engages a different kind of memory than speaking. Writing prompts us to be more logical, coherent, and complete. Written reviews reveal gaps in knowledge that oral reviews miss, just as oral reviews reveal gaps that written reviews miss.

Another advantage of written reviews is that they more closely match the way you're asked to remember

Discovery Statements   Intention Statements

Discovery Statements
- Describe specific thoughts
- Describe specific feelings
- Describe current and past behaviors

(overlap)
- Are a type of journal entry
- Are based on telling the truth
- Can be written at any time on any topic
- Can lead to action

Intention Statements
- Describe future behaviors
- Can include timelines
- Can include rewards

Figure 3.4 Venn Diagram

materials in school. During your academic career, you'll probably take far more written exams than oral exams. Writing can be an effective way to prepare for such tests.

Finally, writing is physical. Your arm, your hand, and your fingers join in. Remember, learning is an active process—you remember what you *do*.

USE YOUR BRAIN

9 Engage your emotions. One powerful way to enhance your memory is to make friends with your amygdala. This area of your brain lights up with extra neural activity each time you feel a strong emotion. When a topic excites love, laughter, or fear, the amygdala sends a flurry of chemical messages that say, in effect, *This information is important and useful. Don't forget it.*

You're more likely to remember course material when you relate it to a goal—whether academic, personal, or career—that you feel strongly about. This is one reason why it pays to be specific about what you want. The more goals you have and the more clearly they are defined, the more channels you create for incoming information.

You can use this strategy even when a subject seems boring at first. If you're not naturally interested in a topic, then create interest. Find a study partner in the class—if possible, someone you know and like—or form a study group. Also consider getting to know the instructor personally. When a course creates a bridge to human relationships, you engage the content in a more emotional way.

10 Overlearn. One way to fight mental fuzziness is to learn more than you need to know about a subject simply to pass a test. You can pick a subject apart, examine it, add to it, and go over it until it becomes second nature.

This technique is especially effective for problem solving. Do the assigned problems and then do more problems. Find another textbook and work similar problems. Then make up your own problems and solve them. When you pretest yourself in this way,

the potential rewards are speed, accuracy, and greater confidence at exam time. Being well prepared can help you prevent test anxiety.

11 Escape the short-term memory trap. Short-term memory is different from the kind of memory you'll need during exam week. For example, most of us can look at an unfamiliar seven-digit phone number once and remember it long enough to dial it. See whether you can recall that number the next day.

Short-term memory can fade after a few minutes, and it rarely lasts more than several hours. A short review within minutes or hours of a study session can move material from short-term memory into long-term memory. That quick mini-review can save you hours of study time when exams roll around.

12 Use your times of peak energy. Study your most difficult subjects during the times when your energy peaks. Some people can concentrate more effectively during daylight hours. The early morning hours can be especially productive, even for those who hate to get up with the sun. Observe the peaks and valleys in your energy flow during the day, and adjust study times accordingly. Perhaps you experience surges in memory power during the late afternoon or evening.

13 Distribute learning. As an alternative to marathon study sessions, experiment with several shorter sessions spaced out over time. You might find that you can get far more done in three 2-hour sessions than in one 6-hour session.

For example, when you are preparing for your American history exam, study for an hour or two and then wash the dishes. While you are washing the dishes, part of your mind will be reviewing what you studied. Return to American history for a while, then call a friend. Even when you are deep in conversation, part of your mind will be reviewing history.

You can get more done if you take regular breaks. You can even use the breaks as mini-rewards. After a productive study session, give yourself permission to log on and check your e-mail, listen to a song, or play 10 minutes of hide-and-seek with your kids.

Distributing your learning is a brain-friendly activity. You cannot absorb new information and ideas during all of your waking hours. If you overload your brain, it will find a way to shut down for a rest—whether you plan for it or not. By taking periodic breaks while studying, you allow information to sink in. During these breaks, your brain is taking the time to rewire itself by growing new connections between cells. Psychologists call this process *consolidation*.[4]

The idea of allowing time for consolidation does have an exception. When you are so engrossed in a textbook that you cannot put it down, when you are consumed by an idea for a term paper and cannot think of anything else—keep going. The master student within you has taken over. Enjoy the ride.

14 Be aware of attitudes. People who think history is boring tend to have trouble remembering dates and historical events. People who believe math is difficult often have a hard time recalling mathematical equations and formulas. All of us can forget information that contradicts our opinions.

If you think a subject is boring, remind yourself that everything is related to everything else. Look for connections that relate to your own interests.

For example, consider a person who is fanatical about cars. He can rebuild a motor in a weekend and has a good time doing so. From this apparently specialized interest, he can explore a wide realm of knowledge. He can relate the workings of an engine to principles of physics, math, and chemistry. Computerized parts in newer cars can lead him to the study of data processing. He can research how the automobile industry has changed our cities and helped create suburbs, a topic that relates to urban planning, sociology, business, economics, psychology, and history.

Being aware of your attitudes is not the same as fighting them or struggling to give them up. Just notice your attitudes and be willing to put them on hold. For more ideas, see the Power Process: "Notice your pictures and let them go" on page 126.

15 Elaborate. According to Harvard psychologist Daniel Schacter, all courses in memory improvement are based on a single technique—elaboration. *Elaboration* means consciously encoding new information. Repetition is one basic way to elaborate. However, current brain research indicates that other types of elaboration are more effective for long-term memory.[5]

One way to elaborate is to ask yourself questions about incoming information: "Does this remind me of something or someone I already know?" "Is this similar to a technique that I already use?" and "Where and when can I use this information?"

When you learned to recognize Italy on a world map, your teacher probably pointed out that the country is shaped like a boot. This is a simple form of elaboration.

The same idea applies to more complex material. When you meet someone new, for example, ask yourself, "Does she remind me of someone else?" Or when reading this book, preview the material using the Master Student Map that opens each chapter.

16 Intend to remember. To instantly enhance your memory, form the simple intention to *learn it now* rather than later. The intention to remember can be more powerful than any single memory technique.

You can build on your intention with simple tricks. During a lecture, for example, pretend that you'll be quizzed on the key points at the end of the period. Imagine that you'll get a $5 reward for every correct answer.

Also pay attention to your attention. Each time your mind wanders during class, make a tick mark in the margins of your notes. The act of writing reengages your attention.

If your mind keeps returning to an urgent or incomplete task, then write an Intention Statement about how you will handle it. With your intention safely recorded, return to what's important in the present moment.

USE YOUR COMPUTER TO
enhance memory

The outlining feature of a word-processing program offers a way to combine some of the memory techniques in this chapter. Outlining allows you to organize information in a meaningful way. Stating key points in your own words also helps you learn actively. To create outlined summaries of your textbooks and lecture notes:

- Divide a book chapter or set of handwritten notes into sections.

- Open up a new document in your word-processing program, and list the main points from each section.

- Shift to the outline view of your document, and turn each point into a level-one heading.

- Enter key facts and other details as normal text under the appropriate heading.

- When reviewing for a test, shift your document into outline view so that only the headings are displayed. Scan them as you would scan the headlines in a newspaper.

- In the outline view, see whether you can recall the details you included. Then open up the normal text underneath each headline to check the accuracy of your memory.

RECALL IT

17 Remember something else. When you are stuck and can't remember something that you're sure you know, remember something else that is related to it.

If you can't remember your great-aunt's name, remember your great-uncle's name. During an economics exam, if you can't remember anything about the aggregate demand curve, recall what you do know about the aggregate supply curve. If you cannot recall specific facts, remember the example that the instructor used during her lecture. Any piece of information is encoded in the same area of the brain as a similar piece of information. You can unblock your recall by stimulating that area of your memory.

A brainstorm is a good memory jog. If you are stumped when taking a test, start writing down lots of answers to related questions, and—pop!—the answer you need is likely to appear.

18 Notice when you do remember. Everyone has a different memory style. Some people are best at recalling information they've read. Others have an easier time remembering what they've heard, seen, or done.

To develop your memory, notice when you recall information easily, and ask yourself what memory techniques you're using naturally. Also notice when you find it difficult to recall information. Be a reporter. Get the facts and then adjust your learning techniques. And remember to congratulate yourself when you remember.

The memory strategies that work best for you might relate to the preferred learning style that you identified in Chapter 1. See whether you can combine those strategies with new ones that are based on a different learning style. This approach might increase your effectiveness in the same way that cross-training works for athletes.

19 Use it before you lose it. Even information encoded in long-term memory becomes difficult to recall when we don't use it regularly. The pathways to the information become faint with disuse. For example, you can probably remember your current phone number. What was your phone number 10 years ago?

This example points to a powerful memory technique. To remember something, access it a lot. Read it, write it, speak it, listen to it, apply it—find some way to make contact with the material regularly. Each time you do so, you widen the neural pathway to the material and make it easier to recall the next time.

One classic technique for this purpose is making flash cards. Write a sample test question on one side of a 3×5 card and the answer to that question on the other side of the card. Use these cards to quiz yourself. Or ask someone else to read the questions, listen to your answers, and compare them to the answers on the card.

You can also use PowerPoint or other presentation software to create flash cards. Add illustrations, color, and other visual effects—a simple and fun way to activate your visual intelligence. A related option is to go online. Do an Internet search with the words *flash, card,* and *online.* You'll find a list of sites that allow you to select from a library of printable flash cards—or create and print your own cards. You can get flash card apps for your smart phone too.

Another way to make contact with the material is to teach it. Teaching demands mastery. When you explain the function of the pancreas to a fellow student, you discover quickly whether you really understand it yourself. Study groups are especially effective because they put you on stage. The friendly pressure of knowing that you'll teach the group helps focus your attention.

20 Adopt the attitude that you never forget. You might not believe that an idea or a thought never leaves your memory. That's okay. In fact, it doesn't matter whether you agree with the idea or not. It can work for you anyway.

Test the concept. Instead of saying, "I don't remember," you can say, "It will come to me." The latter statement implies that the information you want is encoded in your brain and that you can retrieve it—just not right now. You might be surprised to find that the information obediently pops into mind. ■

You're One Click Away...
from finding more memory strategies online.

Your mind,
online

Imagine how useful—and fun—it would be to download everything you've ever read or thought and then instantly locate what you know about a particular topic. Something like this is possible with digital tools. Web sites and computer applications give you a variety of ways to store text and images, organize, search them, and even share them. These applications fall into three major categories.

Social bookmarking. Some Web sites allow you to store, tag, share, and search links to specific pages. Examples are Delicious (www.delicious.com), Diigo (www.diigo.com), and Pinboard (pinboard.in).

Online notebooks. Evernote (www.evernote.com), Springpad (springpadit.com), Zoho Notebook (notebook.zoho.com), and similar Web sites allow you to "clip" images and text from various Web pages, categorize all this content, search it, and add your own notes.

Personal information managers. Examples of personal information managers include Evernote, Zotero, and Yojimbo. These applications share many features with online notebooks. However, some of them allow you to add "offline" content such as digital photos of business cards and receipts. You can search through all this content by using tags and key words.

3

EXERCISE 12

Use Q-Cards to reinforce memory

One memory strategy you might find useful involves a special kind of flash card. It's called a *Question Card*, or *Q-Card* for short.

To create a standard flash card, you write a question on one side of a 3 × 5 card, and its answer on the other side. Q-Cards have a question on *both* sides. Here's the trick: The question on one side of the card contains the answer to the question on the other side.

The questions you write on Q-Cards can draw on both lower- and higher-order thinking skills. Writing these questions forces you to encode material in different ways. You activate more areas of your brain and burn the concepts even deeper into your memory.

For example, say that you want to remember the subject of the Eighteenth Amendment to the U.S. Constitution—the one that prohibited the sale of alcohol. On one side of a 3 × 5 card, write *Which amendment prohibited the sale of alcohol?* Turn the card over, and write *What did the Eighteenth Amendment do?*

To get the most from Q-Cards:

• Add a picture to each side of the card. Doing so helps you learn concepts faster and develop a more visual learning style.

• Read the questions and recite the answers out loud. Two keys to memory are repetition and novelty, so use a different voice whenever you read and recite. Whisper the first time you go through your cards, then shout or sing the next time. Doing this develops an auditory learning style.

• Carry Q-Cards with you, and pull them out during waiting times. To develop a kinesthetic learning style, handle your cards often.

• Create a Q-Card for each new and important concept within 24 hours after attending a class or completing an assignment. This is your *active stack* of cards. Keep answering the questions on these cards until you learn each new concept.

• Review all of the cards for a certain subject on one day each week. For example, on Monday, review all cards from biology; on Tuesday, review all cards from history. These cards make up your *review stacks*.

Get started with Q-Cards right now. Use the blanks below. One blank represents the front of the card; the other blank represents the back. Start by creating a Q-Card about remembering how to use Q-Cards!

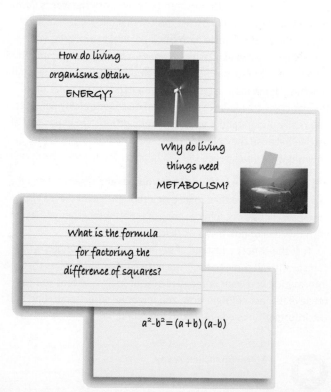

SET A TRAP FOR
your memory

When you want to remind yourself to do something, link this activity to another event you know will take place. The key is to "trap" your memory by picking events that are certain to occur.

Say that you're walking to class and suddenly remember that your accounting assignment is due tomorrow. If you wear a ring, then switch it to a finger on the opposite hand. Now you're "trapped." Every time you glance at your hand and notice that you switched the ring, you get a reminder that you were supposed to remember something else. If you empty your pockets every night, put an unusual item in your pocket in the morning to remind yourself to do something before you go to bed. For example, to remember to call your younger sister on her birthday, pick an object that reminds you of her—a photograph, perhaps—and put it in your pocket. When you empty your pocket that evening and find the photo, you're more likely to make the call.

Everyday rituals that you seldom neglect, such as feeding a pet or unlacing your shoes, provide opportunities for setting traps. For example, tie a triple knot in your shoelace as a reminder to set the alarm for your early morning study group meeting.

You can even use imaginary traps. To remember to pay your phone bill, visualize a big, burly bill collector knocking on your front door to talk to you about how much you owe. The next time your arrive at your front door, you'll be glad that you got there before he did. You still have time to make your payment!

Mobile devices work well for setting memory traps. To remind yourself to bring your textbook to class, for example, set an alarm on your cell phone to go off 10 minutes before you leave the house. Visualize yourself picking up the book when the alarm goes off.

Link two activities together, and make the association unusual. ■

©Istockphoto.com/Tatiana Popova

✔ EXERCISE 13

Remembering your car keys—or anything else

Pick something you frequently forget. Some people chronically lose their car keys or forget to pay their bills on time. Others let anniversaries and birthdays slip by.

Pick an item or a task you're prone to forget. Then design a strategy for remembering it. Use any of the techniques from this chapter, research others, or make up your own from scratch. Describe your technique and the results in the space provided.

In this exercise, as in most of the exercises in this book, a failure is also a success. Don't be concerned with whether your technique will work. Design it, and then find out whether it works. If it doesn't work for you this time, use another method.

_____

_____

_____

_____

_____

_____

_____

_____

_____

_____

_____

_____

_____

YOUR BRAIN—
its care and feeding

When asked about brain-based learning, skeptics might say: "Well, obviously—how could learning be based anywhere other than the brain?"

That's a fair question. One answer is this: Although all learning involves the brain, some learning strategies use more of the brain's unique capacities.

BRAINS THRIVE ON MEANINGFUL PATTERNS

Your brain is a pattern-making machine. It excels at taking random bits of information and translating them into meaningful wholes. Build on this capacity with *elaborative rehearsal*. For example:

- *Use your journal*. Write Discovery and Intention Statements like the ones in this book. Journal Entries prompt you to

> Your brain is a pattern-making machine. It excels at taking random bits of information and translating them into meaningful wholes. Build on this capacity with *elaborative rehearsal*.

elaborate on what you hear in class and read in your textbooks. You can create your own writing prompts. For example: "In class today, I discovered that . . . ." "In order to overcome my confusion about this topic, I intend to . . . ."

- *Send yourself a message.* Imagine that an absent classmate has asked you to send her an e-mail about what happened in class today. Write up a reply and send this e-mail to yourself. You'll actively process your recent learning—and create a summary that you can use to review for tests.

- *Play with ideas.* Copy your notes on to 3 × 5 cards, one fact or idea per card. Then see whether you can arrange them into new patterns—chronological order, order of importance, or main ideas and supporting details.

BRAINS THRIVE ON RICH SENSORY EXPERIENCE

Your brain's contact with the world comes through your five senses. So, anchor your learning in as many senses as possible. Beyond seeing and hearing, this can include touch, movement, smell, and taste:

- *Create images.* Draw mind map summaries of your readings and lecture notes. Include visual images. Put main ideas in larger letters and brighter colors.

- *Translate ideas in physical objects.* If one of your career goals is to work from a home office, for example, then create a model of your ideal workspace. Visit an art supplies store to find appropriate materials.

- *Immerse yourself in concrete experiences.* Say that you're in a music appreciation class and learning about jazz. Go to a local jazz club or concert to see and hear a live performance.

BRAINS THRIVE ON LONG-TERM CARE

Starting now, adopt habits to keep your brain lean and fit for life. Consider these research-based suggestions from the Alzheimer's Association.[6]

- *Stay mentally active.* If you sit at a desk most of the workday, take a hiking class or start a garden. If you seldom travel, start reading maps of new locations and plan a cross-country trip. Play challenging games and work crossword puzzles. Seek out museums, theaters, concerts, and other cultural

Even after you graduate, consider learning another language or taking up a musical instrument. Learning gives your brain a workout, much like sit-ups condition your abs.

3

events. Even after you graduate, consider learning another language or taking up a musical instrument. Learning gives your brain a workout, much like sit-ups condition your abs.

- *Stay socially active.* Having a network of supportive friends can reduce stress levels. In turn, stress management helps to maintain connections between brain cells. Stay socially active by working, volunteering, and joining clubs.

- *Stay physically active.* Physical activity promotes blood flow to the brain. It also reduces the risk of diabetes, cardiovascular disease, and other diseases that can impair brain function. Exercise that includes mental activity—such as planning a jogging route and watching for traffic signals—offers added benefits.

- *Adopt a brain-healthy diet.* A diet rich in dark-skinned fruits and vegetables boosts your supply of antioxidants—natural chemicals that nourish your brain. Examples of these foods are raisins, blueberries, blackberries, strawberries, raspberries, kale, spinach, brussels sprouts, alfalfa sprouts, and broccoli. Avoid foods that are high in saturated fat and cholesterol, which may increase the risk of Alzheimer's disease.

- *Protect your heart.* In general, what's good for your heart is good for your brain. Protect both organs by eating well, exercising regularly, managing your weight, staying tobacco-free, and getting plenty of sleep. These habits reduce your risk of heart attack, stroke, and other cardiovascular conditions that interfere with blood flow to the brain. ■

MNEMONIC DEVICES

It's pronounced "ne-MON-ik." The word refers to tricks that can increase your ability to recall everything from grocery lists to speeches.

Some entertainers use mnemonic devices to perform "impossible" feats of memory, such as recalling the names of everyone in a large audience after hearing them just once. Using mnemonic devices, speakers can go for hours without looking at their notes. The possibilities for students are endless.

There is a catch, though. Mnemonic devices have three serious limitations:

- They don't always help you understand or digest material. Mnemonics rely only on rote memorization.
- The mnemonic device itself is sometimes complicated to learn and time-consuming to develop.
- Mnemonic devices can be forgotten.

In spite of their limitations, mnemonic devices can be powerful. There are five general categories: new words, creative sentences, rhymes and songs, the loci system, and the peg system.

Make up new words. Acronyms are words created from the initial letters of a series of words. Examples include NASA (**N**ational **A**eronautics and **S**pace **A**dministration) and laser (**l**ight **a**mplification by **s**timulated **e**mission of **r**adiation).

You can make up your own acronyms to recall a series of facts. A common mnemonic acronym is Roy G. Biv, which has helped millions of students remember the colors of the visible spectrum (**r**ed, **o**range, **y**ellow, **g**reen, **b**lue, **i**ndigo, and **v**iolet). IPMAT helps biology students remember the stages of cell division (**i**nterphase, **p**rophase, **m**etaphase, **a**naphase, and **t**elophase). OCEAN helps psychology students recall the five major personality factors: **o**pen-mindedness, **c**onscientiousness, **e**xtraversion, **a**greeableness, and **n**euroticism.

Use creative sentences. Acrostics are sentences that help you remember a series of letters that stand for something. For example, the first letters of the words in the sentence *Every good boy does fine* (E, G, B, D, and F) are the music notes of the lines of the treble clef staff.

Create rhymes and songs. Madison Avenue advertising executives spend billions of dollars a year on advertisements designed to burn their messages into your memory. The song "It's the Real Thing" was used to market Coca-Cola, despite the soda's artificial ingredients.

Rhymes have been used for centuries to teach basic facts. "*I before e, except after c*" has helped many a student on spelling tests.

Use the loci system. The word *loci* is the plural of *locus,* a synonym for *place* or *location.* Use the loci system to create visual associations with familiar locations. Unusual associations are the easiest to remember.

The loci system is an old one. Ancient Greek orators used it to remember long speeches, and politicians use it today. For example, if a politician's position were that road taxes must be raised to pay for school equipment, his loci visualizations before a speech might look like the following.

First, as he walks in the door of his house, he imagines a large *porpoise* jumping through a hoop. This reminds him to begin by telling the audience the *purpose* of his speech.

Next, he visualizes his living room floor covered with paving stones, forming a road leading into the kitchen. In the kitchen, he pictures dozens of schoolchildren sitting on the floor because they have no desks.

Now it's the day of the big speech. The politician is nervous. He's perspiring so much that his clothes stick to his body. He stands up to give his speech and his mind goes blank. Then he starts thinking to himself:

I can remember the rooms in my house. Let's see, I'm walking in the front door and—wow!—I see a porpoise. That reminds me to talk about the purpose of my speech. And then there's that road leading to the kitchen. Say, what are all those kids doing there on the floor? Oh, yeah, now I remember—they have no desks! We need to raise taxes on roads to pay for their desks and the other stuff they need in classrooms.

Use the peg system. The peg system is a technique that employs key words that are paired with numbers. Each word forms a "peg" on which you can "hang" mental associations. To use this system effectively, learn the following peg words and their associated numbers well:

bun goes with 1	*sticks* goes with 6
shoe goes with 2	*heaven* goes with 7
tree goes with 3	*gate* goes with 8
door goes with 4	*wine* goes with 9
hive goes with 5	*hen* goes with 10

You can use the peg system to remember the Bill of Rights (the first ten amendments to the U.S. Constitution). For example, amendment number *four* is about protection from unlawful search and seizure. Imagine people knocking at your *door* who are demanding to search your home. This amendment means that you do not have to open your door unless those people have a proper search warrant. ■

Congress of the United States

4th Amendment
protection from unlawful search and seizure

✓ EXERCISE 14

Get creative

Construct your own mnemonic device for remembering some of the memory techniques in this chapter. Make up a poem, jingle, acronym, or acrostic. Or use another mnemonic system. Describe your mnemonic device in the space below.

_____

_____

_____

_____

_____

_____

_____

3

Notable failures

As you experiment with memory techniques, you may try a few that fail at crucial moments—such as during a test. Just remember that many people before you have failed miserably before succeeding brilliantly. Consider a few examples.

In his first professional race, cyclist **Lance Armstrong** finished last.

The first time **Jerry Seinfeld** walked onstage at a comedy club as a professional comic, he looked out at the audience and froze.

When **Lucille Ball** began studying to be an actress in 1927, she was told by the head instructor of the John Murray Anderson Drama School, "Try any other profession."

In high school, actor and comic **Robin Williams** was voted "Least Likely to Succeed."

Walt Disney was fired by a newspaper editor because "he lacked imagination and had no good ideas."

R. H. Macy failed seven times before his store in New York City caught on.

Emily Dickinson had only seven poems published in her lifetime.

Decca Records turned down a recording contract with the **Beatles** with an unprophetic evaluation: "We don't like their sound. Groups of guitars are on their way out."

In 1954, Jimmy Denny, manager of the Grand Ole Opry, fired **Elvis Presley** after one performance.

Babe Ruth is famous for his past home run record, but for decades he also held the record for strikeouts. **Mark McGwire** broke that record.

After **Carl Lewis** won the gold medal for the long jump in the 1996 Olympic Games, he was asked to what he attributed his longevity, having competed for almost 20 years. He said, "Remembering that you have both wins and losses along the way. I don't take either one too seriously."

"I've missed more than 9,000 shots in my career," **Michael Jordan** said. "I've lost almost 300 games. Twenty-six times I've been trusted to take the game winning shot . . . and missed. I've failed over and over and over again in my life. That is why I succeed."

Adapted from "But They Did Not Give Up," Division of Educational Studies, Emory University, accessed January 20, 2011, from www.des.emory.edu/mfp/OnFailingG.html.

You're One Click Away...
from finding more notable failures online.

PRACTICING
critical thinking 3

Memory skills connect to several qualities of a master student—being inquisitive, competent, and able to focus attention. Use this exercise as a way to further develop those qualities in yourself.

First, review the six levels of thinking described by Benjamin Bloom:

Level 1: Remembering—recalling an idea.

Level 2: Understanding—explaining an idea in your own words and giving examples from your own experience.

Level 3: Applying—using an idea to produced a desired result.

Level 4: Analyzing—dividing an idea into parts or steps.

Level 5: Evaluating—rating the truth, usefulness, or quality of an idea—and giving reasons for your rating.

Level 6: Creating—inventing something new based on an idea.

This exercise is about **Level 4: Analyzing**. For example, recall the "memory jungle" described in the article on page 104. This is an idea with four parts. Each part includes a visualization and related feature about memory. These can all be summarized in a chart:

Visualization #1: A well-worn path	Memory feature: Thoughts create "paths" of connected cell in the brain.
Visualization #2: A herd of thoughts	Memory feature: Thoughts that are grouped together ("herded") are easier to recall.
Visualization #3: Turning your back	Memory feature: We quickly forget ("turn our back") on new material unless we review it.
Visualization #4: Directing the animal traffic	Memory feature: You can direct new thoughts ("animals") into your long-term memory by actively using memory techniques.

Creating a chart is one way to analyze an idea. This level of thinking can also involve making lists, drawing maps, and sorting things into groups or categories. On a test, questions that call for analysis might also ask you to *compare* (state how things are alike) and *contrast* (state how things differ).

Now it's your turn. Choose another idea from this chapter (**Level 1: Remembering**) and think about it at **Level 4: Analyzing**. In the space below, summarize the idea and then demonstrate your higher-level thinking. Continue on additional paper as needed.

_____

_____

_____

_____

_____

_____

_____

_____

_____

_____

_____

_____

_____

_____

_____

_____

_____

_____

_____

_____

For more information on the six levels of thinking, see "Becoming a critical thinker" in Chapter 7.

EXERCISE 15

Move from problems to solutions

Many students find it easy to complain about school and to dwell on problems. This exercise gives you an opportunity to change that habit and respond creatively to any problem you're currently experiencing—whether it be with memorizing or some other aspect of school or life.

The key is to dwell more on solutions than on problems. Do that by inventing as many solutions as possible for any given problem. See whether you can turn a problem into a *project* (a plan of action) or a *promise* to change some aspect of your life. Shifting the emphasis of your conversation from problems to solutions can raise your sense of possibility and unleash the master learner within you.

In the space below, describe at least three problems that could interfere with your success as a student. The problems can be related to courses, teachers, personal relationships, finances, or anything else that might get in the way of your success.

My problem is that . . .

_____

_____

My problem is that . . .

_____

_____

My problem is that . . .

_____

_____

Next, brainstorm at least five possible solutions to each of those problems. Ten solutions would be even better. (You can continue brainstorming on a separate piece of paper or on a computer.) You might find it hard to come up with that many ideas. That's okay. Stick with it. Stay in the inquiry, give yourself time, and ask other people for ideas.

I can solve my problem by . . .

_____

_____

I can solve my problem by . . .

_____

_____

I can solve my problem by . . .

_____

_____

JOURNAL ENTRY 7
Discovery Statement

Revisit your memory skills

Take a minute to reflect on the memory techniques in this chapter. You probably use some of them already without being aware of it. In the space below, list at least three memory techniques you have used in the past, and describe how you have used them.

3

_____

_____

_____

_____

_____

_____

_____

_____

_____

_____

_____

_____

_____

_____

_____

_____

_____

_____

_____

_____

_____

_____

_____

_____

_____

_____

_____

REMEMBERING
names

New friendships, job contacts, and business relationships all start with remembering names. Here are some suggestions for remembering them.

Recite and repeat in conversation. When you hear a person's name, repeat it. Immediately say it to yourself several times without moving your lips. You can also repeat the name out loud in a way that does not sound forced or artificial: "I'm pleased to meet you, Maria."

Ask the other person to recite and repeat. You can let other people help you remember their names. After you've been introduced to someone, ask that person to spell her name and pronounce it correctly for you. Most people will be flattered by the effort you're making to learn their names.

While you're at it, verify what name people want to be called. "Bob" may actually prefer "Robert."

Visualize. After the conversation, construct a brief visual image of the person. For a memorable image, make it unusual. Imagine the name painted in hot pink fluorescent letters on the person's forehead.

Admit you don't know. Admitting that you can't remember someone's name can actually put people at ease. Most of them will sympathize if you say, "I'm working to remember names better. Yours is right on the tip of my tongue. What is it again?"

Introduce yourself again. Most of the time we assume introductions are one-shot affairs. If we miss a name the first time around, our hopes for remembering it are dashed. Instead of giving up, reintroduce yourself: "We met earlier. I'm Jesse. Please tell me your name again."

Use associations. Link each person you meet with one characteristic that you find interesting or unusual. For example, you could make a mental note: "Vicki Cheng—long, black hair" or "James Washington—horn-rimmed glasses." To reinforce your associations, write them on 3 × 5 cards as soon as you can.

Limit the number of new names you learn at one time. Occasionally, we find ourselves in situations where we're introduced to several people at the same time: "Dad, these are all the people in my Boy Scout troop." "Let's take a tour so you can meet all 32 people in this department."

When meeting a large group of people, concentrate on remembering just two or three names. Free yourself from feeling obligated to remember everyone. Few of the people in mass introductions expect you to remember their names. Another way to avoid memory overload is to limit yourself to learning just first names. Last names can come later.

Ask for photos. In some cases, you might be able to get photos of all the people you meet. For example, a small business where you work might have a brochure with pictures of all the employees. If you're having trouble remembering names the first week of work, ask for individual or group photos, and write in the names if they're not included. You can use these photos as flash cards to drill yourself on names.

Go early. Consider going early to conventions, parties, and classes. Sometimes just a few people show up on time for these occasions. That's fewer names for you to remember. And as more people arrive, you can overhear them being introduced to others—an automatic review for you.

Make it a game. In situations where many people are new to one another, consider pairing up with another person and staging a contest. Challenge each other to remember as many new names as possible. Then choose an award—such as a movie ticket or free meal—for the person who wins.

Use technology. After you meet new people, enter their names as contacts in your e-mail, add them to a database, or enter them into your cell phone. If you get business cards, enter phone numbers, e-mail addresses, and other contact information as well.

Intend to remember. The simple act of focusing your attention at key moments can do wonders for your memory. Test this idea for yourself. The next time you're introduced to someone, direct 100 percent of your attention to hearing that person's name. Do this consistently, and see what happens to your ability to remember names. ∎

masterstudentprofile

Pablo Alvarado

(1954–) Executive director of the National Day Laborer Organizing Network. Alvarado uses soccer, music, and coalition building to foster humane conditions for day laborers.

As an immigrant worker from El Salvador, Pablo Alvarado has a special connection to the Latin American immigrants who have traveled far from their homes in search of work to support their families. These are the people who wait on street corners, in parking lots, or in parks hoping for temporary employment—which is usually hard physical labor. Their average monthly earnings range from $350 to $1,000. They suffer discrimination, unsafe working conditions, and underpayment or nonpayment for their work, and many live in fear of deportation. Also, in many parts of the country, new civic ordinances prevent day laborers from soliciting work in public places, which makes finding work even more difficult. In addition, day laborers are frequent targets of violence and law enforcement hostility.

In El Salvador, Alvarado's family members were farmers who grew beans, corn, and coffee for their own use. Every day, his father hauled water from a nearby town to sell in their village. At harvest time, young Alvarado worked 10 hours a day at nearby coffee plantations to have money to buy his clothes and school supplies. Although Alvarado's mother never went to school and his father only attended as far as the third grade, his parents insisted that he and his siblings get an education.

In the midst of civil war, when he was 12 years old, Alvarado became a teaching assistant for a literacy class that served his neighbors, and he witnessed the power of education to bring social improvement and better living conditions. "On my way to and from school, I would walk over bodies, which were left on the side of the road. When I was in eighth grade, several teachers were killed and others fled because they were accused of being guerrilla sympathizers," Alvarado recalls.

At age 16, Alvarado used his communications skills to serve as a lay preacher. His teachings contained elements of Liberation Theology, applying the Gospels to current socioeconomic and political struggles. He earned high school teaching credentials in 1989 from Universidad de El Salvador, but "just as many

immigrants have done, I fled my country because of political and economic reasons."

Working as an undocumented immigrant in the United States, Alvarado toiled as a gardener, factory assembly line worker, driver, and painter, and he experienced the pain of isolation and discrimination. While working at a studio-equipment factory, he witnessed hostility between Salvadorans and Mexicans. "Drawing on my childhood experiences, I engaged other coworkers and organized a soccer team that greatly improved relations among workers." That was the beginning of Alvarado's leadership in the United States. "The soccer experience is now part of the national movement, as day laborers in Los Angeles and Washington, D.C., have created their own soccer leagues," he says.

Some of his organizing techniques are unusual, but effective. Besides soccer teams, his organization also sponsors chess teams, marathon races, and popular theater. "On the street corners, workers start by relating to each other as competition (for jobs)," Alvarado explains. "When brought together on a soccer field, their dynamic changes to camaraderie, which then extends back to organizing on the street corners."

Photo by Misha Erwt

PABLO ALVARADO . . . is caring.

YOU . . . can care for people by sharing your memories of their lives.

"Pablo Alvarado, National Day Laborer Organizing Network (NDLON)—Los Angeles, CA: 2004 Award Recipients," Institute for Sustainable Communities, Leadership for a Changing World, Institute for Sustainable Communities, 2009, www. leadershipforchange.org/awardees/awardee.php3?ID=201.

 You're One Click Away...
from learning more about Pablo Alvarado online at the Master Student Profiles. You can also visit the Master Student Hall of Fame to learn about other master students.

© istockphoto.com/pagadesign

PUT THIS CHAPTER TO
W⊕RK

Use your memory skills to succeed in the workplace. Retain information from workshops, training sessions, and business books. Recall details about products and services. And remember the names of your coworkers and job-hunting contacts. Start with the following suggestions:

USE MEMORY TECHNIQUES TO PREPARE FOR JOB INTERVIEWS. Before any job interview, make a short list of things you want to mention. Start with key facts from the research you've done about your prospective employer—company history, products, and services. Also list key points from your skills analysis and résumé. (For more on these topics, see Chapter 12.) Round out your list with the questions *you* want to ask the interviewer. Here are two to consider: What happens next in the hiring process? Do you have any reservations about hiring me?

REMEMBER NAMES AT WORK. Start with the suggestions in "Remembering names" on page 120. Then consider these additional tips:

Comment on the name. This technique acts as a conversation starter while allowing you to recite and repeat the person's name: "I have a cousin named Theresa, so that will be easy to remember." "You're the second person named James that I've met today."

Ask for the spelling. This allows you to hear the name again. It also helps you distinguish between common names with different spellings: *Stephen* versus *Steven*; *Joanne* versus *Joann*. Once you get the spelling, visualize yourself writing it on a blank sheet of paper in big, bold letters.

Break the name down into simpler parts and then say them to yourself. Exaggerate the key sounds. For Tina, say *teeeeee-na*. For Jamal, say *ja-maaaaaal*.

Take notes. Keep a pen and a few 3 × 5 cards in your purse or pocket. After meeting someone, jot the person's name on a card, along with a notable fact: "Sophie works in accounting." "Melissa started working here on the same day I did."

File names for future reference. Gather up all your handwritten notes about people you've met. Then key this information into a document that you can access with your computer or other digital device.

Look for visual cues. If nametags are required in your workplace, then you've got a handy tool for remembering names. Also look for name cards posted on cubicles and workstations.

Be sensitive to cultural norms. In workplaces with a more formal tone, you might be wise to refer to people by their last name: for example, Mr. Hassad or Ms. Washington. Notice how your experienced coworkers handle this situation.

Give yourself a break. Stop saying things such as "I'm bad at names." Instead, say: "I'm *getting better* with names." Notice whether this new way of speaking affects your ability to remember.

NOW CREATE A CAREER CONNECTION OF YOUR OWN. Review this chapter, looking for a memory strategy that you will commit to use while working or looking for a job. In a sentence or two, describe exactly what you plan to do and the primary benefit you want to gain. For example: "I will use an online bookmarking service to clip Web pages about career planning and job hunting. This will help me create a personal library of articles that I can use to improve my next job search."

State your strategy and desired benefit in the space below:

_____

_____

_____

_____

_____

_____

_____

_____

_____

CHAPTER 3 QUIZ

Name _____

Date _____

1. Briefly define the word *love* as it is used in the Power Process: "Love your problems (and experience your barriers)."

2. According to the latest research, memory is:
   (a) A process rather than a thing.
   (b) A process of encoding and decoding.
   (c) Not something you *have*, but something you *do*.
   (d) All of the above.

3. In the article about the memory jungle, the meadow:
   (a) Is a place that every animal (thought or perception) must pass through.
   (b) Represents short-term memory.
   (c) Represents the idea that one type of memory has a limited capacity.
   (d) All of the above.

4. Give two examples of ways in which you can organize a long list of items.

5. Memorization on a deep level can take place if you:
   (a) Repeat the idea.
   (b) Repeat the idea.
   (c) Repeat the idea.
   (d) Do all of the above.

6. The article "20 memory techniques" is divided into four categories. What are those categories?

7. Define the term *graphic organizer* and give two examples.

8. Define *acronym* and give an example of one.

9. Mnemonic devices are the most efficient ways to memorize facts and ideas. True or false? Explain your answer.

10. List three techniques that can be used to remember the names of three specific people you've recently met.

3 SKILLS *Snapshot*

CHAPTER 3

U se this exercise to monitor the Master Student qualities that you're developing—especially those related to memory. Begin by reflecting on some recent experiences. Then take the next step toward memory mastery by committing to a specific action in the near future.

DISCOVERY

My score on the Memory section of the Discovery Wheel on page 37 was . . .

Recalling key facts more quickly and accurately could help me be more effective in the following situations . . .

Memory techniques that I already use include . . .

INTENTION

I'll know that I've reached a new level of mastery with remembering ideas and information when . . .

Stated as goal, my intention is. . .

ACTION

To achieve the goal I just wrote, the most important thing I can do next is to . . .

At the end of this course, I would like my Memory score on the Discovery Wheel to be . . .

Reading

Use this **Master Student Map** to ask yourself,

WHY THIS CHAPTER MATTERS . . .

- Higher education requires extensive reading of complex material.

WHAT IS INCLUDED . . .

- Power Process: Notice your pictures and let them go   126
- Muscle Reading   127
- How Muscle Reading works   128
- Phase 1: Before you read   129
- Phase 2: While you read   130
- Phase 3: After you read   132
- When reading is tough   134
- Getting past roadblocks to reading   135
- Reading faster   137
- Word power—expanding your vocabulary   139
- Mastering the English language   140
- Developing information literacy   142
- Muscle Reading for ebooks   145
- Master Student Profile: Matias Manzano   147

HOW CAN I USE THIS CHAPTER . . .

- Analyze what effective readers do and experiment with new techniques.
- Increase your vocabulary and adjust your reading speed for different types of material.
- Comprehend difficult texts with more ease.

WHAT IF . . .

- I could finish my reading with time to spare and easily recall the key points?

JOURNAL ENTRY 8
Intention Statement

Declare what you want from this chapter

Recall a time when you encountered problems with reading, such as finding words you didn't understand or pausing to reread paragraphs more than once. Then list at least three specific reading skills you want to gain from this chapter.

I intend to . . .

_____

_____

_____

_____

_____

_____

_____

_____

_____

_____

_____

_____

_____

_____

_____

© Ruslan Ivantsov/Shutterstock.com

POWER process

Notice your pictures and let them go

One of the brain's primary jobs is to manufacture images. We use mental pictures to make predictions about the world, and we base much of our behavior on those predictions.

Pictures can sometimes get in our way. Take the student who plans to attend a school he hasn't visited. He chose this school for its strong curriculum and good academic standing, but his brain didn't stop there. In his mind, the campus has historic buildings with ivy-covered walls and tree-lined avenues. The professors, he imagines, will be as articulate as Barack Obama and as entertaining as Conan O'Brien. The cafeteria will be a cozy nook serving everything from delicate quiche to strong coffee. He will gather there with fellow students for hours of stimulating, intellectual conversation. The library will have every book, while the computer lab will boast the newest technology.

The school turns out to be four gray buildings downtown, next to the bus station. The first class he attends is taught by an overweight, balding professor wearing a purple and orange bird-of-paradise tie. The cafeteria is a nondescript hall with machine-dispensed food, and the student's apartment is barely large enough to accommodate his roommate's tuba. This hypothetical student gets depressed. He begins to think about dropping out of school.

The problem with pictures is that they can prevent us from seeing what is really there. That is what happened to the student in this story. His pictures prevented him from noticing that his school is in the heart of a culturally vital city—close to theaters, museums, government offices, clubs, and all kinds of stores. The professor with the weird tie is not only an expert in his field but also a superior teacher. The school cafeteria is skimpy because it can't compete with the variety of inexpensive restaurants in the area.

Our pictures often lead to our being angry or disappointed. We set up expectations of events before they occur. Sometimes we don't even realize that we have these expectations. The next time you discover you are angry, disappointed, or frustrated, look to see which of your pictures aren't being fulfilled.

When you notice that pictures are getting in your way, in the gentlest manner possible let your pictures go. Let them drift away like wisps of smoke picked up by a gentle wind.

This Power Process can be a lifesaver when it comes to reading. Some students enter higher education with pictures about all the reading they'll be required to do before they graduate. They see themselves feeling bored, confused, and worried about keeping up with assignments. If you have such pictures, be willing to let them go. This chapter can help you recreate your whole experience of reading, which is crucial to your success.

Sometimes when we let go of old pictures, it's helpful to replace them with new, positive pictures. These new images can help you take a fresh perspective. Your new pictures might not feel as comfortable and genuine as your old ones. That's okay. Give it time. It's your head, and you're ultimately in charge of the pictures that live there.

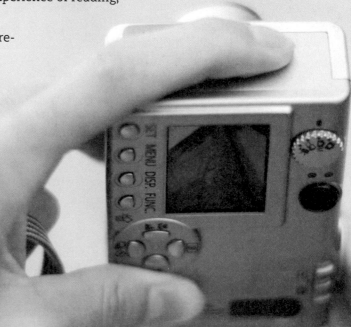

istockphoto.com/Tim Ashton

You're One Click Away...
from accessing Power Process Media online and finding out more about how to "notice your pictures and let them go."

Picture yourself sitting at a desk, a book in your hands. Your eyes are open, and it looks as if you're reading. Suddenly your head jerks up. You blink. You realize your eyes have been scanning the page for 10 minutes, and you can't remember a single thing you have read.

MUSCLE READING 4

Or picture this: You've had a hard day. You were up at 6:00 A.M. to get the kids ready for school. A coworker called in sick, and you missed your lunch trying to do his job as well as your own. You picked up the kids, then had to shop for dinner. Dinner was late, of course, and the kids were grumpy.

Finally, you get to your books at 8:00 P.M. You begin a reading assignment on something called "the equity method of accounting for common stock investments." "I am preparing for the future," you tell yourself, as you plod through two paragraphs and begin the third. Suddenly, everything in the room looks different. Your head is resting on your elbow, which is resting on the equity method of accounting. The clock reads 11:00 P.M. Say good-bye to 3 hours.

Sometimes the only difference between a sleeping pill and a textbook is that the textbook doesn't have a warning on the label about operating heavy machinery.

Contrast this scenario with the image of an active reader, who exhibits the following behaviors:

- Stays alert, poses questions about what she reads, and searches for the answers.
- Recognizes levels of information within the text, separating the main points and general principles from supporting details.
- Quizzes herself about the material, makes written notes, and lists unanswered questions.
- Instantly spots key terms and takes the time to find the definitions of unfamiliar words.
- Thinks critically about the ideas in the text and looks for ways to apply them.

That sounds like a lot to do. Yet skilled readers routinely accomplish all these things and more—while enjoying the process.

Master students engage actively with reading material. They're willing to grapple with even the most challenging texts. They wrestle meaning from each page. They fill the margins with handwritten questions. They underline, highlight, annotate, and nearly rewrite some books to make them their own.

Master students also commit to change their lives based on what they read. Of every chapter, they ask, "What's the point? And what's the payoff? How can I use this to live my purpose and achieve my goals?" These students are just as likely to create to-do lists as to take notes on their reading. And when they're done with a useful book, master students share it with others for continuing conversation. Reading becomes a creative act and a tool for building community.

One way to experience this kind of success is to approach reading with a system in mind. An example is Muscle Reading. You can use Muscle Reading to avoid mental minivacations and reduce the number of unscheduled naps during study time, even after a hard day. Muscle Reading is a way to decrease difficulty and struggle by increasing energy and skill. Once you learn this system, you might actually spend less time on your reading and get more out of it.

Boosting your reading skills will promote your success in school. It can also boost your income. According to a report from the National Endowment for the Arts, proficient readers earn more than people with only basic reading skills. In addition, better readers are more likely to work as managers or other professionals.[1]

This is not to say that Muscle Reading will make your job or education a breeze. Muscle Reading might even look like more work at first. Effective textbook reading is an active, energy-consuming, sit-on-the-edge-of-your-seat business. That's why this strategy is called Muscle Reading. ∎

How Muscle Reading WORKS

Muscle Reading is a three-phase technique you can use to extract the ideas and information you want.

- Phase 1 includes steps to take *before* you read.
- Phase 2 includes steps to take *while* you read.
- Phase 3 includes steps to take *after* you read.

Each phase has specific steps.

PHASE ONE:
Before you read
Step 1: **Preview**
Step 2: **Outline**
Step 3: **Question**

PHASE TWO:
While you read
Step 4: **Focus**
Step 5: **Flag Answers**

PHASE THREE:
After you read
Step 6: **Recite**
Step 7: **Review**
Step 8: **Review again**

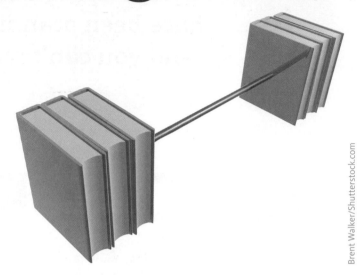

To jog your memory, write the first letters of the Muscle Reading acrostic in a margin or at the top of your notes. Then check off the steps you intend to follow.

To assist your recall of Muscle Reading strategies, memorize three short sentences:

$P_{ry} O_{ut} Q_{uestions.}$

$F_{ocus} and F_{lag} A_{nswers.}$

$R_{ecite,} R_{eview,} and R_{eview again.}$

These three sentences correspond to the three phases of the Muscle Reading technique. Each sentence is an acrostic. The first letter of each word stands for one of the steps listed above.

Take a moment to invent images for each of those sentences.

For *Phase 1*, visualize or feel yourself prying out questions from a text. These questions are ones you want answered based on a brief survey of the assignment. Make a mental picture of yourself scanning the material, spotting a question, and reaching into the text to pry it out. Hear yourself saying, "I've got it. Here's my question."

Then for *Phase 2*, focus on finding answers to your questions. Feel free to underline, highlight, or mark up your text in other ways. Make the answers so obvious that they lift up from the page.

Finally, you enter *Phase 3*. Hear your voice reciting what you have learned. Listen to yourself making a speech or singing a song about the material as you review it.

To jog your memory, write the first letters of the Muscle Reading acrostic in a margin or at the top of your notes. Then check off the steps you intend to follow. Or write the Muscle Reading steps on 3 × 5 cards and then use them for bookmarks.

Muscle Reading might take a little time to learn. At first you might feel it's slowing you down. That's natural when you're gaining a new skill. Mastery comes with time and practice.

PHASE 1 Before you read

STEP 1 PREVIEW

Before you start reading, preview the entire assignment. You don't have to memorize what you preview to get value from this step. Previewing sets the stage for incoming information by warming up a space in your mental storage area.

If you are starting a new book, look over the table of contents and flip through the text page by page. If you're going to read one chapter, flip through the pages of that chapter. Even if your assignment is merely a few pages in a book, you can benefit from a brief preview of the table of contents.

Read all chapter headings and subheadings. Like the headlines in a newspaper, these are usually printed in large, bold type. Often headings are brief summaries in themselves.

Keep an eye out for summary statements. If the assignment is long or complex, read the summary first. Many textbooks have summaries in the introduction or at the end of each chapter.

When previewing, seek out familiar concepts, facts, or ideas. These items can help increase comprehension by linking new information to previously learned material. Take a few moments to reflect on what you already know about the subject—even if you think you know nothing. This technique prepares your brain to accept new information.

Look for ideas that spark your imagination or curiosity. Inspect drawings, diagrams, charts, tables, graphs, and photographs.

Imagine what kinds of questions will show up on a test. Previewing helps to clarify your purpose for reading. Ask yourself what you will do with this material and how it can relate to your long-term goals. Will you be reading just to get the main points? Key supporting details? Additional details? All of the above? Your answers will guide what you do with each step that follows.

Keep your preview short. If the entire reading assignment will take less than an hour, your preview might take 5 minutes. Previewing is also a way to get yourself started when an assignment looks too big to handle. It is an easy way to step into the material.

STEP 2 OUTLINE

With complex material, take time to understand the structure of what you are about to read. Outlining actively organizes your thoughts about the assignment and can help make complex information easier to understand.

If your textbook provides chapter outlines, spend some time studying them. When an outline is not provided, sketch a brief one in the margin of your book or at the beginning of your notes on a separate sheet of paper. Later, as you read and take notes, you can add to your outline.

Headings in the text can serve as major and minor entries in your outline. For example, the heading for this article is "Phase 1: Before you read," and the subheadings list the three steps in this phase. When you outline, feel free to rewrite headings so that they are more meaningful to you.

The amount of time you spend on this outlining step will vary. For some assignments, a 10-second mental outline is all you might need. For other assignments (fiction and poetry, for example), you can skip this step altogether.

STEP 3 QUESTION

Before you begin a careful reading, determine what you want from the assignment. Then write down a list of questions, including any questions that resulted from your preview of the materials.

Another useful technique is to turn chapter headings and subheadings into questions. For example, if a heading is "Transference and Suggestion," you can ask yourself, "What are *transference* and *suggestion?* How does *transference* relate to *suggestion?*" Make up a quiz as if you were teaching this subject to your classmates.

If there are no headings, look for key sentences and turn them into questions. These sentences usually show up at the beginnings or ends of paragraphs and sections.

Have fun with this technique. Make the questions playful or creative. You don't need to answer every question that you ask. The purpose of making up questions is to get your brain involved in the assignment. Take your unanswered questions to class, where they can be springboards for class discussion.

Demand your money's worth from your textbook. If you do not understand a concept, write specific questions about it. The more detailed your questions, the more powerful this technique becomes.

• •

> **Have fun with this technique. Make the questions playful or creative. You don't need to answer every question that you ask. The purpose of making up questions is to get your brain involved in the assignment. Take your unanswered questions to class, where they can be springboards for class discussion.**

• •

 You're One Click Away...
from finding examples of Phase 1 strategies online.

4

PHASE 2 While you read

STEP 4 FOCUS

You have previewed the reading assignment, organized it in your mind or on paper, and formulated questions. Now you are ready to begin reading.

It's easy to fool yourself about reading. Just having an open book in your hand and moving your eyes across a page doesn't mean that you are reading effectively. Reading takes mental focus.

As you read, be conscious of where you are and what you are doing. Use the Power Process: "Be here now" in Chapter 2. When you notice your attention wandering, gently bring it back to the present moment. There are many ways to do this.

To begin, get in a position to stay focused. If you observe chief executive officers, you'll find that some of them wear out the front of their chair first. They're literally on the edge of their seat. Approach your reading assignment in the same way. Sit up. Keep your spine straight. Avoid reading in bed, except for fun.

Avoid marathon reading sessions. Schedule breaks and set a reasonable goal for the entire session. Then reward

FIVE SMART WAYS
to highlight a text

Step 5 in Muscle Reading mentions a powerful tool: highlighting. It also presents a danger—the ever-present temptation to highlight too much text. Excessive highlighting leads to wasted time during reviews. Get the most out of all that money you pay for books and the time you spend reading. Highlight in an efficient way that leaves texts readable for years to come and provides you with an easy reviewing method.

Read carefully first.
Read an entire chapter or section at least once before you begin highlighting. Don't be in a hurry to mark up your book. Get to know the text first. Make two or three passes through difficult sections before you highlight.

Make choices up front about what to highlight.
Perhaps you can accomplish your purposes by highlighting only certain chapters or sections of a text. When you highlight, remember to look for passages that directly answer the questions you posed during Step 3 of Muscle Reading. Within these passages, highlight individual words, phrases, or sentences rather than whole paragraphs. The important thing is to choose an overall strategy before you put highlighter to paper.

Recite first.
You might want to apply Step 6 of Muscle Reading before you highlight. Talking about what you read—to yourself or with other people—can help you grasp the essence of a text. Recite first; then go back and highlight. You'll probably highlight more selectively.

Underline, then highlight.
Underline key passages lightly in pencil. Then close your text and come back to it later. Assess your underlining. Perhaps you can highlight less than you underlined and still capture the key points.

Use highlighting to monitor your comprehension.
Critical thinking plays a role in underlining and highlighting. When highlighting, you're making moment by moment decisions about what you want to remember from a text. You're also making inferences about what material might be included on a test. Take your critical thinking a step further by using highlighting to check your comprehension. Stop reading periodically and look back over the sentences you've highlighted. See whether you are making accurate distinctions between main points and supporting material. Highlighting too much—more than 10 percent of the text—can be a sign that you're not making this distinction and that you don't fully understand what you're reading. See the article "When Reading Is Tough" later in this chapter for suggestions that can help.

 You're One Click Away...
from finding an example of smart highlighting online.

> # It's easy to fool yourself about reading. Just having an open book in your hand and moving your eyes across a page doesn't mean that you are reading effectively. Reading takes mental focus.

yourself with an enjoyable activity for 10 or 15 minutes every hour or two.

For difficult reading, set more limited goals. Read for a half hour and then take a break. Most students find that shorter periods of reading distributed throughout the day and week can be more effective than long sessions.

Visualize the material. Form mental pictures of the concepts as they are presented. If you read that a voucher system can help control cash disbursements, picture a voucher handing out dollar bills. Using visual imagery in this way can help deepen your understanding of the text while allowing information to be transferred into your long-term memory.

Read material out loud, especially if it is complicated. Some of us remember better and understand more quickly when we hear an idea.

Get a "feel" for the subject. For example, let's say you are reading about a microorganism—a paramecium—in your biology text. Imagine what it would feel like to run your finger around the long, cigar-shaped body of the organism. Imagine feeling the large fold of its gullet on one side and the tickle of the hairy little cilia as they wiggle in your hand.

In addition, predict how the author will answer your key questions. Then read to find out if your predictions were accurate.

STEP 5 FLAG ANSWERS

As you read, seek out the answers to your questions. You are a detective, watching for every clue. When you do find an answer, flag it so that it stands out on the page.

Deface your books. Have fun. Flag answers by highlighting, underlining, writing comments, filling in your outline, or marking up pages in any other way that helps you. Indulge yourself as you never could with your grade school books.

Marking up your books offers other benefits. When you read with a highlighter, pen, or pencil in your hand, you involve your kinesthetic senses of touch and motion. Being physical with your books can help build strong neural pathways in your memory.

You can mark up a text in many ways. For example:

- Place an asterisk (*) or an exclamation point (!) in the margin next to an especially important sentence or term.
- Circle key terms and words to look up later in a dictionary.
- Write short definitions of key terms in the margin.
- Write a *Q* in the margin to highlight possible test questions, passages you don't understand, and questions to ask in class.
- Write personal comments in the margin—points of agreement or disagreement with the author.
- Write mini-indexes in the margin—that is, the numbers of other pages in the book where the same topic is discussed.
- Write summaries in your own words.
- Rewrite chapter titles, headings, and subheadings so that they're more meaningful to you.
- Draw diagrams, pictures, tables, or maps that translate text into visual terms.
- Number each step in a list or series of related points.
- In the margins, write notes about the relationships between elements in your reading. For instance, note connections between an idea and examples of that idea.
- If you infer an answer to a question or come up with another idea of your own, write that down as well.

Avoid marking up a text too soon. Wait until you complete a chapter or section to make sure you know the key points. Then mark up the text. Sometimes, flagging answers after you read each paragraph works best.

Also remember that the purpose of making marks in a text is to call out important concepts or information that you will review later. Flagging key information can save lots of time when you are studying for tests. With this in mind, highlight or underline sparingly—usually less than 10 percent of the text. If you mark up too much on a page, you defeat the purpose: to flag the most important material for review.

Finally, jot down new questions, and note when you don't find the answers you are looking for. Ask these questions in class, or see your instructor personally. Demand that your textbooks give you what you want—answers.

You're One Click Away...
from finding examples of Phase 2 strategies online.

PHASE 3 After you read

STEP 6 RECITE

Talk to yourself about what you've read. Or talk to someone else. When you finish a reading assignment, make a speech about it. When you recite, you practice an important aspect of metacognition—synthesis, or combining individual ideas and facts into a meaningful whole.

One way to get yourself to recite is to look at each underlined point. Note what you marked; then put the book down and start talking out loud. Explain as much as you can about that particular point.

To make this technique more effective, do it in front of a mirror. It might seem silly, but the benefits can be enormous. Reap them at exam time.

A related technique is to stop reading periodically and write a short, free-form summary of what you just read. In one study, this informal "retrieval practice" helped students recall information better than other study techniques.[2]

Classmates are even better than mirrors. Form a group and practice teaching one another what you have read. One of the best ways to learn anything is to teach it to someone else.

In addition, talk about your reading whenever you can. Tell friends and family members what you're learning from your textbooks.

Talking about your reading reinforces a valuable skill—the ability to summarize. To practice this skill, pick one chapter (or one section of one chapter) from any of your textbooks. State the main topic covered in this chapter. Then state the main points that the author makes about this topic.

For example, the main topic up to this point in this chapter is Muscle Reading. The main point about this topic is that Muscle Reading includes three phases—steps to take before you read, while you read, and after you read. For a more detailed summary, you could name each of the steps.

Note: This topic-point method does not work so well when you want to summarize short stories, novels, plays, and other works of fiction. Instead, focus on action. In most stories, the main character confronts a major problem and takes a series of actions to solve it. Describe that problem and talk about the character's key actions—the turning points in the story.

STEP 7 REVIEW

Plan to do your first complete review within 24 hours of reading the material. Sound the trumpets! This point is critical: A review within 24 hours moves information from your short-term memory to your long-term memory.

Review within 1 day. If you read it on Wednesday, review it on Thursday. During this review, look over your notes and clear up anything you don't understand. Recite some of the main points again.

This review can be short. You might spend as little as 15 minutes reviewing a difficult 2-hour reading assignment. Investing

Muscle Reading—
a leaner approach

Keep in mind that Muscle Reading is an overall approach, not a rigid, step-by-step procedure. Here's a shorter variation that students have found helpful. Practice it with any chapter in this book:

- **Preview and question.** Flip through the pages, looking at anything that catches your eye—headings, subheadings, illustrations, photographs. Turn the title of each article into a question. For example, "How Muscle Reading works" can become "How does Muscle Reading work?" List your questions on a separate sheet of paper, or write each question on a 3 × 5 card.

- **Read to answer your questions.** Read each article. Then go back over the text and underline or highlight answers to the appropriate questions on your list.

- **Recite and review.** When you're done with the chapter, close the book. Recite by reading each question—and answering it—out loud. Review the chapter by looking up the answers to your questions. (It's easy—they're already highlighted.) Review again by quizzing yourself one more time with your list of questions.

that time now can save you hours later when studying for exams.

STEP 8 REVIEW AGAIN

The final step in Muscle Reading is the weekly or monthly review. This step can be very short—perhaps only 4 or 5 minutes per assignment. Simply go over your notes. Read the high-lighted parts of your text. Recite one or two of the more complicated points.

The purpose of these reviews is to keep the neural pathways to the information open and to make them more distinct. That way, the information can be easier to recall. You can accomplish these short reviews anytime, anywhere, if you are prepared.

Conduct a 5-minute review while you are waiting for a bus, for your socks to dry, or for the water to boil. Three-by-five cards are a handy review tool. Write ideas, formulas, concepts, and facts on cards, and carry them with you. These short review periods can be effortless and fun.

Sometimes longer review periods are appropriate. For example, if you found an assignment difficult, consider rereading it. Start over, as if you had never seen the material before. Sometimes a second reading will provide you with surprising insights.

Decades ago, psychologists identified the primacy-recency effect, which suggests that we most easily remember the first and last items in any presentation.[3] Previewing and reviewing your reading can put this theory to work for you. ∎

You're One Click Away...
from finding examples of Phase 3 strategies online.

4

JOURNAL ENTRY 9 *Discovery/Intention Statement*

Experimenting with Muscle Reading

After reading the steps included in Muscle Reading, reflect on your reading skills. Are you a more effective reader than you thought you were? Less effective? Record your observations below.

I discovered that I . . .

_____

_____

_____

_____

_____

_____

_____

_____

_____

_____

_____

_____

_____

_____

_____

_____

Many students find that they only do the "read" step with their textbooks. You've just read about the advantages of eight additional steps you should perform. Depending on the text, reading assignment, your available time, and your commitment level to the material, you may discover through practice which additional steps work best for you. Right now, make a commitment to yourself to experiment with all or several of the additional Muscle Reading steps by completing the following Intention Statement.

I intend to use the following Muscle Reading steps for the next 2 weeks in my _____ class:

❑ Preview

❑ Outline

❑ Question

❑ Focus

❑ Flag answers

❑ Recite

❑ Review

❑ Review again

When reading is
TOUGH

© Graham Bell/Corbis

Sometimes ordinary reading methods are not enough. It's easy to get bogged down in a murky reading assignment. The solution starts with a First Step: When you are confused, tell the truth about it. Successful readers monitor their understanding of reading material. They do not see confusion as a mistake or a personal shortcoming. Instead, they take it as a cue to change reading strategies and process ideas at a deeper level.

Read it again. Somehow, students get the idea that reading means opening a book and dutifully slogging through the text—line by line, page by page—moving in a straight line from the first word until the last. Actually, this method can be an ineffective way to read much of the published material you'll encounter in college.

Feel free to shake up your routine. Make several passes through tough reading material. During a preview, for example, just scan the text to look for key words and highlighted material. Next, skim the entire chapter or article again, spending a little more time and taking in more than you did during your preview. Finally, read in more depth, proceeding word by word through some or all of the text. Difficult material—such as the technical writing in science texts—is often easier the second time around. Isolate difficult passages and read them again, slowly.

This suggestion comes with one caution. If you find yourself doing a lot of rereading, then consider a change in reading strategies. For example, you might benefit from reciting after each paragraph or section rather than after each chapter. For more ideas, review the steps of Muscle Reading and consider the following suggestions.

Look for essential words. If you are stuck on a paragraph, mentally cross out all of the adjectives and adverbs, and then read the sentences without them. Find the important words—usually verbs and nouns.

Hold a mini-review. Pause briefly to summarize—either verbally or in writing—what you've read so far. Stop at the end of a paragraph and recite, in your own words, what you have just read. Jot down some notes, or create a short outline or summary.

Read it out loud. Make noise. Read a passage out loud several times, each time using a different inflection and emphasizing a different part of the sentence. Be creative. Imagine that you are the author talking.

Talk to someone who can help. Admit when you are stuck. Then bring questions about reading assignments to classmates and members of your study group. Also make an appointment with your instructor. Most teachers welcome the opportunity to work individually with students. Be specific about your confusion. Point out the paragraph that you found toughest to understand.

Stand up. Changing positions periodically can combat fatigue. Experiment with standing as you read, especially if you get stuck on a tough passage and decide to read it out loud.

Skip around. Jump to the next section or to the end of a tough article or chapter. You might have lost the big picture. Simply seeing the next step, the next main point, or a summary might be all you need to put the details in context. Retrace the steps in a chain of ideas, and look for examples. Absorb facts and ideas in whatever order works for you—which may be different than the author's presentation.

Find a tutor. Many schools provide free tutoring services. If your school does not, other students who have completed the course can assist you.

Use another text. Find a similar text in the library. Sometimes a concept is easier to understand if it is expressed another way. Children's books—especially children's encyclopedias—can provide useful overviews of baffling subjects.

Note where you get stuck. When you feel stuck, stop reading for a moment and diagnose what's happening. At these stop points, mark your place in the margin of the page with a penciled S for *Stuck*. A pattern to your marks over several pages might indicate a question you want to answer before going further.

Stop reading. When none of the above suggestions work, do not despair. Admit your confusion and then take a break. Catch a movie, go for a walk, study another subject, or sleep on it. The concepts you've already absorbed might come together at a subconscious level as you move on to other activities. Allow some time for that process. When you return to the reading material, see it with fresh eyes. ■

Getting past ROADBLOCKS *to* READING

Even your favorite strategies for reading can fail when you're dealing with bigger issues. Those roadblocks to getting your reading done can come from three major sources:

- Finding enough time to keep up with your reading.
- Making choices about what to read once you find the time.
- Getting interrupted by other people while you're reading.

For solutions to each of these problems, read on.

SCHEDULING TIME FOR READING

Planning dispels panic (*I've got 300 pages to read before tomorrow morning!*) and helps you finish off your entire reading load for a term. Creating a reading plan is relatively simple if you use the following steps.

Step 1. Estimate the total number of pages that you'll read. To arrive at this figure, check the course syllabus for each class that you're taking. Look for lists of reading assignments. Based on what you find, estimate the total number of pages that you'll read for all your classes.

Step 2. Estimate how many pages you can read during 1 hour. Remember that your reading speed will be different for various materials. It depends on everything from the layout of the pages to the difficulty of the text. To give your estimate some credibility, base it on actual experience. During your first reading assignment in each course, keep track of how many pages you read per hour.

Step 3. Estimate your total number of reading hours. Divide the total number of pages from Step 1 by your pages-per-hour from Step 2. For example, look at this calculation:

600 (total pages for all courses this term) ÷ 10 (pages read per hour) = 60 (total reading hours needed for the term)

The result is the total number of hours you'll need to complete your reading assignments this term. Remember to give yourself some "wiggle room." Allow extra hours for rereading and unplanned events. Consider taking your initial number of projected hours and doubling it. You can always back off from there to an estimate that seems more reasonable.

Step 4. Schedule reading time. Take the total number of hours from Step 3 and divide it by the number of weeks in your current term. That will give you the number of hours to schedule for reading each week.

60 (total reading hours needed for the term) ÷ 16 (weeks in the term) = 3.75 (hours per week to schedule for reading)

Now, go to your calendar or long-term planner and reflect on it for a few minutes. Look for ways to block out those hours next week. For ideas, review Chapter 2.

Step 5. Refine your reading plan. Scheduling your reading takes time. The potential benefits are beyond calculation. With a plan, you can be more confident that you'll actually get your reading done. Even if your estimates are off, you'll still go beyond blind guessing or leaving the whole thing to chance. Your reading matters too much for that.

MAKING CHOICES ABOUT WHAT TO READ

Books about time management often mention the "80/20" principle. According to this principle, 80 percent of the value created by any group derives from only 20 percent of its members. If you have a to-do list of 10 items, for example, you'll get 80 percent of your desired results by doing only 2 items on the list.

The point is not to take these figures literally but to remember the underlying principle: *Focus on what creates the most*

4

value. Look at your reading in light of the 80/20 principle. For instance:

- In a 10-paragraph article, you might find 80 percent of the crucial facts in the headline and first paragraph. (In fact, journalists are *taught* to write this way.)
- If you have a 50-page assignment, you may find that the most important facts and ideas in 10 pages of that total.
- If you're asked to read five books for a course, you may find that most exam questions come from just one of them.

A caution is in order here. The 80/20 principle is not a suggestion to complete only 20 percent of your reading assignments. That choice can undermine your education. To find the most important parts of anything you read, first get familiar with the whole. Only then can you make sound choices about where to focus.

Skilled readers constantly make choices about what to read and what *not* to read. They realize that some texts are more valuable for their purposes than others and that some passages within a single text are more crucial than the rest. When reading, they instantly ask, "What's most important here?"

The answer to this question varies from assignment to assignment, and even from page to page within a single assignment. Pose this question each time that you read, and look for clues to the answers. Pay special attention to the following:

- Any readings that your instructor refers to in class
- Readings that are emphasized in a class syllabus
- Readings that generate the most questions on quizzes and tests
- Parts of a text that directly answer the questions you generated while previewing
- Chapter previews and summaries (usually found at the beginning and end of a chapter or section)

DEALING WITH INTERRUPTIONS

Sometimes the people you live with and care about the most—a friend, roommate, spouse, or child—can become a temporary roadblock to reading. The following strategies can help you stay focused on your reading:

Attend to people first. When you first come home from school, keep your books out of sight. Spend some time with your roommates or family members before you settle in to study. Make small talk and ask them about their day. Give the important people in your life a short period of full, focused attention rather than a longer period of partial attention. Then explain that you have some work to do. Set some ground rules for the amount of time you need to focus on studying. You could be rewarded with extra minutes or hours of quiet time.

Plan for interruptions. It's possible that you'll be interrupted even if you set up guidelines for your study time in advance. If so, schedule the kind of studying that can be interrupted. For instance, you could write out or review flash cards with key terms and definitions. Save the tasks that require sustained attention for more quiet times.

Use "pockets" of time. See whether you can arrange a study time in a quiet place at school before you come home. If you arrive at school 15 minutes earlier and stay 15 minutes later, you can squeeze in an extra half hour of reading that day. Also look for opportunities to study on campus between classes.

When you can't read everything, read something. Even if you can't absorb an entire chapter while your roommates are blasting music, you can skim a chapter. Or you can just read the introduction and summary. When you can't get it *all* done, get *something* done.

Caution: If you always read this way, your education will be compromised. Supplement this strategy with others from this chapter so that you can get your most important reading done.

Read with children underfoot. It is possible to have both effective study time and quality time with your children. The following suggestions come mostly from students who are also parents. The specific strategies you use will depend on your schedule and the ages of your children.

- *Find a regular playmate for your child.* Some children can pair off with close friends and safely retreat to their rooms for hours of private play. You can check on them occasionally and still get lots of reading done.
- *Create a special space for your child.* Set aside one room or area of your home as a play space. Childproof this space. The goal is to create a place where children can roam freely and play with minimal supervision. Consider allowing your child in this area *only* when you study. Your homework time then becomes your child's reward. If you're cramped for space, just set aside some special toys for your child to play with during your study time.
- *Use television responsibly.* Whenever possible, select educational programs that keep your child's mind active and engaged. Also see whether your child can use headphones while watching television. That way, the house stays quiet while you study.
- *Schedule time to be with your children when you've finished studying.* Let your children in on the plan: "I'll be done reading at 7:30. That gives us a whole hour to play before you go to bed."
- *Ask other adults for help.* Getting help can be as simple as asking your spouse, partner, neighbor, or fellow student to take care of the children while you study. Offer to trade child care with a neighbor: You will take his kids and yours for 2 hours on Thursday night if he'll take them for 2 hours on Saturday morning.
- *Find community activities and services.* Ask whether your school provides a day care service. In some cases, these services are available to students at a reduced cost. ■

Reading faster

One way to read faster is to read faster. This idea might sound like double-talk, but it is a serious suggestion. The fact is, you can probably read faster—without any loss in comprehension—simply by making a conscious effort to do so. Your comprehension might even improve.

Experiment with the "just do it" method right now. Read the rest of this article as fast as you can. After you finish, come back and reread the same paragraphs at your usual rate. Note how much you remember from your first sprint through the text. You might be surprised to find out how well you comprehend material even at dramatically increased speeds. Build on that success by experimenting with the following guidelines.

Get your body ready. Gear up for reading faster. Get off the couch. Sit up straight at a desk or table, on the edge of your chair, with your feet flat on the floor. If you're feeling adventurous, read standing up.

Set a time limit. When you read, use a clock, cell phone, or a digital watch with a stopwatch feature to time yourself. You are not aiming to set speed records, so be realistic. For example, set a goal to read two or three sections of a chapter in an hour, using all of the Muscle Reading steps. If that works, set a goal of 50 minutes for reading the same number of sections. Test your limits. The idea is to give yourself a gentle push, increasing your reading speed without sacrificing comprehension.

Relax. It's not only possible to read fast when you're relaxed; it's easier. Relaxation promotes concentration. And remember, relaxation is not the same as sleep. You can be relaxed *and* alert at the same time.

Move your eyes faster. When we read, our eyes leap across the page in short bursts called *saccades* (pronounced "să-käds"). A saccade is also a sharp jerk on the reins of a horse—a violent pull to stop the animal quickly. Our eyes stop like that too, in pauses called *fixations*.

Although we experience the illusion of continuously scanning each line, our eyes actually take in groups of words, usually about three at a time. For more than 90 percent of reading time, our eyes are at a dead stop, in those fixations.

One way to decrease saccades is to follow your finger as you read. The faster your finger moves, the faster your eyes move. You can also use a pen, pencil, or 3 × 5 card as a guide.

Your eyes can move faster if they take in more words with each burst—for example, six instead of three. To practice taking in more words between fixations, find a newspaper with narrow columns. Then read down one column at a time, and fixate only once per line.

In addition to using the above techniques, simply make a conscious effort to fixate less. You might feel a little uncomfortable at first. That's normal. Just practice often, for short periods of time.

Notice and release ineffective habits. Our eyes make regressions; that is, they back up and reread words. You can reduce regressions by paying attention to them. Use a handy 3 × 5 card to cover words and lines that you have just read. You can then note how often you stop and move the card back to reread the text. Don't be discouraged if you stop often at first. Being aware of it helps you regress less frequently.

Also notice vocalizing. You are more likely to read faster if you don't read out loud or move your lips. You can also increase your speed if you don't subvocalize—that is, if you don't mentally "hear" the words as you read them. To stop doing it, just be aware of it.

Another habit to release is reading letter by letter. When we first learn to read, we do it one letter at a time. By now you have memorized many words by their shape, so you don't have to focus on the letters at all. Read this example: "Rasrhcers at Cbmrigae Uivnretisy funod taht eprxert raeedrs dno't eevn look at the lteters." You get the point. Skilled readers recognize many words and phrases in this way, taking them in at a single glance.

When you first attempt to release these habits, choose simpler reading material. That way, you can pay closer attention to your reading technique. Gradually work your way up to more complex material.

If you're pressed for time, skim. When you're in a hurry, experiment by skimming the assignment instead of reading the whole thing. Read the headings, subheadings, lists, charts, graphs, and summary paragraphs. Summaries are especially important. They are usually found at the beginning or end of a chapter or section.

This suggestion is not about reading faster, but reading smarter. In many cases, you can read for main points and let go of the rest. You might not need to process all the facts, examples, and quotations that are used to *support* those main points. Ask

4

© Chris Pancewicz/Alamy

whether you can meet your purpose for reading by skimming or skipping that supporting material.

The essence of many nonfiction books can be summarized in just a few pages. That core message may be all you want from an author.

Stay flexible. Remember that speed isn't everything. Skillful readers vary their reading rate according to their purpose and the nature of the material. An advanced text in analytic geometry usually calls for a different reading rate than the Sunday comics.

You also can use different reading rates on the same material. For example, you might first sprint through an assignment for the key words and ideas, and then return to the difficult parts for a slower and more thorough reading.

Another option is to divide a large reading assignment into smaller sections and use different reading strategies for each one. You might choose to read the first and last sections in detail, for example, and skim the middle sections.

As a general guideline, slow down your reading pace for material that's technical and unfamiliar to you. Speed up for material that's familiar, staying alert for anything that seems new or significant.

Also remember that reading faster *without comprehension* can actually increase the amount of time that you study. Balance a desire for speed with the need for understanding what you read.

Explore more resources. You can find many books about speed-reading. Ask a librarian to help you find a few. Using them can be a lot of fun. For more possibilities, including courses and workshops, go to your favorite search engine on the Internet, and key in the word *speed-reading.*

In your research, you might discover people who offer to take you beyond speed-reading. According to some teachers, you can learn to flip through a book and "mentally photograph" each page—hundreds or even thousands of words at once. To prepare for this feat, you first do relaxation exercises to release tension while remaining alert. In this state, you can theoretically process vast quantities of information at a level other than with your conscious mind.

You might find these ideas controversial. Approach them in the spirit of the Power Process: "Ideas are tools." Also remember that you can use more conventional reading techniques at any time.

One word of caution: Courses and workshops in speed-reading range from free to expensive. Before you lay out any money, check the instructor's credentials and talk to people who've taken the course. Also find out whether the instructor offers free "sampler sessions" and whether you can cancel at some point in the course for a full refund.

Finally, remember the first rule of reading fast: Just do it! ■

Master Students
IN ACTION

" *One night when I was reading, I had so much on my mind that I reread the page probably five times. I finally just put the book down and cleared my mind. I put on some of my favorite music, and I took a fantasy trip by thinking about all my upcoming exciting things that I would be doing. When I was done, I got back to my reading with no trouble at all.* "

—Lindsey Giblin, Central Piedmont Community College

 You're One Click Away...
from a video about Master Students in Action.

 # EXERCISE 16

Relax

Eyestrain can be the result of continuous stress. Take a break from your reading and use this exercise to release tension.

1. Sit on a chair or lie down, and take a few moments to breathe deeply.

2. Close your eyes, place your palms over them, and visualize a perfect field of black.

3. Continue to be aware of the blackness for 2 or 3 minutes while you breathe deeply.

4. Now remove your hands from your eyes, and open your eyes slowly.

5. Relax for a minute more; then continue reading.

WORD POWER—expanding your VOCABULARY

Having a large vocabulary makes reading more enjoyable and increases the range of materials you can explore. In addition, building your vocabulary gives you more options for self-expression when speaking or writing. With a larger vocabulary, you can think more precisely by making finer distinctions between ideas. And you won't have to stop to search for words at crucial times—such as a job interview.

Strengthen your vocabulary by taking delight in words. Look up unfamiliar terms. Pay special attention to words that arouse your curiosity.

Before the age of the Internet, students used two kinds of printed dictionaries: the desk dictionary and the unabridged dictionary. A desk dictionary is an easy-to-handle abridged dictionary that you can use many times in the course of a day. You can keep this book within easy reach (maybe in your lap) so you can look up unfamiliar words while reading.

In contrast, an unabridged dictionary is large and not made for you to carry around. It provides more complete information about words and definitions not included in your desk dictionary, as well as synonyms, usage notes, and word histories. Look for unabridged dictionaries in libraries and bookstores.

You might prefer using one of several online dictionaries, such as Dictionary.com. Another common option is to search for definitions by using a search engine such as Google.com. If you do this, inspect the results carefully. They can vary in quality and be less useful than the definitions you'd find in a good dictionary or thesaurus.

Construct a word stack. When you come across an unfamiliar word, write it down on a 3 × 5 card. Below the word, copy the sentence in which it was used, along with the page number. You can look up each word immediately, or you can accumulate a stack of these cards and look up the words later. Write the definition of each word on the back of the 3 × 5 card, adding the diacritics—marks that tell you how to pronounce it.

To expand your vocabulary and learn the history behind the words, take your stack of cards to an unabridged dictionary. As you find related words in the dictionary, add them to your stack. These cards become a portable study aid that you can review in your spare moments.

Learn—even when your dictionary is across town. When you are listening to a lecture and hear an unusual word or when you are reading on the bus and encounter a word you don't know, you can still build your word stack. Pull out a 3 × 5 card and write down the word and its sentence. Later, you can look up the definition and write it on the back of the card.

Divide words into parts. Another suggestion for building your vocabulary is to divide an unfamiliar word into syllables and look for familiar parts. This strategy works well if you make it a point to learn common prefixes (beginning syllables) and suffixes (ending syllables). For example, the suffix *-tude* usually refers to a condition or state of being. Knowing this makes it easier to conclude that *habitude* refers to a usual way of doing something and that *similitude* means being similar or having a quality of resemblance.

Infer the meaning of words from their context. You can often deduce the meaning of an unfamiliar word simply by paying attention to its context—the surrounding words, phrases, sentences, paragraphs, or images. Later, you can confirm your deduction by consulting a dictionary.

Practice looking for context clues such as these:

- *Definitions*. A key word might be defined right in the text. Look for phrases such as *defined as* or *in other words*.

- *Examples*. Authors often provide examples to clarify a word meaning. If the word is not explicitly defined, then study the examples. They're often preceded by the phrases *for example, for instance,* or *such as*.

- *Lists*. When a word is listed in a series, pay attention to the other items in the series. They might define the unfamiliar word through association.

- *Comparisons*. You might find a new word surrounded by synonyms—words with a similar meaning. Look for synonyms after words such as *like* and *as*.

- *Contrasts*. A writer might juxtapose a word with its antonym. Look for phrases such as *on the contrary* and *on the other hand*. ∎

4

Mastering the English LANGUAGE

The complexity of English makes it a challenge for people who grew up with another language—and for native speakers of English as well. To get the most benefit from your education, analyze the ways that you speak and write English. Look for patterns that might block your success. Then take steps to increase your mastery.

LEARN TO USE STANDARD ENGLISH WHEN IT COUNTS

Standard English (also called *standard written English*) is the form of the language used by educated speakers and writers. It is the form most likely to be understood by speakers and writers of English, no matter where they live.

Using non-standard English in the classroom or workplace might lead people to doubt your skills, your intentions, or your level of education. Non-standard English comes in many forms, including these:

- *Slang*. These informal expressions often create vivid images. When students talk about "acing" a test or "hanging loose" over spring break, for example, they're using slang.

- *Idioms*. These are colorful expressions with meanings that are not always obvious. For instance, a "fork in the road" does not refer to an eating utensil discarded on a street but rather to a place where a part of the road branches off. Even native speakers of English can find idioms hard to understand.

- *Dialects*. A sentence such as "I bought me a new phone" is common in certain areas of the United States. If you use such an expression in a paper or presentation, however, your audience might form a negative impression of you.

- *Jargon*. Some terms are used mainly by people who work in certain professions. If you talk about "hacking a site" or finding a "workaround," for example, then only students majoring in software engineering might understand you.

Any community of English speakers and writers can reshape the language for its own purposes. People who send text messages are doing that now. So are people who post on Twitter.com, a Web site that limits updates to 140 characters. Even your family, friends, and coworkers might develop expressions that no one else comprehends.

Learning when and how to use non-standard English is part of mastering the language. However, save non-standard expressions for informal conversations with friends. In that context, you can safely try out new words and ask for feedback about how you're using them. If you're not sure whether a particular expression is standard English, then talk to an instructor. And if someone points out that you're using non-standard English, be willing to learn from that experience. You can do this even when the feedback is not given with skill or sensitivity.

BUILD CONFIDENCE

Students who grew up with a language other than English might fall under the category of English as a Second Language (ESL) student, or English Language Learner (ELL). Many ESL/ELL students feel insecure about using English in social settings, including the classroom. Choosing not to speak, however, can delay your mastery of English and isolate you from other students.

As an alternative, make it your intention to speak up in class. List several questions beforehand and plan to ask them. Also schedule a time to meet with your instructors during office hours to discuss any material that you find confusing. These strategies can help you build relationships while developing English skills.

In addition, start a conversation with at least one native speaker of English in each of your classes. For openers, ask about their favorite instructors or ideas for future courses to take.

English is a complex language. Whenever you extend your vocabulary and range of expression, the likelihood of making mistakes increases. The person who wants to master English yet seldom makes mistakes is probably being too careful. Do not look upon mistakes as a sign of weakness. Mistakes can be your best teachers—if you are willing to learn from them.

Remember that the terms *English as a Second Language* and *English Language Learner* describe a difference—not a deficiency. The fact that you've entered a new culture and are mastering another language gives you a broader perspective than people who speak only one language. And if you currently speak two or more languages, you've already demonstrated your ability to learn.

ANALYZE ERRORS IN USING ENGLISH

To learn from your errors, make a list of those that are most common for you. Next to the error, write a corrected version. For examples, see the chart below. Remember that native speakers of English also use this technique—for instance, by making lists of words they frequently misspell.

Errors	Corrections
Sun is bright.	The sun is bright.
He cheerful.	He is cheerful.
I enjoy to play chess.	I enjoy playing chess.
Good gifts received everyone.	Everyone received good gifts.
I knew what would present the teachers.	I knew what the teachers would present.
I like very much burritos.	I like burritos very much.
I want that you stay.	I want you to stay.
Is raining.	It is raining.
My mother, she lives in Iowa.	My mother lives in Iowa.
I gave the paper to she.	I gave the paper to her.
They felt safety in the car.	They felt safe in the car.
He has three car.	He has three cars.
I have helpfuls family members.	I have helpful family members.
She don't know nothing.	She knows nothing.

LEARN BY SPEAKING AND LISTENING

You probably started your English studies by using textbooks. Writing and reading in English are important. Both can help you add to your English vocabulary and master grammar. To gain greater fluency and improve your pronunciation, also make it your goal to *hear* and *speak* standard English.

For example, listen to radio talk shows hosted by educated speakers with a wide audience. Imitate the speaker's pronunciation by repeating phrases and sentences that you hear. During TV shows and personal conversations, notice the facial expressions and gestures that accompany certain English words and phrases.

If you speak English with an accent, do not be concerned. Many people speak clear, accented English. Work on your accent only if you can't be easily understood.

Take advantage of opportunities to read and hear English at the same time. For instance, turn on English subtitles when watching

a film on DVD. Also, check your library for books on tape or CD. Check out the printed book, and follow along as you listen.

USE COMPUTER RESOURCES

Some online dictionaries allow you to hear words pronounced. They include Answers.com (www.answers.com) and Merriam-Webster Online (www.m-w.com).

Other resources include online book sites with a read-aloud feature. An example is Project Gutenberg (www.gutenberg.org; search on *audio books*). Speaks for Itself (www.speaksforitself.com) is a free download that allows you to hear text from Web sites read aloud.

Also, check general Web sites for ESL students. A popular one is Dave's ESL Café (www.eslcafe.com), which will lead you to others.

GAIN SKILLS IN NOTE TAKING AND TESTING

When taking notes, remember that you don't have to capture everything that an instructor says. To a large extent, the art of note taking consists of choosing what *not* to record. Listen for key words, main points, and important examples. Remember that instructors will often repeat these things. You'll have more than one chance to pick up on the important material. When you're in doubt, ask for repetition or clarification. For additional suggestions, see Chapter 5: Notes.

Taking tests is a related challenge. You may find that certain kinds of test questions—such as multiple-choice items—are more common in the United States than in your native country. Chapter 6: Tests can help you master these and many other types of tests.

CREATE A COMMUNITY OF ENGLISH LEARNERS

Learning as part of a community can increase your mastery. For example, when completing a writing assignment in English, get together with other people who are learning the language. Read each other's papers and suggest revisions. Plan on revising your paper a number of times based on feedback from your peers.

You might feel awkward about sharing your writing with other people. Accept that feeling—and then remind yourself of everything you have to gain by learning from a group. In addition to learning English more quickly, you can raise your grades and make new friends.

Native speakers of English might be willing to assist your group. Ask your instructors to suggest someone. This person can benefit from the exchange of ideas and the chance to learn about other cultures.

CELEBRATE YOUR GAINS

Every time you analyze and correct an error in English, you make a small gain. Celebrate those gains. Taken together over time, they add up to major progress in mastering English as a second language. ■

4

Developing information literacy

Masterfile (Royalty-Free Div.)

Information literacy is a set of skills to use whenever you want to answer questions or find information. For example, you might want to learn more about a product, a service, a vacation spot, or a potential job. You might want to follow up on something you heard on the radio or saw on TV. Or you might want to develop a topic for a paper or speech.

In any case, the fruit of curiosity is research. And research involves finding information, which means reading—sometimes *lots* of reading.

An important quality of master students is curiosity. To answer questions, these students find information from appropriate sources, evaluate the information, organize it, and use it to achieve a purpose. The ability to do this in a world where data is literally at your fingertips is called information literacy.

DISCOVER YOUR PURPOSE

One of the early steps in Muscle Reading involves asking questions. Research means asking questions as well.

Discover your *main question*. This is the thing that sparked your curiosity in the first place. Answering it is your purpose for doing research.

Your main question will raise a number of smaller, related questions. These are *supporting questions*. They also call for answers.

Suppose that your main question is: "During the mortgage credit crisis of 2007 to 2010, what led banks to lend money to people with poor credit histories?" Your list of supporting questions might include these:

- What banks were involved in the mortgage credit crisis?
- How do banks discover a person's credit history?
- What are the signs of a poor credit history?

Listing your main and supporting questions can save hours of time. If you ever feel overwhelmed or get sidetracked, pull out your list of questions. When the information you're finding answers one of those questions, then you're on track. If you're wading through material that's not answering your questions, then it's time to find another source of information or revise your questions.

CONSIDER PRIMARY AND SECONDARY SOURCES OF INFORMATION

Consider the variety of information sources that are available to you: billions of Web pages, books, magazines, newspapers, and audio and video recordings. You can reduce this vast range of materials to a few manageable categories. Start with the distinction between primary and secondary sources.

Primary sources. These can lead to information treasures. Primary sources are firsthand materials—personal journals, letters, speeches, government documents, scientific experiments, field observations, interviews with recognized experts, archeological digs, artifacts, and original works of art.

Primary sources can also include scholarly publications such as the *New England Journal of Medicine*, *Contemporary Literary Criticism*, and similar publications. One clue that you're dealing with primary source is the title. If it includes the word *journal*, then you're probably reading a primary source. Signs of scholarly articles include these:

- Names of authors with their credentials and academic affiliations
- A brief abstract (summary) of the article, along with a section on research methods (how the authors tested their ideas and reached their conclusions)
- Lengthy articles with detailed treatment of the main topic and definitions of key terms

- Conclusions based on an extensive review of relevant publications, survey research, data collected in a laboratory experiment, or a combination of these

- Extensive bibliographies and references to the work of other scholars in the form of footnotes (at the bottom of each page) or endnotes (at the end of the article)

If you pick up a magazine with pages of full-color advertisements and photos of celebrities, you're not reading a scholarly journal. Though some scholarly articles run just a few pages, many run to 10, 20, or even more. While that's a lot to read, you get more information to use for your assignment or to answer your questions.

Though many kinds of publications can be useful, scholarly journals and other primary sources are unmatched in depth and credibility. In addition, journal articles are often peer reviewed. This means that other experts in the field read and review the articles to make sure that they are accurate.

Secondary sources. These sources summarize, explain, and comment on primary sources:

- Popular magazines such as *Time* and *Newsweek*.

- Magazines—such as the *Atlantic Monthly* and *Scientific American*—with wide circulation and long articles.

- Nationally circulated newspapers such as the *Washington Post, New York Times,* and *Los Angeles Times*.

- General reference works such as the *Encyclopaedia Britannica* and the *Oxford Companion to English Literature*.

Secondary sources are useful places to start your research. Use them to get an overview of your topic. Depending on the assignment, these may be all you need for informal research.

GET TO KNOW YOUR LIBRARY

Remember that many published materials are available in print as well as online. For a full range of sources, head to your campus library.

Ask a librarian. One reason for a trip to the library is to find a reference librarian. Tell this person about the questions you want to answer, and ask for good sources of information.

Take a tour. Libraries—from the smallest one in your hometown to the Smithsonian in Washington, D.C.—consist of just three basic elements:

- *Catalogs*—online databases that list all of the library's accessible sources.

- *Collections*—materials, such as periodicals (magazines, journals and newspapers), books, pamphlets, audiovisual materials, and materials available from other libraries via interlibrary loan.

- *Computer resources*—Internet access; connections to campuswide computer networks; and databases stored on CD-ROMs, CDs, DVDs, or online. Online databases—which allow you to look at full-text articles from magazines, journals, and newspapers—are sometimes available from your personal computer or smartphone

with a password. Many libraries have access to special databases that are not available on the Internet. Also ask about ebooks that can be delivered straight to your computer.

Before you start your next research project, take some time to investigate all three elements of your school's library.

Dig in to the collection. When inspecting a library's collections, look for materials such as the following, making sure to ask about both print and online versions:

- *Encyclopedias.* Use leading print and online encyclopedias, such as *Encyclopaedia Britannica*. Specialized encyclopedias can cover many fields and include, for example, *Encyclopedia of Psychology, Encyclopedia of the Biological Sciences, Encyclopedia of Asian History, Violence in America* and *McGraw-Hill Encyclopedia of Science and Technology.*

- *Biographies.* Read accounts of people's lives in biographical works such as *Who's Who, Dictionary of American Biography, Contemporary Musicians,* and *Biography Index: A Cumulative Index to Biographical Material in Books and Magazines.*

- *Critical works.* Read what scholars have to say about works of art and literature in Oxford Companion volumes (such as *Oxford Companion to Art, Masterplots, Poetry Criticism, Novels for Students,* and *Oxford Companion to African American Literature*).

- *Statistics and government documents.* Among the many useful sources are *Statistical Abstract of the United States, Handbook of Labor Statistics, Occupational Outlook Handbook,* and U.S. Census Bureau publications.

- *Almanacs, atlases, and gazetteers.* For population statistics and boundary changes, see the *World Almanac and Book of Facts, Atlas of Crime,* the *New York Times Almanac,* or the *CIA World Factbook.*

- *Dictionaries.* Consult the *American Heritage Dictionary of the English Language, Oxford English Dictionary,* and other specialized dictionaries such as the *Penguin Dictionary of Literary Terms and Literary Theory, The New Grove Dictionary of Music and Musicians,* and the *Dictionary of the Social Sciences.*

- *Indexes and databases.* Databases contain publication information and an abstract, or sometimes the full text, of an article available for downloading or printing from your computer. Your library houses print and CD-ROM databases and subscribes to some online databases; others are accessible through online library catalogs or Web links.

- *Reference works in specific subject areas.* These references cover a vast range of material. Examples include *The Oxford Companion to Art,* the *Encyclopedia of the Biological Sciences, Countries and Their Cultures,* and the *Concise Oxford Companion to Classical Literature.* Ask a librarian for more information.

- *Periodical articles.* Find articles in periodicals (works issued periodically, such as scholarly journals, popular magazines, and newspapers) by using a periodical index. Some indexes, such as Lexis-Nexis Academic Universe, InfoTrac, OCLC FirstSearch, and New York Times Ondisc, provide the full text of articles.[4]

SEARCH FOR INFORMATION WITH KEY WORDS

One crucial skill for information literacy is using key words. Key words are the main terms in your main and supporting questions. These are the words that you enter into a library database or online search box. Your choice of key words determines the quality of results that you get from Internet search engines such as google.com, and from library catalogs. For better search results:

- *Use specific key words.* Entering *firefox* or *safari* will give you more focused results than entering *web browser*. *Reading strategies* or *note-taking strategies* will get more specific results than *study strategies*. Do not type in your whole research question as a sentence. The search engine will look for each word and give you a lot of useless results.

- *Use unique key words.* Whenever possible, use proper names. Enter *Beatles* or *Radiohead* rather than *British rock bands*. If you're looking for nearby restaurants, enter *restaurant* and your zip code rather than the name of your city.

- *Use quotation marks if you're looking for certain words in a certain order.* "Audacity of hope" will return a list of pages with that exact phrase.

- *Search within a site.* If you're looking only for articles about college tuition from the *New York Times*, then add *new york times* or *nytimes.com* to the search box.

- *Remember to think of synonyms.* For example, "hypertension" is often called "high blood pressure."

- *When you're not sure of a key word, add a wild card character.* In most search engines, that character is the asterisk (*). If you're looking for the title of a film directed by Clint Eastwood and just can't remember the name, enter *clint eastwood directed *.

- *Look for more search options.* Many search engines also offer advanced search features and explain how to use them. Look for the word *advanced* or *more* on the site's home page, and click on the link. If in doubt about how to use your library's search engines, ask a librarian for help.

TURN TO PEOPLE AS SOURCES OF INFORMATION

Making direct contact with people can offer a welcome relief from hours of solitary research time and give you valuable hands-on involvement. Your initial research will uncover the names of experts

on your chosen topic. Consider doing an interview with one of these people—in person, over the phone, or via e-mail. To get the most from interviews:

- Schedule a specific time for the interview—and a specific place, if you're meeting the expert in person.

- Agree on the length of the interview in advance and work within that timeframe.

- Enter the interview with a short list of questions to ask.

- Allow time for additional questions that occur to you during the interview.

- If you want to record the interview, ask for permission in advance.

- When working with people who don't want to be recorded, be prepared to take handwritten notes.

- Ask experts for permission to quote their comments.

- Be courteous before, during, and after the interview; thank the person for taking time with you.

- End the interview at your agreed time.

- Follow up on interviews with a thank-you note.

EVALUATE INFORMATION

Some students assume that anything that's published in print or on the Internet is true. Unfortunately, that's not the case. Some sources of information are more reliable than others, and some published information is misleading or mistaken.

Before evaluating any source of information, make sure that you understand what it says. Use the techniques of Muscle Reading to comprehend an author's message. Then think critically about the information. Chapter 7 offers many suggestions for doing this. Some things you should be sure to look for:

- *Currency.* Notice the published date of your source material. If your topic is time-sensitive, then set some guidelines about how current you want your sources to be—for example, that they were published during the last 5 years.

- *Credibility.* Scan the source for biographical information about the author. Look for educational degrees, training, and work experience that qualify this person to publish on the topic of your research.

- *Bias.* Determine what the Web site or other source is "selling"—the product, service, or point of view it promotes. Political affiliations or funding sources might color the author's point of view. For instance, you can predict that a pamphlet on gun control policies that's printed with funding from the National Rifle Association will promote certain points of view. Round out your research with other sources on the topic.

Evaluate Internet sources with extra care. Ask the following questions:

- *Who pays for the site?* Carefully check information from an organization that sells advertising. Look for an "About This Site" link—a clue to sources of funding.

- *Who runs the site?* Look for a clear description of the person or organization responsible for the content. If the sponsoring person or organization did not create the site's content, then find out who did.

> Some students assume that anything that's published in print or on the Internet is true. Unfortunately, that's not the case.

- *How is the site's content selected?* Look for a link that lists members of an editorial board or other qualified reviewers.

- *Does the site separate fact from opinion?* Reliable sites often follow a newspaper model, which separates reports about current events from editorials.

- *Does the site support claims with evidence?* Credible sites base their editorial stands on expert opinion and facts from scientific studies. Look for references to primary sources. If you find grandiose claims supported only by testimonials, beware. When something sounds too good to be true, it probably is.

- *Does the site link to other sites?* Think critically about these sites as well.

- *How can readers connect with the site?* Look for a way to contact the site's publisher with questions and comments. See whether you can find a physical address, e-mail address, and phone number. Sites that conceal this information might conceal other facts. Also inspect reader comments on the site to see whether a variety of opinions are expressed.

Many Web sites from government agencies and nonprofit organizations have strict and clearly stated editorial policies. These are often good places to start your research.

USE INFORMATION

Many students use information to write a paper or create a presentation. See Chapter 8 of this book for suggestions. In addition, take careful notes on your sources using the techniques explained in Chapter 5. Remember to keep a list of all your sources of information and avoid plagiarism. Be prepared to cite your sources in footnotes or endnotes, and a bibliography.

Also make time to digest all the information you gather. Ask yourself:

- Do I have answers to my main question?

- Do I have answers to my supporting questions?

- What are the main ideas from my sources?

- Do I have personal experiences that can help me answer these questions?

- If a television talk show host asked me these questions, how would I answer?

- On what points do my sources agree?

- On what points do my sources disagree?

- Do I have statistics and other facts that I can use to support my ideas?

- What new questions do I have?

The beauty of these questions is that they stimulate *your* thinking. Discover the pleasures of emerging insights and sudden inspiration. You just might get hooked on the adventure of information literacy.

MUSCLE READING FOR EBOOKS

Today you can read ebooks on many platforms—computers, mobile phones, and dedicated devices such as the Amazon Kindle and Sony Reader. Muscle your way into this new medium by using features that are not available with printed books. Though ebook features vary, see whether you can do the following.

Use navigation tools. To flip electronic pages, look for *previous* and *next* buttons or arrows on the right and left borders of each page. Many ebooks also offer a "go to page" feature that allows you to key in a specific page number.

For a bigger picture of the text, look for a table of contents that lists chapter headings and subheadings. Click on any of these headings to expand the text for that part of the book. Note that charts, illustrations, photos, tables, diagrams and other visuals might be listed separately in the table of contents.

Search. Look for a search box that allows you to enter key words and find all the places in the text where those words are mentioned.

Customize page appearance. For more readable text, adjust the font size or zoom in on a page.

Follow links to related information. Many ebook readers will supply a definition of any word in the text. All you need to do is highlight a word and click on it. Also find out if your ebook reader will connect you to Web sites related to the topic of your ebook.

Mark it up. Look for ways to electronically underline or highlight text. In addition, see whether you can annotate the book by keying in your own notes tied to specific pages. You might be able to tag each note with a key word and then sort your notes into categories based on these words.

Print. See whether you can connect your ebook device to a printer. You might find it easier to study difficult passages on paper. Note that some ebook publishers impose a limit on how much text you can print.

Sit back and listen. Some ebook readers will convert highlighted text into speech. Let your book read itself out loud.

Monitor battery life. Recharge the battery for your ebook device or laptop computer so that it has enough power to last throughout your work or school day. Seeing your screen go dark when you're in the middle of a paragraph could be a one-way ticket to confusion.

Generate notes and citations automatically. Some ebooks will summarize any text that you highlight. Though these are no substitute for your own written summaries, they can be useful starting points. Also, some ebooks will create citations—items you include in the "references" or "works cited" page of a paper.

Copy and paste. See whether you can copy and paste highlighted text to a word-processing file. This is a fast way to create summaries of a reading assignment and take notes while writing papers or creating presentations. To avoid plagiarism, put quotation marks around the text that you copy and paste. Also record the source for each copied passage.

Consult the print version. Sometimes it's hard to beat a good old-fashioned book—especially for dense tables, complex illustrations, and large, color-coded charts. These might not translate well to a small screen. Go to the library or bookstore to see whether you can find those pages in a printed copy of your ebook. ∎

PRACTICING
critical thinking 4

By thinking deeply about your reading, you can make an immediate difference in your ability to learn anything.

Psychologist Benjamin Bloom described six levels of thinking.

Level 1: Remembering—recalling an idea.

Level 2: Understanding—explaining an idea in your own words and giving examples from your own experience.

Level 3: Applying—using an idea to produced a desired result.

Level 4: Analyzing—dividing an idea into parts or steps.

Level 5: Evaluating—rating the truth, usefulness, or quality of an idea—and giving reasons for your rating.

Level 6: Creating—inventing something new based on an idea.

The purpose of this exercise is to practice thinking at **Level 5: Evaluating**. This means rating the truth, usefulness, or quality of an idea—and giving reasons for your rating.

Following is a sample evaluation of the method of Muscle Reading:

The steps of Muscle Reading are useful. Applying all the steps of this method does lead me to actively preview and review as well as read. Doing this consistently would me stay on top of material throughout the whole term rather than relying on cramming during the night before a test. The disadvantage is that eight steps are a lot to remember. For this reason, I prefer the three-step "leaner approach" to Muscle Reading (see page 132). This approach is easier to remember. Because it only includes three major steps, I am also more likely to use it.

Evaluating often means answering questions such as these:

- Do you agree? If not, why?
- How effective is this idea?
- Would you recommend a different options?
- What makes this option better than the others?

Now it's your turn. Recall any idea from this chapter (**Level 1: Remembering**) and think about it at **Level 5: Evaluating**. In the space below, summarize the idea and then demonstrate your higher-level thinking. Continue on additional paper as needed.

_____

_____

_____

_____

_____

_____

_____

_____

_____

_____

_____

_____

_____

_____

_____

_____

_____

_____

_____

_____

_____

_____

_____

For more information on the six levels of thinking, see "Becoming a critical thinker" in Chapter 7.

masterstudentprofile

Matias Manzano

(1985–) One of five finalists for Rookie Teacher of the Year in Miami-Dade County, Florida, the fourth largest school district in America.

I struggled early on with reading. In fourth grade, I scored a 23 percent on a reading proficiency assessment. Many people would have written me off at that young age—a poor, Latino, illegal immigrant who ended up in New York and was destined to fail.

I remember thinking in elementary school that it wasn't fair that the other kids spoke English at home and for that reason, they were better readers than I was. There were times when I would try to read something, and the words would float around the page as if they didn't want to be understood.

I had a teacher in fifth grade, Ms. Leventhaul, who really made me want to improve my reading. She was inspirational. There was something about her demeanor, the way that she carried herself, which was both intimidating and motivational at the same time. She treated me as if she knew that I could achieve greatness.

My brother also challenged me to just read more books. I read at least 20 R. L. Stine *Goosebumps* books in a competition that I had one year with him. We used to have conversations after reading the books. I didn't realize it at the time, but having those conversations allowed me to develop reading skills like making comparisons, identifying main ideas, describing settings, and identifying foreshadowing. By sixth grade, I had scored a 99 percent on the reading assessment.

After high school, I decided to follow in my brother's footsteps and attend Stony Brook University in New York. Money was tight. We would roam around the college, staying with different friends who allowed us to sleep on their floor for the night. I guess I was, in a way, homeless.

Toward the end of my sophomore year, the letter came that our application for legal residence was accepted. I was able to receive financial aid. I no longer had to work 40 hours a week to pay for tuition. I could focus my energy on academics.

The reading skills that I started developing in elementary school became the foundation for my success in college. As a history major and Latin American Caribbean studies minor, I found that my assignments were based on reading scholarly journals and books. My vocabulary improved exponentially. I learned to read entire books in just a few hours.

I can tell you first-hand what research says is true: The greatest factor impacting the education of our nation's poorest children is the quality of the teacher that they get. I joined Teach for America and the staff at Jose De Diego Middle School in Miami because I know that the children living in poverty can achieve at the highest rates. All of my students have talents. All of my students have a spark.

If I had taken certain tests in Florida when I was in fourth grade, the state would have projected me as a future prison inmate. My apologies to the statisticians who use elementary student achievement scores to predict future prison needs. Soon I will finish my master's degree in educational leadership. I am driven by a desire to be the best and to achieve greatness in all aspects of my life, because I believe that no task is insurmountable.

Courtesy of Matias Manzano

MATIAS MANZANO . . . is self-directed.

YOU . . . can be self-directed by focusing your energy on what matters most to you.

You're One Click Away...
from learning more about Matias Manzano online at the Master Student Profiles. You can also visit the Master Student Hall of Fame to learn about other master students.

© Istockphoto.com/pagadesign

PUT THIS CHAPTER TO
WORK

You can use research and reading skills to discover employers that interest you and make the best impression on them during your job search. Once you've got a job, use reading skills to gain skills and advance your career.

USE INFORMATION LITERACY FOR EFFECTIVE JOB HUNTING. Get to know the reference librarians at your school library and public library. These specialists are your allies in discovering who's hiring in your area and what kind of skills they want to see in new employees. Uncovering this kind of information usually calls for going beyond company Web sites. Librarians can help.

DEVELOP INFORMATION LITERACY FOR THE WORK WORLD. Your supervisor might ask, "Have we priced our products above or below the going rate in our region?" Or "What's unique about our line of services, compared to our competitors?" Use the research skills suggested in "Developing information literacy" on page 142 to answer those questions quickly and accurately.

This is another area where reference librarians can help. Some specialize in doing research for certain types of businesses and nonprofit organizations.

EXPAND YOUR VOCABULARY. One key to workplace success is expanding your vocabulary. Learn the key terms used by people in your industry or profession. Find out which publications and Web sites are popular with your coworkers. Start reading these sources, making special note of words and concepts that are new to you.

READ E-MAILS EFFICIENTLY. Scan each new message and file it right away in an appropriate place. If a message requires some kind of response, send it to a folder titled *action.* Review this folder daily. If no response is required but you might refer to the message again, then send it to a folder named *archives.* You can search this folder any time you want to retrieve a message. If the message requires no response and there's little chance that you will ever refer to it, then trash it.

READ WITH A PURPOSE. At work, you're probably reading in order to produce an outcome. Determine your purpose in reading each document and extract what you need to effect that outcome. Look for executive summaries at the front of long documents. Everything you want to know might be there, all in a few pages.

READ WITH A BIAS TOWARD ACTION. Your reading might include passages that call for action on your part. Mark these passages with an appropriate symbol in the margin. For example, write a big letter "A" for *action* next to the relevant paragraph. Or draw a small box there and check off the box after taking the appropriate action. Another option is to enter actionable items directly in your calendar or add them to your to-do list.

CREATE "READ ANYTIME" FILES. Many of the paper-based documents that people get at work consist of basic background material. Often these items are important to read but not urgent. Place these documents in a folder and dig into them when you have a few spare moments.

NOW CREATE A CAREER CONNECTION OF YOUR OWN. Commit to using a suggestion from this chapter at work. Also describe the benefit you want to gain. For example: "I will regularly read the business section of the *New York Times* and *Wall Street Journal*, looking for news about companies that I'd like to work for someday."

State your strategy and desired benefit in the space below:

_____

_____

_____

_____

_____

_____

_____

_____

Name _____

Date _____

1. Briefly explain the problem with holding on to mental pictures, as suggested by the Power Process in this chapter.

2. Name the acrostic that can help you remember the steps of Muscle Reading.

3. You must complete all the steps of Muscle Reading to get the most out of any reading assignment. True or false? Explain your answer.

4. Give three examples of what to look for when previewing a reading assignment.

5. Briefly explain how to use headings in a text to create an outline.

6. In addition to underlining and highlighting, there are other ways to mark up a text. List three possibilities.

7. To get the most benefit from marking a book, underline at least 20 percent of the text. True or false? Explain your answer.

8. Compare the steps of Muscle Reading with the approach described in "Muscle Reading—a leaner approach." How do these two methods differ?

9. Explain at least three strategies you can use when reading is tough.

10. Define the term *information literacy*.

4 SKILLS *Snapshot*

After studying this chapter, you might want to make some changes in the way you read. First, take a snapshot of your current reading habits and reflect on the reading skills you've already developed. Complete the following sentences:

DISCOVERY

My score on the Reading section of the Discovery Wheel on page 37 was . . .

If someone asked me how well I keep up with my assigned reading, I would say that . . .

To get the most out of a long reading assignment, I start by . . .

When I take notes on my reading, my usual method is to . . .

When it's important for me to remember what I read, I . . .

When I don't understand something that I've read, I overcome confusion by . . .

INTENTION

I'll know that I've reached a new level of mastery with reading when . . .

Stated as a goal, my intention is to . . .

ACTION

To reach my goal, the most important thing I can do next is to . . .

At the end of this course, I would like my Reading score on the Discovery Wheel to be . . .

Notes

Use this **Master Student Map** to ask yourself,

WHY THIS CHAPTER MATTERS . . .

- Note taking helps you remember information and influences how well you do on tests.

WHAT IS INCLUDED . . .

- Power Process: I create it all   152
- The note-taking process flows   153
- Observe   154
- Record   157
- Review   162
- Turn PowerPoints into powerful notes   164
- When your instructor talks *quickly*   165
- Taking notes while reading   166
- Get to the bones of your book with concept maps   169
- Taking effective notes for online coursework   170
- Master Student Profile: Harvey Milk   173

HOW CAN I USE THIS CHAPTER . . .

- Experiment with several formats for note taking.
- Create a note-taking format that works especially well for you.
- Take effective notes in special situations—such as while reading, and when instructors talk quickly.

WHAT IF . . .

- You could take notes that remain informative and useful for weeks, months, or even years to come?

JOURNAL ENTRY 10
Intention Statement

Get what you want from this chapter

Recall a recent incident in which you had difficulty taking notes. Perhaps you were listening to an instructor who talked fast, or you got confused and stopped taking notes altogether. Then preview this chapter to find at least three strategies that you can use right away to help you take better notes.

Strategy	Page number

© Ruslan Ivantsov/Shutterstock.com

POWER process

I create it all

This article describes a powerful tool for times of trouble. In a crisis, "I create it all" can lead the way to solutions. The main point of this Power Process is to treat experiences, events, and circumstances in your life *as if* you created them.

"I create it all" is one of the most unusual and bizarre suggestions in this book. It certainly is not a belief. Use it when it works. Don't when it doesn't.

Keeping that in mind, consider how powerful this Power Process can be. It is really about the difference between two distinct positions in life: being a victim or being responsible.

A victim of circumstances is controlled by outside forces. We've all felt like victims at one time or another. Sometimes we felt helpless.

In contrast, we can take responsibility. Responsibility is "response-ability"—the ability to choose a *response* to any event. You can choose your *response* to any event, even when the event itself is beyond your control.

Many students approach grades from the position of being victims. When the student who sees the world this way gets an "F," she reacts something like this:

"Another 'F'! That teacher couldn't teach her way out of a wet paper bag. She can't teach English for anything. There's no way to take notes in that class. And that textbook—what a bore!"

The problem with this viewpoint is that in looking for excuses, the student is robbing herself of the power to get any grade other than an "F." She's giving all of her power to a bad teacher and a boring textbook.

There is another way, called *taking responsibility*. You can recognize that you choose your grades by choosing your actions. Then you are the source, rather than the result, of the grades you get. The student who got an "F" could react like this:

"Another 'F'! Oh, shoot! Well, hmmm . . . What did I do to create it?"

Now, that's power. By asking, "How did I contribute to this outcome?" you are no longer the victim. This student might continue by saying, "Well, let's see. I didn't review my notes after class. That might have done it." Or "I went out with my friends the night before the test. Well, that probably helped me fulfill some of the requirements for getting an 'F.'"

The point is this: When the "F" is the result of your friends, the book, or the teacher, you probably can't do anything about it. However, if you *chose* the "F," you can choose a different grade next time. You are in charge.

You're One Click Away...
from accessing Power Process Media online and finding out more about how to "create it all."

The **Note-Taking** **Process** FLOWS

One way to understand note taking is to realize that taking notes is just one part of the process. Effective note taking consists of three parts: observing, recording, and reviewing. First, you **observe** an "event." This can be a statement by an instructor, a lab experiment, a slide show of an artist's works, or a chapter of required reading.

Then you **record** your observations of that event. That is, you "take notes."

Finally, you **review** what you have recorded. You memorize, reflect, apply, and rehearse what you're learning. This step lifts ideas off the page and turns them into a working part of your mind.

Each part of the note-taking process is essential, and each depends on the other. Your observations determine what you record. What you record determines what you review. And the quality of your review can determine how effective your next observations will be. If you review your notes on the Sino-Japanese War of 1894, for example, the next day's lecture on the Boxer Rebellion of 1900 will make more sense.

Legible and speedy handwriting is also useful in taking notes. Knowledge of outlining is handy too. A nifty pen, a new notebook, and a laptop computer are all great note-taking devices.

And they're all worthless—unless you participate as an energetic observer *in* class and regularly review your notes *after* class. If you take those two steps, you can turn even the most disorganized chicken scratches into a powerful tool.

This is a well-researched aspect of student success in higher education. Study after study points to the benefits of taking notes. The value is added in two ways. First, you create a set of materials that refreshes your memory and helps you prepare for tests. Second, taking notes prompts you to listen effectively during class. You translate new ideas into your own words and images. You impose a personal and meaningful structure on what you see, read, and hear. You move from passive observer to active participant.[1] It's not that you take notes so that you can learn from them later. Instead, you learn *while* taking notes.

Computer technology takes traditional note taking to a whole new level. You can capture key notes with word-processing, outlining, database, and publishing software. Your notes become living documents that you can search, bookmark, tag, and archive like other digital files.

Sometimes note taking looks like a passive affair, especially in large lecture classes. One person at the front of the room does most of the talking. Everyone else is seated and silent, taking notes. The lecturer seems to be doing all of the work.

Don't be deceived.

Look more closely. You'll see some students taking notes in a way that radiates energy. They're awake and alert, poised on the edge of their seats. They're writing—a physical activity that expresses mental engagement. These students listen for levels of ideas and information, make choices about what to record, and compile materials to review.

In higher education, you might spend hundreds of hours taking notes. Making them more effective is a direct investment in your success.

Think of your notes as a textbook that *you* create—one that's more current and more in tune with your learning preferences than any textbook you could buy. ∎

OBSERVE

The note-taking process flows

OBSERVE

Woman in red: © Getty/Frame: Shutterstock

Sherlock Holmes, a fictional master detective and student of the obvious, could track down a villain by observing the fold of his scarf and the mud on his shoes. In real life, a doctor can save a life by observing a mole—one a patient has always had—that undergoes a rapid change.

An accountant can save a client thousands of dollars by observing the details of a spreadsheet. A student can save hours of study time by observing that she gets twice as much done at a particular time of day.

Keen observers see facts and relationships. They know ways to focus their attention on the details and then tap their creative energy to discover patterns. To sharpen your classroom observation skills, experiment with the following techniques, and continue to use those that you find most valuable. Many of these strategies can be adapted to the notes you take while reading.

SET THE STAGE

Complete outside assignments. Nothing is more discouraging (or boring) than sitting through a lecture about the relationship of Le Chatelier's principle to the principle of kinetics if you've never heard of Henri Louis Le Chatelier or kinetics. The more familiar you are with a subject, the more easily you can absorb important information during class lectures. Instructors usually assume that students complete assignments, and they construct their lectures accordingly.

Bring the right materials. A good pen does not make you a good observer, but the lack of a pen or notebook can be distracting enough to take the fine edge off your concentration. Make sure you have a pen, pencil, notebook, or any other materials you need. Bring your textbook to class, especially if the lectures relate closely to the text.

If you are consistently unprepared for a class, that might be a message about your intentions concerning the course. Find out if it is. The next time you're in a frantic scramble to borrow pen and paper 37 seconds before the class begins, notice the cost. Use the borrowed pen and paper to write a Discovery Statement about your lack of preparation. Consider whether you intend to be successful in the course.

Sit front and center. Students who get as close as possible to the front and center of the classroom often do better on tests for several reasons. The closer you sit to the lecturer, the harder it is to fall asleep. The closer you sit to the front, the fewer interesting or distracting classmates are situated between you and the instructor. Material on the board is easier to read from up front. Also, the instructor can see you more easily when you have a question.

Instructors are usually not trained to perform. Some can project their energy to a large audience, but some cannot. A professor who sounds boring from the back of the room might sound more interesting up close.

Sitting up front enables you to become a constructive force in the classroom. By returning the positive energy that an engaged teacher gives out, you can reinforce the teacher's enthusiasm and enhance your experience of the class.

In addition, sound waves from the human voice begin to degrade at a distance of 8 to 12 feet. If you sit more than 15 feet from the speaker, your ability to hear and take effective notes might be compromised. Get close to the source of the sound. Get close to the energy.

Sitting close to the front is a way to commit yourself to getting what you want out of school. One reason students gravitate to the back of the classroom is that they think the instructor is less likely to call on them. Sitting in back can signal a lack of commitment. When you sit up front, you are declaring your willingness to take a risk and participate.

Conduct a short preclass review. Arrive early, and then put your brain in gear by reviewing your notes from the previous class. Scan your reading assignment. Look at the sections you have underlined or highlighted. Review assigned problems and exercises. Note questions you intend to ask.

Clarify your intentions. Take a 3 × 5 card to class with you. On that card, write a short Intention Statement about what you plan to get from the class. Describe your intended level of participation or the quality of attention you will bring to the subject. Be specific. If you found your previous class notes to be inadequate, write down what you intend to do to make your notes from this class session more useful.

"BE HERE NOW" IN CLASS

Accept your wandering mind. The techniques in Chapter 2's Power Process: "Be here now" can be especially useful when your head soars into the clouds. Don't fight daydreaming. When you notice your mind wandering during class, look at it as an opportunity to refocus your attention. If thermodynamics is losing out to beach parties, let go of the beach.

Notice your writing. When you discover yourself slipping into a fantasyland, feel the weight of your pen in your hand. Notice how your notes look. Paying attention to the act of writing can bring you back to the here and now.

You also can use writing in a more direct way to clear your mind of distracting thoughts. Pause for a few seconds, and write those thoughts down. If you're distracted by thoughts of errands you need to run after class, list them on a 3 × 5 card and stick it in your pocket. Or simply put a symbol, such as an arrow or asterisk, in your notes to mark the places where your mind started to wander. Once your distractions are out of your mind and safely stored on paper, you can gently return your attention to taking notes.

Be with the instructor. In your mind, put yourself right up front with the instructor. Imagine that you and the instructor are the only ones in the room and that the lecture is a personal conversation between the two of you. Pay attention to the instructor's body language and facial expressions. Look the instructor in the eye.

Remember that the power of this suggestion is immediately reduced by digital distractions—Web surfing, e-mail checking, or text messaging. Taking notes is a way to stay focused. The physical act of taking notes signals your mind to stay in the same room as the instructor.

Notice your environment. When you become aware of yourself daydreaming, bring yourself back to class by paying attention to the temperature in the room, the feel of your chair, or the quality of light coming through the window. Run your hand along the surface of your desk. Listen to the chalk on the blackboard or the sound of the teacher's voice. Be in that environment. Once your attention is back in the room, you can focus on what's happening in class.

Postpone debate. When you hear something you disagree with, note your disagreement and let it go. Don't allow your internal dialogue to drown out subsequent material. If your disagreement is persistent and strong, make note of it and then move on. Internal debate can prevent you from absorbing new

What to do when you miss a class

For most courses, you'll benefit by attending every class session. This allows you to observe and actively participate. If you miss a class, then catch up as quickly as possible. Find additional ways to observe class content.

Clarify policies on missed classes.

On the first day of classes, find out about your instructors' policies on absences. See whether you will be allowed to make up assignments, quizzes, and tests. Also inquire about doing extra-credit assignments.

Contact a classmate.

Early in the semester, identify a student in each class who seems responsible and dependable. Exchange e-mail addresses and phone numbers. If you know you won't be in class, contact this student ahead of time. When you notice that your classmate is absent, pick up extra copies of handouts, make assignments lists, and offer copies of your notes.

Contact your instructor.

If you miss a class, e-mail or call your instructor, or put a note in his mailbox. Ask whether he has another section of the same course that you can attend so you won't miss the lecture information. Also ask about getting handouts you might need before the next class meeting.

Consider technology.

If there is a Web site for your class, check it for assignments and the availability of handouts you missed. Free online services such as NoteMesh allow students to share notes with one another. These services use wiki software, which allows you to create and edit Web pages using any browser. Before using such tools, however, check with instructors for their policies on note sharing.

5

information. It's okay to absorb information you don't agree with. Just absorb it with the mental tag "My instructor says . . . , and I don't agree with it."

Let go of judgments about lecture styles. Human beings are judgment machines. We evaluate everything, especially other people. If another person's eyebrows are too close together (or too far apart), if she walks a certain way or speaks with an unusual accent, we instantly make up a story about her. We do this so quickly that the process is usually not a conscious one.

Don't let your attitude about an instructor's lecture style, habits, or appearance get in the way of your education. You can decrease the power of your judgments if you pay attention to them and let them go.

You can even let go of judgments about rambling, unorganized lectures. Turn them to your advantage. Take the initiative and organize the material yourself. While taking notes, separate the key points from the examples and supporting evidence. Note the places where you got confused, and make a list of questions to ask.

Participate in class activities. Ask questions. Volunteer for demonstrations. Join in class discussions. Be willing to take a risk or look foolish, if that's what it takes for you to learn. Chances are, the question you think is dumb is also on the minds of several of your classmates.

Relate the class to your goals. If you have trouble staying awake in a particular class, write at the top of your notes how that class relates to a specific goal. Identify the reward or payoff for reaching that goal.

Think critically about what you hear. This suggestion might seem contrary to the previously mentioned technique "postpone debate." It's not. You might choose not to think critically about the instructor's ideas during the lecture. That's fine. Do it later, as you review and edit your notes. This is the time to list questions or write down your agreements and disagreements.

WATCH FOR CLUES

Be alert to repetition. When an instructor repeats a phrase or an idea, make a note of it. Repetition is a signal that the instructor thinks the information is important.

Listen for introductory, concluding, and transition words and phrases. Introductory, concluding, and transition words and phrases include phrases such as *the following three factors, in conclusion, the most important consideration, in addition to,* and *on the other hand.* These phrases and others signal relationships, definitions, new subjects, conclusions, cause and effect, and examples. They reveal the structure of the lecture. You can use these phrases to organize your notes.

Watch the board or PowerPoint presentation. If an instructor takes the time to write something down on the board or show a PowerPoint presentation, consider the material to be important.

Copy all diagrams and drawings, equations, names, places, dates, statistics, and definitions.

Watch the instructor's eyes. If an instructor glances at her notes and then makes a point, it is probably a signal that the information is especially important. Anything she reads from her notes is a potential test question.

Highlight the obvious clues. Instructors often hint strongly or tell students point-blank that certain information is likely to appear on an exam. Make stars or other special marks in your notes next to this information. Instructors are not trying to hide what's important.

Notice the instructor's interest level. If the instructor is excited about a topic, it is more likely to appear on an exam. Pay attention when she seems more animated than usual. ■

 You're One Click Away...
from finding more strategies for observing online.

JOURNAL ENTRY 11
Discovery/Intention Statement

Create more value from lectures

Think back on the last few lectures you have attended. How do you currently observe (listen to) lectures? What specific behaviors do you have as you sit and listen? Do you listen more closely in some classes than others? Briefly describe your responses in the space below.

I discovered that I . . .

_____

_____

_____

_____

Now write an Intention Statement about any changes you want to make in the way you respond to lectures.

I intend to . . .

_____

_____

_____

_____

RECORD

The note-taking process flows

Woman in white: © Getty/Frame: Shutterstock

The format and structure of your notes are more important than how fast you write or how elegant your handwriting is. The following techniques can improve the effectiveness of your notes.

GENERAL TECHNIQUES FOR NOTE TAKING

Use key words. An easy way to sort the extraneous material from the important points is to take notes using key words. Key words or phrases contain the essence of communication. They include these:

- Concepts, technical terms, names, and numbers
- Linking words, including words that describe action, relationship, and degree (for example, *most, least,* and *faster*)

Key words evoke images and associations with other words and ideas. They trigger your memory. That characteristic makes them powerful review tools. One key word can initiate the recall of a whole cluster of ideas. A few key words can form a chain from which you can reconstruct an entire lecture.

To see how key words work, take yourself to an imaginary classroom. You are now in the middle of an anatomy lecture. Picture what the room looks like, what it feels like, how it smells. You hear the instructor say:

> *Okay, what happens when we look directly over our heads and see a piano falling out of the sky? How do we take that signal and translate it into the action of getting out of the way? The first thing that happens is that a stimulus is generated in the neurons—receptor neurons—of the eye. Light reflected from the piano reaches our eyes. In other words, we see the piano.*
>
> *The receptor neurons in the eye transmit that sensory signal—the sight of the piano—to the body's nervous system. That's all they can do—pass on information. So we've got a sensory signal coming into the nervous system. But the neurons that initiate movement in our legs are effector neurons. The information from the sensory neurons must be transmitted to effector neurons, or we will get squashed by the piano. There must be some kind of interconnection between receptor and effector neurons. What happens between the two? What is the connection?*

Key words you might note in this example include *stimulus, generated, receptor neurons, transmit, sensory signals, nervous system, effector neurons,* and *connection.* You can reduce the instructor's 163 words to these 12 key words. With a few transitional words, your notes might look like this:

Stimulus (piano) generated in receptor neurons (eye)

Sensory signals transmitted by nervous system to effector neurons (legs)

What connects receptor to effector?

Note the last key word of the lecture: *connection.* This word is part of the instructor's question and leads to the next point in the lecture. Be on the lookout for questions like this. They can help you organize your notes and are often clues for test questions.

5

Use pictures and diagrams. Make relationships visual. Copy all diagrams from the board, and invent your own. A drawing of a piano falling on someone who is looking up, for example, might be used to demonstrate the relationship of receptor neurons to effector neurons. Label the eyes "receptor" and the feet "effector." This picture implies that the sight of the piano must be translated into a motor response. By connecting the explanation of the process with the unusual picture of the piano falling, you can link the elements of the process together.

Write notes in paragraphs. When it is difficult to follow the organization of a lecture or put information into outline form, create a series of informal paragraphs. These paragraphs should contain few complete sentences. Reserve complete sentences for precise definitions, direct quotations, and important points that the instructor emphasizes by repetition or other signals—such as the phrase "This is an important point."

Copy material from the board or a PowerPoint presentation. Record key formulas, diagrams, and problems that the teacher presents on the board or in a PowerPoint presentation. Copy dates, numbers, names, places, and other facts. You can even use your own signal or code to flag important material.

Use a three-ring binder. Three-ring binders have several advantages over other kinds of notebooks. First, pages can be removed and spread out when you review. This way, you can get the whole picture of a lecture. Second, the three-ring-binder format allows you to insert handouts right into your notes. Third, you can insert your own out-of-class notes in the correct order.

Use only one side of a piece of paper. When you use one side of a page, you can review and organize all your notes by spreading them out side by side. Most students find the benefit well worth the cost of the paper. Perhaps you're concerned about the environmental impact of consuming more paper. If so, you can use the blank side of old notes and use recycled paper.

Use 3 × 5 cards. As an alternative to using notebook paper, use 3 × 5 cards to take lecture notes. Copy each new concept onto a separate 3 × 5 card.

Keep your own thoughts separate. For the most part, avoid making editorial comments in your lecture notes. The danger is that when you return to your notes, you might mistake your own ideas for those of the instructor. If you want to make a comment, clearly label it as your own.

Use an "I'm lost" signal. No matter how attentive and alert you are, you might get lost and confused in a lecture. If it is inappropriate to ask a question, record in your notes that you were lost. Invent your own signal—for example, a circled question mark. When you write down your code for "I'm lost," leave space for the explanation or clarification that you will get later. The space will also be a signal that you missed something. Later, you can speak to your instructor or ask to see a fellow student's notes.

Label, number, and date all notes. Develop the habit of labeling and dating your notes at the beginning of each class. Number the page too. Sometimes the sequence of material in a lecture is important. Write your name and phone number in each notebook in case you lose it.

Use standard abbreviations. Be consistent with your abbreviations. If you make up your own abbreviations or symbols, write a key explaining them in your notes. Avoid vague abbreviations. When you use an abbreviation such as *comm.* for *committee*, you run the risk of not being able to remember whether you meant *committee, commission, common,* or *commit*. One way to abbreviate is to leave out vowels. For example, *talk* becomes *tlk*, *said* becomes *sd*, *American* becomes *Amrcn*.

Leave blank space. Notes tightly crammed into every corner of the page are hard to read and difficult to use for review. Give your eyes a break by leaving plenty of space.

Later, when you review, you can use the blank spaces in your notes to clarify points, write questions, or add other material.

Take notes in different colors. You can use colors as highly visible organizers. For example, you can signal important points with red. Or use one color of ink for notes about the text and another color for lecture notes.

Use graphic signals. The following ideas can be used with any note-taking format:

- Use brackets, parentheses, circles, and squares to group information that belongs together.
- Use stars, arrows, and underlining to indicate important points. Flag the most important points with double stars, double arrows, or double underlines.
- Use arrows and connecting lines to link related groups.
- Use equal signs and greater-than and less-than signs to indicate compared quantities.

To avoid creating confusion with graphic symbols, use them carefully and consistently. Write a "dictionary" of your symbols in the front of your notebooks; an example is shown here.

I I, ( ), ◯, ▭ = info
        that belongs together

*, ↘, ═ = important

**, ↘↘, ☰, !!! = extra important

> = greater than < = less than
═ = equal to

⟶ = leads to, becomes
    Ex: school → job → money

? = huh?, lost

?? = big trouble, clear up
     immediately

Use recorders effectively. Some students record lectures with audio or digital recorders, but there are persuasive arguments against doing so. When you record a lecture, there is a strong temptation to daydream. After all, you can always listen to the lecture again later on. Unfortunately, if you let the recorder do all of the work, you are skipping a valuable part of the learning process.

There are other potential problems as well. Listening to recorded lectures can take a lot of time—more time than reviewing written notes. Recorders can't answer the questions you didn't ask in class. Also, recording devices malfunction. In fact, the unscientific Hypothesis of Recording Glitches states that the tendency of recorders to malfunction is directly proportional to the importance of the material. With those warnings in mind, you can use a recorder effectively if you choose. For example, you can use recordings as backups to written notes. (Check with your instructor first. Some prefer not to be recorded.) Turn the recorder on; then take notes as if it weren't there. Recordings can be especially useful if an instructor speaks fast.

THE CORNELL METHOD

A note-taking system that has worked for students around the world is the *Cornell method*.[2] Originally developed by Walter Pauk at Cornell University during the 1950s, this approach continues to be taught across the United States and in other countries as well.

The cornerstone of this method is what Pauk calls the *cue column*—a wide margin on the left-hand side of the paper. The cue column is the key to the Cornell method's many benefits. Here's how to use it.

Format your paper. On each sheet of your notepaper, draw a vertical line, top to bottom, about 2 inches from the left edge of

the paper. This line creates the cue column—the space to the left of the line. You can also find Web sites that allow you to print out pages in this format. Just do an Internet search using the key words *cornell method pdf*.

Take notes, leaving the cue column blank. As you read an assignment or listen to a lecture, take notes on the right-hand side of the paper. Fill up this column with sentences, paragraphs, outlines, charts, or drawings. Do not write in the cue column. You'll use this space later, as you do the next steps.

Condense your notes in the cue column. Think of the notes you took on the right-hand side of the paper as a set of answers. In the cue column, list potential test questions that correspond to your notes. Write one question for each major term or point.

As an alternative to questions, you can list key words from your notes. Yet another option is to pretend that your notes are a series of articles on different topics. In the cue column, write a newspaper-style headline for each "article." In any case, be brief. If you cram the cue column full of words, you defeat its purpose—to reduce the number and length of your notes.

Write a summary. Pauk recommends that you reduce your notes even more by writing a brief summary at the bottom of each page. This step offers you another way to engage actively with the material.

Cue column	Notes
What are the 3 phases of Muscle Reading?	Phase 1: Before you read Phase 2: While you read Phase 3: After you read
What are the steps in phase 1?	1. Preview 2. Outline 3. Question
What are the steps in phase 2?	4. Focus 5. Flag answers
What are the steps in phase 3?	6. Recite 7. Review 8. Review again
What is an acronym for Muscle Reading?	Pry = preview Out = outline Questions = question Focus Flag Answers Recite Review Review again

Summary
Muscle Reading includes 3 phases: before, during, and after reading. Each phase includes specific steps. Use the acronym to recall all the steps.

5

Use the cue column to recite. Cover the right-hand side of your notes with a blank sheet of paper. Leave only the cue column showing. Then look at each item you wrote in the cue column and talk about it. If you wrote questions, answer each question. If you wrote key words, define each word and talk about why it's important. If you wrote headlines in the cue column, explain what each one means and offer supporting details. After reciting, uncover your notes and look for any important points you missed.

MIND MAPPING

Mind mapping, a system developed by Tony Buzan,[3] can be used in conjunction with the Cornell method to take notes. In some circumstances, you might want to use mind maps exclusively.

To understand mind maps, first review the features of traditional note taking. Outlines (explained in the next section) divide major topics into minor topics, which in turn are subdivided further. They organize information in a sequential, linear way.

The traditional outline reflects only a limited range of brain function—a point that is often made in discussions about "left-brain" and "right-brain" activities. People often use the term *right brain* when referring to creative, pattern-making, visual, intuitive brain activity. They use the term *left brain* when talking about orderly, logical, step-by-step characteristics of thought. Writing teacher Gabrielle Rico uses another metaphor. She refers to the left-brain mode as our "sign mind" (concerned with words) and the right-brain mode as our "design mind" (concerned with visuals).[4] A mind map uses both kinds of brain functions. Mind maps can contain lists and sequences and show relationships. They can also provide a picture of a subject. They work on both verbal and nonverbal levels.

One benefit of mind maps is that they quickly, vividly, and accurately show the relationships between ideas. Also, mind mapping helps you think from general to specific. By choosing a main topic, you focus first on the big picture, then zero in on subordinate details. And by using only key words, you can condense a large subject into a small area on a mind map. You can review more quickly by looking at the key words on a mind map than by reading notes word for word.

Give yourself plenty of room. To create a mind map, use blank paper that measures at least 11 by 17 inches. If that's not available, turn regular notebook paper on its side so that you can take notes in a horizontal (instead of vertical) format. If you use a computer in class to take notes, consider

software that allows you to create digital mind maps that can include graphics, photos, and URL links.

Determine the main concept of the lecture, article, or chapter. As you listen to a lecture or read, figure out the main concept. Write it in the center of the paper and circle it, underline it, or highlight it with color. You can also write the concept in large letters. Record concepts related to the main concept on lines that radiate outward from the center. An alternative is to circle or box in these concepts.

Use key words only. Whenever possible, reduce each concept to a single word per line or circle or box in your mind map. Although this reduction might seem awkward at first, it prompts you to summarize and to condense ideas to their essence. That means fewer words for you to write now and fewer to review when it's time to prepare for tests. (Using shorthand symbols and abbreviations can help.) Key words are usually nouns and verbs that communicate the bulk of the speaker's ideas. Choose words that are rich in associations and that can help you recreate the lecture.

Create links. A single mind map doesn't have to include all of the ideas in a lecture, book, or article. Instead, you can link mind maps. For example, draw a mind map that sums up the five key points in a chapter, and then make a separate, more detailed mind map for each of those key points. Within each mind map, include references to the other mind maps. This technique helps explain and reinforce the relationships among many ideas. Some students pin several mind maps next to one another on a bulletin board or tape them to a wall. This allows for a dramatic—and effective—look at the big picture.

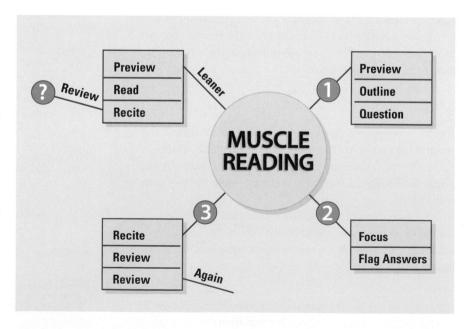

OUTLINING

A traditional outline shows the relationships among major points and supporting ideas. One benefit of taking notes in the outline format is that doing so can totally occupy your attention. You are recording ideas and also organizing them. This process can be an advantage if the material has been presented in a disorganized way. By playing with variations, you can discover the power of outlining to reveal relationships among ideas. Technically, each word, phrase, or sentence that appears in an outline is called a *heading*. Headings are arranged in different levels:

- In the first, or top, level of headings, note the major topics presented in a lecture or reading assignment.

- In the second level of headings, record the key points that relate to each topic in the first-level headings.

- In the third level of headings, record specific facts and details that support or explain each of your second-level headings. Each additional level of subordinate heading supports the ideas in the previous level of heading.

Roman numerals offer one way to illustrate the difference between levels of headings. See the following examples.

First-level heading

Second-level heading

Third-level heading

I. Muscle Reading includes 3 phases.
   A. Phase 1: Before you read
      1. Preview
      2. Outline
      3. Question
   B. Phase 2: While you read
      4. Focus
      5. Flag answers
   C. Phase 3: After you read
      6. Recite
      7. Review
      8. Review again

COMBINING FORMATS

Feel free to use different note-taking systems for different subjects and to combine formats. Do what works for you.

Distinguish levels with indentations only:

Muscle Reading includes 3 phases
   Phase 1: Before you read
      Preview

Distinguish levels with bullets and dashes:

MUSCLE READING INCLUDES 3 PHASES
   • Phase 1: Before you read
     – Preview

Distinguish headings by size:

MUSCLE READING INCLUDES 3 PHASES

Phase 1: Before you read

Preview

For example, combine mind maps along with the Cornell method. You can modify the Cornell format by dividing your notepaper in half. Reserve one half for mind maps and the other for linear information such as lists, graphs, and outlines, as well as equations, long explanations, and word-for-word definitions. You can incorporate a mind map into your paragraph-style notes whenever you feel one is appropriate. Minds maps are also useful for summarizing notes taken in the Cornell format.

John Sperry, a teacher at Utah Valley State College, developed a note-taking system that can include all of the formats discussed in this article:

- Fill up a three-ring binder with fresh paper. Open your notebook so that you see two blank pages—one on the left and one on the right. Plan to take notes across this entire two-page spread.

- During class or while reading, write your notes only on the left-hand page. Place a large dash next to each main topic or point. If your instructor skips a step or switches topics unexpectedly, just keep writing.

- Later, use the right-hand page to review and elaborate on the notes that you took earlier. This page is for anything you want. For example, add visuals such as mind maps. Write review questions, headlines, possible test questions, summaries, outlines, mnemonics, or analogies that link new concepts to your current knowledge.

- To keep ideas in sequence, place appropriate numbers on top of the dashes in your notes on the left-hand page. Even if concepts are presented out of order during class, they'll still be numbered correctly in your notes. ■

You're One Click Away...
from seeing more examples of notes in various formats online.

REVIEW

The note-taking process flows

Woman in red: © Getty/Frame: Shutterstock

Think of reviewing as an integral part of note taking rather than an added task. To make new information useful, encode it in a way that connects it to your long-term memory. The key is reviewing.

Review within 24 hours. In Chapter 4, when you read the suggestion to review what you've read within 24 hours, you were asked to sound the trumpet. If you have one, get it out and sound it again. This note-taking technique might be the most powerful one you can use. It might save you hours of review time later in the term.

Many students are surprised that they can remember the content of a lecture in the minutes and hours after class. They are even more surprised by how well they can read the sloppiest of notes at that time. Unfortunately, short-term memory deteriorates quickly. The good news is that if you review your notes soon enough, you can move that information from short-term to long-term memory. And you can do it in just a few minutes—often 10 minutes or less.

The sooner you review your notes, the better, especially if the content is difficult. In fact, you can start reviewing during class. When your instructor pauses to set up the overhead display or erase the board, scan your notes. Dot the *i*'s, cross the *t*'s, and write out unclear abbreviations. Another way to use this technique is to get to your next class as quickly as you can. Then use the 4 or 5 minutes before the lecture begins to review the notes you just took in the previous class. If you do not get to your notes immediately after class, you can still benefit by reviewing them later in the day. A review right before you go to sleep can also be valuable.

Think of the day's unreviewed notes as leaky faucets, constantly dripping and losing precious information until you shut them off with a quick review. Remember, it's possible to forget most of the material within 24 hours—unless you review.

Edit your notes. During your first review, fix words that are illegible. Write out abbreviated words that might be unclear to you later. Make sure you can read everything. If you can't read something or don't understand something you *can* read, mark it, and make a note to ask your instructor or another student about it. Check to see that your notes are labeled with the date and class and that the pages are numbered.

Fill in key words in the left-hand column. This task is important if you are to get the full benefit of using the Cornell method. Using the key word principles described earlier in this chapter, go through your notes and write key words or phrases in the left-hand column. These key words will speed up the review process later. As you read your notes, focus on extracting important concepts.

Use your key words as cues to recite. Cover your notes with a blank sheet of paper so that you can see only the key words in the left-hand margin. Take each key word in order, and recite as much as you can about the point. Then uncover your notes and look for any important points you missed.

Conduct short weekly review periods. Once a week, review all of your notes again. These review sessions don't need to take a lot of time. Even a 20-minute weekly review period is valuable. Some students find that a weekend review—say, on Sunday afternoon—helps them stay in continuous touch with the material. Scheduling regular review sessions on your calendar helps develop the habit.

As you review, step back to see the larger picture. In addition to reciting or repeating the material to yourself, ask questions about it: Does this relate to my goals? How does this compare to information I already know, in this field or another? Will I be tested on this material? What will I do with this material? How can I associate it with something that deeply interests me?

Consider typing your notes. Some students type up their handwritten notes on the computer. The argument for doing so is threefold. First, typed notes are easier to read. Second, they take up less space. Third, the process of typing them forces you to review the material.

Another alternative is to bypass handwriting altogether and take notes in class on a laptop. This solution has a potential drawback, though: Computer errors can wipe out your notes files. If you like using this method of taking notes, save your files frequently, and back up your work onto a jump drive, external hard drive, or online backup service.

Create summaries. Mind mapping is an excellent way to summarize large sections of your course notes or reading assignments. Create one map that shows all the main topics you want to remember. Then create another map about each main topic. After drawing your maps, look at your original notes, and fill in anything you missed. This system is fun and quick.

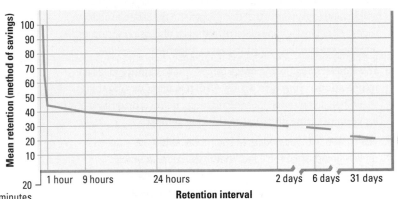

While you're reviewing, evaluate your notes. Review sessions are excellent times to look beyond the *content* of your notes and reflect on your note-taking *process*. Remember these common goals of taking notes in the first place:

- *Reduce* course content to its essentials.
- *Organize* the content.
- Demonstrate that you *understand* the content.

If your notes consistently fall short on one of these points, then review this chapter for a strategy that can help.

Hermann Ebbinghaus, a psychologist, discovered that most forgetting occurs during the first 9 hours after we learn new information—especially during the first hour. Use the strategies in this chapter to prevent forgetting and reverse this "Ebbinghaus curve." ∎

Another option is to create a "cheat sheet." There's only one guideline: Fit all your review notes on a single sheet of paper. Use any note-taking format that you want—mind map, outline, Cornell method, or a combination of all of them. The beauty of this technique is that it forces you to pick out main ideas and key details. There's not enough room for anything else!

If you're feeling adventurous, create your cheat sheet on a single index card. Start with the larger sizes (5 × 7 or 4 × 6) and then work down to a 3 × 5 card.

Some instructors might let you use a summary sheet during an exam. But even if you can't use it, you'll benefit from creating one while you study for the test. Summarizing is a powerful way to review.

You're One Click Away...
from finding more strategies for reviewing online.

JOURNAL ENTRY 12 *Discovery Statement*

Reflect on your review habits

Respond to the following statements by checking "Always," "Often," "Sometimes," "Seldom," or "Never" after each.

1. I review my notes immediately after class.
   _____ Always _____ Often _____ Sometimes _____ Seldom _____ Never

2. I conduct weekly reviews of my notes.
   _____ Always _____ Often _____ Sometimes _____ Seldom _____ Never

3. I make summary sheets of my notes.
   _____ Always _____ Often _____ Sometimes _____ Seldom _____ Never

4. I edit my notes within 24 hours.
   _____ Always _____ Often _____ Sometimes _____ Seldom _____ Never

5. Before class, I conduct a brief review of the notes I took in the previous class.
   _____ Always _____ Often _____ Sometimes _____ Seldom _____ Never

Turn POWERPOINTS into POWERFUL NOTES

PowerPoint presentations are common. They can also be lethal for students who want to master course content or those who simply want to stay awake.

Some students stop taking notes during a PowerPoint presentation. This choice can be hazardous to your academic health for three major reasons:

- *PowerPoint presentations don't include everything.* Instructors and other speakers use PowerPoint to organize their presentations. Topics covered in the slides make up an outline of what your instructor considers important. Slides are created to flag the main points and signal transitions between points. However, speakers usually add examples and explanations that don't appear on the slides. In addition, slides will not include any material from class discussion, including any answers that the instructor gives in response to questions.

- *You stop learning.* Taking notes forces you to capture ideas and information in your own words. Also, the act of writing things down helps you remember the material. If you stop writing and let your attention drift, you can quickly get lost.

- *You end up with major gaps in your notes.* When it's time to review your notes, you'll find that material from PowerPoint presentations is missing. This can be a major pain at exam time.

To create value from PowerPoint presentations, take notes on them. Continue to observe, record, and review. See PowerPoint as a way to *guide* rather than to *replace* your own note taking. Even the slickest, smartest presentation is no substitute for your own thinking.

Experiment with the following suggestions. They include ideas about what to do before, during, and after a PowerPoint presentation.

BEFORE THE PRESENTATION

Sometimes instructors make PowerPoint slides available before a lecture. If you have computer access, download these files. Scan the slides, just as you would preview a reading assignment.

Consider printing out the slides and bringing them along to class. (If you own a copy of PowerPoint, then choose the "handouts" option when printing. This will save paper and ink.) You can take notes directly on the pages that you print out as in the figure below. Be sure to add the slide numbers if they are missing.

If you use a laptop computer for taking notes during class, then you might not want to bother with printing. Just open up the PowerPoint file and type your notes in the window that appears at the bottom of each slide. After class, you can print out the slides in note view. This will show the original slides plus any text that you added.

DURING THE PRESENTATION

In many cases, PowerPoint slides are presented visually by the instructor *only during class.* The slides are not provided as handouts, and they are not available online for students to print out.

This makes it even more important to take effective notes in class. Capture the main points and key details as you normally would. Use your preferred note-taking strategies.

Be selective in what you write down. Determine what kind of material is on each slide. Stay alert for new topics, main points, and important details. Taking too many notes makes it hard to keep up with a speaker and separate main points from minor details.

In any case, go *beyond* the slides. Record valuable questions and answers that come up during a discussion, even if they are not a planned part of the presentation.

AFTER THE PRESENTATION

If you printed out slides before class and took notes on those pages, then find a way to integrate them with the rest of your notes. For example, add references in your notebook to specific slides. Or create summary notes that include the major topics and points from readings, class meetings, and PowerPoint presentations.

Printouts of slides can provide review tools. Use them as cues to recite. Cover up your notes so that only the main image or words on each slide are visible. See whether you can remember what else appears on the slide, along with the key points from any notes you added.

Also consider "editing" the presentation. If you have the PowerPoint file on your computer, make another copy of it. Open up this copy, and see whether you can condense the presentation. Cut slides that don't include anything you want to remember. Also rearrange slides so that the order makes more sense to you. Remember that you can open up the original file later if you want to see exactly what your instructor presented. ■

How Muscle Reading Works

▸ Phase 1 — Before You Read
  ▪ **P**ry **O**ut **Q**uestions

▸ Phase 2 — While You Read
  ▪ **F**ocus and **F**lag **A**nswers

▸ Phase 3 — After You Read
  ▪ **R**ecite, **R**eview, and **R**eview Again

_____
_____
_____
_____
_____
_____
_____
_____
_____

When your instructor talks QUICKLY

Take more time to prepare for class. Familiarity with a subject increases your ability to pick up on key points. If an instructor lectures quickly or is difficult to understand, conduct a thorough preview of the material to be covered.

Be willing to make choices. Focus your attention on key points. Instead of trying to write everything down, choose what you think is important. Occasionally, you will make a less than perfect choice or even neglect an important point. Worse things could happen. Stay with the lecture, write down key words, and revise your notes immediately after class.

Exchange photocopies of notes with classmates. Your fellow students might write down something you missed. At the same time, your notes might help them. Exchanging photocopies can fill in the gaps.

Leave large empty spaces in your notes. Leave plenty of room for filling in information you missed. Use a symbol that signals you've missed something, so you can remember to come back to it.

See the instructor after class. Take your class notes with you, and show the instructor what you missed.

Use an audio recorder. Recording a lecture gives you a chance to hear it again whenever you choose. Some audio recording software allows you to vary the speed of the recording. With this feature, you can perform magic and actually slow down the instructor's speech.

Before class, take notes on your reading assignment. You can take detailed notes on the text before class. Leave plenty of blank space. Take these notes with you to class, and simply add your lecture notes to them.

Go to the lecture again. Many classes are taught in multiple sections. That gives you the chance to hear a lecture at least twice—once in your regular class and again in another section of the class.

Learn shorthand. Some note-taking systems, known as shorthand, are specifically designed for getting ideas down fast. Books and courses are available to help you learn these systems. You can also devise your own shorthand method by inventing one- or two-letter symbols for common words and phrases.

Ask questions—even if you're totally lost. Many instructors allow a question session. This is the time to ask about the points you missed.

At times you might feel so lost that you can't even formulate a question. That's okay. One option is to report this fact to the instructor. He can often guide you to a clear question. Another option is to ask a related question. Doing so might lead you to the question you really wanted to ask.

Ask the instructor to slow down. This solution is the most obvious. If asking the instructor to slow down doesn't work, ask her to repeat what you missed. ■

✓ EXERCISE 17

Taking notes under pressure

With note taking, as with other skills, the more you practice, the better you become. You can use TV programs and videos to practice listening for key words, writing quickly, focusing your attention, and reviewing. Programs that feature speeches and panel discussions work well for this purpose. So do documentary films.

The next time you watch such a program, use pen and paper to jot down key words and information. If you fall behind, relax. Just leave a space in your notes and return your attention to the program. If a program includes commercial breaks, use them to review and revise your notes.

At the end of the program, spend 5 minutes reviewing all of your notes. Create a mind map based on your notes. Then sum up the main points of the program for a friend.

This exercise will help you develop an ear for key words. Because you can't ask questions or request that speakers slow down, you train yourself to stay totally in the moment.

Don't be discouraged if you miss a lot the first time around. Do this exercise several times, and observe how your mind works.

Another option is to record a program and then take notes. You can stop the recording at any point to review what you've written.

Ask a classmate to do this exercise with you. Compare your notes and look for any points that either of you missed.

Taking notes
WHILE READING

Taking notes while reading requires the same skills that apply to taking class notes: observing, recording, and reviewing. Use these skills to take notes for review and for research.

REVIEW NOTES

Review notes will look like the notes you take in class. Take review notes when you want more detailed notes than writing in the margin of your text allows. You might want to single out a particularly difficult section of a text and make separate notes. Or make summaries of overlapping lecture and text material. Because you can't underline or make notes in library books, these sources will require separate notes, too. To take more effective review notes, use the following suggestions.

Set priorities. Single out a particularly difficult section of a text and make separate notes. Or make summaries of overlapping lecture and text material.

Use a variety of formats. Translate text into Cornell notes, mind maps, or outlines. Combine these formats to create your own. Translate diagrams, charts, and other visual elements into words. Then reverse the process by translating straight text into visual elements.

However, don't let the creation of formats get in your way. Even a simple list of key points and examples can become a powerful review tool. Another option is to close your book and just start writing. Write quickly about what you intend to remember from the text, and don't worry about following any format.

Condense a passage to key quotes. Authors embed their essential ideas in key sentences. As you read, continually ask yourself, "What's the point?" Then see whether you can point to a specific sentence on the page to answer your question. Look especially at headings, subheadings, and topic sentences of paragraphs. Write these key sentences word for word in your notes, and put them within quotation marks. Copy as few sentences as you can and still retain the core meaning of the passage.

Condense by paraphrasing. Pretend that you have to summarize a chapter, article, or book on a postcard. Limit yourself to a single paragraph—or a single sentence—and use your own words. This is a great way to test your understanding of the material.

Take a cue from the table of contents. Look at the table of contents in your book. Write each major heading on a piece of paper, or key those headings into a word-processing file on your computer. Include page numbers. Next, see whether you can improve on the table of contents. Substitute your own headings for those that appear in the book. Turn single words or phrases into complete sentences, and use words that are meaningful to you.

Adapt to special cases. The style of your notes can vary according to the nature of the reading material. If you are assigned a short story or poem, for example, then read the entire work once without taking any notes. On your first reading, simply enjoy the piece. When you finish, write down your immediate impressions. Then go over the piece again. Make brief notes on characters, images, symbols, settings, plot, point of view, or other aspects of the work.

Note key concepts in math and science. When you read mathematical, scientific, or other technical materials, copy important formulas or equations. Recreate important diagrams, and draw your own visual representations of concepts. Also write down data that might appear on an exam.

RESEARCH NOTES

Take research notes when preparing to write a paper or deliver a speech. One traditional method of research is to take notes on index cards. You write *one* idea, fact, or quotation per card, along with a note about the source (where you found it). The advantage of limiting each card to one item is that you can easily arrange cards according to the sequence of ideas in your outline. If you change your outline, no problem. Just resort your cards.

Taking notes on a computer offers the same flexibility as index cards. Just include one idea, fact, or quotation per paragraph along with the source. Think of each paragraph as a separate "card." When you're ready to create the first draft of your paper or presentation, just move paragraphs around so that they fit your outline.

Include your sources. No matter whether you use cards or a computer, be sure to *include a source for each note that you take*.

Say, for example, that you find a useful quotation from a book. You want to include that quotation in your paper. Copy the quotation word for word onto a card, or key the quotation into a computer file. Along with the quotation, note the book's author, title, date and place of publication, and publisher. You'll need such information later when you create a formal list of your sources—a bibliography, or a list of endnotes or footnotes.

For guidelines on what information to record about each type of source, see the sidebar to this article as a place to start. Your instructors might have different preferences, so ask them for guidance as well.

Note this information about
YOUR SOURCES

Following are checklists of the information to record about various types of sources. Whenever possible, print out or make photocopies of each source. For books, include a copy of the title page and copyright page, both of which are found in the front matter. For magazines and scholarly journals, copy the table of contents.

For each *book* you consult, record the following:

- Author
- Editor (if listed)
- Translator (if listed)
- Edition number (if listed)
- Full title, including the subtitle
- Name and location of the publisher
- Copyright date
- Page numbers for passages that you quote, summarize, or paraphrase

For each *article* you consult, record the following:

- Author
- Editor (if listed)
- Translator (if listed)
- Full title, including the subtitle
- Name of the periodical
- Volume number
- Issue number
- Issue date
- Page numbers for passages that you quote, summarize, or paraphrase

For each *computer-based source* you consult (CD-ROMs and Internet documents), record the following:

- Author
- Editor (if listed)
- Translator (if listed)
- Full title of the page or article, including the subtitle
- Name of the organization that posted the site or published the CD-ROM
- Dates when the page or other document was published and revised
- Date when you accessed the source
- URL for Web pages (the uniform resource locator, or Web site address, which often starts with http://)
- Version number (for CD-ROMs)
- Volume, issue number, and date for online journals

Note: Computer-based sources may not list all the above information. For Web pages, at a minimum record the date you accessed the source and the URL.

For each *interview* you conduct, record the following:

- Name of the person you interviewed
- Professional title of the person you interviewed
- Contact information for the person you interviewed—mailing address, phone number, e-mail address
- Date of the interview

5

Avoid plagiarism. When people take material from a source and fail to acknowledge that source, they are committing plagiarism. Even when plagiarism is accidental, the consequences can be harsh. For essential information on this topic, see "Academic integrity: Avoiding plagiarism" on page 260.

Many cases of plagiarism occur during the process of taking research notes. To prevent this problem, remember that a major goal of taking research notes is to *clearly separate your own words and images from words and images created by someone else.* To meet this goal, develop the following habits:

- If you take a direct quote from one of your sources, then enclose those words in quotation marks and note information about that source.

- If you take an image (photo, illustration, chart, or diagram) from one of your sources, then note information about that source.

- If you summarize or paraphrase *a specific passage* from one of your sources, then use your own words and note information about that source.

- If your notes include any idea that is closely identified with a particular person, then note information about the source.

- When you include one of your own ideas in your notes, then simply note the source as "me."

If you're taking notes on a computer and using Internet sources, be especially careful to avoid plagiarism. When you copy text or images from a Web site, separate those notes from your own ideas. Use a different font for copied material, or enclose it in quotation marks.

You do *not* need to note a source for these:

- Facts that are considered common knowledge ("The history of the twentieth century includes two world wars").

- Facts that can be easily verified ("The United States Constitution includes a group of amendments known as the Bill of Rights").

- Your own opinion ("Hip-hop artists are the most important poets of our age").

The bottom line: Always present your own work—not materials that have been created or revised by someone else. If you're ever in doubt about what to do, then take the safest course: Cite a source. Give credit where credit is due.

The bottom line: Always present your own work— not materials that have been created or revised by someone else. If you're ever in doubt about what to do, then take the safest course: Cite a source. Give credit where credit is due.

Reflect on your notes. Schedule time to review all the information and ideas that your research has produced. By allowing time for rereading and reflecting on all the notes you've taken, you create the conditions for genuine understanding.

Start by summarizing major points of view on your topic. Note points of agreement and disagreement among your sources.

Also see whether you can find direct answers to the questions that you had when you started researching. These answers could become headings in your paper.

Look for connections in your material, including ideas, facts, and examples that occur in several sources. Also look for connections between your research and your life—ideas that you can verify based on personal experience. ■

You're One Click Away...
from finding examples of effective research and review notes online.

Get to the BONES of your BOOK with CONCEPT MAPS

oncept mapping, pioneered by Joseph Novak and D. Bob Gowin, is a tool to make major ideas in a book leap off the page.[5] In creating a concept map, you reduce an author's message to its essence—its bare bones. Concept maps can also be used to display the organization of lectures and discussions.

Concepts and links are the building blocks of knowledge. A *concept* is a name for a group of related things or ideas. *Links* are words or phrases that describe the relationship between concepts. Consider the following paragraph:

Muscle Reading consists of three phases. Phase 1 includes tasks to complete before reading. Phase 2 tasks take place during reading. Finally, Phase 3 includes tasks to complete after reading.

In this paragraph, examples of concepts are Muscle Reading, reading, phases, tasks, Phase 1, Phase 2, and Phase 3. Links include consists of, includes, before, during, and after.

To create a concept map, list concepts and then arrange them in a meaningful order from general to specific. Then fill in the links between concepts, forming meaningful statements.

Concept mapping promotes critical thinking. It alerts you to missing concepts or faulty links between concepts. In addition, concept mapping mirrors the way that your brain learns—that is, by linking new concepts to concepts that you already know.

To create a concept map, use the following steps:

1. **List the key concepts in the text.** Aim to express each concept in three words or less. Most concept words are nouns, including terms and proper names. At this point, you can list the concepts in any order.

2. **Rank the concepts so that they flow from general to specific.** On a large sheet of paper, write the main concept at the top of the page. Place the most specific concepts near the bottom. Arrange the rest of the concepts in appropriate positions throughout the middle of the page. Circle each concept.

3. **Draw lines that connect the concepts.** On these connecting lines, add words that describe the relationship between the concepts. Again, limit yourself to the fewest words needed to make an accurate link—three words or less. Linking words are often verbs, verb phrases, or prepositions.

4. **Finally, review your map.** Look for any concepts that are repeated in several places on the map. You can avoid these repetitions by adding more links between concepts. ■

You're One Click Away...
from seeing more examples of concept maps online.

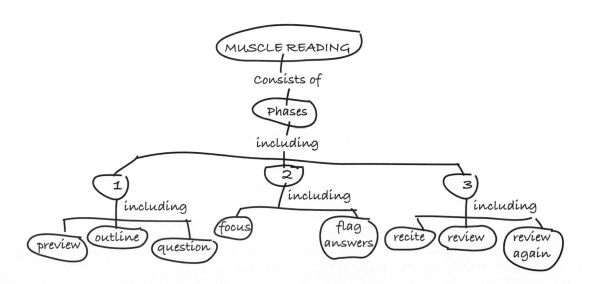

Taking *effective notes* for *online coursework*

If you are taking an online course, or a course that is heavily supported by online materials, then get ready for new challenges to note taking. You can use a variety of strategies to succeed.

Do a trial run with technology. Verify your access to course Web sites, including online tutorials, PowerPoint presentations, readings, quizzes, tests, assignments, bulletin boards, and chat rooms. Ask your instructors for Web site addresses, e-mail addresses, and passwords. Work out any bugs when you start the course and well before that first assignment is due.

If you're planning to use a computer lab on campus, find one that meets course requirements. Remember that on-campus computer labs may not allow you to install all the software needed to access Web sites for your courses or textbooks.

Develop a contingency plan. Murphy's Law of Computer Crashes states that technology tends to break down at the moment of greatest inconvenience. You might not believe this piece of folklore, but it's still wise to prepare for it:

- Find a "technology buddy" in each of your classes—someone who can contact the instructor if you lose Internet access or experience other computer problems.
- Every day, make backup copies of files created for your courses.
- Keep extra printer supplies—paper and toner or ink cartridges—on hand at all times. Don't run out of necessary supplies on the day a paper is due.

Get actively involved with the course. Your online course will include a page that lists homework assignments and test dates. That's only the beginning. Look for ways to engage with the material by submitting questions, completing assignments, and interacting with the instructor and other students.

Take notes on course material. You can print out anything that appears on a computer screen. This includes online course materials—articles, books, manuscripts, e-mail messages, chat room sessions, and more.

The potential problem is that you might skip the note-taking process altogether. ("I can just print out everything!") You would then miss the chance to internalize a new idea by restating it in your own words—a principal benefit of note taking. Result: Material passes from computer to printer without ever intersecting with your brain.

To prevent this problem, take notes in Cornell, mind map, concept map, or outline format. Write Discovery and Intention Statements to capture key insights from the materials and next actions to take. Also talk about what you're learning. Recite key points out loud, and discuss what you find online with other students.

iStockphoto.com/Andrew Rich

Of course, it's fine to print out online material. If you do, treat your printouts like mini-textbooks. Apply the steps of Muscle Reading as explained in Chapter 4.

Another potential problem with online courses is the physical absence of the teacher. In a classroom, you get lots of visual and verbal clues to what kinds of questions will appear on a test. Those clues are often missing from an online course, which means that they could be missing from your notes. Ask your online instructor about what material she considers to be most important.

Set up folders and files for easy reference. Create a separate folder for each class on your computer's hard drive. Give each folder a meaningful name, such as *biology—spring2009*. Place all files related to a course in the appropriate folder. Doing this can save you from one of the main technology-related time wasters: searching for lost files.

Also name individual files with care. Avoid changing extensions that identify different types of files, such as .ppt for PowerPoint presentations or .pdf for files in the Adobe Reader portable document format. Changing extensions might lead to problems when you're looking for files later or sharing them with other users.

Take responsibility. If you register for an online course with no class meetings, you might miss the motivating presence of an instructor and classmates. Instead, manufacture your own motivation. Be clear about what you'll gain by doing well in the course. Relate course content to your major and career goals. Don't wait to be contacted by your classmates and instructor. Initiate that contact on your own.

Ask for help. If you feel confused about anything you're learning online, ask for help right away. This is especially important when you don't see the instructor face-to-face in class. Some students simply drop online courses rather than seek help. E-mail or call the instructor before you make that choice. If the instructor is on campus, you might be able to arrange for a meeting during office hours.

Manage time and tasks carefully. Courses that take place mostly or totally online can become invisible in your weekly academic schedule. This reinforces the temptation to put off dealing with these courses until late in the term.

Avoid this mistake! Consider the real possibility that an online course can take *more* time than a traditional, face-to-face lecture class. Online courses tend to embrace lots of activities—sending and receiving e-mails, joining discussion forums, commenting on blog posts, and more. New content might appear every day. One key to keeping up with the course is frequent contact and careful time management:

- Early in the term, create a detailed schedule for online courses. In your calendar, list a due date for each assignment. Break big assignments into smaller steps, and schedule a due date for each step.

- Schedule times in your calendar to complete online course work. Give these scheduled sessions the same priority as regular classroom meetings. At these times, check for online announcements relating to assignments, tests, and other course events. Check for course-related e-mails daily.

- If the class includes discussion forums, check those daily as well. Look for new posts and add your replies. The point of these tools is to create a lively conversation that starts early and continues throughout the term.

· ·

> Consider the real possibility that an online course can take *more* time than a traditional, face-to-face lecture class. Online courses tend to embrace lots of activities—sending and receiving e-mails, joining discussion forums, commenting on blog posts, and more.

· ·

- When you receive an online assignment, e-mail any questions immediately. If you want to meet with an instructor in person, request an appointment several days in advance.

- Give online instructors plenty of time to respond. They are not always online. Many online instructors have traditional courses to teach, along with administration and research duties.

- Download or print out online course materials as soon as they're posted on the class Web site. These materials might not be available later in the term.

- If possible, submit online assignments early. Staying ahead of the game will help you avoid an all-nighter at the computer during finals week.

Find tools that help with online courses. BlackBoard and other portals for online courses offer tools to help you access the content. See whether there are any created specifically for your class.

These tools might include "apps"—software programs designed to run on smart phones, iPods, iPads, and similar devices. Most apps have specific, limited features. They're designed to just do one or two things well. Look for apps that allow you to manage to-do lists, maintain a calendar, create flash cards, take notes, make voice recordings, read ebooks, and listen to audio books.

Many apps are free. Others cost just a few dollars or come in trial versions that you can use for free.

Focus your attention. Some students are used to visiting Web sites while watching television, listening to loud music, or using instant messaging software. When applied to online learning, these habits can reduce your learning and endanger your grades. To succeed with technology, turn off the television, quit online chat sessions, and turn down the music. Whenever you go online, stay in charge of your attention.

Ask for feedback. To get the most from online learning, request feedback from your instructor via e-mail. When appropriate, also ask for conferences by phone or in person.

Sharing files offers another source of feedback. For example, Microsoft Word has a Track Changes feature that allows other people to insert comments into your documents and make suggested revisions. These edits are highlighted on the screen. Use such tools to get feedback on your writing from instructors and peers.

Note: Be sure to check with your instructors to see how they want students enrolled in their online courses to address and label their e-mails. Many teachers ask their online students to use a standard format for the subject area so they can quickly recognize e-mails from them.

Contact other students. Make personal contact with at least one other student in each of your classes—especially classes that involve lots of online course work. Create study groups to share notes, quiz each other, critique papers, and do other cooperative learning tasks. This kind of support can help you succeed as an online learner. ■

5

PRACTICING
critical thinking 5

The purpose of this exercise is to practice thinking about note-taking at **Level 6: Creating**. This means inventing something new based on an idea or strategy that you've learned.

According to psychologist Benjamin Bloom, creating is the highest level of thinking. At the same time, you can set the stage for creativity by thinking at any of the other levels—remembering, understanding, applying, analyzing, and evaluating.

Level 1: Remembering—recalling an idea.

Level 2: Understanding—explaining an idea in your own words and giving examples from your own experience.

Level 3: Applying—using an idea to produced a desired result.

Level 4: Analyzing—dividing an idea into parts or steps.

Level 5: Evaluating—rating the truth, usefulness, or quality of an idea—and giving reasons for your rating.

Level 6: Creating—inventing something new based on an idea.

This chapter presents three major formats for taking notes: the Cornell method, mind mapping, and outlining. These formats can be modified and combined. For example, you could take notes during class with the Cornell method. After class, you could expand on your notes by capturing some of the main points in mind maps and outlines. Combining all three formats is an example of creative thinking.

Now, based on your experience with this chapter, create a note-taking format of your own. Describe this format in the space provided to the right. Or, use additional paper and other materials to create a detailed example or model of your format.

For more information on the six levels of thinking, see "Becoming a critical thinker" in Chapter 7.

masterstudentprofile

Harvey Milk

(1930–1978) One of America's first openly gay men to win political office, Harvey Milk was assassinated by a former San Francisco city supervisor.

People told Harvey Milk that no openly gay man could win political office. Fortunately, he ignored them.

There was a time when it was impossible for people—straight or gay—even to imagine a Harvey Milk. The funny thing about Milk is that he didn't seem to care that he lived in such a time. After he defied the governing class of San Francisco in 1977 to become a member of its board of supervisors, many people—straight and gay—had to adjust to a new reality he embodied: that a gay person could live an honest life and succeed. That laborious adjustment plods on—now forward, now backward—though with every gay character to emerge on TV and with every presidential speech to a gay group, its eventual outcome favoring equality seems clear.

The few gays who had scratched their way into the city's [San Francisco's] establishment blanched when Milk announced his first run for supervisor in 1973, but Milk had a powerful idea: he would reach downward, not upward, for support. He convinced the growing gay masses of "Sodom by the Sea" that they could have a role in city leadership, and they turned out to form "human billboards" for him along major thoroughfares. In doing so, they outed themselves in a way once unthinkable. It was invigorating.

While his first three tries for office failed, they lent Milk the credibility and positive media focus that probably no openly gay person ever had. Not everyone cheered, of course, and death threats multiplied. Milk spoke often of his ineluctable assassination, even recording a will naming acceptable successors to his seat and containing the famous line: "If a bullet should enter my brain, let that bullet destroy every closet door."

Two bullets actually entered his brain. It was Nov. 27, 1978, in city hall, and Mayor George Moscone was also killed. Fellow supervisor Daniel White, a troubled anti-gay conservative, had left the board, and he became unhinged when Moscone denied his request to return. White admitted the murders within hours. . . .

A jury gave him just five years with parole. Defense lawyers had barred anyone remotely pro-gay from the jury and brought a psychologist to testify that junk food had exacerbated White's depression. (The so-called Twinkie defense was later banned.) Milk's words had averted gay riots before, but after the verdict, the city erupted. More than 160 people ended up in the hospital.

Milk's killing probably awakened as many gay people as his election had. His death inspired many associates—most notably Cleve Jones, who later envisioned the greatest work of American folk art, the AIDS quilt. But while assassination offered Milk something then rare for openly gay men—mainstream empathy—it would have been thrilling to see how far he could have gone as a leader. He had sworn off gay bathhouses when he entered public life, and he may have eluded the virus that killed so many of his contemporaries. He could have guided gay America through the confused start of the AIDS horror. Instead, he remains frozen in time, a symbol of what gays can accomplish and the dangers they face in doing so.

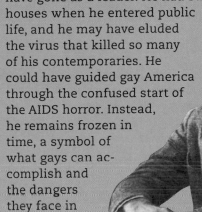

© Bettmann/CORBIS

HARVEY MILK . . . was courageous.

YOU . . . can demonstrate courage by choosing your response to any event.

Source: John Cloud, "The Pioneer," Time, June 14, 1999, Copyright © 1999, Time Inc. All rights reserved. Reprinted by permission.

You're One Click Away...
from learning more about Harvey Milk online at the Master Student Profiles. You can also visit the Master Student Hall of Fame to learn about other master students.

5

PUT THIS CHAPTER TO WORK

The ability to take clear and accurate notes is the key to success in many careers. Doctors, nurses, and counselors take notes about their patients and clients. Managers take notes during performance reviews. And anyone who attends a meeting or interview can benefit from note-taking skills. Following are some ways to apply what you've learned from this chapter.

WHEN APPROPRIATE, TAKE NOTES DURING JOB INTERVIEWS. The obvious reason for taking notes is to record your discoveries—and your intentions to follow up with appropriate action. Taking notes also keeps you focused and engaged during the interview. It might even impress the interviewer.

OBSERVE AND RECORD AT WORK. During meetings, training sessions, and workshops, experiment with taking notes in several formats: Cornell, mind mapping, outlining, concept mapping, or some combination.

REVIEW AND EDIT YOUR NOTES. Schedule time each week to review any notes you take at work. Edit or rewrite them for clarity. Underline or highlight the main points and items for follow up.

FOCUS ON ESSENTIALS. During a presentation or training session at work, let go of any judgments about the presenter's speaking style or appearance. Focus on the content of this person's message. Look for ideas to remember and use. Capture those ideas fully and accurately in your notes.

KEEP UP WITH SPEAKERS. You might find yourself taking notes during fast-paced meetings or conference calls. Use suggestions from the article "When your instructor talks *fast*" in this chapter. Immediately after the call or meeting, review and edit your notes.

RECORD DISCOVERIES AND INTENTIONS. In your personal journal, write Discovery Statements about your current skills and ways to be more effective at work. State a work-related problem and brainstorm to come up with possible solutions. Also list career goals and write Intention Statements about how you plan to achieve them.

APPLY THE POWER PROCESS: "I CREATE IT ALL." This can be a lifesaver when dealing with people and problems at work. Before blaming a snafu on a coworker, think about this Power Process. Look for any ways that you might have contributed to the problem.

Even if you did *not* contribute to the problem, look for ways that you can contribute to the solution. Write Intention Statements to clarify what you will think, say, and do in the future to create a more positive work environment. In the workplace, problem solvers are valued.

One of the ideas behind "I create it all" is to create a gap between stimulus and response. See whether you can fill this gap with a conscious *choice* rather than an unconscious *reaction*.

For example, if a coworker reprimands you, that's a stimulus. You can wait anywhere from a few seconds to few days before choosing your response. Slow down and carefully plan what to say or do next. Make your point in a way that serves everybody and tones down the conflict.

NOW CREATE A CAREER CONNECTION OF YOUR OWN. Review this chapter, looking for a suggestion that you will commit to use while working or looking for a job. In a sentence or two, describe exactly what you plan to do and the primary benefit you want to gain. For example: "When writing notes at work, I will transfer action reminders to my calendar or to-do list. This will help me stay on top of my workload."

State your strategy and desired benefit in the space below:

_____

_____

_____

_____

_____

_____

_____

_____

_____

Name _____

Date _____

1. Define the word *responsibility* as it is used in the Power Process: "I create it all."

2. What are the three major parts of effective note taking as explained in this chapter? Summarize each step in one sentence.

3. According to the text, neat handwriting and a knowledge of outlining are the only requirements for effective notes. True or false? Explain your answer.

4. What are some advantages of sitting in the front and center of the classroom?

5. Describe a way to apply the Power Process: "Be here now" to the job of taking notes in class.

6. Instructors sometimes give clues that the material they are presenting is important. List at least three of these clues.

7. Postponing judgment while taking notes means that you have to agree with everything that the instructor says. True or false? Explain your answer.

8. Describe the two main types of key words. Then write down at least five key words from this chapter.

9. Graphic signals include which of the following?
   (a) Brackets and parentheses
   (b) Stars and arrows
   (c) Underlining and connecting lines
   (d) Equal signs and greater-than and less-than signs
   (e) All of the above

10. Describe at least three strategies for reviewing notes.

CHAPTER 5 SKILLS Snapshot

Take a snapshot of your note-taking skills as they exist today, after reading and doing this chapter. Begin by reflecting on some of your recent experiences with note taking. Then take the next step toward mastery by committing to a specific action in the near future.

DISCOVERY

My score on the Notes section of the Discovery Wheel on page 37 was . . .

If my attention wanders while taking notes, I refocus by . . .

When I strongly disagree with the opinion of a speaker or author, I respond by . . .

If asked to rate the overall quality of the notes that I've taken in the last week, I would say that . . .

In general, I find my notes to be most useful when they . . .

INTENTION

I'll know that I've reached a new level of mastery with note taking when . . .

My main goal for note taking is . . .

ACTION

The most important thing I can do next to meet my goal is . . .

By the time I finish this course, I would like my Notes score on the Discovery Wheel to be . . .

Tests

 Use this **Master Student Map** to ask yourself,

WHY THIS CHAPTER MATTERS . . .

- Adopting a few simple techniques can make a major difference in how you feel about tests—and how you perform on them.

WHAT IS INCLUDED . . .

- Power Process: Detach   178
- Disarm tests   179
- What to do *before* the test   181
- Ways to predict test questions   183
- Cooperative learning: Studying in groups   184
- What to do during the test   186
- The test isn't over until . . .   189
- The high costs of cheating   190
- Let go of test anxiety   191
- Getting ready for math tests   193
- Studying across the curriculum   197
- Celebrate mistakes   198
- Master Student Profile: Bert and John Jacobs   199

HOW CAN I USE THIS CHAPTER . . .

- Predict test questions and use your study time more effectively.
- Harness the power of cooperative learning by studying with other people.
- Gain strategies for raising your scores on tests.
- Separate your self-image from your test scores.

WHAT IF . . .

- I could let go of anxiety about tests—or anything else?

JOURNAL ENTRY 13
Intention Statement

Use this chapter to transform your experience with tests

Think about how you want your experience of test taking to change. For example, you might want to walk into every test feeling well rested and thoroughly prepared. Next, preview this chapter to find at least three strategies to accomplish your goal. List those strategies below, and note the page numbers where you can find out more about each one.

Strategy	Page number
_____	_____
_____	_____
_____	_____
_____	_____
_____	_____
_____	_____
_____	_____
_____	_____
_____	_____
_____	_____
_____	_____
_____	_____

© Ruslan Ivantsov/Shutterstock.com

POWER process

DETACH

This Power Process helps you release the powerful, natural student within you. It is especially useful whenever negative emotions are getting in your way.

Attachments are addictions. When we are attached to something, we think we cannot live without it, just as a drug addict feels he cannot live without drugs. We believe our well-being depends on maintaining our attachments.

We can be attached to just about anything: beliefs, emotions, people, roles, objects. The list is endless.

One person, for example, might be so attached to his car that he takes an accident as a personal attack. Pity the poor unfortunate who backs into this person's car. He might as well have backed into the owner himself.

Another person might be attached to her job. Her identity and sense of well-being depend on it. She could become depressed if she got fired.

When we are attached and things don't go our way, we can feel angry, sad, afraid, or confused.

Suppose you are attached to getting an "A" on your physics test. You feel as though your success in life depends on getting that "A." As the clock ticks away, you work harder on the test, getting more stuck. That voice in your head gets louder: "I must get an 'A.' I MUST get an 'A.' I MUST GET AN 'A!'"

Now is a time to detach. See whether you can just *observe* what's going on, letting go of all your judgments. When you just observe, you reach a quiet state above and beyond your usual thoughts. This is a place where you can be aware of being aware. It's a tranquil spot, apart from your emotions. From here, you can see yourself objectively, as if you were watching someone else.

That place of detachment might sound far away and hard to reach. You can get there in three ways.

First, pay attention to your thoughts and physical sensations. If you are confused and feeling stuck, tell yourself, "Here I am, confused and stuck." If your palms are sweaty and your stomach is one big knot, admit it.

Second, practice relaxation. Start by simply noticing your breathing. Then breathe more slowly and more deeply. See whether you can breathe the relaxing feeling into your whole body.

Third, practice seeing current events from a broader perspective. In your mind, zoom out to a bigger picture. Ask yourself how much today's test score will matter to you in one week, one month, one year, or one decade from today. You can apply this technique to any challenge in life.

Caution: Giving up an *attachment* to being an "A" student does not mean giving up *being* an "A" student. Giving up an attachment to a job doesn't mean giving up the job. When you detach, you get to keep your values and goals. However, you know that you will be okay even if you fail to achieve a goal.

Remember that you are more than your goals. You are more than your thoughts and feelings. These things come and go. Meanwhile, the part of you that can *just observe* is always there and always safe, no matter what happens.

Behind your attachments is a master student. Release that mastery. Detach.

You're One Click Away...
*from accessing Power Process Media online
and finding out more about how to "detach."*

DISARM TESTS

On the surface, tests don't look dangerous. Maybe that's why we sometimes treat them as if they were land mines. Suppose a stranger walked up to you on the street and asked, "Does a finite abelian P-group have a basis?" Would you break out in a cold sweat? Would your muscles tense up? Would your breathing become shallow?

Probably not. Even if you had never heard of a finite abelian P-group, you probably would remain coolly detached. However, if you find the same question on a test and you have never heard of a finite abelian P-group, your hands might get clammy.

Grades (A to F) are what we use to give power to tests. And there are lots of misconceptions about what grades are. Grades are not a measure of intelligence or creativity. They are not an indication of our ability to contribute to society. Grades are simply a measure of how well we do on tests.

Some people think that a test score measures what a student has accomplished in a course. This idea is false. A test score is a measure of what a student scored on a test. If you are anxious about a test and blank out, the grade cannot measure what you've learned. The reverse is also true: If you are good at taking tests and you are a lucky guesser, the score won't be an accurate reflection of what you know.

Grades are not a measure of self-worth. Yet we tend to give test scores the power to determine how we feel about ourselves. Common thoughts include "If I fail a test, I am a failure" or "If I do badly on a test, I am a bad person." The truth is that if you do badly on a test, you are a person who did badly on a test. That's all.

If you experience test anxiety, then you might find this line of reasoning hard to swallow. Test anxiety is a common problem among students. And it can surface in many ways, masquerading as a variety of emotions. Here are some examples:

- *Anger:* "The teacher never wanted me to pass this stupid course anyway."
- *Blame:* "If only the class were not so boring."
- *Fear:* "I'll never have enough time to study."

Believing in any of these statements leaves us powerless. We become victims of things that we don't control—the teacher, the textbook, or the wording of the test questions.

Another option is to ask: What can *I* do to experience my next test differently? How can I prepare more effectively? How can I manage stress before, during, and after the test? When you answer such questions, you take back your power.

Carrying around misconceptions about tests and grades can put undue pressure on your performance. It's like balancing on a railroad track. Many people can walk along the rail and stay balanced for long periods. Yet the task seems entirely different if the rail is placed between two buildings, 52 stories up.

It is easier to do well on exams if you don't put too much pressure on yourself. Don't give the test some magical power over your own worth as a human being. Academic tests are not a matter of life and death. Scoring low on important tests—standardized tests or medical school exams, bar exams, CPA exams—usually means only a delay.

Whether the chance of doing poorly is real or exaggerated, worrying about it can become paralyzing. The way to deal with tests is to keep them in perspective. Keep the railroad track on the ground. ■

6

PRACTICING
critical thinking 6

You might find the Power Process: "Detach" to be one of the more challenging ideas in *Becoming a Master Student*. Use your thinking skills to unlock the power in this Power Process.

One way to demonstrate an understanding of this Power Process is to give an example of it:

A man dying from lung cancer spent his last days celebrating his long life. One day his son asked him how he was feeling.

"Oh, I'm great," said the man with cancer. "Your mom and I have been having a wonderful time just rejoicing in the life that we have had together."

"Oh, I'm glad you're doing well," said the man's son. "The prednisone you have been taking must have kicked in again and helped your breathing."

"Well, not exactly. Actually, my body is in terrible shape. My breathing has been a struggle these last few days.

I guess what I'm saying is that my body is not working well at all, but I am still great."

This dying man was painfully aware of his body. He also thought of himself as *more* than his body. Above all, he celebrated his marriage. He saw the most important fact about himself to be love, not cancer. This man gave his son—who just happens to be the author of this book—an unforgettable lesson in detachment.

Now do your own thinking about detachment. First, think at **Level 1: Remembering**. Review the Power Process on page 178. You might want to underline or highlight key words or sentences.

Next, move up to **Level 2: Understanding**. Imagine that you are going to explain this Power Process to someone who has not read this book. What would you say? Answer this question by writing a short paragraph. Be sure to use your own words rather than quoting the article directly. Include an example of how you practiced detachment in the past or could practice it in the future.

JOURNAL ENTRY 14
Discovery Statement

Explore your feelings about tests

Complete the following sentences:

As exam time gets closer, one thing I notice that I do is . . .

_____
_____
_____

When it comes to taking tests, I have trouble . . .

_____
_____
_____

The night before a test, I usually feel . . .

_____
_____
_____

The morning of a test, I usually feel . . .

_____
_____
_____

During a test, I usually feel . . .

_____
_____
_____

After a test, I usually feel . . .

_____
_____
_____

When I learn a test score, I usually feel . . .

_____
_____
_____

You're One Click Away...
from accessing and completing this Journal Entry online under Success Tools in Becoming a Master Student's College Success CourseMate.

JOURNAL ENTRY 15
Discovery/Intention Statement

Notice your excuses and let them go

Do a timed, 4-minute brainstorm of all the reasons, rationalizations, justifications, and excuses you have used to avoid studying. Be creative. Write your list of excuses in the space below. Use additional paper as needed.

Review your list. Then write a Discovery Statement about patterns that you see in your excuses.

I discovered that I . . .

Next, review your list, pick the excuse that you use the most, and circle it. In the space below, write an Intention Statement about what you will do to begin eliminating your favorite excuse. Make this Intention Statement one that you can keep, with a time line and a reward.

I intend to . . .

_____
_____
_____
_____
_____
_____
_____
_____
_____
_____
_____
_____
_____
_____
_____
_____
_____
_____
_____
_____
_____

WHAT TO DO
BEFORE THE TEST

Do daily reviews. Daily reviews include short preclass and post-class reviews of lecture notes. Also conduct brief daily reviews with textbooks: Before reading a new assignment, scan your notes and the sections you underlined or highlighted in the previous assignment. In addition, use the time you spend waiting for the bus or doing the laundry to conduct short reviews.

Concentrate daily reviews on two kinds of material. One is material you have just learned, either in class or in your reading. Second is material that involves simple memorization—equations, formulas, dates, definitions.

Begin to review on the first day of class. Most instructors outline the whole course at that time. You can even start reviewing within seconds after learning. During a lull in class, go over the notes you just took. Immediately after class, review your notes again.

Do weekly reviews. Review each subject at least once a week, allowing about 1 hour per subject. Include reviews of assigned reading and lecture notes. Look over any mind map summaries or flash cards you have created. Also practice working on sample problems.

Do major reviews. Major reviews are usually most helpful when conducted the week before finals or other critical exams. They help you integrate concepts and deepen your understanding of material presented throughout the term. These are longer review periods—2 to 5 hours at a stretch, with sufficient breaks. Remember that the effectiveness of your review begins to drop after an hour or so unless you give yourself a short rest.

After a certain point, short breaks every hour might not be enough to refresh you. That's when it's time to quit. Learn your limits by being conscious of the quality of your concentration.

During long sessions, study the most difficult subjects when you are the most alert: at the beginning of the session.

Schedule reviews. Schedule specific times in your calendar for reviews. Start reviewing key topics at least 5 days before you'll be tested on them. This allows plenty of time to find the answers to questions and close any gaps in your understanding.

Create study checklists. You can use study checklists the way a pilot uses a preflight checklist. Pilots go through a standard routine before they take off. They physically mark off each item: test flaps, check magnetos, check fuel tanks, adjust instruments, check rudder. A written list helps them to be sure they don't miss anything. Once they are in the air, it's too late. Taking an exam is like flying a plane. Once the test begins, it's too late to memorize that one equation you forgot to include in your review.

Make a checklist for each subject. List reading assignments by chapters or page numbers. List dates of lecture notes. Write down various types of problems you will need to solve. Write down other skills to master. Include major ideas, definitions, theories, formulas, and equations. For math and science tests, choose some problems and do them over again as a way to review for the test.

A.BACALL

"'How To Do Well In School Without Studying' is over there in the fiction section."

6

Remember that a study checklist is not a review sheet; it is a to-do list. Checklists contain the briefest possible description of each item to study.

Instead of a checklist, you may want to use a test prep plan. This written plan goes beyond a study checklist to include the following:

- The date and time of each test, along with the name of the course and instructor.

- The type of items—such as essay or multiple choice—that are likely to appear on each test.

- Specific dates and times that you intend to study for each test (which you then enter on your calendar).

- Specific strategies that you intend to use while studying for each test.

Create mind map summary sheets. There are several ways to make a mind map as you study for tests. Start by creating a map totally from memory. You might be surprised by how much you already know. After you have gone as far as you can using recall alone, go over your notes and text, and fill in the rest of the map. Another option is to go through your notes and write down key words as you pick them out. Then, without looking at your notes, create a mind map of everything you can recall about each key word. Finally, go back to your notes, and fill in material you left out.

Create flash cards. Flash cards are like portable test questions. On one side of some 3 × 5 cards, write questions. On the other side, write the answers. It's that simple. Always carry a pack of flash cards with you, and review them whenever you have a minute to spare. Use flash cards for formulas, definitions, theories, key words from your notes, axioms, dates, foreign language phrases, hypotheses, and sample problems. Create flash cards regularly as the term progresses. Buy an inexpensive card file to keep your flash cards arranged by subject.

Monitor your reviews. Each day that you prepare for a test, assess what you have learned and what you still want to learn. See how many items you've covered from your study checklist. Look at the tables of contents in your textbooks, and mark an X next to the sections that you've summarized. This helps you gauge the thoroughness of your reviews and alerts you to areas that still need attention.

Take a practice test. Write up your own questions based on course material—a good activity for study groups. Take your practice test several times before the actual exam. You might type this "test" so that it looks like the real thing. If possible, take your practice test in the same room where you will take the actual test.

Also meet with your instructor to go over your practice test. Ask whether your questions focus on appropriate topics and represent the kind of items you can expect to see. The instructor might decline to give you any of this information. More often, though, instructors will answer some or all of your questions about an upcoming test.

Get copies of old exams. Copies of previous exams for the class might be available from the instructor, the instructor's department, the library, or the counseling office. Old tests can help you plan a review strategy. One caution: If you rely on old tests exclusively, you might gloss over material the instructor has added since the last test. Also, check your school's policy about making past tests available to students. Some schools might not allow it. ■

 You're One Click Away...
from seeing examples of mind map summary sheets and other review tools online.

How to cram (even though you "shouldn't")

Know the limitations of cramming, and be aware of its costs. Cramming won't work if you've neglected all of the reading assignments or if you've skipped most of the lectures and daydreamed through the rest. The more courses you have to cram for, the less effective cramming will be. Also, cramming is not the same as learning: You won't remember what you cram.

If you are going to cram, however, then avoid telling yourself that you *should* have studied earlier, you *should* have read the assignments, or you *should* have been more conscientious. All those *shoulds* get you nowhere. Instead, write an Intention Statement about how you will change your study habits. Give yourself permission to be the fallible human being you are. Then make the best of the situation.

Make choices Pick out a *few* of the most important elements of the course and learn them backward, forward, and upside down. For example, devote most of your attention to the topic sentences, tables, and charts in a long reading assignment.

Make a plan After you've chosen what elements you want to study, determine how much time to spend on each one.

Recite and recite again The key to cramming is repetition. Go over your material again and again.

Ways to
PREDICT TEST QUESTIONS

Predicting test questions can do more than get you a better grade. It can also keep you focused on the purpose of a course and help you design your learning strategies. Making predictions can be fun too—especially when they turn out to be accurate.

Ask about the nature of the test. Eliminate as much guesswork as possible. Ask your instructor to describe upcoming tests. Do this early in the term so you can be alert for possible test questions throughout the course. Here are some questions to ask:

- What course material will the test cover—readings, lectures, lab sessions, or a combination?
- Will the test be cumulative, or will it cover just the most recent material you've studied?
- Will the test focus on facts and details or major themes and relationships?
- Will the test call on you to solve problems or apply concepts?
- Will you have choices about which questions to answer?
- What types of questions will be on the test—true/false, multiple choice, short answer, essay?

Note: In order to study appropriately for essay tests, find out how much detail the instructor wants in your answers. Ask how much time you'll be allowed for the test and about the length of essay answers (number of pages, blue books, or word limit). Having that information before you begin studying will help you gauge your depth for learning the material.

Put yourself in your instructor's shoes. If you were teaching the course, what kinds of questions would you put on an exam? You can also brainstorm test questions with other students—a great activity for study groups.

Look for possible test questions in your notes and readings. Have a separate section in your notebook labeled "Test questions." Add several questions to this section after every lecture and assignment. You can also create your own code or graphic signal—such as a "*T!*" in a circle—to flag possible test questions in your notes. Use the same symbol to flag review questions and problems in your textbooks that could appear on a test.

Remember that textbook authors have many ways of pointing you to potential test items. Look for clues in chapter overviews and summaries, headings, lists of key words, and review questions. Some textbooks have related Web sites where you can take practice tests.

Look for clues to possible questions during class. During lectures, you can predict test questions by observing what an instructor says and how he says it. Instructors often give clues. They might repeat important points several times, write them on the board, or return to them in later classes.

Gestures can indicate critical points. For example, your instructor might pause, look at notes, or read passages word for word.

Notice whether your teacher has any strong points of view on certain issues. Questions on those issues are likely to appear on a test. Also pay attention to questions the instructor poses to students, and note questions that other students ask.

When material from reading assignments is covered extensively in class, it is likely to be on a test. For science courses and other courses involving problem solving, work on sample problems using different variables.

Save all quizzes, papers, lab sheets, and graded materials of any kind. Quiz questions have a way of reappearing, in slightly altered form, on final exams. If copies of previous exams and other graded materials are available, use them to predict test questions.

Apply your predictions. To get the most value from your predictions, use them to guide your review sessions.

Remember the obvious. Be on the lookout for these words: *This material will be on the test.* ■

6

Yuri Arcurs/Shutterstock.com

Study groups can lift your mood on days when you just don't feel like working. If you skip a solo study session, no one else will know. If you declare your intention to study with others who are depending on you, your intention gains strength.

Study groups are especially important if going to school has thrown you into a new culture. Joining a study group with people you already know can help ease the transition. To multiply the benefits of working with study groups, seek out people of other backgrounds, cultures, races, and ethnic groups. You can get a whole new perspective on the world, along with some valued new friends.

Joining a study group also helps you to develop a number of skills for working on teams in the workplace. Effective teams consist of people who know how to resolve conflict, give each other constructive feedback, collaborate to reach a common goal, and build consensus based on creative and critical thinking. None of us is born with these skills. You can start learning them now and use them to advance your career in the future.

FORM A STUDY GROUP

Choose a focus for your group. Many students assume that the purpose of a study group is to help its members prepare for a test. That's one valid purpose—and there are others.

Through his research on cooperative learning, psychologist Joe Cuseo has identified several kinds of study groups.[1] For instance, members of *test review* groups compare answers and help one another discover sources of errors. *Note-taking* groups focus on comparing and editing notes, often meeting directly after the day's class. Members of *research* groups meet to help one another find, evaluate, and take notes on background materials for papers and presentations. *Reading* groups can be useful for courses in which test questions are based largely on textbooks. Meet with classmates to compare the passages you underlined or highlighted and the notes you made in the margins of your books.

Look for dedicated students. Find people you are comfortable with and who share your academic goals. Look for students who pay attention, participate in class, and actively take notes. Invite them to join your group.

Of course, you can recruit members in other ways. One way is to make an announcement during class. Another option is to post signs asking interested students to contact you. Or pass around a sign-up sheet before class. These methods can reach many people, but they do take more time to achieve results. And you have less control over who applies to join the group.

Limit groups to four people. Research on cooperative learning indicates that four people are an ideal group size.[2] Larger groups can be unwieldy.

Studying with friends is fine, but if your common interests are pizza and jokes, you might find it hard to focus.

Hold a planning session. Ask two or three people to get together for a snack and talk about group goals, meeting times, and other logistics. You don't have to make an immediate commitment.

As you brainstorm about places to meet, aim for a quiet meeting room with plenty of room to spread out materials. Your campus library probably has study rooms. Campus tutoring services might also have space and other resources for study groups.

Do a trial run. Test the group first by planning a one-time session. If that session works, plan another. After a few successful sessions, you can schedule regular meetings.

CONDUCT YOUR GROUP

Ask your instructor for guidelines on study group activity. Many instructors welcome and encourage study groups. However, they have different ideas about what kinds of collaboration are acceptable. Some activities—such as sharing test items or writing papers from a shared outline—are considered cheating and can have serious consequences. Let your instructor know that you're forming a group, and ask for clear guidelines.

Set an agenda for each meeting. At the beginning of each meeting, reach agreement on what you intend to do. Set a time limit for each agenda item, and determine a quitting time. End each meeting with assignments for all members to complete before the next meeting.

Assign roles. To make the most of your time, ask one member to lead each group meeting. The leader's role is to keep the discussion focused on the agenda and ask for contributions from all members. Assign another person to act as recorder. This person will take notes on the meeting, recording possible test questions, answers, and main points from group discussions. Rotate both of these roles so that every group member takes a turn.

Cycle through learning styles. As you assign roles, think about the learning styles present in your group. Some people excel at raising questions and creating lots of ideas. Others prefer to gather information and think critically. Some like to answer questions and make decisions, while others excel at taking action. Each of these distinct modes of learning are explained in Chapter 1 on pages 41, LSI-6, and 43–46. To create an effective group, match people with their preferred activities. Also change roles periodically. This gives group members a chance to explore new learning styles.

Teach each other. Teaching is a great way to learn something. Turn the material you're studying into a list of topics and assign a specific topic to each person, who will then teach it to the group. When you're done presenting your topic, ask for questions or comments. Prompt each other to explain ideas more clearly, find gaps in understanding, consider other points of view, and apply concepts to settings outside the classroom.

Test one another. During your meeting, take a practice test created from questions contributed by group members. When you're finished, compare answers. Or turn testing into a game by pretending you're on a television game show. Use sample test questions to quiz one another.

Compare notes. Make sure that all the group's members heard the same thing in class and that you all recorded the important information. Ask others to help explain material in your notes that is confusing to you.

Create wall-size mind maps or concept maps to summarize a textbook or series of lectures. Work on large sheets of butcher paper, or tape together pieces of construction paper. When creating a mind map, assign one branch to each member of the study group. Use a different colored pen or marker for each branch of the mind map. (For more information on concept maps and mind maps, see Chapter 5: "Notes.")

Monitor effectiveness. On your meeting agenda, include an occasional discussion about your group's effectiveness. Are you meeting consistently? Is the group helping members succeed in class?

Use this time to address any issues that are affecting the group as a whole. If certain members are routinely unprepared for study sessions, brainstorm ways to get them involved. If one person tends to dominate meetings, reel her in by reminding her that everyone's voice needs to be heard.

To resolve conflict among group members, keep the conversation constructive. Focus on solutions. Move from vague complaints ("You're never prepared") to specific requests ("Will you commit to bringing ten sample test questions next time?"). Asking a "problem" member to lead the next meeting might make an immediate difference.

Use technology to collaborate. Web-based applications allow you to create virtual study groups and collaborate online. For example, create and revise documents with sites such as Google Docs (www.docs.google.com) and Zoho Writer (www.writer.zoho.com).

Create and share PowerPoint and keynote presentations with tools such as SlideShare (www.slideshare.net).

Use Basecamp (www.basecamphq.com), Joint Contact (www.jointcontact.com), or 5pm (www.5pmweb.com) to manage projects. You can share files, create a group calendar, assign tasks, chat online, post messages, and track progress toward milestones (key due dates).

Create group mind maps with MindMeister (www.mindmeister.com) and Mindomo (www.mindomo.com).

For more options, do an Internet search with the key words *collaborate online*.

If your course has an online component, look for collaboration tools there. For example, Blackboard has some handy features for this purpose—chat, e-mail, and discussion groups. ■

Master Students
IN ACTION

"*When studying for a test, the first thing I usually do is to read over my notes. Sometimes I reread the chapter just to make sure I comprehend what the chapter is saying. I find it very helpful to go online to the publisher's Web site and do the practice exams. By doing the practice exams, I get a better perspective of what the critical points are in the chapters. I like to go through the chapter outline because sometimes the answers are in the outlines.*"

—Lea Dean,
Central Michigan
University

You're One Click Away...
*from a video about
Master Students in Action.*

6

What to do during the test

iStockphoto.com/Darko Novakovic

Prepare yourself for the test by arriving early. Being early often leaves time to do a relaxation exercise. While you're waiting for the test to begin and talking with classmates, avoid asking the question "How much did you study for the test?" This question might fuel anxious thoughts that you didn't study enough.

AS YOU BEGIN

Ask the teacher or test administrator if you can use scratch paper during the test. (If you use a separate sheet of paper without permission, you might appear to be cheating.) If you *do* get permission, use this paper to jot down memory aids, formulas, equations, definitions, facts, or other material you know you'll need and might forget. An alternative is to make quick notes in the margins of the test sheet.

Pay attention to verbal directions given as a test is distributed. Then scan the whole test immediately. Evaluate the importance of each section. Notice how many points each part of the test is worth; then estimate how much time you'll need for each section, using its point value as your guide. For example, don't budget 20 percent of your time for a section that is worth only 10 percent of the points.

Read the directions slowly. Then reread them. It can be agonizing to discover that you lost points on a test merely because you failed to follow the directions. When the directions are confusing, ask to have them clarified.

Now you are ready to begin the test. If necessary, allow yourself a minute or two of "panic" time. Notice any tension you feel, and apply one of the techniques explained in the article "Let Go of Test Anxiety" later in this chapter.

Answer the easiest, shortest questions first. This gives you the experience of success. It also stimulates associations and prepares you for more difficult questions. Pace yourself, and watch the time. If you can't think of an answer, move on. Follow your time plan.

If you are unable to determine the answer to a test question, keep an eye out throughout the test for context clues that may remind you of the correct answer or provide you with evidence to eliminate wrong answers.

MULTIPLE-CHOICE QUESTIONS

- **Answer each question in your head first.** Do this step before you look at the possible answers. If you come up with an answer that you're confident is right, look for that answer in the list of choices.

- **Read all possible answers before selecting one.** Sometimes two answers will be similar and only one will be correct.

- **Test each possible answer.** Remember that multiple-choice questions consist of two parts: the stem (an incomplete statement or question at the beginning) and a list of possible answers. Each answer, when combined with the stem, makes a complete statement or question-and-answer pair that is either true or false. When you combine the stem with each possible answer, you are turning each multiple-choice question into a small series of true/false questions. Choose the answer that makes a true statement.

- **Eliminate incorrect answers.** Cross off the answers that are clearly not correct. The answer you cannot eliminate is probably the best choice.

TRUE/FALSE QUESTIONS

- **Read the entire question.** Separate the statement into its grammatical parts—individual clauses and phrases—and then test each part. If any part is false, the entire statement is false.

- **Look for qualifiers.** Qualifiers include words such as *all, most, sometimes,* or *rarely.* Absolute qualifiers such as *always* or *never* generally indicate a false statement.

- **Find the devil in the details.** Double-check each number, fact, and date in a true/false statement. Look for numbers that have been transposed or facts that have been slightly altered. These are signals of a false statement.

- **Watch for negatives.** Look for words such as *not* and *cannot.* Read the sentence without these words and see whether you come up with a true/false statement. Then reinsert the negative words and see whether the statement makes more sense. Watch especially for sentences with two negative words. As in math operations, two negatives cancel each other out: *We cannot say that Chekhov never succeeded at short story writing* means the same as *Chekhov succeeded at short story writing*.

COMPUTER-GRADED TESTS

- Make sure that the answer you mark corresponds to the question you are answering.
- Check the test booklet against the answer sheet whenever you switch sections and whenever you come to the top of a column.
- Watch for stray marks on the answer sheet; they can look like answers.
- If you change an answer, be sure to erase the wrong answer thoroughly, removing all pencil marks completely.

OPEN-BOOK TEST

- Carefully organize your notes, readings, and any other materials you plan to consult when writing answers.
- Write down any formulas you will need on a separate sheet of paper.
- Bookmark the table of contents and index in each of your textbooks. Place sticky notes and stick-on tabs or paper clips on other important pages of books (pages with tables, for instance).
- Create an informal table of contents or index for the notes you took in class.
- Predict which material will be covered on the test, and highlight relevant sections in your readings and notes.

SHORT-ANSWER/FILL-IN-THE-BLANK TESTS

- Concentrate on key words and facts. Be brief.
- Overlearning material can really pay off. When you know a subject backward and forward, you can answer this type of question almost as fast as you can write.

MATCHING TESTS

- Begin by reading through each column, starting with the one with fewer items. Check the number of items in each column to see whether they're equal. If they're not, look for an item in one column that you can match with two or more items in the other column.
- Look for any items with similar wording, and make special note of the differences between these items.
- Match words that are similar grammatically. For example, match verbs with verbs and nouns with nouns.

- When matching individual words with phrases, first read a phrase. Then look for the word that logically completes the phrase.
- Cross out items in each column when you are through with them.

ESSAY QUESTIONS

Managing your time is crucial in answering essay questions. Note how many questions you have to answer, and monitor your progress during the test period. Writing shorter answers and completing all of the questions on an essay test will probably yield a better score than leaving some questions blank.

Find out what an essay question is asking—precisely. If a question asks you to *compare* the ideas of Sigmund Freud and Karl Marx, no matter how eloquently you *explain* them, you are on a one-way trip to No Credit City.

Before you write, make a quick outline. An outline can help speed up the writing of your detailed answer; you're less likely to leave out important facts; and if you don't have time to finish your answer, your outline could win you some points. To use test time efficiently, keep your outline brief. Focus on key words to use in your answer.

Introduce your answer by getting to the point. General statements such as "There are many interesting facets to this difficult question" can cause irritation to teachers grading dozens of tests.

One way to get to the point is to begin your answer with part of the question. Suppose the question is "Discuss how increasing the city police budget might or might not contribute to a decrease in street crime." Your first sentence might be this: "An increase in police expenditures will not have a significant effect on street crime for the following reasons." Your position is clear. You are on your way to an answer.

Then expand your answer with supporting ideas and facts. Start out with the most solid points. Be brief and avoid filler sentences.

Write legibly. Grading essay questions is in large part a subjective process. Sloppy, difficult-to-read handwriting might actually lower your grade.

Write on one side of the paper only. If you write on both sides of the paper, writing may show through and obscure the words on the other side. If necessary, use the blank side to add points you missed. Leave a generous left-hand margin and plenty of space between your answers, in case you want to add points that you missed later on.

Finally, if you have time, review your answers for grammar and spelling errors, clarity, and legibility. ■

6

Words to watch for in
ESSAY QUESTIONS

The following words are commonly found in essay test questions. They give you precise directions about what to include in your answer. Get to know these words well. When you see them on a test, underline them. Also look for them in your notes. Locating such key words can help you predict test questions.

Analyze: Break into separate parts and discuss, examine, or interpret each part. Then give your opinion.

Compare: Examine two or more items. Identify similarities and differences.

Contrast: Show differences. Set in opposition.

Criticize: Make judgments about accuracy, quality, or both. Evaluate comparative worth. Criticism often involves analysis.

Define: Explain the exact meaning—usually, a meaning specific to the course or subject. Definitions are usually short.

Describe: Give a detailed account. Make a picture with words. List characteristics, qualities, and parts.

Diagram: Create a drawing, chart, or other visual element. Label and explain key parts.

Discuss: Consider and debate or argue the pros and cons of an issue. Write about any conflict. Compare and contrast.

Enumerate: List the main parts or features in a meaningful order and briefly describe each one.

Evaluate: Make judgments about accuracy, quality, or both (similar to *criticize*).

Explain: Make an idea clear. Show logically how a concept is developed. Give the reasons for an event.

Illustrate: Clarify an idea by giving examples of it. Illustration often involves comparison and contrast. Read the test directions to see whether the question calls for actually drawing a diagram as well.

Interpret: Explain the meaning of a new idea or event by showing how it relates to more familiar ideas or events. Interpretation can involve evaluation.

List: Write a series of concise statements (similar to *enumerate*).

Outline: List the main topics, points, features, or events and briefly describe each one. (This does not necessarily mean creating a traditional outline with Roman numerals, numbers, and letters.)

Prove: Support with facts, examples, and quotations from credible sources (especially those presented in class or in the text).

Relate: Show the connections between ideas or events. Provide a larger context for seeing the big picture.

State: Explain precisely and clearly.

Summarize: Give a brief, condensed account. Include main ideas and conclusions. Avoid supporting details, or include only significant details.

Trace: Show the order of events or the progress of a subject or event.

Notice how these words differ. For example, *compare* asks you to do something different from *contrast*. Likewise, *criticize* and *explain* call for different responses.

If any of these terms are still unclear to you, look them up in an unabridged dictionary.

During a test, you might be allowed to ask for an explanation of a key word. Check with instructors for policies.

 You're One Click Away...
from reviewing these key words and other helpful vocabulary terms by using online flash cards.

The test isn't over *UNTIL . . .*

Many students believe that a test is over as soon as they turn in the answer sheet. Consider another point of view: You're not done with a test until you know the answer to any question that you missed—and why you missed it.

This point of view offers major benefits. Tests in many courses are cumulative. In other words, the content included on the first test is assumed to be working knowledge for the second test, midterm, or final exam. When you discover what questions you missed and understand the reasons for lost points, you learn something—and you greatly increase your odds of achieving better scores later in the course.

To get the most value from any test, take control of what you do at two critical points: the time immediately following the test and the time when the test is returned to you.

Immediately following the test. After finishing a test, your first thought might be to nap, snack, or go out with friends to celebrate. Restrain those impulses for a short while so that you can reflect on the test. The time you invest now carries the potential to raise your grades in the future.

To begin with, sit down in a quiet place. Take a few minutes to write some Discovery Statements related to your experience of taking the test. Describe how you felt about taking the test, how effective your review strategies were, and whether you accurately predicted the questions that appeared on the test.

Follow up with an Intention Statement or two. State what, if anything, you will do differently to prepare for the next test. The more specific you are, the better.

When the test is returned. When a returned test includes a teacher's comments, view this document as a treasure trove of intellectual gold.

First, make sure that the point totals add up correctly, and double-check for any other errors in grading. Even the best teachers make an occasional mistake.

Next, look at the test items that you missed. Ask these questions:

- On what material did the teacher base test questions—readings, lectures, discussions, or other class activities?

- What types of questions appeared in the test—objective (such as matching items, true/false questions, or multiple choice), short answer, or essay?

- What types of questions did you miss?

- Can you learn anything from the instructor's comments that will help you prepare for the next test?

- What strategies did you use to prepare for this test? What would you do differently to prepare for your next test?

Also see whether you can correct any answers that lost points. To do this, carefully analyze the source of your errors, and find a solution. Consult the chart below for help. ■

Source of test error	Possible solutions
Study errors—studying material that was not included on the test, or spending too little time on material that did appear on the test	• Ask your teacher about specific topics that will be included on a test. • Practice predicting test questions. • Form a study group with class members to create mock tests.
Careless errors, such as skipping or misreading directions	• Read and follow directions more carefully—especially when tests are divided into several sections with different directions. • Set aside time during the next test to proofread your answers.
Concept errors—mistakes made when you do not understand the underlying principles needed to answer a question or solve a problem	• Look for patterns in the questions you missed. • Make sure that you complete all assigned readings, attend all lectures, and show up for laboratory sessions. • Ask your teacher for help with specific questions.
Application errors—mistakes made when you understand underlying principles but fail to apply them correctly	• Rewrite your answers correctly. • When studying, spend more time on solving sample problems. • Predict application questions that will appear on future tests, and practice answering them.
Test mechanics errors—missing more questions in certain parts of the test than others, changing correct answers to incorrect ones at the last minute, leaving items blank, miscopying answers from scratch paper to the answer sheet	• Set time limits for taking each section of a test, and stick to them. • Proofread your test answers carefully. • Look for patterns in the kind of answers you change at the last minute. • Change answers only if you can state a clear and compelling reason to do so.

6

The HIGH COSTS of cheating

Cheating on tests can be a tempting strategy. It offers the chance to get a good grade without having to study.

Instead of studying, you could spend more time watching TV, partying, sleeping, or doing anything that seems like more fun. Another benefit is that you could avoid the risk of doing poorly on a test—which could happen even if you *do* study.

Remember that cheating carries costs. Here are some consequences to consider.

You risk failing the course or getting expelled from college. The consequences for cheating are serious. Cheating can result in failing the assignment, failing the entire course, getting suspended, or getting expelled from college entirely. Documentation of cheating may also prevent you from being accepted to other colleges.

You learn less. Although you might think that some courses offer little or no value, you can create value from any course. If you look deeply enough, you can discover some idea or acquire some skill to prepare you for future courses or a career after graduation.

You lose time and money. Getting an education costs a lot of money. It also calls for years of sustained effort. Cheating sabotages your purchase. You pay full tuition and invest your energy without getting full value for it. You shortchange yourself and possibly your future coworkers, customers, and clients. Think about it: You probably don't want a surgeon who cheated in medical school to operate on you.

Fear of getting caught promotes stress. When you're fully aware of your emotions about cheating, you might discover intense stress. Even if you're not fully aware of your emotions, you're likely to feel some level of discomfort about getting caught.

Violating your values promotes stress. Even if you don't get caught cheating, you can feel stress about violating your own ethical standards. Stress can compromise your physical health and overall quality of life.

Cheating on tests can make it easier to violate your integrity again. Human beings become comfortable with behaviors that they repeat. Cheating is no exception.

Think about the first time you drove a car. You might have felt excited—even a little frightened. Now driving is probably second nature, and you don't give it much thought. Repeated experience with driving creates familiarity, which lessens the intense feelings you had during your first time at the wheel.

You can experience the same process with almost any behavior. Cheating once will make it easier to cheat again. And if you become comfortable with compromising your integrity in one area of life, you might find it easier to compromise in other areas.

Cheating lowers your self-concept. Whether or not you are fully aware of it, cheating sends the message that you are not smart enough or responsible enough to make it on your own. You deny yourself the celebration and satisfaction of authentic success.

An alternative to cheating is to become a master student. Ways to do this are described on every page of this book. ∎

Perils of high-tech CHEATING

Digital technology offers many blessings, but it also expands the options for cheating during a test. For example, one student loaded class notes onto a smartphone and tried to read them. Another student dictated his class notes into files stored on his iPod and tried to listen to them. At one school, students used cell phones to take photos of test questions. They sent the photos to classmates outside the testing room, who responded by text-messaging the answers.[3]

All of these students were caught. Schools are becoming sophisticated about detecting high-tech cheating. Some install cameras in exam rooms. Others use software that monitors the programs running on students' computers during tests. And some schools simply ban all digital devices during tests.

The bottom line: If you cheat on a test, you are more likely than ever before to get caught.

There's no need to learn the hard way—through painful consequences—about the high costs of high-tech cheating. Using the suggestions in this chapter can help you succeed on tests *and* preserve your academic integrity.

> ### If you freeze during tests and flub questions when you know the answers, you might be dealing with test anxiety.

Masterfile (Royalty-Free Div.)

Let go of
TEST ANXIETY

A little tension before a test is fine. That tingly, butterflies-in-the-stomach feeling you get from extra adrenaline can sharpen your awareness and keep you alert. You can enjoy the benefits of a little tension while you stay confident and relaxed.

Yell "Stop!" If you notice that your mind is consumed with worries and fears—that your thoughts are spinning out of control—mentally yell "Stop!" If you're in a situation that allows it, yell it out loud. This action can allow you to redirect your thoughts. Once you've broken the cycle of worry or panic, you can use any of the following techniques.

Describe your thoughts in writing. Certain thoughts tend to increase test anxiety. One way to defuse them is to simply acknowledge them. To get the full benefit of this technique, take the time to make a list. Write down what you think and feel about an upcoming test. Capture everything that's on your mind, and don't stop to edit. One study indicates that this technique can relieve anxiety and potentially raise your test score.[4]

Dispute your thoughts. You can take the above technique one step further. Do some critical thinking. Remember that anxiety-creating thoughts about tests often boil down to this statement: *Getting a low grade on a test is a disaster.* Do the math, however: A 4-year degree often involves taking about 32 courses (8 courses per year over 4 years for a full-time student). This means that your final grade on any one course amounts to about only 3 percent of your total grade point average. This is *not* an excuse to avoid studying. It is simply a reason to keep tests in perspective.

Praise yourself. Many of us take the first opportunity to belittle ourselves: "Way to go, dummy! You don't even know the answer to the first question on the test." We wouldn't dream of treating a friend this way, yet we do it to ourselves. An alternative is to give yourself some encouragement. Treat yourself as if you were your own best friend. Prepare carefully for each test. Then remind yourself, "I am ready. I can do a great job on this test."

Consider the worst. Rather than trying to put a stop to your worrying, consider the very worst thing that could happen. Take your fear to the limit of absurdity. Imagine the catastrophic problems that might occur if you were to fail the test. You might say to yourself, "Well, if I fail this test, I might fail the course, lose my financial aid, and get kicked out of school. Then I won't be able to get a job, so the bank will repossess my car, and I'll start drinking." Keep going until you see the absurdity of your predictions. After you stop chuckling, you can backtrack to discover a reasonable level of concern.

Breathe. You can calm physical sensations within your body by focusing your attention on your breathing. Concentrate on the air going in and out of your lungs. Experience it as it passes through your nose and mouth. Do this exercise for 2 to 5 minutes. If you notice that you are taking short, shallow breaths, begin to take longer and deeper breaths. Imagine your lungs to be a pair of bagpipes. Expand your chest to bring in as much air as possible. Then listen to the plaintive chords as you slowly release the air. ■

6

Have some **FUN!**

Contrary to popular belief, finals week does not have to be a drag. In fact, if you have used techniques in this chapter, exam week can be fun. You will have done most of your studying long before finals arrive.

When you are well prepared for tests, you can even use fun as a technique to enhance your performance. The day before a final, go for a run or play a game of basketball. Take in a movie or a concert. A relaxed brain is a more effective brain. If you have studied for a test, your mind will continue to prepare itself even while you're at the movies. Get plenty of rest too. There's no need to cram until 3:00 A.M. when you have reviewed material throughout the term.

EXERCISE 18

Twenty things I like to do

One way to relieve tension is to mentally yell "Stop!" and substitute a pleasant daydream for the stressful thoughts and emotions you are experiencing.

To create a supply of pleasant images to recall during times of stress, conduct an 8-minute brainstorm about things you like to do. Your goal is to generate at least twenty ideas. Time yourself, and write as fast as you can in the space below.

When you have completed your list, study it. Pick out two activities that seem especially pleasant, and elaborate on them by creating a mind map in the space below. Write down all of the memories you have about that activity.

You can use these images to calm yourself in stressful situations.

Getting ready for math tests

Many students who could succeed in math shy away from the subject. Some had negative experiences in past courses. Others believe that math is only for gifted students.

At some level, however, math is open to all students. There's more to this subject than memorizing formulas and manipulating numbers. Imagination, creativity, and problem-solving skills are important too.

Consider a three-part program for math success. Begin with strategies for overcoming math anxiety. Next, boost your study skills. Finally, let your knowledge shine during tests.

OVERCOME MATH ANXIETY

Many schools offer courses in overcoming math anxiety. Ask your advisor about resources on your campus. Also experiment with the following suggestions.

Connect math to life. Think of the benefits of mastering math courses. You'll have more options for choosing a major and a career. Math skills can also put you at ease in everyday situations—calculating the tip for a waiter, balancing your checkbook, working with a spreadsheet on a computer. If you follow baseball statistics, cook, do construction work, or snap pictures with a camera, you'll use math. And speaking the language of math can help you feel at home in a world driven by technology.

Pause occasionally to get an overview of the branch of math that you're studying. What's it all about? What basic problems is it designed to solve? How do people apply this knowledge in daily life? For example, many architects, engineers, and space scientists use calculus daily.

Take a First Step. Math is cumulative. Concepts build upon each other in a certain order. If you struggled with algebra, you may have trouble with trigonometry or calculus.

To ensure that you have an adequate base of knowledge, tell the truth about your current level of knowledge and skill. Before you register for a math course, locate assigned texts for the prerequisite courses. If the material in those books seems new or difficult for you, see the instructor. Ask for suggestions on ways to prepare for the course.

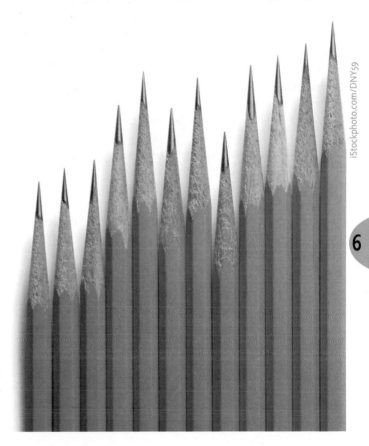

iStockphoto.com/DNY59

6

Notice your pictures about math. Sometimes what keeps people from succeeding at math is their mental picture of mathematicians. They see a man dressed in a baggy plaid shirt and brown wingtip shoes. He's got a calculator on his belt and six pencils jammed in his shirt pocket.

These pictures are far from realistic. Succeeding in math won't turn you into a nerd. Actually, you'll be able to enjoy school more, and your friends will still like you.

Mental pictures about math can be funny, but they can have serious effects. If math is seen as a field for white males, then women and people of color are likely to get excluded. Promoting math success for all students helps to overcome racism and sexism.

Change your conversation about math. When students fear math, they often say negative things to themselves about their abilities in this subject. Many times this self-talk includes statements such as *I'll never be fast enough at solving math problems* or *I'm good with words, so I can't be good with numbers.*

Get such statements out in the open, and apply some emergency critical thinking. You'll find two self-defeating assumptions lurking there: *Everybody else is better at math and science than I am* and *Since I don't understand a math concept right now, I'll never understand it.* Both of these statements are illogical.

Replace negative beliefs with logical, realistic statements that affirm your ability to succeed in math: *Any confusion I feel now can be resolved. I learn math without comparing myself to others.* And *I ask whatever questions are needed to aid my understanding.*

Choose your response to stress. Math anxiety is seldom just "in your head." It can also register as sweaty palms, shallow breathing, tightness in the chest, or a mild headache. Instead of trying to ignore these sensations, just notice them without judgment. Over time, simple awareness decreases their power.

In addition, use stress management techniques. "Let Go of Test Anxiety" on page 191 offers a bundle of them.

No matter what you do, remember to breathe. You can relax in any moment just by making your breath slower and deeper. Practice doing this while you study math. It will come in handy at test time.

BOOST STUDY SKILLS FOR MATH

Choose teachers with care. Whenever possible, find a math teacher whose approach to math matches your learning style. Talk with several teachers until you find one you enjoy.

Another option is to ask around. Maybe your academic advisor can recommend math teachers. Also ask classmates to name their favorite math teachers—and to explain the reasons for their choices.

In some cases, only one teacher will be offering the math course you need. The suggestions that follow can be used to learn from a teacher regardless of her teaching style.

Take math courses back to back. Approach math in the same way that you learn a foreign language. If you take a year off in between Spanish I and Spanish II, you won't gain much fluency. To master a language, you take courses back to back. It works the same way with math, which is a language in itself.

Avoid short courses. Courses that you take during summer school or another shortened term are condensed. You might find yourself doing far more reading and homework each week than you do in longer courses. If you enjoy math, the extra intensity can provide a stimulus to learn. But if math is not your favorite subject, give yourself extra time. Enroll in courses spread out over more calendar days.

Form a study group. During the first week of each math course, organize a study group. Ask each member to bring five problems to group meetings, along with solutions. Also exchange contact information so that you can stay in touch via e-mail, phone, and text messaging.

Make your text top priority. Math courses are often text driven. Budget for math textbooks and buy them as early as possible. Class activities usually closely follow the book. This fact underscores the importance of completing your reading assignments. Master one concept before going on to the next, and stay current with your reading. Be willing to read slowly and reread sections as needed.

Do homework consistently. Students who succeed in math do their homework daily—from beginning to end, and from the easy problems all the way through the hard problems. If you do homework consistently, you're not likely to be surprised on a test.

When doing homework, use a common process to solve similar problems. There's comfort in rituals, and using familiar steps can help to reduce math anxiety.

Take notes that promote success in math. Though math courses are often text-driven, you might find that the content and organization of your notes makes a big difference as well. Take notes during every class and organize them by date. Also number the pages of your notes. Create a table of contents or index for them so that you can locate key concepts quickly.

In addition, make separate notes to integrate material from class meetings and reading assignments. Paul Nolting, author of the *Math Study Skills Workbook*, suggests that you create a large table with three columns: Key Words/Rules, Examples, and Explanation.[5] Updating this table weekly is a way to review for tests, uncover questions, and monitor your understanding.

Participate in class. Success in math depends on your active involvement. Attend class regularly. Complete homework assignments *when they're due*—not just before the test. If you're

1: Prepare

- Read each problem two or three times, slowly and out loud whenever possible.
- Consider creating a chart with three columns labeled *What I already know, What I want to find out,* and *What connects the two.* The third column is the place to record a formula that can help you solve the problem.
- Determine which arithmetic operations (addition, subtraction, multiplication, division) or formulas you will use to solve the problem.
- See if you can estimate the answer before you compute it.

2: Compute

- Reduce the number of unknowns as much as you can. Consider creating a separate equation to solve each unknown.
- When solving equations, carry out the algebra as far as you can before plugging in the actual numbers.
- Cancel and combine. For example, if the same term appears in both dividend and divisor, they will cancel each other out.
- Remember that it's OK to make several attempts at solving the problem before you find an answer.

3: Check

- Plug your answer back into the original equation or problem and see if it works out correctly.
- Ask yourself if your answer seems likely when compared with your estimate. For example, if you're asked to apply a discount to an item, that item should cost less in your solution.
- Perform opposite operations. If a problem involves multiplication, check your work by division; add, then subtract; factor, then multiply; find the square root, then the square; differentiate, then integrate.
- Keep units of measurement clear. Say that you're calculating the velocity of an object. If you're measuring distance in meters and time in seconds, the final velocity should be in meters per second.

6

confused, get help right away from an instructor, tutor, or study group. Instructors' office hours, free on-campus tutoring, and classmates are just a few of the resources available to you. Also support class participation with time for homework. Make daily contact with math.

Math tests often involve lists of problems to solve. Ask your instructor about what type of tests to expect. Then prepare for the tests using strategies from this chapter.

Ask questions fearlessly. It's a cliché, and it's true: In math, there are no dumb questions. Ask whatever questions will aid your understanding. Keep a running list of them, and bring the list to class.

Read actively. To get the most out of your math texts, read with paper and pencil in hand. Work out examples. Copy diagrams, formulas, and equations. Use chapter summaries and introductory outlines to organize your learning. From time to time, stop, close your book, and mentally reconstruct the steps in solving a problem. Before you memorize a formula, understand the basic concepts behind it.

USE TESTS TO SHOW WHAT YOU KNOW

Practice problem solving. To get ready for math tests, work *lots* of problems. Find out whether practice problems or previous tests are on file in the library, in the math department, or with your math teacher.

Isolate the types of problems that you find the most difficult. Practice them more often. Be sure to get help with these kinds of problems *before* exhaustion or frustration sets in.

To prepare for tests, practice working problems fast. Time yourself. This activity is a great one for math study groups.

Approach problem solving with a three-step process, as shown in the chart on this page. During each step, apply an appropriate strategy.

Practice test taking. In addition to solving problems, create practice tests:

- Print out a set of problems, and set a timer for the same length of time as your testing period.
- Whenever possible, work on these problems in the same room where you will take the actual test.

- Use only the kinds of supporting materials—such as scratch paper or lists of formulas—that will be allowed during the test.

- As you work problems, use deep breathing or another technique to enter a more relaxed state.

To get the most value from practice tests, use them to supplement—not replace—your daily homework.

Ask appropriate questions. If you don't understand a test item, ask for clarification. The worst that can happen is that an instructor or proctor will politely decline to answer your question.

Write legibly. Put yourself in the instructor's place. Imagine the prospect of grading stacks of illegible answer sheets. Make your answers easy to read. If you show your work, underline key sections and circle your answer.

Do your best. There are no secrets involved in getting ready for math tests. Master some stress management techniques, do your homework, get answers to your questions, and work sample problems. If you've done those things, you're ready for the test and deserve to do well. If you haven't done all those things, just do the best you can.

Remember that your personal best can vary from test to test, and even from day to day. Even if you don't answer all test questions correctly, you can demonstrate what you *do* know right now.

During the test, notice when solutions come easily. Savor the times when you feel relaxed and confident. If you ever feel math anxiety in the future, these are the times to remember.[6] ■

✔ EXERCISE 19

Use learning styles for math success

Review the articles about learning styles in Chapter 1: First Steps. Look for strategies that could promote your success in math. Modify any of the suggested strategies so that they work for you, or invent new techniques of your own.

If you're a visual learner, for example, you might color code your notes by writing key terms and formulas in red ink. If you like to learn by speaking and listening, consider reading key passages in your textbooks out loud. And if you're a kinesthetic learner, use "manipulatives"—such as magnetic boards with letters and numbers—when you study math.

Whatever you choose, commit to using at least one new strategy. In the space below, describe what you will do.

_____

_____

_____

_____

_____

_____

_____

_____

_____

_____

_____

_____

Studying across the CURRICULUM

Think for a moment about the range of subjects that you're asked to study in higher education. Schools offer courses in everything from algebra to zoology, and you'll sample a variety of them. The challenge is to shift intellectual gears so that you can succeed in all those different subjects.

Some of the subjects you'll study in higher education share a single purpose—to *propose theories based on observations*. Physics, biology, and chemistry offer theories to explain and predict events in the natural world. Social sciences, such as psychology and sociology, offer theories to predict and explain events in the human world.

Other subjects go beyond theory to *define problems and offer solutions*. Their subjects range from the abstract problems of pure mathematics to the practical problems of engineering and computer science.

Courses in the arts do not propose carefully reasoned theories. Nor do they focus on solving problems. Instead, they *teach through vicarious experience*. When you read a novel, see a play, or watch a film, you view the world through another human being's eyes. Just as you learn from your own experience, you can learn from the experience of others.

To deal with all those differences in subjects, pull out a full toolbox of strategies. When preparing for tests in specific subjects, consider the suggestions in the following chart. Then create more strategies of your own. ■

Subject Area	Strategies for Test Preparation
Humanities: English, literature, public speaking, history, religion, philosophy, fine arts	• Deepen your reading skills by previewing and reviewing each assignment (see Chapter 4: Reading). • Keep a dictionary handy, and create an updated list of new words and their definitions. • Experiment with several different formats for taking notes (see Chapter 5: Notes). • Keep a personal journal in which you practice writing and make connections between the authors and ideas that you're studying. • Take part in class discussions, and welcome chances to speak in front of groups.
Math and natural sciences: algebra, geometry, calculus, chemistry, biology, physics	• Before registering for a course, make sure that you are adequately prepared through prior course work. • In your notes, highlight basic principles—definitions, assumptions, and axioms. • Learn concepts in the sequence presented by your instructor. • If you feel confused, ask a question immediately. • Attend all classes, practice solving problems every day, and check your work carefully. • Translate word problems into images or symbols; translate images and symbols into words. • Balance abstract ideas with concrete experiences, including laboratory sessions and study groups. • Take math courses back to back so you can apply what you learn in one level of a math course immediately to the next level.
Social sciences: sociology, psychology, economics, political science, anthropology, geography	• Pay special attention to theories—statements that are used to explain relationships between observations and predict events. • Expect to encounter complex and contradictory theories, and ask your instructor about ways to resolve disagreements among experts in the field. • Ask your instructor to explain the scientific method and how it is used to arrive at theories in each of the social sciences. • Ask about current issues in the social sciences. • Ask for examples of a theory, and look for them in your daily life.
Foreign languages: learning to speak, read, and write any language that is new to you	• Pay special attention to the "rules"—principles of grammar, noun forms, and verb tenses. For each principle, list correct and incorrect examples. • Spend some time reading, writing, or speaking the language every day. • Welcome the opportunity to practice speaking in class, where you can get immediate feedback. • Start or join a study group in each of your language classes. • Spend time with people who are already skilled in speaking the language. • Travel to a country where the language is widely spoken. • Take your language courses back to back to ensure fluency.

6

Celebrate mistakes

Yuri Shirokov/Shutterstock.com

PKruger/Shutterstock

The title of this article is no mistake. And, it is not a suggestion that you purposely set out to *make* mistakes. Rather, the goal is to shine a light on mistakes so that we can examine them and fix them. Mistakes that are hidden cannot be corrected and are often worth celebrating for the following reasons.

Mistakes are valuable feedback. Mistakes are part of the learning process. In fact, mistakes are often more interesting and more instructive than are successes.

Mistakes demonstrate that we're taking risks. People who play it safe make few mistakes.

Making mistakes can be evidence that we're stretching to the limit of our abilities—growing, risking, and learning.

Celebrating mistakes gets them out into the open. When we celebrate a mistake, we remind ourselves that the person who made the mistake is not bad—just human. Everyone makes mistakes. And hiding mistakes takes a lot of energy that could be channeled into correcting errors. This is not a recommendation that you purposely set out to make mistakes. Mistakes are not an end in themselves. Rather, their value lies in what we learn from them. When we make a mistake, we can admit it and correct it.

Mistakes happen only when we're committed to making things work. Imagine a school where teachers usually come to class late. Residence halls are never cleaned, and scholarship checks are always late. The administration is in chronic debt, students seldom pay tuition on time, and no one cares. In this school, the word *mistake* would have little meaning. Mistakes become apparent only when people are committed to quality. ■

"F" is for feedback

When some students get an "F" on an assignment, they interpret that letter as a message: "You are a failure." That interpretation is not accurate. Getting an "F" means only that you failed a test—not that you failed your life.

From now on, imagine that the letter "F" when used as a grade represents another word: *feedback*. An "F" is an indication that you didn't understand the material well enough. It's a message to do something differently before the next test or assignment. If you interpret "F" as *failure*, you don't get to change anything. But if you

interpret "F" as *feedback*, you can change your thinking and behavior in ways that promote your success. You can choose a new learning strategy, or let go of an excuse about not having the time to study.

Getting prompt and meaningful feedback on your performance is a powerful strategy for learning *anything*. Tests are not the only source of feedback. Make a habit of asking for feedback from your instructors, advisors, classmates, coworkers, friends, family members, and anyone else who knows you. Just determine what you want to improve and ask, "How am I doing?"

masterstudentprofile

Bert and John Jacobs

Bert Jacobs (1965–) and John Jacobs (1968–), whose job titles are "chief executive optimist" and "chief creative optimist," started their business by selling T-shirts out of the back of a van.

"Life is good" says the T-shirt, the hoodie, the baseball cap, and the onesie, to which one might reasonably respond in these days of doom and gloom, "Really?"

When Bert and John Jacobs launched their self-described optimistic apparel company out of a Boston apartment 15 years ago, we were smack in the middle of the go-go '90s, and those three little words—part lifestyle, part mantra, part last ditch effort by a pair of struggling T-shirt entrepreneurs to make rent money—seemed to mirror the national mood.

Today, not so much. Which oddly enough might makes this something of a golden moment for the Life is good company.

"It is generally people who face the greatest adversity who embrace this message the most," says Bert Jacobs, whose company Web site features a section of "inspiring letters that fuel us all to keep spreading good vibes." The letters include testimonials from survivors of a grizzly bear attack, a young amputee, and a soldier stationed in Iraq. "People have a higher sense and appreciation of the simple things when they've been through something difficult. It's our job to see the glass half full."

Life is good doesn't have a demographic, the brothers like to say, but rather a psychographic: the optimists. And while one might imagine that their numbers are dwindling at roughly the same rate as their retirement accounts, some observers suggest otherwise.

That's not to say Life is good is immune to the downturn, but in this company's case it's all relative.

Until last year, the company, whose annual sales top $100 million, had never had a year with less than 30 percent growth. In 2008, it grew only 10 percent, a slowdown that Jacobs notes (in apropos parlance) is "not exactly something you bum out about." Especially since the company hasn't spent a dime on advertising.

Life is good was tested once before, not by the company's customers, but its employees. In the days following 9/11, a number of managers approached Bert Jacobs and said that they weren't feeling right about spreading the company's signature tidings. Some had lost friends in the attacks. The news was all about anthrax and terrorism and tips on turning your basement into a bunker. Maybe life wasn't so good, and maybe this was not the message the American people wanted to hear.

But the company forged ahead, launching its first (wildly successful) nationwide fund-raiser. Jacobs calls it the pivotal moment in his business life.

"Our company has this fantastic positive energy, and our brand is capable of bringing people together," he says. "We know there's trauma and violence and hardship. Life is good isn't the land of Willy Wonka. We're not throwing Frisbees all day. We live in the real world. But you can look around you and find good things any time."

BERT AND JOHN JACOBS . . .
are positive.

YOU . . . can detach from negative thoughts and open up to other perspectives.

Source: Joan Anderman, "A Positive Outlook? Apparel Company Says Bad Times Make Its Message More Vital," *The Boston Globe*, March 17, 2009, The Boston Globe. All rights reserved. Used by permission and protected by the Copyright Laws of the United States. The printing, copying, redistribution, or retransmission of this Content without express written permission is prohibited.

You're One Click Away...
from learning more about Bert and John Jacobs online at the Master Student Profiles. You can also visit the Master Student Hall of Fame to learn about other master students.

PUT THIS CHAPTER TO WORK

You are not necessarily done with tests, appraisals, or assessments once you graduate. People in many careers prepare for licensing tests and certification exams. You might even go back to school for another degree. Use the ideas in this chapter to make peace with tests at any stage of your life.

LET GO OF INTERVIEW ANXIETY. The same techniques that help you manage text anxiety can also help you approach job interviews with confidence. If you feel nervous before an interview, experiment with disputing your thoughts, praising yourself, accepting the worst possible outcome, and yelling "stop" when stressful thoughts arise. Also apply strategies for relaxing and dealing with emotions. For more details, review "Let go of test anxiety" on page 191.

MAKE PERFORMANCE REVIEWS WORK FOR YOU. Like tests, performance reviews offer feedback. These usually take place in a meeting with your direct supervisor at work. Reviews follow various formats, and organizations have their own systems for rating performance. To get the most from these meetings, focus on answering three questions: "What am I doing well? What could I do better? What skills are most important for me to develop right now?"

CELEBRATE MISTAKES. Recall a mistake you made at work and then write about it. In a Discovery Statement, describe what you did to create a result you didn't want ("I discovered that I tend to underestimate the number of hours projects take"). Then write an Intention Statement describing something you can do differently in the future ("I intend to keep track of my actual hours on each project so that I can give more accurate estimates").

GO FOR FUN. Finally, see whether you can adapt suggestions from "Have some FUN!" to cultivate enjoyment at work. One benefit of career planning (see Chapter 12) is finding a job that allows you to follow your interests—in other words, to have fun. Successful people often eliminate the distinction between work and play in their lives. You're more likely to excel professionally when you're having a blast at your job.

SEIZE OPPORTUNITIES TO LEARN COOPERATIVELY. Teamwork is often required in the workplace. Almost every job is accomplished by the combined efforts of many people. For example, manufacturing a single car calls for the contribution of designers, welders, painters, electricians, marketing executives, computer programmers, and many others.

Joining study groups now, while you are in school, can help you expand your learning styles and develop the skills of a successful team player. Many of those skills center on outcome-based and action-oriented thinking. During your first meeting, set clear goals to achieve as a group. End each meeting with a clear list of actions to complete before the next meeting, along with who will take each action.

NOW CREATE A CAREER CONNECTION OF YOUR OWN. Review this chapter, looking for a suggestion that you will commit to use while working or looking for a job. In a sentence or two, describe exactly what you plan to do and the primary benefit you want to gain. For example: "I will practice noticing my breathing when things get stressful at work. This will help me slow down and think carefully before I choose what to do and say next."

State your strategy and desired benefit in the space below:

_____

_____

_____

_____

_____

_____

_____

_____

Name _____

Date _____

1. Describe how using the Power Process: "Detach" differs from giving up.

2. According to the text, test scores measure your accomplishments in a course. True or false? Explain your answer.

3. Briefly explain the difference between a daily review and a major review.

4. Define the term *study checklist,* and give three examples of what to include on such checklists.

5. Study groups can focus on which of the following?
   (a) Comparing and editing class notes
   (b) Doing research to prepare for papers and presentations
   (c) Finding and understanding key passages in assigned readings
   (d) Creating and taking practice tests
   (e) All of the above

6. When answering multiple-choice questions, the recommended strategy is to read all of the possible answers before answering the question in your head. True or false? Explain your answer.

7. The presence of absolute qualifiers, such as always or never, generally indicates a false statement. True or false? Explain your answer.

8. Describe three techniques for dealing with test anxiety.

9. The text offers a three-step process for solving math problems. Name these steps, and list a strategy related to each one.

10. According to the text, learning from mistakes is so powerful that we should deliberately set out to *make* mistakes. True or false? Explain your answer.

Take a minute to reflect on your responses to the Tests section of the Discovery Wheel on page 37. Then take your discoveries and intentions about tests to the next level by completing the following sentences.

DISCOVERY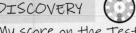

My score on the Tests section of the Discovery Wheel on page 37 was . . .

To study for a test, what I usually do is to . . .

One strategy that really helps me with taking tests is . . .

If I feel stressed about a test, I respond by . . .

INTENTION

I'll know that I've reached a new level of mastery with tests when . . .

My main goal related to test taking is . . .

ACTION

To reach my goal, the most important thing I can do next is to . . .

By the time I finish this course, I would like my Tests score on the Discovery Wheel to be . . .

Thinking

 Use this **Master Student Map** to ask yourself,

 WHY THIS CHAPTER MATTERS . . .

- The ability to think creatively and critically helps you succeed in any course.

WHAT IS INCLUDED . . .

- Power Process: Find a bigger problem   204
- Critical thinking: A survival skill   205
- Becoming a critical thinker   207
- Finding "aha!"—creativity fuels critical thinking   211
- Ways to create ideas   212
- Don't fool yourself: Fifteen common mistakes in logic   216
- Uncovering assumptions   219
- Think critically about information on the Internet   220
- Gaining skill at decision making   221
- Four ways to solve problems   222
- Asking questions—learning through inquiry   224
- Thinking about your major   226
- Service-learning: The art of learning by contributing   228
- Master Student Profile: Twyla Tharp   231

 HOW CAN I USE THIS CHAPTER . . .

- Read, write, speak, and listen more effectively.
- Learn strategies to enhance your success in problem solving.
- Apply thinking skills to practical decisions, such as choosing a major.

WHAT IF . . .

- I could solve problems more creatively and make decisions in every area of life with more confidence?

JOURNAL ENTRY 16
Intention Statement

Choose to create value from this chapter

Remember a time in your life when you felt unable to choose among several different solutions to a problem or struggled with making a decision. Then scan this chapter to find useful suggestions for decision making, problem solving, and critical thinking. Below, note three techniques that you definitely intend to use.

Strategy	Page number
_____	_____
_____	_____
_____	_____
_____	_____
_____	_____
_____	_____
_____	_____
_____	_____
_____	_____
_____	_____
_____	_____
_____	_____
_____	_____

© Ruslan Ivantsov/Shutterstock.com

POWER process

Find a bigger problem

It is impossible to live a life that's free of problems. Besides, problems serve a purpose. They provide opportunities to participate in life. Problems stimulate us and pull us forward.

Seen from this perspective, our goal becomes not to eliminate problems, but to find problems that are worthy of us. Worthy problems are those that challenge us to think, consider our values, and define our goals. Solving the biggest problems offers the greatest potential benefits for others and ourselves. Engaging with big problems changes us for the better. Bigger problems give more meaning to our lives.

Problems expand to fill whatever space is available. Suppose that your only problem for today is to write a thank-you letter to a job interview. You could spend the entire day thinking about what you're going to say, writing the letter, finding a stamp, going to the post office—and then thinking about all of the things you forgot to say.

Now suppose that you get a phone call with an urgent message: A close friend has been admitted to the hospital and wants you to come right away. It's amazing how quickly and easily that letter can get finished when there's a bigger problem on your plate.

True, the smaller problems that enter our lives still need to be solved. The goal is simply to solve them in less time and with less energy.

Bigger problems are easy to find—world hunger, child abuse, environmental pollution, terrorism, human rights violations, drug abuse, street crime, energy shortages, poverty, and wars. These problems await your attention and involvement.

Tackling a bigger problem does not have to be depressing. In fact, it can be energizing—a reason for getting up in the morning. A huge project can channel your passion and purpose.

When we take on a bigger problem, we play full out. We do justice to our potentials. We start to love what we do and do what we love. We're awake, alert, and engaged. Playing full out means living our lives as if our lives depended on it.

Perhaps a little voice in your mind is saying, "That's crazy. I can't do anything about global problems." In the spirit of critical thinking, put that idea to the test. Get involved in solving a bigger problem. Then notice the difference that you *can* make. And just as important, notice how your other problems dwindle—or even vanish.

You're One Click Away...
from accessing Power Process Media online and finding out more about how to "find bigger problems."

Jan Martin Will/Shutterstock.com

204 *Chapter 7 • Thinking*

CRITICAL THINKING:
a survival skill

Society depends on persuasion. Advertisers want us to spend money on their products. Political candidates want us to "buy" their stands on the issues. Teachers want us to agree that their classes are vital to our success. Parents want us to accept their values. Authors want us to read their books. Broadcasters want us to spend our time in front of the radio or television, consuming their programs and not those of the competition. The business of persuasion has an impact on all of us.

A typical American sees thousands of television commercials each year—and TV is just one medium of communication. Add to that the writers and speakers who enter our lives through radio shows, magazines, books, billboards, brochures, Internet sites, and fund-raising appeals—all with a product, service, cause, or opinion for us to embrace.

This flood of appeals leaves us with hundreds of choices about what to buy, where to go, and who to be. It's easy to lose our heads in the crosscurrent of competing ideas—unless we develop skills in critical thinking. When we think critically, we can make choices with open eyes.

It has been said that human beings are rational creatures. Yet no one is born as an effective thinker. Critical thinking is a learned skill. This is one reason that you study so many subjects in higher education—math, science, history, psychology, literature, and more. A broad base of courses helps you develop as a thinker. You see how people

. . . .

This flood of appeals leaves us with hundreds of choices about what to buy, where to go, and who to be. It's easy to lose our heads in the crosscurrent of competing ideas—unless we develop skills in critical thinking.

. . . .

with different viewpoints arrive at conclusions, make decisions, and solve problems. This gives you a foundation for dealing with complex challenges in your career, your relationships, and your community.

Critical thinking frees us from nonsense. Novelist Ernest Hemingway once said that anyone who wants to be a great writer must have a built-in, shockproof "crap" detector.[1] That inelegant comment points to a basic truth: As critical thinkers, we are constantly on the lookout for thinking that's inaccurate, sloppy, or misleading.

Critical thinking is a skill that will never go out of style. At various times in human history, nonsense has been taken for the truth. For example, people have believed the following:

- Illness results from an imbalance in the four vital fluids: blood, phlegm, water, and bile.
- Racial integration of the armed forces will lead to destruction of soldiers' morale.
- Women are incapable of voting intelligently.
- We will never invent anything smaller than a transistor. (That was before the computer chip.)

The critical thinkers of history arose to challenge short-sighted ideas such as those above. These courageous men and women held their peers to higher standards of critical thinking.

Even in mathematics and the hard sciences, the greatest advances take place when people reexamine age-old beliefs. Scientists continually uncover things that contradict everyday certainties. For example, physics presents us with a world where solid objects are made of atoms spinning around in empty space—where matter and energy are two forms of the same substance. At a moment's notice, the world can deviate from the "laws of nature." That is because those "laws" exist in our heads—not in the world.

Critical thinking frees us from self-deception. Critical thinking is a path to freedom from half-truths and deception. You have the right to question everything that you see, hear, and read. Acquiring this ability is a major goal of a college education.

One of the reasons that critical thinking is so challenging—and so rewarding—is that we have a remarkable capacity to fool ourselves. Some of our ill-formed thoughts and half-truths have a source that hits a little close to home. That source is ourselves.

If you take a course in psychology, you might hear about the theory of cognitive dissonance.[2] This is a term for the tension

7

we feel when we encounter a fact that contradicts our deeply-held beliefs. To reduce the discomfort, we might deny the fact or explain it away with deceptive thinking.

For example, consider someone who stakes her identity on the fact that she is a valued employee. During a recession, she gets laid off. On her last day at work, she learns that her refusal to take part in on-the-job training sessions was the major reason that the company let her go. This brute fact contradicts her belief in her value. Her response: "I didn't need that training. I already knew that stuff anyway. Nobody at that company could teach me anything."

A skilled critical thinker would go beyond such self-justifying statements and ask questions instead: "What training sessions did I miss? Could I have learned something from them? Were there any signs that I was about to be laid off, and did I overlook them? What can I do to prevent this from happening again?"

Master students are willing to admit the truth when they discover that their thinking is fuzzy, lazy, based on a false assumption, or dishonest. These students value facts. When a solid fact contradicts a cherished belief, they are willing to change the belief.

More uses of critical thinking. Clear thinking promotes your success inside and outside the classroom. Any time that you are faced with a choice about what to believe or what to do, your thinking skills come in to play. Consider the following applications.

Critical thinking informs reading, writing, speaking, and listening. These elements are the basis of communication—a process that occupies most of our waking hours.

> Master students are willing to admit the truth when they discover that their thinking is fuzzy, lazy, based on a false assumption, or dishonest. These students value facts. When a solid fact contradicts a cherished belief, they are willing to change the belief.

Critical thinking promotes social change. The institutions in any society—courts, governments, schools, businesses, nonprofit groups—are the products of cultural customs and trends. All social movements—from the American Revolution to the Civil Rights movement—come about through the work of engaged individuals who actively participated in their communities and questioned what was going on around them. As critical thinkers, we strive to understand and influence the institutions in our society.

Critical thinking uncovers bias and prejudice. Working through our preconceived notions is a first step toward communicating with people of other races, ethnic backgrounds, and cultures.

Critical thinking reveals long-term consequences. Crises occur when our thinking fails to keep pace with reality. An example is the world's ecological crisis, which arose when people polluted the earth, air, and water without considering the long-term consequences. Imagine how different our world would be if our leaders had thought like the first female chief of the Cherokees. Asked about the best advice her elders had given her, she replied, "Look forward. Turn what has been done into a better path. If you are a leader, think about the impact of your decision on seven generations into the future."

Critical thinking as thorough thinking. For some people, the term *critical thinking* has negative connotations. If you prefer, use *thorough thinking* instead. Both terms point to the same activities: sorting out conflicting claims, weighing the evidence, letting go of personal biases, and arriving at reasonable conclusions. These activities add up to an ongoing conversation—a constant process, not a final product.

We live in a culture that values quick answers and certainty. These concepts are often at odds with effective thinking. Thorough thinking is the ability to examine and reexamine ideas that might seem obvious. This kind of thinking takes time and the willingness to say three subversive words: *I don't know.*

Thorough thinking is also the willingness to change our opinions as we continue to examine a problem. This calls for courage and detachment. Just ask anyone who has given up a cherished point of view in light of new evidence.

Thorough thinking is the basis for much of what you do in school—reading, writing, speaking, listening, note taking, test taking, problem solving, and other forms of decision making. Skilled students have strategies for accomplishing all these tasks. They distinguish between opinion and fact. They ask probing questions and make detailed observations. They uncover assumptions and define their terms. They make assertions carefully, basing them on sound logic and solid evidence. Almost everything that we call *knowledge* is a result of these activities. This means that critical thinking and learning are intimately linked.

Another kind of thorough thinking—planning—has the power to lift the quality of your daily life. When you plan, you are the equal of the greatest sculptor, painter, or playwright. More than creating a work of art, you are designing your life. *Becoming a Master Student* invites you to participate in this form of thinking by choosing your major, planning your career, and setting long-term goals.

Use the suggestions in this chapter to claim the thinking powers that are your birthright. The critical thinker is one aspect of the master student who lives inside you. ∎

Becoming a
CRITICAL THINKER

Thinking is a path to intellectual adventure. Although there are dozens of possible approaches to thinking well, the process boils down to asking and answering questions.

One quality of a master student is the ability to ask questions that lead to deeper learning. Your mind is an obedient servant. It will deliver answers at the same level as your questions. Becoming a critical thinker means being flexible and asking a wide range of questions.

GETTING READY FOR CRITICAL THINKING

A psychologist named Benjamin Bloom named six levels of thinking. (He called them *educational objectives*, or goals for learning).[3] Each level of thinking calls for asking and answering different kinds of questions.

LEVEL 1: Remembering. At this level of thinking, the key question is *Can I recall the key terms, facts, or events?* To prompt level 1 thinking, an instructor might ask you to do the following:

- List the nine steps of Muscle Reading.
- State the primary features of a mind map.
- Name the master student profiled in Chapter 6 of this book.

To study for a test with level 1 questions, you could create flash cards to review ideas from your readings and class notes. You could also read a book with a set of questions in mind and underline the answers to those questions in the text. Or, you could memorize a list of definitions so that you can recite them exactly. These are just a few examples.

Although remembering is important, this is a relatively low level of learning. No critical or creative thinking is involved. You simply recognize or recall something that you've observed in the past.

LEVEL 2: Understanding. At this level, the main question is *Can I explain this idea in my own words?* Often this means giving examples of an idea based on your own experience.

Suppose that your instructor asks you to do the following:

- Explain the main point of the Power Process: "I create it all."
- Summarize the steps involved in creating a concept map.
- Compare mind mapping with concept mapping, stating how they're alike and how they differ.

Other key words in level 2 questions are *discuss, estimate,* and *restate.* All of these are cues to go one step beyond remembering and to show that you truly *comprehend* an idea.

LEVEL 3: Applying. Learning at level 3 means asking: *Can I use this idea to produce a desired result?* That result might include completing a task, meeting a goal, making a decision, or solving a problem.

Some examples of level 3 thinking are listed here:

- Write an affirmation about succeeding in school, based on the guidelines in this text.
- Write an effective goal statement.
- Choose a mnemonic to remember the names of the Great Lakes.

Some key words in level 3 questions include *apply*, *solve*, *construct*, *plan*, *predict*, and *produce*.

LEVEL 4: Analyzing. Questions at this level boil down to this: *Can I divide this idea into parts or steps?* For example, you could do the following:

- Divide the steps of Muscle Reading into three major phases.
- Take a list of key events in the Vietnam War and arrange them in chronological order.
- Organize the 20 memory techniques from Chapter 3 into different categories.

Other key words in level 4 questions are *classify*, *separate*, *distinguish*, and *outline*.

LEVEL 5: Evaluating. Learning at level 5 means asking, *Can I rate the truth, usefulness, or quality of this idea—and give reasons for my rating?* This is the level of thinking you would use to do the following:

- Judge the effectiveness of an Intention Statement.
- Recommend a method for taking lecture notes when an instructor talks fast.
- Rank the Power Processes in order of importance to you—from most useful to least useful.

Level 5 involves genuine critical thinking. At this level you agree with an idea, disagree with it, or suspend judgment until you get more information. In addition, you give reasons for your opinion and offer supporting evidence.

Some key words in level 5 questions are *critique*, *defend*, and *comment*.

LEVEL 6: Creating. To think at this level, ask, *Can I invent something new based on this idea?* For instance, you might do the following:

- Invent your own format for taking lecture notes.
- Prepare a list of topics that you would cover if you were teaching a student success course.

- Imagine that you now have enough money to retire and then write goals you would like to accomplish with your extra time.
- Create a Power Point presentation based on ideas found in this chapter. Put the material in your own words, and use visual elements to enhance the points.

Creative thinking often involves analyzing an idea into parts and then combining those parts in a new way. Another source of creativity is taking several ideas and finding an unexpected connection among them. In either case, you are thinking at a very high level. You are going beyond agreement and disagreement to offer something unique—an original contribution of your own.

Questions for creative thinking often start with words such as *adapt*, *change*, *collaborate*, *compose*, *construct*, *create*, *design*, and *develop*. You might also notice phrases such as *What changes would you make...? How could you improve...? Can you think of another way to...? What would happen if...?*

GAINING SKILL AS A CRITICAL THINKER

Critical and creative thinking are exciting. The potential rewards are many, and the stakes are high. Your major decisions in life—from choosing a major to choosing a spouse—depend on your skills at critical and creative thinking.

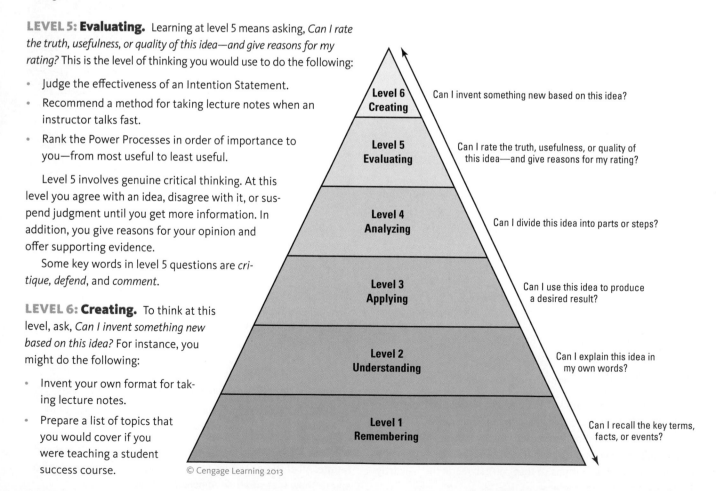

Level 6 Creating — Can I invent something new based on this idea?

Level 5 Evaluating — Can I rate the truth, usefulness, or quality of this idea—and give reasons for my rating?

Level 4 Analyzing — Can I divide this idea into parts or steps?

Level 3 Applying — Can I use this idea to produce a desired result?

Level 2 Understanding — Can I explain this idea in my own words?

Level 1 Remembering — Can I recall the key terms, facts, or events?

© Cengage Learning 2013

All levels of thinking are useful. Notice that the lower levels of thinking (1 to 3) give you fewer options than the highest levels (4 to 6). Lower levels of thinking are sometimes about finding the "right" answer to a question. At levels 4, 5, and 6, you might discover several valid answers or create several workable solutions.

Also notice that the levels build on each other. Before you agree or disagree with an idea, make sure that you *remember* it accurately and truly *understand* it. Your understanding will go deeper if you can *apply* and *analyze* the idea as well. Master students stay aware of their current level of thinking. They can also move to other levels with a clear intention.

Remember that the highest levels of thinking call for the highest investments of time and energy. Also, moving from a lower level of thinking to a higher level often requires courage, along with an ability to tolerate discomfort. Give yourself permission to experiment, practice, and learn from mistakes.

The suggestions here will help you to deepen your skills at critical thinking. To learn more about creative thinking, see "Finding 'aha!'—Creativity fuels critical thinking" on page 211 and "Ways to create ideas" on page 212.

Find various points of view on any issue. Imagine George Bush, Cesar Chavez, and Barack Obama assembled in one room to debate the most desirable way to reshape our government. Picture Madonna, Oprah Winfrey, and Mark Zuckerberg leading a workshop on how to plan your career. When seeking out alternative points of view, let scenes like these unfold in your mind.

Dozens of viewpoints exist on every important issue—reducing crime, ending world hunger, preventing war, educating our children, and countless other concerns. In fact, few problems have any single, permanent solution. Each generation produces its own answers to critical questions, based on current conditions. Our search for answers is a conversation that spans centuries. On each question, many voices are waiting to be heard.

You can take advantage of this diversity by seeking out alternative views with an open mind. When talking to another person, be willing to walk away with a new point of view—even if it's the one you brought to the table, supported with new evidence.

Examining different points of view is an exercise in analysis, which you can do with the suggestions that follow.

Define terms. Imagine two people arguing about whether an employer should limit health care benefits to members of a family. To one person, the word *family* means a mother, father, and children; to the other person, the word *family* applies to any individuals who live together in a long-term, supportive relationship. Chances are the debate will go nowhere until these two people realize that they're defining the same word in different ways.

Conflicts of opinion can often be resolved—or at least clarified—when we define our key terms up front. This is especially true with abstract, emotion-laden terms such as *freedom*, *peace*, *progress*, or *justice*. Blood has been shed over the meaning of those words. Define terms with care.

Look for assertions. Speakers and writers present their key terms in a larger context called an *assertion*. An assertion is a complete sentence that directly answers a key question. For example, consider this sentence from the article "Master student qualities" in the Introduction to this book: "Mastery means attaining a level of skill that goes beyond technique." This sentence is an assertion that answers an important question: How do we recognize mastery?

Look for at least three viewpoints. When asking questions, let go of the temptation to settle for just a single answer. Once you have come up with an answer, say to yourself, "Yes, that is one answer. Now what's another?" Using this approach can sustain honest inquiry, fuel creativity, and lead to conceptual breakthroughs. Be prepared: The world is complicated, and critical thinking is a complex business. Some of your answers might contradict others. Resist the temptation to have all of your ideas in a neat, orderly bundle.

Practice tolerance. One path to critical thinking is tolerance for a wide range of opinions. Taking a position on important issues is natural. When we stop having an opinion on things, we've probably stopped breathing.

Problems occur when we become so attached to our current viewpoints that we refuse to consider alternatives. Likewise, it can be disastrous when we blindly follow everything any person

7

Each generation produces its own answers to critical questions, based on current conditions. Our search for answers is a conversation that spans centuries. On each question, many voices are waiting to be heard.

009

013 Cengage Learning. All Rights Reserved. May not be scanned, copied or duplicated, or posted to a publicly accessible website, in whole or in part.

Becoming a Master Student **209**

or group believes without questioning its validity. Many ideas that are widely accepted in Western cultures—for example, civil liberties for people of color and the right of women to vote—were once considered dangerous. Viewpoints that seem outlandish today might become widely accepted a century, a decade, or even a year from now. Remembering this idea can help us practice tolerance for differing beliefs and, in doing so, make room for new ideas that might alter our lives.

Look for logic and evidence. Uncritical thinkers shield themselves from new information and ideas. As an alternative, you can follow the example of scientists, who constantly search for evidence that contradicts their theories. The following suggestions can help you do so.

The aim of using logic is to make statements that are clear, consistent, and coherent. As you examine a speaker's or writer's assertions, you might find errors in logic—assertions that contradict each other or assumptions that are unfounded.

Also assess the evidence used to support points of view. Evidence comes in several forms, including facts, expert testimony, and examples. To think critically about evidence, ask questions such as these:

- Are all or most of the relevant facts presented?
- Are the facts consistent with one another?
- Are facts presented accurately—or in a misleading way?
- Are opinions mistakenly being presented as facts?
- Are enough examples included to make a solid case for the viewpoint?
- Do the examples truly support the viewpoint?
- Are the examples typical? That is, could the author or speaker support the assertion with other examples that are similar?
- Is the expert credible—truly knowledgeable about the topic?
- Does this evidence affirm or contradict something that I already know?

Consider the source. Look again at that article on the problems of manufacturing cars powered by natural gas. It might have been written by an executive from an oil company. Check out the expert who disputes the connection between smoking and lung cancer. That "expert" might be the president of a tobacco company.

This is not to say that we should dismiss the ideas of people who have a vested interest in stating their opinions. Rather, we should take their self-interest into account as we consider their ideas.

Understand before criticizing. Polished debaters are good at summing up their opponents' viewpoints—often better than the people who support those viewpoints themselves. Likewise, critical thinkers take the time to understand a statement of opinion before agreeing or disagreeing with it.

Effective understanding calls for listening without judgment. Enter another person's world by expressing her viewpoint in your own words. If you're conversing with that person, keep revising your summary until she agrees that you've stated her position accurately. If you're reading an article, write a short summary of it. Then scan the article again, checking to see whether your synopsis is on target.

Watch for hot spots. Many people have mental "hot spots"—topics that provoke strong opinions and feelings. Examples are abortion, homosexuality, gun control, and the death penalty.

To become more skilled at examining various points of view, notice your own particular hot spots. Make a clear intention to accept your feelings about these topics and to continue using critical thinking techniques in relation to them.

One way to cool down our hot spots is to remember that we can change or even give up our current opinions without giving up ourselves. That's a key message behind the Power Processes: "Ideas are tools" and "Detach." These articles remind us that human beings are much more than the sum of their current opinions.

Be willing to be uncertain. Some of the most profound thinkers have practiced the art of thinking by using a magic sentence: "I'm not sure yet."

Those are words that many people do not like to hear. Our society rewards quick answers and quotable sound bites. We're under considerable pressure to utter the truth in 10 seconds or less.

In such a society, it is courageous and unusual to take the time to pause, to look, to examine, to be thoughtful, to consider many points of view—and to be unsure. When a society adopts half-truths in a blind rush for certainty, a willingness to embrace uncertainty can move us forward.

Write about it. Thoughts can move at blinding speed. Writing slows down that process. Gaps in logic that slip by us in thought or speech are often exposed when we commit the same ideas to paper. Writing down our thoughts allows us to compare, contrast, and combine points of view more clearly—and therefore to think more thoroughly.

Notice your changing perspectives. Researcher William Perry found that students in higher education move through stages of intellectual development.[4] In earlier stages, students tend to think there is only one correct viewpoint on each issue, and they look to their instructors to reveal that truth. Later, students acknowledge a variety of opinions on issues and construct their own viewpoints.

Remember that the process of becoming a critical thinker will take you through a variety of stages. Give yourself time, and celebrate your growing mastery. ■

Finding "aha!"— *creativity fuels* critical thinking

This chapter offers you a chance to practice two types of thinking: convergent thinking and divergent thinking.

Convergent thinking involves a narrowing-down process. Out of all the possible viewpoints on an issue or alternative solutions to a problem, you choose the one that is the most reasonable or that provides the most logical basis for action. This is the essence of *critical thinking*.

Some people see convergent thinking and critical thinking as the same thing. However, convergent thinking is just one part of critical thinking. Before you choose among viewpoints, generate as many of them as possible. Open up alternatives, and consider all of your options. Define problems in different ways. Keep asking questions and looking for answers. This opening-up process is called *divergent thinking* or *creative thinking*.

Creative thinking provides the basis for convergent thinking. In other words, one path toward having good ideas is to have *lots* of ideas. Then you can pick and choose from among them, combining and refining them as you see fit.

Choose when to think creatively. The key is to make conscious choices about what kind of thinking to do in any given moment. Generally speaking, creative thinking is more appropriate in the early stages of planning and problem solving. Feel free to dwell in this domain for a while. If you narrow down your options too soon, you run the risk of missing an exciting solution or of neglecting a novel viewpoint.

Remember that creative thinking and convergent thinking take place in a continuous cycle. After you've used convergent thinking to narrow down your options, you can return to creative thinking at any time to generate new ones.

Cultivate "aha!" Central to creative thinking is something called the "aha!" experience. Nineteenth-century poet Emily Dickinson described aha! this way: "If I feel physically as if the top of my head were taken off, I know that is poetry." Aha! is the burst of creative energy heralded by the arrival of a new, original idea. It is the sudden emergence of an unfamiliar pattern, a previously undetected relationship, or an unusual combination of familiar elements. It is an exhilarating experience.

Aha! does not always result in a timeless poem or a Nobel Prize. It can be inspired by anything from playing a new riff on a guitar to figuring out why your car's fuel pump doesn't work. A nurse might notice a patient's symptom that everyone else missed. That's an aha! An accountant might discover a tax break for a client. That's an aha! A teacher might devise a way to reach a difficult student. Aha!

Follow through. The flip side of aha! is following through. Thinking is both fun and work. It is both effortless and uncomfortable. It's the result of luck and persistence. It involves spontaneity and step-by-step procedures, planning and action, convergent and creative thinking.

Companies that depend on developing new products and services need people who can find aha! and do something with it. The necessary skills include the ability to spot assumptions, weigh evidence, separate fact from opinion, organize thoughts, and avoid errors in logic. All these skills involve demanding work. Just as often, they can be energizing and fun. ■

7

Tangram

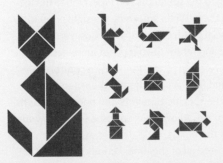

A tangram is an ancient Chinese puzzle game that stimulates the play instinct so critical to creative thinking. The cat figure here was created by rearranging seven sections of a square. Hundreds of images can be devised in this manner. Playing with

tangrams allows us to see relationships we didn't notice before.

The rules of the game are simple: Use these seven pieces to create something that wasn't there before. Be sure to use all seven. You might start by mixing up the pieces and seeing whether you can put them back together to form a square. Make your own tangram by cutting pieces like these out of poster board. When you come up with a pattern you like, trace around the outside edges of it, and see whether a friend can discover how you did it.

WAYS TO CREATE IDEAS

Anyone can think creatively. Use the following techniques to generate ideas about anything—whether you're studying math problems, remodeling a house, or writing a best seller.

Conduct a brainstorm. Brainstorming is a technique for creating plans, finding solutions, and discovering new ideas. When you are stuck on a problem, brainstorming can break the logjam. For example, if you run out of money 2 days before payday every week, you can brainstorm ways to make your money last longer. You can brainstorm ways to pay for your education. You can brainstorm ways to find a job.

The overall purpose of brainstorming is to generate as many solutions as possible. Sometimes the craziest, most outlandish ideas, while unworkable in themselves, can lead to new ways to solve problems. Use the following steps to try out the brainstorming process:

- *Focus on a single problem or issue.* State your focus as a question. Open-ended questions that start with the words *what, how, who, where,* and *when* often make effective focusing questions. For example, What is my ideal career? What is my ideal major? How can I raise the quality of relationships? What is the single most important change I can make in my life right now?

- *Relax.* Creativity is enhanced by a state of relaxed alertness. If you are tense or anxious, use relaxation techniques such as those described in "Let Go of Test Anxiety" in Chapter 6.

- *Set a quota or goal for the number of solutions you want to generate.* Goals give your subconscious mind something to aim for.

- *Set a time limit.* Use a clock to time it to the minute. Digital sports watches with built-in stopwatches work well. Experiment with various lengths of time. Both short and long brainstorms can be powerful.

- *Allow all answers.* Brainstorming is based on attitudes of permissiveness and patience. Accept every idea. At this stage, there are no wrong answers. If it pops into your head, put it

down on paper. Quantity, not quality, is the goal. Avoid making judgments and evaluations during the brainstorming session. If you get stuck, think of an outlandish idea, and write it down. One crazy idea can unleash a flood of other, more workable solutions.

- *Brainstorm with others.* Group brainstorming is a powerful technique. Group brainstorms take on lives of their own. Assign one member of the group to write down solutions. Feed off the ideas of others, and remember to avoid evaluating or judging anyone's ideas during the brainstorm.

After your brainstorming session, evaluate the results. Toss out any truly nutty ideas, but not before you give them a chance.

Focus and let go. Focusing and letting go are alternating parts of the same process. Intense focus taps the resources of your conscious mind. Letting go gives your subconscious mind time to work. When you focus for intense periods and then let go for a while, the conscious and subconscious parts of your brain work in harmony.

Focusing attention means being in the here and now. To focus your attention on a project, notice when you pay attention and when your mind starts to wander. And involve all of your senses. For example, if you are having difficulty writing a paper at a computer, practice focusing by listening to the sounds as you type. Notice the feel of the keys as you strike them. When you know the sights, sounds, and sensations you associate with being truly in focus, you'll be able to repeat the experience and return to your paper more easily.

Be willing to recognize conflict, tension, and discomfort in yourself. Notice them and fully accept them rather than fight against them. Look for the specific thoughts and body sensations that make up the discomfort. Allow them to come fully into your awareness, and then let them pass.

You might not be focused all of the time. Periods of inspiration might last only seconds. Be gentle with yourself when you notice that your concentration has lapsed. In fact, that might be a time to let go. *Letting go* means not forcing yourself to be creative. Practice focusing for short periods at first, and then give yourself a break. Play a board game. Go outside and look for shapes in the clouds. Switch to a new location. Take a nap when you are tired. Thomas Edison, the inventor, took frequent naps. Then the lightbulb clicked on.

Cultivate creative serendipity.

The word *serendipity* was coined by the English author Horace Walpole from the title of an ancient Persian fairy tale, "The Three Princes of Serendip." The princes had a knack for making lucky discoveries. Serendipity is that knack, and it involves more than luck. It is the ability to see something valuable that you weren't looking for.

History is full of people who make serendipitous discoveries. Country doctor Edward Jenner noticed "by accident" that milkmaids seldom got smallpox. The result was his discovery that mild cases of cowpox immunized them. Penicillin was also discovered "by accident." Scottish scientist Alexander Fleming was growing bacteria in a laboratory petri dish. A spore of *Penicillium notatum*, a kind of mold, blew in the window and landed in the dish, killing the bacteria. Fleming isolated the active ingredient. A few years later, during World War II, it saved thousands of lives. Had Fleming not been alert to the possibility, the discovery might never have been made.

Keep your eyes open. You might find a solution to an accounting problem in a Saturday morning cartoon. You might discover a topic for your term paper at the corner convenience store. Multiply your contacts with the world. Resolve to meet new people. Join a study or discussion group. Read. Go to plays, concerts, art shows, lectures, and movies. Watch television programs you normally wouldn't watch.

Also expect discoveries. One secret for success is being prepared to recognize "luck" when you see it.

Keep idea files.

We all have ideas. People who treat their ideas with care are often labeled "creative." They not only recognize ideas but also record them and follow up on them.

One way to keep track of ideas is to write them down on 3 × 5 cards. Invent your own categories, and number the cards so you can cross-reference them. For example, if you have an idea about making a new kind of bookshelf, you might file a card under "Remodeling." A second card might also be filed under "Marketable Ideas." On the first card, you can write down your ideas, and on the second, you can write, "See card #321—Remodeling."

Include in your files powerful quotations, random insights, notes on your reading, and useful ideas that you encounter in class. Collect jokes too.

> We all have ideas. People who treat their ideas with care are often labeled "creative." They not only recognize ideas but also record them and follow up on them.

7

CREATE on your feet

A popular trend in executive offices is the stand-up desk—a raised working surface at which you stand rather than sit.

Standing has advantages over sitting for long periods. You can stay more alert and creative when you're on your feet. One theory is that our problem-solving ability improves when we stand, due to increased heart rate and blood flow to the brain.

Standing can ease lower-back pain too. Sitting for too long aggravates the spine and its supporting muscles.

Photo courtesy of David Ellis

Standing while working is a technique with tradition. If you search the Web for stand-up desks, you'll find models based on desks used by Thomas Jefferson, Winston Churchill, and writer Virginia Woolf. Consider setting your desk up on blocks or putting a box on top of your desk so that you can stand while writing, preparing speeches, or studying. Discover how long you can stand comfortably while working, and whether this approach works for you.

Keep a journal. Journals don't have to be exclusively about your own thoughts and feelings. You can record observations about the world around you, conversations with friends, important or offbeat ideas—anything.

To fuel your creativity, read voraciously, including newspapers, magazines, blogs, and other Web sites. Explore beyond mainstream journalism. Hundreds of low-circulation specialty magazines and online news journals cover almost any subject you can imagine. Keep letter-size file folders of important documents. Bookmark Web sites in your browser. Use an online service such as Evernote, Delicious, or Pinboard to save articles that you want to read and refer to later. Create idea files on your computer.

Safeguard your ideas, even if you're pressed for time. Jotting down four or five words is enough to capture the essence of an idea. You can write down one quotation in a minute or two. And if you carry 3 × 5 cards in a pocket or purse, you can record ideas while standing in line or sitting in a waiting room.

Review your files regularly. Some amusing thought that came to you in November might be the perfect solution to a problem in March.

Collect and play with data. Look from all sides at the data you collect. Switch your attention from one aspect to another. Examine each fact, and avoid getting stuck on one particular part of a problem. Turn a problem upside down by picking a solution first and then working backward. Ask other people to look at the data. Solicit opinions.

Living with the problem invites a solution. Write down data, possible solutions, or a formulation of the problem on 3 × 5 cards, and carry them with you. Look at them before you go to bed at night. Review them when you are waiting for the bus. Make them part of your life, and think about them frequently.

Look for the obvious solutions or the obvious "truths" about the problem—then toss them out. Ask yourself, "Well, I know X is true, but if X were *not* true, what would happen?" Or ask the reverse: "If that *were* true, what would follow next?"

Put unrelated facts next to each other and invent a relationship between them, even if it seems absurd at first. In *The Act of Creation,* novelist Arthur Koestler says that finding a context in which to combine opposites is the essence of creativity.[5]

Make imaginary pictures with the data. Condense it. Categorize it. Put it in chronological order. Put it in alphabetical order. Put it in random order. Order it from most to least complex. Reverse all of those orders. Look for opposites.

It has been said that there are no new ideas—only new ways to combine old ideas. Creativity is the ability to discover those new combinations.

Create while you sleep. A part of our mind works as we sleep. You've experienced this fact directly if you've ever fallen asleep with a problem on your mind and awakened the next morning with a solution. For some of us, the solution appears in a dream or just before we fall asleep or wake up.

You can experiment with this process. Ask yourself a question as you fall asleep. Keep pencil and paper or a recorder near your bed. The moment you wake up, begin writing or speaking, and see whether an answer to your question emerges.

Many of us have awakened from a dream with a great idea, only to fall asleep again and lose it forever. To capture your ideas, keep a notebook by your bed at all times. Put the notebook where you can find it easily.

There is a story about how Benjamin Franklin used this suggestion. Late in the evenings, as he was becoming drowsy, he would sit in his rocking chair with a rock in his right hand and a metal bucket on the floor beneath the rock. The moment he fell asleep, the rock would fall from his grip into the bottom of the bucket, making a loud noise that awakened him. Having placed a pen and paper nearby, he immediately wrote down what he was thinking. Experience taught him that his thoughts at these moments were often insightful and creative.

Promote creative thinking in groups. Sometimes creative thinking dies in committee. People are afraid to disagree with a forceful leader and instead keep their mouths shut. Or a longstanding group ignores new members with new ideas. The result can be "group think," where no one questions the prevailing opinion. To stimulate creative thinking in groups, try these strategies:

- *Put your opinion on hold.* If you're leading a meeting, ask other people to speak up first. Then look for the potential value in *any* idea. Avoid nonverbal language that signals a negative reaction, such as frowning or rolling your eyes.

- *Rotate group leadership.* Ask group members to take turns. This strategy can work well in groups where people have a wide range of opinions.

- *Divide larger groups into several teams.* People might be more willing to share their ideas in a smaller group.

- *Assign a devil's advocate.* Give one person free permission to poke holes in any proposal.

- *Invite a guest expert.* A fresh perspective from someone outside the group can spark an aha!

- *Set up a suggestion box.* Let people submit ideas anonymously, in writing.

Refine ideas and follow through. Many of us ignore the part of the creative process that involves refining ideas and following through. How many great moneymaking schemes have we had that we never pursued? How many good ideas have we had for short stories that we never wrote? How many times have we said to ourselves, "You know, what they ought to do is attach two handles to one of those things, paint it orange, and sell it to police departments. They'd make a fortune." And we never realize that we are "they."

Genius resides in the follow-through—the application of perspiration to inspiration. One powerful tool you can use to follow through is the Discovery and Intention Journal Entry system. First

> Learn to trust the creative process—even when no answers are in sight. We are often reluctant to look at problems if no immediate solution is at hand. Trust that a solution will show up.

Another way to refine an idea is to simplify it. And if that doesn't work, mess it up. Make it more complex.

Finally, keep a separate file in your ideas folder for your own inspirations. Return to it regularly to see whether there is anything you can use. Today's defunct term paper idea could be next year's "A" in speech class.

Trust the process. Learn to trust the creative process—even when no answers are in sight. We are often reluctant to look at problems if no immediate solution is at hand. Trust that a solution will show up. Frustration and a feeling of being stuck are often signals that a solution is imminent.

Sometimes solutions break through in a giant AHA! More often they come in a series of little aha!s. Be aware of what your aha!s look, feel, and sound like. This understanding sets the stage for even more flights of creative thinking. ■

write down your idea in a Discovery Statement, and then write what you intend to do about it in an Intention Statement. You also can explore the writing techniques discussed in Chapter 8: Communicating as a guide for refining your ideas.

You're One Click Away...
from finding more strategies online for creative thinking.

EXERCISE 20

Explore emotional reactions

Each of us has certain "hot spots"—issues that trigger strong emotional reactions. These topics may include abortion, gay and lesbian rights, capital punishment, and funding for welfare programs. There are many other examples, varying from person to person. Examine your own hot spots below by writing a word or short phrase summarizing each issue about which you feel very strongly. Then describe what you typically say or do when each issue comes up in conversation.

After you have completed your list, think about what you can do to become a more effective thinker when you encounter one of these issues. For example, you could breathe deeply and count to five before you offer your own point of view. Or you might preface your opinion with an objective statement such as "There are many valid points of view on this issue. Here's the way I see it, and I'm open to your ideas."

_____

_____

_____

_____

_____

_____

_____

_____

_____

DON'T FOOL YOURSELF: *fifteen common mistakes* IN LOGIC

Rich Reid/National Geographic/Getty Images

Logic is a branch of philosophy that seeks to distinguish between effective and ineffective reasoning. Students of logic look for valid steps in an *argument*, or a series of statements. The opening statements of the argument are the premises, and the final statement is the conclusion.

Effective reasoning is not just an idle pastime for unemployed philosophers. Learning to think logically offers many benefits: When you think logically, you take your reading, writing, speaking, and listening skills to a higher level. You avoid costly mistakes in decision making. You can join discussions and debates with more confidence, cast your election votes with a clear head, and become a better-informed citizen. People have even improved their mental health by learning to dispute illogical beliefs.[6]

Over the last 2,500 years, specialists have listed some classic land mines in the field of logic—common mistakes in thinking that are called *fallacies*. The study of fallacies could fill a yearlong course. Following are 15 examples to get you started. Knowing about them before you string together a bunch of assertions can help you avoid getting fooled.

1 Jumping to conclusions. Jumping to conclusions is the only exercise that some lazy thinkers get. This fallacy involves drawing conclusions without sufficient evidence. Take the bank officer who hears about a student's failing to pay back an education loan. After that, the officer turns down all loan applications from students. This person has formed a rigid opinion on the basis of hearsay. Jumping to conclusions—also called *hasty generalization*—is at work here.

Following are more examples of this fallacy:

* *When I went to Mexico for spring break, I felt sick the whole time. Mexican food makes people sick.*

* *Google's mission is to "organize the world's information." Their employees must be on a real power trip.*

* *During a recession, more people go to the movies. People just want to sit in the dark and forget about their money problems.*

Each item in the above list includes two statements, and the second statement does not necessarily follow from the first. More evidence is needed to make any possible connection.

2 Attacking the person. The mistake of attacking the person is common at election time. An example is the candidate who claims that her opponent has failed to attend church regularly during the campaign. People who indulge in personal attacks are attempting an intellectual sleight of hand to divert our attention away from the truly relevant issues.

3 Appealing to authority. A professional athlete endorses a brand of breakfast cereal. A famous musician features a soft drink company's product in a rock video. The promotional brochure for an advertising agency lists all of the large companies that have used its services.

In each case, the people involved are trying to win your confidence—and your dollars—by citing authorities. The underlying assumption is usually this: *Famous people and organizations buy our product. Therefore, you should buy it too.* Or: *You should accept this idea merely because someone who's well-known says it's true.*

Appealing to authority is usually a substitute for producing real evidence. It invites sloppy thinking. When our only evidence for a viewpoint is an appeal to authority, it's time to think more thoroughly.

4 Pointing to a false cause. The fact that one event follows another does not necessarily mean that the two events have a cause-and-effect relationship. All we can actually say is that the events might be correlated. For example, as children's vocabularies improve, they can get more cavities. This does not mean that cavities are the result of an improved vocabulary. Instead, the increase in cavities is due to other factors, such as physical maturation and changes in diet or personal care.

Suppose that you see this newspaper headline: "Student tries to commit suicide after failing to pass bar exam." Seeing this headline, you might conclude that the student's failure to pass the exam lead to a depression that caused his suicide attempt. However, this is simply an assumption that can be stated in the following way: *When two events occur closely together in time, the first event is the cause of the second event.* Perhaps the student's depression was in fact caused by another traumatic event not mentioned in the headline, such as breaking up with a longtime girlfriend.

5 Thinking in all-or-nothing terms. Consider these statements: *Doctors are greedy. You can't trust politicians. Students these days are in school just to get high-paying jobs; they lack idealism. Homeless people don't want to work.*

These opinions imply the word *all*. They gloss over individual differences, claiming that all members of a group are exactly alike. They also ignore key facts—for instance, that some doctors volunteer their time at free medical clinics and that many homeless people are children who are too young to work.

All-or-nothing thinking is one of the most common errors in logic. To avoid this fallacy, watch out for words such as *all, everyone, no one, none, always,* and *never.* Statements that include these words often make sweeping claims that require a lot of evidence. See whether words such as *usually, some, many, few,* and *sometimes* lead to more accurate statements. Sometimes the words are implied. For example, the implication in the claim "Doctors are greedy" is that *all* doctors are greedy.

6 Basing arguments on emotion. The politician who ends every campaign speech with flag waving and slides of his mother eating apple pie is staking his future on appeals to emotion. So is the candidate who paints a grim scenario of the disaster and ruination that will transpire unless she is elected. Get past the fluff and histrionics to see whether you can uncover any worthwhile ideas.

7 Using a faulty analogy. An *analogy* states a similarity between two things or events. Some arguments rest on analogies that hide significant differences. On June 25, 1987, the Associated Press reported an example: U.S. representative Tom DeLay opposed a bill to ban chlordane, a pesticide that causes cancer in laboratory animals. Supporting this bill, he argued, would be like banning cars because they kill people. DeLay's analogy was faulty. Banning automobiles would have a far greater impact on society than banning a single pesticide, especially if safer pesticides are available.

8 Creating a straw man. The name of this fallacy comes from the scarecrows traditionally placed in gardens to ward off birds. A scarecrow works because it looks like a man. Likewise, a person can attack ideas that *sound like* his opponent's ideas but are actually absurd. For example, some legislators attacked the Equal Rights Amendment by describing it as a measure to abolish separate bathrooms for men and women. In fact, supporters of this amendment proposed no such thing.

9 Begging the question. Speakers and writers beg the question when their colorful language glosses over an idea that is unclear or unproven. Consider this statement: *Support the American tradition of individual liberty and oppose mandatory seat belt laws!* Anyone who makes such a statement "begs" (fails to answer) a key question: Are laws that require drivers to use seat belts actually a violation of individual liberty?

10 Confusing fact and opinion. Facts are statements verified by direct observation or compelling evidence that creates widespread agreement. In recent years, some politicians argued for tax cuts on the grounds that the American economy needed to create more jobs. However, it's not a fact that tax cuts automatically create more jobs. This statement is almost impossible to verify by direct observation, and there's actually evidence against it.

11 Creating a red herring. When hunters want to throw a dog off a trail, they can drag a smoked red herring (or some other food with a strong odor) over the ground in the opposite direction. This distracts the dog, who is fooled into following a false trail. Likewise, people can send our thinking on false trails by raising irrelevant issues. Case in point: In 2006, some people who opposed a presidential campaign by U.S. Senator Barack Obama emphasized his middle name: Hussein. This was an irrelevant attempt to link the senator to Saddam Hussein, the dictator and former ruler of Iraq.

12 Appealing to tradition. Arguments based on an appeal to tradition take a classic form: *Our current beliefs and behaviors have a long history; therefore, they are correct.* This argument has been used to justify the divine right of kings, feudalism, witch burnings, slavery, child labor, and a host of other traditions that are now rejected in most parts of the world. Appeals to tradition ignore the fact that unsound ideas can survive for centuries before human beings realize that they are being fooled.

13 Appealing to "the people." Consider this statement: *Millions of people use Wikipedia as their main source of factual information. Wikipedia must be the best reference work in the world.* This is a perfect example of the *ad populum* fallacy. (In Latin, that phrase means "to the people.") The essential error is assuming that popularity, quality, and accuracy are the same.

Appealing to "the people" taps into our universal desire to be liked and to associate with a group of people who agree with us.

7

No wonder this fallacy is also called "jumping on the bandwagon." Following are more examples:

- *Internet Explorer is the most widely used Web browser. It must be the best one.*

- *Dan Brown's books, including* The Da Vinci Code, *did not sell as well as the Harry Potter books by J. K. Rowling. I guess we know who's the better writer.*

- *Same-sex marriages must be immoral. Most Americans think so.*

You can refute such statements by offering a single example: Many Americans once believed that slavery was moral and that people of color should not be allowed to vote. That did not make either belief right.

14 Distracting from the real issue. The fallacy of distracting from the real issue occurs when a speaker or writer makes an irrelevant statement and then draws a conclusion based on that statement. For example: *The most recent recession was caused by people who borrowed too much money and bankers who loaned too much money. Therefore, you should never borrow money to go to school.* This argument ignores the fact that a primary source of the recession was loans to finance housing—not loans to finance education. Two separate topics are mentioned, and statements about one do not necessarily apply to the other.

15 Sliding a slippery slope. The fallacy of sliding a slippery slope implies that if one undesired event occurs, then other, far more serious events will follow: *If we restrict our right to own guns, then all of our rights will soon be taken away. If people keep downloading music for free, pretty soon they'll demand to get everything online for free. I notice that more independent bookstores are closing; it's just a matter of time before people stop reading.*

When people slide a slippery slope, they assume that different types of events have a single cause. They also assume that a particular cause will operate indefinitely. In reality, the world is far more complex. Grand predictions about the future often prove to be wrong.

Finding fallacies before they become a fatal flaw (bonus suggestions). Human beings have a long history of fooling themselves. This article presents just a partial list of logical fallacies. You can prevent them and many more by following a few suggestions:

- When outlining a paper or speech, create a two-column chart. In one column, make a list of your main points. In the other column, summarize the evidence for each point. If you have no evidence for a point, a logical fallacy may be lurking in the wings.

- Go back to some of your recent writing—assigned papers, essay tests, journal entries, and anything else you can find. Look for examples of logical fallacies. Note any patterns, such as repetition of one particular fallacy. Write an Intention Statement about avoiding this fallacy.

- Be careful when making claims about people who disagree with you. One attitude of a critical thinker is treating everyone with fairness and respect. ■

You're One Click Away...
from practicing hunting for fallacies online.

Master Students
IN ACTION

You're One Click Away...
from viewing a video about Master Students in Action.

"*I think critical thinking is when you're presented with a problem or a scenario and you just don't go with your gut reaction. You have to look at the problem from many different angles and weigh different options before you decide what is the right answer.*"

—*Lauren Swidler,*
Providence College

Photo courtesy of Lauren Swidler

Uncovering ASSUMPTIONS

Consider the following argument:

- Orcas (killer whales) mate for life.
- Orcas travel in family groups.
- Science has revealed that orcas are intelligent.
- Therefore, orcas should be saved from extinction.

One idea—or assumption—underlies this line of thought: *Any animal that displays significant human characteristics deserves special protection.* Whether or not you agree with this argument, consider for a moment the process of making assumptions.

Assumptions are invisible and powerful. Assumptions are ideas that guide our thinking and behavior. Often assumptions are unconscious. People can remain unaware of their most basic and far-reaching assumptions—the very ideas that shape their lives.

Spotting assumptions can be tricky because they are usually unstated and offered without evidence. And scores of assumptions can be held at the same time. Those assumptions might even contradict each other, resulting in muddled thinking and confused behavior. This makes uncovering assumptions a feat worthy of the greatest detective.

Assumptions drive our attitudes and actions. Letting assumptions remain in our subconscious can erect barriers to our success. Take the person who says, "I don't worry about saving money for the future. I think life is meant to be enjoyed today—not later." This statement rests on at least two assumptions: *Saving money is not enjoyable* and *we can enjoy ourselves only when we're spending money.*

It would be no surprise to find out that this person runs out of money near the end of each month and depends on cash advances from high-interest credit cards. He is shielding himself from some ideas that could erase his debt: Saving money can be a source of satisfaction, and many enjoyable activities cost nothing.

The stakes in uncovering assumptions are high. Prejudice thrives on the beliefs that certain people are inferior or dangerous due to their skin color, ethnic background, or sexual orientation. Those beliefs have led to flawed assumptions such as *mixing the blood of the races will lead to genetically inferior offspring* and *racial integration of the armed forces will lead to the destruction of morale.*

When we remain ignorant of our assumptions, we also make it easier for people with hidden agendas to do our thinking for us. Demagogues and unethical advertisers know that unchallenged assumptions are potent tools for influencing our attitudes and behavior.

Assumptions can create conflict. Heated conflict and hard feelings often result when people argue on the level of opinions—forgetting that the real conflict lies at the level of their assumptions.

An example is the question about whether the government should fund public works programs that create jobs during a recession. People who advocate such programs might assume that creating such jobs is an appropriate task for the federal government. In contrast, people who argue against such programs might assume that the government has no business interfering with the free workings of the economy. There's little hope of resolving this conflict of opinion unless we deal with something more basic: our assumptions about the proper role of government.

> ## Letting assumptions remain in our subconscious can erect barriers to our success.

Look for assumptions. You can follow a three-step method for testing the validity of any viewpoint. First, look for the assumptions—the assertions implied by that viewpoint. Second, write down these assumptions. Third, see whether you can find any exceptions to the assumptions.

Consider this statement: "My mother and father have a good marriage—after all, they're still together after 35 years." Behind this statement is a big assumption: *Good marriages are those that last a long time.* Yet there are possible exceptions. For example, you may know of married couples who stay together for decades, even though they confess to be unhappy in the relationship.

Uncovering assumptions and looking for exceptions can help you detect many errors in logic. This is a tool you can pull out any time you want to experience the benefits of critical thinking. ■

7

THINK CRITICALLY about information on the *INTERNET*

Sources of information on the Internet range from the reputable (such as the Library of Congress) to the flamboyant (such as the *National Enquirer*). People are free to post *anything* on the Internet, including outdated facts as well as intentional misinformation.

Newspaper, magazine, and book publishers often employ fact checkers, editors, and lawyers to screen out errors and scrutinize questionable material before publication. Authors of Web pages and other Internet sources might not have these resources or choose to use them.

Taking a few simple precautions when you surf the Internet can keep you from crashing onto the rocky shore of misinformation.

Distinguish between *ideas* and *information*. To think more powerfully about what you find on the Internet, remember the difference between information and ideas. For example, consider the following sentence: *Nelson Mandela became president of South Africa in 1994*. That statement provides information about South Africa. In contrast, the following sentence states an idea: *Nelson Mandela's presidency means that apartheid has no future in South Africa.*

Information refers to facts that can be verified by independent observers. *Ideas* are interpretations or opinions based on facts. These include statements of opinion and value judgments. Several people with the same information might adopt different ideas based on that information.

People who speak of the Internet as the "information superhighway" often forget to make the distinction between information and ideas. Don't assume that an idea is more current, reasonable,

> People who speak of the Internet as the "information superhighway" often forget to make the distinction between information and ideas. Don't assume that an idea is more current, reasonable, or accurate just because you find it on the Internet.

or accurate just because you find it on the Internet. Apply your critical thinking skills to all published material—print and online.

Look for overall quality. Examine the features of a Web site in general. Notice the effectiveness of the text and visuals as a whole. Also note how well the site is organized and whether you can navigate the site's features with ease. Look for the date that crucial information was posted, and determine how often the site is updated.

Next, get an overview of the site's content. Examine several of the site's pages, and look for consistency of facts, quality of information, and competency with grammar and spelling. Are the links within the site easy to navigate?

Also evaluate the site's links to related Web pages. Look for links to pages of reputable organizations. Click on a few of those links. If they lead you to dead ends, it might indicate that the site you're evaluating is not updated often—a clue that it's not a reliable source for late-breaking information.

Look at the source. Find a clear description of the person or organization responsible for the Web site. Many sites include this information in an "About" link.

The domain in the uniform resource locator (URL) for a Web site gives you clues about sources of information and possible bias. For example, distinguish among information from a for-profit commercial enterprise (URL ending in .com); a nonprofit organization (.org); a government agency (.gov); and a school, college, or university (.edu).

If the site asks you to subscribe or become a member, then find out what it does with the personal information that you provide. Look for a way to contact the site's publisher with questions and comments.

Look for documentation. When you encounter an assertion on a Web page or some other Internet resource, note the types and quality of the evidence offered. Look for credible examples, quotations from authorities in the field, documented statistics, or summaries of scientific studies.

Remember that wikis (peer-edited sites) such as Wikipedia do not employ editors to screen out errors or scrutinize questionable material before publication. Do not rely on these sites when researching a paper or presentation. Also, be cautious about citing blogs, which often are not reviewed for accuracy. Such sources may, however, provide you with key words and concepts that help lead you to scholarly research on your topic.

Set an example. In the midst of the Internet's chaotic growth, you can light a path of rationality. Whether you're sending a short e-mail message or building a massive Web site, bring your own critical thinking skills into play. Every word and image that you send down the wires to the Web can display the hallmarks of critical thinking—sound logic, credible evidence, and respect for your audience. ■

Gaining skill at DECISION MAKING

© Mike Baldwin. Reproduction rights available from www.CartoonStock.com

We make decisions all the time, whether we realize it or not. Even avoiding decisions is a form of decision making. The student who puts off studying for a test until the last minute might really be saying, "I've decided this course is not important" or "I've decided not to give this course much time." In order to escape such a fate, decide right now to experiment with the following suggestions.

Recognize decisions. Decisions are more than wishes or desires. There's a world of difference between "I wish I could be a better student" and "I will take more powerful notes, read with greater retention, and review my class notes daily." Decisions are specific and lead to focused action. When we decide, we narrow down. We give up actions that are inconsistent with our decision. Deciding to eat fruit for dessert instead of ice cream rules out the next trip to the ice cream store.

Establish priorities. Some decisions are trivial. No matter what the outcome, your life is not affected much. Other decisions can shape your circumstances for years. Devote more time and energy to the decisions with big outcomes.

Base your decisions on a life plan. The benefit of having long-term goals for our lives is that they provide a basis for many of our daily decisions. Being certain about what we want to accomplish this year and this month makes today's choices more clear.

Balance learning styles in decision making. To make decisions more effectively, use all four modes of learning explained in Chapter 1: First Steps. The key is to balance reflection with action, and thinking with experience. First, take the time to think creatively, and generate many options. Then think critically about the possible consequences of each option before choosing one. Remember, however, that thinking is no substitute for experience. Act on your chosen option, and notice what happens. If you're not getting the results that you want, then quickly return to creative thinking to invent new options.

Choose an overall strategy. Every time you make a decision, you choose a strategy—even when you're not aware of it. Effective decision makers can articulate and choose from among several strategies. For example:

- *Find all of the available options, and choose one deliberately.* Save this strategy for times when you have a relatively small number of options, each of which leads to noticeably different results.

- *Find all of the available options, and choose one randomly.* This strategy can be risky. Save it for times when your options are basically similar and fairness is the main issue.

- *Limit the options, and then choose.* When deciding which search engine to use on the World Wide Web, visit many sites and then narrow the list down to two or three that you choose.

Use time as an ally. Sometimes we face dilemmas—situations in which any course of action leads to undesirable consequences. In such cases, consider putting a decision on hold. Wait it out. Do nothing until the circumstances change, making one alternative clearly preferable to another.

Use intuition. Some decisions seem to make themselves. A solution pops into our mind, and we gain newfound clarity. Using intuition is not the same as forgetting about the decision or refusing to make it. Intuitive decisions usually arrive after we've gathered the relevant facts and faced a problem for some time.

Evaluate your decision. Hindsight is a source of insight. After you act on a decision, observe the consequences over time. Reflect on how well your decision worked and what you might have done differently.

Think choices. This final suggestion involves some creative thinking. Consider that the word *decide* derives from the same roots as *suicide* and *homicide*. In the spirit of those words, a decision forever "kills" all other options. That's kind of heavy. Instead, use the word *choice,* and see whether it frees up your thinking. When you *choose,* you express a preference for one option over others. However, those options remain live possibilities for the future. Choose for today, knowing that as you gain more wisdom and experience, you can choose again. ■

You're One Click Away...
from finding more strategies online for making decisions.

Four ways to solve problems

Think of problem solving as a process with four P's: Define the *problem*, generate *possibilities*, create a *plan*, and *perform* your plan.

1 Define the problem. To define a problem effectively, understand what a problem is—a mismatch between what you want and what you have. Problem solving is all about reducing the gap between these two factors.

Tell the truth about what's present in your life right now, without shame or blame. For example: "I often get sleepy while reading my physics assignments, and after closing the book I cannot remember what I just read."

Next, describe in detail what you want. Go for specifics: "I want to remain alert as I read about physics. I also want to accurately summarize each chapter I read."

Remember that when we define a problem in limiting ways, our solutions merely generate new problems. As Albert Einstein said, "The world we have made is a result of the level of thinking we have done thus far. We cannot solve problems at the same level at which we created them."[7]

Define the **problem**	**What** is the problem?	
Generate **possibilities**	**What if** there are several possible solutions?	
Create a **plan**	**How** would this possible solution work?	
Perform your plan	**Why** is one solution more workable than another?	

This idea has many applications for success in school. An example is the student who struggles with note taking. The problem, she thinks, is that her notes are too sketchy. The logical solution, she decides, is to take more notes, and her new goal is to write down almost everything her instructors say. No matter how fast and furiously she writes, she cannot capture all of the instructors' comments.

Consider what happens when this student defines the problem in a new way. After more thought, she decides that her dilemma is not the *quantity* of her notes but their *quality*. She adopts a new format for taking notes, dividing her notepaper into two columns. In the right-hand column, she writes down only the main points of each lecture. And in the left-hand column, she notes two or three supporting details for each point.

Over time, this student makes the joyous discovery that there are usually just three or four core ideas to remember from each lecture. She originally thought the solution was to take more notes. What really worked was taking notes in a new way.

2 Generate possibilities. Now put on your creative thinking hat. Open up. Brainstorm as many possible solutions to the problem as you can. At this stage, quantity counts. As you generate possibilities, gather relevant facts. For example, when you're faced with a dilemma about what courses to take next term, get information on class times, locations, and instructors. If you haven't decided which summer job offer to accept, gather information on salary, benefits, and working conditions.

3 Create a plan. After rereading your problem definition and list of possible solutions, choose the solution that seems most workable. Think about specific actions that will reduce the gap between what you have and what you want. Visualize the steps you will take to make this solution a reality, and arrange them in chronological order. To make your plan even more powerful, put it in writing.

4 Perform your plan. This step gets you off your chair and out into the world. Now you actually *do* what you have planned.

Ultimately, your skill in solving problems lies in how well you perform your plan. Through the quality of your actions, you become the architect of your own success.

When facing problems, experiment with these four P's, and remember that the order of steps is not absolute. Also remember that any solution has the potential to create new problems. If that happens, cycle through the four P's of problem solving again. ■

You're One Click Away...
from finding more strategies online for problem solving.

Asking questions— learning through **inquiry**

Thinking is born of questions. Questions wake us up. Questions alert us to hidden assumptions. Questions promote curiosity and create new distinctions. Questions open up options that otherwise go unexplored. Besides, teachers love questions.

There's a saying: "Tell me, and I forget; show me, and I remember; involve me, and I understand." Asking questions is a way to stay involved. One of the main reasons you are in school is to ask questions—a process called *inquiry-based learning*. This process takes you beyond memorizing facts and passing tests. Asking questions turns you into a lifelong learner.

One of the main reasons you are in school is to ask questions. This kind of learning goes beyond memorizing facts and passing tests. Educated people do more than answer questions. They also *ask* questions. They continually search for better questions, including questions that have never been asked before.

Questions have practical power. Asking for directions can shave hours off a trip. Asking a librarian for help can save hours of research time. Asking how to address an instructor, whether by first name or formal title, can change your relationship with that person. Asking your academic advisor a question can alter your entire education. Asking people about their career plans can alter *your* career plans.

Asking questions is also a way to improve relationships with friends and coworkers. When you ask a question, you offer a huge gift to people—an opportunity for them to speak their brilliance and for you to listen to their answers.

George Bernard Shaw, the playwright, knew the power of questions. "Some men see things as they are, and say, Why?" he wrote. "I dream of things that never were, and say, Why not?"

Students often say, "I don't know what to ask." If you have ever been at a loss for questions, here are some ways to discover them. Apply these strategies to any subject you study in school or to any area of your life that you choose to examine.

Ask questions that create possibilities. In Japan, there is a method called *Naikan* that is sometimes used in treating alcoholism. This program is based on asking three questions: "What have I received from others? What have I given to others? And what troubles and difficulties have I caused others?"[8] Taking the time to answer these questions in detail, and with rigorous honesty, can turn someone's life around.

Asking questions is also a way to help people release rigid, unrealistic beliefs: "Everyone should be kind to me." "If I make a mistake, it's terrible." "Children should always do what I say." In her book *Loving What Is*, Byron Katie recommends that you ask four questions about such beliefs: Is it true? Can you absolutely know that it's true? How do you react when you believe that thought? And, who would you be *without* that thought?[9]

At any moment you can ask a question that opens up a new possibility for someone. Suppose a friend walks up to you and says, "People just never listen to me."

You listen carefully. Then you say, "Let me make sure I understand. Who, specifically, doesn't listen to you? And how do you know they're not listening?"

Another friend comes up to you and says, "I just lost my job to someone who has less experience. That should never happen."

"Wow, that's hard," you say. "I'm sorry you lost your job. Who can help you find another job?"

Then a relative seeks your advice. "My mother-in-law makes me mad," she says.

"You're having a hard time with this person," you say. "What does she say and do when you feel mad at her? And are there times when you *don't* get mad at her?"

These kinds of questions—asked with compassion and a sense of timing—can help people move from complaining about problems to solving them.

7

Ask questions for critical thinking. In their classic *How to Read a Book*, Mortimer Adler and Charles Van Doren list four different questions to sum up the whole task of thinking critically about any body of ideas:[10]

What is this piece of writing about as a whole? To answer this question, state the main topic in one sentence. Then list the related subtopics.

What is being said in detail, and how? List the main terms, assertions, and arguments. Also state what problems the writer or speaker is trying to solve.

Is it true? Examine the logic and evidence behind the ideas. Look for missing information, faulty information, and errors in reasoning. Also determine which problems were solved and which remain unsolved.

What of it? After answering the first three questions, prepare to change your thinking or behavior as a result of encountering new ideas.

Discover your own questions. Students sometimes say, "I don't know what questions to ask." Consider the following ways to create questions about any subject you want to study, or about any area of your life that you want to change.

Let your pen start moving. Sometimes you can access a deeper level of knowledge by taking out your pen, putting it on a piece of paper, and writing down questions—even before you know what to write. Don't think. Just watch the pen move across the paper. Notice what appears. The results might be surprising.

Ask about what's missing. Another way to invent useful questions is to notice what's missing from your life and then ask how to supply it. For example, if you want to take better notes, you can write, "What's missing is skill in note taking. How can I gain more skill in taking notes?" If you always feel rushed, you can write, "What's missing is time. How do I create enough time in my day to actually do the things that I say I want to do?"

Pretend to be someone else. Another way to invent questions is first to think of someone you greatly respect. Then pretend you're that person. Ask the questions you think she would ask.

Begin a general question; then brainstorm endings. By starting with a general question and then brainstorming a long list of endings, you can invent a question that you've never asked before. For example:

- What can I do when . . . an instructor calls on me in class and I have no idea what to say? When a teacher doesn't show up for class on time? When I feel overwhelmed with assignments?

- How can I . . . take the kind of courses that I want? Expand my career options? Become much more effective as a student, starting today?

- When do I . . . decide on a major? Transfer to another school? Meet with an instructor to discuss an upcoming term paper?

- What else do I want to know about . . . my academic plan? My career plan? My options for job hunting? My friends? My relatives? My spouse?

- Who can I ask about . . . my career options? My major? My love life? My values and purpose in life?

Ask questions to promote social change. If your friends are laughing at racist jokes, you have a right to ask why. If you're legally registered to vote and denied access to a voting booth, you have a right to ask for an explanation. Asking questions can advance justice.

Ask what else you want to know. Many times you can quickly generate questions by simply asking yourself, "What else do I want to know?" Ask this question immediately after you read a paragraph in a book or listen to someone speak.

Start from the assumption that you are brilliant. Then ask questions to unlock your brilliance. ■

15 questions to try on for size

1. What is the most important problem in my life to solve right now?
2. What am I willing to do to solve this problem?
3. How can I benefit from solving this problem?
4. Who can I ask for help?
5. What are the facts in this situation?
6. What are my options in this situation?
7. What can I learn from this situation?
8. What do I want?
9. What am I willing to do to get what I want?
10. What will be the consequences of my decision in one week? One month? One year?
11. What is the most important thing for me to accomplish today?
12. What's the best possible use of my time right now?
13. What am I grateful for?
14. Who loves me?
15. Who do I love?

Thinking about your major

One decision that troubles many students in higher education is the choice of a major. Weighing the benefits, costs, and outcomes of a possible major is an intellectual challenge. This choice is an opportunity to apply your critical thinking, decision making, and problem solving skills. The following suggestions will guide you through this seemingly overwhelming process.

1. DISCOVER OPTIONS

Follow the fun. Perhaps you look forward to attending one of your classes and even like completing the assignments. This is a clue to your choice of major.

See whether you can find lasting patterns in the subjects and extracurricular activities that you've enjoyed over the years. Look for a major that allows you to continue and expand on these experiences.

Also, sit down with a stack of 3 × 5 cards and brainstorm answers to the following questions:

- What do you enjoy doing most with your unscheduled time?

- Imagine that you're at a party and having a fascinating conversation. What is this conversation about?

- What kind of problems do you enjoy solving—those that involve people? Products? Ideas?

- What interests are revealed by your choices of reading material, television shows, and other entertainment?

- What would an ideal day look like for you? Describe where you'd live, who would be with you, and what you'd do throughout the day. Do any of these visions suggest a possible major?

Questions like these can uncover a "fun factor" that energizes you to finish the work of completing a major.

Consider your abilities. In choosing a major, ability counts as much as interest. In addition to considering what you enjoy, think about times and places when you excelled. List the courses that you aced, the work assignments that you mastered, and the hobbies that led to rewards or recognition. Let your choice of a major reflect a discovery of your passions *and* potentials.

Use formal techniques for self-discovery. Explore questionnaires and inventories that are designed to correlate your interests with specific majors. Examples include the Strong Interest Inventory and the Self-Directed Search. Your academic advisor or someone in your school's career planning office can give you more details about these and related inventories. For some fun, take several of them and meet with an advisor to interpret the results. Remember inventories can help you gain self-knowledge, and

Boy with remote control: © Ron Chapple; Airplane: © Corbis; Forehead: Masterfile (Royalty-Free Div.)

other people can offer valuable perspectives. However, what you *do* with all this input is entirely up to you.

Link to long-term goals. Your choice of a major can fall into place once you determine what you want in life. Before you choose a major, back up to a bigger picture. List your core values, such as contributing to society, achieving financial security and professional recognition, enjoying good health, or making time for fun. Also write down specific goals that you want to accomplish 5 years, 10 years, or even 50 years from today.

Many students find that the prospect of getting what they want in life justifies all of the time, money, and day-to-day effort invested in going to school. Having a major gives you a powerful incentive for attending classes, taking part in discussions, reading textbooks, writing papers, and completing other assignments. When you see a clear connection between finishing school and creating the life of your dreams, the daily tasks of higher education become charged with meaning.

Ask other people. Key people in your life might have valuable suggestions about your choice of major. Ask for their ideas, and

7

listen with an open mind. At the same time, distance yourself from any pressure to choose a major or career that fails to interest you. If you make a choice based solely on the expectations of other people, you could end up with a major or even a career you don't enjoy.

Gather information. Check your school's catalog or Web site for a list of available majors. Here is a gold mine of information. Take a quick glance, and highlight all the majors that interest you. Then talk to students who have declared them. Also read descriptions of courses required for these majors. Do you get excited about the chance to enroll in them? Pay attention to your "gut feelings."

Also chat with instructors who teach courses in a specific major. Ask for copies of their class syllabi. Go the bookstore and browse the required texts. Based on all this information, write a list of prospective majors. Discuss them with an academic advisor and someone at your school's career-planning center.

Invent a major. When choosing a major, you might not need to limit yourself to those listed in your school catalog. Many schools now have flexible programs that allow for independent study. Through such programs you might be able to combine two existing majors or invent an entirely new one of your own.

Consider a complementary minor. You can add flexibility to your academic program by choosing a minor to complement or contrast with your major. The student who wants to be a minister could opt for a minor in English; all of those courses in composition can help in writing sermons. Or the student with a major in psychology might choose a minor in business administration, with the idea of managing a counseling service some day. An effective choice of a minor can expand your skills and career options.

Think critically about the link between your major and your career. Your career goals might have a significant impact on your choice of major. For an overview of career planning and an immediate chance to put ideas down on paper, see Chapter 12: What's Next?

You might be able to pursue a rewarding career by choosing among *several* different majors. Even students planning to apply for law school or medical school have flexibility in their choice of majors. In addition, after graduation, many people are employed in jobs with little relationship to their major. And you might choose a career in the future that is unrelated to any currently available major.

2. MAKE A TRIAL CHOICE

Pretend that you have to choose a major today. Based on the options for a major that you've already discovered, write down the first three ideas that come to mind. Review the list for a few minutes, and then just choose one.

3. EVALUATE YOUR TRIAL CHOICE

When you've made a trial choice of major, take on the role of a scientist. Treat your choice as a hypothesis, and then design a series of experiments to evaluate and test it. For example:

- Schedule office meetings with instructors who teach courses in the major. Ask about required course work and career options in the field.

- Discuss your trial choice with an academic advisor or career counselor.

- Enroll in a course related to your possible major. Remember that introductory courses might not give you a realistic picture of the workloads involved in advanced courses. Also, you might not be able to register for certain courses until you've actually declared a related major.

- Find a volunteer experience, internship, part-time job, or service-learning experience related to the major.

- Interview students who have declared the same major. Ask them in detail about their experiences and suggestions for success.

- Interview people who work in a field related to the major and "shadow" them—that is, spend time with those people during their workday.

- Think about whether you can complete your major given the amount of time and money that you plan to invest in higher education.

- Consider whether declaring this major would require a transfer to another program or even another school.

If your "experiments" confirm your choice of major, celebrate that fact. If they result in choosing a new major, celebrate that outcome as well.

Also remember that higher education represents a safe place to test your choice of major—and to change your mind. As you sort through your options, help is always available from administrators, instructors, advisors, and peers.

4. CHOOSE AGAIN

Keep your choice of a major in perspective. There is probably no single "correct" choice. Your unique collection of skills is likely to provide the basis for majoring in several fields.

Odds are that you'll change your major at least once—and that you'll change careers several times during your life. One benefit of higher education is mobility. You gain the general skills and knowledge that can help you move into a new major or career field at any time.

Viewing a major as a one-time choice that determines your entire future can raise your stress levels. Instead, look at choosing a major as the start of a continuing path that involves discovery, choice, and passionate action. ■

You're One Click Away...
from finding more strategies online for choosing a major.

JOURNAL ENTRY 17 *Discovery/Intention Statement*

Reflect on choosing a major

Follow up on the suggestions given in "Thinking about your major" on page 225. If you had already chosen a major, did any of these suggestions confirm that choice? Did you uncover any new or surprising possibilities for declaring a major?

I discovered that I . . .

_____

_____

_____

_____

_____

_____

Now consider the major that is your current top choice. Think of publications you expect to find, resources you plan to investigate, and people you intend to consult in order to gather more information about this major.

I intend to . . .

_____

_____

_____

_____

_____

Plan to repeat this Journal Entry several times. You might find yourself researching several majors and changing your mind. That's fine. The aim is to start thinking about your major now.

EXERCISE 21

Translating goals into action

Goal setting is an exercise in decision making and problem solving. Choose one long-range goal, such as a personal project or a social change you'd like to help bring about. Examples include learning to scuba dive, eating a more healthful diet, studying to be an astronaut, improving health care for chronically ill children, inventing an energy-saving technology, increasing the effectiveness of American schools, and becoming a better parent.

Review the suggestions for writing and setting goals in Chapter 2. Then write one long-range goal here:

_____

_____

_____

_____

_____

Next, ask yourself, "What specific actions are needed in the short term to meet my long-range goal?" Brainstorm a list of actions here:

_____

_____

_____

_____

_____

_____

_____

_____

Finally, from the above list, choose at least one action that you can take during the next 24 hours. Add that action to your to-do list or calendar.

7

SERVICE-LEARNING:
The art of learning by
CONTRIBUTING

As part of a service-learning project for a sociology course, students volunteer at a community center for older adults. For another service-learning project, history students interview people in veterans' hospitals about their war experiences. These students plan to share their interview results with a psychiatrist on the hospital staff.

Meanwhile, business students provide free tax-preparation help at a center for low-income people. Students in graphic arts classes create free promotional materials for charities. Other students staff a food cooperative and a community credit union.

These examples of actual projects from the National Service-Learning Clearinghouse demonstrate the working premise of service-learning: Volunteer work and other forms of contributing can become a vehicle for higher education.

Fill yourself up and give it back. In the spirit of the Power Process included earlier in this chapter, think of service-learning as a way to "find a bigger problem." This suggestion is based on one of the core values behind this book—making a positive contribution to the lives of other people.

Becoming a Master Student is about filling yourself up, taking care of yourself, being selfish, and meeting your needs. The techniques and suggestions in these pages focus on ways to get what you want out of school, work, and the rest of your life.

One of the results of all this successful selfishness is the capacity to contribute. This means giving back to your community in ways that enhance the lives of other people.

People who are satisfied with life can share that satisfaction with others. It is hard to contribute to another person's joy until you experience joy yourself. The same is true for love. When people are filled with love, they can more easily contribute love to others. Contributing is what's left to do when your needs are met. It completes the circle of giving and receiving.

Elements of service-learning. Service-learning generally includes three elements: meaningful community service, a formal academic curriculum, and time for students to reflect on what they learn from service. That reflection can include speeches, journal writing, and research papers.

> People who are satisfied with life can share that satisfaction with others. It is hard to contribute to another person's joy until you experience joy yourself. Contributing is what's left to do when your needs are met. It completes the circle of giving and receiving.

Service-learning creates a win–win scenario. For one thing, students gain the satisfaction of contributing. They also gain experiences that can guide their career choices and help them develop job skills.

At the same time, service-learning adds to the community a resource with a handsome return on investment. For example, participants in the Learn and Serve America program (administered by the Corporation for National and Community Service) provided community services valued at four times the program cost.[11]

Find service-learning courses. Many schools offer service-learning programs. Look in the index of your school catalog under "service-learning," and search your school's Web site using those key words. There might be a service-learning office on your campus.

Also turn to national organizations that keep track of service-learning opportunities. One is the Corporation for National and Community Service, a federal government agency (www.nationalservice.gov, 202-606-5000). You can also contact the National Service-Learning Clearinghouse (www.servicelearning.org, 866-245-7378). These resources can lead you to others, including service-learning programs in your state.

GETTING THE MOST FROM SERVICE-LEARNING

When you design a service-learning project, consider the following suggestions.

Follow your interests. Think of the persistent problems in the world—illiteracy, hunger, obesity, addictions, unemployment, poverty, and more. Which of them generate the strongest feelings in you? Which of them link to your possible career plans and choice of major? The place where passion intersects with planning often creates a useful opportunity for service-learning.

Choose partners carefully. Work with a community organization that has experience with students. Make sure that the organization has liability insurance to cover volunteers.

Learn about the organization. Once you connect with community organization, learn everything you can about it. Find its mission statement and explore its history. Find out what makes this organization unique. If the organization partners with others in the community, learn about those other organizations as well.

Handle logistics. Integrating service-learning into your schedule can call for detailed planning. If your volunteer work takes place off campus, arrange for transportation and allow for travel time.

Include ways to evaluate your project. From your Intention Statements, create action goals and outcome goals. *Action goals* state what you plan to do and how many people you intend to serve; for instance, "We plan to provide 100 hours of literacy tutoring to 10 people in the community." *Outcome goals* describe the actual impact that your project will have: "At the end of our project, 60 percent of the people we tutor will be able to write a résumé and fill out a job application." Build numbers into your goals whenever possible. That makes it easier to evaluate the success of your project.

Build long-term impact into your project. One potential pitfall of service-learning is that the programs are often short-lived. After students pack up and return to campus, programs can die. To avoid this outcome, make sure that other students or community members are willing to step in and take over for you when the semester ends.

Build transferable skills. Review the list of 65 transferable skills on page 355. Use this list as a way to stimulate your thinking. List the specific skills that you're developing through service-learning.

Keep this list. It will come in handy when you write a résumé and fill out job applications. And before you plan to do another service-learning project, think about the skills you'd like to develop from that experience.

Make use of mistakes. If your project fails to meet its goals, then turn this result into an opportunity to learn. State—in writing—the obstacles you encountered and possible ways to overcome them. The solutions you offer will be worth gold to the people who follow in your footsteps. Sharing the lessons learned from mistakes is an act of service in itself.

Connect service-learning to critical thinking. Remember that a *service* activity does not necessarily become a *service* attitude. Students can engage in service-learning merely to meet academic requirements and add a line to their résumé. Or students can engage in service-learning as a way to make long-term changes in their beliefs and behavior.

The idea behind service-learning is that community action is a strategy for academic achievement. This is what distinguishes service-learning from other forms of volunteer activity. A service-learning course combines work in the community with activities in the classroom. Contributing to others becomes a powerful and effective way to learn.

Turn to a tool you've used throughout this book—the Discovery and Intention Journal Entry system. Write Discovery Statements about what you gain from service-learning and how you feel about what you're doing. Follow up with Intention Statements about what you'll do differently for your next service-learning experience.

To think critically and creatively about your service-learning project, also ask questions such as these:

- What service did you perform?
- What roles did your service project include, and who filled those roles?
- What knowledge and skills did you bring to this project?
- After being involved in this project, what new knowledge and skills do you want to gain?
- What did you learn from this experience that can make another service-learning project more successful?
- Will this service-learning project affect your choice of a major? If so, how?
- Will this service-learning project affect your career plans? If so, how?

Service-learning provides an opportunity to combine theory and practice, reflection and action, "book learning" and "real-world" experience. Education takes place as we reflect on our experiences and turn them into new insights and intentions. Use service-learning as a way to take your thinking skills to a whole new level. ■

You're One Click Away...
from finding more strategies online for effective service-learning.

7

Recall an idea or suggestion from the chapter that you'd like to explore in more detail. Summarize it, and include the page number where it appears:

_____

_____

_____

_____

You've just done some thinking at **Level 1: Remembering**—Now, take your thinking about this idea or suggestion to **one** of the higher levels:

Level 2: Understanding—Explain this idea in your own words and give examples from your own experience.

Level 3: Applying—Use the idea to produce a desired result.

Level 4: Analyzing—Divide this idea into parts or steps.

Level 5: Evaluating—Rate the truth, usefulness or quality of the idea—and give reasons for your rating.

Level 6: Creating—Invent something new based on the idea.

Demonstrate your higher-level thinking by writing a brief paragraph in the space below. If you want to show your thinking in another way, then check with your instructor. In either case, clearly state your intended level of thinking (For example, "To *apply* this idea, I would . . . .")

_____

_____

_____

_____

_____

_____

masterstudentprofile

Twyla Tharp

(1941–) A choreographer who has worked with her own company, the Joffrey Ballet, the Paris Opera Ballet, London's Royal Ballet, and the American Ballet Theatre. She also created dances for the films *Hair, Ragtime,* and *Amadeus.*

Every creative person has to learn to deal with failure, because failure, like death and taxes, is inescapable. If Leonardo and Beethoven and Goethe failed on occasion, what makes you think you'll be the exception?

I don't mean to romanticize failure. . . . Believe me, success is preferable to failure. But there is a therapeutic power to failure. It cleanses. It helps you put aside who you aren't and reminds you of who you are. Failure humbles. . . .

When I tape a 3-hour improvisational session with a dancer and find only 30 seconds of useful material in the tape, I am earning straight A's in failure. Do the math: I have rejected 99.7 percent of my work that day. It would be like a writer knocking out a 2,000-word chapter and upon rereading deciding that only three words were worth keeping. Painful, yes, but for me absolutely necessary.

What's so wonderful about wasting that kind of time? It's simple: The more you fail in private, the less you will fail in public. In many ways, the creative act is editing. You're editing out all the lame ideas that won't resonate with the public. It's not pandering. It's exercising your judgment. It's setting the bar a little higher for yourself, and therefore for your audience. . . .

Some of my favorite dancers at New York City Ballet were the ones who fell the most. I always loved watching Mimi Paul; she took big risks onstage and went down often. Her falls reminded you that the dancers were doing superhuman things onstage, and when she fell, I would realize, "Damn, she's human." And hitting the ground seemed to transform Mimi: It was as though the stage absorbed the energy of her fall and injected it back into her with an extra dose of fearlessness. Mimi would bounce back up, ignore the fall, and right before my eyes would become superhuman again. I thought, "Go, Mimi!" She became greater because she had fallen. Failure enlarged her dancing.

That should be your model for dealing with failure.

When you fail in public, you are forcing yourself to learn a whole new set of skills, skills that have nothing to do with creating and everything to do with surviving.

Jerome Robbins liked to say that you do your best work after your biggest disasters. For one thing, it's so painful that it almost guarantees that you won't make those mistakes again. Also, you have nothing to lose; you've hit bottom and the only place to go is up. A fiasco compels you to change dramatically. The golfer Bobby Jones said, "I never learned anything from a match I won." He respected defeat and profited from it. . . .

My heroes in *The Odyssey* are the older warriors who have been through many wars. They don't hide their scars, they wear them proudly as a kind of armor. When you fail—when your short film induces yawns or your photographs inspire people to say, "That's nice" (ouch!), or your novel is trashed in a journal of opinion that matters to you—the best thing to do is acknowledge your battle scars and gird yourself for the next round. Tell yourself, "This is a deep wound. But it's going to heal and I will remember the wound. When I go back into the fray, it will serve me well."

7

TWYLA THARP . . . is creative.

YOU . . . can be more creative by seeing failure as a chance to learn.

Source: Reprinted with the permission of Simon & Schuster, Inc., from *The Creative Habit: Learn It and Use It for Life* by Twyla Tharp with Mark Reiter. Copyright © 2003 W.A.T. Ltd. All rights reserved.

You're One Click Away...
from learning more about Twyla Tharp online at the Master Student Profiles. You can also visit the Master Student Hall of Fame to learn about other master students.

© Istockphoto.com/pagadesign

PUT THIS CHAPTER TO
W●RK

For a recent survey, IBM's Institute for Business Value asked 1,500 chief executive officers to name the leadership skill they considered most important. The top answer was creativity.[12] Use suggestions from this chapter to unleash new ideas in the work place. Follow up with critical thinking strategies to turn those ideas into reality.

THINK THROUGH ANSWERS TO COMMON INTERVIEW QUESTIONS. One place to display creative thinking is during a job interview. Job interviewers have many standard questions. Most of them boil down to a few major concerns:

- How did you find out about us?
- Would we be comfortable working with you?
- How can you help us?
- Will you learn this job quickly?
- What makes you different from other applicants?

Before your interview, prepare some answers to these questions.

If you get turned down for the job after your interview, don't take it personally. Every interview is a source of feedback about what works—and what doesn't work—in contacting employers. Use that feedback to interview more effectively next time.

DEVELOP EXPERT THINKING SKILLS. In their book *The New Division of Labor: How Computers Are Creating the Next Job Market*, Frank Levy and Richard J. Murname argue that prospering in a global economy calls for *expert thinking*. This means "solving new problems for which there are no routine solutions."[13]

The chef who creates a new meal without increasing restaurant costs shows expert thinking. So does a car mechanic who solves a problem not covered in the owner's manual, and the web designer who creates a new application for blogging.

Jobs that do not involve expert thinking are more likely to be outsourced or automated. For example, travel agents and underwriters (people who determine eligibility for an insurance policy or loan) traditionally made decisions according to step-by-step formulas. Those kinds of decisions are now made by computers.

An expert has deep knowledge about a field along with an ability to identify new relationships between ideas. Develop expert thinking by taking advanced courses in your major and seizing opportunities to work on project teams.

ASK QUESTIONS TO CREATE PROJECT PLANS. When your team meets, start by brainstorming answers to key questions: "Why are we doing this project? What would a successful outcome look like? How will we measure our results? What are the next actions to take? Who will take them? By when?"

NOW CREATE A CAREER CONNECTION OF YOUR OWN. Review this chapter, looking for a suggestion that you will commit to use while working or looking for a job. In a sentence or two, describe exactly what you plan to do and the primary benefit you want to gain. For example: "I will talk to people who are working in my career field to find out what they majored in and why. This will help me choose my own major."

State your strategy and desired benefit in the space below:

_____

_____

_____

_____

_____

_____

_____

_____

_____

_____

_____

Name _____

Date _____

1. List the six levels of thinking described by Benjamin Bloom.

2. List the key question associated with each level of thinking of Bloom's taxonomy.

3. Briefly explain the difference between convergent and divergent thinking.

4. Discuss what is meant in this chapter by *aha!*

5. Briefly describe three strategies for creative thinking.

6. List three types of logical fallacies, and give an example of each type.

7. Name at least one logical fallacy involved in this statement: "Everyone who's ever visited this school agrees that it's the best in the state."

8. List an assumption that underlies the following statement: "Why save money? I want to enjoy life today."

9. According to the text, the words *choose* and *decide* have the same meaning. True or false? Explain your answer.

10. Summarize the four steps in the process of choosing a major, as explained in this chapter.

7 SKILLS *Snapshot*

Take a minute to reflect on your responses to the Thinking section of the Discovery Wheel on page 38. Then take your discoveries and intentions about creative and critical thinking to the next level by completing the following sentences.

DISCOVERY

My score on the Thinking section of the Discovery Wheel on page 38 was . . .

When I'm asked to come up with a topic for a paper or speech, the first thing I do is . . .

When I get involved in a conversation and hear an idea I disagree with, my first response is often to . . .

When I face a major choice in my life, the way that I usually make a decision is . . .

INTENTION

One of the biggest problems I face right now is . . .

To come up with a solution for this problem, I will . . .

In declaring my major, the steps I plan to take include . . .

ACTION

To reach that level of mastery, the most important thing I can do next is to . . .

I'll know that I've reached a new level of mastery with critical and creative thinking skills when . . .

By the time I finish this course, I would like my Thinking score on the Discovery Wheel to be . . .

Communicating

 Use this **Master Student Map** to ask yourself,

 ## WHY THIS CHAPTER MATTERS . . .

- Your communication abilities—including your skills in listening, speaking, and writing—are as important to your success as your technical skills.

 ## WHAT IS INCLUDED . . .

- Power Process: Employ your word   236
- Communicating creates our world   237
- Communication—keeping the channels open   238
- Choosing to *listen*   239
- Choosing to speak   241
- Developing emotional intelligence   245
- Collaborating for success   246
- Managing conflict   247
- Five ways to say no . . . respectfully   250
- Five steps to effective complaints   252
- Mastering social networks   253
- Three phases of effective writing   255
- Academic integrity: Avoid plagiarism   260
- Mastering public speaking   262
- Master Student Profile: Mark Zuckerberg   267

 ## HOW CAN I USE THIS CHAPTER . . .

- Listen, speak, and write in ways that promote your success.
- Prevent and resolve conflict with other people.
- Make and keep agreements as a tool for creating your future.

 ## WHAT IF . . .

- I could consistently create the kind of relationships that I've always wanted?

JOURNAL ENTRY 18
Intention Statement

Commit to create value from this chapter

Think of a time when you experienced an emotionally charged conflict with another person. Then scan this chapter for ideas that can help you get your feelings and ideas across more skillfully in similar situations. List at least three ideas below, along with the page numbers where you intend to read more about them.

Strategy	Page number
_____	_____
_____	_____
_____	_____
_____	_____
_____	_____
_____	_____
_____	_____
_____	_____
_____	_____
_____	_____
_____	_____
_____	_____
_____	_____
_____	_____
_____	_____
_____	_____

© Ruslan Ivantsov/Shutterstock.com

POWER process

Employ your word

When you give your word, you are creating—literally. The person you are is, for the most part, a result of the agreements you make. Others know who you are by your words and your commitments. And you can learn who you are by observing which commitments you choose to keep and which ones you choose to avoid.

Relationships are built on agreements. When we break a promise to be faithful to a spouse, to help a friend move to a new apartment, or to pay a bill on time, relationships are strained.

The words we use to make agreements can be placed into six different levels. We can think of each level as one rung on a ladder—the ladder of powerful speaking. As we move up the ladder, our speaking becomes more effective.

The first and lowest rung on the ladder is *obligation*. Words used at this level include *I should, he ought to, someone had better, they need to, I must,* and *I had to.* Speaking this way implies that something other than ourselves is in control of our lives. When we live at the level of obligation, we speak as if we are victims.

The second rung is *possibility*. At this level, we examine new options. We play with new ideas, possible solutions, and alternative courses of action. As we do, we learn that we can make choices that dramatically affect the quality of our lives. We are not the victims of circumstance. Phrases that signal this level include *I might, I could, I'll consider, I hope to,* and *maybe.*

From possibility, we can move up to the third level—*preference.* Here we begin the process of choice. The words *I prefer* signal that we're moving toward one set of possibilities over another, perhaps setting the stage for eventual action.

Above preference is a fourth rung called *passion.* Again, certain words signal this level: *I want to, I'm really excited to do that,* and *I can't wait.*

Action comes with the fifth rung—*planning.* When people use phrases such as *I intend to, my goal is to, I plan to,* and *I'll try like mad to,* they're at the level of planning. The Intention Statements you write in this book are examples of planning.

The sixth and highest rung on the ladder is *promising.* This is where the power of your word really comes into play. At this level, it's common to use phrases such as these: *I will, I promise to, I am committed,* and *you can count on it.* Promising is where we bridge from possibility and planning to action. Promising brings with it all of the rewards of employing your word.

You're One Click Away...
from accessing Power Process Media online and finding out more about how to "employ your word.".

iStockphoto.com/Clayton Hansen

Communicating creates our world

Certain things are real for us because we can see them, touch them, hear them, smell them, or taste them. Books, pencils, tables, chairs, and food all are real in this sense. They enter our world in a straightforward, uncomplicated way.

Many other aspects of our lives, however, do not have this kind of observable reality. None of us can point to a *purpose,* for example. Nor would a purpose step up and introduce itself or buy us lunch. The same is true about other abstract concepts, such as *quality, intelligence, trust, human rights,* or *student success.*

Concepts such as these shape our experience of life. Yet they don't really exist until we talk about them. These concepts come alive for us only to the degree that we have conversations about them. Communicating brings our world into being.

According to communication theorist Lee Thayer, there are two basic life processes. One is acquiring and processing energy. The other is acquiring and processing information, also known as *communication.*[1] From this point of view, communicating is just as fundamental to life as eating.

Through communication, we take raw impressions and organize them into patterns. With our senses, we perceive sights, sounds, and other sensations. However, none of our sense organs is capable of perceiving *meaning.* We create meaning by finding patterns in our sensations and sharing them through conversation.

Communication can be defined as the process of creating shared meaning. When two people agree about the meaning of an event, they've communicated. However, communication is a constant challenge. Each of us creates meaning in a way that is unique.

When people speak or listen, they don't exchange meaning. They exchange symbols—words, images, gestures. And symbols are open to interpretation. This means that communication is always flawed to some extent. We can never be sure that the message we send is the message that others receive. This creates a constant challenge in our relationships.

Much of this chapter is about two low-tech methods for creating shared meaning—speaking and listening, face-to-face.

Often we can make an immediate difference in the quality of a relationship by starting with the way we listen. "You have two ears and one mouth," author Paula Bern reminds us. "Remember to use them in more or less that proportion."

Then, when it's your turn to speak, consider the benefits of open and honest communication. Sometimes it's tempting to hold back—to say only a fraction of what you're thinking or feeling. This can be one more way to keep a conflict alive. An alternative is to "empty your bucket." There are times when you can benefit everyone by letting your words and feelings flow spontaneously. Don't worry about speaking perfectly. Just reveal what's on your mind. Get all of your cards on the table. This too calls for balance. Sometimes people say *too* much. And they take a lot of time to lay the groundwork for their main point, making their listeners wait in suspense. This technique works well for actors on a stage who want to add drama to a scene. It doesn't work so well off-stage, especially when people are in conflict. When people feel forced to listen, they can become impatient and irritable. To prevent this problem, get to your point right away. Then elaborate. Provide supporting details while respecting everyone's time.

Another powerful way to boost your communication skills is to remember that disagreement can be positive. Breakdowns in communication are going to happen. Most of them can be resolved. Managing conflict in effective ways can actually bring people closer together.

With practice we can overcome many of the challenges inherent in human communication. That's what this chapter is about. As you enhance your skills at listening, speaking, and writing, you can create a new world. ■

8

In our daily contact with other people and the mass media, we are exposed to hundreds of messages. Yet the obstacles to receiving those messages accurately are numerous.

Communication— keeping the channels open

For one thing, only a small percentage of communication is verbal. We also send messages with our bodies and with the tone of our voices. Throw in a few other factors, such as a hot room or background noise, and it's a wonder we can communicate at all.

Written communication adds a whole other set of variables. When you speak, you supplement the meaning of your words with the power of body language and voice inflection. When you write, those nonverbal elements are absent. Instead, you depend on your skills at word choice, sentence construction, and punctuation to get your message across. The choices that you make in these areas can aid—or hinder—communication.

In communication theory, the term *noise* refers to any factor that distorts meaning. When noise is present, the channels of communication start to close. Noise can be external (a lawn mower outside a classroom) or internal (the emotions of the sender or receiver, such as speech anxiety). To a large extent, skillful communication means reducing noise and keeping channels open.

© Moodboard/Corbis; static: © Paul Edmondson/Corbis; ear: © Masterfile Royalty Free

One powerful technique for doing these crucial things is to separate the roles of sending and receiving. Communication channels get blocked when we try to send and receive messages at the same time. Instead, be aware of when you are the receiver and when you are the sender. If you are receiving (listening or reading), just receive; avoid switching into the sending (speaking or writing) mode. When you are sending, stick with it until you are finished.

Communication works best when each of us has plenty of time to receive what others send *and* the opportunity to send a complete message when it's our turn. Communication is a two-way street. When someone else talks, just listen. Then switch roles so that you can be the sender for a while. Keep this up until you do a reasonably complete job of creating shared meaning. ■

✔ EXERCISE 22

Practice sending or receiving

The purpose of this exercise is to help you slow down the pace of communication and clearly separate the roles of sending and receiving. Begin by applying the following steps to conversations on neutral topics. With some practice, you'll be ready to use this technique in situations that could escalate into an argument.

First, find a partner, and choose a topic for a conversation. Also set a time limit for doing this exercise. Then complete the following steps:

1. Get two 3 × 5 cards. Label one of them *sender*. Label the other *receiver*. Choose one card, and give the other one to your partner.

2. If you chose the *sender* card, then start speaking. If you chose the *receiver* card, then listen to your partner without saying a word.

3. When the sender is done speaking, exchange cards and switch roles. The person who listened in Step 2 now gets to speak. However, *do not exchange cards until the sender in Step 2 declares that she has expressed everything she wants to say.*

4. Keep switching cards and roles until your time is up.

After completing these steps, reflect on the experience. What has this exercise taught you about your current skills as a speaker and listener?

Choosing to LISTEN

Effective listening is not easy. It calls for concentration and energy. But it's worth the trouble. People love a good listener. The best salespeople, managers, coworkers, teachers, parents, and friends are the best listeners.

Through skilled listening, you can gain insight into other people and yourself. You can also promote your success in school through more powerful notes, more productive study groups, and better relationships with students and instructors.

To listen well, begin from a clear intention. *Choose* to listen well. Once you've made this choice, you can use the following techniques to be even more effective at listening. Notice that these techniques start with suggestions for nonverbal listening, which involves remaining silent while another person talks. The second set of suggestions is about verbal listening, where you occasionally speak up in ways that help you fully receive a speaker's message.

NONVERBAL LISTENING

Be quiet. Silence is more than staying quiet while someone is speaking. Allowing several seconds to pass before you begin to talk gives the speaker time to catch her breath and gather her thoughts. She might want to continue. Someone who talks nonstop might fear she will lose the floor if she pauses.

If the message being sent is complete, this short break gives you time to form your response and helps you avoid the biggest barrier to listening—listening with your answer running. If you make up a response before the person is finished, you might miss the end of the message, which is often the main point.

In some circumstances, pausing for several seconds might be inappropriate. Ignore this suggestion completely in an emergency, where immediate action is usually necessary.

Maintain eye contact. Look at the other person while he speaks. Maintaining eye contact demonstrates your attentiveness and helps keep your mind from wandering. Your eyes also let you observe the speaker's body language and behavior. If you avoid eye contact, you can fail to see *and* fail to listen.

This idea is not an absolute. Maintaining eye contact is valued more in some cultures than others. Also, some people learn primarily by hearing; they can listen more effectively by turning off the visual input once in a while.

Display openness. You can display openness through your facial expression and body position. Uncross your arms and legs. Sit up straight. Face the other person, and remove any physical barriers between you, such as a pile of books.

> Observe a person in a conversation who is not talking. Is he listening? Maybe. Maybe not. Is he focusing on the speaker? Preparing his response? Daydreaming?

Send acknowledgments. Let the speaker know periodically that you are still there. Words and nonverbal gestures of acknowledgment convey to the speaker that you are interested and that you are receiving his message. These words and gestures include "Umhum," "Okay," "Yes," and head nods.

These acknowledgments do not imply your agreement. When people tell you what they don't like about you, your head nod doesn't mean that you agree. It just indicates that you are listening.

Release distractions. Even when your intention is to listen, you might find your mind wandering. Thoughts about what *you* want to say or something you want to do later might claim your attention. There's a simple solution: Notice your wandering mind without judgment. Then bring your attention back to the act of listening.

You can also set up your immediate environment to release distractions. Turn off or silence your cell phone. Stash your laptop and other digital devices. Send the message that your sole intention in the moment is to listen.

Another option is to ask for a quick break so that you can make a written note about what's on your mind. Tell the speaker that you're writing so that you can clear your mind and return to full listening.

Suspend judgments. Listening and agreeing are two different activities. As listeners, our goal is to fully receive another person's message. This does not mean that we're obligated to agree with the message. Once you're confident that you accurately understand a speaker's point of view, you are free to agree or disagree with it. The key to effective listening is understanding *before* evaluating.

8

VERBAL LISTENING

Choose when to speak. When we listen to another person, we often interrupt with our own stories, opinions, suggestions, and comments. Consider the following dialogue:

"Oh, I'm so excited! I just found out that I've been nominated to be in *Who's Who in American Musicians.*"

"Yeah, that's neat. My Uncle Elmer got into *Who's Who in American Veterinarians.* He sure has an interesting job. One time I went along when he was treating a cow, and you'll never believe what happened next. . . ."

To avoid this kind of one-sided conversation, delay your verbal responses. This does not mean that you remain totally silent while listening. It means that you wait for an *appropriate* moment to respond.

Watch your nonverbal responses too. A look of "Good grief!" from you can deter the other person from finishing his message.

Feed back meaning. Sometimes you can help a speaker clarify her message by paraphrasing it. This does not mean parroting what she says. Instead, briefly summarize. Psychotherapist Carl Rogers referred to this technique as *reflection.*[2]

Feed back what you see as the essence of the person's message: "Let me see whether I understood what you said. . . ." or "What I'm hearing you say is. . . ." Often, the other person will say, "No, that's not what I meant. What I said was. . . ."

There will be no doubt when you get it right. The sender will say, "Yeah, that's it," and either continue with another message or stop sending when he knows you understand.

When you feed back meaning, be concise. This is not a time to stop the other person by talking on and on about what you think you heard.

Notice verbal *and* nonverbal messages. You might point out that the speaker's body language seems to convey the exact opposite of what her words do. For example: "I noticed you said you are excited, but you look bored."

Keep in mind that the same nonverbal behavior can have various meanings across cultures. Someone who looks bored might simply be listening in a different way.

Listen for requests and intentions. An effective way to listen to complaints is to look for the request hidden in them. "This class is a waste of my time" can be heard as "Please tell me what I'll gain if I participate actively in class." "The instructor talks too fast" might be asking "What strategies can I use to take notes when the instructor covers material rapidly?"

We can even transform complaints into intentions. Take this complaint: "The parking lot by the dorms is so dark at night that I'm afraid to go to my car." This complaint can result in having a light installed in the parking lot.

Viewing complaints as requests gives us more choices. Rather than responding with defensiveness ("What does he know anyway?"), resignation ("It's always been this way and always will be"), or indifference ("It's not my job"), we can decide whether to grant the request (do what will alleviate the other's difficulty) or help the person translate his own complaint into an action plan.

Allow emotion. In the presence of full listening, some people will share things that they feel deeply about. They might shed a few tears, cry, shake, or sob. If you feel uncomfortable when this happens, see whether you can accept the discomfort for a little while longer. Emotional release can bring relief and trigger unexpected insights.

Ask for more. Full listening with unconditional acceptance is a rare gift. Many people have never experienced it. They are used to being greeted with resistance, so they habitually stop short of saying what they truly think and feel. Help them shed this habit by routinely asking, "Is there anything more you want to say about that?" This question sends the speaker a message that you truly value what she has to say.

Be careful with questions and advice. Questions are directive. They can take conversations in a new direction, which may not be where the speaker wants to go. Ask questions only to clarify the speaker's message. Later, when it's your turn to speak, you can introduce any topic that you want.

Also be cautious about giving advice. Unsolicited advice can be taken as condescending or even insulting. Skilled listeners recognize that people are different, and they do not assume that they know what's best for someone else.

Take care of yourself. People seek good listeners, and there are times when you don't want to listen. You might be distracted with your own concerns. Be honest. Don't pretend to listen. You can say, "What you're telling me is important, but I'm pressed for time right now. Can we set aside another time to talk about this?" It's okay not to listen.

Stay open to the adventure of listening. Receiving what another person has to say is an act of courage. Listening fully—truly opening yourself to the way another person sees the world—means taking risks. Your opinions may be challenged. You may be less certain or less comfortable than you were before.

Along with the risks come rewards. Listening in an unguarded way can take your relationships to a new depth and level of honesty. This kind of listening can open up new possibilities for thinking, feeling, and behaving. And when you practice full listening, other people are more likely to receive when it's your turn to send. ■

You're One Click Away...
from finding more strategies online for full listening.

Choosing to SPEAK

You have been talking with people for most of your life, and you usually manage to get your messages across. There are times, though, when you don't. Often, these times are emotionally charged.

We all have this problem. Sometimes we feel wonderful or rotten or sad or scared, and we want to express it. Emotions, though, can get in the way of the message. And although you can send almost any message through tears, laughter, fist pounding, or hugging, sometimes words are better. Begin with a sincere intention to reach common ground with your listener. Then experiment with the suggestions that follow.

Replace "you" messages with "I" messages. It can be difficult to disagree with someone without his becoming angry or your becoming upset. When conflict occurs, we often make statements about the other person, or "you" messages:

"You are rude."
"You make me mad."
"You must be crazy."
"You don't love me anymore."

This kind of communication results in defensiveness. The responses might be similar to these:

"I am not rude."
"I don't care."
"No, *you* are crazy."
"No, *you* don't love *me!*"

"You" messages are hard to listen to. They label, judge, blame, and assume things that may or may not be true. They demand rebuttal. Even praise can sometimes be an ineffective "you" message. "You" messages don't work.

Psychologist Thomas Gordon suggests that when communication is emotionally charged, consider limiting your statements to descriptions about yourself.[3] Replace "you" messages with "I" messages:

"You are rude" might become "I feel upset."
"You make me mad" could be "I feel angry."
"You must be crazy" can be "I don't understand."
"You don't love me anymore" could become "I'm afraid we're drifting apart."

Suppose a friend asks you to pick him up at the airport. You drive 20 miles and wait for the plane. No friend. You decide your friend missed her plane, so you wait 3 hours for the next flight. No

friend. Perplexed and worried, you drive home. The next day, you see your friend downtown.

"What happened?" you ask.
"Oh, I caught an earlier flight."
"You are a rude person," you reply.

Look for and talk about the facts—the observable behavior. Everyone will agree that your friend asked you to pick her up, that she did take an earlier flight, and that you did not receive a call from her. But the idea that she is rude is not a fact—it's a judgment.

She might go on to say, "I called your home, and no one answered. My mom had a stroke and was rushed to Valley View. I caught the earliest flight I could get." Your judgment no longer fits.

When you saw your friend, you might have said, "I waited and waited at the airport. I was worried about you. I didn't get a call. I feel angry and hurt. I don't want to waste my time. Next time, you can call me when your flight arrives, and I'll be happy to pick you up."

"I" messages don't judge, blame, criticize, or insult. They don't invite the other person to counterattack with more of the same. "I" messages are also more accurate. They report our own thoughts and feelings.

At first, "I" messages might feel uncomfortable or seem forced. That's okay. Use the "Five ways to say 'I'" explained on page 242.

Remember that questions are not always questions. You've heard these "questions" before. A parent asks, "Don't you want to look nice?" Translation: "I wish you'd cut your hair, lose the blue jeans, and put on a tie." Or how about this question from a spouse: "Honey, wouldn't you love to go to an exciting hockey game tonight?" Translation: "I've already bought tickets."

We use questions that aren't questions to sneak our opinions and requests into conversations. "Doesn't it upset you?" means "It upsets me," and "Shouldn't we hang the picture over here?" means "I want to hang the picture over here."

Communication improves when we say, "I'm upset" and "Let's hang the picture over here."

Choose your nonverbal messages. How you say something can be more important than what you say. Your tone of voice and gestures add up to a silent message that you send. This message can support, modify, or contradict your words. Your posture, the way

8

you dress, how often you shower, and even the poster hanging on your wall can negate your words before you say them.

Most nonverbal behavior is unconscious. We can learn to be aware of it and choose our nonverbal messages. The key is to be clear about our intention and purpose. When we know what we want to say and are committed to getting it across, our inflections, gestures, and words work together and send a unified message.

Notice barriers to sending messages. Sometimes fear stops us from sending messages. We are afraid of other people's reactions, sometimes justifiably. Being truthful doesn't mean being insensitive to the impact that our messages have on others. Tact is a virtue; letting fear prevent communication is not.

Assumptions can also be used as excuses for not sending messages. "He already knows this," we tell ourselves.

Predictions of failure can be barriers to sending too. "He won't listen," we assure ourselves. That statement might be inaccurate. Perhaps the other person senses that we're angry and listens in a guarded way. Or perhaps he is listening and sending nonverbal messages we don't understand.

Or we might predict, "He'll never do anything about it, even if I tell him." Again, making assumptions can defeat your message before you send it.

It's easy to make excuses for not communicating. If you have fear or some other concern about sending a message, be aware of it. Don't expect the concern to go away. Realize that you can communicate even with your concerns. You can choose to make them part of the message: "I am going to tell you how I feel, but I'm afraid that you will think it's stupid."

Talking to someone when you don't want to could be a matter of educational survival. Sometimes a short talk with an advisor, a teacher, a friend, or a family member can solve a problem that otherwise could jeopardize your education.

Speak candidly. When we brood on negative thoughts and refuse to speak them out loud, we lose perspective. And when we keep joys to ourselves, we diminish our satisfaction. A solution is to share regularly what we think and feel. Psychotherapist Sidney Jourard referred to such openness and honesty as *transparency* and wrote eloquently about how it can heal and deepen relationships.[4]

Sometimes candid speaking can save a life. For example, if you think a friend is addicted to drugs, telling her so in a supportive, nonjudgmental way is a sign of friendship.

Imagine a community in which people freely and lovingly speak their minds—without fear or defensiveness. That can be your community.

This suggestion comes with a couple of caveats. First, there is a big difference between speaking candidly about your problems and griping about them. Gripers usually don't seek solutions. They just want everyone to know how unhappy they are. Instead, talk about problems as a way to start searching for solutions.

Second, avoid bragging. Other people are turned off by constant references to how much money you have, how great your partner is, how numerous your social successes are, or how much status your family enjoys. There is a difference between sharing excitement and being obnoxious.

Offer "feedforward." Giving people feedback about their past performance can be a powerful way to help them learn. Equally useful is "feedforward," which means exploring new options for the future.

Marshall Goldsmith, a management consultant, suggests a way to do this. First, talk about a specific, high-impact behavior that you'd like to change—for example, "I want to be a better listener."

FIVE WAYS to say "I"

An "I" message can include any or all of the following five elements. Be careful when including the last two elements, though, because they can contain hidden judgments or threats.

Observations. Describe the facts—the indisputable, observable realities. Talk about what you—or anyone else—can see, hear, smell, taste, or touch. Avoid judgments, interpretations, or opinions. Instead of saying, "You're a slob," say, "Last night's lasagna pan was still on the stove this morning."

Feelings. Describe your own feelings. It is easier to listen to "I feel frustrated" than to "You never help me." Stating how you feel about another's actions can be valuable feedback for that person.

Wants. You are far more likely to get what you want if you say what you want. If someone doesn't know what you want, she doesn't have a chance to help you get it. Ask clearly. Avoid demanding or using the word *need*. Most people like to feel helpful, not obligated. Instead of saying, "Do the dishes when it's your turn, or else!" say, "I want to divide the housework fairly."

Thoughts. Communicate your thoughts, but use caution. Beginning your statement with the word "I" doesn't automatically make it an "I" message. "I think you are a slob" is a "you" judgment in disguise. Instead, say, "I'd have more time to study if I didn't have to clean up so often."

Intentions. The last part of an "I" message is a statement about what you intend to do. Have a plan that doesn't depend on the other person. For example, instead of "From now on, we're going to split the dishwashing evenly," you could say, "I intend to do my share of the housework and leave the rest."

Then gather with a small group of trusted friends and ask for suggestions about ways to accomplish your goal. To make this process work, avoid any conversation about what's happened in the past. Focus instead on next actions you intend to take. Also listen to what others suggest without criticizing their ideas.[5]

Speak up! Look for opportunities to practice speaking strategies. Join class discussions, and keep a running list of questions and comments to share. Start conversations about topics that excite you. Ask for information and clarification. Ask for feedback on your skills.

Also speak up when you want support. Consider creating a team of people who help one another succeed. Such a team can develop naturally from a study group that works well. Ask members whether they would be willing to accept and receive support in achieving a wide range of academic and personal goals. Meet regularly to do goal-setting exercises from this book and brainstorm success strategies.

After you have a clear statement of your goals and a plan for achieving them, let family members and friends know. When appropriate, let them know how they can help. You may be surprised at how often people respond to a genuine request for support. ■

 You're One Click Away...
from finding more strategies online for speaking your mind.

Master Students
IN ACTION

"Dealing with conflict online is totally different from dealing with it in person. I find that even if something is "resolved" online, it will probably come up in person anyway, so why not just talk face-to-face?"

–Cat Salerno, University of New Hampshire

Cat Salerno

 You're One Click Away...
from viewing a video about Master Students in Action.

✓ EXERCISE 23

Write an "I" message

Pick something about school that irritates you. Then pretend that you are talking to a person who is associated with this irritation. Write down what you would say to this person as a "you" message.

_____

_____

_____

_____

_____

_____

_____

_____

Now write the same complaint as an "I" message. Include at least the first three elements suggested in "Five Ways to Say 'I.'"

_____

_____

_____

_____

_____

_____

_____

8

Discover communication styles

The concept of *communication styles* can be useful when you want to discover sources of conflict with another person—or when you're in a conversation with someone from a different culture.

Consider the many ways in which people express themselves verbally. These characteristics can reflect an individual's preferred communication style:

- *Extroversion*—talking to others as a way to explore possibilities for taking action.
- *Introversion*—thinking through possibilities alone before talking to others.
- *Dialogue*—engaging in a discussion to hear many points of view before coming to a conclusion or decision.
- *Debate*—arguing for a particular point of view from the outset of a discussion.
- *Openness*—being ready to express personal thoughts and feelings early in a relationship.
- *Reserve*—holding back on self-expression until a deeper friendship develops.
- A *faster pace* of conversation—allowing people to speak quickly and forcefully while filling any gaps in conversation.
- A *slower pace* of conversation—allowing people to speak slowly and quietly while taking time to formulate their thoughts.

These are just a few examples of differences in communication styles. You might be able to think of others.

The point is that people with different communication styles can make negative assumptions about each other. For example, those who prefer fast-paced conversations might assume that people who talk slowly are indecisive. And people who prefer slower-paced conversations might assume that people who talk quickly are pushy and un-interested in anyone else's opinion.

Take this opportunity to think about your preferred communication styles and assumptions. Do they enhance or block your relationships with other people? Think back over the conversations you've had during the past week. Then complete the following sentences, using additional paper as needed.

1. I discovered that I prefer conversations that allow me to. . .

_____

_____

_____

2. I discovered that I usually feel uncomfortable in conversations when other people. . .

_____

_____

_____

3. When people do the things listed in Item 2, I tend to make certain assumptions, such as. . .

_____

_____

_____

4. As an alternative to making the assumptions listed in Item 3, I intend to. . .

_____

_____

_____

Developing EMOTIONAL INTELLIGENCE

In his book *Working with Emotional Intelligence*, Daniel Goleman defines emotional intelligence as a cluster of traits:

- *Self-awareness*—recognizing your full range of emotions and knowing your strengths and limitations.
- *Self-regulation*—responding skillfully to strong emotions, practicing honesty and integrity, and staying open to new ideas.
- *Motivation*—persisting to achieve goals and meet standards of excellence.
- *Empathy*—sensing other people's emotions and taking an active interest in their concerns.
- *Skill in relationships*—listening fully, speaking persuasively, resolving conflict, and leading people through times of change.

Goleman concludes that "IQ washes out when it comes to predicting who among a talented pool of candidates *within* an intellectually demanding profession will become the strongest leader." At that point, emotional intelligence starts to become more important.[6]

If you're emotionally intelligent, you're probably described as someone with good "people skills." You're aware of your feelings. You act in thoughtful ways, show concern for others, resolve conflict, and make responsible decisions.

Your emotional intelligence skills will serve you in school and in the workplace, especially when you collaborate on project teams. You can deepen your skills with the following strategies.

RECOGNIZE THREE ELEMENTS OF EMOTION

Even the strongest emotion consists of just three elements: physical sensations, thoughts, and action. Usually they happen so fast that you can barely distinguish them. Separating them out is a first step toward emotional intelligence.

Imagine that you suddenly perceive a threat—such as a supervisor who's screaming at you. Immediately your heart starts beating in double-time and your stomach muscles clench (physical sensations). Then thoughts race through your head: *This is a disaster. She hates me. And everyone's watching.* Finally, you take action, which could mean staring at her, yelling back, or running away.

NAME YOUR EMOTIONS

Naming your emotions is a first step to going beyond the "fight or flight" reaction to any emotion. Naming gives you power. The second that you attach a word to an emotion, you start to gain perspective. People with emotional intelligence have a rich vocabulary to describe a wide range of emotions. For example, do an Internet search with the key words *feeling list*. Read through the lists you find for examples of ways that you can name your feelings in the future.

ACCEPT YOUR EMOTIONS

Another step toward emotional intelligence is accepting your emotions—*all* of them. This can be challenging if you've been taught that some emotions are "good," whereas others are "bad." Experiment with another viewpoint: You do not choose your emotional reactions. However, you can choose what you *do* in response to any emotion.

EXPRESS YOUR EMOTIONS

One possible response to any emotion is expressing it. The key is to speak without blaming others for the way you feel. The basic tool for doing so is using "I" messages, as described on page 242.

RESPOND RATHER THAN REACT

The heart of emotional intelligence is moving from mindless reaction to mindful action. See whether you can introduce an intentional gap between sensations and thoughts on the one hand and your next action on the other hand. To do this more often:

- *Run a "mood meter."* Check in with your moods several times each day. On a 3 × 5 card, note the time of day and your emotional state at that point. Rate your mood on a scale of 1 (relaxed and positive) to 10 (very angry, very sad, or very afraid).
- *Write Discovery Statements.* In your journal, write about situations in daily life that trigger strong emotions. Describe these events—and your usual responses to them—in detail.
- *Write Intention Statements.* After seeing patterns in your emotions, you can consciously choose to behave in new ways. Instead of yelling back at the angry supervisor, for example, make it your intention to simply remain silent and breathe deeply until he finishes. Then say, "I'll wait to respond until we've both had a chance to cool down."

MAKE DECISIONS WITH EMOTIONAL INTELLIGENCE

When considering a possible choice, ask yourself, "How am I likely to feel if I do this?" You can use "gut feelings" to tell when an action might violate your values or hurt someone.

Think of emotions as energy. Anger, sadness, and fear send currents of sensation through your whole body. Ask yourself how you can channel that energy into constructive action. ■

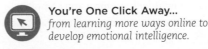

You're One Click Away...
from learning more ways online to develop emotional intelligence.

8

Collaborating
for success

In the classroom and in the workplace, projects get done by people who collaborate on teams. Yet not all teams are created equal. Some produce long-term, positive change. Other teams produce bland reports that make a direct trip to the recycling bin. Use the following strategies to create collaborations that make a difference.

DRAW LESSONS FROM THE PAST

During your team's first meeting, set aside time to talk about everyone's past experience with teams. Share your best and worst experiences. Based on this discussion, create your own list of what makes a successful team. Then make some basic agreements about ways to prevent the problems you've experienced with teams in the past.

APPLY THE CYCLE OF LEARNING TO TEAMS

Your team is likely to include people with a variety of learning styles. Turn this diversity into a source of strength. Let teams members choose tasks based on their preferences.

Chapter 1 of this book explains David Kolb's theory—that people learn from experience by cycling through four kinds of activity. Teams learn in a similar way. Encourage members to:

- Get fully involved with the team and actively commit to its purpose (feeling).
- Think critically about which agreements and actions will achieve the team's purpose (thinking).
- Listen carefully to what other team members say and stay open to new ideas (watching).
- Make clear decisions and take prompt action (doing).

SHARE ROLES

Teams often begin by choosing a leader with a vision, charisma, and expertise. As your team matures, however, consider letting other members take turns in a leadership role. This is one way to encourage a diversity of viewpoints and help people expand their learning styles.

EVEN OUT THE WORKLOAD

One potential trap for teams is that one person ends up doing most of the work. This person might feel resentful and complain. If you find yourself in this situation, transform your complaint into a request. Instead of scolding team members for being lazy, request help. Ask team members to take over tasks that you've been doing. Delegate specific jobs.

ENCOURAGE NEW IDEAS

Sometimes creative thinking dies in committee. Team members stop asking questions. People feel afraid to disagree with a forceful leader. They keep their mouths shut. Longstanding teams ignore new members with new ideas. To prevent these outcomes:

- *Put your opinions on hold.* If you're leading a meeting, pose a question and ask other people to contribute answers. Then look for the potential value in *any* idea. Avoid nonverbal language that signals a negative reaction, such as frowning or rolling your eyes.
- *Divide larger groups into several teams.* People might be more willing to ask questions and volunteer answers in a smaller group.
- *Assign a "devil's advocate."* Give one person free permission to ask tough questions and poke holes in any proposal.
- *Invite a guest expert.* A fresh perspective from someone outside the group can stimulate fresh questions and spark insights.
- *Set up a suggestion box.* Let team members submit questions and ideas anonymously, in writing.

ASK THESE QUESTIONS EVERY TIME THAT YOUR TEAM MEETS

Two questions, recommended by David Allen in his *Productive Living* newsletter, lead to team meetings that actually produce results.[7]

First: "What's the successful outcome?" If no one on your team can visualize a successful outcome for a meeting, then save everybody some frustration. Ask that the meeting be postponed until your team can create a clear agenda.

Second: "What's the next action to make it happen?" Too many meetings end with no clear agreement about the next actions to be taken, who will take them, and by what date. To get clarity and accountability, ask each team member to state what he or she will do before the next meeting. ■

You're One Click Away...
from finding more strategies online for constructive collaboration.

MANAGING CONFLICT

Conflict management is one of the most practical skills you'll ever learn. Here are strategies that can help.

The first five strategies discussed are about dealing with the *content* of a conflict—defining the problem, exploring viewpoints, and discovering solutions. The remaining strategies are about finding a *process* for resolving any conflict, no matter what the content.

To bring these strategies to life, think of ways to use them in managing a conflict that you face right now.

FOCUS ON CONTENT

Back up to common ground. Conflict heightens the differences between people. When this happens, it's easy to forget how much we still agree with each other.

As a first step in managing conflict, back up to common ground. List all of the points on which you are *not* in conflict: "I know that we disagree about how much to spend on a new car, but we do agree that the old one needs to be replaced." Often, such comments put the problem in perspective and pave the way for a solution.

State the problem. Using "I" messages, as explained earlier in this chapter, state the problem. Tell people what you observe, feel, think, want, and intend to do. Allow the other people in a particular conflict to do the same.

Each person might have a different perception of the problem. That's fine. Let the conflict come into clear focus. It's hard to fix something unless people agree on what's broken.

Remember that the way you state the problem largely determines the solution. Defining the problem in a new way can open up a world of possibilities. For example, "I need a new roommate" is a problem statement that dictates one solution. "We could use some agreements about who cleans the apartment" opens up more options, such as resolving a conflict about who will wash the dishes tonight.

State all points of view. If you want to defuse tension or defensiveness, set aside your opinions for a moment. Take the time to understand the other points of view. Sum up those viewpoints in words that the other parties can accept. When people feel that they've been heard, they're often more willing to listen.

Ask for complete communication. In times of conflict, we often say one thing and mean another. So before responding to what the other person says, use active listening. Check to see whether you have correctly received that person's message by saying, "What I'm hearing you say is. . . . Did I get it correctly?"

Focus on solutions. After stating the problem, dream up as many solutions as you can. Be outrageous. Don't hold back. Quantity—not quality—is the key. If you get stuck, restate the problem and continue brainstorming.

Next, evaluate the solutions you brainstormed. Discard the unacceptable ones. Talk about which solutions will work and how difficult they will be to implement. You might hit upon a totally new solution.

Choose one solution that is most acceptable to everyone involved, and implement it. Agree on who is going to do what by when. Then keep your agreements.

Finally, evaluate the effectiveness of your solution. If it works, pat yourselves on the back. If not, make changes or implement a new solution.

Focus on the future. Instead of rehashing the past, talk about new possibilities. Think about what you can do to prevent problems in the future. State how you intend to change, and ask others for their contributions to the solution.

FOCUS ON PROCESS

Commit to the relationship. The thorniest conflicts usually arise between people who genuinely care for each other. Begin by affirming your commitment to the other person: "I care about you, and I want this relationship to last. So I'm willing to do whatever it

8

takes to resolve this problem." Also ask the other person for a similar commitment.

Allow strong feelings. Permitting conflict can also mean permitting emotion. Being upset is all right. Feeling angry is often appropriate. Crying is okay. Allowing other people to see the strength of our feelings can help resolve the conflict. This suggestion can be especially useful during times when differences are so extreme that reaching common ground seems impossible.

Expressing the full range of your feelings can transform the conflict. Often what's on the far side of anger is love. When we express and release resentment, we might discover genuine compassion in its place.

Notice your need to be "right." Some people approach conflict as a situation where only one person wins. That person has the "right" point of view. Everyone else loses.

When this happens, step back. See whether you can approach the situation in a neutral way. Define the conflict as a problem to be solved, not as a contest to be won. Explore the possibility that you might be mistaken. There might be more than one acceptable solution. The other person might simply have a different learning style than yours. Let go of being "right," and aim for being effective at resolving conflict instead.

Sometimes this means apologizing. Conflict sometimes arises from our own errors. Others might move quickly to end the conflict when we acknowledge this fact and ask for forgiveness.

Slow down the communication. In times of great conflict, people often talk all at once. Words fly like speeding bullets, and no one listens. Chances for resolving the conflict take a nosedive.

When everyone is talking at once, choose either to listen or to talk—not both at the same time. Just send your message. Or just receive the other person's message. Usually, this technique slows down the pace and allows everyone to become more levelheaded.

To slow down the communication even more, take a break. Depending on the level of conflict, this might mean anything from a few minutes to a few days.

A related suggestion is to do something nonthreatening together. Share an activity with the others involved that's not a source of conflict.

Pete Saloutos/Shutterstock.com

Communicate in writing. What can be difficult to say to another person face-to-face might be effectively communicated in writing. When people in conflict write letters or e-mails to each other, they automatically apply many of the suggestions in this article. Writing is a way to slow down the communication and ensure that only one person at a time is sending a message.

There is a drawback to this tactic, though: It's possible for people to misunderstand what you say in a letter or e-mail. To avoid further problems, make clear what you are *not* saying: "I am saying that I want to be alone for a few days. I am *not* saying that I want you to stay away forever." Saying what you are *not* saying is often useful in face-to-face communication as well.

Before you send your letter or e-mail, put yourself in the shoes of the person who will receive it. Imagine how your comments could be misinterpreted. Then rewrite your note, correcting any wording that might be open to misinterpretation.

Resolve conflicts with
roommates

People who live together share a delicate bond. Relationships with even best friends or closest relatives can quickly deteriorate over disagreements about who pays the bills or washes the dishes.

You can prevent conflicts with roommates by negotiating agreements now. For example, adopt a policy about borrowing. Loaning your roommate a book or a tennis racket might seem like a small thing. Yet these small loans can become a sore point in a relationship. Some people have difficulty saying no and resent lending things. If so, keep borrowing to a minimum.

Meet with your roommates to discuss the following:

- What you will do about sharing belongings such as computers, audio and video equipment, food, or clothing
- How you will create a study environment at home
- How you will split household costs and make sure that bills get paid on time
- How you will resolve conflicts when someone thinks that a roommate is not keeping your agreements

Expand this list to include other issues that matter to you. For maximum clarity, put your agreements in writing.

There's another way to get the problem off your chest, especially when strong, negative feelings are involved: Write the nastiest, meanest e-mail response you can imagine, leaving off the address of the recipient so you don't accidentally send it. Let all of your frustration, anger, and venom flow onto the page. Be as mean and blaming as possible. When you have cooled off, see whether there is anything else you want to add.

Then destroy the letter or delete the e-mail. Your writing has served its purpose. Chances are that you've calmed down and are ready to engage in skillful conflict management.

Get an objective viewpoint. With the agreement of everyone involved, set up a video camera, and record a conversation about the conflict. In the midst of a raging argument, when emotions run high, it's almost impossible to see ourselves objectively. Let the camera be your unbiased observer. Another way to get an objective viewpoint is to use a mediator—an objective, unbiased third party. Even an untrained mediator—as long as it's someone who is not a party to the conflict—can do much to decrease tension. Mediators can help everyone get their point of view across. The mediator's role is not to give advice, but to keep the discussion on track and moving toward a solution.

Allow for cultural differences. People respond to conflict in different ways, depending on their cultural background. Some stand close, speak loudly, and make direct eye contact. Other people avert their eyes, mute their voices, and increase physical distance.

When it seems to you that other people are sidestepping or escalating a conflict, consider whether your reaction is based on cultural bias.

Agree to disagree. Sometimes we say all we have to say on an issue. We do all of the problem solving we can do. We get all points of view across. And the conflict still remains, staring us right in the face.

What's left is to recognize that honest disagreement is a fact of life. We can peacefully coexist with other people—and respect them—even though we don't agree on fundamental issues. Conflict can be accepted even when it is not resolved.

See the conflict within you. Sometimes the turmoil we see in the outside world has its source in our own inner world. A cofounder of Alcoholics Anonymous put it this way: "It is a spiritual axiom that every time we are disturbed, no matter what the cause, there is something awry with us."

When we're angry or upset, we can take a minute to look inside. Perhaps we are ready to take offense—waiting to pounce on something the other person said. Perhaps, without realizing it, we did something to create the conflict. Or maybe the other person is simply saying what we don't want to admit is true.

When these things happen, we can shine a light on our own thinking. A simple spot-check might help the conflict disappear—right before our eyes. ■

You're One Click Away...
from discovering more ways online to manage conflict.

© 2013 Cengage Learning. All Rights Reserved. May not be scanned, copied or duplicated, or posted to a publicly accessible website, in whole or in part.

JOURNAL ENTRY 20
Discovery/Intention Statement

Recreate a relationship

Think about one of your relationships for a few minutes. It can involve a parent, sibling, spouse, child, friend, hairdresser, or anyone else. In the space below, write down some things that are not working in the relationship. What bugs you? What do you find irritating or unsatisfying?

I discovered that . . .

_____

_____

_____

_____

_____

_____

_____

Now think for a moment about what you want from this relationship. More attention? Less nagging? More openness, trust, financial security, or freedom? Choose a suggestion from this chapter, and describe how you could use it to make the relationship work.

I intend to . . .

_____

_____

_____

_____

_____

_____

_____

_____

8

Becoming a Master Student **249**

Five ways to say no . . .
RESPECTFULLY

All your study plans can go down the drain when a friend says, "Time to party!" Sometimes, succeeding in school means replying with a graceful and firm no.

Students in higher education tend to have many commitments. Saying no helps you to prevent an overloaded schedule that compromises your health and grade point average. You can use five strategies to say no in a respectful way—gracefully.

Think critically about your assumptions. An inability to say no can spring from the assumption that you'll lose friends if you state what you really want. But consider this: If you cannot say no, then you are not in charge of your time. You've given that right to whoever wants to interrupt you. This is not a friendship based on equality. True friends will respect your wishes.

Plan your refusal. You might find it easier to say no when you don't have to grasp for words. Choose some key words and phrases in advance—for example, "I'd love to, but not today"; "Thanks for asking. I have a huge test tomorrow and want to study"; or "I'd prefer not to do anything tonight; do you want to grab lunch tomorrow instead?"

When you refuse, align your verbal and nonverbal messages. Reinforce your words with a firm voice and a posture that communicates confidence.

Avoid apologies or qualifiers. People give away their power when they couch their no's in phrases such as "I'm sorry, but I just don't know whether I want to" or "Would you get upset if I said no?"

You don't have to apologize for being in charge of your life. It's okay to say no.

Wait for the request. People who worry about saying no often give in to a request before it's actually been made. Wait until you

Masterfile (Royalty-Free Div.)

hear a question. "Time to party!" is not a question. Nor is it a call to action. Save your response until you hear a specific request, such as "Would you go to a party with me?"

Remember that one *no* leads to another *yes*. *Yes* and *no* are complementary, not contradictory. Saying no to one activity allows you to say yes to something that's more important right now. Saying no to a movie allows you to say yes to outlining a paper or reading a textbook chapter. You can say an unqualified yes to the next social activity—and enjoy it more—after you've completed some key tasks on your to-do list. ■

You're One Click Away...
from discovering more online about the power of saying no.

You deserve compliments

Some people find it more difficult to accept compliments than criticisms. Here are some hints for handling compliments.

Accept the compliment. People sometimes respond to praise with "Oh, it's really nothing" or "This old thing? I've had it for years." This type of response undermines both you and the person who sent the compliment.

Choose another time to deliver your own compliments. Automatically returning a compliment can appear suspiciously polite and insincere.

Let the compliment stand. "Do you really think so?" questions the integrity of the message. It can also sound as if you're fishing for more compliments.

Accepting compliments is not the same as being conceited. If you're in doubt about how to respond, just smile and say, "Thank you!" This simple response affirms the compliment, along with the person who delivered it.

You are worthy and capable. Allow people to acknowledge that fact.

✓ EXERCISE 24

VIPs (Very Important Persons)

STEP 1 Under the column below titled "Name," write the names of at least seven people who have positively influenced your life. They might be relatives, friends, teachers, or perhaps persons you have never met. (Complete each step before moving on.)

STEP 2 In the next column, rate your gratitude for this person's influence (from 1 to 5, with 1 being a little grateful and 5 being extremely grateful).

STEP 3 In the third column, rate how fully you have communicated your appreciation to this person (again, 1 to 5, with 1 being not communicated and 5 being fully communicated).

STEP 4 In the final column, put a "U" to indicate the persons with whom you have unfinished business (such as an important communication that you have not yet sent).

	Name	Grateful (1–5)	Communicated (1–5)	U
1.				
2.				
3.				
4.				
5.				
6.				
7.				

STEP 5 Now select two persons with "U's" beside their names, and write each of them a letter. Express the love, tenderness, and joy you feel toward them. Tell them exactly how they have helped change your life and how glad you are that they did.

STEP 6 You also have an impact on others. Write below the names of people whose lives you have influenced. Consider sharing with these people why you enjoy being a part of their lives.

_____

_____

_____

_____

_____

_____

_____

_____

_____

_____

_____

_____

_____

8

Five steps to effective complaints

Sometimes relationship building means making a complaint. Whining, blaming, pouting, screaming, and yelling insults usually don't get results. Consider the following suggestions instead.

1 Go to the source. Start with the person who is most directly involved with the problem. When you're in school, that person is usually an instructor. Give this person the first chance to resolve an issue. Instructors usually appreciate feedback, and they can't always read a student's mind to know when a problem occurs.

2 Present the facts without blaming anyone. Consider how it might feel to receive complaints like these: "I put a lot of work into this project, but you gave me a 'C.'" "Your class is boring." "I just can't trust you."

Your complaint will carry more weight if you document the facts instead. Keep track of names and dates. Note what actions were promised and what results actually occurred.

3 Learn about other options. Schools have policies and procedures related to student complaints. Look for them in your school's catalog and Web site. Student government is also a potential resource.

At many schools you can talk to a student or staff ombudsman—someone who is trained to help resolve conflicts between students and instructors.

4 Ask for commitments. When you find someone who is willing to solve your problem, get him to say exactly what he is going to do, and when.

5 Persist. Assume that others are on your team. Many people are out there to help you. State what you intend to do, and ask for their partnership. ■

© Photodisc/Fotosearch

Criticism is constructive

Although receiving criticism is rarely fun, it is often educational. Here are some ways to get the most value from it.

Avoid finding fault. When your mind is occupied with finding fault in others, you aren't open to hearing constructive comments about yourself.

Take criticism seriously. Some people laugh or joke to cover up their anger or embarrassment at being criticized. A humorous reaction on your part can be mistaken for a lack of concern.

React to criticism with acceptance. Most people don't enjoy pointing out another's faults. Your denial, argument, or joking makes it more difficult for them to give honest feedback. You can disagree with criticism and still accept it calmly.

Keep criticism in perspective. Avoid blowing the criticism out of proportion. The purpose of criticism is to generate positive change and self-improvement. There's no need to overreact to it.

Listen without defensiveness. You can't hear the criticism if you're busy framing your rebuttal.

Mastering

social NETWORKS

Social networks create value. Web sites such as Facebook and LinkedIn are known as places to share news, photos, and personal profiles. You can also use such sites to form study groups, promote special events, and make job contacts. Microblogging services such as Twitter allow hour-by-hour and even minute-to-minute contact.

Activity in online communities can also have unexpected consequences. For some students, social networking takes time away from studying and other activities that connect to long-term goals. Other people get involved in "cyberbullying"—hate speech or threats of violence. And, some people find that embarrassing details from their online profiles come back to haunt them years later.

You can use simple strategies to stay in charge of your safety, reputation, and integrity any time you connect with people online.

Post only what you want made public and permanent. The Internet as a whole is a public medium. This is true of its online communities as well. Post only the kind of information about yourself that you *want* to be made public.

Friends, relatives, university administrators, potential employers, and police officers might be able to access your online profile. Don't post anything that could embarrass you later. Act today to protect the person that you want to be 4 or 5 years from now.

Remember that there is no delete key for the Internet. Web sites such as the Internet Archive and its "Wayback Machine" almost guarantee that anything you post online will stay online for a long time. Anyone with Internet access can take your words and images and post them on a Web site or distribute them via e-mail to damage your reputation. In the virtual world, you never know who's following you.

. . . .

Don't post anything that could embarrass you later. Act today to protect the person that you want to be 4 or 5 years from now.

. . . .

To avoid unwanted encounters with members of online communities, also avoid posting the following:

- Your home address
- Your school address
- Your phone number
- Your birth date
- Your screen name for instant messaging
- Your class schedule
- Your financial information, such as bank account numbers, credit card numbers, your social security number, or information about an eBay or PayPal account
- Information about places that you regularly go at certain times of the day
- Information about places you plan to visit in the future
- Provocative pictures or messages with sexual innuendos
- Pictures of yourself at school or at work
- Plans for vacation or out-of-town visits

To further protect your safety, don't add strangers to your list of online friends.

Use similar caution and common sense when joining groups. Signing up for a group with a name like *Binge Drinking Forever* can have consequences for years to come.

Be honest. After you've chosen what information to post, make sure that it's accurate. False information can lead to expulsion from a community. For example, MySpace administrators delete profiles of people who lie about their age.[8]

Also avoid flirting while you're online. People may not be who they say they are.

Use privacy features. Many online communities offer options for blocking messages from strangers, including instant messages and friendship invitations. Several social networking sites allow you to create both private and public profiles. (Look for a link on each site titled "Frequently Asked Questions," "Security Features," "Account Settings," or "Privacy Settings.") For further protection, review and update your list of contacts on a regular basis. In addition, respect the privacy of other members.

"Friend" people with care. You do not have to accept every friend request or "follow" every person who chooses to follow you. Remember that many instructors will not connect with students in social networks, and some schools have policies to discourage this. Networks

8

such as Facebook are by definition social Web sites. The relationship between students and instructors is professional—not social.

Be cautious about meeting community members in person. Because people can give misleading or false information about themselves online, avoid meeting them in person. If you do opt for a face-to-face meeting, choose a public place and bring along a friend you trust.

Report malicious content. If you find online content that you consider offensive or dangerous, report it to site administrators. In many online communities, you can do this anonymously. You can help to prevent online forms of intolerance, prejudice, and discrimination. Set a positive counterexample by posting messages that demonstrate acceptance of diversity.

Remember netiquette. The word *etiquette* refers to common courtesy in interpersonal relationships. Its online equivalent is called *netiquette*—a set of guidelines for using computers, cell phones, or any other form of technology.

Certain kinds of exchanges can send the tone of online communications—including social networking, e-mail messages, and blog postings—into the gutter. To promote a cordial online community, abide by the following guidelines:

- Respect others' time. People often turn to the Internet with the hope of saving time—not wasting it. You can accommodate their desires by typing concise messages. Adopt the habit of getting to your point, sticking to it, and getting to the end.

- Fine-tune the mechanics. Proofread your message for spelling and grammar—just as you would a printed message. Some e-mail programs have built-in spelling checkers as an optional tool. Give your readers the gift of clarity and precision. Use electronic communications as a chance to hone your writing skills.

- Avoid typing passages in ALL UPPERCASE LETTERS. This is the online equivalent of shouting.

- Design your messages for fast retrieval. Avoid graphics and attachments that take a long time to download, tying up your recipient's computer.

- Remember that the message is missing the emotion. When you communicate online, the people who receive your e-mail will miss out on voice inflection and nonverbal cues that are present in face-to-face communication. Without these cues, words can be easily misinterpreted. Reread your message before sending it to be sure you have clarified what you want to say and how you feel.

The cornerstone of netiquette is to remember that the recipient on the other end is a human being. Whenever you're at a keyboard or cell phone typing up messages, ask yourself one question: "Would I say this to the person's face?"

Use social networks to learn. Learning naturally occurs in social networks—that is, among groups of teachers and students.

With technology, you can extend your network across the reach of the Internet. For example:

- Choose a topic that interests you, and search for related Web sites and podcasts.

- Use an RSS reader such as Google Reader or NetNewsWire to get updated lists of articles on the Web sites you'd like to follow.

- Search Twitter, Facebook, and other social networking sites to see whether you can connect with the authors of those articles.

- Use direct messages and e-mail to connect with those authors.

- Use videoconferencing Web sites to converse in real time with people across the world.

- Pay special attention to well-written blogs, and join the discussion by commenting on the postings.

- Create your own blog to document your learning, and welcome comments from others. ▪

You're One Click Away...
from learning more online about smart social networking.

Text message etiquette— five key points

1. **Keep it short.** Limit text messages to about 150 characters. That's two to three sentences. If you go longer, your phone might split the message in two or even drop the last few words. In addition, long texts can be confusing. Send an e-mail or make a phone call instead.

2. **Double-check the outgoing number.** If a message intended for your boyfriend or girlfriend ends up going to your boss, the results can be alarming.

3. **At work and in other public places, set your phone on vibrate.** No one else wants to hear how many text messages you're getting.

4. **Keep the time in mind.** Save 2:00 a.m. text messages for special circumstances and your closest friends. A text can ring at the same volume as a phone call and wake people up.

5. **Reflect on the number of messages you send to each person.** Replacing in-person and phone contact with texting might send a message that the relationship is a low priority.

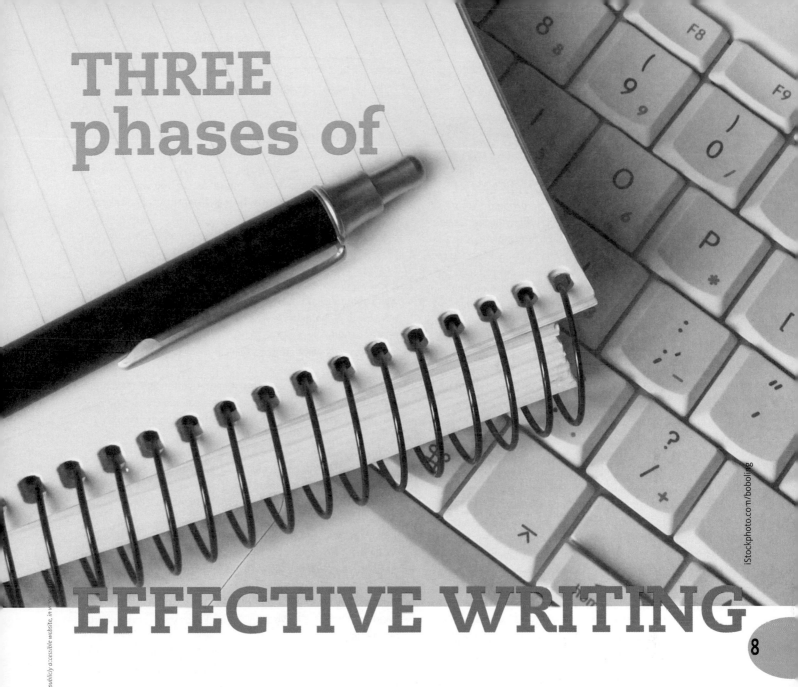

THREE phases of EFFECTIVE WRITING

8

Effective writing is essential to your success. Papers, presentations, essay tests, e-mail, social networking sites—and even the occasional text message—call for your ability to communicate ideas with force and clarity.

iStockphoto.com/boboling

This chapter outlines a three-phase process for writing anything:

1. Getting ready to write
2. Writing a first draft
3. Revising your draft

PHASE 1: GETTING READY TO WRITE

Schedule and list writing tasks. You can divide the ultimate goal—a finished paper—into smaller steps that you can tackle right away. Estimate how long it will take to complete each step. Start with the date your paper is due and work backward to the present. Say that the due date is December 1, and you have about 3 months to write the paper. To give yourself a cushion, schedule November 20 as your targeted completion date. Plan what you want to get done by November 1, and then list what you want to get done by October 1.

Choose a topic. It's easy to put off writing if you have a hard time choosing a topic. However, it is almost impossible to make a wrong choice of topic at this stage. You can choose a different topic later if you find the one you've chosen isn't working out.

Using your instructor's guidelines for the paper or speech, write down the list of possible topics that you created earlier. Then choose one. If you can't decide, use scissors to cut your list into single items, put them in a box, and pull one out. To avoid getting stuck on this step, set a precise time line: "I will choose a topic by 4:00 p.m. on Wednesday."

There's no need to brainstorm topics in isolation. You can harness the energy and the natural creative power of a group to assist you in creating topics for your paper. For ideas about ways to brainstorm, see Chapter 7: Thinking.

Narrow your topic. The most common pitfall is selecting a topic that's too broad. "Harriet Tubman" is not a useful topic for your American history paper because it's too broad. Covering that topic would take hundreds of pages. Instead, consider "Harriet Tubman's activities as a Union spy during the Civil War." Your topic statement can function as a working title.

Write a thesis statement. Clarify what you want to say by summarizing it in one concise sentence. This sentence, called a *thesis statement,* refines your working title. It also helps in making a preliminary outline.

You might write a thesis statement such as "Harriet Tubman's activities with the Underground Railroad led to a relationship with the Union army during the Civil War." A thesis statement that's clear and to the point can make your paper easier to write. Remember, you can always rewrite your thesis statement as you learn more about your topic.

A thesis statement is different from a topic. Like newspaper headlines, a thesis statement makes an assertion or describes an action. It is expressed in a complete sentence, including a verb. "Diversity" is a topic. "Cultural diversity is valuable" is a thesis statement.

Consider your purpose. Effective writing flows from a purpose. Discuss the purpose of your assignment with your instructor. Also think about how you'd like your reader or listener to respond after considering your ideas. Do you want your audience to think differently, to feel differently, or to take a certain action?

How you answer these questions greatly affects your writing strategy. If you want someone to think differently, make your writing clear and logical. Support your assertions with evidence. If you want someone to feel differently, consider crafting a story. Write about a character your audience can empathize with, and tell how that character resolves a problem that the audience can relate to. And if your purpose is to move the reader into action, explain exactly what steps to take, and offer solid benefits for doing so.

To clarify your purpose, state it in one sentence. For example, "I will define the term *success* in such a clear and convincing way that I win a scholarship from the publisher of this textbook."

Do initial research. At the initial stage, the objective of your research is not to uncover specific facts about your topic. That comes later. First, you want to gain an overview of the subject. Discover the structure of your topic—its major divisions and branches.

Say that you want to persuade the reader to vote for a certain candidate. You must first learn enough about this person to summarize his background and state his stands on key issues.

Outline. An outline is a kind of map. When you follow a map, you avoid getting lost. Likewise, an outline keeps you from wandering off the topic.

To start an outline, gather a stack of 3 × 5 cards. Brainstorm ideas you want to include in your paper. Write one phrase or sentence per card. Then experiment with the cards. Group them into separate stacks, each stack representing one major category. After that, arrange the stacks in order. Finally, arrange the cards within each stack in a logical order. Rearrange them until you discover an organization that you like. If you write on a computer, consider using the outlining feature of your word-processing software.

Do in-depth research. You can find information about research skills in Chapter 4: Reading and Chapter 5: Notes. The following are further suggestions.

Use 3 × 5 cards. If they haven't found their way into your life by now, joy awaits you. These cards work wonders when you conduct research. Just write down one idea per card. This makes it easy to organize—and reorganize—your ideas.

Organizing research cards as you create them saves time. Use rubber bands to keep source cards—cards that include the bibliographical information for a source—separate from information cards—cards that include nuggets of information from a source—and to maintain general categories.

You can also save time in two other ways. First, copy all of the information correctly. Always include the source code and page number on information cards. Second, be neat and organized. Write legibly, using the same format for all of your cards.

In addition to source cards and information cards, generate idea cards. If you have a thought while you are researching, write it down on a card. Label these cards clearly as containing your own ideas.

An alternative to 3 × 5 cards is a computer outlining or database program. Some word-processing packages also include features that can be used for outlining and note taking.

☐ Avoid ~~at all costs and at all times~~ the ~~really, really~~ terrible mistake of using ~~way too many~~ unnecessary words, ~~a mistake that some student writers often make when they sit down to write papers for the various courses in which they participate at the fine institutions of higher learning which they are fortunate to attend.~~

Many writers prefer to get their first draft down quickly. Their advice is just to keep writing. Of course, you may pause occasionally to glance at your notes and outline. The idea is to avoid stopping to edit your work. You can save that for the next step.

Speak it. To get ideas flowing, start talking. Admit your confusion or lack of clear ideas. Then just speak. By putting your thoughts into words, you'll start thinking more clearly. Novelist E. M. Forster said, "'Speak before you think' is creation's motto."[9]

Use free writing. Free writing, a technique championed by writing teacher Peter Elbow, sends a depth probe into your creative mind.[10] There's only one rule in free writing: Write without stopping. Set a time limit—say, 10 minutes—and keep your pencil in motion or your fingers dancing across the keyboard the whole time. Give yourself permission to keep writing. Ignore the urge to stop and rewrite, even if you think what you've written isn't very good. There's no need to worry about spelling, punctuation, or grammar. It's okay if you stray from the initial subject. Just keep writing, and let the ideas flow. Experiment with free writing as soon as your instructor assigns a paper.

PHASE 2: WRITING A FIRST DRAFT

Gather your notes and outline. If you've planned your writing project and completed your research, you've already done much of the hard work. Now you can relax into writing your first draft. To create your draft, gather your notes and arrange them to follow your outline. Then write about the ideas in your notes. Write in paragraphs, with one idea per paragraph. If you have organized your notes logically, related facts will appear close to one another.

Ease into it. Some people find that it works well to forget the word *writing*. Instead, they ease into the task with activities that help generate ideas. You can free associate, cluster, meditate, daydream, doodle, draw diagrams, visualize the event you want to describe, talk into a voice recorder—anything that gets you started.

Remember that the first draft is not for keeps. You can worry about quality later, when you revise. Your goal at this point is simply to generate lots of material.

Make writing a habit. The word *inspiration* is not in the working vocabulary for many professional writers. Instead of waiting for inspiration to strike, they simply make a habit of writing at a certain time each day. You can use the same strategy. Schedule a block of time to write your first draft. The very act of writing can breed inspiration.

Respect your deep mind. Part of the process of writing takes place outside our awareness. There's nothing mysterious about this process. Many people report that ideas come to them while they're doing something totally unrelated to writing. Often this happens after they've been grappling with a question and have reached a point where they feel stuck. It's like the composer who said, "There I was, sitting and eating a sandwich, and all of a sudden this darn tune pops into my head." You can trust your deep mind. It's writing while you eat, sleep, and brush your teeth.

8

Get physical. Writing, like jogging or playing tennis, is a physical activity. You can move your body in ways that are in tune with the flow of your ideas. While working on the first draft, take breaks. Go for a walk. Speak or sing your ideas out loud. From time to time, practice relaxation techniques and breathe deeply.

PHASE 3: REVISING YOUR DRAFT

Plan to revise a paper two or three times. Make a clean copy of each revision, and then let the last revised draft sit for at least 3 or 4 days.

Schedule time for rewrites before you begin, and schedule at least 1 day between revisions so that you can let the material sit. On Tuesday night, you might think your writing sings the song of beautiful language. On Wednesday, you will see that those same words, such as the phrase "sings the song of beautiful language," belong in the trash basket.

Keep in mind the saying "Write in haste; revise at leisure." When you edit and revise, slow down and take a microscope to your work. One guideline is to allow 50 percent of writing time for planning, researching, and writing the first draft. Then give the remaining 50 percent to revising.

While you're in the revising phase, consider making an appointment to see your instructor during office hours. Bring along a current draft of your paper. Be willing to share your thesis and outline. Ask for revision tips. If your school has a writing assistance center, see someone there as well.

One effective way to revise your paper is to read it out loud. The eyes tend to fill in the blanks in our own writing. The combination of voice and ears forces us to pay attention to the details.

Another technique is to ask other people to review your paper. If you do this in class, it's called peer editing. This is never a substitute for your own review, but other people can often see mistakes you miss. Remember, when other people criticize or review your work, they're not attacking you. They're just commenting on your paper. With a little practice, you can actually learn to welcome feedback.

When it's your turn to edit someone else's writing, remember two guidelines: First, be positive. Find something that you like about the paper and talk about that. Second, offer a specific suggestion. Begin this statement with words such as: "I think your paper would be even stronger if...."

After getting feedback on your draft, revise it while keeping the following suggestions in mind.

Cut. Look for excess baggage. Avoid at all costs and at all times the really, really terrible mistake of using way too many unnecessary words, a mistake that some student writers often make when they sit down to write papers for the various courses in which they participate at the fine institutions

> Approach your rough draft as if it were a chunk of granite from which you will chisel the final product. In the end, much of your first draft will be lying on the floor. What is left will be the clean, clear, polished product. Sometimes the revisions are painful.

of higher learning that they are fortunate enough to attend. (Example: The previous sentence could be edited to "Avoid unnecessary words.")

Approach your rough draft as if it were a chunk of granite from which you will chisel the final product. In the end, much of your first draft will be lying on the floor. What is left will be the clean, clear, polished product. Sometimes the revisions are painful. Sooner or later, every writer invents a phrase that is truly clever but makes no contribution to the purpose of the paper. Grit your teeth and let it go.

Note: For maximum efficiency, make the larger cuts first—sections, chapters, pages. Then go for the smaller cuts—paragraphs, sentences, phrases, words. Stay within the word limit that your instructor assigns.

Paste. In deleting both larger and smaller passages in your first draft, you've probably removed some of the original transitions and connecting ideas. The next task is to rearrange what's left of your paper or speech so that it flows logically. Look for consistency within paragraphs and for transitions from paragraph to paragraph and section to section.

If all or part of your draft doesn't hang together, reorder your ideas. Imagine yourself with scissors and glue, cutting the paper into scraps—one scrap for each point. Then paste these points down in a new, more logical order.

Fix. Now it's time to look at individual words and phrases. Define any terms that the reader might not know, putting them in plain English whenever you can. Scan your paper for any passages that are written in the language of texting or instant messaging. Rewrite those into full sentences.

In general, rely on vivid nouns and verbs. Using too many adjectives and adverbs weakens your message and adds unnecessary bulk to your writing. Write about the details, and be specific. Also, use the active rather than the passive voice.

> Instead of writing in the passive voice:
>> *A project was initiated.*
> You can use the active voice:
>> *The research team began a project.*

> Instead of writing verbosely:
>> *After making a timely arrival and perspicaciously observing the unfolding events, I emerged totally and gloriously victorious.*
> You can write to the point, as Julius Caesar did:
>> *I came, I saw, I conquered.*
> Instead of writing vaguely:
>> *The speaker made effective use of the television medium, asking in no uncertain terms that we change our belief systems.*
> You can write specifically:
>> *The reformed criminal stared straight into the television camera and shouted, "Take a good look at what you're doing! Will it get you what you really want?"*

Prepare. In a sense, any paper is a sales effort. If you hand in a paper that is wearing wrinkled jeans, its hair tangled and unwashed and its shoes untied, your instructor is less likely to buy it. To avoid this situation, format your paper following accepted standards for margin widths, endnotes, title pages, and other details.

Ask your instructor for specific instructions on how to cite the sources used in writing your paper. You can find useful guidelines in the *MLA Handbook for Writers of Research Papers,* a book from the Modern Language Association. Also visit the MLA Web site at www.mla.org/style.

If you cut and paste material from a Web page directly into your paper, be sure to place that material in quotation marks and cite the source. And before referencing an e-mail message, verify the sender's identity. Remember that anyone sending e-mail can pretend to be someone else.

Use quality paper for your final version. For an even more professional appearance, bind your paper with a plastic or paper cover.

> In a sense, any paper is a sales effort. If you hand in a paper that is wearing wrinkled jeans, its hair tangled and unwashed and its shoes untied, your instructor is less likely to buy it.

Proof. As you ease down the homestretch, read your revised paper one more time. This time, go for the big picture and look for the following:

- A clear thesis statement
- Sentences that introduce your topic, guide the reader through the major sections of your paper, and summarize your conclusions
- Details—such as quotations, examples, and statistics—that support your conclusions
- Lean sentences that have been purged of needless words
- Plenty of action verbs and concrete, specific nouns

Finally, look over your paper with an eye for spelling and grammar mistakes. If you're writing with software that checks for such errors, take advantage of this feature. Also keep in mind that even the best software will miss some mistakes. Computers still cannot replace a skilled human proofreader.

When you're through proofreading, take a minute to savor the result. You've just witnessed something of a miracle—the mind attaining clarity and resolution. That's the *aha!* in writing. ∎

 You're One Click Away...
from finding more paths online to effective writing.

8

ACADEMIC INTEGRITY:
Avoid plagiarism

Using another person's words, images, or other original creations without giving proper credit is called *plagiarism*. Plagiarism amounts to taking someone else's work and presenting it as your own—the equivalent of cheating on a test.

Higher education consists of a community of scholars who trust one another to speak and write with integrity. Plagiarism undermines this trust. The consequences of plagiarism can range from a failing grade to expulsion from school.

Plagiarism can be unintentional. Some students don't understand the research process. Sometimes they leave writing until the last minute and don't take the time to organize their sources of information. Also, some people are raised in cultures where identity is based on group membership rather than individual achievement. These students may find it hard to understand how an individual can own creative work. Remember, however, that even accidental plagiarism can lead to a lowered grade and other penalties.

To avoid plagiarism, ask an instructor where you can find your school's written policy on this issue. Read this document carefully, and ask questions about *anything* you don't understand.

> Higher education consists of a community of scholars who trust one another to speak and write with integrity. Plagiarism undermines this trust. The consequences of plagiarism can range from a failing grade to expulsion from school.

The basic guideline for preventing plagiarism is to cite a source for any fact or idea that is new to you. These include words and images created by another person. The overall goal is to clearly distinguish your own work from the work of others. A secondary goal is to give enough information about your sources so that they are easy to find. There are several ways to ensure that you meet both of these goals consistently.

Know the perils of "paper mills." A big part of the problem is misuse of the Internet. Anyone with a computer can access thousands of Web pages on a given topic. Images and text from those sources are easily copied and pasted into another document. Technology makes it easy to forget that some information is free for the taking—and some is privately owned.

Plagiarism is now a growth industry. A quick Web search will uncover hundreds of online business that sell term papers, essays, and book reports. These businesses are often called "paper mills." Some of them offer to customize their products for an additional fee. Even so, these services are based on plagiarism.

Students who use these services might answer, "When I buy a paper online, it's not plagiarism. I paid for those words, so now they're mine." But in fact, those words were still created by someone else. Plagiarism is more than merely copying words from another source: It's turning in thoughts and work that you did not produce.

Also remember that plagiarism includes turning in a paper—or portions of a paper—that you have already written for another class. If you want to draw on prior research, talk to your instructor first.

Identify direct quotes. If you use a direct quote from another writer or speaker, put that person's words in quotation marks. If you do research online, you might find yourself copying sentences or paragraphs from a Web page and pasting them directly into your notes. *This is the same as taking direct quotes from your source.* To avoid plagiarism, identify such passages in an obvious way. Besides enclosing them in quotation marks, you could format them in a different font or color to help you remember that these are quotes from other sources. Just remember to reverse the formatting before turning in your paper.

Paraphrase carefully. Instead of using a direct quote, you might choose to paraphrase an author's words. Paraphrasing means restating the original passage in your own words, usually making it shorter and simpler. Students who copy a passage word for word and then just rearrange or delete a few phrases are running a serious risk of plagiarism. Consider this paragraph:

Higher education also offers you the chance to learn how to learn. In fact, that's the subject of this book. Employers value the person who is a "quick study" when it comes to learning a new job. That makes your ability to learn a marketable skill.

Following is an improper paraphrase of that passage:

With higher education comes the chance to learn how to learn. Employers value the person who is a "quick study" when it comes to learning a new job. Your ability to learn is a marketable skill.

A better paraphrase of the same passage would be this one:

The author notes that when we learn how to learn, we gain a skill that is valued by employers.

Remember to cite a source for paraphrases, just as you do for direct quotes.

When you use the same sequence of ideas as one of your sources—even if you have not paraphrased or directly quoted—cite that source.

Summarize carefully. For some of your notes, you may simply want to summarize your source in a few sentences or paragraphs. To do this effectively:

- Read your source several times for understanding.
- Put your source away; then write a summary in your own words.
- In your summary, include only the author's major points.
- Check your summary against your source for accuracy.

Identify distinctive terms and phrases. Some ideas are closely identified with their individual creators. Students who present such ideas without mentioning the individual are plagiarizing. This is true even if they do not copy words, sentence structure, or overall organization of ideas.

For example, the phrase "seven habits of highly effective people" is closely linked to Stephen Covey, author of several books based on this idea. A student might write a paper titled "Habits of Effective People," using words, sentences, and a list of habits that differ completely from Covey's. However, the originality of this student's thinking could still be called into question. This student would be wise to directly mention Covey in the paper and acknowledge Covey's idea that effectiveness and habits are closely linked.

Note details about each source. Identify the source of any material that you quote, paraphrase, or summarize. For books, details about each source include the author, title, publisher, publication date, location of publisher, and page number. For articles from print sources, record the article title and the name of the magazine or journal as well. If you found the article in an academic or technical journal, also record the volume and number of the publication. A librarian can help identify these details.

If your source is a Web page, record as many identifying details as you can find—author, title, sponsoring organization, URL, publication date, and revision date. In addition, list the date that you accessed the page.

Cite your sources as endnotes or footnotes to your paper. Ask your instructor for examples of the format to use.

Submit only your own work. Turning in materials that have been written or revised by someone else puts your education at risk.

Allow time to digest your research. If you view research as a task that you can squeeze into a few hours, then you may end up more confused than enlightened. Instead, allow for time to reread and reflect on the facts you gather. This creates conditions for genuine understanding and original thinking.

In particular, take the time to do these things:

- Read over all your notes without feeling immediate pressure to write.
- Summarize major points of view on your topic, noting points of agreement and disagreement.
- Look for connections in your material—ideas, facts, and examples that occur in several sources.
- Note direct answers to your main and supporting research.
- Revise your thesis statement, based on discoveries from your research.
- Put all your notes away and write informally about what you want to say about your topic.
- Look for connections between your research and your life—ideas that you can verify based on personal experience. ■

You're One Click Away...
from finding examples online of the suggestions in this article.

8

> Some people tune out during a speech. Just think of all the times you have listened to instructors, lecturers, and politicians. Remember all the wonderful daydreams you had during their speeches.

James Steidl/Shutterstock.com

Mastering PUBLIC SPEAKING

Your audiences are like you. The way you plan and present your speech can determine the number of audience members who will stay with you until the end. Polishing your speaking and presentation skills can also help you think on your feet and communicate clearly. You can use these skills in any course and in any career you choose.

Creating a presentation is much like writing a paper. Divide the project into three phases:

1. Preparing your presentation
2. Delivering your presentation
3. Reflecting on your presentation

PHASE 1: PREPARING YOUR PRESENTATION

Start from your passions. If your instructor allows you to choose the topic of presentation, then choose one that you find interesting. Imagine that the first words in your presentation will be: "I'm here to talk to you because I feel passionately about...." How would you complete the sentence? Turn your answer into your main topic.

Consider a "process speech." In this type of presentation, your purpose is to explain a way to do or make something. Examples are changing a tire, planting asparagus, or preparing a healthy meal in 15 minutes. Choose a short, step-by-step process with a concrete outcome. This makes it easier to organize, practice, and deliver your first presentation.

In the introduction to your process speech, get the audience's attention and establish rapport. State the topic and purpose of your speech. Relate the topic to something that audience members care about. During the body of your speech, explain each step in the process, following a logical order. To conclude, quickly summarize the process and remind your audience of its usefulness.

Analyze your audience. Developing a speech is similar to writing a paper. Begin by writing out your topic, purpose, and thesis statement as described in "Phase 1: Getting ready to write" on page 255. Then carefully analyze your audience by using the strategies in the chart on page 263.

Remember that audiences want to know that your presentation relates to their needs and desires. To convince people that you have something worthwhile to say, think of your main topic or point. Then see whether you can complete this sentence: *I'm telling you this because....*

Organize your presentation. List three to five questions that your audience members are likely to ask about your topic. Put those questions in logical order. Organize your presentation so that it directly answers those questions.

Also consider the length of your presentation. As a general guideline, plan on delivering about a hundred words per minute. Remember that you could lose points if your presentation goes over the assigned time limit.

Aim for a lean presentation—enough words to make your point but not so many as to make your audience restless. Leave your listeners wanting more. When you speak, be brief and then be seated.

Speeches are usually organized in three main parts: the introduction, the main body, and the conclusion.

If your topic is new to listeners . . .	• Explain why your topic matters to them. • Relate the topic to something that listeners already know and care about. • Define any terms that listeners might not know.
If listeners already know about your topic . . .	• Acknowledge this fact at the beginning of your speech. • Find a narrow aspect of the topic that may be new to listeners. • Offer a new perspective on the topic, or connect it to an unfamiliar topic.
If listeners disagree with your thesis . . .	• Tactfully admit your differences of opinion. • Reinforce points on which you and your audience agree. • Build credibility by explaining your qualifications to speak on your topic. • Quote expert figures that agree with your thesis—people whom your audience is likely to admire. • Explain that their current viewpoint has costs for them, and that a slight adjustment in their thinking will bring significant benefits.
If listeners may be uninterested in your topic . . .	• Explain how listening to your speech can help them gain something that matters deeply to them. • Explain ways to apply your ideas in daily life.

Write the introduction. Rambling speeches with no clear point or organization put audiences to sleep. Solve this problem with your introduction. The following introduction, for example, reveals the thesis and exactly what's coming. It reveals that the speech will have three distinct parts, each in logical order:

Dog fighting is a cruel sport. I intend to describe exactly what happens to the animals, tell you who is doing this, and show you how you can stop this inhumane practice.

Whenever possible, talk about things that hold your interest. Include your personal experiences and start with a bang. Consider this introduction to a speech on the subject of world hunger:

I'm very honored to be here with you today. I intend to talk about malnutrition and starvation. First, I want to outline the extent of these problems, then I will discuss some basic assumptions concerning world hunger, and finally I will propose some solutions.

You can almost hear the snores from the audience. Following is a rewrite:

More people have died from hunger in the past 5 years than have been killed in all of the wars, revolutions, and murders in the past 150 years. Yet there is enough food to go around. I'm honored to be here with you today to discuss solutions to this problem.

Some members of an audience will begin to drift during any speech, but most people pay attention for at least the first few seconds. Highlight your main points in the beginning sentences of your speech.

A related option is to simply announce the questions you intend to answer. You can number these questions and write them on a flip chart. Or create an overview slide with the list of questions.

People might tell you to start your introduction with a joke. Humor is tricky. You run the risk of falling flat or offending somebody. Save jokes until you have plenty of experience with public speaking and know your audiences well.

Also avoid long, flowery introductions in which you tell people how much you like them, how thrilled you are to address them, and how humble you feel standing in front of them. If you lay it on too thick, your audience won't believe a word of it.

Draft your introduction, and then come back to it after you've written the rest of your speech. In the process of creating the main body and conclusion, your thoughts about the purpose and main points of your speech might change. You might even want to write the introduction last.

Write the main body. The main body of your speech is the content, which accounts for 70 to 90 percent of most speeches. In the main body, you develop your ideas in much the same way that you develop a written paper. If you raised questions in your introduction, be sure to directly answer them.

Transitions are especially important. Give your audience a signal when you change points. Do so by using meaningful pauses and verbal emphasis as well as transitional phrases: "On the other hand, until the public realizes what is happening to children in these countries…" or "The second reason hunger persists is…."

In long speeches, recap from time to time. Also preview what's to come. Hold your audience's attention by using facts, descriptions, expert opinions, and statistics.

Write the conclusion. At the end of the speech, summarize your points and draw your conclusion. You started with a bang; now finish with drama. The first and last parts of a speech are the most important. Make it clear to your audience when you've reached the end. Avoid endings such as "This is the end of my speech." A simple standby is "So in conclusion, I want to reiterate three points: First, …" When you are finished, stop talking.

Create speaking notes. Some professional speakers recommend writing out your speech in full, and then putting key words or main points on a few 3 × 5 cards. Number the cards so that if you drop them, you can quickly put them in order again. As you finish the information on each card, move it to the back of the pile. Write information clearly and in letters large enough to be seen from a distance.

The disadvantage of the 3 × 5 card system is that it involves card shuffling. Some speakers prefer to use standard outlined notes. Another option is mind mapping. Even an hour-long speech can be mapped on one sheet of paper. You can also use memory techniques to memorize the outline of your speech.

8

Create supporting visuals. Presentations often include visuals such as PowerPoint slides and posters. With PowerPoint, you can also add video clips from your computer or cell phone. These visuals can reinforce your main points and help your audience understand how your presentation is organized.

Use visuals to *complement* rather than *replace* your speaking. If you use too many visuals—or visuals that are too complex—your audience might focus on them and forget about you.

To use PowerPoint and similar software to full advantage:

- Ask your instructor whether it's acceptable to use technology in your presentation.

- Ask yourself whether slides will actually benefit your presentation. If you use PowerPoint simply because you *can*, you run the risk of letting the technology overshadow your message.

- Use fewer slides rather than more. For a 15-minute presentation, 10 slides is enough.

- Use slides to *show* rather than *tell*. Save them for illustrations, photos, charts, and concepts that are hard to express in words. Don't expect your audience to read a lot of text.

- Limit the amount of text on each visual. Stick to key words presented in short sentences or phrases.

- Use a consistent set of plain fonts that are large enough for all audience members to see. Avoid using more than two fonts, and avoid UPPERCASE letters.

- Stick with a simple consistent color scheme. Use dark text on a light background. Keep backgrounds consistent, and avoid colors that compete with each other.

Overcome fear of public speaking. You may not be able to eliminate fear of public speaking entirely, but you can take three steps to reduce and manage it.

© Nick Bland. www.panicfreepublicspeaking.com.au

First, prepare thoroughly. Research your topic thoroughly. Knowing your topic inside and out can create a baseline of confidence. To make a strong start, memorize the first four sentences that you plan to deliver, and practice them many times. Delivering them flawlessly when you're in front of an audience can build your confidence for the rest of your speech.

Second, accept your physical sensations. You've probably experienced physical sensations that are commonly associated with stage fright: dry mouth, a pounding heart, sweaty hands, muscle jitters, shortness of breath, and a shaky voice. One immediate way to deal with such sensations is to simply notice them. Tell yourself, "Yes, my hands are clammy. Yes, my stomach is upset. Also, my face feels numb." Trying to deny or ignore such facts can increase your fear. When you fully accept sensations, however, they start to lose power.

Third, focus on content, not delivery. Michael Motley, a professor at the University of California–Davis, distinguishes between two orientations to speaking. People with a *performance orientation* believe that the speaker must captivate the audience by using formal techniques that differ from normal conversation. In contrast, speakers with a *communication orientation* see public speaking simply as an extension of one-to-one conversation. The goal is not to perform but to communicate your ideas to an audience in the same ways that you would explain them to a friend.[11]

Adopting a communication orientation can reduce your fear of public speaking. Instead of thinking about yourself, focus on your message. Your audience is more interested in *what* you have to say than *how* you say it. Forget about giving a "speech." Just give people valuable ideas and information that they can use.

Practice your presentation. The key to successful public speaking is practice. Do this with your "speaker's voice." Your voice sounds different when you talk loudly, and this fact can be unnerving. Get used to it early on.

Practice in the room in which you will deliver your speech. Keep an eye on the time to make sure that you stay within the limit.

Hear what your voice sounds like over a sound system. If you can't practice your speech in the actual room, at least visit the site ahead of time. Also make sure that the materials you will need for your speech, including any audio-visual equipment, will be available when you want them.

Whenever possible, make a recording. Many schools have video recording equipment available for student use. Use it while you practice. Then view the finished recording to evaluate your presentation.

Listen for repeated words and phrases. Examples include *you know, kind of,* and *really,* plus any little *uh's, umm's,* and *ah's.* To get rid of them, tell yourself that you intend to notice every time they pop up in your daily speech. When you hear them, remind yourself that you don't use those words anymore.

Keep practicing. Avoid speaking word for word, as if you were reading a script. When you know your material well, you can deliver it in a natural way. Practice your presentation until you could deliver it in your sleep. Then run through it a few more times.

PHASE 2: DELIVERING YOUR PRESENTATION

Before you begin, get the audience's attention. If people are still filing into the room or adjusting their seats, they're not ready to listen. When all eyes are on you, then begin.

Dress for the occasion. The clothing you choose to wear on the day of your speech delivers a message that's as loud as your words. Consider how your audience will be dressed, and then choose a wardrobe based on the impression you want to make.

Project your voice. When you speak, talk loudly enough to be heard. Avoid leaning over your notes or the podium.

Maintain eye contact. When you look at people, they become less frightening. Also, remember that it is easier for the audience to listen to someone when that person is looking at them. Find a few friendly faces around the room, and imagine that you are talking to each of these people individually.

Notice your nonverbal communication. Be aware of what your body is telling your audience. Contrived or staged gestures will look dishonest. Be natural. If you don't know what to do with your hands, notice that. Then don't do anything with them.

Notice the time. You can increase the impact of your words by keeping track of the time during your speech. It's better to end early than to run late.

Pause when appropriate. Beginners sometimes feel that they have to fill every moment with the sound of their voice. Release that expectation. Give your listeners a chance to make notes and absorb what you say.

Have fun. Chances are that if you lighten up and enjoy your presentation, so will your listeners.

PHASE 3: REFLECTING ON YOUR PRESENTATION

Many students are tempted to sigh with relief when their presentation is done and put the event behind them. Resist this temptation. If you want to get better at making presentations, then take time to reflect on each performance. Did you finish on time? Did you cover all of the points you intended to cover? Was the audience attentive? Did you handle any nervousness effectively?

Write Journal Entries about what you discovered and intend to do differently for your next presentation. Remember to be as kind to yourself as you would be to someone else after a presentation. In addition to noting areas for improvement, note what you did well. Congratulate yourself on getting up in front of an audience and completing your presentation.

Also welcome feedback from others. Most of us find it difficult to hear criticism about our speaking. Be aware of resisting such criticism, and then let go of your resistance. Listening to feedback will increase your skill. ■

You're One Click Away...
from finding more strategies online for stunning speaking.

Making the grade in group presentations

When preparing group presentations, you can use three strategies for making a memorable impression.

Get organized.
As soon as you get the assignment, select a group leader and exchange contact information. Schedule specific times and places for planning, researching, writing, and practicing your presentation.

At your first meeting, write a to-do list that includes all of the tasks involved in completing the assignment. Distribute tasks fairly, paying attention to the strengths of individuals in your group. For example, some people excel at brainstorming, whereas others prefer researching.

One powerful way to get started is to define clearly the topic and thesis, or main point, of your presentation. Then support your thesis by looking for the most powerful facts, quotations, and anecdotes you can find.

As you get organized, remember how your presentation will be evaluated. If the instructor doesn't give grading criteria, create your own.

Get coordinated.
Get together several times to practice your presentation before it's scheduled to be given in class. Develop smooth, short transitions between individual speakers. Keep track of the time so that you stay within the guidelines for the assignment.

Also practice using visuals such as flip charts, posters, DVDs, videotapes, or slides. To give visuals their full impact, make them appropriate for the room where you will present. Make sure that text is large enough to be seen from the back of the room. For bigger rooms, consider using presentation software or making overhead transparencies.

Get cooperation.
Presentations that get top scores take teamwork and planning—not egos. Communicate with group members in an open and sensitive way. Contribute your ideas, and be responsive to the viewpoints of other members. When you cooperate, your group is on the way to an effective presentation.

8

PRACTICING
critical thinking 8

Throughout this book, you've practiced the six levels of thinking described in "Becoming a critical thinker" on page 207. Doing this exercise will give you additional practice with **Level 2: Understanding**.

At this level of thinking, you comprehend information and ideas well enough to explain them in your own words. Test questions that call for understanding begin with terms such as these:

- Compare
- Contrast
- Discuss
- Estimate
- Explain
- Give an example
- Illustrate
- Infer
- Interpret
- Paraphrase
- Predict
- Summarize
- Translate

You can do this level of thinking in any of your courses. In a science class, for example, an instructor might ask you to name the various types of clouds and then **explain** the factors that cause each kind of cloud to form. In a literature class, the instructor might ask you to **summarize** the plot of a short story.

This level of thinking is especially useful when you want to clarify your intentions. In the space below, list one of your personal values or goals. Then demonstrate how well you understand it. **Give an example** of how you put the value into action. Or **explain** how you will know when you've reached the goal.

_____

_____

_____

_____

_____

_____

_____

_____

_____

_____

_____

_____

_____

_____

_____

master**student**profile

Mark Zuckerberg

In a report for *60 Minutes*, the CBS TV program, Lesley Stahl interviewed the founder and CEO of a company that began in a Harvard dorm room and is now estimated to be worth $15 billion.

The face of Facebook is Mark Zuckerberg, the mogul who's guiding its extraordinary growth. What everyone wants to know is: Is he old enough to be running a company some people say is the biggest thing since Google?

"I'm 23 right now," Zuckerberg tells Stahl when asked how old he is.

"And you're running this huge company," Stahl remarks.

"It's not that big," Zuckerberg says. . . .

"It used to be the case, like you'd switch jobs. And then maybe you wouldn't keep in touch with all the people that you knew from that old job. Just 'cause it was too hard," Zuckerberg explains. "But one of the things that Facebook does is it makes it really easy to just stay in touch with all these people."…

Facebook's headquarters in downtown Palo Alto look like a dorm room; the 400 employees, who get free food and laundry, show up late, stay late, and party really late.

Zuckerberg, who's made the cover of *Newsweek* and is reportedly worth $3 billion, sits at a desk like the other software engineers, writing computer code.

"Have you changed your lifestyle? You don't look like you're buyin' really expensive clothes," Stahl asks Zuckerberg, who showed up to the interview in a sweatshirt and sandals. . . .

"I have a little, like one bedroom apartment with a mattress on the floor. That's where I live," Zuckerberg says.

Like the founders of Google, Larry Page and Sergey Brin, Mark Zuckerberg is looked up to in Silicon Valley as a visionary. . . .

He expanded access to Facebook from college students to high schoolers, then in 2006 to adults, his fastest growing demographic. Now he's inviting everyone on the site to create new software and pocket the profits themselves. It's a way to keep the next big thing on Facebook. New programs emerge daily, like Facebook Scrabble.

"I actually have a couple games going on now with my grandparents," Zuckerberg says, laughing. "So, they got on Facebook and we started playing Scrabble together."

So Facebook is changing the way we communicate with our friends, and with our grandparents. It's also changing politics. Every major candidate has a page. Zuckerberg says there seem to be more Republicans on the site than Democrats, and among them, Barack Obama—with his young persons following—is hugely popular. . . .

"It used to be, first you went on *Face The Nation* if you were a candidate. Then you went on *Letterman*. Now it seems the candidates have to be on Facebook. Are you changing the way candidates are running for president?" Stahl asks.

"Well, I think because politicians can communicate with tens of thousands of people at the same time, it's pretty effective for them in campaigning," Zuckerberg explains. . . .

Asked if he thinks his age is an asset or a liability, Zuckerberg says, "There's probably a little bit of both, right? I mean there are definitely elements of experience and stuff that someone who's my age wouldn't have. But there are also things that I can do that other people wouldn't necessarily be able to."

While *60 Minutes* was working on this story, associate producer Ros Menon lost her wallet in a New York City cab. The good Samaritan who found it tracked her down by searching for her—you guessed it—on Facebook.

MARK ZUCKERBERG . . . is willing to change.

YOU . . . can change by giving yourself permission to achieve big goals.

Source: Adapted from "The Face Behind Facebook," January 13, 2008, Copyright (c) 2008 by CBS News. Reproduced by permission. http://www.cbsnews.com/stories/2008/01/10/60minutes/main3697442.shtml

You're One Click Away...
from learning more about Mark Zuckerberg online at the Master Student Profiles. You can also visit the Master Student Hall of Fame to learn about other master students.

© Istockphoto.com/pagadesign

PUT THIS CHAPTER TO WORK

The techniques described in this chapter have direct applications in the workplace. According to the National Association of Colleges and Employers, verbal communication tops the list of "soft" skills that companies look for in new college graduates.[12]

The ability to write is also in demand. To verify this, scan job postings and notice how many of them call for it. Proposals, reports, e-mail messages, Web pages, and other documents are essential to the flow of ideas and information. People without writing skills can only influence people through direct contact. If you can write a persuasive memo, however, your ideas can spread to hundreds of people. Most new products and services—especially those that involve high budgets—begin with a written proposal.

USE STORYTELLING TECHNIQUES. During a job search, emphasize your communication skills. Talk about times when you demonstrated these skills in work and academic experiences.

In particular, draw on one of the most powerful forms of human communication—stories. In essence, a story is a series of events that occur when a person faces a significant problem and solves it. Practice talking about your experiences with this definition in mind.

DEVELOP CONVERSATION SKILLS. One of the most practical communication skills you can develop is the ability to hold one-on-one conversations. In the workplace, you will regularly meet new coworkers, customers, and clients. The ability to put people at ease through "small talk" makes you valuable to an employer. In a business context, this is a high-level skill that depends on the ability to listen closely, suspend judgment, and sympathize with another person's experiences.

DEVELOP COMPLEX COMMUNICATION SKILLS. In their book *The New Division of Labor: How Computers Are Creating the Next Job Market*, Frank Levy and Richard J. Murname emphasize the value of *complex communication*. This is the ability to acquire information, explain it, and persuade coworkers that your explanation implies a definite course of action. A supervisor who wants her employees to adopt a new procedure needs complex communication skills. So does an engineer who submits a new prototype for a disk drive, a marketing manager

who wants her company to develop a new product, and a sales person who confronts a skeptical customer.

Complex communication is required for any job that involves direct teaching, persuasion, or negotiation. People who develop this set of skills are less likely to lose their jobs due to automation or outsourcing. Start now by seizing every opportunity to write papers and make presentations that persuade people to adopt new ideas and take action on them.

EDIT YOUR WRITING FOR THE WORKPLACE. Jakob Nielsen, author of *Designing Web Usability: The Practice of Simplicity*, suggests that effectively written Web pages are:

- *Concise*—free of needless words and organized so that the main point of each section and paragraph comes at the beginning.

- *Scannable*—prepared with subheadings and visuals that allow readers to skim and quickly find what they need.

- *Objective*—packed with credible facts and free of "hype"—vague or exaggerated claims presented without evidence.[13]

These three guidelines can assist you in *all* forms of business writing.

MANAGE CONFLICT WITHIN TEAMS. If you get into a personal conflict with a coworker, reread the article "Managing conflict" on page 247 and choose a suggestion to apply. Simply by remembering to separate the processes of sending and receiving, you can immediately improve your relationships with both supervisors and employees.

NOW CREATE A CAREER CONNECTION OF YOUR OWN. Review this chapter, looking for a suggestion that you will commit to use while working or looking for a job. In a sentence or two, describe exactly what you plan to do and the primary benefit you want to gain. For example: "I will join a site for professional networking such as LinkedIn. Developing an online profile for this site will give me a head start on creating my résumé."

State your strategy and desired benefit in the space below:

_____

_____

_____

Name _____

Date _____

1. Name the six rungs on the ladder of powerful speaking from the Power Process: "Employ your word."

2. Write one example of a statement on the lowest rung of the ladder of powerful speaking—and another example of a statement on the highest rung.

3. One strategy for effective communication is to separate the roles of sending and receiving. Briefly explain how to do this.

4. This chapter suggests techniques for nonverbal and verbal listening. Briefly explain the difference between these two approaches to listening, and give one example of each approach.

5. You can listen skillfully to a speaker even when you disagree with that person's viewpoint. True or false? Explain your answer.

6. Reword the following complaint as a request: "You always interrupt when I talk!"

7. List the five parts of an "I" message (the five ways to say "I").

8. Briefly explain how teams can build the cycle of learning into their work.

9. Define *plagiarism*, and explain ways to avoid it.

10. Describe at least three techniques for practicing and delivering a speech.

8 SKILLS *Snapshot*

CHAPTER

Take a minute to reflect on your responses to the Communicating section of the Discovery Wheel on page 38. Reflect on the progress you've made, and clarify your intentions to develop further mastery. Complete the following sentences.

DISCOVERY

My score on the Communicating section of the Discovery Wheel on page 38 was . . .

The technique that has made the biggest difference in my skill at listening is . . .

When I feel angry with people, the way I usually express it is to . . .

When I'm effective at managing conflict, I remember to . . .

When I hear an accomplished public speaker, the skill that I would most like to acquire is . . .

INTENTION

I'll know that I've reached a new level of mastery with my communication skills when . . .

My main goal for communicating is . . .

ACTION

To reach that level of mastery, the most important thing I can do next is to . . .

At the end of this course, I would like my Communicating score on the Discovery Wheel to be . . .

Dixersity

 Use this **Master Student Map** to ask yourself,

 WHY THIS CHAPTER MATTERS . . .
- You're likely to learn and work with people from many different cultures.

WHAT IS INCLUDED . . .

- Power Process: Choose your conversations and your community   272
- Waking up to diversity   273
- Diversity is real—and valuable   274
- Building relationships across cultures   276
- Overcome stereotypes with critical thinking   281
- Students with disabilities: Know your rights   282
- Dealing with sexism and sexual harassment   284
- Leadership in a diverse world   286
- Master Student Profile: Sampson Davis   291

 HOW CAN I USE THIS CHAPTER . . .
- Study effectively with people from many different cultures.
- Gain skills to succeed in a multicultural workforce.
- Choose conversations that promote your success.

 WHAT IF . . .
- I could create positive relationships with people from any culture?

JOURNAL ENTRY 21
Intention Statement

Commit to create value from this chapter

Recall a time when you felt included in a group of people, even though the group was diverse. Next, scan this chapter for ideas that can help you recreate that kind of a supportive environment. List three ideas that you intend to explore in more detail, along with their associated page numbers.

Strategy	Page number

© Ruslan Ivantsov/Shutterstock.com

process

Choose your conversations and your community

Conversations can exist in many forms. One form involves people talking out loud to each other. At other times, the conversation takes place inside our own heads, and we call it *thinking*. We are even having a conversation when we read a magazine or a book, watch television or a movie, or write a letter or a report. These observations have three implications that wind their way through every aspect of our lives.

One implication is that conversations exercise incredible power over what we think, feel, and do. They shape our attitudes, our decisions, our opinions, our emotions, and our actions. If you want clues as to what a person will be like tomorrow, listen to what she's talking about today.

Second, given that conversations are so powerful, it's amazing that few people act on this fact. Most of us swim in a constant sea of conversations, almost none of which we carefully and thoughtfully choose.

The real power of this process lies in a third discovery: We can choose our conversations. Certain conversations create real value for us. They give us fuel for reaching our goals. Other conversations distract us from what we want. They might even create lasting unhappiness and frustration.

Suppose that you meet with an instructor to ask about some guidelines for writing a term paper. She launches into a tirade about your writing skills and lack of preparation for higher education. This presents you with several options. One possibility is to talk about what a jerk the instructor is and give up on the idea of learning to write well. Another option is to refocus the conversation on what you can do to improve your writing skills, such as working with a writing tutor or taking a basic composition class. These two sets of conversations will have vastly different consequences for your success in school.

Another important fact about conversations is that the people you associate with influence them dramatically. If you want to change your attitudes about anything—prejudice, politics, religion, humor—choose your conversations by choosing your community. Spend time with people who speak about and live consistently with the attitudes you value. Use conversations to change habits. Use conversations to explore new ways of seeing the world and to create new options in your life.

When we choose our conversations, we discover a tool of unsurpassed power. This tool has the capacity to remake our thoughts—and thus our lives. It's as simple as choosing the next article you read or the next topic you discuss with a friend.

Start choosing your conversations today, and watch what happens.

You're One Click Away...
from accessing Power Process Media online and finding out more about how to "choose your conversations."

WAKING UP TO *diversity*

Learning about diversity is an education in itself. This process can be frightening, frustrating, and even painful. It can also be exciting and enriching.

Consider that the people referred to as "minorities" in the United States are a numerical majority in other parts of the world. To make this idea more real, imagine the human race represented in a single village of just 100 people. If these villagers accurately reflected the Earth's total population, then only 18 would be white, and just 31 would describe themselves as Christian. In addition, 80 would live in substandard housing, 67 would be illiterate, and only 7 would have Internet access.[1]

The diverse cultures of our planet are meeting daily through a growing world economy and a global network of computers. Discussions of diversity often focus on characteristics commonly linked to race—differences in skin tone, facial features, and hair texture. But grouping people according to such differences is arbitrary. We could just as easily classify them on the basis of height, weight, foot size, fingernail length, or a hundred other physical traits.

In this chapter, the word *diversity* refers to differences of any type. From this perspective, diversity can be compared to an iceberg. Only the top of an iceberg is visible; most of it is hidden under water. Likewise, only a few aspects of diversity are visible, such as obvious differences in physical appearance, language, social and economic background, and behavior. Much remains hidden from our awareness—different ideas about relationships, decision making, and problem solving; different assumptions about the meaning of love and duty, beauty and friendship, justice and injustice; and much more.

This chapter is titled "Diversity" because that term is widely accepted. You might gain more value from thinking about *cultural competence* instead. This term reminds us that even in the most culturally sensitive environment, people can fail at understanding each other and working toward shared goals. *Cultural competence* refers to gaining skills in these areas and actively using those skills in daily life.

You'll learn most by stepping outside your comfort zone and taking risks. Get involved in a study group or campus organization with people from different countries. Keep asking yourself, "What is the next action I could take to live and work more effectively in our global village?" The answers could change your life. ■

JOURNAL ENTRY 22
Discovery Statement

Reflect on the quality of a recent conversation

Review the Power Process: "Choose your conversations and your community" on page 272. Then, in the space below, describe a conversation you had today. Summarize what was said, and reflect on whether the conversations aligned with your values and goals.

I discovered that …

_____

_____

_____

_____

_____

_____

_____

_____

_____

_____

_____

_____

_____

_____

9

Diversity is
REAL—AND VALUABLE

Think about a common daily routine. A typical American citizen awakens in a bed (an invention from the Near East). After dressing in clothes (possibly designed in Italy), she slices a banana (grown in Honduras) on her bowl (made in China) of cereal, and then brews coffee (shipped from Nicaragua). After breakfast, she reads the morning newspaper (printed by a process invented in Germany, on paper, which was first made in China). Then she turns on her portable media player (made in Taiwan) and listens to music (possibly by a band from Cuba). This scenario presents just a few examples of how the cultures of the world meet in our daily lives.

The word *culture* embraces many kinds of differences. We can speak of the culture of large corporations or the culture of the fine arts. There are the cultures of men and women; heterosexual, homosexual, and bisexual people; and older and younger people. There are the cultures of urban and rural dwellers, the cultures of able-bodied people and people with disabilities, and the cultures of two-parent families and single-parent families. There are cultures defined by differences in standards of living and differences in religion.

Higher education might bring you into the most diverse environment that you will ever encounter. Your fellow students could come from many ethnic groups and countries. In addition, consider faculty members, staff members, alumni, donors, and their families. Think of all the possible differences in their family backgrounds, education, job experiences, religion, marital status, sexual orientation, and political viewpoints. Few institutions in our society can match the level of diversity found on many campuses.

A First Step to living effectively in a diverse world is to remember that many dimensions of culture are alive in you and in the people you meet every day. Once you recognize that such diversity is a fact, you can practice a new level of tolerance and respect for individual differences.

Discrimination is also real. The ability to live with diversity is now more critical than ever. Racism, homophobia, and other forms of discrimination exist in many settings, including higher education. According to the Federal Bureau of Investigation (FBI), nearly half of the hate crimes that took place in the United States during 2009 were motivated by racial bias.[2] Each year, thousands of bias-motivated threats and physical assaults occur on college campuses in the United States.[3]

Of course, discrimination can be far more subtle than hate crimes. Consider how you would respond to the following situations:

- Members of a sociology class are debating the merits of reforming the state's welfare system. The instructor calls on a student who grew up on a reservation and says, "Tell us: What's the Native American perspective on this issue anyway?" Here the student is being typecast as a spokesperson for her entire ethnic group.

- Students in a mass media communications class are learning to think critically about television programs. They're talking about a situation comedy set in an urban high-rise apartment building with mostly African American residents. "Man, they really whitewashed that show," says one student. "It's mostly about inner-city black people, but they didn't show anybody on welfare, doing drugs, or joining gangs." The student's comment perpetuates common racial stereotypes.

- On the first day of the term, students taking English Composition enter a class taught by a professor from Puerto Rico. One of the students asks the professor, "Am I in the right class? Maybe there's been a mistake. I thought this was supposed to be an English class, not a Spanish class." The student assumed that only white people are qualified to teach English courses.

Forrest Toms, of Training Research and Development, defines racism as "prejudice plus power"—the power to define reality, to enshrine one culture as the "correct" set of lenses for viewing the world. The operating assumption is that differences mean deficits. When racism and other forms of intolerance live, we all lose—even if we belong to a group with social and political power. We lose the ability to make friends and to function effectively on teams. We crush human potential. And people without the skills to bridge cultures are already at a disadvantage.

Higher education offers a chance to change this situation. Campuses can become cultural laboratories—places where people of diverse cultures meet in an atmosphere of tolerance. Students who create alliances outside their familiar group memberships are preparing to succeed in both school and work.

Diversity is valuable. Synergy rests on the idea that the whole is more than the sum of its parts. A symphony orchestra consists of many different instruments; when played together, their effect is multiplied many times. A football team has members with different specialties; when their talents are combined, they can win a league championship.

Today we are waking up not only to the *fact* of diversity but also to the *value* of diversity. Biologists tell us that diversity of animal species benefits our ecology. The same idea applies to the human species. Our goal in education can be to see that we are all part of a complex world—that our own culture is different from, not better than, other cultures. Knowing this, we can stop saying, "Ours is the way to work, learn, relate to others, and view the world." Instead, we can say, "Here is the way I have been doing it. I would also like to see your way."

The fact of diversity also presents opportunities in the workplace. Understanding cultural differences will help you to embrace others' viewpoints that lead to profitable solutions. Organizations that are attuned to diversity are more likely to prosper in the global marketplace.

It takes no more energy to believe that differences enrich us than it does to believe that differences endanger us. Embracing diversity adds value to any organization and can be far more exciting than just meeting the minimum requirements for affirmative action.

Accepting diversity does not mean ignoring the differences among cultures so that we all become part of an anonymous "melting pot." Instead, we can become more like a mosaic—a piece of art in which each element both maintains its individuality and blends with others to form a harmonious whole.

The more you can embrace diversity, the more friends you can make in school and the better prepared you'll be for the workforce of the twenty-first century. If you plan to pursue a career in health care, for example, you can prepare to work with patients from many ethnic groups. If you choose to start a business, you can prepare to sell to customers from many demographic groups. And if you plan to teach, you can prepare to assist every student who walks into your classroom.

Learning to thrive with diversity is a process of returning to "beginner's mind"—a place where we discover diversity as if for the first time. It is a magical place—a place of new beginnings and fresh options. It takes courage to dwell in beginner's mind—courage to go outside the confines of our own culture and worldview. It can feel uncomfortable at first. Yet there are lasting rewards to be gained.

Even if you've already attended diversity workshops in high school or at work, see whether you can return to beginner's mind. Entering higher education can take your experience of diversity to a whole new level. ■

✓ EXERCISE 25

Explore the influence of stereotypes

A stereotype is an assumption that all members of a group are the same. Stereotypes ignore the differences among people.

To discover how stereotypes can enter your mind, do a short thinking experiment. List the first words that come to mind when you see or hear the following terms. Write quickly and don't stop to think about your responses.

musician . . .

homeless people . . . .

football players . . .

Eskimo . . . .

mathematicians . . .

computer programmers . . .

Now reflect on your lists. Do you see any evidence of stereotypes? Explain your answer:

_____

_____

_____

_____

_____

_____

You'll learn more about stereotypes as you read and use the rest of this chapter.

Building relationships across cultures

Communicating with people of other cultures is a learned skill—a habit. According to Stephen R. Covey, author of *The Seven Habits of Highly Effective People*, a habit is the point at which desire, knowledge, and skill meet:[4]

- Desire is about *wanting* to do something.
- Knowledge is *understanding* what to do.
- And skill is the *ability* to do it.

Peter Dazeley/Photographer's Choice/Getty

© Sven Hagolani/zefa/Corbis

Master students merge these qualities in the way that they relate to people of different cultures.

Knowing techniques for communicating across cultures is valuable. And what gives them power is a sincere desire and commitment to create understanding. If you truly value cultural diversity, then you can discover ways to build bridges between people. Use the following suggestions and invent more of your own.

Start with self-discovery. One step to developing diversity skills is to learn about yourself and understand the lenses through which you see the world. One way to do this is to intentionally switch lenses—that is, to consciously perceive familiar events in a new way.

For example, think of a situation in your life that involved an emotionally charged conflict among several people. Now mentally put yourself inside the skin of another person in that conflict. Ask yourself, "How would I view this situation if I were that person?"

You can also learn by asking, "What if I were a person of the opposite gender? Or if I were member of a different racial or ethnic group? Or if I were older or younger?" Do this exercise consistently, and you'll discover that we live in a world of multiple realities. There are many different ways to interpret any event—and just as many ways to respond, given our individual differences.

Also reflect on how people can have experiences of privilege *and* prejudice. For example, someone might tell you that he's more likely to be promoted at work because he's white and male—*and* that he's been called "white trash" because he lives in a trailer park.

See whether you can recall incidents such as these from your own life. Think of times when you were favored because of your gender, race, or age—and times when you were excluded or ridiculed based on one of those same characteristics. In doing this, you'll discover ways to identify with a wider range of people.

Learn about other cultures. People from different cultures read differently, write differently, think differently, eat differently, and learn differently than you. If you know this from the beginning, you can be more effective with your classmates, coworkers, and neighbors.

One key to understanding styles is to look for several possible interpretations of any behavior. For example:[5]

- Consider the hand signal that signifies *okay* to many Americans—thumb and index finger forming a circle. In France, that signal denotes the number zero. In Japan, it is a symbol for money. And in Brazil, it is considered an obscene gesture.

- When Americans see a speaker who puts her hands in her pockets, they seldom attribute any meaning to this behavior. But in many countries—such as Germany, Indonesia, and Austria—this gesture is considered rude.

- During a conversation, you might prefer having a little distance between yourself and another person. But in Iran, people may often get so close to you that you can feel their breath.

These examples could be extended to cover many areas—posture, eye contact, physical contact, facial expressions, and more. And the various ways of interpreting these behaviors are neither right nor wrong. They simply represent differing styles in making meaning out of what we see.

You might find yourself fascinated by the styles that make up a particular culture. Consider learning as much about that culture as possible. Immerse yourself in it. Read novels, see plays, go to concerts, listen to music, look at art, take courses, learn the language.

Look for differences between individualist and collectivist cultures. Individualist cultures flourish in the United States, Canada, and Western Europe. If your family has deep roots in one of these areas, you were probably raised to value personal fulfillment and personal success. You received recognition or rewards when you stood out from your peers by earning the highest grades in your class, scoring the most points during a basketball season, or demonstrating another form of individual achievement.

In contrast, collectivist cultures value cooperation over competition. Group progress is more important than individual success. Credit for an achievement is widely shared. If you were raised in such a culture, you probably place a high value on your family and were taught to respect your elders. Collectivist cultures dominate Asia, Africa, and Latin America.

In short, individualist cultures often emphasize "I." Collectivist cultures tend to emphasize "we." Forgetting about the differences between them can strain a friendship or wreck an international business deal.

If you were raised in an individualist culture:

- *Remember that someone from a collectivist culture may place a high value on "saving face."* This idea involves more than simply avoiding embarrassment. This person may *not* want to be singled out from other members of a group, even for a positive achievement. If you have a direct request for this person or want to share something that could be taken as a personal criticism, save it for a private conversation.

- *Respect titles and last names.* Although Americans often like to use first names immediately after meeting someone, in some cultures this practice is acceptable only among family members. Especially in work settings, use last names and job titles during your first meetings. Allow time for informal relationships to develop.

- *Put messages in context.* For members of collectivist cultures, words convey only part of an intended message. Notice gestures and other nonverbal communication as well.

If you were raised in a collectivist culture, you can creatively "reverse" the above list. Keep in mind that direct questions from an American student or coworker are meant not to offend, but only to clarify, an idea. Don't be surprised if you are called by a nickname, if no one asks about your family, or if you are rewarded for a personal achievement. In social situations, remember that indirect cues might not get another person's attention. Practice asking clearly and directly for what you want.

Reach out. If carrying out any of these suggestions feels awkward, just apply the Power Process: "Be here now." Then use the suggestions in this article. By intentionally expanding your comfort zone over time, you can break down social barriers and gain a new level of ease at being with people.

A more formal option is to arrange an intergroup dialogue—a *"facilitated,* face-to-face meeting between students from two or more social identity groups that have a history of conflict or potential conflict." Examples are Christians and Muslims, blacks and whites, and people with disabilities and those without disabilities. The goal is sustained and meaningful conversation about controversial issues.[6] Groups typically gather for 2-hour meetings over 6 to 12 weeks.

The format for intergroup dialogues was developed at the University of Michigan and is now being used at campuses across the country. Ask your academic advisor whether such a program is available at your school.

Look for common ground. Students in higher education often find that they worry about many of the same things—including tuition bills, the quality of dormitory food, and the shortage of on-campus parking spaces. More important, our fundamental goals as human beings—such as health, physical safety, and economic security—cross culture lines.

9

> The key is to honor the differences among people while remembering what we have in common. Diversity is not just about our differences—it's also about our similarities.

The key is to honor the differences among people while remembering what we have in common. Diversity is not just about our differences—it's also about our similarities. On a biological level, less than 1 percent of the human genome accounts for visible characteristics such as skin color. In terms of our genetic blueprint, we are more than 99 percent the same.[7]

Speak and listen with cultural sensitivity. After first speaking with someone from another culture, don't assume that you've been understood or that you fully understand the other person. The same action can have different meanings at different times, even for members of the same culture. Check it out. Verify what you think you have heard. Listen to see whether what you spoke is what the other person received.

If you're speaking with someone who doesn't understand English well, keep the following ideas in mind:

- Speak slowly, distinctly, and patiently.

- To clarify your statement, don't repeat individual words over and over again. Restate your entire message with simple, direct language and short sentences.

- Avoid slang and figures of speech.

- Use gestures to accompany your words.

- English courses for nonnative speakers often emphasize written English, so write down what you're saying. Print your message in capital letters.

- Stay calm, and avoid sending nonverbal messages that you're frustrated.

If you're unsure about how well you're communicating, ask questions: "I don't know how to make this idea clear to you. How might I communicate better?" "When you look away from me during our conversation, I feel uneasy. Is there something else we need to talk about?" "When you don't ask questions, I wonder whether I am being clear. Do you want any more explanation?" Questions such as these can get cultural differences out in the open in a constructive way.

Look for individuals, not group representatives. Sometimes the way we speak glosses over differences among individuals and reinforces stereotypes. For example, a student worried about her grade in math expresses concern over "all those Asian students who are skewing the class curve." Or a white music major assumes that her black classmate knows a lot about jazz or hip-hop music. We can avoid such errors by seeing people as individuals—not spokespersons for an entire group.

Find a translator, mediator, or model. People who move with ease in two or more cultures can help us greatly. Diane de Anda, a professor at the University of California, Los Angeles, speaks of three kinds of people who can communicate across cultures. She calls them *translators, mediators,* and *models.*[8]

A *translator* is someone who is truly bicultural—a person who relates naturally to both people in a mainstream culture and people from a contrasting culture. This person can share her own experiences in overcoming discrimination, learning another language or dialect, and coping with stress.

Mediators are people who belong to the dominant or mainstream culture. Unlike translators, they might not be bicultural. However, mediators value diversity and are committed to cultural understanding. Often they are teachers, counselors, tutors, mentors, or social workers.

Models are members of a culture who are positive examples. Models include students from any racial or cultural group who participate in class and demonstrate effective study habits. Models can also include entertainers, athletes, and community leaders.

Your school might have people who serve these functions, even if they're not labeled translators, mediators, or models. Some schools have mentor or "bridge" programs that pair new students with teachers of the same race or culture. Ask your student counseling service about such programs.

Develop support systems. Many students find that their social adjustment affects their academic performance. Students with strong support systems—such as families, friends, churches, self-help groups, and mentors—are using a powerful strategy for success in school. As an exercise, list the support systems that you rely on right now. Also list new support systems you could develop.

Support systems can help you bridge culture gaps. With a strong base of support in your own group, you can feel more confident in meeting people outside that group.

Be willing to accept feedback. Members of another culture might let you know that some of your words or actions had a meaning other than what you intended. For example, perhaps a comment that seems harmless to you is offensive to them. And they may tell you directly about it.

Avoid responding to such feedback with comments such as "Don't get me wrong," "You're taking this way too seriously," or "You're too sensitive." Instead, listen without resistance. Open yourself to what others have to say. Remember to distinguish between the *intention* of your behavior and its actual *impact* on other people. Then take the feedback you receive and ask yourself how you can use it to communicate more effectively in the future.

You can also interpret such feedback positively—a sign that others believe you can change and that they see the possibility of a better relationship with you.

If you are new at responding to diversity, expect to make some mistakes along the way. As long as you approach people in a spirit of tolerance, your words and actions can always be changed.

Speak up against discrimination. You might find yourself in the presence of someone who tells a racist joke, makes a homophobic comment, or utters an ethnic slur. When this happens, you have a right to state what you observe, share what you think, and communicate how you feel. Depending on the circumstance, you might say:

- "That's a stereotype, and we don't have to fall for it."
- "Other people are going to take offense at that. Let's tell jokes that don't put people down."
- "I realize that you don't mean to offend anybody, but I feel hurt and angry by what you just said."
- "I know that an African American person told you that story, but I still think it's racist and creates an atmosphere that I don't want to be in."

This kind of speaking may be the most difficult communicating you ever do. However, if you *don't* do it, you give the impression that you agree with biased speech.

In response to your candid comments, many people will apologize and express their willingness to change. Even if they don't, you can still know that you practiced integrity by aligning your words with your values.

Change the institution. None of us lives in isolation. We all live in systems, and these systems do not always tolerate diversity. As a student, you might see people of color ignored in class. You might see people of a certain ethnic group passed over in job hiring or underrepresented in school organizations. And you might see gay and lesbian students ridiculed or even threatened with violence. One way to stop these actions is to point them out.

You can speak more effectively about what you believe by making some key distinctions. Remember the following:

- *Stereotypes* are errors in thinking—inaccurate ideas about members of another culture.
- *Prejudice* refers to positive or negative feelings about others, which are often based on stereotypes.
- *Discrimination* takes places when stereotypes or prejudice gets expressed in policies and laws that undermine equal opportunities for all cultures.

Federal civil rights laws, as well as the written policies of most schools, ban racial and ethnic discrimination. If your school receives federal aid, it must set up procedures that protect students against such discrimination.

Throughout recent history, students have fueled social change. Student action helped to shift Americans' attitudes toward segregated universities, the Vietnam War, the military draft, and the invasion of Iraq. When it comes to ending discrimination, you are in an environment where you can make a difference. Run for student government. Write for school publications. Speak at rallies. Express your viewpoint. This is training for citizenship in a multicultural world. ■

You're One Click Away...
from gaining more strategies online for building relationships across cultures.

You're One Click Away...
from viewing a video about Master Students in Action.

Master Students
IN ACTION

"*You have to fill in bubbles for your race, and I remember raising my hand and asking the teacher what I should put because I wasn't sure (it said to only fill in one). . . . I just said, "My father is black and my mother is white; what should I put?" She leaned over, nodded knowingly, and just tapped the black option. . . . It was the first time I realized that despite how I might identify myself, that might not be how others perceive me.*"

—Danielle Ciccone,
Brown University

9

EXERCISE 26

Becoming a culture learner

To learn about other cultures in depth, actively move through the cycle of learning described by psychologist David Kolb (and explained more fully when you completed your Learning Styles Inventory beginning on page LSI-1). This exercise, which has three parts, illustrates one way to apply the cycle of learning. Use additional paper as needed to complete each part.

Part 1: Feeling

Think of a specific way to interact with people from a culture different from your own. For example, attend a meeting for a campus group that you normally would not attend. Or sit in a campus cafeteria with a new group of people. In the space below, describe what you will do to create your experience of a different culture.

_____

_____

_____

_____

_____

Part 2: Watching

Describe the experience you had while doing Part 1 of this exercise. Be sure to separate your observations—what you saw, heard, or did—from your interpretations. In addition, see whether you can think of other ways to interpret each of your observations. Use the table below for this part of the exercise. An example is included to get you started.

Part 3: Thinking

Next, see whether you can refine your initial interpretations and develop them into some informed conclusions about your experience in Part 1. Do some research about other cultures, looking specifically for information that can help you understand the experience. (Your instructor and a librarian can suggest ways to find such information.) Whenever possible, speak directly to people of various cultures. Share your observations from Part 1, and ask for *their* interpretations. Reflect on the information you gather. Does it reinforce any of the interpretations you listed in Part 2? Does it call for a change in your thinking? Summarize your conclusions in the space below.

_____

_____

_____

_____

_____

Observation	Your Initial Interpretation	Other Possible Interpretations
For 30 minutes starting at noon on Tuesday, I sat alone in the northeast section of the cafeteria in our student union. During this time, all of the conversations I overheard were conducted in Spanish.	I sat alone because the Spanish-speaking students did not want to talk to me. They are unfriendly.	The Spanish-speaking students are actually friendly. They were just not sure how to start a conversation with me. Perhaps they thought I wanted to eat alone or study. Also, I could have taken the initiative to start a conversation.

OVERCOME STEREOTYPES
with critical thinking

Consider assertions such as these: "College students like to drink heavily," "People who speak English as a second language are hard to understand," and "Americans who criticize the president are unpatriotic."

These assertions are examples of stereotyping—generalizing about a group of people based on the behavior of isolated group members. The word *stereotype* originally referred to a method used by printers to produce duplicate pages of text. This usage still rings true. When we stereotype, we gloss over individual differences and assume that every member of a group is a "duplicate." These assumptions are learned, and they can be changed.

Stereotypes infiltrate every dimension of human individuality. People are stereotyped on the basis of their race, ethnic group, religion, political affiliation, geographic location, birthplace, accent, job, economic status, age, gender, sexual orientation, IQ, height, hair color, or hobbies.

Stereotypes have many possible sources: fear of the unknown, uncritical thinking, and negative encounters between individual members of different groups. Whatever their cause, stereotypes abound.

In themselves, generalizations are neither good nor bad. In fact, they are essential. Mentally sorting people, events, and objects into groups allows us to make sense of the world. But when we consciously or unconsciously make generalizations that rigidly divide the people of the world into "us" versus "them," we create stereotypes and put on the blinders of prejudice.

You can take several steps to free yourself from stereotypes.

Look for errors in thinking. Some of the most common errors in thinking are the following:

- *Selective perception.* Stereotypes can literally change the way we see the world. If we assume that homeless people are lazy, for instance, we tend to notice only the examples that support our opinion. Stories about homeless people who are too young or too ill to work will probably escape our attention.

- *Self-fulfilling prophecy.* When we interact with people based on stereotypes, we set them up in ways that confirm our thinking. For example, when people of color were denied access to higher education based on stereotypes about their intelligence, they were deprived of opportunities to demonstrate their intellectual gifts.

- *Self-justification.* Stereotypes can allow people to assume the role of victim and to avoid taking responsibility for their own lives. An unemployed white male might believe that affirmative action programs are making it impossible for him to get a job—even as he overlooks his own lack of experience or qualifications.

Create categories in a more flexible way. Stereotyping has been described as a case of "hardening of the categories." Avoid this problem by making your categories broader. Instead of seeing

> **The word *stereotype* originally referred to a method used by printers to produce duplicate pages of text. This usage still rings true. When we stereotype, we gloss over individual differences and assume that every member of a group is a "duplicate."**

people based on their skin color, you could look at them on the basis of their heredity. (People of all races share most of the same genes.) Or you could make your categories narrower. Instead of talking about "religious extremists," look for subgroups among the people who adopt a certain religion. Distinguish between groups that advocate violence and those that shun it.

Test your generalizations about people through action. You can test your generalizations by actually meeting people of other cultures. It's easy to believe almost anything about certain groups of people as long as we never deal directly with individuals. Inaccurate pictures tend to die when people from different cultures study together, work together, and live together. Consider joining a school or community organization that will put you in contact with people of other cultures. Your rewards will include a more global perspective and an ability to thrive in a multicultural world.

Be willing to see your own stereotypes. The Power Process: "Notice your pictures and let them go" can help you see your own stereotypes. One belief about yourself that you can shed is *I have no pictures about people from other cultures.* Even people with the best of intentions can harbor subtle biases. Admitting this possibility allows you to look inward even more deeply for stereotypes.

Every time we notice an inaccurate picture buried in our mind and let it go, we take a personal step toward embracing diversity. ∎

You're One Click Away...
from finding more examples online of stereotypes and critical responses to them.

9

Andersen Ross/Getty Images

STUDENTS WITH DISABILITIES:
Know your rights

Even the most well-intentioned instructors can forget about assisting people with disabilities. One reason is that disabilities vary so much. For example, some disabilities are visible. Other disabilities—such as hyperactivity disorders and learning disabilities—are invisible. Some disabilities are permanent. Others—such as a broken leg from last weekend's ski trip—are temporary.

At one time, students with disabilities faced a restricted set of choices in school. New technology, such as computers and calculators operated with voice commands, changed that. Students with disabilities can now choose from almost any course or major offered in higher education.

To protect your rights when dealing with any kind of disability, speak up. Ask for what you want. Begin by reviewing the "Five ways to say 'I'" presented in Chapter 8 on page 242. Develop your skills at using "I" messages and listening actively when people respond. Also use the following strategies.

LEARN ABOUT LAWS THAT APPLY TO YOU

Equal opportunity for people with disabilities is the law. In the United States, both the Civil Rights Act of 1964 and the Rehabilitation Act of 1973 offer legal protection. The Americans with Disabilities Act of 1990 extends earlier legislation.

These laws give you the right to ask for academic adjustments based on your needs. Some examples are listed here:

- Arranging for priority registration
- Reducing a course load
- Substituting one course for another

- Providing note takers, recording devices, and sign language interpreters
- Equipping school computers with screen-reading, voice recognition, or other adaptive software or hardware
- Installing a telecommunications device for the hearing impaired (TTY/TDD) in your dorm room if telephones are provided there

In making an adjustment, your school is *not* obligated to change the essential requirements for a course. For example, you can ask for extra testing time. However, your instructor is not required to change the content of the test.

LEARN ABOUT SERVICES AT YOUR SCHOOL

Visit the disability services office at your school. Ask about the adjustments listed previously and other options, such as these:

- Permits that allow you to park a car closer to classrooms
- Lecture transcriptions
- Textbook-reading services
- Assistants for laboratory courses in science
- Shuttle buses for transportation between classes
- Closed captioning for instructional television programs
- Interpreters for the hearing impaired
- Books and other course materials in braille or on audio

The student health center may also offer certain services to people with disabilities. In addition, the Job Accommodation Network offers help in placing employees with learning or physical disabilities. For more information, call (800) 526-7234, or go online to askjan.org.

ASK FOR AN ADJUSTMENT

You do not have to reveal that you have a disability. If you want an adjustment or choose to use disability services, however, then you will need to disclose the facts about your condition.

You will probably be asked to document that you have a disability and that you need an adjustment. This documentation might include a written evaluation from a physician, psychologist, or other professional who has worked with you.

To get the adjustment that you want, be prepared to describe the challenges that your disability has created in the past. Help instructors and administrators understand how your education has been affected. Also describe possible solutions, and be as specific as possible.

Ask for adjustments and services as early as possible. These will not be provided automatically. In higher education, you are expected to advocate for yourself.

USE TECHNOLOGY TO YOUR ADVANTAGE

If you have a disability, then gain as many computer skills as possible. Also set up your computer to promote your success. For example, find out how to do the following:

- Enlarge the cursor and adjust its blink rate.
- Enlarge all fonts and icons.
- Zoom in on all or a portion of the screen image.
- Adjust the screen display to remove all color and render images in black and white or gray scale.
- Use voice recognition rather than the keyboard for menu options.
- Turn on text-to-speech capabilities so that a computer-generated voice reads menu options, alerts, and web pages out loud.
- Choose a keyboard layout that's more convenient for typing with one hand or finger.

To access such features in the Windows operating system, select the Windows Control Panel or use the Accessibility Wizard. In Mac OS X, click on the Apple menu in the upper-left corner of the screen and select "System Preferences." In the System Preferences panel, click "Universal Access."

SPEAK ASSERTIVELY

Tell instructors when it's appropriate to consider your disability. If you use a wheelchair, for example, ask for appropriate transportation on field trips. If you have a visual disability, request that instructors speak as they write on the chalkboard. Also ask them to use high-contrast colors and to write legibly.

PLAN AHEAD

Meet with your counselor or advisor to design an educational plan—one that takes your disability into account. A key part of this plan is choosing instructors. Ask for recommendations before registering for classes. Interview prospective instructors, and ask to sit in on their classes. Express an interest in the class, ask to see a course outline, and discuss any adjustments that could help you complete the course.

USE EMPOWERING WORDS

Changing just a few words can make the difference between asking for what you want and apologizing for it. When people refer to disabilities, you might hear words such as *special treatment, accommodation,* and *adaptation.* Experiment with using the terms *adjustment* and *alternative* instead. The difference between these two groups of terms involves equality. Asking for an adjustment in an assignment or for an alternative assignment is asking for the right to produce equal work—not for special treatment that waters down the assignment.

ASK FOR APPROPRIATE TREATMENT

Many instructors will be eager to help you. In fact, at times they might go overboard. For example, a student who has trouble writing by hand might ask to complete in-class writing assignments on a computer. "Okay," the teacher might reply, "and take a little extra time. For you, there's no rush."

For some students this is a welcome response. Others, who have no need for an extended time line, can reply, "Thank you for thinking of me. I'd prefer to finish the assignment in the time frame allotted for the rest of the class."

FOLLOW UP WHEN NECESSARY

If the academic adjustment that you requested is not working, let your school know right away. Talk to the person who helped set up the adjustment. Remember that schools usually have grievance procedures for resolving conflicts about the services you're receiving.

Almost every school has a person who monitors compliance with disability laws. This person is often called the Section 504 coordinator, ADA coordinator, or disability services coordinator. If you think a school is discriminating against you because of your disability, this is the person to contact. You can also file a complaint against the school with the Office for Civil Rights. For more information, do an Internet search with the key words *contact OCR,* or call (800) 421-3481.

TAKE CARE OF YOURSELF

Many students with chronic illnesses or disabilities find that rest breaks are essential. If this is true for you, write such breaks into your daily or weekly plan.

A related suggestion is to treat yourself with respect. If your health changes in a way that you don't like, avoid berating yourself. Focus on finding an effective medical treatment or other solution.

It's important to accept compliments and periodically review your accomplishments in school. Fill yourself with affirmation. As you educate yourself, you are attaining mastery. ■

Dealing with sexism and
SEXUAL HARASSMENT

Until the early nineteenth century, women in the United States were banned from attending colleges and universities. Today, women make up the majority of first-year students in higher education, yet they still encounter bias based on gender. Although men also can be subjects of sexism and sexual harassment, women are more likely to experience this form of discrimination.

Bias based on gender can take many forms. For example, instructors might gloss over the contributions of women. Students in philosophy class might never hear of a woman named Hypatia, an ancient Greek philosopher and mathematician. Those majoring in computer science might never learn about Rear Admiral Grace Murray Hopper, who pioneered the development of a computer language named COBOL. And your art history textbook might not mention the Mexican painter Frida Kahlo or the American painter Georgia O'Keeffe.

Even the most well-intentioned people might behave in ways that hurt or discount women. Sexism is a factor in these situations:

- Instructors use only masculine pronouns—*he, his,* and *him*—to refer to both men and women.

- Career counselors hint that careers in mathematics and science are not appropriate for women.

- Students pay more attention to feedback from a male teacher than from a female teacher.

- Women are not called on in class, their comments are ignored, or they are overly praised for answering the simplest questions.

- People assume that middle-aged women who return to school have too many family commitments to study adequately or do well in their classes.

Many kinds of behavior—both verbal and physical—can be categorized as sexual harassment. This kind of discrimination involves unwelcome sexual conduct. Examples of such conduct in a school setting include the following:

- Sexual advances

- Any other unwanted touch

- Displaying or distributing sexually explicit materials

- Sexual gestures or jokes

- Pressure for sexual favors

- Spreading rumors about someone's sexual activity or rating someone's sexual performance

Sexual Harassment: It's Not Academic, a pamphlet from the U. S. Department of Education, quotes a woman who experienced sexual

> ## Sexism and sexual harassment are real. Incidents that are illegal or violate organizational policies occur throughout the year at schools and in workplaces.

harassment in higher education: "The financial officer made it clear that I could get the money I needed if I slept with him."[9] That's an example of *quid pro quo harassment*. This legal term applies when students believe that an educational decision depends on submitting to unwelcome sexual conduct. *Hostile environment harassment* takes place when such incidents are severe, persistent, or pervasive.

The feminist movement has raised awareness about all forms of harassment. We can now respond to such incidents in the places we live, work, and go to school. Specific strategies follow.

Point out sexist language and behavior. When you see examples of sexism, point them out. Your message can be more effective if you use "I" messages instead of personal attacks, as explained in Chapter 8: Communicating.

Indicate the specific statements and behaviors that you consider sexist. To help others understand sexism, you might rephrase a sexist comment so that it targets another group, such as Jews or African Americans. People sometimes spot anti-Semitism or racism more readily than sexism.

Keep in mind that men can also be subjected to sexism, ranging from antagonistic humor to exclusion from jobs that have traditionally been done by women.

Observe your own language and behavior. Looking for sexist behavior in others is a good first step in dealing with it. Detecting it in yourself can be just as powerful. Write a Discovery Statement about specific comments that could be interpreted as sexist. Then notice whether you say any of these things. Also, ask people you know to point out occasions when you use similar statements. Follow up with an Intention Statement that describes how you plan to change your speaking or behavior.

You can also write Discovery Statements about the current level of intimacy (physical and verbal) in any of your relationships at home, work, or school. Be sure that any increase in the level of intimacy is mutually agreed upon.

Encourage support for women. Through networks, women can work to overcome the effects of sexism. Strategies include study groups for women, women's job networks, and professional organizations, such as the Association for Women in Communications. Other examples are counseling services and health centers for women, family planning agencies, and rape prevention centers.

If your school does not have the women's networks you want, you can help form them. Help set up a 1-day or 1-week conference on women's issues. Create a discussion or reading group for the women in your class, department, residence hall, union, or neighborhood.

Take action. If you are sexually harassed, take action. Title IX of the Education Amendments of 1972 prohibits sexual harassment and other forms of sex discrimination. The law also requires schools to have grievance procedures in place for dealing with such discrimination. If you believe that you've been sexually harassed, report the incident to a school official. This person can be a teacher, administrator, or campus security officer. Check to see whether your school has someone specially designated to handle your complaint, such as an affirmative action officer or Title IX coordinator.

You can also file a complaint with the Office for Civil Rights (OCR), a federal agency that makes sure schools and workplaces comply with Title IX. In your complaint, include your name, address, and daytime phone number, along with the date of the incident and a description of it. Do this within 180 days of the incident. You can contact the OCR at (800) 421-3481. Or do an Internet search with the key words *contact OCR*.

Your community might offer more resources to protect against sexual discrimination. Examples are public interest law firms, legal aid societies, and unions that employ lawyers to represent students. ■

You're One Click Away...
from finding more examples online of sexual harassment and prevention strategies.

SEVEN STRATEGIES
for nonsexist communication

Following are tools you can use to speak and write in ways that are gender fair—without twisting yourself into verbal knots.

1 Use gender-neutral terms. Instead of writing *policeman* or *chairman*, for example, use *police officer* or *chairperson*. In many cases there's no need to identify the gender or marital status of a person. This allows us to dispose of expressions such as *female driver* and *lady doctor*.

2 Use examples that include both men and women. Good writing thrives on examples and illustrations. As you search for details to support the main points in your paper, include the stories and accomplishments of women as well as men.

3 Alternate pronoun gender. In an attempt to be gender fair, some writers make a point of mentioning both sexes whenever they refer to gender. Another method is to alternate the gender of pronouns throughout your writing. Still another option is to alternate male and female pronouns—the strategy used in this book. This allows you to avoid using awkward wording such as "He/she should open his/her book."

4 Switch to plural. Because plural pronouns in English are not gender specific, a sentence such as *The writer has many tools at her disposal* becomes *Writers have many tools at their disposal*.

5 Avoid words that imply sexist stereotypes. Included here are terms such as *tomboy, sissy, office boy, advertising man, man-eater, mama's boy, old lady,* and *powder puff*.

6 Use parallel names. When referring to men and women, use first and last names consistently. Within the same paper, for instance, avoid the phrase *President Barack Obama and his wife*. Instead, write the First Lady's full name: *Michelle Obama*.

7 Visualize a world of gender equality. Our writing is a direct reflection of the way we perceive the world. As we make a habit of recognizing women in roles of leadership, our writing can reflect this shift in viewpoint. That's a powerful step toward gender-fair writing.

9

Jeff Hunter/Getty Images

LEADERSHIP in a DIVERSE world

Many people mistakenly think that the only people who are leaders are those with formal titles such as *supervisor* or *manager*. In fact, though, some leaders have no such titles. Some have never supervised others. Like Mahatma Gandhi, some people change the face of the world without ever reaching a formal leadership position.

No one is born knowing how to lead. We acquire the skills over time. Begin now, while you are in higher education. Campuses offer continual opportunities to gain leadership skills. Volunteer for clubs, organizations, and student government. Look for opportunities to tutor or to become a peer advisor or mentor. No matter what you do, take on big projects—those that are worthy of your time and talents.

The U. S. Census Bureau predicts that the groups once classified as minorities—Hispanics, African Americans, East Asians, and South Asians—will become the majority by the year 2042. For Americans under age 18, this shift will take place in 2023.[10] Translation: Your next boss or coworker could be a person whose life experiences and views of the world differ radically from yours.

We live in a world where Barack Obama, a man with ancestors from Kenya and Kansas, became president of the United States; where Bobby Jindal, the son of immigrants from India, became governor of Louisiana; and where Oprah Winfrey, an African American woman, can propel a book to the top of the best seller list simply by recommending it on her television show. These people set examples of diversity in leadership that many others will follow.

Although many of us will never become so well-known, we all have the capacity to make significant changes in the world around us. Through our actions and words, we constantly influence what happens in our classrooms, offices, communities, and families. We are all leaders, even if sometimes we are unconscious of that fact.

To become a more effective leader, understand the many ways you naturally influence others. This kind of self-awareness—and the ability to harness that influence for positive goals—are qualities of master students. Also prepare to apply your leadership skills in a multicultural world.

> To become a more effective leader, understand the many ways you naturally influence others. This kind of self-awareness—and the ability to harness that influence for positive goals—are qualities of master students.

The following strategies can help you have a positive impact on your relationships with your friends and family members. Also use them when you join study groups and project teams in the workplace.

Own your leadership. Let go of the reluctance that many of us feel toward assuming leadership. It's impossible to escape leadership. Every time you speak, you lead others in some small or large way. Every time you take action, you lead others through your example. Every time you ask someone to do something, you are in essence leading that person. Leadership becomes more effective when it is consciously applied.

Be willing to be uncomfortable. Leadership is a courageous act. Leaders often are not appreciated or even liked. They can feel isolated—cut off from their colleagues. This isolation can sometimes lead to self-doubt and even fear. Before you take on a leadership role, be aware that you might experience such feelings. Also remember that none of these feelings has to stop you from leading.

Allow huge mistakes. The more important and influential you are, the more likely it is that your mistakes will have huge consequences. The chief financial officer for a large company can make a mistake that costs thousands or even millions of dollars. A physician's error could cost a life. As commander-in-chief of the armed forces, the president of a country can make a decision that costs thousands of lives. At the same time, these people are in a position to make huge changes for the better—to save thousands of dollars or lives through their power, skill, and influence.

People in leadership positions can become paralyzed and ineffective if they fear making a mistake. It's necessary for them to act even when information is incomplete or when they know a catastrophic mistake is a possible outcome.

Take on big projects. Leaders make promises. And effective leaders make big promises. These words—*I will do it* and *You can count on me*—distinguish a leader.

Look around your world to see what needs to be done, and then take it on. Consider taking on the biggest project you can think of—ending world hunger, eliminating nuclear weapons, wiping out poverty, promoting universal literacy. Think about how you'd spend your life if you knew that you could make a difference regarding these overwhelming problems. Then take the actions you considered. See what a difference they can make for you and for others.

Tackle projects that stretch you to your limits—projects that are worthy of your time and talents.

Provide feedback. An effective leader is a mirror to others. Share what you see. Talk with others about what they are doing effectively—and what they are doing ineffectively.

Keep in mind that people might not enjoy your feedback. Some would probably rather not hear it at all. Two things can help. One is to let people know up front that if they sign on to work with you, they can expect feedback. Also give your feedback with skill. Use "I" messages as explained in Chapter 8: Communicating. Back up any criticisms with specific observations and facts. And when people complete a task with exceptional skill, point that out too.

Paint a vision. Help others see the big picture—the ultimate purpose of a project. Speak a lot about the end result and the potential value of what you're doing.

There's a biblical saying: "Without vision, the people perish." Long-term goals usually involve many intermediate steps. Unless we're reminded of the purpose for those day-to-day actions, our work can feel like a grind. Leadership is the art of helping others lift their eyes to the horizon—keeping them in touch with the ultimate value and purpose of a project. Keeping the vision alive helps spirits soar.

Model your values. "Be the change you want to see" is a useful motto for leaders. Perhaps you want to see integrity, focused attention, and productivity in the people around you. Begin by modeling these qualities yourself. It's easy to excite others about a goal when you are enthusiastic about it yourself. Having fun while being productive is contagious. If you bring these qualities to a project, others might follow suit.

Make requests—lots of them. An effective leader is a request machine. Making requests—both large and small—is an act of respect. When we ask a lot from others, we demonstrate our respect for them and our confidence in their abilities.

9

At first, some people might get angry when we make requests of them. Over time, however, many will see that requests are compliments and opportunities to expand their skills. Ask a lot from others, and they might appreciate you because of it.

Follow up. What we don't inspect, people don't respect. When other people agree to do a job for you, follow up to see how it is going. You can do so in a way that communicates your respect and interest—not your fear that the project might flounder. When you display a genuine interest in other people and their work, they are more likely to view you as a partner in achieving a shared goal.

Focus on problems, not people. Sometimes projects do not go as planned. Big mistakes occur. If this happens, focus on the project and the mistakes—not the personal faults of your colleagues. People do not make mistakes on purpose. If they did, we would call them "on-purposes," not mistakes. Most people will join you in solving a problem if your focus is on the problem, not on what they did wrong.

Acknowledge others. Express genuine appreciation for the energy and creativity that others have put into their work. Take the time to be interested in what others have done and to care about the results they have accomplished. Thank and acknowledge them with your eyes, your words, and the tone of your voice.

Share credit. As a leader, constantly give away the praise and acknowledgment that you receive. When you're congratulated for your performance, pass the praise on to others. Share the credit with the group.

When you're a leader, the results you achieve depend on the efforts of many others. Acknowledging that fact often is more than telling the truth—it's essential if you want to continue to count on the support of others in the future.

Delegate. Ask a coworker or classmate to take on a job that you'd like to see done. Ask the same of your family or friends. Delegate tasks to the mayor of your town, the governor of your state, and the leaders of your country.

Take on projects that are important to you. Then find people who can lead the effort. You can do this even when you have no formal role as a leader.

We often see delegation as a tool that's available only to those above us in the chain of command. Actually, delegating up or across an organization can be just as effective. Consider delegating a project to your boss. That is, ask him to take on a job that you'd like to see accomplished. It might be a job that you cannot do, given your position in the company.

Balance styles. Think for a moment about your own learning style. To lead effectively, assess your strengths, and look for people who can complement them. If you excel at gathering

information and setting goals, for example, then recruit people who like to make decisions and take action. Also enlist people who think creatively and generate different points of view.

Look for different styles in the people who work with you. Remember that learning results from a balance between feeling, watching, thinking, and doing. (For more information, see Chapter 1: First Steps.) The people you lead will combine these characteristics in infinite variety. Welcome that variety, and accommodate it.

You can defuse and prevent many conflicts simply by acknowledging differences in style. Doing so opens up more options than blaming the differences on "politics" or "personality problems."

Listen. As a leader, be aware of what other people are thinking, feeling, and wanting. Listen fully to their concerns and joys. Before you criticize their views or make personal judgments, take the time to understand what's going on inside them. This is not merely a personal favor to the people you work with. The more you know about your coworkers or classmates, the more effectively you can lead them.

Communicate assertively—not aggressively or passively. *Aggressive* communication is ineffective. People who act aggressively are domineering. They often get what they want by putting down other people or using strong-arm methods. When aggressive people win, other people lose.

Assertive communication is asking directly and confidently for what you want *and* showing respect for others at the same time. This is one sign of an effective leader. Assertive people are committed to win–win solutions.

Some of us don't act assertively out of fear that we will appear aggressive. This is *passive* communication—neither assertive nor aggressive—that gets us nowhere. By remaining quiet and submissive, we allow others to infringe on our rights. When others run our lives, we fail to have the lives we want.

For more on how to speak assertively, see the suggestions for speaking with "I" messages in Chapter 8.

Practice. Leadership is an acquired skill. No one is born knowing how to make requests, give feedback, create budgets, do long-range planning, or delegate tasks. We learn these things over time, with practice, by seeing what works and what doesn't.

As a process of constant learning, leadership calls for all of the skills of master students. Look for areas in which you can make a difference, and experiment with these strategies. Right now there's something worth doing that calls for your leadership. Take action, and others will join you. ■

You're One Click Away...
from gaining more perspectives online on leadership.

Removing barriers to communication

E ffective leaders act as a mirror to others. They talk with others about what they are doing effectively—*and* what they are doing ineffectively.

People might not enjoy your feedback. Some would probably rather not hear it at all. Two things can help. One is to let people know up front that if they work with you, they can expect feedback. Also, give your feedback with skill.

Whenever you serve as a leader, examine your relationships. Then complete the following statements:

I discovered that I am not communicating about ...

_____

_____

with ...

_____

I discovered that I am not communicating about ...

_____

_____

with ...

_____

I discovered that I am not communicating about ...

_____

_____

with ...

_____

Now choose one idea from the article "Leadership in a diverse world" that can open communication with these people in these areas. Describe below how you will use this idea.

I intend to ...

_____

_____

_____

_____

_____

_____

_____

_____

_____

_____

9

PRACTICING
critical thinking 9

Throughout this book you've practiced the six levels of thinking described in "Becoming a critical thinker" on page 207.

Level 1: Remembering—recalling an idea.

Level 2: Understanding— explaining an idea in your own words and giving examples from your own experience.

Level 3: Applying—using an idea to produce a desired result.

Level 4: Analyzing—dividing an idea into parts or steps.

Level 5: Evaluating—rating the truth, usefulness, or quality of an idea—and giving reasons for your rating.

Level 6: Creating—inventing something new based on an idea.

Doing this exercise will give you additional practice with **Level 3: Applying**. At this level of thinking, you use an idea or suggestion to complete a task or produce another desired result. Test questions that call for understanding begin with terms such as these:

• Apply
• Complete
• Compute
• Construct
• Demonstrate
• Make use of
• Show
• Solve
• Use

You can do this level of thinking in any of your courses. For example, assignments in math courses ask you to apply formulas to **solve** problems and **calculate** answers. In a public speaking course, an instructor might ask you to **demonstrate** the difference between effective PowerPoint slides and ineffective slides.

The value you get from *Becoming a Master Student* and your student success course depends greatly on your skills at **Level 3: Applying**. In the space provided, describe how you applied an idea from this book or course. Or write a paragraph about how you intend to **apply** a suggestion from this chapter. First, summarize that suggestion. Then describe the specific steps you will take to **make use of** the suggestion so that it actually makes a difference in your life.

_____

_____

_____

_____

_____

_____

_____

_____

_____

_____

_____

_____

_____

_____

_____

_____

_____

_____

_____

_____

_____

_____

_____

_____

_____

_____

masterstudentprofile

Sampson Davis

(1973–) As a teenager growing up in Newark, New Jersey, Sampson made a pact with two of his friends to "beat the street," attend college, and become a physician.

Medical school was one of the roughest periods of my life. Something unexpected was always threatening to knock me out of the game: family distractions, the results of my first state board exam, the outcome of my initial search for a residency. But through determination, discipline, and dedication, I was able to persevere.

I call them my three "D's", and I believe that they are the perfect formula for survival, no matter what you are going through.

Determination is simply fixing your mind on a desired outcome, and I believe it is the first step to a successful end in practically any situation. When I made the pact with George and Rameck at the age of 17, I was desperate to change my life. Going to college and medical school with my friends seemed the best way to make that happen.

But, of course, I had no idea of the challenges awaiting me, and many times over the years I felt like giving up. Trust me, even if you're the most dedicated person, you can get weary when setbacks halt or interfere with your progress. But determination means nothing without the discipline to go through the steps necessary to reach your goal—whether you're trying to lose weight or finish college—and the dedication to stick with it.

When I failed the state board exam, the light in the tunnel disappeared. But I just kept crawling toward my goal. I sought counseling when I needed it, and I found at least one person with whom I could share the range of emotions I was experiencing. If you're going through a difficult time and can't see your way out alone, you should consider asking for help. I know how difficult that is for most guys . . . . But reaching out to counselors I had come to trust over the years and talking to my roommate Camille helped me unload some of the weight I was carrying. Only then was I able to focus clearly on what I needed to do to change my circumstances.

I'm grateful that I took kung fu lessons as a kid, because the discipline I learned back then really helped me to stay consistent once I started meditating, working out, and studying every single day. . . .

Another important ingredient of perseverance is surrounding yourself with friends who support your endeavor. I can't tell you how much it helped me to have George and Rameck in my life to help me reach my goal. Even though things were awkward between us for a while after I failed the state boards, just knowing they were there and that they expected me to succeed motivated me.

I found motivation wherever I could. One of my college professors once told me that I didn't have what it takes to be a doctor, and I even used that to motivate me. I love being the underdog. I love it when someone expects me to fail. That, like nothing else, can ignite my three "D's."

And when success comes, I'm the one who's not surprised.

© Michael Cidyoung/Retna Ltc./Corbis

SAMPSON DAVIS . . . is determined.

YOU . . . can be determined by defining goals that make a huge difference in your life.

9

You're One Click Away...
from learning more about Sampson Davis online at the Master Student Profiles. You can also visit the Master Student Hall of Fame to learn about other master students.

PUT THIS CHAPTER TO WORK

TALK ABOUT CULTURAL COMPETENCE. In the workplace, the term *cultural competence* is starting to replace *diversity skills*. The reason is simple: It's one thing to create a workplace that includes people of various cultural backgrounds. It's another thing to create a workplace where all those people feel welcome. During job interviews, be prepared to give evidence of your cultural competence. Talk about cooperative learning projects with diverse members—and how you involved everyone on the team.

EXPECT DIFFERENCES. Most of us unconsciously judge others by a single set of cultural standards—our own. That can lead to communication breakdown. Consider some examples:

- A man in Costa Rica works for a company that's based in the United States and has offices around the world. He turns down a promotion that would take his family to California. This choice mystifies the company's executives. Yet the man has grandparents who are in ill health, and leaving them behind would be taboo in his country.

- A Caucasian woman from Ohio travels to Mexico City on business. She shows up promptly for a 9:00 A.M. meeting and finds that it starts 30 minutes late and goes an hour beyond its scheduled ending time. She's entered a culture with a flexible sense of time.

- An American executive schedules a meeting over dinner with people from his company's office in Italy. As soon as the group orders food, the executive launches into a discussion of his agenda items. He notices that his coworkers from Italy seem unusually silent and wonders whether they feel offended. He forgets that they come from a culture where people phase in to business discussions slowly—only after building a relationship through "small talk."

To prevent misunderstandings, remember that culture touches every aspect of human behavior, ranging from the ways that people greet each to the ways they resolve conflict. Expecting differences up-front helps you keep an open mind.

USE LANGUAGE WITH CARE. Even people who speak the same language can use simple words that can be confusing to others. For instance, giving someone a "mickey" can mean pulling a practical joke—or slipping a drug into someone's drink. We can find it tough to communicate simple observations, let alone abstract concepts.

You can help by communicating simply and directly. When meeting with people who speak English as a second language, think twice before using figures of speech or slang expressions. Stick to standard English and enunciate clearly. Fight the common urge to speak louder. Speak slowly and clearly, not loudly.

Also remember that nonverbal language differs across cultures. For example, people from India may shake their head from side to side to indicate agreement, not disagreement.

PUT MESSAGES IN CONTEXT. When speaking to people of another culture, you might find that words carry only part of an intended message. In many countries, strong networks of shared assumptions form a context for communication. As an example, people from some Asian and Arabic countries might not include every detail of an agreement in a written contract. These people often place a high value on keeping verbal promises. Spelling out all the details in writing might be considered an insult. Knowing such facts can help you prevent and resolve conflicts in the workplace.

NOW CREATE A CAREER CONNECTION OF YOUR OWN. Review this chapter, looking for a suggestion that you will commit to use while working or looking for a job. In a sentence or two, describe exactly what you plan to do and the primary benefit you want to gain. For example: "I will form a study group and set an agenda for our first session. This will help me develop leadership skills."

State your strategy and desired benefit in the space below.

_____

_____

_____

_____

_____

Name _____

Date _____

1. Explain a strategy for taking charge of the conversations in your life.

2. Give two examples of differences between individualist and collectivist cultures.

3. Briefly describe three strategies for building relationships across cultures.

4. Explain the differences among *stereotypes*, *prejudice*, and *discrimination*.

5. Define the terms *translator*, *mediator*, and *model* as explained in this chapter.

6. The text suggests looking for individuals rather than group representatives. Explain this suggestion in your own words.

7. Describe an error in thinking that helps to create stereotypes.

8. Briefly explain the difference between *quid pro quo harassment* and *hostile environment harassment*.

9. Rewrite the following sentence so that it is gender neutral: "Any writer can benefit from honing his skill at observing people."

10. According to the text, few of us get the chance to be leaders. True or false? Explain your answer.

9

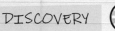

9 SKILLS *Snapshot*

CHAPTER

Now that you've reflected on the ideas in this chapter and experimented with some new strategies, revisit your responses to the Diversity section of the Discovery Wheel exercise on page 38. Complete the following sentences.

DISCOVERY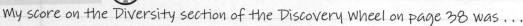

My score on the Diversity section of the Discovery Wheel on page 38 was ...

If I talk to people who express racial and ethnic stereotypes, I respond by ...

When I meet someone whose culture differs in a major way from mine, my first
reaction is often to ...

Other ways I could respond include ...

INTENTION

I'll know that I've reached a new level of mastery with diversity when ...

ACTION

To reach that level of mastery, the most important thing I can do next is to ...

At the end of this course, I would like my Diversity score on the Discovery Wheel to be ...

Money

 Use this **Master Student Map** to ask yourself,

 WHY THIS CHAPTER MATTERS . . .

- Money does not have to be a barrier to getting what you want from school—and from your life.

WHAT IS INCLUDED . . .

- Power Process: Risk being a fool   296
- The end of money worries   297
- Make more money   304
- Spend less money   305
- Managing money during tough times   307
- Take charge of your credit   309
- Education is worth it—and you can pay for it   313
- Your learning styles and your money   314
- Your money and your values   315
- Master Student Profile: Lisa Price   317

 HOW CAN I USE THIS CHAPTER . . .

- Discover the details about how money flows in and out of your life.
- Experiment with ways to increase your income and decrease expenses.
- Gain strategies for saving, investing, and reducing debt.
- Find ways to pay for your education.

 WHAT IF . . .

- I could adopt habits that would free me from money worries for the rest of my life?

© Ruslan Ivantsov/Shutterstock.com

JOURNAL ENTRY 24
Intention Statement

Commit to a new experience of money

Scan this chapter with an eye for strategies that could help you increase your income, decrease your expenses, or both. List three money strategies that you'd like to use right away.

I intend to . . .

_____

_____

_____

_____

_____

_____

_____

_____

_____

_____

_____

_____

POWER process

Risk being a fool

Noam Armonn/Shutterstock.com

A master student has the courage to take risks. And taking risks means being willing to fail sometimes—even being willing to be a fool.

Don't be upset. All of us are fools at one time or another. If you doubt it, think back to that stupid thing you did just a few days ago. You know the one. Yes . . . *that* one. It was embarrassing, and you tried to hide it. You pretended you weren't a fool. This happens to everyone.

We are all fallible human beings. Most of us, however, spend too much time and energy trying to hide our foolhood. No one is really tricked by this—not even ourselves. It's okay to look ridiculous while dancing. It's all right to sound silly when singing to your kids. Sometimes it's okay to be absurd. It comes with taking risks.

This Power Process comes with a warning label: Taking risks does *not* mean escaping responsibility for our actions. "Risk being a fool" is not a suggestion to get drunk at a party and make a fool of yourself. It is not a suggestion to fool around or do things badly. Mediocrity is not the goal.

The point is that mastery in most activities calls for the willingness to do something new, to fail, to make corrections, to fail again, and so on.

Take money, for example. This chapter asks you to consider an outrageous idea—that you can end money worries. If you share this idea with someone, they might even call you a fool. If you're okay with those reactions, then nobody's criticism will stop you. You're free to explore any idea and even make a few mistakes. In the process, you could learn something that changes your whole experience of money.

There's one sure-fire way to avoid any risk of being a fool, and that's to avoid life. The center fielder who sits out every game is safe from making any errors. The comedian who never performs in front of an audience is certain to avoid telling jokes that fall flat. The possibility of succeeding at any venture increases when we're comfortable with making mistakes— that is, with the risk of being a fool.

You're One Click Away...
from accessing Power process Media online and finding out more about how to "risk being a fool."

The end of *money worries*

M ost money problems result from spending more than is available. It's that simple, even though we often do everything we can to make the problem much more complicated.

The solution also is simple: *Don't spend more than you have.* If you are spending more than you have, then increase your income, decrease your spending, or do both. This idea has never won a Nobel Prize in Economics, but you won't go broke applying it to your life.

Money produces more unnecessary conflict and worry than almost anything else. And it doesn't seem to matter how much money a person has. People who earn $10,000 a year never have enough. People who earn $100,000 a year might also say that they never have enough.

Let's say they earned $1 million a year. Then they'd have enough, right? Not necessarily. Money worries can upset people no matter how much they have, especially when the economy dips into recession.

Money management may be based on a simple idea, but there is a big incentive for us to make it seem more complicated and scarier than it really is. If we don't understand money, then we don't have to be responsible for it. After all, if you don't know how to change a flat tire, then you don't have to be the one responsible for fixing it.

"I can't afford it" is a common reason that students give for dropping out of school. Actually, "I don't know how to pay for it" or "I don't think it's worth it" are probably more accurate ways to state the problem.

Using the strategies in this chapter could help you create financial peace of mind. That's a bold statement—perhaps even an outrageous one. But what if it's true? Approach this idea as a possibility. Then experiment with it, using your own life as the laboratory.

This chapter can benefit you even during a recession. Although the state of the overall economy matters as well, your financial fate depends far more on the small choices you make every day about spending and earning money.

The strategies you're about to learn are not complicated. In fact, they're not even new. The strategies are all based on the cycle of discovery, intention, and action that you've already practiced with the Journal Entries in this book. With these strategies—and the abilities to add and subtract—you have everything you need to manage your money.

There are three main steps in money management:

- First, tell the truth about how much money you have and how much you spend (discovery).
- Second, commit to spend less than you have (intention).
- Finally, apply the suggestions for earning more money, spending less money, or both (action).

If you do these three things consistently, you can eventually say goodbye to most money worries. For example, the single habit of paying off your entire credit card balance each month might be enough to transform your financial life.

This chapter about money does not tell you how to become a millionaire, though you can certainly adopt that as a goal if you choose. Instead, the following pages reveal what many millionaires know—ways to control money instead of letting money control you. ■

You're One Click Away...
from finding more perspectives online on the nature of financial freedom.

This book is worth $1,000

C engage Learning is proud to present three students each year with a $1,000 scholarship for tuition reimbursement. Any post-secondary school in the United States and Canada can nominate one student for the scholarship. To be considered, write an essay that answers the question "How do you define success?"

You're One Click Away...
from finding more details online at the College Success CourseMate for Becoming a Master Student.

10

✓ EXERCISE 27

The Money Monitor/Money Plan

Many of us find it easy to lose track of money. It likes to escape when no one is looking. And usually, no one is looking. That's why the simple act of noticing the details about money can be so useful—even if this is the only idea from the chapter that you ever apply.

Use this exercise as a chance to discover how money flows into and out of your life. The goal is to record all the money you receive and spend over the course of 1 month. This sounds like a big task, but it's simpler than you might think. Besides, there's a big payoff for this action. With increased awareness of income and expenses, you can make choices about money that will change your life. Here's how to begin.

STEP 1 Tear out the Money Monitor/Money Plan form on page 301. Make photocopies of this form to use each month. The form helps you do two things. One is to get a big picture of the money that flows in and out of your life. The other is to plan specific and immediate changes in how you earn and spend money.

STEP 2 Keep track of your income and expenses. Use your creativity to figure out how you want to carry out this step. The goal is to create a record of exactly how much you earn and spend each month. Use any method that works for you. And keep it simple. Following are some options:

- **Carry 3 × 5 cards in your pocket, purse, backpack, or briefcase.** Every time you buy something or get paid, record a few details on a card. List the date. Add a description of what you bought or what you got paid. Note whether the item is a source of income (money coming in) or an expense (money going out). Be sure to use a separate card for each item. This makes it easier to sort your cards into categories at the end of the month and fill out your Money Monitor/Money Plan.

- **Save all receipts and file them.** This method does not require you to carry any 3 × 5 cards. But it does require that you faithfully hang on to every receipt and record of payment. Every time you buy

something, ask for a receipt. Then stick it in your wallet, purse, or pocket. When you get home, make notes about the purchase on the receipt. Then file the receipts in a folder labeled with the current month and year (for example, January 2011). Every time you get a paycheck during that month, save the stub and add it to the folder. If you do not get a receipt or record of payment, whip out a 3 × 5 card and create one of your own. Detailed receipts will help you later on when you file taxes, categorize expenses (such as food and entertainment), and check your purchases against credit card statements.

- **Use personal finance software.** Learn to use Quicken or a similar product that allows you to record income and expenses on your computer and to sort them into categories.

- **Use online banking services.** If you have a checking account that offers online services, take advantage of the records that the bank is already keeping for you. Every time you write a check, use a debit card, or make a deposit, the transaction will show up online. You can use a computer to log in to your account and view these transactions at any time. If you're unclear about how to use online banking, go in to your bank and ask for help.

- **Experiment with several of the above options.** Settle into one that feels most comfortable to you. Or create a method of your own. Anything will work, as long as you end each month with an *exact and accurate* record of your income and expenses.

STEP 3 On the last day of the month, fill out your Money Monitor/Money Plan. Pull out a blank Money Monitor/Money Plan. Label it with the current month and year. Fill out this form using the records of your income and expenses for the month.

Notice that the far left column of the Money Monitor/Money Plan includes categories of income and expenses. (You can use the blank rows for categories of income and expenses that are not already included.) Write your total for each category in the middle column.

For example, if you spent $300 at the grocery store this month, write that amount in the middle column next to *Groceries*. If you work a part-time job and received two paychecks for the month, write the total in the middle column next to *Employment*. See the sample Money Monitor/Money Plan on page 300 for more examples.

Remember to split expenses when necessary. For example, you might write one check each month to pay the balance due on your credit card. The purchases listed on your credit card bill might fall into several categories. Total up your expenses in each category, and list them separately.

Suppose that you used your credit card to buy music online, purchase a sweater, pay for three restaurant meals, and buy two tanks of gas for your car. Write the online music expense next to *Entertainment*. Write the amount you paid for the sweater next to *Clothes*. Write the total you spent at the restaurants next to *Eating Out*. Finally, write the total for your gas stops next to *Gas*.

Now look at the column on the far right of the Money Monitor/Money Plan. This column is where the magic happens. Review each category of income and expense. If you plan to reduce your spending in a certain category during the next month, write a minus sign (−) in the far right column. If you plan a spending increase in

any category next month, write a plus sign (+) in the far right column. If you think that a category of income or expense will remain the same next month, leave the column blank.

Look again at the sample Money Monitor/Money Plan on page 300. This student plans to reduce her spending for clothes, eating out, and entertainment (which for her includes movies and DVD rentals). She plans to increase the total she spends on groceries. She figures that even so, she'll save money by cooking more food at home and eating out less.

STEP 4 After you've filled out your first Money Monitor/Money Plan, take a moment to congratulate yourself. You have actively collected and analyzed the data needed to take charge of your financial life. No matter how the numbers add up, you are now in conscious control of your money. Repeat this exercise every month. It will keep you on a steady path to financial freedom.

You're One Click Away...
from doing this exercise online at your College Success CourseMate.

No budgeting required

Notice one more thing about the Money Monitor/Money Plan: It does not require you to create a budget. Budgets—like diets—often fail. Many people cringe at the mere mention of the word *budget*. To them it is associated with scarcity, drudgery, and guilt. The idea of creating a budget conjures up images of a penny-pinching Ebenezer Scrooge shaking a bony, wrinkled finger at them and screaming, "You spent too much, you loser!"

That's not the idea behind the Money Monitor/Money Plan. In fact, there is no budget worksheet for you to complete each month. And no one is pointing a finger at you. Instead of budgeting, you simply write a plus sign or a minus sign next to each expense or income category that you *freely choose* to increase or decrease next month. There's no extra paperwork, no shame, and no blame.

10

Sample Money Monitor/Money Plan

Income	This Month	Next Month
Employment	500	
Grants	100	
Interest from Savings		
Loans	300	
Scholarships	100	
Total Income	1000	

Expenses	This Month	Next Month
Books and Supplies		
Car Maintenance		
Car Payment		
Clothes		–
Deposits into Savings Account		
Eating Out	50	–
Entertainment	50	–
Gas	100	
Groceries	300	+
Insurance (Car, Life, Health, Home)		
Laundry	20	
Phone	55	
Rent/Mortgage Payment	400	
Tuition and Fees		
Utilities	50	
Total Expenses	1025	–

Money Monitor/Money Plan
Month_____ Year_____

Income	This Month	Next Month	Expenses	This Month	Next Month
Employment			Books and Supplies		
Grants			Car Maintenance		
Interest from Savings			Car Payment		
Loans			Clothes		
Scholarships			Deposits into Savings Account		
			Eating Out		
			Entertainment		
			Gas		
			Groceries		
			Insurance (Car, Life, Health, Home)		
			Laundry		
			Phone		
			Rent/Mortgage Payment		
			Tuition and Fees		
			Utilities		
Total Income			Total Expenses		

10

Money Monitor/Money Plan
Month_____ Year_____

Income	This Month	Next Month
Employment		
Grants		
Interest from Savings		
Loans		
Scholarships		
Total Income		

Expenses	This Month	Next Month
Books and Supplies		
Car Maintenance		
Car Payment		
Clothes		
Deposits into Savings Account		
Eating Out		
Entertainment		
Gas		
Groceries		
Insurance (Car, Life, Health, Home)		
Laundry		
Phone		
Rent/Mortgage Payment		
Tuition and Fees		
Utilities		
Total Expenses		

JOURNAL ENTRY 25 *Discovery/Intention Statement*

Reflect on your Money Monitor/Money Plan

Now that you've experimented with the Money Monitor/Money Plan process, reflect on what you're learning. To start creating a new future with money, complete the following statements:

After monitoring my income and expenses for 1 month, I was surprised to discover that . . .

_____

_____

_____

_____

When it comes to money, I am skilled at . . .

_____

_____

_____

_____

When it comes to money, I am *not* so skilled at . . .

_____

_____

_____

_____

I could increase my income by . . .

_____

_____

_____

_____

I could spend less money on . . .

_____

_____

_____

_____

After thinking about the most powerful step I can take right now to improve my finances, I intend to . . .

_____

_____

_____

_____

10

MAKE MORE MONEY

For many people, finding a way to increase income is the most appealing way to fix a money problem. This approach is reasonable, but it has a potential problem: When their income increases, many people continue to spend more than they make. This means that money problems persist even at higher incomes. To avoid this problem, manage your expenses no matter how much money you make.

If you do succeed at controlling your expenses over the long term, then increasing your income is definitely a way to build wealth. Among the ways to make more money are to focus on your education, consider financial aid, work while you're in school, and do your best at every job.

Focus on your education. Your most important assets are not your bank accounts, your car, or your house—they are your skills. As Henry Ford said, "The only real security that a person can have in this world is a reserve of knowledge, experience, and ability. Without these qualities, money is practically useless."[1]

That's why your education is so important. Right now, you're developing knowledge, experience, and abilities that you can use to create income for the rest of your life.

Once you graduate and land a job in your chosen field, continue your education. Look for ways to gain additional skills or certifications that lead to higher earnings and more fulfilling work assignments.

Consider financial aid. Student grants and loans can play a major role in your college success by freeing you up from having to work full-time or even part-time. Many students erroneously assume they don't qualify for educational grants or low-interest student loans. Visit the financial aid office at your school to discover your options.

Work while you're in school. If you work while you're in school, you earn more than money. You gain experience, establish references, interact with a variety of people, and make contact with people who might hire you in the future. Also, regular income in any amount can make a difference in your monthly cash flow.

Many students work full-time or part-time jobs. Work and school don't have to conflict, especially if you plan carefully (see Chapter 2: Time) and ask for your employer's support.

On most campuses, the financial aid office employs a person whose job it is to help students find work while they're in school. See that person.

Some part-time jobs are just made for students. Serving or delivering food may not be glamorous, but the tips can make a real difference in your monthly income. Other jobs, such as working the reference desk at the campus library or monitoring the front desk in a dorm, can offer quiet times that are ideal for doing some extra studying.

Another option is to start your own business. Consider a service you could offer—anything from lawn mowing to computer consulting. Students can boost their income in many other ways, such as running errands, giving guitar lessons, walking pets, and house sitting. Charge reasonable rates, provide impeccable service, and ask your clients for referrals.

See whether you can find a job related to your chosen career. Even an entry-level job in your field can provide valuable experience. Once you've been in such a job for a while, explore the possibilities for getting a promotion.

Do your best at every job. Once you get a job, make it your intention to excel as an employee. A positive work experience can pay off for years by leading to other jobs, recommendations, and contacts.

To maximize your earning power, keep honing your job-hunting and career-planning skills. You can find a wealth of ideas on these topics in Chapter 12: What's Next.

Finally, keep things in perspective. If your job is lucrative and rewarding, great. If not, remember that almost any job can support you in becoming a master student and reaching your educational goals. ∎

You're One Click Away...
from discovering more ways online to increase your income.

Master Students **IN ACTION**

" *My money management strategies include waiting until I have the money to buy something and searching for the best deal. I'm a fiend when it comes to searching for coupons online. I could spend less money on food if I went out to eat less. I figured I could save $100–$150 a month by packing a lunch.* "

—Jake Zucker, The University of Rochester

Courtesy of Jake Zucker

You're One Click Away...
from viewing a video about Master Students in Action.

SPEND LESS MONEY

Controlling your expenses is something you can do right away, and it's usually easier than increasing your income. Use ideas from the following list, and invent more of your own.

Look to big-ticket items. When you look for places to cut expenses, start with the items that cost the most. Choices about where to live, for example, can save you thousands of dollars. Sometimes a place a little farther from campus, or a smaller house or apartment, will be much less expensive. You can also keep your housing costs down by finding a roommate. Offer to do repairs or maintenance in exchange for reduced rent. Pay your rent on time, and treat property with respect.

Another high-ticket item is a car. Take the cost of buying or leasing and then add expenses for parking, insurance, repairs, gas, maintenance, and tires. You might find that it makes more sense to walk, bike, use public transportation, ride a campus shuttle, and call for an occasional taxi ride. Or carpool. Find friends with a car, and chip in for gas.

Use Exercise 27: "The Money Monitor/Money Plan" on page 298 to discover the main drains on your finances. Then focus on one or two areas where you can reduce spending while continuing to pay your fixed monthly bills such as rent and tuition.

Look to small-ticket items. Reducing or eliminating the money you spend on low-cost purchases can make the difference between saving money or going into debt. For example, $3 spent at the coffee shop every day adds up to $1,095 over a year. That kind of spending can give anyone the jitters.

Ask for student discounts. Movie theaters, restaurants, bars, shopping centers, and other businesses sometimes discount prices for students. Also ask your bank whether you can open a student checking and savings account with online banking. The fees and minimum required amounts could be lower. Go online to check your balances weekly so that you avoid overdraft fees.

Do comparison shopping. Prices vary dramatically. Shop around, wait for off-season sales, and use coupons. Check out secondhand stores, thrift stores, and garage sales. Before plunking down the full retail price for a new item, consider whether you could buy it used. You can find "preowned" clothes, CDs, furniture, sports equipment, audio equipment, and computer hardware in retail stores and on the Internet.

Also go online to find Web sites that will compare prices for you. Examples include Yahoo! Shopping (shopping.yahoo.com) and Google Product Search (www.google.com/prdhp).

Be aware of quality. The cheapest product is not always the least expensive over the long run. Sometimes, a slightly more expensive item is the best buy because it will last longer.

Remember, there is no correlation between the value of something and the amount of money spent to advertise it. Carefully inspect things you are considering to buy to see whether they are well made.

Save money on eating and drinking. This single suggestion could significantly lower your expenses. Instead of hitting a restaurant or bar, head to the grocery store. In addition, clip food coupons. Sign up for a shopper's discount card.

Cooking for yourself doesn't need to take much time if you do a little menu planning. Create a list of your five favorite home-cooked meals. Learn how to prepare them. Then keep ingredients for these meals always on hand. To reduce grocery bills, buy these ingredients in bulk.

If you live in a dorm, review the different meal plans you can buy. Some schools offer meal plans for students who live off campus. These plans might be cheaper than eating in restaurants while you're on campus.

More deals are online. Find coupons at Web sites such as Groupon (www.groupon.com) and Living Social (www.livingsocial.com).

Lower your phone bills. If you use a cell phone, pull out a copy of your latest bill. Review how many minutes you used last month. Perhaps you could get by with a less expensive phone, fewer minutes, fewer text messages, and a cheaper plan.

Do an Internet search on *cell phone plan comparison,* and see whether you could save money by switching providers. Also consider a family calling plan, which might cost less than a separate plan for each person. In addition, consider whether you need a home phone (a land line) *and* a cell phone. Dropping the home phone could save you money right away.

Keep an eye on Web-based options for turning your voice into a digital signal that travels over the Internet. This technology is called Voice over Internet Protocol (VoIP), and Skype (www.skype.com) is just one example of it. Using VoIP can be cheaper than making international phone calls.

Go "green." To conserve energy and save money on utility bills, turn out the lights when you leave a room. Keep windows and doors closed in winter. In summer, keep windows open early in the day to invite lots of cool air into your living space. Then close up the apartment or house to keep it cool during the hotter hours of the day. Leave air-conditioning set at 72 degrees or above. In cool weather, dress warmly and keep the house at 68 degrees or less. In hot weather, take shorter, cooler showers.

Unplug any electric appliances that are not in use. Appliances like microwaves, audio systems, and cell phone chargers use energy when plugged in even when they're not in use. Also, plug computer equipment into power strips that you can turn off while you sleep.

10

Explore budget plans for monthly payments that fluctuate, such as those for heating your home. These plans average your yearly expenses so you pay the same amount each month.

Pay cash. To avoid interest charges, deal in cash. If you don't have the cash, don't buy. Buying on credit makes it more difficult to monitor spending. You can easily bust next month's money plan with this month's credit card purchases.

Postpone purchases. If you plan to buy something, leave your checkbook or credit card at home when you first go shopping. Look at all the possibilities. Then go home and make your decision when you don't feel pressured. When you are ready to buy, wait a week, even if the salesperson pressures you. What seems like a necessity today may not even cross your mind the day after tomorrow.

Notice what you spend on "fun." Blowing your money on fun is fun. It is also a fast way to blow your savings. When you spend money on entertainment, ask yourself what the benefits will be and whether you could get the same benefits for less money. You can read magazines for free at the library, for example. Most libraries also loan CDs and DVDs for free.

Use the envelope system. After reviewing your monthly income and expenses, put a certain amount of cash each week in an envelope labeled *Entertainment/Eating Out*. When the envelope is empty, stop spending money on these items for the rest of the week. If you use online banking, see whether you can create separate accounts for various spending categories. Then deposit

a fixed amount of money into each of those accounts. This is an electronic version of the envelope system.

Don't compete with big spenders. When you watch other people spend their money, remember that you don't know the whole story. Some students have parents with deep pockets. Others head to Mexico every year for spring break but finance the trips with high-interest credit cards. If you find yourself feeling pressured to spend money so that you can keep up with other people, stop to think about how much it will cost over the long run. Maybe it's time to shop around for some new friends.

Use the money you save to prepare for emergencies and reduce debt. If you apply strategies such as those listed here, you might see your savings account swell nicely. Congratulate yourself. Then choose what to do with the extra money. To protect yourself during tough times, create an emergency fund. Then reduce your debt by paying more than the minimum on credit card bills and loan payments (see "Take charge of your credit" on page 309).

Spend less, and feel the power. Cutting your spending might be challenging at first. Give it time. Spending less is not about sacrificing pleasure. It's about something that money can't buy—the satisfaction of choosing exactly where your money goes and building a secure financial future. Every dollar that you save on a frivolous expense is a dollar you can invest in something that truly matters to you. ∎

You're One Click Away...
from discovering more cost-cutting strategies online.

✓ EXERCISE 28

Show me the money

See whether you can use *Becoming a Master Student* to create a financial gain that is many times more than the cost of the book. Scan the entire text, and look for suggestions that could help you save money or increase income in significant ways; for example:

- Use suggestions for career planning and job hunting in Chapter 12: What's Next to find your next job more quickly—and start earning money sooner.

- Get a higher-paying job with strategies from the articles "Build an irresistible résumé" on page 366 and "Use job interviews to hire an employer" on page 369.

- Use suggestions from this chapter to reduce your monthly expenses and fatten up your savings account.

In the space below, write your ideas for creating more money from your experience of this book. Use additional paper as needed.

_____

_____

_____

_____

_____

_____

_____

Managing money during tough times

A short-term crisis in the overall economy can reduce your income and increase your expenses. So can the decision to go back to school. The biggest factor in your long-term financial well-being, though, is your daily behavior. Habits that help you survive during tough times will also help you prosper after you graduate and when the economy rebounds. Taking informed action is a way to cut through financial confusion and move beyond fear.

Start by doing Exercise 27: "Money Monitor/Money Plan" on page 298. This exercise will give you the details about what you're spending and earning right now. With that knowledge, you can choose your next strategy from among the following.

TAKE A FIRST STEP

If the economy tanks, we can benefit by telling the truth about it. We can also tell the truth about ourselves. It's one thing to condemn the dishonesty of mortgage bankers and hedge fund managers. It's another thing to have an unpaid balance on a credit card or wipe out a savings accounts and still believe that we are in charge of our money. The first step to changing such behaviors is simply to admit that they don't work.

SPEND LESS AND SAVE MORE

The less you spend, the more money you'll have on hand. Use that money to pay your monthly bills, pay off your credit cards, and create an emergency fund to use in case you lose your job or a source of financial aid. See "Spend less money" on page 305 for ideas.

Author Suze Orman recommends three actions to show that you can reduce spending at any time: (1) Do not spend money for 1 day, (2) do not use your credit card for 1 week, and (3) do not eat out for 1 month. Success with any of these strategies can open up your mind to other possibilities for spending less and saving more.[2]

MAKE SURE THAT YOUR SAVINGS ARE PROTECTED

The Federal Deposit Insurance Corporation (FDIC) backs individual saving accounts. The National Credit Union Administration (NCUA) offers similar protection for credit union members. If your savings are protected by these programs, every penny you deposit is safe. Check your statements to find out, or go online to www.myfdicinsurance.gov.

10

PAY OFF YOUR CREDIT CARDS

If you have more than one credit card with an outstanding balance, then find out which one has the highest interest rate. Put as much money as you can toward paying off that balance while making the minimum payment on the other cards. Repeat this process until all unpaid balances are erased.

INVEST ONLY AFTER SAVING

The stock market is only for money that you can afford to lose. Before you speculate, first save enough money to live on for at least 6 months in case you're unemployed. Then consider what you'll need over the next 5 years to finish your schooling and handle other major expenses. Save for these expenses before taking any risks with your money.

DO STELLAR WORK AT YOUR CURRENT JOB

The threat of layoffs increases during a recession. However, companies will hesitate to shed their star employees. If you're working right now, then think about ways to become indispensable. Gain skills and experience that will make you more valuable to your employer.

No matter what job you have, be as productive as possible. Look for ways to boost sales, increase quality, or accomplish tasks in less time. Ask yourself every day how you can create extra value by solving a problem, reducing costs, improving service, or attracting new clients or customers.

THINK ABOUT YOUR NEXT JOB

Create a career plan that describes the next job you want, the skills that you'll develop to get it, and the next steps you'll take to gain those skills. Stay informed about the latest developments in your field. Find people who are already working in this area, and contact them for information interviews.

You might want to start an active job hunt now, even if you have a job. Find time to build your network, go to job-related conferences, and stay on top of current job openings in your field. For related ideas, see Chapter 12.

RESEARCH UNEMPLOYMENT BENEFITS

Unemployment benefits have limits and may not replace your lost wages. However, they can cushion the blow of losing a job while you put other strategies in place. To learn about the benefits offered in your state, go online to www.servicelocator.org. Click "Unemployment Benefits." Then enter your state.

GET HEALTH INSURANCE

A sudden illness or lengthy hospital stay can drain your savings. Health insurance can pick up all or most of the costs instead. If possible, get health insurance through your school or employer. Another option is private health insurance. This can be cheaper than extending an employer's policy if you lose your job. To find coverage, go online to the Web site of the National Association of Health Underwriters (www.nahu.org) and www.ehealthinsurance.com.

GET HELP THAT YOU CAN TRUST

Avoid debt consolidators that offer schemes to wipe out your debt. What they don't tell you is that their fees are high, and that using them can lower your credit rating. Turn instead to the National Foundation for Credit Counseling (www.nfcc.org). Find a credit counselor that is accredited by this organization. Work with someone who is open about fees and willing to work with all your creditors. Don't pay any fees up front, before you actually get help.

PUT YOUR PLAN IN WRITING

List the specific ways that you will reduce spending and increase income. If you have a family, consider posting this list for everyone to see. The act of putting your plan in writing can help you feel in control of your money. Review your plan regularly to make sure that it's working and that everyone who's affected is on board.

COPE WITH STRESS IN POSITIVE WAYS

When times get tough, some people are tempted to reduce stress with unhealthy behaviors like smoking, drinking, and overeating. Find better ways to cope. Exercise, meditation, and a sound sleep can do wonders. For specific suggestions, see Chapter 11: Health.

Social support is one of the best stress busters. If you're unemployed or worried about money, connect with family members and friends often. Turn healthy habits such as exercising and preparing healthy meals into social affairs.

CHOOSE YOUR MONEY CONVERSATIONS

When the economy tanks, the news is filled with gloomy reports and dire predictions. Remember that reports are constantly competing for your attention. Sometimes they use gloom-and-doom headlines to boost their ratings.

Keep financial news in perspective. Recessions can be painful. And they eventually end. The mortgage credit crisis in recent years was due to speculation, not to a lack of innovation. Our economy will continue to reward people who create valuable new products and services.

To manage stress, limit how much attention you pay to fear-based articles and programs. You can do this even while staying informed about news. Avoid conversations that focus on problems. Instead, talk about ways to take charge of your money and open up job prospects. Even when the economy takes a nosedive, there is always at least one more thing you can do to manage stress and get on a firmer financial footing.

Talk about what gives your life meaning beyond spending money. Eating at home instead of going out can bring your family closer together and save you money weekly, monthly, and annually. Avoiding loud bars and making time for quiet conversation can deepen your friendships. Finding free sources of entertainment can lead you to unexpected sources of pleasure. Letting go of an expensive vacation can allow you to pay down your debts and find time for a fun hobby. Keeping your old car for another year might allow you to invest in extra skills training.

When tough times happen, use them as a chance to embrace the truth about your money life rather than resist it. Live from conscious choice rather than unconscious habit. Learning to live within your means is a skill that can bring financial peace of mind for the rest of your life. ■

You're One Click Away...
from finding more ways online to thrive during tough times.

Take charge of
your credit

A good credit rating will serve you for a lifetime. With this asset, you'll be able to borrow money any time you need it. A poor credit rating, however, can keep you from getting a car or a house in the future. You might also have to pay higher insurance rates, and you could even be turned down for a job.

To take charge of your credit, borrow money only when truly necessary. If you do borrow, make all of your payments, and make them on time. This is especially important for managing credit cards and student loans.

USE CREDIT CARDS WITH CAUTION

A credit card is compact and convenient. That piece of plastic seems to promise peace of mind. Low on cash this month? Just whip out your credit card, slide it across the counter, and relax. Your worries are over—that is, until you get the bill. Credit cards often come with a hefty interest rate—sometimes as high as 30 percent.

A 2009 report by Sallie Mae, a student loan corporation, reveals that the average credit card debt among undergraduate students is $3,173.[3] However, many students are carrying higher amounts of debt, with costs that can soar over time. Suppose that a student owes $7,000 on a credit card with an annual percentage rate (APR) of 18.9 percent. Also suppose that he pays only the minimum balance due each month and charges nothing else to the account. He'll need to make payments for 16 years and pay $7,173 in interest.[4]

Credit cards do offer potential benefits, of course. Having one means that you don't have to carry around a checkbook or large amounts of cash, and they're pretty handy in emergencies. Getting a card is one way to establish a credit record. Some cards offer rewards, such as frequent flier miles and car rental discounts.

Used unwisely, however, credit cards can create a debt that takes decades to repay. This debt can seriously delay other goals—paying off student loans, financing a new car, buying a home, or saving for retirement.

Use the following strategies to take control of your credit cards. Write these ideas on a 3 × 5 card, and don't leave home without it.

Pay off the balance each month. An unpaid credit card balance is a sure sign that you are spending more money than you have. To avoid this outcome, keep track of how much you spend with credit cards each month. Pay off the card balance each month, on time, and avoid finance or late charges.

If you do accumulate a large credit card balance, go to your bank and ask about ways to get a loan with a lower interest rate. Use this loan to pay off your credit cards. Then promise yourself never to accumulate credit card debt again.

Scrutinize credit card offers. Finding a card with a lower interest rate can make a dramatic difference. Suppose that you have an $8,000 balance on a card with a 16 percent APR. Your interest charges would be $1,280 per year. If you have the same balance on a card with a 4.9 percent APR, your annual interest charges would be $392. It pays to shop around.[5]

However, look carefully at credit card offers. Low rates might be temporary. After a few months, they could double or even triple. Also look for annual fees, late fees, and other charges buried in the fine print.

Be especially wary of credit card offers made to students. Remember that the companies who willingly dispense cards on campus are not there to offer an educational service. They are in business to make money by charging you interest.

Avoid cash advances. Due to their high interest rates and fees, credit cards are not a great source of spare cash. Even when you get cash advances on these cards from an ATM, it's still borrowed money. As an alternative, get a debit card tied to a checking account, and use that card when you need cash on the go.

10

Check statements against your records. File your credit card receipts each month. When you get the bill for each card, check it against your receipts for accuracy. Mistakes in billing are rare, but they can happen. In addition, checking your statement reveals the interest rate and fees that are being applied to your account.

Credit card companies can change the terms of your agreement with little or no warning. Check bills carefully for any changes in late fees, service charges, and credit limits. When you get letters about changes in your credit card policies, read them carefully. Cancel cards from companies that routinely raise fees.

Use just one credit card. To simplify your financial life and take charge of your credit, consider using only one card. Choose one with no annual fee and the lowest interest rate. Consider the bottom line, and be selective. If you do have more than one credit card, pay off the one with the highest interest rate first. Then consider cancelling that card.

Get a copy of your credit report. A credit report is a record of your payment history and other credit-related items. You are entitled to get a free copy each year. Go to your bank and ask someone there how to do this. You can also request a copy of your credit report online at https://www.annualcreditreport.com. This site was created by three nationwide consumer credit-reporting companies—Equifax, Experian, and TransUnion. Check your report carefully for errors or accounts that you did not open. Do this now, before you're in financial trouble.

Protect your credit score. Whenever you apply for a loan, the first thing a lender will do is check your credit score. The higher

Common
credit terms

Annual fee—a yearly charge for using a credit card, sometimes called a membership fee or participation fee.

Annual percentage rate (APR)—the interest that you owe on unpaid balances in your account. The APR equals the periodic rate times the number of billing periods in a year.

Balance due—the remaining amount of money that you owe a credit card company or other lender.

Balance transfer—the process of moving an unpaid debt from one lender to another lender.

Bankruptcy—a legal process that allows borrowers to declare their inability to pay their debts. People who declare bankruptcy transfer all their assets to a court-appointed trustee and create a plan to repay some or all of their borrowed money. Bankruptcy protects people from harassment by their creditors and lowers their credit scores.

Credit score—a three-digit number that reflects your history of repaying borrowed money and paying other bills on time (also called a FICO score—an acronym for the Fair Isaac Corporation, which was the first company to create credit ratings.) This number ranges from 300 to 850. The higher the number, the better your credit rating.

Default—state of a loan when the borrower fails to make required payments or otherwise violates the terms of the agreement. Default may prompt the creditor to turn the loan over to a collection agency, which can severely harm the borrower's credit score.

Finance charge—the total fee for using a credit card, which includes the interest rate, periodic rate, and other fees. Finance charges for cash advances and balance transfers can be different from finance charges for unpaid balances.

Grace period—for a credit card user who pays off the entire balance due, a period of time when no interest is charged on a purchase. When there is no grace period, finance charges apply immediately to a purchase.

Interest rate—an annual fee that borrowers pay to use someone else's money, normally a percentage of the balance due.

Minimum payment—the amount you must pay to keep from defaulting on an account; usually 2 percent of the unpaid balance due.

Payment due date—the day that a lender must receive your payment—not the postmarked date or the date you make a payment online. Check your statements carefully, as credit card companies sometimes change the due dates.

Periodic rate—an interest rate based on a certain period of time, such as a day or a month.

your score, the more money you can borrow at lower interest rates. To protect your credit score:

- Pay all your bills on time.
- Hold on to credit cards that you've had for a while.
- Avoid applying for new credit cards.
- Pay off your credit card balance every month—especially for the cards that you've had the longest.
- If you can't pay off the entire balance, then pay as much as you can above the minimum monthly payment.
- Never charge more than your limit.
- Avoid using a credit card as a source of cash.
- Avoid any actions that could lead a credit card company to reduce your credit limit.

MANAGE STUDENT LOANS

A college degree is one of the best investments you can make. But you don't have to go broke to get that education. You can make that investment with the lowest debt possible.

Choose schools with costs in mind. If you decide to transfer to another school, you can save thousands of dollars the moment you sign your application for admission. In addition to choosing schools on the basis of reputation, consider how much they cost and the financial aid packages that they offer.

Avoid debt when possible. The surest way to manage debt is to avoid it altogether. If you do take out loans, borrow only the

> A college degree is one of the best investments you can make. But you don't have to go broke to get that education. You can make that investment with the lowest debt possible.

amount that you cannot get from other sources—scholarships, grants, employment, gifts from relatives, and personal savings. Predict what your income will be when the first loan payments are due, and whether you'll make enough money to manage continuing payments.

Also set a target date for graduation, and stick to it. The fewer years you go to school, the lower your debt.

Shop carefully for loans. Go the financial aid office and ask whether you can get a Stafford loan. These are fixed-rate, low-interest loans from the federal government. If you qualify for a subsidized Stafford loan, the government pays the interest due while you're in school. Unsubsidized Stafford loans do not offer this benefit, but they are still one of the cheapest student loans you can get. Remember that *anyone* can apply for a Stafford loan. Take full advantage of this program before you look into other loans. For more information on the loans that are available to you, visit www.studentaid.ed.gov.

If your parents are helping to pay for your education, they can apply for a PLUS loan. There is no income limit, and parents can borrow up to the total cost of their children's education. With these loans, your parents—not you—are the borrowers. A new option allows borrowers to defer repayment until after you graduate.

If at all possible, avoid loans from privately-owned companies. These companies often charge higher interest rates and impose terms that are less favorable to students.

While you're shopping around, ask about options for repaying your loans. Lenders might allow you to extend the payments over a longer period or adjust the amount of your monthly payment based on your income.

Some lenders will forgive part of a student loan if you agree to take a certain type of job for a few years—for example, teaching in a public school in a low-income neighborhood or working as a nurse in a rural community.

Repay your loans. If you take out student loans, find out exactly when the first payment is due on each of them. Make all your payments, and make them on time. Don't assume that you can wait to start repayment until you find a job. Any bill payments that you miss will hammer your credit score.

Also ask your financial aid office about whether you can consolidate your loans. This means that you lump them all together and owe just one payment every month. Loan consolidation makes it easier to stay on top of your payments and protect your credit score. ■

10

You're One Click Away...
from finding more strategies online for credit mastery.

EXERCISE 29

Start setting money goals

You can begin setting and achieving financial goals now. This is true even if you are in debt and living in a dorm on a diet of macaroni. If you're not convinced, then read on.

Remember that there are two major types of goals.

Outcome goals are commitments to produce a certain result in the future. In terms of money, these are some examples of outcomes goals:

- Saving $2,000 to buy a new computer by December 31 of this year
- Saving $5,000 for a car down payment by January 1, 2015
- Saving $10,000 for a house down payment by July 1, 2020

Process goals are the second type. They are not tied to a particular outcome such as having a specific amount of money in hand by a certain date. Process goals are about things you do on a daily, weekly, or monthly basis. They are commitments to change your behavior *now* rather than produce a certain result in the future.

Examples of process goals related to money are listed here:

- Saving 5 percent of every paycheck received and depositing that in a savings account to use for emergency expenses.
- Reducing restaurant expenses by splitting meals and skipping desserts.
- Reducing entertainment expenses by streaming movies with a computer rather than going to a theater.

Outcome goals can involve large amounts of money and often depend on your having a certain level of income.

In contrast, process goals can involve any amount of money, and they are not tied to any income level. You can set a goal to save 5 percent of your monthly income whether that amount is $5, $50, or $500.

Process goals are all about adopting new habits. Those habits might produce only modest results in the near future. When sustained over decades, however, they can make a major difference in your net worth.

In the space below write at least three money goals. Clearly label each one as an outcome or process goal. When setting a process goal, write down a habit that you will adopt immediately. Be sure to describe an observable behavior.

Goal #1:

_____

_____

_____

Goal #2:

_____

_____

_____

Goal #3:

_____

_____

_____

IF YOU'RE IN

trouble . . .

You might face obstacles to meeting your financial goals. Money problems are common. Solve them in ways that protect you for the future.

Get specific data. Complete Exercise 27: "The Money Monitor/Money Plan," included earlier in this chapter.

Be honest with creditors. Determine the amount that you are sure you can repay each month, and ask the creditor whether that would work for your case.

Go for credit counseling. Most cities have agencies with professional advisors who can help straighten out your financial problems.

Change your spending patterns. If you have a history of overspending (or underearning), change is possible. This chapter is full of suggestions.

Keep your money secure. To prevent other security breaches when managing money, regularly monitor online bank accounts. Use Web sites with an address (URL) that begins with https:// rather than http://. The extra s stands for secure, meaning that any data you send will be encrypted.

Education is worth it—
and you can pay for it

Education is one of the few things you can buy that will last a lifetime. It can't rust, corrode, break down, or wear out. It can't be stolen, repossessed, or destroyed. Once you have a degree, no one can take it away. That makes your education a safer investment than real estate, gold, oil, diamonds, or stocks.

Higher levels of education are associated with the following:[6]

- Greater likelihood of being employed
- Greater likelihood of having health insurance
- Higher income
- Higher job satisfaction
- Higher tax revenues for governments, which fund libraries, schools, parks, and other public goods
- Lower dependence on income support services, such as food stamps
- Higher involvement in volunteer activities

In short, education is a good deal for you and for society. It's worth investing in it periodically to update your skills, reach your goals, and get more of what you want in life.

Millions of dollars are waiting for people who take part in higher education. The funds flow to students who know how to find them. There are many ways to pay for school. The kind of help you get depends on your financial need. In general, *financial need* equals the cost of your schooling minus what you can reasonably be expected to pay. A financial aid package includes three major types of assistance:

- Money you do not pay back (grants and scholarships)
- Money you *do* pay back (loans)
- Work-study programs

Many students who get financial aid receive a package that includes all of the above elements.

To find out more, visit your school's financial aid office on a regular basis. Also go online. Start with Student Aid on the Web at http://studentaid.ed.gov. ■

 You're One Click Away...
from discovering more ways online to pay for school.

 EXERCISE 30

Education by the hour

Determine exactly what it costs you to go to school. Fill in the blanks, using totals for a semester, quarter, or whatever term system your school uses. **Note:** Include only the costs that relate directly to going to school. For example, under "Transportation," list only the amount that you pay for gas to drive back and forth to school—not the total amount you spend on gas for a semester.

Tuition	$_____
Books	$_____
Fees	$_____
Transportation	$_____
Clothing	$_____
Food	$_____
Housing	$_____
Entertainment	$_____
Other expenses (such as insurance, medical costs, and child care)	$_____
Subtotal	$_____
Salary you could earn per term if you weren't in school	$_____
Total (A)	$_____

Now figure out how many classes you attend in one term. This is the number of your scheduled class periods per week multiplied by the number of weeks in your school term. Put that figure below:

Total (B) $_____

Divide the **Total (B)** into the
Total (A), and put that amount here: $_____

This is what it costs you to go to one class one time.

On a separate sheet of paper, describe your responses to discovering this figure. Also list anything you will do differently as a result of knowing the hourly cost of your education.

 You're One Click Away...
from completing this exercise online under Exercises.

10

From top left clockwise: Michael Shake/Shutterstock.com; Tomislav Forgo/Shutterstock.com; Sebastian Kaulitzki/Shutterstock.com; Alexey Fursov/Shutterstock.com; Edd Westmacott/ Shutterstock.com; PhotoAlto/Michele Constantini/Getty Images

Why   What   How   What if

Your learning styles and your money

"The Learning Style Inventory from Chapter 1 explains four learning styles—unique ways of perceiving and processing our experiences. You can see these different styles at work in the ways that people spend and earn money. For example:

- Some people buy quickly once they find a product or service that connects to something they care about deeply (*doing*).
- Others take the time to shop around and compare prices before they spend (*watching*).
- Some people are curious about how the stock and bond markets work and will take the time to analyze the field (*thinking*).
- Others want to jump right in and experiment with ways to make more money (*feeling*).

Recognizing and accepting such differences can help you prevent and solve conflict that centers on money.

When you make financial decisions that involve family members or friends, ask the following four questions. These questions can be especially useful when you're considering a major purchase, such as a car or house. The goal is to honor everyone's learning styles—and their money.

***Why* am I considering spending this money?** We buy when we see something to be gained. This could involve a small benefit, such as spending a couple of dollars on a soft drink to satisfy your thirst. Or it could be a larger benefit, like spending thousands of dollars on a car to satisfy your desire for convenience and mobility. Before you hand over your cash or credit card, be clear about what you want to gain.

***What* are the facts I need to know?** The answer to this question is useful even with small purchases. In the case of the soft drink, for example, check out the ingredients on the label. Then think about whether you want to put that stuff in your body. If you're buying a car, find out exactly how much it will cost beyond the sticker price. If you plan to borrow money, research the available options. Your bank or credit union may offer a better interest rate than the car dealer. Or maybe a relative would consider giving you a no-interest loan.

***How* would this purchase affect my life?** Many purchases come with a cost that goes beyond money. That soft drink might come with hidden costs—excess sugar and calories. Buying or renting a bigger home could tie you into higher payments. And that might require you to work more hours or see less of your family. When you spend your time, energy, and money for one purpose, those resources are not available for other purposes.

***What if* I could get the same benefit without spending money?** You could save a couple dollars, reduce calories, *and* quench your thirst by using a drinking fountain instead of buying an overpriced drink. You could get around town *and* save thousands of dollars by getting a used car, or by using public transportation and paying for an occasional taxi ride. And you could gain more living space by building a small addition to your current home or by simply cleaning out some cluttered rooms.

Before you spend a dime, ask whether you can get the same benefit for no money down—or no money at all. ■

Your money and your values

Want a clue to your values? Look at the way you handle money. The amount you spend on fast food shows how much you value convenience. The amount you spend on clothes shows how much you value appearance. And the amount you spend on tuition shows how much you value education. You might not think about values when you pull out a credit card or put cash on the counter. Even so, your values are at work.

Think of any value as having two aspects. One is invisible—a belief about what matters most in life. You can define this belief by naming something you want and asking, "*Why* do I want that?" Keep asking until you reach a point where the question no longer makes sense. At that point, you'll bump into one of your values.

Suppose that you want to start dating. Why do you want that? Perhaps you want to find someone who will really listen to you and also share his deepest feelings. Why do you want *that*? Perhaps because you want to love and be loved. If someone asks why you want *that*, you might say, "I want that because . . . well, I just want it." At that point, the *why?* question no longer applies. To you, love is an end in itself. You desire love simply for its own sake. Love is one of your values.

The second aspect of any value is a behavior. If you value love, you will take action to meet new people. You'll develop close friendships. You'll look for a spouse or life partner and build a long-term relationship. These behaviors are visible signs that you value love.

We experience peace of mind when our behaviors align with our values. However, this is not always the case. If you ever suspect that there's a conflict between your values and your behavior, then look at your money life for clues.

For example, someone says that he values health. After monitoring his expenses, he discovers that he spent $200 last month on fast food. He's discovered a clear source of conflict. He can resolve that conflict by redefining his values or changing his behavior. We sometimes work to buy more things that we have no time to enjoy . . . because we work so much. This can be a vicious cycle.

Sometimes we live values that are not our own. Values creep into our lives due to peer pressure or advertising. Movies, TV, and magazines pump us full of images about the value of owning more *stuff*—bigger houses, bigger cars, better clothes. All that stuff costs a lot of money. The process of acquiring it can drive us into debt—and into jobs that pay well but deny our values.

Money gives us plenty of opportunities for critical thinking. For example, think about the wisdom of choosing to spend money on the latest video game or digital gadget rather than a textbook or other resource needed for your education. Games and gadgets can deliver many hours of entertainment before they break down. Compare that to the value of doing well in a course, graduating with better grades, and acquiring skills that increase your earning power for the rest of your career.

One way to align your behaviors with your beliefs is to ask one question whenever you spend money: *Is this expense consistent with my values?* Over time, this question can lead to daily changes in your behavior that make a big difference in your peace of mind.

Keeping track of your income and expenses allows you to make choices about money with your eyes open. It's all about handling money on purpose and living with integrity. With the financial facts at hand, you can spend and earn money in ways that demonstrate your values. ■

FREE FUN

Sometimes it seems that the only way to have fun is to spend money. Not true. Search out free entertainment on campus and in your community. Beyond this, your imagination is the only limit. Some suggestions are listed below. If you think they're silly or boring, create better ideas of your own.

Browse a bookstore.

Volunteer at a child care center.

Draw.

Exercise.

Find other people who share your hobby, and start a club.

Give a massage.

Do yoga with a friend.

Play Frisbee golf.

Make dinner for your date.

Picnic in the park.

Take a long walk.

Ride your bike.

Listen to music that you already own but haven't heard for a while.

Take a candlelight bath.

Play board games.

Have an egg toss.

Test-drive new cars.

Donate blood.

Make yourself breakfast in bed.

 You're One Click Away... *from finding more options online for free fun.*

10

PRACTICING
critical thinking 10

Throughout this book you've practiced the six levels of thinking described in "Becoming a critical thinker" on page 207.

Level 1: Remembering—recalling an idea.

Level 2: Understanding—explaining an idea in your own words and giving examples from your own experience.

Level 3: Applying—using an idea to produced a desired result.

Level 4: Analyzing—dividing an idea into parts or steps.

Level 5: Evaluating—rating the truth, usefulness, or quality of an idea—and giving reasons for your rating.

Level 6: Creating—inventing something new based on an idea.

Doing this exercise will give you additional practice with **Level 4: Analyzing**. At this level of thinking, you break down a large idea into smaller parts and then sort those parts into categories. You might also list the various causes of an event or the factors that contribute to a problem. On a test, questions that call for analysis begin with key words such as these:

- Analyze
- Arrange
- Categorize
- Classify
- Differentiate
- Distinguish
- Divide
- List
- Organize

Any of your courses can call for analysis. In a chemistry course, for example, an instructor might ask you to list the factors that cause metal to rust. In an American history course, you might discuss the events that lead up to the Civil War.

This level of thinking is especially useful in solving problems related to money. When discussing personal finances, you might hear people say, "The money I make just seems to disappear. I don't know where it all goes."

Imagine that a friend has just said this to you. She's also asked you to help her **analyze** her money problems. In the space provided, **list** the questions you would ask about how she handles money. Or **list** a series of steps that she could take to **organize** her financial life and **arrange** those steps in order.

_____

_____

_____

_____

_____

_____

_____

_____

_____

_____

_____

_____

_____

_____

_____

_____

_____

_____

_____

_____

_____

_____

_____

_____

_____

_____

_____

_____

masterstudentprofile

Lisa Price

(1962–) Lisa transformed Carol's Daughter, a line of all-natural body care products, from a hobby into a multimillion-dollar business.

I have loved fragrance since I was a small child. I used my allowance to buy perfume, not clothes. I was a huge Prince fan, and I read that he had a fragrance bar on his dresser so he could mix scents. So I found a way to make my own fragrances blending perfume oils.

Over the years, it became something I did to relax. My mother was the one who suggested I start selling my body cream at a church flea market in the summer of 1993.

By the end of that first day, I was pretty much sold out. I made another batch and spent most of that summer at street fairs and flea markets, paying close attention to my customers. I noticed that they were looking for hair products. So I started making things for hair to keep them from walking away from my table.

My day job was in television and film production, but customers started to call me for refills. The weather was too cold for flea markets, so I had them come to my apartment. I continued selling out of my home until 1996, when I was expecting my first child. I quit TV because I knew I couldn't do that—be a mom, be a wife, and do this business.

I came up with the name at the very beginning. I made a list of things that I was and a list of things I wanted to become. There were other things on the list, like Robert's daughter and Gordon's girlfriend. But when I said Carol's daughter, I got goose bumps. It sounded right.

My mother and I used to joke about it over the years. She would say, "Have you made enough money for me to sue you for using my name?" When she died, someone at her wake said to me, "It's so wonderful that you honored your mother while she was still here." My mother spent most of her adult life sick. When she was in her early 20s, she was diagnosed with polymyositis. It's a collagen vascular disease, and it attacks the muscles and the nervous system. She never complained, but I can remember times when I would hear her scream because her legs had cramped up. We would have to massage her legs and help her breathe through it.

As I was growing the business, I would sometimes feel overwhelmed. But my mother taught me to smile through adversity, to know that I wouldn't be given the job if I couldn't do it. It's appropriate that the company is named after her. . . .

Carol's Daughter has made other people in the beauty business look at African American consumers in a different way. When I first started to do this, the black products were always at the back of the drugstore on the lower shelves. They were always dusty, dirty, and sticky; they looked like nobody ever touched them. That's changing. . . . It's great to be part of that shift.

Bennett Faglin/WireImage

LISA PRICE . . . is willing to take risks.

YOU . . . can take risks with more confidence when you are skilled with money.

10

Source: Adapted with permission from "The Sweet Smell of Success: What Mom Taught Lisa Price, Founder of Carol's Daughter," *Newsweek*, October 13, 2008, accessed February 6, 2011, from www.newsweek.com/id/162352.

You're One Click Away...
from learning more about Lisa Price online at Master Student Profiles. You can also visit the Master Student Hall of Fame to learn about other master students.

PUT THIS CHAPTER TO WORK

MANAGE YOUR MONEY DURING A JOB SEARCH. As a student, you can get practical experience in monitoring money, reducing expenses, and avoiding credit card debt. These skills will serve you well when the time comes to apply for jobs after you graduate. This is especially true during a recession, where a job hunt can last 20 weeks or more. During your job search, review and do Exercise 27: "The Money Monitor/Money Plan."

DEVELOP FINANCIAL LITERACY FOR THE WORKPLACE. Your next job may require you to prepare budgets, keep money records, make financial forecasts, and adjust income and expenses in order to meet an organization's financial goals. The ability to handle such tasks successfully is called *workplace financial literacy*. To get the most from your education, create a detailed plan for gaining this form of literacy.

Think about the ways you'll be handling money in your chosen career. If you plan to become an architect, for example, you'll need to estimate costs for a building project, request bids from contractors, and then evaluate those bids. Find out more by interviewing people who work in your field and asking them about how they handle money on the job.

After listing the financial skills that you need, consider which courses you'll take to develop them. You might benefit from classes in business management or accounting.

LEARN SPREADSHEET SOFTWARE. With spreadsheet programs such as Microsoft's Excel, you can enter data into charts with rows and columns and then apply various formulas. This makes it possible to create budgets, income reports, expense records, and investment projections. Many organizations use spreadsheets to track their finances. Master this software now and you'll have a marketable skill to add to your résumé.

KEEP RECORDS OF YOUR FINANCIAL SUCCESS AT WORK. Throughout your career, keep track of the positive outcomes you produce at work, including financial successes. Summarize these results in a sentence or two and add them to your résumé as well. Whenever you deliver a project on time and on budget, write Discovery Statements about how you created that result. Follow up with Intention Statements about ways to be even more effective on your next project.

CONSIDER INCOME AND EXPENSES RELATED TO YOUR CAREER CHOICES. Your career plan can include estimates of how much money you'll earn in various jobs in your field. In addition, think about the possible expenses involved in your career choice. If you're planning a career that requires graduate school, for example, then consider how you will pay for that education. Perhaps advancement in your career calls for additional certifications or coursework. Examples are continuing education credits for teachers and board certifications for nurses and physicians. Start thinking now about how you'll meet such requirements.

An equally important consideration is your choice about where to locate after graduating from school. Given the high cost of living in certain cities, this choice can have a big impact on your personal finances. A starting salary of $40,000 won't take you as far in New York City or Boston as it will in Kansas City or Des Moines. Consider whether your career calls for living in a major metropolitan area with high housing and transportation costs. If so, then set salary goals that will help you cover such costs with money to spare.

NOW CREATE A CAREER CONNECTION OF YOUR OWN. Review this chapter, looking for a suggestion that you will commit to use while working or looking for a job. In a sentence or two, describe exactly what you plan to do and the primary benefit you want to gain. For example: "I will look for work-study assignments and internships that allow me to create budgets. This will help me develop financial skills for the workplace."

State your strategy and desired benefit in the space below:

_____

_____

_____

_____

Name _____

Date _____

1. The Power Process: "Risk being a fool" suggests that sometimes you should take action without considering the consequences. True or false? Explain your answer.

2. Summarize the three main steps in money management, as explained in this chapter.

3. Describe a strategy for increasing your income while you are in school.

4. List three ways to decrease your expenses while you are in school.

5. According to the text, what is the biggest factor in your long-term financial well-being?
   (a) The state of the overall economy   (b) The interest rates on your credit cards
   (c) The federal deficit   (d) Your daily behavior
   (e) None of the above

6. What are three ways that you can avoid getting into financial trouble when you use credit cards?

7. Privately owned companies generally offer better student loans than the federal government. True or false? Explain your answer.

8. List three sources of money to help students pay for their education.

9. The text asserts that investing in your education is safer than investing in real estate, gold, oil, diamonds, or stocks. List the reasons given for this statement.

10. What is a question that you can ask to align your expenses with your values?

10

10 SKILLS *Snapshot*

CHAPTER 10

Now that you've reflected on the ideas in this chapter and experimented with some new strategies, revisit your responses to the Money section of the Discovery Wheel exercise on page 38. Think about the most powerful action you could take in the near future toward financial mastery. Complete the following sentences.

DISCOVERY

My score on the Money section of the Discovery Wheel on page 38 was . . .

Right now my main sources of income are . . .

My three biggest expenses each month are . . .

One monthly expense that I could reduce right away is . . .

INTENTION

To begin reducing the expense I just listed, I could . . .

I plan to graduate by (month and year) . . .

I plan to pay for my education next year by . . .

I'll know that I've reached a new level of mastery with money when . . .

ACTION

To reach that level of mastery, the most important thing I can do next is to . . .

At the end of this course, I would like my Money score on the Discovery Wheel to be . . .

Health

Use this **Master Student Map** to ask yourself,

WHY THIS CHAPTER MATTERS . . .

- Succeeding in higher education calls for a baseline of physical and emotional well-being.

WHAT IS INCLUDED . . .

- Power Process: Surrender   322
- Wake up to health   323
- Choose your fuel   324
- Choose to exercise   325
- Choose emotional health   326
- Developing a strong self-image   329
- Asking for help   331
- Suicide is no solution   332
- Choose to stay safe   333
- Choose sexual health: Prevent infection   334
- Choose sexual health: Prevent unwanted pregnancy   335
- Alcohol, tobacco, and drugs: The truth   339
- From dependence to recovery   342
- Warning: Advertising can be dangerous to your health   344
- Master Student Profile: Randy Pausch   347

HOW CAN I USE THIS CHAPTER . . .

- Maintain your physical and mental energy.
- Enhance your self-esteem.
- Make decisions about alcohol and other drugs in a way that supports your success.

WHAT IF . . .

- I could meet the demands of daily life with energy and optimism to spare?

© Ruslan Ivantsov/Shutterstock.com

JOURNAL ENTRY 26
Discovery Statement

Take a First Step about your health

This chapter allows you to look closely at your health. Aim to change your behavior in specific ways that make a dramatic, positive difference in your life. Start with a one-sentence First Step:

What concerns me more than anything else about my health right now is . . .

_____

_____

_____

_____

_____

_____

_____

_____

_____

_____

_____

_____

Note: You can expand on your response—and keep it private—by writing it on a separate piece of paper.

POWER process

Surrender

Life can be magnificent and satisfying. It can also be devastating. Sometimes there is too much pain or confusion. Problems can be too big and too numerous. Life can bring us to our knees in a pitiful, helpless, and hopeless state. A broken relationship, a sudden diagnosis of cancer, a dependence on drugs, or a stress-filled job can leave us feeling overwhelmed—powerless.

In these troubling situations, the first thing we can do is to admit that we don't have the resources to handle the problem. No matter how hard we try and no matter what skills we bring to bear, some problems remain out of our control. When this is the case, we can tell the truth: "It's too big and too mean. I can't handle it." In that moment, we take a step toward greater health.

Desperately struggling to control a problem can easily result in the problem controlling us. Surrender is letting go of being the master in order to avoid becoming the slave.

Many traditions make note of this idea. Western religions speak of surrendering to God. Hindus say surrender to the Self. Members of Alcoholics Anonymous talk about turning their lives over to a Higher Power. Agnostics might suggest surrendering to their intellect, their intuition, or their conscience.

In any case, surrender means being receptive. Once we admit that we're at the end of our rope, we open ourselves up to help. We learn that we don't have to go it alone. We find out that other people have faced similar problems and survived. We give up our old habits of thinking and behaving as if we have to be in control of everything. We stop acting as general manager of the universe. We surrender. And that creates a space for something new in our lives.

Surrender is not "giving up." It is not a suggestion to quit and do nothing about your problems. Giving up is fatalistic and accomplishes nothing. You have many skills and resources. Use them. You can apply all of your energy to handling a situation and still surrender at the same time. You can surrender to weight gain even as you step up your exercise program. You can surrender to a toothache even as you go to the dentist. You can surrender to the past while adopting new habits for a healthy future.

Surrender includes doing whatever you can in a positive, trusting spirit. Let go, keep going, and know when a source of help lies beyond you.

You're One Click Away...
from accessing Power Process Media online and finding out more about how to "surrender."

Hannamariah/Shutterstock.com

Wake up TO HEALTH

Some people see health as just a matter of common sense. These people might see little value in reading a health chapter. After all, they already know how to take care of themselves.

Yet *knowing* and *doing* are two different things. Health information does not always translate into healthy habits.

We expect to experience health challenges as we age. Even youth, though, is no guarantee of good health. Over the last 3 decades, obesity among young adults has tripled. Twenty-nine percent of young men smoke. And 70 percent of deaths among adults ages 18 to 29 result from unintentional injuries, accidents, homicide, and suicide.[1]

As a student, your success in school is directly tied to your health. Lack of sleep and exercise have been associated with lower grade point averages among undergraduate students. So have alcohol use, tobacco use, gambling, and chronic health conditions.[2] And any health habit that undermines your success in school can also undermine your success in later life.

On the other hand, we can adopt habits that sustain our well-being. One study found that people lengthened their lives an average of 14 years by adopting just four habits: staying tobacco-free, eating more fruits and vegetables, exercising regularly, and drinking alcohol in moderation if at all.[3]

Health also hinges on a habit of exercising some tissue that lies between your ears—the organ called your brain. One path to greater health starts not with new food or a new form of exercise, but with new ideas.

Olena Pivnenko/Shutterstock.com

Consider the power of beliefs. Some of them create barriers to higher levels of health: "Your health is programmed by your heredity." "Some people are just low on energy." "Healthy food doesn't taste very good." "Over the long run, people just don't change their habits." Be willing to test these ideas and change them when it serves you.

People often misunderstand what the word *health* means. Remember that this word is similar in origin to *whole, hale, hardy,* and even *holy*. Implied in these words are qualities that most of us associate with healthy people: alertness, vitality, vigor. Healthy people meet the demands of daily life with energy to spare. Illness or stress might slow them down for a while, but then they bounce back. They know how to relax, create loving relationships, and find satisfaction in their work.

To open up your inquiry into health—and to open up new possibilities for your life—consider three ideas.

First, health is a continuum. On one end of that continuum is a death that comes too early. On the other end is a long life filled with satisfying work and fulfilling relationships. Many of us exist between those extremes at a point we might call average. Most of the time we're not sick. And most of the time we're not truly thriving either.

Second, health changes. Health is not a fixed state. In fact, health fluctuates from year to year, day to day, and moment to moment. Those changes can occur largely by chance. Or they can occur more often by choice, as we take conscious control of our thinking and behavior.

Third, even when faced with health challenges, we have choices. We can choose attitudes and habits that promote a higher quality of life. For example, people with diabetes can often manage the disease by exercising more and changing their diet.

Health is one of those rich, multilayered concepts that we can never define completely. In the end, your definition of *health* comes from your own experience. The proof lies not on these pages but in your life—in the level of health that you create, starting now.

You have choices. You can remain unaware of habits that have major consequences for your health. Or you can become aware of current habits (discovery), choose new habits (intention), and take appropriate action.

Health is a choice you make every moment, with each thought and behavior. Wake up to this possibility by experimenting with the suggestions in this chapter. ■

11

Choose Your FUEL

Food is your primary fuel for body and mind. And even though you've been eating all your life, entering higher education is bound to change the way that you fuel yourself.

There have been hundreds of books written about nutrition. One says don't drink milk. Another says the calcium provided by milk is an essential nutrient we need daily. Although such debate seems confusing, take comfort. There is actually wide agreement about how to fuel yourself for health.

Today, federal nutrition guidelines are summarized visually as a *dinner plate*. The idea is to eat more of the foods shown in the bigger sections of the dinner plate. To see an example and build your personal food pyramid, go online to www.choosemyplate.gov.

The various food guidelines available agree on several core principles:[4]

- Emphasize fruits, vegetables, whole grains, and fat-free or low-fat milk and milk products.

- Include lean meats, poultry, fish, beans, eggs, and nuts.

- Choose foods that are low in saturated fats, trans fats, cholesterol, salt (sodium), and added sugars.

Michael Pollan, a writer for the *New York Times Magazine,* spent several years sorting out the scientific literature on nutrition.[5] He boiled the key guidelines down to seven words in three sentences:

- *Eat food.* In other words, choose whole, fresh foods over processed products with a lot of ingredients.

- *Not too much.* If you want to manage your weight, then control how much you eat. Notice portion sizes. Pass on snacks, seconds, and desserts—or indulge just occasionally.

- *Mostly plants.* Fruits, vegetables, and grains are loaded with chemicals that help to prevent disease. Plant-based foods, on the whole, are also lower in calories than foods from animals (meat and dairy products).

Finally, forget diets. *How* you eat can matter more than *what* you eat. If you want to eat less, then eat slowly. Savor each bite. Stop when you're satisfied instead of when you feel full. Use meal times as a chance to relax, reduce stress, and connect with people. ■

iStockphoto.com/james steidl

You're One Click Away...
from discovering more strategies online for fueling your body.

Prevent and treat eating disorders

Eating disorders affect many students. These disorders involve serious disturbances in eating behavior. Examples are overeating or extreme reduction of food intake, as well as irrational concern about body shape or weight. Women are much more likely to develop these disorders than are men, though cases are on the rise among males.

Bulimia involves cycles of excessive eating and forced purges. A person with this disorder might gorge on a pizza, doughnuts, and ice cream and then force herself to vomit. Or she might compensate for overeating with excessive use of laxatives, enemas, or diuretics.

Anorexia nervosa is a potentially fatal illness marked by self-starvation. People with anorexia may practice extended fasting or eat only one kind of food for weeks at a time.

These disorders are not due to a failure of willpower. They are real illnesses in which harmful patterns of eating take on a life of their own.

Eating disorders can lead to many complications, including life-threatening heart conditions and kidney failure. Many people with eating disorders also struggle with depression, substance abuse, and anxiety. They need immediate treatment to stabilize their health. This is usually followed by continuing medical care, counseling, and medication to promote a full recovery.

If you're worried you might have an eating disorder, visit a doctor, campus health service, or local public health clinic. If you see signs of an eating disorder in someone else, express your concern with "I" messages, as explained in Chapter 8: Communicating.

For more information, contact the National Eating Disorders Association at 1-800-931-2237 or online at www.nationaleatingdisorders.org.

Choose to EXERCISE

Our bodies need to be exercised. The world ran on muscle power back in the era when we had to hunt down a woolly mammoth every few weeks and drag it back to the cave. Now we can grab a burger at a drive-up window. Today we need to make a special effort to exercise.

Exercise promotes weight control and reduces the symptoms of depression. It also helps to prevent heart attack, diabetes, and several forms of cancer.[6] Exercise also refreshes your body and your mind. If you're stuck on a math problem or blocked on writing a paper, take an exercise break. Chances are that you'll come back with a fresh perspective and some new ideas.

If you get moving, you'll create lean muscles, a strong heart, and an alert brain. If the word *exercise* turns you off, think *physical activity* instead. Here are some things you can do:

Stay active throughout the day. Park a little farther from work or school. Do your heart a favor by walking some extra blocks. Take the stairs instead of riding elevators. For an extra workout, climb two stairs at a time.

An hour of daily activity is ideal, but do whatever you can. Some activity is better than none.

No matter what you do, ease into it. For example, start by walking briskly for at least 15 minutes every day. Increase that time gradually, and add a little jogging.

Adapt to your campus environment. Look for exercise facilities on campus. Search for classes in aerobics, swimming, volleyball, basketball, golf, tennis, and other sports. Intramural sports are another option. School can be a great place to get in shape.

Do what you enjoy. Stay active with aerobic activities that you enjoy. You might like martial arts, kickboxing, yoga, ballroom dance classes, stage combat classes, or mountain climbing. Check your school catalog for such courses.

Vary your routine. Find several activities that you like to do, and rotate them throughout the year. Your main form of activity during winter might be ballroom dancing, riding an exercise bike, or skiing. In summer, you could switch to outdoor sports. Whenever possible, choose weight-bearing activities such as walking, running, or stair climbing.

Get active early. Work out first thing in the morning. Then it's done for the day. Make it part of your daily routine, just like brushing your teeth.

Exercise with other people. Making exercise a social affair can add a fun factor and raise your level of commitment.

Join a gym without fear. Many health clubs welcome people who are just starting to get in shape.

Look for gradual results. If your goal is to lose weight, be patient. Because 1 pound equals 3,500 calories, you might feel tempted to reduce weight loss to a simple formula: *Let's see … if I burn away just 100 calories each day through exercise, I should lose 1 pound every 35 days.*

Actually, the relationship between exercise and weight loss is complex. Many factors—including individual differences in metabolism and the type of exercise you do—affect the amount of weight you actually lose.[7]

When you step on the bathroom scale, look for small changes over time rather than sudden, dramatic losses. Gradual weight loss is more healthy, anyway—and easier to sustain over the long term.

Weight loss is just one potential benefit of exercise. Choosing to exercise can lift your mood, increase your stamina, strengthen your bones, stabilize your joints, and help prevent heart disease. It can also reduce your risk of high blood pressure, diabetes, and several forms of cancer. If you do resistance training—such as weight machines or elastic-band workouts—you'll strengthen your muscles as well. For a complete fitness program, add stretching exercises to enjoy increased flexibility.[8]

Before beginning any vigorous exercise program, consult a health care professional. This is critical if you are overweight, over age 60, in poor condition, or a heavy smoker, or if you have a history of health problems. ■

You're One Click Away...
from discovering more ways online to follow through on your exercise goals.

11

CHOOSE EMOTIONAL HEALTH

The number of students in higher education who have emotional health problems is steadily increasing.[9] According to the American College Health Association, 31 percent of college students report that they have felt so depressed that it was difficult to function. Almost half of students say that they've felt overwhelming anxiety, and 60 percent report that they've felt very lonely.[10]

Emotional health includes many factors: your skill at managing stress, your ability to build loving relationships, your capacity to meet the demands of school and work, and your beliefs about your ability to succeed. People with mental illness have thoughts, emotions, or behaviors that consistently interfere with these areas of life.

You can take simple and immediate steps to prevent emotional health problems or cope with them if they do occur. Remember that strategies for managing test-related stress can help you manage *any* form of stress. (See "Let go of test anxiety" on page 191.) Here are some other suggestions to promote your emotional health.

Take care of your body. Your thoughts and emotions can get scrambled if you go too long feeling hungry or tired. Follow the suggestions in this chapter for eating, exercise, and sleep.

Solve problems. Although you can't "fix" a bad feeling in the same way that you can fix a machine, you can choose to change a situation associated with that feeling. There might be a problem that needs a solution. You can use feeling bad as your motivation to solve that problem.

Sometimes an intense feeling of sadness, anger, or fear is related to a specific situation in your life. Describe the problem. Then brainstorm solutions and choose one to implement. Reducing your course load, cutting back on hours at work, getting more financial aid, delegating a task, or taking some other concrete action might solve the problem and help you feel better.

Stay active. A related strategy is to do something—*anything* that's constructive, even if it's not a solution to a specific problem.

For example, mop the kitchen floor. Clean out your dresser drawers. Iron your shirts. This sounds silly, but it works.

The basic principle is that you can separate emotions from actions. It is appropriate to feel miserable when you do. It's normal to cry and express your feelings. It is also possible to go to class, study, work, eat, and feel miserable at the same time. Unless you have a diagnosable problem with anxiety or depression, you can continue your normal activities until the misery passes.

Japanese psychiatrist Morita Masatake, a contemporary of Sigmund Freud, based his whole approach to treatment on this insight: We can face our emotional pain directly and still take constructive action. One of Masatake's favorite suggestions for people who felt depressed was that they tend a garden.[11]

Focus on one task at a time. It's easy to feel stressed if you dwell on how much you have to accomplish this year, this term, this month, or even this week. One solution is to plan using the suggestions in Chapter 2: Time.

Remember that an effective plan for the day does two things. First, it clarifies what you're choosing *not* to do today. (Tasks that you plan to do in the future are listed on your calendar or to-do list.) Second, an effective plan reduces your day to a series of concrete tasks—such as making phone calls, going to classes, running errands, or reading chapters—that you can do one at a time.

If you feel overwhelmed, just find the highest-priority task on your to-do list. Do it with total attention until it's done. Then go back to your list for the next high-priority task. Do *it* with total attention. Savor the feeling of mastery and control that comes with crossing each task off your list.

Don't believe everything you think. According to Albert Ellis and other cognitive psychologists, stress results not from events in our lives, but from the way we *think* about those events.[12] If we believe that people should always behave in exactly the way we expect them to, for instance, we set ourselves up for misery. The same happens if we believe that events should always turn out exactly as we want.

There are two main ways to deal with such thoughts. First, don't believe them. Dispute such thoughts and replace them with more realistic ones: *I can control my own behavior, but not the behavior of others.* And: *Some events are beyond my control.* Changing our beliefs can reduce our stress significantly.

Second, you can just release stress-producing thoughts without disputing them. Meditation is a way to do this. While meditating, you simply notice your thoughts as they arise and pass. Instead of reacting to them, you observe them. Eventually, your stream of thinking slows down. You might enter a state of deep relaxation that also yields life-changing insights.

Many religious organizations offer meditation classes. You can also find meditation instruction through health maintenance organizations, YMCAs or YWCAs, and community education programs.

Remember that emotional pain is not a sickness. Emotional pain has gotten a bad name. This reputation is undeserved. There

Choose to rest

A lack of rest can decrease your immunity to illness and impair your performance in school. You still might be tempted to cut back drastically on your sleep once in a while for an all-night study session. Instead, read Chapter 2: Time for some time management ideas. Depriving yourself of sleep is a choice you can avoid.

If you have trouble falling asleep, experiment with the following suggestions:

- Exercise daily. For many people, regular exercise promotes sounder sleep. However, finish exercising several hours before you want to go to sleep.
- Avoid naps during the daytime.
- Monitor your caffeine intake, especially in the afternoon and evening.
- Avoid using alcohol to feel sleepy. Drinking alcohol late in the evening can disrupt your sleep during the night.

- Develop a sleep ritual—a regular sequence of calming activities that end your day. You might take a warm bath and do some light reading. Turn off the TV and computer at least 1 hour before you go to bed.
- Keep your sleeping room cool.
- Keep a regular schedule for going to sleep and waking up.
- Sleep in the same place each night. When you're there, your body gets the message: "It's time to go to sleep."
- Practice relaxation techniques while lying in bed. A simple one is to count your breaths and release distracting thoughts as they arise.
- Make tomorrow's to-do list before you go to sleep so you won't lie there worrying that tomorrow you'll forget about something you need to do.
- Get up and study or do something else until you're tired.
- See a doctor if sleeplessness persists.

11

is nothing wrong with feeling bad. It's okay to feel miserable, depressed, sad, upset, angry, dejected, gloomy, or unhappy.

It might not be pleasant to feel bad, but it can be good for you. Often, bad is an appropriate way to feel. When you leave a place you love, sadness is natural. When you lose a friend or lover, misery might be in order. When someone treats you badly, it is probably appropriate to feel angry. When a loved one dies, it is necessary to grieve. The grief might appear in the form of depression, sadness, or anger.

There is nothing wrong with extreme emotional pain. If depression, sadness, or anger persists, then get help. Otherwise, allow yourself to experience these emotions. They're often appropriate.

Sometimes we allow ourselves to feel bad only if we have a good reason. For example: "Well, I feel very sad, but that is because I just found out my best friend is moving to Europe." It's all right to know the reason why you are sad. It's also fine not to know. You can feel bad for no apparent reason. The reason doesn't matter. Because you cannot directly control any feeling, simply accept it.

There's no way to predict how long emotional pain will last. The main point is that it does not last forever. There's no need to let a broken heart stop your life. Although you can find abundant advice on the subject, just remember a simple and powerful idea: This too shall pass.

Sometimes other people—friends or family members, for example—have a hard time letting you feel bad. They might be worried that they did something wrong and want to make it better. They want you to quit feeling bad. Tell them you will—eventually. Assure them that you will feel good again, but that for right now you just want to feel bad.

Share what you're thinking and feeling. Revealing your inner world with a family member or friend is a powerful way to gain perspective. The simple act of describing a problem can sometimes reveal a solution or give you a fresh perspective.

Get help. Remember a basic guideline about *when* to seek help: whenever problems with your thinking, moods, or behavior consistently interfere with your ability to sleep, eat, go to class, work, or create positive relationships.

You can get help at the student health center on campus. This is not just a service for treating colds, allergies, and flu symptoms. Counselors expect to help students deal with adjustment to campus, changes in mood, academic problems, and drug abuse and dependence.

Students with anxiety disorders, clinical depression, bipolar disorder, and other diagnoses might get referred to a professional outside the student health center. The referral process can take time, so seek help right away. Your tuition helps to pay for these services. It's smart to use them now.

You can find resources to promote emotional health even if your campus doesn't offer counseling services. Start with a personal physician—one person who can coordinate all of your health care. (For suggestions, go to your school's health center.) A personal physician can refer you to another health professional if it seems appropriate.

These two suggestions can also work after you graduate. Promoting emotional health is a skill to use for the rest of your life. ■

You're One Click Away...
from finding more pathways to robust emotional health online.

Master Students
IN ACTION

You're One Click Away...
from viewing a video about Master Students in Action.

"*I start every week with my Success Triangle: (1) Prioritize what needs to be done now and what can be done by others; (2) make a schedule, and check it daily (or more often as needed); and (3) reward myself—eat right, exercise, and get more rest. When I stick to my plan, there's less stress in my life.*"

—Karen Grajeda,
Boise State University

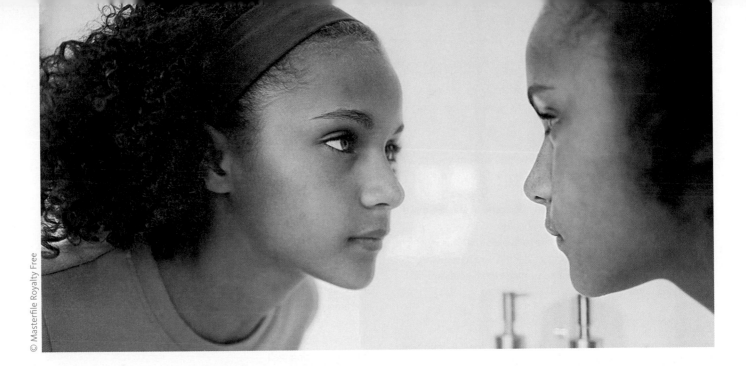

Developing a strong
SELF-IMAGE

Your *self-image* is the way you see yourself. It includes beliefs and feelings about your potential to succeed.

Self-image can erode in ways that are imperceptible to us. Over time, we can gradually buy into a reduced sense of our own possibilities in life. These views make it less likely that

The challenge of higher education often puts our self-image at risk. The rigors of class work, financial pressures, and new social settings can test our ability to adapt and change.

we'll take risks, create a vision for the future, and set and achieve goals.

Self-image is related to what psychologists call *self-efficacy*. This field of research is closely associated with psychologist Albert Bandura of Stanford University.[13] *Efficacy* refers to the ability to produce a desired effect. *Self-efficacy* refers to your belief in your ability to determine the outcomes of events—especially outcomes that are strongly influenced by your own behavior.

A strong self-image allows you to tackle problems with confidence, set long-term goals, and see difficult tasks as creative challenges rather than potential disasters. With a strong self-image, you believe that your action counts. You see yourself as someone who can make a positive difference in the world.

No one has to live with a poor self-image. Your self-image is flexible. It changes over time, and you can influence it with the following strategies.

SET UP SITUATIONS IN WHICH YOU CAN WIN

Start by planning scenarios in which you can succeed. Bandura calls these "mastery situations." For example, set yourself up for success by breaking a big project down into small, doable tasks.

11

Then tackle and complete the first task. This accomplishment can help you move on to the next task with higher self-efficacy. Success breeds more success.

SET GOALS WITH CARE

If you want to boost your self-image, be picky about your goals. According to the research, goals that you find easy to meet will not make much of a difference in the way you see yourself. Instead, set goals that call on you to overcome obstacles, make persistent effort, and even fail occasionally.

At the same time, it is important to avoid situations in which you are *often* likely to fail. Setting goals that you have little chance of meeting can undermine your self-image. Ideal goals are both challenging *and* achievable.

ADOPT A MODEL

In self-efficacy research, the word *model* has a special definition. This term refers to someone who is similar to you in key ways and who succeeds in the kinds of situations in which you want to succeed. To find a model, gather with people who share your interests. Look for people with whom you have a lot in common—and who have mastered the skills that you want to acquire. Besides demonstrating strategies and techniques for you to use, these people hold out a real possibility of success for you.

CHANGE THE CONVERSATION ABOUT YOURSELF

Monitor what you say and think about yourself. Remember that your self-talk might be so habitual that you don't even notice it. Whether or not you are fully aware of these thoughts, they can make or break your sense of self-image.

Pay close attention. Notice when you speak or think negatively about yourself. Telling the truth about your weaknesses is one thing. Consistently underrating yourself is another. In the conversation about yourself, go for balance. Tell the truth about the times you set a goal and missed it. Also take the time to write and speak about the goals you meet and what works well in your life.

People with a strong self-image attribute their failures to skills that they currently lack—and that they can acquire in the future. This approach chooses not to look on failures as permanent, personal defects. Rather than saying, "I just don't have what it takes to become a skilled test taker," say, "I can adopt techniques to help me remember key facts even when I feel stressed."

INTERPRET STRESS IN A NEW WAY

Achieving your goals might place you right in the middle of situations in which you feel stress. You might find yourself meeting new people, leading a meeting, speaking in public, or doing something else that you've never done before. That can feel scary.

Remember that stress comes in two forms—thoughts and physical sensations. Thoughts can include mental pictures of yourself making mistakes or being publicly humiliated. They also

can be statements such as "This is the worst possible thing that could happen to me." Sensations can include shortness of breath, dry mouth, knots in the stomach, tingling feelings, headaches, and other forms of discomfort.

The way you interpret stress as you become aware of it can make a big difference in your self-image. During moments when you want to do well, you might rely on a stream of personal impressions to judge your performance. In those moments, see whether you can focus your attention. Rather than attaching negative interpretations to your experience of stress, simply notice your thoughts and sensations. Release them instead of dwelling on them or trying to resist them. As you observe yourself over time, you might find that the physical sensations associated with your sense of stress and your sense of excitement are largely the same. Instead of viewing these sensations as signs of impending doom when they are caused by stress, see them as a boost of energy and enthusiasm that you can channel into performing well.

COMPARE YOURSELF TO YOURSELF

Our own failures are often more dramatic to us than the failures of others. Our own successes are often more invisible to us. When we're unsure of ourselves, we can look in any direction and see people who seem more competent and more confident than we do. When we start the comparison game, we open the door to self-doubt.

There is a way to play the comparison game and win: Instead of comparing yourself with others, compare yourself to yourself. Measure success in terms of self-improvement rather than in terms of triumphs over others. Take time to note any progress you've made toward your goals over time. Write Discovery Statements about that progress. Celebrate your success in any area of life, no matter how small that success might seem.

SURROUND YOURSELF WITH SUPPORT

Seek out people who share your values and support your goals. This might mean going beyond your family. If you are the first student in your family to attend college, for example, your family might support you and still not understand your experiences. Find additional support by joining a study group, getting to know instructors, meeting with your advisor, and getting involved in a campus organization.

When you find supportive people, be willing to receive their encouragement. Instead of deflecting compliments ("It was nothing"), fully receive the positive things that others say about you ("Thank you"). Also, take public credit for your successes. "Well, I was just lucky" can change to "I worked hard to achieve that goal." ◼

 You're One Click Away...
*from learning more ways to change
your self-image online.*

ASKING FOR HELP

The world responds to people who ask. If you're not consistently getting what you want in life, then consider the power of asking for help.

"Ask and you shall receive" is a gem of wisdom from many spiritual traditions. Yet acting on this simple idea can be challenging.

Some people see asking for help as a sign of weakness. Actually, it's a sign of strength. Focus on the potential rewards. When you're willing to receive and others are willing to give, resources become available. Circumstances fall into place. Dreams that once seemed too big become goals that you can actually achieve. You benefit, and so do other people.

Remember that asking for help pays someone a compliment. It means that you value what people have to offer. Many will be happy to respond. The key is asking with skill.

ASK WITH CLARITY

Before asking for help, think about your request. Take time to prepare, and consider putting it in writing before you ask in person.

The way you ask has a great influence on the answers you get. For example, "I need help with money" is a big statement. People might not know how to respond. Be more specific: "Do you know any sources of financial aid that I might have missed?" Or: "My expenses exceed my income by $200 each month. I don't want to work more hours while I'm in school. How can I fill the gap?"

ASK WITH SINCERITY

People can tell when a request comes straight from your heart. Although clarity is important, remember that you're asking for help—not making a speech. Keep it simple and direct. Just tell the truth about your current situation, what you want, and the gap between the two. It's okay to be less than perfect.

ASK WIDELY

Consider the variety of people who can offer help. They include parents, friends, classmates, coworkers, mentors, and sponsors. People such as counselors, advisors, and librarians are *paid* to help you.

Also be willing to ask for help with tough issues in any area of life—sex, health, money, career decisions, and more. If you consistently ask for help only in one area, you limit your potential.

To get the most value from this suggestion, direct your request to an appropriate person. For example, you wouldn't ask your instructors for advice about sex. However, you can share any concern with a professional counselor.

ASK WITH AN OPEN MIND

When you ask for help, see whether you can truly open up. If an idea seems strange or unworkable, put your objections on hold for the moment. If you feel threatened or defensive, just notice the feeling. Then return to listening. Discomfort can be a sign that you're about to make a valuable discovery. If people only confirm what you already think and feel, you miss the chance to learn.

ASK WITH RESPONSIBILITY

If you want people to offer help, then avoid statements such as "You know that suggestion you gave me last time? Wow, that really bombed!"

When you act on an idea and it doesn't work, the reason may have nothing to do with the other person. Perhaps you misunderstood or forgot a key point. Ask again for clarity. In any case, the choice about what to do—and the responsibility for the consequences—is still yours.

ASK WITH AN OPENING FOR MORE IDEAS

Approaching people with a specific, limited request can work wonders. So can asking in a way that takes the conversation to a new place. You can do this with creative questions: "Do you have any other ideas for me?" "Would it help if I approached this problem from a different angle?" "Could I be asking a better question?"

ASK AGAIN

People who make a living by selling things know the power of a repeated request. Some people habitually respond to a first request with "no." They might not get to "yes" until the second or third request.

Some cultures place a value on competition, success, and "making it on your own." In this environment, asking for help is not always valued. Sometimes people say no because they're surprised or not sure how to respond. Give them more time and another chance to come around. ■

11

SUICIDE is no solution

While preparing for and entering higher education, people typically face major changes. The stress they feel can lead to depression and anxiety. Both are risk factors for suicide—the second leading cause of death on college campuses.[14]

To prevent suicide, start by recognizing danger signals:

- **Talking about suicide.** People who attempt suicide often talk about it first. They might say, "I just don't want to live anymore." Or "I want you to know that no matter what happens, I've always loved you." Or "Tomorrow night at 7:30, I'm going to end it all with a gun."

- **Planning for it.** People planning suicide will sometimes put their affairs in order. They might close bank accounts, give away or sell precious possessions, or make or update a will. They might even develop specific plans on how to kill themselves.

- **Having a history of previous attempts.** The American Foundation for Suicide Prevention estimates that up to 50 percent of the people who kill themselves have attempted suicide at least once before.[15]

- **Dwelling on problems.** Expressing extreme helplessness or hopelessness about solving problems can indicate that someone might be considering suicide.

- **Feeling depressed.** Although not everyone who is depressed attempts suicide, almost everyone who attempts suicide feels depressed.

TAKE PROMPT ACTION

Most often, suicide can be prevented. If you suspect that someone you know is considering suicide, do whatever it takes to ensure the person's safety. Let this person know that you will persist until you are certain that she's safe. Any of the following actions can help:

- **Take it seriously.** Taking suicidal comments seriously is especially important when you hear them from young adults. Suicide threats are more common in this age group and might be dismissed as normal. Err on the side of being too careful rather than negligent.

- **Listen fully.** Encourage the person at risk to express thoughts and feelings appropriately. If he claims that he doesn't want to talk, be inviting, be assertive, and be persistent. Be totally committed to listening.

- **Speak powerfully.** Let the person at risk know that you care. Trying to talk someone out of suicide or minimizing problems is generally useless. Acknowledge that problems are serious and that they can be solved. Point out that suicide is a permanent solution to a temporary problem—and that help is available.

- **Get professional help.** Suggest that the person see a mental health professional. If she resists help, offer to schedule the appointment for her and to take her to it. If this fails, get others involved, including the depressed person's family or school personnel.

> Trying to talk someone out of suicide or minimizing problems is generally useless. Acknowledge that problems are serious and that they can be solved. Point out that suicide is a permanent solution to a temporary problem.

- **Remove access to firearms.** Most suicides are attempted with guns. Get rid of any guns that might be around. Also remove all drugs and razors.

- **Ask the person to sign a "no-suicide contract."** Get a promise, in writing, that the person will not hurt himself before speaking to you. A written promise can provide the "excuse" he needs not to take action.

- **Handle the event as an emergency.** If a situation becomes a crisis, do not leave the person alone. Call a crisis hotline, 911, or a social service agency. If necessary, take the person to the nearest hospital emergency room, clinic, or police station.

- **Follow up.** Someone in danger of attempting suicide might resist further help even if your first intervention succeeds. Ask the person whether she's keeping counseling appointments and taking prescribed medication. Help this person apply strategies for solving problems. Stay in touch.

TAKE CARE OF YOURSELF

If you ever begin to think about committing suicide, remember that you can apply any of the above suggestions to yourself. For example, look for warning signs and take them seriously. Seek out someone you trust. Tell this person how you feel. If necessary, make an appointment to see a counselor, and ask someone to accompany you. When you're at risk, you deserve the same compassion that you'd willingly extend to another person.

Find out more from the American Foundation for Suicide Prevention at 1-800-273-8255 or www.afsp.org. Another excellent resource is the It Gets Better Project at www.itgetsbetter.org. ■

Choose to STAY SAFE

TAKE GENERAL PRECAUTIONS

Three simple actions can significantly increase your personal safety. One is to always lock doors when you're away from home. If you live in a dorm, follow the policies for keeping the front doors secure. Don't let an unauthorized person walk in behind you. If you commute to school or have a car on campus, keep your car doors locked.

The second action is to avoid walking alone, especially at night. Many schools offer shuttle buses to central campus locations. Use them. As a backup, carry enough spare cash for a taxi ride.

Third, be prepared for a crisis. Ask your instructors about what to do in classroom emergencies. Look for emergency phones along the campus routes that you normally walk. You can always use your cell phone to call 911 for help.

Also, be willing to make that call when you see other people in unsafe situations. For example, you might be at a party with a friend who drinks too much and collapses. In this situation, some underage students might hesitate to call for help. They fear getting charged with illegal alcohol possession. Don't make this mistake. Every minute that you delay calling 911 puts your friend at further risk.

PREVENT SEXUAL ASSAULT

You need to know how to prevent sexual assault while you're on campus. This problem could be more common at your school than you

iStockphoto.com/Sherwin McGehee

think. People often hesitate to report rape for many reasons, such as fear, embarrassment, and concerns that others won't believe them.

Both women and men can take steps to prevent rape from occurring in the first place:

- Get together with a group of people for a tour of the campus. Make a special note of danger spots, such as unlighted paths and unguarded buildings. Keep in mind that rape can occur during daylight and in well-lit places.

- Ask whether your school has escort services for people taking evening classes. These might include personal escorts, car escorts, or both. If you do take an evening class, ask whether there are security officers on duty before and after the class.

- Take a course or seminar on self-defense and rape prevention. To find these courses, check with your student counseling service, community education center, or local library.

If you are raped, get medical care right away. Go to the nearest rape crisis center, hospital, student health service, or police station. Also arrange for follow-up counseling. It's your decision whether to report the crime. Filing a report does not mean that you have to press charges. And if you do choose to press charges later, having a report on file can help your case. ∎

Observe thyself

You are an expert on your body. You are more likely to notice changes before anyone else does. Pay attention to these changes. They are often your first clue about the need for medical treatment or intervention. Watch for signs such as the following:

- Weight loss of more than 10 pounds in 10 weeks with no apparent cause
- A sore, scab, or ulcer that does not heal in 3 weeks
- A skin blemish or mole that bleeds, itches, or changes size, shape, or color
- Persistent or severe headaches
- Sudden vomiting that is not preceded by nausea
- Fainting spells

- Double vision
- Blood that is coughed up or vomited
- Black and tarry bowel movements
- Rectal bleeding
- Pink, red, or unusually cloudy urine
- Discomfort or difficulty when urinating or during sexual intercourse
- Lumps or thickening in a breast
- Vaginal bleeding between menstrual periods or after menopause

If you are experiencing any of these symptoms, get help from your doctor or campus health service—*before* a minor illness or injury leads to more-serious problems.

11

Choose sexual health:
PREVENT INFECTION

People with a sexually transmitted infection (STI) might feel no symptoms for years and not even discover that they are infected. Know how to protect yourself.

STIs can result from vaginal sex, oral sex, anal sex, or any other way that people contact semen, vaginal secretions, and blood. Without treatment, some of these infections can lead to blindness, infertility, cancer, heart disease, or even death.[16]

There are at least 25 kinds of STIs. Common examples are chlamydia, gonorrhea, and syphilis. Sexual contact can also spread the human papillomavirus (HPV, the most common cause of cervical cancer) and the human immunodeficiency virus (HIV, the virus that causes AIDS).

Most STIs can be cured if treated early. (Herpes and AIDS are important exceptions.) Prevention is better. Some guidelines for prevention follow.

Abstain from sex. Abstain from sex, or have sex exclusively with one person who is free of infection and has no other sex partners. These are the only ways to be absolutely safe from STIs.

Talk to your partner. Before you have sex with someone, talk about the risk of STIs. If you are infected, tell your partner.

Use condoms. Male condoms are thin membranes stretched over the penis prior to intercourse. Condoms prevent semen from entering the vagina. For the most protection, use latex condoms—not ones made of lambskin or polyurethane. Use a condom every time you have sex, and for any type of sex.

Condoms are not guaranteed to work all of the time. They can break, leak, or slip off. In addition, condoms cannot protect you from STIs that are spread by contact with herpes sores or warts.

Talk to your doctor before using condoms, lubricants, spermicides, and other products that contain nonoxynol-9. This chemical can irritate a woman's vagina and cervix and can actually increase the risk of STIs.

Stay sober. People are more likely to have unsafe sex when drunk or high.

Do not share needles. Sharing needles or other paraphernalia with other drug users can spread STIs.

Take action soon after you have sex. Urinate soon after you have sex. Wash your genitals with soap and water.

Get vaccinated. Vaccines are available to prevent hepatitis B and HPV infection. See your doctor.

Get screened for STIs. The only way to find out whether you're infected is to be tested by a health care professional. If you have sex with more than one person, get screened for STIs at least once each year. Do this even if you have no symptoms. Remember that many schools offer free STI screening.

The more people you have sex with, the greater your risk of STIs. You are at risk even if you have sex only once with one person who is infected.

The U.S. Centers for Disease Control and Prevention recommends chlamydia screening for all sexually active women under age 26. Women age 25 and older should be screened if they have a new sex partner or multiple sex partners.[17]

Recognize the symptoms of STIs. Symptoms include swollen glands with fever and aching; itching around the vagina; vaginal discharge; pain during sex or when urinating; sore throat following oral sex; anal pain after anal sex; sores, blisters, scabs, or warts on the genitals, anus, tongue, or throat; rashes on the palms of your hands or soles of your feet; dark urine; loose and light-colored stools; and unexplained fatigue, weight loss, and night sweats.

Get treated right away. If you think you have an STI, go to your doctor, campus health service, or local public health clinic. Early treatment might prevent serious health problems. To avoid infecting other people, abstain from sex until you are treated and cured. ■

You're One Click Away...
from learning more about preventing sexually transmitted infections online.

Choose sexual health:
PREVENT UNWANTED PREGNANCY

You and your partner can avoid unwanted pregnancy. There are many options. But choosing among them can be a challenge. Think about whether you want to have children someday, the number of sexual partners you have, your comfort with using a birth control method, possible side effects, and your overall health.

Even birth control methods that are usually effective can fail when used incorrectly. To prevent pregnancy, make sure you understand your chosen method. Then use it *every* time you have sex. Start with the ideas listed below. Also talk to your doctor.

Abstinence. Abstinence is choosing *not* to have sex—vaginal, oral, or anal. You might feel pressured to change your mind about this choice. However, many people exist happily without having sex. Abstinence, when practiced without exception, is the only sure way to prevent pregnancy and sexually transmitted infections (STIs).

Natural family planning. Natural family planning is based on abstaining from sex when a woman is most fertile (likely to become pregnant). It is sometimes called the "rhythm method." For women with a regular menstrual cycle, this fertile time is about 9 days each month. It includes the days right before and after ovulation. There are no side effects with natural family planning. However, it is difficult to know for sure when a woman is ovulating. Before you consider natural family planning, talk to a qualified instructor.

Barrier methods. Several methods of birth control create barriers that prevent sperm from reaching a woman's egg. One is the sponge. This is a soft disk made of polyurethane that contains nonoxynol-9—a spermicide (chemical that kills sperm). To use a sponge, a woman runs it under water and then places it inside her vagina to cover the cervix (the opening to the womb). If you choose to use the sponge, ask your doctor for instructions on when to remove it after you have intercourse. Keep in mind that nonoxynol-9 can irritate tissue in the vagina and anus with frequent use, making it easier for STIs to enter the body. Some women are sensitive to nonoxynol-9, so the sponge is not an option for them.

Other barrier methods include the diaphragm, cervical cap (FemCap), and cervical shield (Lea's Shield). These are cups made out of silicone or latex. The woman fills them with a spermicide and then places them inside her vagina to cover the cervix before having sex. The diaphragm and cervical cap come in various sizes, meaning that a woman has to see her doctor to get fitted for one. The cervical shield comes in only one size. Again, ask a doctor about when to remove these devices.

Male condoms, another type of barrier, are wrapped over an erect penis before sex. For better protection, use them with a spermicide. Also, use a new condom every time you have sex. The male latex condom is the only form of birth control known to protect against STIs.

If you use male condoms, keep some precautions in mind. Do not use them with oil-based lubricants such as petroleum jelly, lotions, baby oil, or massage oils. All of these can cause condoms to break. Instead, use lubricated condoms or add a water-based lubricant, such as K-Y Jelly. Remember that "natural" condoms—condoms made from lambskin—do not prevent STIs. Also, storing condoms in a warm place—such as a car or wallet—can weaken them and lead to breakage.

Female condoms are made of polyurethane. They are lubricated and placed inside the woman's vagina. Carefully follow the instructions about when to insert the female condom. Use a new condom each time you have sex. Do not use a female condom and a male condom at the same time.

Spermicides come in several forms: tablets, suppositories, cream, film, gel, and foam. They work best with a barrier method, such as a condom, cervical cap, or diaphragm. Note that some spermicides include nonoxynol-9, which can irritate tissue in the vagina and anus and make it easier for STIs to enter the body. Also, vaginal yeast infections can make spermicides less effective.

Hormonal methods. There are several hormonal methods for preventing pregnancy. These methods work by preventing ovulation, fertilization, or implantation of a fertilized egg.

11

An oral contraceptive—the *Pill*—is a synthetic hormone that "tells" a woman's body not to produce eggs. Many kinds are available. Talk to your doctor to make an informed choice. You might be advised to avoid the Pill if you are older than 35 and smoke, if you've had blood clots, or if you've had cancer. Antibiotics can interfere with the Pill, so ask your doctor about other methods of birth control when you're taking this medication.

Women can choose from several methods that release hormones to stop ovulation. These include a skin patch (Ortho Evra), an injection (Depo-Provera), and a vaginal ring (NuvaRing). Again, ask your doctor about possible side effects and for specific instructions on how to use these methods.

Implants. Some devices for preventing pregnancy are placed inside a woman's body and left there for several years. These devices release a hormone that prevents sperm from reaching an egg. They can also prevent a fertilized egg from implanting in the lining of the uterus. The rod (Implanon) goes under the skin of the upper arm. Intrauterine devices (IUDs) go inside a woman's uterus. They include the copper IUD (ParaGard) and the hormonal IUD (Mirena).

Talk to your doctor about how implants are inserted, how long they stay inside you, and which option would be most effective for you.

Emergency contraceptives. When women have vaginal sex without using birth control, or when they use birth control that fails, they can take "morning-after" pills. These pills are taken in two doses, 12 hours apart. The pills release hormones that stop ovulation or stop sperm from fertilizing an egg. This method works best when the pills are taken within 72 hours after sex.

Permanent methods. Some birth control methods are only for people who do not want to have children, or want to stop having children. One method is surgical sterilization. For women this means cutting, tying, or sealing the fallopian tubes (where eggs travel to get implanted in the uterus). Men get a vasectomy, which prevents sperm from going to the penis. Remember that sperm can stay in a man's body for about 3 months after surgery. Use another form of birth control during this time.

Women can also be sterilized without surgery. The doctor inserts an implant (Essure) that causes scar tissue to form in the fallopian tubes. Until the scarring appears—usually in about 3 months—another form of birth control is needed.

Where to get birth control. You can buy condoms, sponges, and spermicides over the counter at a store. Other birth control devices—including morning-after pills for women under age 18—require a prescription.

> Be sure you know how to use your chosen method of birth control. A doctor might assume that you already have this knowledge. If you don't, ask questions freely. Remember that some methods require practice and special techniques.

Note: **Withdrawal does not work.** Withdrawal happens when a man takes his penis out of the woman's vagina before he has an orgasm. Don't rely on this method for birth control. It requires extraordinary self-control. In addition, men can release some sperm before they have an orgasm. This can lead to pregnancy. If the man has an STI, the withdrawal method can pass the infection on to the woman as well.

Evaluate birth control methods. Be sure you know how to use your chosen method of birth control. A doctor might assume that you already have this knowledge. If you don't, ask questions freely. Remember that some methods require practice and special techniques. For example, male condoms have an inside and outside surface, and they work best when there's a little space left at the tip for fluid.

The following chart summarizes the effectiveness of various birth control methods and possible side effects. However, effectiveness rates can only be estimated. The estimates depend on many factors—for example, the health of the people using them, their number of sex partners, and how often they have sex. *Remember that a method can work only if used consistently and correctly.* ■

Method	Failure Rate (number of pregnancies expected per 100 women)	Some Side Effects and Risks
Sterilization surgery for women	Less than 1	• Pain • Bleeding • Complications from surgery • Ectopic (tubal) pregnancy
Sterilization implant for women (Essure)	Less than 1	• Pain • Ectopic (tubal) pregnancy
Sterilization surgery for men	Less than 1	• Pain • Bleeding • Complications from surgery
Implantable rod (Implanon)	Less than 1 Might not work as well for women who are overweight or obese.	• Acne • Weight gain • Ovarian cysts • Mood changes • Depression • Hair loss • Headache • Upset stomach • Dizziness • Sore breasts • Changes in period • Lowered interest in sex
Intrauterine device (ParaGard, Mirena)	Less than 1	• Cramps • Bleeding between periods • Pelvic inflammatory disease • Infertility • Tear or hole in the uterus
Shot/Injection (Depo-Provera)	Less than 1	• Bleeding between periods • Weight gain • Sore breasts • Headaches • Bone loss with long-term use
Oral Contraceptives (combination pill, or "the Pill")	5 Being overweight may increase the chance of getting pregnant while using the Pill.	• Dizziness • Upset stomach • Changes in your period • Changes in mood • Weight gain • High blood pressure • Blood clots • Heart attack • Stroke • New vision problems
Oral contraceptives (continuous/extended use, or "no-period Pill")	5 Being overweight may increase the chance of getting pregnant while using the Pill.	• Same as combination pill • Spotting or bleeding between periods • Hard to know if pregnant
Oral contraceptives (progestin-only pill, or "mini-Pill")	5 Being overweight may increase the chance of getting pregnant while using the Pill.	• Spotting or bleeding between periods • Weight gain • Sore breasts

11

Method	Failure Rate (number of pregnancies expected per 100 women)	Some Side Effects and Risks
Skin patch (Ortho Evra)	5 May not work as well in women weighing more than 198 pounds.	• Similar to side effects for the combination pill • Greater exposure to estrogen than with other methods
Vaginal ring (NuvaRing)	5	• Similar to side effects for the combination pill • Swelling of the vagina • Irritation • Vaginal discharge
Male condom	11-16	• Allergic reactions
Diaphragm with spermicide	15	• Irritation • Allergic reactions • Urinary tract infection • Toxic shock if left in too long
Sponge with spermicide (Today Sponge)	16-32	• Irritation • Allergic reactions • Hard time taking it out • Toxic shock if left in too long
Cervical cap with spermicide	17-23	• Irritation • Allergic reactions • Abnormal Pap smear • Toxic shock if left in too long
Female condom	20	• Irritation • Allergic reactions
Natural family planning (rhythm method)	25	• None
Spermicide alone	30 It works best if used along with a barrier method, such as a condom.	• Irritation • Allergic reactions • Urinary tract infection
Emergency contraception ("morning-after pill," "Plan B")	15 It must be used within 72 hours of having unprotected sex. Should not be used as regular birth control; only in emergencies.	• Upset stomach • Vomiting • Stomach pain • Fatigue • Headache

Source: womenshealth.gov, "Birth Control Methods: Frequently Asked Questions," March 6, 2009, accessed January 9, 2011, from www.4women.gov/faq/birth-control-methods.cfm#b.

Alcohol, tobacco, and drugs:
The Truth

The truth is that getting high can be fun. In our culture, and especially in our media, getting high has become synonymous with having a good time. Even if you don't smoke, drink, or use other drugs, you are certain to come in contact with people who do.

For centuries, human beings have devised ways to change their feelings and thoughts by altering their body chemistry. The Chinese were using marijuana 5,000 years ago. Herodotus, the ancient Greek historian, wrote about a group of people in eastern Europe who threw marijuana on hot stones and inhaled the vapors. More recently, during the American Civil War, customers could buy opium and morphine at neighborhood stores.[18]

Today we are still a drug-using society. Of course, some of those uses are therapeutic and lawful, including taking drugs as prescribed by a doctor or psychiatrist. The problem comes when we turn to drugs as *the* solution to any problem. Are you uncomfortable? Often the first response is "Take something."

We live in times when reaching for instant comfort via chemicals is not only condoned but encouraged. If you're bored, tense, or anxious, you can drink a can of beer, down a glass of wine, or light up a cigarette. If you want to enhance your memory, take a "smart drug," which includes prescription stimulants and caffeine. And these are only the legal options. If you're willing to take risks, you can pick from a large selection of illegal drugs on the street. And if that seems too risky, you can abuse prescription drugs.

There is a big payoff in using alcohol, tobacco, caffeine, cocaine, heroin, or other drugs—or people wouldn't do it. The payoff can be direct, such as relaxation, self-confidence, comfort, excitement, or the ability to pull an all-nighter. At times, the payoff is avoiding rejection or defying authority.

In addition to the payoffs, there are costs. For some people, the cost is much greater than the payoff. Even if drug use doesn't make you broke, it can make you crazy. This is not necessarily the kind of crazy where you dress up like Napoleon. Rather, it is the kind where you care about little else except finding more drugs—friends, school, work, and family be damned.

Substance abuse is only part of the picture. People can also relate to food, gambling, money, sex, and even work in compulsive ways.

Some people will stop abusing a substance or activity when the consequences get serious enough. Other people don't stop. They continue their self-defeating behaviors, no matter the consequences for themselves, their friends, or their families. At that point, the problem goes beyond abuse. It's addiction.

With addiction, the costs can include overdose, infection, and lowered immunity to disease. These can be fatal. Long-term heavy drinking, for example, damages every organ system in the human body. And about 440,000 Americans die annually from the effects of cigarette smoking, including secondhand smoke.[19]

Lectures about the reasons for avoiding alcohol and drug abuse and addiction can be pointless. We don't take care of our bodies because someone says we should. We might take care of ourselves when we see that the costs of using a substance outweigh the benefits.

Acknowledging that alcohol, tobacco, and other drugs can be fun infuriates a lot of people. Remember that this acknowledgment is *not* the same as condoning drug use. The point is this: People are more likely to abstain when they're convinced that using these substances leads to more pain than pleasure over the long run. You choose. It's your body. ■

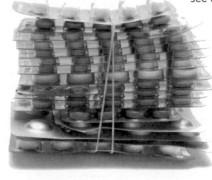

VR Photos/Shutterstock.com

Givaga/Shutterstock.com

iStockphoto.com/Sergey Mostovoy

11

EXERCISE 31

Addiction: How do I know?

People who have problems with drugs and alcohol can hide this fact from themselves and from others. It is also hard to admit that a friend or loved one might have a problem. The purpose of this exercise is to give you an objective way to look at your relationship with drugs or alcohol. There are signals that indicate when drug or alcohol use has become abusive or even addictive. This exercise can also help you determine if a friend might be addicted.

Answer the following questions quickly and honestly with yes, no, or n/a (not applicable). If you are concerned about someone else, rephrase each question using that person's name.

_____ Are you uncomfortable discussing drug abuse or addiction?

_____ Are you worried about your own drug or alcohol use?

_____ Are any of your friends worried about your drug or alcohol use?

_____ Have you ever hidden from a friend, spouse, employer, or coworker the fact that you were drinking? (Pretended you were sober? Covered up alcohol breath?)

_____ Do you sometimes use alcohol or drugs to escape lows rather than to produce highs?

_____ Have you ever gotten angry when confronted about your use?

_____ Do you brag about how much you consume? ("I drank her under the table.")

_____ Do you think about or do drugs when you are alone?

_____ Do you store up alcohol, drugs, cigarettes, or caffeine (in coffee or soft drinks) to be sure you won't run out?

_____ Does having a party almost always include alcohol or drugs?

_____ Do you try to control your drinking so that it won't be a problem? ("I drink only on weekends now." "I never drink before 5:00 p.m." "I drink only beer.")

_____ Do you often explain to other people why you are drinking? ("It's my birthday." "It's my friend's birthday." "It's Veterans Day." "It sure is a hot day.")

_____ Have you changed friends to accommodate your drinking or drug use? ("She's okay, but she isn't excited about getting high.")

_____ Has your behavior changed in the last several months? (Grades down? Lack of interest in a hobby? Change of values or of what you think is moral?)

_____ Do you drink or use drugs to relieve tension? ("What a day! I need a drink.")

_____ Do you have medical problems (stomach trouble, malnutrition, liver problems, anemia) that could be related to drinking or drugs?

_____ Have you ever decided to quit drugs or alcohol and then changed your mind?

_____ Have you had any fights, accidents, or similar incidents related to drinking or drugs in the last year?

_____ Has your drinking or drug use ever caused a problem at home?

_____ Do you envy people who go overboard with alcohol or drugs?

_____ Have you ever told yourself you can quit at any time?

_____ Have you ever been in trouble with the police after or while you were drinking?

_____ Have you ever missed school or work because you had a hangover?

_____ Have you ever had a blackout (a period you can't remember) during or after drinking?

_____ Do you wish that people would mind their own business when it comes to your use of alcohol or drugs?

_____ Is the cost of alcohol or other drugs taxing your budget or resulting in financial stress?

_____ Do you need increasing amounts of the drug to produce the desired effect?

_____ When you stop taking the drug, do you experience withdrawal?

_____ Do you spend a great deal of time obtaining and using alcohol or other drugs?

_____ Have you used alcohol or another drug when it was physically dangerous to do so (such as when driving a car or working with machines)?

_____ Have you been arrested or had other legal problems resulting from the use of a substance?

Now count the number of questions to which you answered yes. If you answered yes more than once, then talk with a professional. This does not necessarily mean that you are addicted. It does point out that alcohol or other drugs are adversely affecting your life. Talk to someone with training in recovery from chemical dependency. Do not rely on the opinion of anyone who lacks such training.

If you filled out this questionnaire about another person and you answered yes two or more times, then your friend might need help. You probably can't provide that help alone. Seek out a counselor or a support group such as Al-Anon. Call the local Alcoholics Anonymous chapter to find out about an Al-Anon meeting near you.

Some facts . . .

The National Institute on Alcohol Abuse and Alcoholism reports the following annual consequences of excessive and underage drinking by college students.[20] For more information, go online to www. collegedrinkingprevention.gov.

Death	1,825 college students between the ages of 18 and 24 die from alcohol-related unintentional injuries, including motor vehicle crashes.
Injury	599,000 students between the ages of 18 and 24 are unintentionally injured under the influence of alcohol.
Assault	696,000 students between the ages of 18 and 24 are assaulted by another student who has been drinking.
Sexual Abuse	97,000 students between the ages of 18 and 24 are victims of alcohol-related sexual assault or date rape.
Unsafe Sex	400,000 students between the ages of 18 and 24 had unprotected sex. More than 100,000 students between the ages of 18 and 24 report having been too intoxicated to know if they consented to having sex.
Academic Problems	About 25 percent of college students report academic consequences of their drinking, including missing class, falling behind, doing poorly on exams or papers, and receiving lower grades overall.
Health Problems/Suicide Attempts	More than 150,000 students develop an alcohol-related health problem, and between 1.2 and 1.5 percent of students indicate that they tried to commit suicide within the past year due to drinking or drug use.
Drunk Driving	3,360,000 students between the ages of 18 and 24 drive under the influence of alcohol.
Vandalism	About 11 percent of college student drinkers report that they have damaged property while under the influence of alcohol.
Property Damage	More than 25 percent of administrators from schools with relatively low drinking levels and over 50 percent from schools with high drinking levels say their campuses have a "moderate" or "major" problem with alcohol-related property damage.
Police Involvement	About 5 percent of 4-year college students are involved with the police or campus security as a result of their drinking, and 110,000 students between the ages of 18 and 24 are arrested for an alcohol-related violation such as public drunkenness or driving under the influence.
Alcohol Abuse and Dependence	31 percent of college students met criteria for a diagnosis of alcohol abuse and 6 percent for a diagnosis of alcohol dependence in the past 12 months, according to questionnaire-based self-reports about their drinking.

11

© Photodisc/Fotosearch

FROM DEPENDENCE TO RECOVERY

The technical term for drug addiction is *drug dependence*. This disease is defined by the following:

- *Loss of control*—continued substance use or activity in spite of adverse consequences.

- *Pattern of relapse*—vowing to quit or limit the activity or substance use and continually failing to do so.

- *Tolerance*—the need to take increasing amounts of a substance to produce the desired effect.

- *Withdrawal*—signs and symptoms of physical and mental discomfort or illness when the substance is taken away.[21]

This list can help you determine whether dependence is a barrier for you right now. The items above can apply to anything from cocaine use to compulsive gambling.

If you have a problem with dependence in any form, get help. Consider the following suggestions.

Use responsibly. Show people that you can have a good time without alcohol or other drugs. If you do choose to drink, consume alcohol with food. Pace yourself. Take time between drinks.

Avoid promotions that encourage excess drinking. "Ladies Drink Free" nights are especially dangerous. Women are affected more quickly by alcohol, making them targets for rape. Also stay out of games that encourage people to guzzle. And avoid people who make fun of you for choosing not to drink.

Pay attention. Whenever you use alcohol or another drug, do so with awareness. Then pay attention to the consequences. Act with deliberate decision rather than out of habit or under pressure from others.

Look at the costs. There is always a tradeoff to dependence. Drinking six beers might result in a temporary high, and you will probably remember that feeling. You might feel terrible the morning after consuming six beers, but some people find it easier to forget *that* pain. Stay aware of how dependence makes you feel.

Before going out to a restaurant or bar, set a limit for the number of drinks you will consume. If you consistently break this promise to yourself and experience negative consequences afterward, then you have a problem.

Admit the problem. People with active dependencies are a varied group—rich and poor, young and old, successful and unsuccessful. Often these people do have one thing in common: They are masters of denial. They deny that they are unhappy. They deny that they have hurt anyone. They are convinced that they can quit any time they want. They sometimes become so adept at hiding the problem from themselves that they die.

Take responsibility for recovery. Nobody plans to become an addict. If you have pneumonia, you seek treatment and recover without guilt or shame. Approach drug dependence in the same way. You can take responsibility for your recovery without blame, shame, or guilt.

Get help. People cannot treat dependence on their own. Behaviors tied to dependence are often symptoms of an illness that needs treatment.

Two broad options exist for getting help. One is the growing self-help movement. The other is formal treatment. People recovering from addiction often combine the two.

Many self-help groups are modeled after Alcoholics Anonymous (AA). AA is made up of recovering alcoholics and addicts. These people understand the problems of abuse firsthand, and they follow a systematic, 12-step approach to living without it. AA is one of the oldest and most successful self-help programs in the world. Chapters of AA welcome people from all walks of life, and you don't have to be an alcoholic to attend most meetings. Programs based on AA principles exist for many other forms of dependence as well.

Some people feel uncomfortable with the AA approach. They can use other options, including private therapy and group therapy. Also investigate organizations such as Women for Sobriety, the Secular Organizations for Sobriety, and Rational Recovery. Use whatever works for you.

Treatment programs are available in almost every community. They might be residential (you live there for weeks or months at a time) or outpatient (you visit several hours a day). Find out where these treatment centers are located by calling a doctor, a mental health professional, or a local hospital. If you don't have insurance, it is usually possible to arrange some other payment program. Cost is no reason to avoid treatment.

Get help for a friend or family member. You might know someone whose behavior meets the criteria for dependence. If so, you have every right to express your concern to that person. Wait until the person is clearheaded. Then mention specific incidents. For example: "Last night you drank five beers when we were at my apartment, and then you wanted to drive home. When I offered to call a cab for you instead, you refused." Also be prepared to offer a source of help, such as the phone number of a local treatment center. ■

You're One Click Away...
from learning more online about recovery from dependence.

Succeed in quitting
SMOKING

© 2013 Cengage Learning. All Rights Reserved. May not be scanned, copied or duplicated, or posted to a publicly accessible website, in whole or in part.

There is no magic formula for becoming tobacco free. However, you can take steps to succeed sooner rather than later. The American Cancer Society suggests the following.[22]

Make a firm choice to quit. All plans for quitting depend on this step. If you're not ready to quit yet, then admit it. Take another look at how smoking affects your health, finances, and relationships.

Set a date. Choose a "quit day" within the next month. That's close enough for a sense of urgency—and time to prepare. Consider a date with special meaning, such as a birthday or anniversary. Let friends and family members know about the big day.

Get personal support. Involve other people. Sign up for a quit smoking class. Attend Nicotine Anonymous or a similar group.

Consider medication. Medication can double your chances of quitting successfully.[23] Options include bupropion hydrochloride (Zyban) and varenicline (Chantix), as well as the nicotine patch, gum, nasal spray, inhaler, and lozenge.

Prepare the environment. Right before your quit day, get rid of all cigarettes and ashtrays at home and at work. Stock up on oral substitutes such as sugarless gum, candy, and low-fat snacks.

Deal with cravings for cigarettes. Distract yourself with exercise or another physical activity. Breathe deeply. Tell yourself that you can wait just a little while longer until the craving passes. Even the strongest urges to smoke will pass. Avoid alcohol use, which can increase cravings.

Learn from relapses. If you break down and light up a cigarette, don't judge yourself. Quitting often requires several attempts. Think back over your past plans for quitting and how to improve on them. Every relapse contains a lesson about how to succeed next time.

11

WARNING:
ADVERTISING
can be dangerous to
YOUR HEALTH

. . . .

The average American is exposed to hundreds of advertising messages per day. Unless you are stranded on a desert island, you are affected by advertising.

. . . .

Advertising serves a useful function. It helps us make choices about how we spend our money. We can choose among thousands of companies that provide goods and services. Advertising makes us aware of the options.

Advertising also plays on our emotions. And some ads are dangerously manipulative.

Consider how advertising can affect your health. Advertising alcohol, tobacco, pain relievers, and other health-related products is a big business. Much of the revenue earned by newspapers, magazines, radio, television, and Web sites comes from ads for these products. This means that advertisers are a major source of information about health and illness.

Advertising influences our food choices. The least nutritious foods often bring in the most advertising money. So, advertisers portray the primary staples of our diet as sugary breakfast cereals, candy bars, and soft drinks.

Ads for alcohol glorify drinking. Advertisers imply that daily drinking is the norm. Pleasant experiences are enhanced by drinking. Holidays naturally include alcohol. Parties are a flop without it. Relationships are more romantic over cocktails. Everybody drinks.

Advertising also targets our emotional health. The message behind many ads is: *Buying our product will make you okay.* This message is used to sell clothes, makeup, and hair products to make us look okay; drugs, alcohol, and food to make us feel okay; perfumes, toothpaste, and deodorants to make us smell okay. According to many ads, buying the right product is essential to having the right relationships in our lives.

A related problem concerns images of women. Ads give us the impression that women love to spend hours discussing floor wax, deodorants, tampons, and laundry detergent—and that they think constantly about losing weight and looking sexy. In some ads, women handle everything from kitchen to bedroom to boardroom—true superwomen.

Images such as these are demeaning to women and damaging to men. Women lose when they allow their self-image to be influenced by ads. Men lose when they expect real-life women to look and act like the women on television.

Advertising creates illusions. The next time you're in a crowd, notice how few people look like those in ads.

Advertising often excludes people of color. If our perceptions were based solely on advertising, we would be hard-pressed to know that our society is racially and ethnically diverse. See how many examples of cultural stereotypes you can find in the ads you encounter this week.

Use advertising as a continual opportunity to develop the qualities of a critical thinker. Every time you're exposed to an ad, ask: What's the main message, and what's the evidence for it?

Stay aware of how a multibillion-dollar industry affects your health. ■

JOURNAL ENTRY 27
Discovery/Intention Statement

Advertisements and your health

Think of a time when—after seeing an advertisement or a commercial—you craved a certain food or drink, or you really wanted to buy something. Describe a specific ad and exactly how it affected you.

I discovered that I . . .

_____

_____

_____

Now describe anything you'd like to do differently in the future when you notice that advertising affects you in the way you just described.

I intend to . . .

_____

_____

_____

This exercise involves thinking at all six levels described in "Becoming a critical thinker" on page 207.

Note: If you'd like to keep your responses to this exercise confidential, then write on separate paper.

Do you **remember** your response to the Journal Entry that opened this chapter? If not, take minute to review what you wrote.

Now, after reading and completing the exercises in this chapter, do you **understand** your current level of health in a different way? Explain your answer:

_____

_____

_____

_____

Also take a minute to page through this chapter again and review the suggested strategies for protecting your health. List five strategies that you'd like to **apply**:

_____

_____

_____

_____

Next, **analyze** your current level of health in more detail. If a statement does not apply to you, then skip it. As with the Discovery Wheel, the usefulness of this writing will be determined by your honesty and courage.

Eating

What I know about the way I eat is . . .

_____

_____

What I would most like to change about my diet is . . .

_____

_____

My eating habits lead me to be . . .

_____

_____

Exercise

The way I usually exercise is . . .

_____

_____

The last time I did 20 minutes or more of heart/lung (aerobic) exercise was . . .

_____

_____

As a result of my physical conditioning, I feel . . .

_____

_____

And I look . . .

_____

_____

It would be easier for me to work out regularly if I . . .

_____

_____

The most important benefit for me in exercising more is . . .

_____

_____

Substances

My history of cigarette smoking is . . .

_____

_____

An objective observer would say that my use of alcohol is . . .

_____

_____

11

In the last 10 days, the number of alcoholic drinks I have had is . . .

_____

_____

_____

I would describe my use of coffee, soda, and other caffeinated drinks as . . .

_____

_____

_____

I have used the following illegal drugs in the past week:

_____

_____

_____

When it comes to drugs, what I am sometimes concerned about is . . .

_____

_____

_____

I take the following prescription drugs:

_____

_____

_____

Relationships

Someone who knows me fairly well would say I am emotionally . . .

_____

_____

_____

The way I look and feel has affected my relationships by . . .

_____

_____

_____

My use of drugs or alcohol has been an issue with the following people . . .

_____

_____

_____

The best thing I could do for myself and my relationships would be to . . .

_____

_____

_____

Sleep

The number of hours I sleep each night is . . .

_____

_____

On weekends I normally sleep . . .

_____

_____

I have trouble sleeping when . . .

_____

_____

Last night I . . .

_____

_____

The quality of my sleep is usually . . .

_____

_____

In light of your analysis, go back to the five strategies you listed earlier. **Evaluate** them by considering the aspect of your health that is most important to you right now. Then choose one strategy that you will definitely commit to use during the next 30 days. Describe that strategy below, making sure it is an action that you can take immediately:

_____

_____

_____

_____

_____

Finally, experiment with the idea that your health is something that you **create** over the long term. Write a larger health-related goal—one that could make a big difference in the quality of your life over the next year. Also list the actions you will take to achieve that goal:

_____

_____

_____

_____

_____

_____

_____

_____

masterstudentprofile

Randy Pausch

(1960–2008) Pausch was a professor at Carnegie Mellon University, who, shortly after being diagnosed with pancreatic cancer, gave a "last lecture"—a reflection on his personal and professional journey—that became a hit on YouTube (this lecture was later adapted into a book of the same title). He devoted the remaining 9 months of his life to creating a legacy.

It's a thrill to fulfill your own childhood dreams, but as you get older, you may find that enabling the dreams of others is even more fun.

When I was teaching at the University of Virginia in 1993, a twenty-two-year-old artist-turned-computer-graphics-wiz named Tommy Burnett wanted a job on my research team. After we talked about his life and goals, he suddenly said, "Oh, and I have always had this childhood dream."

Anyone who uses "childhood" and "dream" in the same sentence usually gets my attention.

"And what is your dream, Tommy?" I asked.

"I want to work on the next Star Wars film," he said.

Remember, this was in 1993. The last Star Wars movie had been made in 1983, and there were no concrete plans to make any more. I explained this. "That's a tough dream to have because it'll be hard to see it through," I told him. "Word is that they're finished making Star Wars films."

"No," he said, "they're going to make more, and when they do, I'm going to work on them. That's my plan."

Tommy was six years old when the first Star Wars film came out in 1977. "Other kids wanted to be Hans Solo," he told me. "Not me. I wanted to be the guy who made the special effects—the space ships, the planets, the robots."

He told me that, as a boy, he read the most technical Star Wars articles he could find. He had all the books that explained how the models were built, and how the special effects were achieved. . . . I figured Tommy's big dream would never happen, but it might serve him well somehow. I could use a dreamer like that. I knew from my NFL desires that even if he didn't achieve his, they could serve him well, so I asked him to join our research team. . . .

When I moved to Carnegie Mellon, every member of my team from the University of Virginia came with me—everyone except Tommy. He couldn't make the move. Why? Because he had been hired by producer/director George Lucas' company, Industrial Light & Magic. And it's worth noting that they didn't hire him for his dream; they hired him for his skills. In his time with our research group, he had become an outstanding programmer in the Python language, which as luck would have it, was the language of choice in their shop. Luck is indeed where preparation meets opportunity.

It's not hard to guess where this story is going. Three new Star Wars films would be made—in 1999, 2002, and 2005—and Tommy ended up working on all of them.

On Star Wars Episode II: Attack of the Clones, Tommy was a lead technical director. There was an incredible fifteen-minute battle scene on a rocky red planet, pitting clones against droids, and Tommy was the guy who planned it all out. He and his team used photos of the Utah desert to create a virtual landscape for the battle. Talk about cool jobs. Tommy had one that let him spend each day on another planet.

RANDY PAUSCH . . . was energetic.

YOU . . . can build energy with effective habits for eating, sleeping, and managing stress.

11

You're One Click Away...
from learning more about Randy Pausch online at the Master Student Profiles. You can also visit the Master Student Hall of Fame to learn about other master students.

© iStockphoto.com/pagadesign

PUT THIS CHAPTER TO WORK

Few students need another lecture about the health risks of drug dependence, unprotected sex, sleep deprivation, and a high-calorie diet. You already know about that. What students might forget, however, is that poor health can hurt their chances for getting a job, keeping a job, and earning more money.

One quality of a master student is a strong work ethic. This implies showing up for work, staying alert, and tackling tasks with energy. Employers reward people with these characteristics, and the strategies in this chapter can help you demonstrate them.

MANAGE YOUR EMOTIONAL HEALTH DURING A JOB SEARCH. Job hunting during a recession can raise anyone's anxiety level. If you face this challenge, adapt the stress management strategies from this chapter to your advantage. For example:

- *Think critically about stress-inducing thoughts.* Despite what people say, it is never true that "there are no jobs out there." Jobs are always opening up as people retire, find new jobs in career field, or change careers. In January 2009—during a recession—4,300,000 people in the U.S. found new jobs. In addition, 3,000,000 jobs went unfilled.[24]

- *Be willing to change your behavior.* When the economy contracts, competition for jobs increases. People who are persistent and flexible in their strategies will gain an edge. The strategy is simple: If one approach to job-hunting fails, then use another one. Reading help-wanted ads and sending out résumés are just a few possibilities. Others are networking, going to state and federal employment agencies, working temporary jobs, volunteering, taking a part-time job while looking for a full-time position, joining a job club, starting a business, and directly approaching companies that interest you. Skilled job hunters stay optimistic by staying flexible.

- *Protect your overall health.* Losing sleep, skipping exercise, and eating poorly can take a toll on your mood. Getting more rest, physical activity, and nutritious food can lift your mood during a long job search.

MANAGE YOUR ENERGY LEVELS AT WORK. Once you've got a job, give it your best. Whenever possible, save demanding tasks for times when your physical and mental energy peaks. Take scheduled breaks and meal times. Rather than heading to the lounge to guzzle coffee or fill up on sweets, consider going outside for a walk and breath of fresh air.

If you sit for long hours at a computer, prevent eyestrain. Turn away from the screen and rest your eyes from time to time. Looking out a window or at a distant object can help.

In addition, pay attention to your posture. Adjust your chair so that you can sit comfortably, with your back relaxed and your spine erect. Place a pillow or small cushion behind your lower back. Also remember that crossing your legs while sitting can reduce circulation and leave you with sore muscles.

TAKE FULL ADVANTAGE OF HEALTH BENEFITS. Your employee health benefits might include screenings for a variety of conditions, paid time off for medical appointments, and discounts for health club memberships. Set up a meeting with someone at work who can explain all the options available to you.

NOW CREATE A CAREER CONNECTION OF YOUR OWN. Review this chapter, looking for a suggestion that you will commit to use while working or looking for a job. In a sentence or two, describe exactly what you plan to do and the primary benefit you want to gain. For example: "I will skip the elevator and climb at least one flight of stairs while I'm at work. This will help me make exercise a regular part of my day."

State your strategy and desired benefit in the space below:

_____

_____

_____

_____

_____

Name _____

Date _____

1. How does the Power Process: "Surrender" differ from giving up?

2. List Michael Pollan's guidelines for nutrition.

3. List two ways you can build more physical activity into your day, outside of a scheduled time for exercise.

4. The text suggests two ways to "not believe everything you think." Briefly summarize those suggestions.

5. According to the text, emotional pain is a sickness that always call for professional help. True or false? Explain your answer.

6. The suggested guidelines for asking for help include these:
   (a) Ask with clarity.
   (b) Ask with sincerity.
   (c) Ask widely.
   (d) Ask with an open mind.
   (e) All of the above

7. Name three behaviors that signal a danger of suicide.

8. Key signs of dependence include the following:
   (a) Loss of control
   (b) A pattern of relapse
   (c) Tolerance
   (d) Withdrawal
   (e) All of the above

9. One of the suggestions for dealing with addiction is "Pay attention." This implies that it's okay to use drugs, as long as you do so with full awareness. True or false? Explain your answer.

10. The only option for long-term recovery from dependence is treatment based on the steps of Alcoholics Anonymous. True or false? Explain your answer.

11

CHAPTER 11 SKILLS *Snapshot*

Now that you've reflected on the ideas in this chapter and experimented with some new strategies, revisit your responses to the Health section of the Discovery Wheel exercise on page 38. Also think about ways to develop more mastery in this area of your life. Complete the following sentences.

DISCOVERY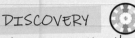

My score on the Health section of the Discovery Wheel on page 38 was . . .

To monitor my current level of health, I look for specific changes in . . .

After reading and doing this chapter, my top three health concerns are . . .

INTENTION

My top three intentions for responding to these concerns are . . .

I'll know that I've reached a new level of mastery with health when . . .

NEXT ACTION

To reach that level of mastery, the most important thing I can do next is to. . .

At the end of this course, I would like my Health score on the Discovery Wheel to be . . .

What's Next?

 Use this **Master Student Map** to ask yourself,

 WHY THIS CHAPTER MATTERS . . .

- You can use the techniques introduced in this book to set and achieve goals for the rest of your life.

WHAT IS INCLUDED . . .

- Power Process: Be it   352
- Define your values; align your actions   353
- Jumpstart your education with transferable skills   354
- Create your career *now*   358
- Sample career plans   361
- Transferring to a new school   364
- Build an irresistible résumé   366
- Use job interviews to "hire" an employer   369
- The Discovery Wheel—coming full circle   372
- Now that you're done—begin   377
- "Use the following suggestions to continue . . ."   378
- Master Student Profile: Lisa Ling   381

 HOW CAN I USE THIS CHAPTER . . .

- Choose the next steps in your education and career.
- Highlight your continuing success on résumés and in interviews.
- Use a Power Process that enhances every technique in this book.

 WHAT IF . . .

- I could begin creating the life of my dreams—starting today?

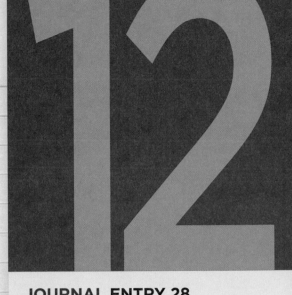

JOURNAL ENTRY 28
Discovery/Intention Statement

Revisiting what you want and how you intend to get it

Review the Power Process: "Discover what you want" on page 2. Then complete the following sentences with the first thoughts that come to mind:

I discovered that what I want most from life is . . .

_____

_____

_____

_____

To get what I want from my life, I intend to . . .

_____

_____

_____

_____

© Ruslan Ivantsov/Shutterstock.com

POWER process Be it

Use this Power Process to enhance all of the techniques in this book.

Consider that most of our choices in life fall into three categories. We can do the following:

• Increase our material wealth (what we have).
• Improve our skills (what we do).
• Develop our "being" (who we are).

Many people devote their entire lifetime to the first two categories. They act as if they are "human havings" instead of human beings. For them, the quality of life hinges on what they have. They devote most of their waking hours to getting more—more clothes, more cars, more relationships, more degrees, more trophies. "Human havings" define themselves by looking at the circumstances in their lives—what they have.

Some people escape this materialist trap by adding another dimension to their identities. In addition to living as "human havings," they also live as "human doings." They thrive on working hard and doing everything well. They define themselves by how efficiently they do their jobs, how effectively they raise their children, and how actively they participate in clubs and organizations. Their thoughts are constantly about methods, techniques, and skills.

In addition to focusing on what we have and what we do, we can also focus on our being. That last word describes how we *see* ourselves.

All of the techniques in this book can be worthless if you operate with the idea that you are an ineffective student. You might do almost everything this book suggests and still never achieve the success in school that you desire.

Instead, picture yourself as a master student right now. Through higher education, you are simply gaining knowledge and skills that reflect and reinforce this view of yourself. Change the way you see yourself. Then watch your actions and results shift as if by magic.

Remember that "Be it" is not positive thinking or mental cheerleading. This Power Process works well when you take a First Step—when you tell the truth about your current abilities. The very act of accepting who you are and what you can do right now unleashes a powerful force for personal change.

If you can first visualize where you want to be, if you can go there in your imagination, if you can *be* it today, then you set yourself up to succeed.

If you want it, be it.

You're One Click Away...
from from accessing Power Process Media online and finding out more about how to "be it."

Define your *values;*
align your *actions*

One way to choose what's next in your life is to define your values. Values are the things in life that you want for their own sake. Values influence and guide your choices, including your moment-by-moment choices of what to do and what to have. Your values define who you are and who you want to be.

Some people are guided by values that they automatically adopt from others or by values that remain largely unconscious. Other people focus on short-term gain and forget about how their behavior violates their values over the long term (a perspective that helped to create the recent economic recession). All these people could be missing the opportunity to live a life that's truly of their own choosing.

The master student qualities explained in this book are based on a specific set of values:

- Focused attention
- Self-responsibility
- Integrity
- Risk taking
- Contributing

You'll find these values and related ones directly stated in the Power Processes throughout the text. For instance:

"Discover what you want" is about the importance of living a purpose-based life.

"Ideas are tools" points to the benefits of being willing to experiment with new ideas.

"Be here now" expresses the value of focused attention.

"Love your problems (and experience your barriers)" is about seeing difficulties as opportunities to develop new skills.

"Notice your pictures and let them go" is about adopting an open-minded attitude.

"I create it all" is about taking responsibility for our beliefs and behaviors.

"Detach" reminds us that our core identity and value as a person does not depend on our possessions, our circumstances, or even our accomplishments.

"Find a bigger problem" is about offering our lives by contributing to others.

"Employ your word" expresses the value of making and keeping agreements.

"Choose your conversations and your community" reminds us of the power of language, and that we can reshape our lives by taking charge of our thoughts.

"Risk being a fool" is about courage—the willingness to take risks for the sake of learning something new.

"Surrender" points to the value of human community and the power of asking for help.

"Be it" is specifically about the power of attitudes—the idea that change proceeds from the inside out as we learn to see ourselves in new ways.

In addition, most of the skills you read about in these pages have their source in values. The Time Monitor process, for example, calls for focused attention. Even the simple act of sharing your notes with a student who missed a class is an example of contributing.

Gaining a liberal education is all about adopting and acting on values. As you begin to define your values, consider the people who have gone before you. In creeds, scriptures, philosophies, myths, and sacred stories, the human race has left a vast and varied record of values. Be willing to look everywhere, including sources that are close to home. The creed of your local church or temple might eloquently describe some of your values. So might the mission statement of your school, company, or club. Another way to define your values is to describe the qualities of people you admire.

Also, translate your values into behavior. Although defining your values is powerful, it doesn't guarantee any results. To achieve your goals, take actions that align with your values. ∎

12

You're One Click Away...
from finding a sample list of values online.

Jumpstart your education with
transferable skills

Few words are as widely misunderstood as *skill*. Defining it carefully can have an immediate and positive impact on your career planning.

IDENTIFY TWO KINDS OF SKILLS

One dictionary defines *skill* as "the ability to do something well, usually gained by training or experience." Some skills—such as the ability to repair fiber-optic cables or do brain surgery—are acquired through formal schooling, on-the-job training, or both. These abilities are called *work-content skills*. People with such skills have mastered a specialized body of knowledge needed to do a specific kind of work.

However, there is another category of skills that we develop through experiences both inside and outside the classroom. These are *transferable skills*. Transferable skills are abilities that help people thrive in any job—no matter what work-content skills they have. You start developing these skills even before you take your first job.

Perhaps you've heard someone described this way: "She's really smart and knows what she's doing, but she's got lousy people skills." People skills—such as *listening* and *negotiating*—are prime examples of transferable skills. Other examples are listed on the next few pages.

SUCCEED IN MANY SITUATIONS

Transferable skills are often invisible to us. The problem begins when we assume that a given skill can be used in only one context, such as being in school or working at a particular job. Thinking in this way places an artificial limit on our possibilities.

As an alternative, think about the things you routinely do to succeed in school. Analyze your activities to isolate specific skills. Then brainstorm a list of jobs where you could use the same skills.

Consider the task of writing a research paper. This calls for the following skills:

- *Planning,* including setting goals for completing your outline, first draft, second draft, and final draft
- *Managing time* to meet your writing goals
- *Interviewing* people who know a lot about the topic of your paper
- *Researching* using the Internet and campus library to discover key facts and ideas to include in your paper
- *Writing* to present those facts and ideas in an original way
- *Editing* your drafts for clarity and correctness

Now consider the kinds of jobs that draw on these skills.

For example, you could transfer your skill at writing papers to a possible career in journalism, technical writing, or advertising copywriting.

You could use your editing skills to work in the field of publishing as a magazine or book editor.

> When meeting with an academic advisor, you may be tempted to say, "I've just been taking general education and liberal arts courses. I don't have any marketable skills." Think again.

Interviewing and research skills could help you enter the field of market research. And the abilities to plan, manage time, and meet deadlines will help you succeed in all the jobs mentioned so far.

Use the same kind of analysis to think about transferring skills from one job to another. Say that you work part-time as an administrative assistant at a computer dealer that sells a variety of hardware and software. You take phone calls from potential customers, help current customers solve problems using their computers, and attend meetings where your coworkers plan ways to market new products. You are developing skills at *selling, serving customers,* and *working on teams.* These skills could help you land a job as a sales representative for a computer manufacturer or software developer.

The basic idea is to take a cue from the word *transferable.* Almost any skill you use to succeed in one situation can *transfer* to success in another situation.

The concept of transferable skills creates a powerful link between higher education and the work world. Skills are the core elements of any job. While taking any course, list the specific skills you are developing and how you can transfer them to the work world. Almost everything you do in school can be applied to your career—if you consistently pursue this line of thought.

ASK FOUR QUESTIONS

To experiment further with this concept of transferable skills, ask and answer four questions derived from the Master Student Map.

Why identify my transferable skills? Getting past the "I-don't-have-any-skills" syndrome means that you can approach job hunting with more confidence. As you uncover these hidden assets, your list of qualifications will grow as if by magic. You won't be padding your résumé. You'll simply be using action words to tell the full truth about what you can do.

Identifying your transferable skills takes a little time. And the payoffs are numerous. A complete and accurate list of transferable skills can help you land jobs that involve more responsibility, more variety, more freedom to structure your time, and more money. Careers can be made—or broken—by the skills that allow you to define your job, manage your workload, and get along with people.

Transferable skills help you thrive in the midst of constant change. Technology will continue to develop. Ongoing discoveries in many fields could render current knowledge obsolete. Jobs that exist today may disappear in a few years, only to be replaced by entirely new ones.

In the economy of the twenty-first century, you might not be able to count on job security. What you *can* count on is "skills security"—abilities that you can carry from one career to another or acquire as needed. Even though he only completed 8 years of formal schooling,[1] Henry Ford said, "The only real security that a person can have in this world is a reserve of knowledge, experience, and ability. Without these qualities, money is practically useless."[2]

***What* are my transferable skills?** Discover your transferable skills by reflecting on key experiences. Recall a time when you performed at the peak of your ability, overcame obstacles, won an award, gained a high grade, or met a significant goal. List the skills you used to create those successes.

For a more complete picture of your transferable skills, describe the object of your action. Say that one of the skills on your list is *organizing*. This could refer to organizing ideas, organizing people, or organizing objects in a room. Specify the kind of organizing that you like to do.

***How* do I perform these skills?** You can bring your transferable skills into even sharper focus by adding adverbs—words that describe *how* you take action. You might say that you edit *accurately* or learn *quickly*.

In summary, you can use a three-column chart to list your transferable skills. For example:

Verb	Object	Adverb
Organizing	Records	Effectively
Serving	Customers	Courteously
Coordinating	Special events	Efficiently

Add a specific example of each transferable skill to your skills list, and you're well on the way to an engaging résumé and a winning job interview.

***What if* I could expand my transferable skills?** In addition to thinking about the skills you already have, consider the skills you'd like to acquire. Describe them in detail. List experiences that can help you develop them. Let your list of transferable skills grow and develop as you do. ■

You're One Click Away...
from learning more about transferable skills online.

65 transferable skills

There are literally hundreds of transferable skills. To learn more, check out O*Net OnLine, a Web site from the federal government at www.onetonline.org/. There you'll find tools for discovering your skills and matching them to specific occupations. Additional information on careers and job hunting is available through CareerOneStop at www.careeronestop.org.

Self-discovery and self-management skills

1. Assessing your current knowledge and skills
2. Seeking out opportunities to acquire new knowledge and skills
3. Choosing and applying learning strategies
4. Showing flexibility by adopting new attitudes and behaviors

For more information about self-discovery skills, review the Introduction to this book and Chapter 1.

Time management skills

5. Scheduling due dates for project outcomes
6. Scheduling time for goal-related tasks
7. Choosing technology and applying it to goal-related tasks
8. Choosing materials and facilities needed to meet goals
9. Designing other processes, procedures, or systems to meet goals
10. Working independently to meet goals
11. Planning projects for teams
12. Managing multiple projects at the same time
13. Monitoring progress toward goals
14. Persisting in order to meet goals
15. Delivering projects and outcomes on schedule

For more information about time management skills, review Chapter 2.

12

(Continued)

Reading skills

16. Reading for key ideas and major themes
17. Reading for detail
18. Reading to synthesize ideas and information from several sources
19. Reading to discover strategies for solving problems or meeting goals
20. Reading to understand and follow instructions

For more information about reading skills, review Chapter 4.

Note-taking skills

21. Taking notes on material presented verbally, in print, or online
22. Creating pictures, graphs, and other visuals to summarize and clarify information
23. Organizing information and ideas in digital and paper-based forms
24. Researching by finding information online or in the library
25. Gathering data through field research or working with primary sources

For more information about note-taking skills, review Chapter 5.

Test-taking and related skills

26. Assessing personal performance at school or at work
27. Using test results and other assessments to improve performance
28. Working cooperatively in study groups and project teams
29. Managing stress
30. Applying scientific findings and methods to solve problems
31. Using mathematics to do basic computations and solve problems

For more information about this group of skills, review Chapters 3, 6, and 11.

Thinking skills

32. Thinking to create new ideas, products, or services
33. Thinking to evaluate ideas, products, or services
34. Evaluating material presented verbally, in print, or online
35. Thinking of ways to improve products, services, or programs
36. Choosing appropriate strategies for making decisions
37. Choosing ethical behaviors
38. Stating problems accurately
39. Diagnosing the sources of problems
40. Generating possible solutions to problems
41. Weighing benefits and costs of potential solutions
42. Choosing and implementing solutions
43. Interpreting information needed for problem solving or decision making

For more information about thinking skills, review Chapter 7.

Communication skills

44. Assigning and delegating tasks
45. Coaching
46. Consulting
47. Counseling
48. Editing publications
49. Giving people feedback about the quality of their performance
50. Interpreting and responding to nonverbal messages
51. Interviewing people
52. Leading meetings
53. Leading project teams
54. Listening fully (without judgment or distraction)
55. Preventing conflicts (defusing a tense situation)
56. Resolving conflicts
57. Responding to complaints
58. Speaking to diverse audiences
59. Writing
60. Editing

For more information about communication skills, review Chapters 8 and 9.

Money skills

61. Monitoring income and expenses
62. Raising funds
63. Decreasing expenses
64. Estimating costs
65. Preparing budgets

For more information about money skills, review Chapter 10.

 You're One Click Away...
from finding an expanded list of transferable skills online.

✔ EXERCISE 32

Recognize your skills

This exercise about discovering your skills includes three steps. Before you begin, gather at least a hundred 3 × 5 cards and a pen or pencil. Or open up a computer file and use any software that allows you to create lists. Allow about 1 hour to complete the exercise.

STEP 1 **List recent activities** Recall your activities during the past week or month. To refresh your memory, review your responses to Exercise 8: "The Time Monitor" in Chapter 2. (You might even benefit from doing that exercise again.)

List down as many of these activities as you can. (If you're using 3 × 5 cards, list each item on a separate card.) Include work-related activities, school activities, and hobbies. Spend 10 minutes on this step.

STEP 2 **List rewards and recognitions** Next, list any rewards you've received, or other recognition of your achievements, during the past year. Examples include scholarship awards, athletic awards, or recognitions for volunteer work. Allow 10 minutes for this step as well.

STEP 3 **List work-content skills** Now review the two lists you just created. Then take another 10 minutes to list any specialized areas of knowledge needed to do those activities, win those awards, and receive those recognitions.

These areas of knowledge indicate your *work-content skills*. For example, tutoring a French class requires a working knowledge of that language.

List all of your skills that fall into this category, labeling each one as "work-content."

STEP 4 **List transferable skills** Go over your list of activities one more time. Spend 10 minutes looking for examples of *transferable skills*—those that can be applied to a variety of situations. For instance, giving a speech or working as a salesperson in a computer store requires the ability to persuade people. Tuning a car means that you can attend to details and troubleshoot.

List all your skills that fall into this category, labeling each one as "transferable."

STEP 5 **Review and plan** You now have a detailed picture of your skills. Review all the lists you created in the previous steps. See whether you can add any new items that occur to you.

Save your lists in a place where you can easily find them again. Plan to update all of them at least once each year. Your lists will come in handy for writing your résumé, preparing for job interviews, and doing other career-planning tasks.

12

Create your CAREER now

There's an old saying: "If you enjoy what you do, you'll never work another day in your life." If you clearly define your career goals and your strategy for reaching them, you can plan your education effectively and create a seamless transition from school to the workplace.

Terry Vine/Getty Images

Career planning involves continuous exploration. There are dozens of effective paths to take. Begin now with the following ideas.

YOU ALREADY KNOW A LOT ABOUT YOUR CAREER PLAN

When people learn study skills and life skills, they usually start with finding out things they don't know. That means discovering new strategies for taking notes, reading, writing, managing time, and the other subjects covered in this book.

Career planning is different. You can begin your career planning education by realizing how much you know right now. You've already made many decisions about your career. This is true for young people who say, "I don't have any idea what I want to be when I grow up." It's also true for midlife career changers.

Consider the student who can't decide whether she wants to be a cost accountant or a tax accountant and then jumps to the conclusion that she is totally lost when it comes to career planning. It's the same with the student who doesn't know whether he wants to be a veterinary assistant or a nurse.

These people forget that they already know a lot about their career choices. The person who couldn't decide between veterinary assistance and nursing had already ruled out becoming a lawyer, computer programmer, or teacher. He just didn't know yet whether he had the right bedside manner for horses or for people. The person who was debating tax accounting versus cost accounting already knew she didn't want to be a doctor, playwright, or taxicab driver. She did know she liked working with numbers and balancing books.

In each case, these people have already narrowed their list of career choices to a number of jobs in the same field—jobs that draw on the same core skills. In general, they already know what they want to be when they grow up.

Demonstrate this for yourself. Find a long list of occupations. (One source is *The Dictionary of Occupational Titles*, a government publication available at many libraries.) Using a stack of 3 × 5 cards, write down about a hundred randomly selected job titles, one title per card. Sort through the cards, and divide them into two piles. Label one pile "Careers I've Definitely Ruled Out for Now." Label the other pile "Possibilities I'm Willing to Consider."

You might go through a stack of a hundred such cards and end up with ninety-five in the "definitely ruled out" pile and five in the "possibilities" pile. This demonstrates that you already have a career in mind.

YOUR CAREER IS A CHOICE, NOT A DISCOVERY

Many people approach career planning as if they were panning for gold. They keep sifting through the dirt, clearing the dust, and throwing out the rocks. They are hoping to strike it rich and discover the perfect career.

Other people believe that they'll wake up one morning, see the heavens part, and suddenly know what they're supposed to do. Many of them are still waiting for that magical day to dawn.

You can approach career planning in a different way. Instead of seeing a career as something you discover, you can see it as something you choose. You don't find the right career. You create it.

There's a big difference between these two approaches. Thinking that there's only one "correct" choice for your career can lead to a lot of anxiety: "Did I choose the right one?" "What if I made a mistake?"

Viewing your career as your creation helps you relax. Instead of anguishing over finding the right career, you can stay open to possibilities. You can choose one career today, knowing that you can choose again later.

Suppose that you've narrowed your list of possible careers to five, and you still can't decide. Then just choose one. Any one. Many people will have five careers in a lifetime anyway. You might be able to pursue all five of your careers, and you can do any one of them first. The important thing is to choose.

One caution is in order. Choosing your career is not something to do in an information vacuum. Rather, choose after you've done a lot of research. That includes research into yourself—your skills and interests—and a thorough knowledge of what careers are available.

After you've gathered all of the data, there's only one person who can choose your career: you. This choice does not have to be a weighty one. In fact, it can be like going into your favorite restaurant and choosing from a menu that includes only your favorite dishes. At that point, it's difficult to make a mistake. Whatever your choice, you know you'll enjoy it.

YOU HAVE A WORLD OF CHOICES

Our society offers a limitless array of careers. You no longer have to confine yourself to a handful of traditional categories, such as business, education, government, or manufacturing. People are constantly creating new products and services to meet emerging demands. The number of job titles is expanding so rapidly that we can barely keep track of them.

In addition, people are constantly creating new goods and services to meet emerging needs. For instance, there are people who work as *ritual consultants,* helping people plan weddings, anniversaries, graduations, and other ceremonies. *Space planners* help

individuals and organizations arrange furniture and equipment efficiently. *Auto brokers* visit dealers, shop around, and buy a car for you. *Professional organizers* will walk into your home or office and advise you on managing time and paperwork. *Pet psychologists* will help you raise a happy and healthy animal. And *life coaches* will assist you in setting and achieving goals relating to your career or anything else.

The global marketplace creates even more options for you. Through Internet connections and communication satellites that bounce phone calls across the planet, you can exchange messages with almost anyone, anywhere. Your customers or clients could be located in Colorado or China, Pennsylvania, or Panama. Your skills in thinking globally and communicating with a diverse world could help you create a new product or service for a new market—and perhaps a career that does not even exist today.

PLAN BY NAMING NAMES

One key to making your career plan real and to ensuring that you can act on it is naming. Go back over your plan to see whether you can include specific names whenever they're called for:

- *Name your job.* List the skills you enjoy using, and find out which jobs use them (the *Occupational Outlook Handbook* is a good resource for this activity). What are those jobs called? List them. Note that the same job might have different names.

- *Name your company—the agency or organization you want to work for.* If you want to be self-employed or start your own business, name the product or service you'd sell. Also list some possible names for your business. If you plan to work for others, name the organizations or agencies that are high on your list.

- *Name your contacts.* Take the list of organizations you just compiled. Find out which people in these organizations are responsible for hiring. List those people, and contact them directly. If you choose self-employment, list the names of possible customers or clients. All of these people are job contacts.

- *Name your location.* Ask whether your career choices are consistent with your preferences about where to live and work. For example, someone who wants to make a living as a studio musician might consider living in a large city such as New York or Toronto. This contrasts with the freelance graphic artist who conducts his business mainly by phone, fax, and e-mail. He might be able to live anywhere and still pursue his career.

Now expand your list of contacts by brainstorming with your family and friends. Come up with a list of names—anyone who can help you with career planning and job hunting. Write each of these names on a 3×5 card. You can also use a spiral-bound notebook, computer, or smartphone.

Next, call the key people on your list. Ask them about their career experiences, tell them about the career path you're considering, and probe their knowledge of the industry you're interested in. After you speak with them, make brief notes about what you discussed. Also jot down any actions you agreed to take, such as a follow-up call.

12

Consider everyone you meet as a potential member of your job network. Be prepared to talk about what you do. Develop a "pitch"—a short statement of your career goal that you can easily share with your contacts. For example: "After I graduate, I plan to work in the travel business. I'm looking for an internship in a travel agency for next summer. Do you know of any agencies that take interns?"

DESCRIBE YOUR IDEAL LIFESTYLE

In addition to choosing the content of your career, you have many options for integrating work into the context of your life. You can work full-time. You can work part-time. You can commute to a cubicle in a major corporation. Or you can work at home and take the 30-second commute from your bedroom to your desk.

Close your eyes. Visualize an ideal day in your life after graduation. Vividly imagine the following:

- Your work setting
- Your coworkers
- Your calendar and to-do list for that day
- Other sights and sounds in your work environment

This visualization emphasizes the importance of finding a match between your career and your lifestyle preferences—the amount of flexibility in your schedule, the number of people you see each day, the variety in your tasks, and the ways that you balance work with other activities.

CONSIDER SELF-EMPLOYMENT

Instead of joining a thriving business, you could create one of your own. If the idea of self-employment seems far-fetched, consider that as a student, you already *are* self-employed. You are setting your own goals, structuring your time, making your own financial decisions, and monitoring your performance. These are all transferable skills that you could use to become your own boss. Remember that many successful businesses—including Facebook and Yahoo!—were started by college students.

TEST YOUR CHOICE—AND BE WILLING TO CHANGE

Career-planning materials and counselors can help you test your choice and change it if you decide to do so. Read books about careers. Search for career-planning Web sites. Ask career counselors about skills assessments that can help you discover more about your skills and identify jobs that call for those skills. Take career-planning courses and workshops sponsored by your school. Visit the career-planning and job placement offices on campus. Once you have a career choice, translate it into workplace experience. For example:

- Contact people who are actually doing the job you're researching, and ask them a lot of questions about what it's like (an *information interview*).
- Choose an internship or volunteer position in a field that interests you.
- Get a part-time or summer job in your career field.

> Career planning is not a once-and-for-all proposition. Rather, career plans are made to be changed and refined as you gain new information about yourself and the world.

If you find that you enjoy such experiences, you've probably made a wise career choice. And the people you meet are possible sources of recommendations, referrals, and employment in the future. If you did *not* enjoy your experiences, celebrate what you learned about yourself. Now you're free to refine your initial career choice or go in a new direction.

Career planning is not a once-and-for-all proposition. Rather, career plans are made to be changed and refined as you gain new information about yourself and the world. You might not walk straight into your dream job right after graduation. And you can approach *any* position in a way that takes you one step closer to your career goal. Do your best at every job, and stay flexible. Career planning never ends, and the process is the same, whether you're choosing your first career or your fifth.

REMEMBER YOUR PURPOSE

While digging deep into the details of career planning, take some time to back up to the big picture. Listing skills, researching jobs, writing résumés—all these activities are necessary and useful. At the same time, though, attending to these tasks can obscure your broadest goals. To get perspective, you need to go back to the basics—a life purpose.

Your deepest desire might be to see that hungry children are fed, to make sure that beautiful music keeps getting heard, or to help alcoholics become sober. When such a large purpose is clear, smaller decisions about what to do are often easier.

A life purpose makes a career plan simpler and more powerful. It cuts through the stacks of job data and employment figures. Your life purpose is like the guidance system for a rocket. It keeps the plan on target while revealing a path for soaring to the heights.[3] ∎

 You're One Click Away...
from finding more strategies online for career planning.

Sample CAREER PLANS

Following are some examples of mind maps, pie charts, and lists that you can use to visually represent your career plan.

Sample 1
A mind map that links personal values to desired skills that could be used in a variety of careers.

Sample 2
A pie chart summarizing the amounts of time devoted to career-related activities.

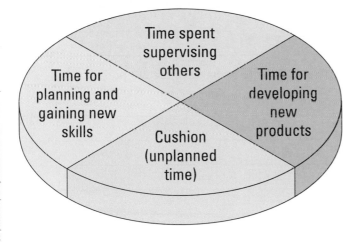

Sample 3
A list of career goals sorted by priority. In this case, each goal is assigned a number from 1 to 100. Higher numbers denote higher priority.

- Consult college career services department on law school options (100)
- Prepare rigorously for LSAT and do well (100)
- Get into top-10 law school (95)
- Get position as editor on Law Review (90)
- Graduate in top of class at law school (85)
- Work for state district attorney's office (80)
- Use my position and influence to gain political and judicial contacts (75)
- Found private law firm focused on protection of workers' rights (70)
- Win major lawsuits in defense of individual liberties in the workplace (60)
- Leave law practice to travel to developing countries in aid of poor for two years (60)
- Found international agency for protection of human rights (50)
- Win Nobel Prize (30)

You're One Click Away...
from finding more sample career plans online.

12

EXERCISE 33

Create your career plan—now

Write your career plan. Now. Start the process of career planning, even if you're not sure where to begin. Your response to this exercise can be just a rough draft of your plan, which you can revise and rewrite many times. The point is to get your ideas in writing.

The final format of your plan is up to you. You might include many details, such as the next job title you'd like to have, the courses required for your major, and other training that you want to complete. You might list companies to research and people that could hire you. You might also include target dates to complete each of these tasks.

Another option is to represent your plan visually through flowcharts, time lines, mind maps, or drawings. You can generate these by hand or use computer software.

For now, experiment with career planning by completing the following sentences. Use the space provided, and continue on additional paper as needed. When answering the first question, write down what first comes to your mind. The goal is to begin the process of discovery. You can always change direction after some investigation.

1. The career I choose for now is . . .

_____

_____

_____

_____

_____

_____

_____

_____

_____

_____

_____

2. The major steps that will guide me to this career are . . .

_____

_____

_____

_____

_____

_____

_____

_____

_____

_____

_____

_____

3. The immediate steps I will take to pursue this career are . . .

_____

_____

_____

_____

_____

_____

_____

_____

_____

✓ EXERCISE 34

Make a trial choice of major

The article "Thinking about your major" on page 225 explains four strategies for choosing a major. Now that you've thought more about what your career plan is, the purpose of this exercise is to take action on the strategies of choosing a major that will support your career plan. First, take a few minutes to review the article on page 225 and your career plan from Exercise 33. Then complete the following steps:

STEP 1 **Discover options** Look at your school's catalog or Web site for a list of majors. Make a photocopy of that list or print it out. Spend at least 5 minutes reading through all the majors that your school offers.

STEP 2 **Make a trial choice** Next, cross out all of the majors that you already know are not right for you. You will probably eliminate well over half the list. Scan the remaining majors. Next to the ones that definitely interest you, write "yes." Next to majors that you're willing to consider and are still unsure about, write "maybe."

Now, focus on your "yes" choices. See whether you can narrow them down to three majors. List those here:

Finally, write an asterisk next to the major that interests you most right now. *This is your trial choice of major.*

STEP 3 **Evaluate your trial choice** Congratulations on making your choice! Now take a few minutes to reflect on it. Does it align with your interests, skills, and career plans? Set a goal to test your choice of major with out-of-classroom experience. Examples are internships, field experiences, study abroad programs, and work-study assignments. Note that these experiences might confirm your trial choice—or lead to a new choice of major.

✓ EXERCISE 35

Create your academic plan

An academic plan is a road map for getting the most out of your education. This document is a list of all the courses you plan to take and *when* you plan to take each one. (At some schools, it is called a *degree plan.*)

STEP 1 You probably started an academic plan when you registered for school. If you have any notes or materials from that experience, then review them. Also review your school's course catalog and Web site.

STEP 2 Using all of the information you've gathered so far, create your list of planned courses on separate paper. Another option is to use your computer and create your list with word-processing, outlining, or spreadsheet software.

Consider formatting your plan as a chart:

- In the first column, list the name of each course.

- Use a second column to write the number of credits for each course.

- In the third column, note the term you plan to take each course (for example, *Spring 2016*). Be sure to check your college catalog for course prerequisites or corequisites.

STEP 3 Now evaluate your academic plan. Make sure that it:

- Gives you the total number of credits you need to graduate.

- Meets your school's requirements for general education.

- Meets the requirements for your major, your minor, or both.

Reach out to instructors and advisors for help. Use available resources to create an academic plan that fuels your success.

12

TRANSFERRING TO A
new school

If you ever choose to change schools, you won't be alone. The *New York Times* reports that about 60 percent of students graduating from college attend more than one school.[4]

© PhotoAlto/Alamy

The way that you choose a new school will have a major impact on your education. This is true if you're transferring from a community or technical college to a 4-year school or if you're choosing a graduate school.

Even if you don't plan to go through the process of choosing schools again, you can use the following ideas to evaluate your current school.

KNOW KEY TERMS

As you begin researching schools, take a few minutes to review some key terms.

Articulation agreements are official documents that spell out the course equivalents that a school accepts.

An *associate of arts (A.A.)* or *associate of science (A.S.)* is the degree title conferred by many 2-year colleges. Having a degree from a 2-year college can make it easier to change schools than transferring without a degree.

Course equivalents are courses you've already taken that another school will accept as meeting its requirements for graduation.

Prerequisites are courses or skills that a school requires students to complete or have before they enter or graduate.

GATHER INFORMATION

To research schools, start with publications. These include print sources, such as school catalogs, and school Web sites. Next,

contact people—academic advisors, counselors, other school staff members, and current or former students from the schools you're considering. Contact the advisor at the new school to find out what the acceptance and graduation requirements will be.

Use your research to dig up key facts such as these about each school you're considering:

- Location
- Number of students
- Class sizes
- Possibilities for contact with instructors outside class
- Percentage of full-time faculty members
- Admissions criteria
- Availability of degrees that interest you
- Tuition and fees
- Housing plans
- Financial aid programs
- Religious affiliation
- Diversity of students and staff
- Course requirements
- Retention rates (how many students come back to school after their freshman year)

To learn the most about a school, go beyond the first statistics you see. For example, a statement that "30 percent of our students are persons of color" doesn't tell you much about the numbers of people from specific ethnic or racial groups.

Also, you could transfer to a school that advertises student–instructor ratios of 15 to 1 and then find yourself in classes with 100 people. Remember that any statement about average class size is just that—an average. To gain more details, ask how often you can expect to enroll in smaller classes, especially during your final terms.

Take trips to the two or three schools that interest you most. Ask for a campus tour and a chance to sit in on classes.

In addition, gather facts about your current academic profile. Include your grades, courses completed, degrees attained, and grade point average (GPA). Standardized test scores are important. They include your scores on the Scholastic Assessment Test (SAT), American College Test (ACT), Graduate Record Examinations (GRE), and any advanced placement (AP) tests you've taken.

CHOOSE YOUR NEW SCHOOL

If you follow the above suggestions, you'll end up with stacks of publications and pages of notes. As you sort through all this information, remember that your impressions of a school will go beyond a dry list of facts. Also pay attention to your instincts and intuitions—your "gut feelings" of attraction to one school or hesitation about another. These impressions can be important to your choice. Allow time for such feelings to emerge.

You can also benefit from putting your choice of schools in a bigger context. Consider the purposes, values, and long-term goals you've generated by doing the exercises and Journal Entries in this book. Consider which school is most likely to support the body of discoveries and intentions that you've created.

As you choose your new school, consider the needs and wishes of your family members and friends. Ask for their guidance and support. If you involve them in the decision, they'll have more stake in your success.

At some point, you'll just choose a school. Remember that there is no one "right" choice. You could probably thrive at many schools—perhaps even at your current one. Use the suggestions in this book to practice self-responsibility. Take charge of your education no matter which school you attend.

SUCCEED AT YOUR NEW SCHOOL

Be willing to begin again. Some students approach a transfer with a "been there, done that" attitude. Having enrolled in higher education before, they assume that they don't need the orientation, advising, or other student services available at their new school.

Consider an alternative. Because your tuition and fees cover all these services, you might as well take advantage of them. By doing so, you could uncover opportunities that you missed while researching schools. At the very least, you'll meet people who will support your transition.

Your prior experience in higher education gives you strengths. Acknowledge them, even as you begin again at your new school.

While celebrating your past accomplishments, you can explore new paths to student success.

Connect to people. At your new school, you'll be in classes with people who have already developed social networks. To avoid feeling left out, seek out chances to meet people. Join study groups, check out extracurricular activities, and consider volunteering for student organizations. Making social connections can ease your transition to a new academic environment.

Check credits. If you plan to transfer, meet with an advisor at your new school as soon as possible. Talk about how the credits that you've already earned will transfer to that school. This can save you a lot of tuition money.

No two schools offer the same sets of courses, so determining credits is often a matter of interpretation. In some cases, you might be able to persuade a registrar or the admissions office to accept some of your previous courses. Keep a folder of syllabuses from your courses for this purpose. Ask your academic advisor for help. Taking care of these details can help you graduate from your new school on time, with the education that you want. ■

 You're One Click Away...
from learning more online about changing schools.

Master Students
IN ACTION

"*The feeling of accomplishment is a feeling like no other. To know what it is like to finish what you started and what it took to get there. . . . I believe that success is not about what you have gained, but what you have gone through.*"

—*Alex Denizard,*
TCI College of Technology

 You're One Click Away...
from viewing a video about Master Students in Action.

12

BUILD AN IRRESISTIBLE résumé

A résumé is much more than a list of your qualifications. This document says a lot about who you are, what you love to do, and how you contribute to the world by using your skills. You can gain a lot from thinking about those things now, even if you don't plan to apply for a job in the near future. Start *building* your résumé now, even if you don't plan to *use* one for a while.

BUILD YOUR RÉSUMÉ FROM A SKILLS PERSPECTIVE

According to one perspective, there's no need to think about a résumé until your last term in school. At that time you go to a career planning workshop or two, check the job listings, and start sending out applications. And if you don't land a job—well, you can always go back to school.

Instead, take a skills perspective. Ask one question about every experience you have in higher education: *How will this help me develop a valuable skill?* Remembering this question will help you choose courses, instructors, and extracurricular activities with a new level of clarity. Then, when it's your time to send out a résumé, you'll be ready to demonstrate your mastery.

An education is much more than a grade point average and list of course credits. The whole point is to become a different person. Graduating means being able to *do* things that you could not do when you started school.

Today you can start developing the ability to think critically, speak persuasively, and write clearly. You can learn to work in teams, solve complex problems, innovate, and act with integrity. These are skills that allow you to prosper in the workplace and find your place in a global economy. From this perspective, a résumé is something that you build during your whole time in higher education.

START BUILDING SKILLS FOR YOUR IDEAL RÉSUMÉ

To get the most from your education, think about the résumé you want to have when you graduate. With that vision of the person you want to be, choose the skills that you want to gain.

If you've actively participated with this course and this book, then you've got a head start. Review "Master student qualities" on page 3. Reread your responses to the Journal Entries and exercises throughout this book. Also review the articles in this chapter about values, transferable skills, declaring a major, and choosing your career.

With those insights fresh in mind, start planning. Write goals to develop specific skills. Then list the actions you will take to develop those skills. Add reminders of these actions to your to-do list and calendar so that you can actually achieve your goals.

Many of your plans will involve taking courses. In addition, look for ways to gain and use skills outside the classroom. Sign up for internships and service learning projects related to your major. Find part-time jobs related to your career plan. Seize every opportunity to take theories and test them in the work world. These experiences will help you develop an expertise, build a job network, and make a seamless transition to your next career.

REMEMBER THE REASON FOR A RÉSUMÉ

When you *do* write a résumé to apply for a job, approach it as a piece of persuasive writing—not a dry recitation of facts or a laundry list of previous jobs. The key purpose of your resume is to get you to the next step in the hiring process.

There is no formula for a great résumé. Employers have many different preferences for what they want to see. Just remember that an effective résumé states how you can benefit a potential employer. Second, it offers evidence that you can deliver those benefits. Make sure that every word in your résumé serves those goals.

To write an effective résumé, consider your audience. Picture a person who has a several hundred résumés to plow through, and almost no time for that task. She may spend only 20 seconds scanning each résumé before making a decision about who to call for interviews. Remember to be concise. Employers will not read long resumes with attachments and pages of details.

Your goal is to get past this first cut. Neatness, organization, and correct grammar and punctuation are essential. Meet these goals, and then make an even stronger impression with the following strategies.

USE THIS RÉSUMÉ CHECKLIST

The following suggestions will guide you through one common résumé format:

- *Let people know how to contact you.* Start your résumé with contact information. This includes your name, mailing address, e-mail address, and phone number. If you have a Web site, add that as well. Make sure that your e-mail address, voice mail greeting, and Web site convey a professional image.

- *State your objective.* This is a description of the job that you want. Keep this to one sentence, and tailor it to the specific position for which you're applying. Craft your objective to get attention. Ask yourself: From an employer's perspective, what kind of person would make an ideal candidate for this job? Then write your objective to directly answer this question with two or three specific qualities that you can demonstrate.

- *Focus the objective on what you can do for the employer.* Here is the first place to state the benefits you can deliver. Avoid self-centered phrases like "a job in the software industry where I can develop my sales skills." Instead, state your objective as "a sales position for a software company that wants to continually generate new customers and exceed its revenue goals."

- *Highlight your experience.* Follow your objective with the body of your résumé. One common heading is *experience*. Write this section carefully. Here is where you give a few relevant details about your past jobs, listed in order starting with your most recent position. This is the heart of a *chronological* résumé. An alternative to the chronological format is the *functional* résumé. It highlights your skills, strengths, and personal achievements rather than past jobs. This format might be useful for people with limited experience or gaps in their work history.

- *Highlight your education.* A second common heading for the body of a résumé is "education." List any degree that you attained beyond high school, along with honors, awards, and significant activities. If you are currently enrolled in classes, note that as well. Include your planned degree and date of graduation.

- *Include references.* Many résumés end with a line such as "references are available on request." Before you add this statement, make sure that you can deliver a list of people who have already agreed to write a reference for you. Ask for their permission and current contact information.

- *Write so that the facts leap off the page.* Whenever possible, use phrases that start with an action verb: "*supervised* three people," "*generated* leads for sales calls," "*wrote* speeches and *edited* annual reports," "*designed* a process that reduced production expenses by 20 percent." Active verbs refer directly to your skills. Make them relevant to the job you're seeking, and tie them to specific accomplishments whenever possible. Be prepared to discuss these accomplishments during a job interview.

- *Cut the fluff.* Leave out information that could possibly eliminate you from the hiring process and send your résumé hurtling into the circular file. Avoid boilerplate language—stock wording or vague phrases such as "proven success in a high-stress environment," "highly motivated self-starter," or "a demonstrated capacity for strategic thinking."

- *Get feedback.* Ask friends and family members if your résumé is persuasive and easy to understand. Also get feedback from someone at your school's career-planning center. Revise your résumé based on their comments. Then revise some more. Create sparkling prose that will intrigue a potential employer enough to call you for an interview.

- *Take charge of your online résumé.* While you're writing a résumé, take a break to check your online presence. Type your name into an Internet search engine such as Google and see what results you get. These search results make up your online résumé.

Employers will check social networking sites such as Facebook, MySpace, and Twitter to learn about you. Review your posts, photos, videos, and files on all social networks you have joined, deleting content as well as unsubscribing from any inactive social network accounts. Be mindful as you post future content. Add updates about your academic achievements, extracurricular activities, and internships.

You can also use social networking to actively support your job search. For example, start a Twitter stream about topics related to your major and career plan. Link your followers to useful articles, and start following people who are working your chosen field.

ROUND OUT YOUR RÉSUMÉ WITH A PORTFOLIO

Photographers, contractors, and designers regularly show portfolios filled with samples of their work. Today, employers and educators increasingly see the portfolio as a tool that's useful for everyone. Some schools require students to create them, and some employers want to see a portfolio before they hire.

Portfolios consist of artifacts. An *artifact* is any object that's important to you and that reveals something about yourself. Examples include awards, recommendation letters, job descriptions for positions you've held, writing samples, presentations, articles about projects you've done, lists of grants or scholarships you've received, programs from performances you've given, and transcripts of your grades. Your portfolio can also include photographs, audio or video recordings, Web sites, or representations of anything else you've created.

To save hours when creating your portfolio, start documenting your artifacts. Record the "five W's" about each one: *who* was involved with it, *what* you did with it, *when* it was created, *where*

12

it was created, and *why* the artifact is important to you. Update this information as you collect new artifacts. Whenever possible, manage this information with a computer, using word-processing or database software.

When you're ready to create a portfolio for a specific audience, write your purpose—for example, to demonstrate your learning or to document your work experience as you prepare for a job interview.

Also think about your audience—the people who will see your portfolio. Predict what questions they will ask and make sure they're answered in your portfolio. Screen artifacts with your purpose and audience in mind. If a beautiful artifact fails to meet your purpose or fit your audience, leave it out for now.

Consider presenting your portfolio online in the form of a personal Web site with an online portfolio of your work or keeping a blog and writing a post every 2 weeks or so. Focus your posts on topics related to your career plan. Search for blogs by people with similar interests and add constructive comments to their posts.

SEE YOUR RÉSUMÉ AS A WORK IN PROGRESS

To create an effective résumé, plan to revise it regularly. Save a copy on a flash drive or computer hard drive in a file you can update. See which version of your résumé leads to the most interviews.

Look at a lot of sample résumés, especially from people in your career field. There is no ideal format for a résumé. Just focus on doing what works.

Also combine your résumé with other strategies. If you just send out résumés and neglect to make personal contacts, you will be disappointed with the results. Instead, research companies and do information interviews. Contact potential employers directly—even if they don't have a job opening at the moment. Find people in organizations who have the power to hire you. Then use every job contact you have to introduce yourself to those people and schedule an interview. To get the most from your résumé, use it to support a variety of job-hunting strategies. ■

FINE TUNE YOUR

cover letter

Remember the primary question in an employer's mind: What do you have to offer us? Using a three-part structure can help you answer this question.

1. Gain attention

In your first sentence, address the person who can hire you and grab that person's attention. Make a statement that appeals directly to her self-interest. Write something that moves a potential employer to say, "We can't afford to pass this person up. Call him right away to set up an appointment."

To come up with ideas for your opening, complete the following sentence: "The main benefits that I can bring to your organization are . . . ." Another option: "My work experience ties directly to several points mentioned in your job description. First, ..."

Perhaps someone the employer knows told you about this job opening. Mention this person in your opening paragraph, especially if she has a positive reputation in the organization.

2. Build interest

Add a fact or two to back up your opening sentence. If you're applying for a specific job opening, state this.

If you're not, then offer an idea that will intrigue the employer enough to respond anyway. Another option is to give a summary of your key qualifications for a specific job. Briefly refer to your experience and highlight a few key achievements.

3. Take care of business

Refer the reader to your résumé. Mention that you'll call at a specific point to follow up. Then make good on your promise.

And don't forget . . .

- Whenever possible, address your letter to a specific person. Make sure to use this person's correct title and mailing address. If you cannot find a specific name, then address your letter to "Dear Hiring Manager for [name of the position]."

- Use a simple typeface that is easy to read.

- Tailor each letter you write to the specific company and position you are applying for. Sending a "stock letter" implies that you don't really care about the job.

- Thank your reader for her time and consideration.

Use job interviews to "hire" an employer

Job interviews are times for an employer to size up applicants and screen most of them out. The reverse is also true: Interviews offer *you* a chance to size up potential employers. Careful preparation and follow-up can help you get the information—and the job—that you want.

PUT INTERVIEWS IN CONTEXT

Mention the phrase *job hunting*, and many people think about poring through the help-wanted sections in newspapers and Web sites, sending out hundreds of résumés, and going to employment agencies. The desired result is an interview that leads to a job offer.

There's a big problem with these typical job-hunting strategies: They don't work well.[5] Many employers turn to help-wanted listings, résumés, and employment agencies only as a last resort. When they have positions to fill, they prefer instead to hire people they already know. Employers also listen closely when friends, family members, and coworkers recommend someone *they* know.

Richard Bolles, author of *What Color Is Your Parachute? A Practical Manual for Job-Hunters and Career-Changers,* recommends the following steps in job hunting:

- Discover which skills you want to use in your career.
- Discover which jobs draw on the skills you want to use.
- Interview people who are doing the kind of jobs you'd want to do.

- Research companies you'd like to work for, and find out what kinds of problems they face on a daily basis.
- Identify a person at each one of these companies who has the power to hire you.
- Arrange an interview with that person, even if the company has no job openings at the moment.
- Stay in contact with the people who interviewed you, knowing that a job opening can occur at any time—even during a recession.[6]

Notice that getting an interview comes toward the bottom of the above list—*after* you take the time to discover a lot about yourself and the work world. Those are keys to unlocking the hidden job market.

START BUILDING YOUR NETWORK—NOW

Networking is often described as the most effective way to get a job. Start by sharing your career plans with friends, relatives, neighbors, coworkers, students, instructors, and advisors. Basically, your network includes *anyone* who can hire you or refer you to an employer.

It's never too early to start building your network. Look for student and professional organizations that relate to your career plan. Go to conferences, conventions, and job fairs. Talk often about your skills and the work you want to do. Even a casual conversation in the grocery store or dentist's office can lead to job

12

> **When you want a job, tell everyone—especially people who have the power to hire you. This sets the stage for getting interviews.**

openings. Keep a list of the people you meet and brief notes about what you discussed.

Also begin networking online. Do this by creating profiles on Web sites such as Twitter, Facebook, and LinkedIn. Develop your online presence with your career goals in mind. Take part in online discussion groups. Read career-related blogs and post comments. Connect with members of your network. Also consider building a personal Web site that can function as an online résumé and portfolio.

Anything about you that appears online can affect your job search. So, post only information that you want to be made public. At least once each year, do an Internet search on your name and review the results. Remove content that could hurt your job prospects.

The bottom line: When you want a job, tell everyone—especially people who have the power to hire you. This sets the stage for getting interviews.

BEFORE YOU GO TO THE INTERVIEW

To get the most from your interviews, learn everything you can about each organization that interests you. Start by searching the Internet. Then head to your campus and public libraries. Tell a reference librarian that you're researching specific companies in preparation for a job interview, and ask for good sources of information.

Before you interview for a job at any organization, learn about:

- The organization's products and services
- Major developments in the organization during the past year
- Directions that the organization plans to go during the upcoming year
- Names of the organization's major divisions
- Names of people who could hire you
- The types of jobs they offer

Next, prepare for common questions. Many interviewers have the following questions on their mind, even if they don't ask them directly:

- How did you find out about us?
- Will we be comfortable working with you?

- How can you help us?
- Will you learn this job quickly?
- What makes you different from other people applying for this job?

Write out brief answers to those questions. Mention personal characteristics such as those listed in "Master student qualities" on page 3. Also describe your skills and specific examples of how you used them to create positive results.

Next, summarize the main points you want to make on a single sheet of paper. Then practice delivering them verbally to the point where you barely refer to the sheet. Your goal is to sound prepared without delivering canned answers.

For extra practice, prepare for the following questions:

What do you want to tell me about yourself? For interviewers, this question serves several purposes. First, it encourages you to open up. The interviewer wants to get a sense of who you are as a person—beyond your cover letter and résumé. The question also tests your ability to think on your feet. A skilled interviewer will pay as much attention to *how* you answer the question as to *what* you say. Focus on the top two to three things that you want the interviewer to recall about you. Talk about aspects of your education and experience that most qualify you for the job. Do *not* give the story of your life.

What are your weaknesses? Interviewers want to know that you have enough self-awareness to spot your limitations. By planning in advance, you will be prepared to share a weakness that points to one of your strengths. For example, you might be slow to complete some tasks because you show a high level of attention to detail. At the same time, declare your intention to improve.

Why should I hire you? The full version is *Why should I hire you instead of any of the other people who are applying for this job?* Take a cue from the field of advertising, and develop your "unique selling proposition." This is the main thing that sets you apart from other job applicants. Focus on a key benefit that you can deliver—one that's unusual or distinctive. Begin your answer with a reference to the interviewer's organization. For example, mention a current development such as new product, service, or initiative. Then talk specifically about how you can enhance that new development.

If you plan to bring examples of work from your portfolio, contact the employer ahead of time to find out how many people will be at the interview so you can bring the correct number of copies.

Also plan to dress appropriately for your interview. Don't choose clothing, shoes, jewelry, or cologne that will clash with an employer's expectations. If you have tattoos, be careful about revealing them.

Round out your preparation by reviewing the Power Process: "Be it." To convince an employer that you can do a job, first convince yourself. Be authentic. Start from a conviction that you already *are* an excellent candidate, and that the job connects with your values. Your passion and personality counts as much as any prepared answer.

DURING THE INTERVIEW

Plan to arrive early for your interview. While you're waiting, observe the workplace. Notice what people are saying and doing. See whether you can "read" the company culture by making informal observations.

Just before the interview begins, remind yourself that you have one goal—to get the *next* interview. The top candidates for a job often talk to several people in a company.

When you meet the interviewer, do three things right away: smile, make eye contact, and give a firm handshake. Nonverbal communication creates a lasting impression.

After making small talk, the interviewer will start asking questions. Draw on the answers you've prepared. At the same time, respond to the *exact* questions that you're asked. Speak naturally and avoid the impression that you're making a speech or avoiding a question.

Stay aware of how much you talk. Avoid answers that are too brief or too long. Respond to each question for a minute or two. If you have more to say, end your answer by saying, "Those are the basics. I can add more if you want."

A skilled interviewer will allow time for *you* to ask questions about the company. Use this time to your full advantage. Some good questions to ask:

- When does the job begin?
- What is a typical day like?
- What would I work on if I were to get the job?
- What training is offered for this job?
- Are there opportunities to advance?
- Who will supervise me in this job?
- Could I take a tour of the workplace?

Save questions about benefits, salary, and vacation days for the second interview. When you get to that point, you know that the employer is interested in you. You might have leverage to negotiate.

Be sure to find out the next step in the hiring process and when it will take place. Also ask interviewers for their business cards and how they want you to follow up. Some people are fine with a phone call, fax, e-mail, or other form of online communication. Others prefer a good, old-fashioned letter.

If you're truly interested in the job and feel comfortable with the interviewer, ask one more question: "Do you have any concerns about hiring me?" Listen carefully to the reply. Then respond to each concern in a polite way.

AFTER THE INTERVIEW

Congratulate yourself for getting as far in the hiring process as an interview. Write a Discovery Statement that describes your strengths, along with what you learned about your potential employer. Also write an Intention Statement about ways to be more effective during your next interview.

Now comes follow-up. This step can give you the edge that leads to a job offer.

Pull out the business cards from the people who interviewed you. Write them thank-you notes, following each person's preference for paper-based or online contact. Do this within 2 business days after the interview. If you talked to several people at the same company, then write a different note to each one.

Besides thanking each person for an interview, mention something that you discussed. Include a reminder of why you're a "fit" for the job. Proofread each note carefully.

Also alert your references that they might get a contact from the interviewers.

Within 5 business days, find a reason to contact the interviewer again. For example, e-mail a link to an interesting article and explain how it might be useful. If you have a Web site with a blog, let them know about a recent post. Reinforce the value you will bring to their team.

If you have permission to make contact by phone, also do so within 10 business days of the interview.

If you get turned down for the job after your interview, don't take it personally. Every interview is a source of feedback about what works—and what doesn't work—in contacting employers. Use that feedback to interview more effectively next time.

Also remember that each person you talked to is now a member of your network. This is true even if you do not get a job offer. Follow up by asking interviewers to keep you in mind for future job openings. Using this approach, you gain from every interview, no matter what the outcome. ∎

> # Stay aware of how much you talk. Avoid answers that are too brief or too long. Respond to each question for a minute or two. If you have more to say, end your answer by saying, "Those are the basics. I can add more if you want."

You're One Click Away...
from discovering more job-hunting strategies online.

THE DISCOVERY WHEEL—COMING FULL CIRCLE

This book doesn't work. It is worthless. Only you can work. Only you can make a difference and use this book to become a more effective student.

The purpose of this book is to give you the opportunity to change your behavior. The fact that something seems like a good idea doesn't necessarily mean that you will put it into practice. This exercise gives you a chance to see what behaviors you have changed on your journey toward becoming a master student.

Answer each question quickly and honestly. Record your results on the Discovery Wheel on this page. Then compare it with the one you completed in Chapter 1.

The scores on this Discovery Wheel indicate your current strengths and weaknesses on your path toward becoming a master student. The last Journal Entry in this chapter provides an opportunity to write about how you intend to change. As you complete this self-evaluation, keep in mind that your commitment to change allows you to become a master student. *Your scores might be lower here than on your earlier Discovery Wheel.* That's okay. Lower scores might result from increased self-awareness and honesty, as well as other valuable assets.

Note: The online version of this exercise does not include number ratings, so the results will be formatted differently from those described here. If you did your previous Discovery Wheel online, do it online again. This will help you compare your two sets of responses more accurately.

5 points = This statement is always or almost always true of me.

4 points = This statement is often true of me.

3 points = This statement is true of me about half the time.

2 points = This statement is seldom true of me.

1 point = This statement is never or almost never true of me.

You're One Click Away...
from having your Discovery Wheel scores calculated automatically for you online.

1. _____ I enjoy learning.

2. _____ I understand and apply the concept of multiple intelligences.

3. _____ I connect my courses to my purpose for being in school.

4. _____ I make a habit of assessing my personal strengths and areas for improvement.

5. _____ I am satisfied with how I am progressing toward achieving my goals.

6. _____ I use my knowledge of learning styles to support my success in school.

7. _____ I am willing to consider any idea that can help me succeed in school—even if I initially disagree with that idea.

8. _____ I regularly remind myself of the benefits I intend to get from my education.

_____ **Total score (1) Attitude**

1. _____ I set long-term goals and periodically review them.

2. _____ I set short-term goals to support my long-term goals.

3. _____ I write a plan for each day and each week.

4. _____ I assign priorities to what I choose to do each day.

5. _____ I plan review time so I don't have to cram before tests.

6. _____ I plan regular recreation time.

7. _____ I adjust my study time to meet the demands of individual courses.

8. _____ I have adequate time each day to accomplish what I plan.

_____ **Total score (2) Time**

1. _____ I am confident of my ability to remember.

2. _____ I can remember people's names.

3. _____ At the end of a lecture, I can summarize what was presented.

4. _____ I apply techniques that enhance my memory skills.

5. _____ I can recall information when I'm under pressure.

6. _____ I remember important information clearly and easily.

7. _____ I can jog my memory when I have difficulty recalling.

8. _____ I can relate new information to what I've already learned.

_____ **Total score (3) Memory**

1. _____ I preview and review reading assignments.

2. _____ When reading, I ask myself questions about the material.

3. _____ I underline or highlight important passages when reading.

4. _____ When I read textbooks, I am alert and awake.

5. _____ I relate what I read to my life.

6. _____ I select a reading strategy to fit the type of material I'm reading.

7. _____ I take effective notes when I read.

8. _____ When I don't understand what I'm reading, I note my questions and find answers.

_____ **Total score (4) Reading**

1. _____ When I am in class, I focus my attention.

2. _____ I take notes in class.

3. _____ I am aware of various methods for taking notes and choose those that work best for me.

4. _____ I distinguish important material and note key phrases in a lecture.

5. _____ I copy down material that the instructor writes on the board or overhead display.

6. _____ I can put important concepts into my own words.

7. _____ My notes are valuable for review.

8. _____ I review class notes within 24 hours.

_____ **Total score (5) Notes**

1. _____ I use techniques to manage stress related to exams.

2. _____ I manage my time during exams and am able to complete them.

3. _____ I am able to predict test questions.

4. _____ I adapt my test-taking strategy to the kind of test I'm taking.

5. _____ I understand what essay questions ask and can answer them completely and accurately.

6. _____ I start reviewing for tests at the beginning of the term.

7. _____ I continue reviewing for tests throughout the term.

8. _____ My sense of personal worth is independent of my test scores.

_____ **Total score (6) Tests**

1. _____ I have flashes of insight and think of solutions to problems at unusual times.

2. _____ I use brainstorming to generate solutions to a variety of problems.

3. _____ When I get stuck on a creative project, I use specific methods to get unstuck.

4. _____ I learn by thinking about ways to contribute to the lives of other people.

5. _____ I am willing to consider different points of view and alternative solutions.

6. _____ I can detect common errors in logic.

7. _____ I construct viewpoints by drawing on information and ideas from many sources.

8. _____ As I share my viewpoints with others, I am open to their feedback.

_____ **Total score (7) Thinking**

1. _____ I am honest with others about who I am, what I feel, and what I want.

2. _____ Other people tell me that I am a good listener.

3. _____ I can communicate my upset and anger without blaming others.

4. _____ I can make friends and create valuable relationships in a new setting.

5. _____ I am open to being with people I don't especially like in order to learn from them.

6. _____ I can effectively plan and research a large writing assignment.

12

7. _____ I create first drafts without criticizing my writing, then edit later for clarity, accuracy, and coherence.

8. _____ I know ways to prepare and deliver effective speeches.

_____ Total score (8) Communicating

1. _____ I build rewarding relationships with people from diverse backgrounds.

2. _____ I use critical thinking to overcome stereotypes.

3. _____ I point out examples of discrimination and sexual harassment and effectively respond to them.

4. _____ I am constantly learning ways to thrive with diversity.

5. _____ I can effectively resolve conflict with people from other cultures.

6. _____ My writing and speaking are free of sexist expressions.

7. _____ I take diversity into account when assuming a leadership role.

8. _____ I respond effectively to changing demographics in my country and community.

_____ Total score (9) Diversity

1. _____ I am in control of my personal finances.

2. _____ I can access a variety of resources to finance my education.

3. _____ I am confident that I will have enough money to complete my education.

4. _____ I take on debts carefully and repay them on time.

5. _____ I have long-range financial goals and a plan to meet them.

6. _____ I make regular deposits to a savings account.

7. _____ I pay off the balance on credit card accounts each month.

8. _____ I can have fun without spending money.

_____ Total score (10) Money

1. _____ I have enough energy to study and work—and still enjoy other areas of my life.

2. _____ If the situation calls for it, I have enough reserve energy to put in a long day.

3. _____ The way I eat supports my long-term health.

4. _____ The way I eat is independent of my feelings of self-worth.

5. _____ I exercise regularly to maintain a healthful weight.

6. _____ My emotional health supports my ability to learn.

7. _____ I notice changes in my physical condition and respond effectively.

8. _____ I am in control of any alcohol or other drugs I put into my body.

_____ Total score (11) Health

1. _____ I see learning as a lifelong process.

2. _____ I relate school to what I plan to do for the rest of my life.

3. _____ I see problems and tough choices as opportunities for learning and personal growth.

4. _____ I have a written career plan and update it regularly.

5. _____ I am gaining skills to support my success in the workplace.

6. _____ I take responsibility for the quality of my education—and my life.

7. _____ I live by a set of values that translates into daily actions.

8. _____ I am willing to accept challenges even when I'm not sure how to meet them.

_____ Total score (12) Purpose

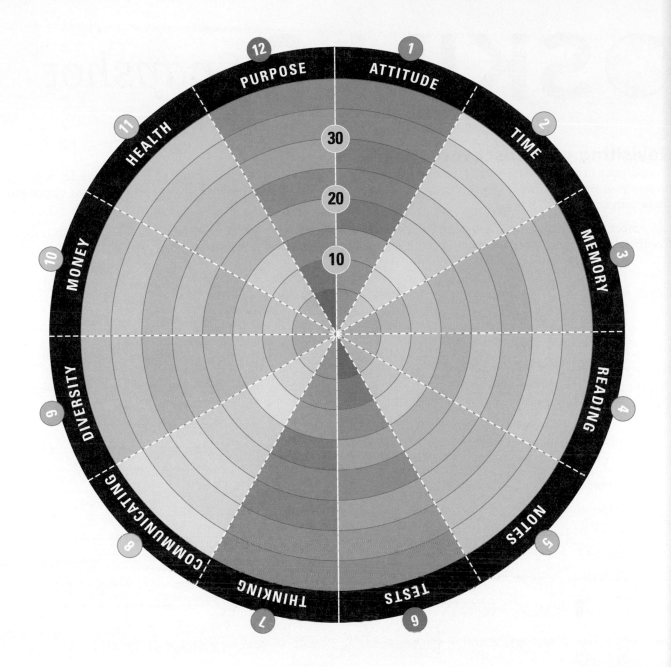

FILLING IN YOUR DISCOVERY WHEEL

Using the total score from each category, shade in each section of the Discovery Wheel on this page. Use different colors, if you want. For example, you could use green to denote areas you want to work on. When you have finished, complete the following Skills Snapshot on the next page. ∎

12

SKILLS *Snapshot*

Revisiting your Discovery Wheels

The purpose of this exercise is to (1) review both of the Discovery Wheels you completed in this book, (2) summarize your insights from doing them, and (3) declare how you will use these insights to promote your continued success in school.

Remember, a lower score on the second Discovery Wheel does not necessarily indicate decreased personal effectiveness. Instead, the lower score could result from increased honesty and greater self-awareness.

Enter your Discovery Wheel scores from both chapters in the space below.

	Chapter 1	Chapter 12
Attitude		
Time		
Memory		
Reading		
Notes		
Tests		
Thinking		
Communicating		
Diversity		
Money		
Health		
Purpose		

Comparing the Discovery Wheel in this chapter with the Discovery Wheel in Chapter 1, I discovered that I . . .

In the next 6 months, I intend to review the following articles from this book for additional suggestions I could use:

Now that you're done—
BEGIN

If you used this book fully—if you actively participated in reading the contents, writing the Journal Entries, doing the exercises, practicing critical thinking, and putting the suggestions to work—you have had quite a journey.

Recall some high points of that journey. The first half of this book is about the nuts and bolts of education—the business of acquiring knowledge. It helps prepare you for making the transition to higher education and suggests that you take a First Step by telling the truth about your skills and setting goals to expand them. Also included are guidelines for planning your time, training your memory, improving your reading skills, taking useful notes, and succeeding at tests.

All of this activity prepares you for another aim of education—generating new knowledge. Meeting this aim leads you to the topics in the second half of this book: thinking for yourself, enhancing your communication skills, embracing diversity, learning to manage money, living with vibrant health, and creating a unique place for yourself in the world. All are steps on the path of becoming a master student.

Now what? What's your next step?

As you answer this question, remember that the process of experimenting with your life never ends. At any moment, you can begin again.

Consider the possibility that you can create the life of your dreams. Your responses to any of the ideas, exercises, and Journal Entries in this book can lead you to think new thoughts, say new things, and do what you never believed you could do. If you're willing to master new ways to learn, the possibilities are endless. This message is more fundamental than any individual tool or technique you'll ever read about.

There are people who scoff at the suggestion that they can create the life of their dreams. These people have a perspective that is widely shared. Please set it aside.

You are on the edge of a universe so miraculous and full of wonder that your imagination, even at its most creative moment, cannot encompass it. Paths are open to lead you to worlds beyond your wildest dreams.

If this sounds like a pitch for the latest recreational drug, it might be. That "drug" is enthusiasm. It is automatically generated by your body when you are learning, planning, taking risks, achieving goals, and discovering new worlds inside and outside your skin.

> The first chapter in this book included articles about transition. You are about to make another transition—not just to another chapter of this book, but to the next chapter of your life.

Even so, we might avoid thinking about what's next in our lives until we're feeling ready for such a big conversation. "Ready" might be next week, next month, next year, or some other time that sounds more convenient. Other people reinforce this notion by telling you that your life will *really* start on the day when you . . . . (Fill in the blank with phrases such as *graduate from college, get married, have kids, get promoted,* or *retire*.)

Agreeing with these statements can condemn us to a life of perpetual waiting. Using this logic, we could wait our whole life to start living. And that doesn't sound like much fun.

However, there is another option: You can give up the myth of "someday." You can start choosing the next steps now. You can start making commitments for the future that change your action in the present. Set goals that might take years to accomplish—and then enjoy every step along the way.

The first chapter in this book included articles about transition. You are about to make another transition—not just to another chapter of this book, but to the next chapter of your life. Engage with what you have learned to explore your skills, choose your major, plan your career, find your place in the global economy, and otherwise create the life of your dreams.

Use these pages to choose what's next for you. ∎

12

"Use the following suggestions to continue . . ."

Keep a journal. Psychotherapist Ira Progoff based his Intensive Journal System on the idea that regular journaling can be a path to life-changing insights.[7] To begin journaling, consider buying a bound notebook in which to record your private reflections and dreams for the future. Get a notebook that will be worthy of your personal discoveries and intentions. Or keep an electronic journal on your computer. Write or type in your journal daily. Record what you are learning about yourself and the world.

Write about your hopes, wishes, and goals. Keep a record of significant events. Consider using the format of Discovery Statements and Intention Statements that you learned in this book.

Take a workshop. Schooling doesn't have to stop at graduation, and it doesn't have to take place on a campus. In most cities, a variety of organizations sponsor ongoing workshops covering topics from cosmetology to cosmology. Take workshops to learn skills, understand the world, and discover yourself. You can be trained in cardiopulmonary resuscitation (CPR), attend a lecture on developing nations, or take a course on assertiveness training.

Read, watch, and listen. Publications related to *Becoming a Master Student* are listed in Additional Reading on page 393. Also, ask friends and instructors what they are reading. Sample a variety of publications. None of them has all of the truth. Most of them have a piece of it.

At any point in your life, you can enroll in "Internet university." Courses from many colleges and universities are available online, often for free. Search for content from reputable instructors, and remember to think critically about everything you find online.

Take an unrelated class. Sign up for a class that is totally unrelated to your major. If you are studying economics, take a physics course. If you are planning to be a doctor, take an accounting course. Take a course that will help you develop new computer skills and expand your possibilities for online learning.

You can discover a lot about yourself and your intended future when you step out of old patterns. In addition to formal courses offered at your school, check into local community education courses. They offer a low-cost alternative that poses no threat to your grade point average.

Travel. See the world. Visit new neighborhoods. Travel to other countries. Explore. Find out what it looks like inside buildings that you normally have no reason to enter, museums that you never found interesting before, cities that are out of the way, forests and mountains that lie beyond your old boundaries, and far-off places that require planning and saving to reach.

Get counseling. Solving emotional problems is not the only reason to visit a counselor, therapist, or psychologist. These people are excellent resources for personal growth. You can use counseling to look at and talk about yourself in ways that might be uncomfortable for anyone except a trained professional. Counseling offers a chance to focus exclusively on yourself—something that is usually not possible in normal social settings.

Form a support group. Just as a well-organized study group can promote your success in school, an organized support group can help you reach goals in other areas of your life.

Today, people in support groups help one another lose weight, stay sober, cope with chronic illness, recover from emotional trauma, and overcome drug addiction.

Groups can also brainstorm possibilities for job hunting, career planning, parenting, solving problems in relationships, promoting spiritual growth—strategies for reaching almost any goal you choose.

Find a mentor—or become one. Seek the counsel of experienced people you respect and admire. Use them as role models. If they are willing, ask them to be sounding boards for your plans and ideas. Many people are flattered to be asked.

You can also become a mentor. If you want to perfect your skills as a master student, teach them to someone else. Offer to coach another student in study skills in exchange for child care, free lunches, or something else you value. A mentor relationship can bridge the boundaries of age, race, and culture.

Consider further education and training. Your career plan might call for continuing education, additional certifications, or an advanced degree. Remember that the strategies in this book can help you gain new knowledge and skills at any point in your life.

Redo this book. If you didn't get everything you wanted from this book, it's not too late. You can read part of it or all of it again at any time. For a review of the main topics, see the "Master Guide to *Becoming a Master Student*" on page 385.

Also redo portions of the book that you found valuable. As you plan your career and hunt for jobs, you might find that the Put This Chapter to Work articles in each chapter acquire new meaning. Redo the quizzes to test your ability to recall certain information. Redo the exercises that were particularly effective for you. They can work again. Many of the exercises in this book can produce a different result after a few months. You are changing, and your responses change too.

The Discovery Wheel can be useful in revealing techniques you have actually put into practice. This exercise is available online. You can redo it as many times as you like. You can also redo the Journal Entries. If you keep your own journal, refer to it as you rewrite the Journal Entries in this book.

As you redo this book or any part of it, reconsider techniques that you skimmed over or skipped before. They might work for you now. Modify the suggestions, or add new ones. Redoing this book can refresh and fine-tune your study habits.

Another way to redo this book is to retake your student success course. People who do this often say that the second time is much different from the first. They pick up ideas and techniques that they missed the first time around and gain deeper insight into things they already know. ∎

You're One Click Away...
from finding more suggestions online for continuing the path toward mastery.

✔ EXERCISE 37

This book shouts, "Use me!"

Becoming a Master Student is designed to be used for years. The success strategies presented here are not likely to become habits overnight. There are more suggestions than can be put into action immediately. Some of what is discussed might not apply to your life right now, but it might be just what you could use in a few months.

Plan to keep this book and use it again. Imagine that your book has a mouth. (Visualize the mouth.) Also imagine that it has arms and legs. (Visualize them.)

Now picture your book sitting on a shelf or table that you see every day. Imagine a time when you are having trouble in school and struggling to be successful as a student. Visualize your book jumping up and down, shouting, "Use me! Read me! I might have the solution to your problem, and I know I can help you solve it."

This is a memory technique to remind you to use a resource. Sometimes when you are stuck, all you need is a small push or a list of possible actions. At those times, hear your book shout, "Use me!"

This exercise will give you practice in thinking at **Level 5: Evaluating**. Test questions that call for this level of thinking begin with words like these:

- Critique
- Evaluate
- Judge
- Justify
- Rank
- Recommend
- Suggest
- Support

Your courses will often involve this level of thinking. For example, an English literature instructor might assign several short stories for you to read and then ask, "Which story did you like best, and why?"

Suppose that a friend says to you, "I want to get the most value from the money and time I invest in higher education. What are the most important things for me to do?" Your answer to this question involves evaluating.

Based on your experience with *Becoming a Master Student*, list the top three strategies that you would **suggest** for your friend that will **support** success in school.

_____

_____

_____

_____

_____

_____

 # EXERCISE 38

Do something you can't

Few significant accomplishments result from people sticking to the familiar. You can accomplish much more than you think you can. Doing something you can't involves taking risks. This exercise has three steps.

STEP 1 Select something that you have never done before, that you don't know how to do, that you are fearful of doing, or that you think you probably can't do. Perhaps you've never learned to play an instrument, or you've never run a marathon. Be smart. Don't pick something that will hurt you physically, such as flying from a third-floor window. Use the space below to describe what you have chosen.

_____

_____

STEP 2 Do it. Of course, this is easier to say than to do. This exercise is not about easy. It is about discovering capabilities that stretch your self-image. To accomplish something that is bigger than your self-perceived abilities, use any of the tools you have gained from this book. Develop a plan. Divide and conquer. Stay focused. Use outside resources. Let go of self-destructive thoughts. Summarize the tools you will use.

_____

_____

_____

STEP 3 Write about your results of this exercise here.

_____

_____

_____

_____

masterstudentprofile

Lisa Ling

(1973–) Lisa Ling, host of National Geographic Channel's *Explorer*, special correspondent for *The Oprah Winfrey Show*, and a former cohost of ABC's *The View*, was one of the youngest reporters for *Channel One News*, whose programming is aimed at middle and high schools.

I had heard about auditions for a teen magazine show called *Scratch*. They were holding auditions in a mall, and one Saturday in Sacramento I showed up along with hundreds of other students. They chose four of us to host this show—a fun teen magazine where I interviewed celebrities and did makeovers and silly things like that. But what was cool was that it was produced by a local news affiliate, and I used that entrée into the station to get an internship in the newsroom. I hung out with the writers and learned to run the teleprompter. I was sort of an eager and aggressive young kid who wanted to learn about the business, and I would show up at the TV station at 4:30 or 5:00 in the morning before classes.

After doing three years on a teen magazine show, I was ready to go to college. Then the director of Channel One called me and said, "We'd like you to come audition." I did and got the job. It was based in Los Angeles, so I ended up going to the University of Southern California while doing Channel One at the same time.

Channel One has been plagued by . . . controversy because it airs commercials within the broadcast. But for me as a reporter it was the most incredible opportunity, and the editorial content of Channel One I would put up against any network news show. I was a 19- and 20-year-old kid covering the civil war in Afghanistan, the Russian referendum elections, the civil war in Algeria, the drug war in Colombia, overpopulation in China, globalization in India. I would work on a series about the democracy movement in Iran in 1995 that would run about twenty-five minutes throughout the course of a week. And at that time what news outlet would cover Iran for twenty-five minutes?

I actually think that was some of my best journalism. While I did do research on the various stories and countries, I kind of went in to them not knowing so much—just being open and not having a lot of preconceived ideas or notions. You know, these days we are almost brainwashed. When our leadership characterizes entire countries as evil, how do you *not* go into stories with preconceived ideas? What we did as young people was pick these places in the world that no one was covering and went there. We didn't tell our viewers what to think. We just gave them an opportunity to experience what *we* were experiencing.

I majored in history because I wanted to have as broad-based an education as I could possibly get. My history background and my political science background and my travels have been my biggest assets as a journalist.

People are always asking me: How did you get your job? And my answer is, I just got it. I just kind of willed it into existence. I just kind of created this situation.

My advice to young people: Before you get hampered by a job and family and financial obligations, try to get out of your comfort zone. If you can, live in another country for a year or so. You won't regret it.

LISA LING . . . is inquisitive.

YOU . . . can keep inquiring about new possibilities for your life.

Source: Excerpted from "Journalist and Correspondent Lisa Ling," broadcast on *Profiles*, a radio program from WFIU, Indiana University, and hosted by Owen Johnson, November 11, 2007, http://wfiu.org/profiles/lisa-ling.

You're One Click Away...
from learning more about Lisa Ling online at the Master Student Profiles. You can also visit the Master Student Hall of Fame to learn about other master students.

12

PUT THIS CHAPTER TO WORK

This chapter offers plenty of strategies for discovering skills, planning your career, and finding a job that you love. Build on everything you've learned by lifting your eyes to the horizon and adopting a long-term perspective.

PLAN FOR CHANGE. Keep up-to-date with breaking changes in the job market as you decide what's next in your career. This is easier to do than ever before, thanks to resources mentioned throughout this book:

- *The Internet.* Use your skills in searching the Internet to find Web sites devoted to your field. Start by keying your job title into a search engine such as Google or Yahoo! Also search for career-related listservs that distribute e-mail messages to groups of people with similar interests.

- *Periodicals.* Read the business sections of the *New York Times* and the *Wall Street Journal*, for example. Most newspapers also have online editions, as do general-interest magazines such as *Time* and *Business Week*.

- *Professional associations.* People in similar jobs like to band together and give each other a heads up on emerging trends—one reason for professional associations. These range from the American Medical Association to the Society of Actuaries. There's bound to be one for people in your field. Ask colleagues and search the Internet. *Note:* Many associations post Web sites and publish newsletters or trade magazines.

- *Conferences and conventions.* Many professional associations sponsor annual meetings. Here's where you can meet people face-to-face and use your networking skills. Print and online publications are powerful sources of news, but sometimes nothing beats plain old schmoozing. Ask people at work what professional organizations they have joined.

MAKE YOURSELF INDISPENSABLE. Look for ways to excel at your job by building relationships, becoming a rock-star collaborator, and consistently delivering results. Whenever possible, exceed your work-related goals. These are strategies for surviving layoffs and increasing job security.

KEEP YOUR CAREER PLAN ALIVE. Write your career goals on 3×5 cards or sticky notes. Post these in places where you can't miss them—your desk, your bathroom mirror, your car. Put your vision for the future in front of your face.

USE TECHNOLOGY TO POWER YOUR JOB SEARCH. Social networking sites such as LinkedIn are designed for people who want to connect with employers. Create a professional profile on these sites and build a network of contacts. Begin this process now. Develop relationships over time, well before you start applying for jobs.

Remember that you can use Facebook, Twitter, and similar sites for professional purposes. Use their search functions to find companies that interest you—and names of people within those companies who could hire you. After "following" these people for a while and establishing a friendly online connection, you might be able to send them a direct message.

In addition, search for blogs related to your career interests. Pay special attention to blogs that include job listings.

Consider launching your own professional blog. Include an online résumé and articles with useful content for people in your field. Be prepared to add new content weekly, or even daily, especially during your job search.

NOW CREATE A CAREER CONNECTION OF YOUR OWN. Review this chapter, looking for at least one suggestion that you will commit to use while working or looking for a job. In a sentence or two, describe exactly what you plan to do and the primary benefits you want to gain. For example: "I will register for workshops and seminars that help me keep my skills up to date. This will help me stay in the career of my choice."

State your strategies and desired benefits in the space below:

_____

_____

_____

_____

_____

Name _____

Date _____

1. List the three categories of choices explained in the Power Process: "Be it."

2. Explain how *work-content skills* and *transferable skills* differ.

3. List two examples of work-content skills.

4. List five examples of transferable skills.

5. According to the text, you can create a career plan through the process of "naming names." True or false? Explain your answer.

6. Give three examples of ways to test your career choice.

7. Explain what is meant in this chapter by building your résumé from a "skills perspective."

8. Describe a problem associated with typical job-hunting strategies. Then briefly describe an alternative approach to job hunting.

9. If your scores are lower on the Discovery Wheel the second time you complete it, this means your skills have not improved. True or false? Explain your answer.

10. List at least three ways in which you can continue on your path of becoming a master student after completing this book.

12

CHAPTER 12 **SKILLS** *Snapshot*

If you fully participated with this chapter, you've got a lot of answers to the opening question: What's next? Reflect on these answers in light of your responses to the Purpose section of the Discovery Wheel in this chapter (page 374).

DISCOVERY

My score on the Purpose section on the Discovery Wheel on page 374 was . . .

Three transferable skills that I've already developed are . . .

In making a trial choice of major, I discovered that . . .

When thinking and talking about my career plan, I feel . . .

INTENTION

Three new transferable skills that I want to develop are . . .

What I want most as a result of completing the requirements for my major is to . . .

What I want most from any career I choose is . . .

What I want most from my education is . . .

ACTION

The three most important things I can do in the next 6 months to achieve my career and educational goals are to . . .

Getting On Course to Your Success

SUCCESSFUL STUDENTS ...	STRUGGLING STUDENTS ...
accept personal responsibility, seeing themselves as the primary cause of their outcomes and experiences.	**see themselves as victims**, believing that what happens to them is determined primarily by external forces such as fate, luck, and powerful others.
discover self-motivation, finding purpose in their lives by discovering personally meaningful goals and dreams.	**have difficulty sustaining motivation**, often feeling depressed, frustrated, and/or resentful about a lack of directionin their lives.
master self-management, consistently planning and taking purposeful actions in pursuit of their goals and dreams.	**seldom identify specific actions needed to accomplish a desired outcome**, and when they do, they tend to procrastinate.
employ interdependence, building mutually supportive relationships that help them achieve their goals and dreams (while helping others do the same).	**are solitary**, seldom requesting, even rejecting, offers of assistance from those who could help.

Taking the First Step

Focus Questions What does "success" mean to you? When you achieve your greatest success, what will you have, what will you be doing, and what kind of person will you be?

Congratulations on choosing to attend college! With this choice, you've begun a journey that can lead to great personal and professional success.

WHAT IS SUCCESS?

I've asked many college graduates, "What did success mean to you when you were an undergraduate?" Here are some typical answers:

When I was in college, success to me was . . .

. . . getting all A's and B's.
. . . making two free-throws to win the conference basketball tournament.
. . . having a great social life.
. . . parenting two great kids and still making the dean's list.
. . . being the first person in my family to earn a college degree.

Notice that each response emphasizes *outer success:* high grades, sports victories, popularity, and college degrees. These successes are public, visible achievements that allow the world to judge one's abilities and worth.

I've also asked college graduates, "If you could repeat your college years, what would you do differently?" Here are some typical answers:

If I had a chance to do college over, I would . . .

. . . focus on learning instead of just getting good grades.
. . . major in engineering, the career I had a passion for.
. . . constantly ask myself how I could use what I was learning to enhance my life and the lives of the people I love.
. . . discover my personal values.
. . . learn more about the world I live in and more about myself . . . especially more about myself!

Notice that the focus some years after graduation often centers on *inner success:* enjoying learning, following personal interests, focusing on personal values, and creating more fulfilling lives. These successes are private, invisible victories that offer a deep sense of personal contentment.

Only with hindsight do most college graduates realize that, to be completely satisfying, success must occur both in the visible world and in the invisible spaces within our minds and hearts. This book, then, is about how to achieve both outer and inner success in college and in life.

To that end, I suggest the following simple definition of success: **Success is staying on course to your desired outcomes and experiences.** Maybe you'd

> College is a place where a student ought to learn not so much how to make a living, but how to live.
>
> *Dr. William A. Nolen*

like to earn a college degree or start your own business or marry and have six kids. Maybe you'd like to experience joy or confidence or love. Maybe you'd like to be seen by others as a "self-made" person who achieved success by your efforts alone. Maybe you'd prefer to experience being a valued member of a group that is loyal and committed to one another. Regardless of what your desired outcomes and experiences may be, following the time-tested strategies presented in *On Course* will help you achieve them.

As a college instructor, I have seen thousands of students arrive on campus with dreams, then struggle, fail, and fade away. I've seen thousands more come to college with dreams, pass their courses, and graduate, having done little more than cram their brains with information that's promptly forgotten after the final exam. They've earned degrees, but in more important ways they have remained unchanged.

Our primary responsibility in life, I suggest, is to realize the incredible potential with which each of us is born. All of our experiences, especially those during college, can contribute to the creation of our best selves.

On Course shows how to use your college experience as a laboratory experiment. In this laboratory you'll learn and apply proven strategies that help you create success—academically, personally, and professionally. I'm not saying it'll be easy, but you're about to learn strategies that have made a difference in the lives of thousands of students before you. So get ready to change the outcomes of your life and the quality of your experiences along the way! Get ready to create success as *you* define it.

To begin, consider a curious puzzle: Two students enter a college class on the first day of the semester. Both appear to have similar intelligence, backgrounds, and abilities. The weeks slide by, and the semester ends. Surprisingly, one student soars and the other sinks. One fulfills his potential; the other falls short. Why do students with similar aptitudes perform so differently? More important, which of these students is you?

Teachers observe this puzzle in every class. I bet you've seen it, too, not only in school, but wherever people gather. Some people have a knack for achievement. Others wander about confused and disappointed, unable to create the success they claim they want. Clearly, having potential does not guarantee success.

What, then, are the essential ingredients of success?

> There is only one success—to be able to spend your life in your own way.
>
> *Christopher Morely*

THE POWER OF CHOICE

The main ingredient in all success is wise choices. That's because the quality of our lives is determined by the quality of the choices we make on a daily basis. Successful people stay on course to their destinations by wisely choosing their beliefs and behaviors.

Do beliefs cause behaviors, or do behaviors lead to beliefs? Like the chicken and the egg, it's hard to say which came first. This much is clear: Once you choose a positive belief or an effective behavior, you usually find yourself in a cycle of success. Positive beliefs lead to effective behaviors. Effective behaviors lead to success. And success reinforces the positive beliefs.

> The deepest personal defeat suffered by human beings is constituted by the difference between what one was capable of becoming and what one has in fact become.
>
> *Ashley Montagu*

Here's an example showing how the choice of beliefs and behaviors determines results. Until 1954, most track-and-field experts believed it was impossible for a person to run a mile in less than four minutes. On May 6, 1954, however, Roger Bannister of England ran a mile in the world-record time of 3:59.4. Once Bannister had proven that running a four-minute mile was possible, within months, many other runners also broke the four-minute barrier. In other words, once runners chose a new belief (a person *can* run a mile in less than four minutes), they pushed their physical abilities, and suddenly the impossible became possible. By the way, the present world's record, set in 1999 by Hicham El Guerrouj of Morocco, is an amazing 3:43.13. So much for limiting beliefs!

Consider another example. After a disappointing test score, a struggling student thinks, "I knew I couldn't do college math!" This belief will likely cause the student to miss classes and neglect assignments. These self-defeating behaviors will lead to even lower test scores, reinforcing the negative beliefs. This student, caught in a cycle of failure, is now in grave danger of failing math.

In that same class, however, someone with no better math ability is passing the course because this student believes she *can* pass college math. Consequently, she chooses positive behaviors such as attending every class, completing all of her assignments, getting a tutor, and asking the instructor for help. Her grades go up, confirming her empowering belief. The cycle of success has this student on course to passing math.

Someone once said, "If you keep doing what you've been doing, you'll keep getting what you've been getting." That's why if you want to improve your life (and why else would you attend college?), you may need to change some of your beliefs and behaviors. Conscious experimentation will teach you which ones are already working well for you and which ones need revision. Once these new beliefs and behaviors become a habit, you'll find yourself in the cycle of success, on course to creating your dreams in college and in life.

Life is a self-fulfilling prophesy . . . in the long run you usually get what you expect.

Denis Waitley

WRITE A GREAT LIFE

College offers the perfect opportunity to design a life worth living. A time-tested tool for this purpose is a journal, a written record of your thoughts and feelings, hopes and dreams. Journal writing is a way to explore your life in depth and discover your best "self." This self-awareness will enable you to make wise choices about what to keep doing and what to change.

Many people who keep journals do what is called "free writing." They simply write whatever thoughts come to mind. This approach can be extremely valuable for exploring issues present in one's mind at any given moment.

In *On Course*, however, you will write a guided journal. This approach is like going on a journey with an experienced guide. Your guide takes you places and shows you sights you might never have discovered on your own.

Before writing each journal entry, you'll read an article about proven success strategies. Then you'll apply the strategies to your own life by completing the guided journal entry that follows the article. Here are five guidelines for creating a meaningful journal:

- **Copy the directions for each step into your journal (just the bold print):** When you find your journal in a drawer or computer file 20 years from now, having the directions in your journal will help you make sense of what you've written. Underline or bold the directions to distinguish them from your answers.

- **Be spontaneous:** Write whatever comes to mind in response to the directions. Imagine pouring liquid thoughts into your journal without pausing to edit or rewrite. Unlike public writings, such as an English composition or a history research paper, your journal is a private document written primarily for your own benefit.

- **Be honest:** As you write, tell yourself the absolute truth; honesty leads to your most significant discoveries about yourself and your success.

- **Be creative:** Add favorite quotations, sayings, and poems. Use color, drawings, clip art, and photographs. Express your best creative "self."

- **Dive deep:** When you think you have exhausted a topic, write more. Your most valuable thoughts will often take the longest to surface. So, most of all—DIVE DEEP!

For easy reference, these five important guidelines are also printed on the inside back cover of this book.

Whether you handwrite your journal or compose it on a computer, I urge you to keep all of your journal entries together in one book or file. If you do, one day many years from now, you'll have the extraordinary pleasure of reading this autobiography of your growing wisdom about creating success in college and in life.

ASSESS YOURSELF

Before we examine the choices of successful students, take a few minutes to complete the self-assessment questionnaire on the next two pages. Your scores will identify behaviors and beliefs that support your success. They'll also point out behaviors and beliefs you may want to change to achieve more of your potential in college and in life. In the last chapter, you will have an opportunity to repeat this self-assessment and compare your two scores. I think you're going to be pleasantly surprised!

This self-assessment is not a test. There are no right or wrong answers. The questions simply give you an opportunity to create an accurate and current self-portrait. Be absolutely honest and have fun with this activity, for it is the first step on an exciting journey to a richer, more personally fulfilling life.

Journal work is an excellent approach to uncovering hidden truths about ourselves.

Marsha Sinetar

SELF-ASSESSMENT

Visit www.cengagebrain.com to access this self-assessment online through CourseMate for *On Course.*

Read the following statements and score each one according to how true or false you believe it is about you. To get an accurate picture of yourself, consider what IS true about you (not what you want to be true). Remember, there are no right or wrong answers. Assign each statement a number from 0 to 10, as follows:

Totally False ← 0 1 2 3 4 5 6 7 8 9 10 → Totally True

1. _____ I control how successful I will be.
2. _____ I'm not sure why I'm in college.
3. _____ I spend most of my time doing important things.
4. _____ When I encounter a challenging problem, I try to solve it by myself.
5. _____ When I get off course from my goals and dreams, I realize it right away.
6. _____ I'm not sure how I prefer to learn.
7. _____ Whether I'm happy or not depends mostly on me.
8. _____ I'll truly accept myself only after I eliminate my faults and weaknesses.
9. _____ Forces out of my control (such as poor teaching) are the cause of low grades I receive in school.
10. _____ I place great value on getting my college degree.
11. _____ I don't need to write things down because I can remember what I need to do.
12. _____ I have a network of people in my life that I can count on for help.
13. _____ If I have habits that hinder my success, I'm not sure what they are.
14. _____ When I don't like the way an instructor teaches, I know how to learn the subject anyway.
15. _____ When I get very angry, sad, or afraid, I do or say things that create a problem for me.
16. _____ When I think about performing an upcoming challenge (such as taking a test), I usually see myself doing well.
17. _____ When I have a problem, I take positive actions to find a solution.
18. _____ I don't know how to set effective short-term and long-term goals.
19. _____ I am organized.
20. _____ When I take a difficult course in school, I study alone.
21. _____ I'm aware of beliefs I have that hinder my success.
22. _____ I'm not sure how to think critically and analytically about complex topics.
23. _____ When choosing between doing an important school assignment or something really fun, I do the school assignment.
24. _____ I break promises that I make to myself or to others.
25. _____ I make poor choices that keep me from getting what I really want in life.
26. _____ I expect to do well in my college classes.
27. _____ I lack self-discipline.
28. _____ I listen carefully when other people are talking.
29. _____ I'm stuck with any habits of mine that hinder my success.
30. _____ My intelligence is something about myself that I can improve.

31. _____ I often feel bored, anxious, or depressed.

32. _____ I feel just as worthwhile as any other person.

33. _____ Forces outside of me (such as luck or other people) control how successful I will be.

34. _____ College is an important step on the way to accomplishing my goals and dreams.

35. _____ I spend most of my time doing unimportant things.

36. _____ I am aware of how to show respect to people who are different from me (race, religion, sexual orientation, age, etc.).

37. _____ I can be off course from my goals and dreams for quite a while without realizing it.

38. _____ I know how I prefer to learn.

39. _____ My happiness depends mostly on what's happened to me lately.

40. _____ I accept myself just as I am, even with my faults and weaknesses.

41. _____ I am the cause of low grades I receive in school.

42. _____ If I lose my motivation in college, I don't know how I'll get it back.

43. _____ I have a written self-management system that helps me get important things done on time.

44. _____ I seldom interact with people who are different from me.

45. _____ I'm aware of the habits I have that hinder my success.

46. _____ If I don't like the way an instructor teaches, I'll probably do poorly in the course.

47. _____ When I'm very angry, sad, or afraid, I know how to manage my emotions so I don't do anything I'll regret later.

48. _____ When I think about performing an upcoming challenge (such as taking a test), I usually see myself doing poorly.

49. _____ When I have a problem, I complain, blame others, or make excuses.

50. _____ I know how to set effective short-term and long-term goals.

51. _____ I am disorganized.

52. _____ When I take a difficult course in school, I find a study partner or join a study group.

53. _____ I'm unaware of beliefs I have that hinder my success.

54. _____ I know how to think critically and analytically about complex topics.

55. _____ I often feel happy and fully alive.

56. _____ I keep promises that I make to myself or to others.

57. _____ When I have an important choice to make, I use a decision-making process that analyzes possible options and their likely outcomes.

58. _____ I don't expect to do well in my college classes.

59. _____ I am a self-disciplined person.

60. _____ I get distracted easily when other people are talking.

61. _____ I know how to change habits of mine that hinder my success.

62. _____ Everyone is born with a certain amount of intelligence, and there's not really much you can do to change that.

63. _____ When choosing between doing an important school assignment or something really fun, I usually do something fun.

64. _____ I feel less worthy than other people.

Transfer your scores to the scoring sheets on the next page. For each of the eight areas, total your scores in columns A and B. Then total your final scores as shown in the sample on the next page.

SELF-ASSESSMENT SCORING SHEET

SAMPLE

A		B	
6. __8__		29. __3__	
14. __5__		35. __3__	
21. __6__		50. __6__	
73. __9__		56. __2__	

__28__ + 40 − __14__ = 54

SCORE #1: ACCEPTING PERSONAL RESPONSIBILITY

A		B	
1. ___		9. ___	
17. ___		25. ___	
41. ___		33. ___	
57. ___		49. ___	

___ + 40 − ___ = ___

SCORE #2: DISCOVERING SELF-MOTIVATION

A		B	
10. ___		2. ___	
26. ___		18. ___	
34. ___		42. ___	
50. ___		58. ___	

___ + 40 − ___ = ___

SCORE #3: MASTERING SELF-MANAGEMENT

A		B	
3. ___		11. ___	
19. ___		27. ___	
43. ___		35. ___	
59. ___		51. ___	

___ + 40 − ___ = ___

SCORE #4: EMPLOYING INTERDEPENDENCE

A		B	
12. ___		4. ___	
28. ___		20. ___	
36. ___		44. ___	
52. ___		60. ___	

___ + 40 − ___ = ___

SCORE #5: GAINING SELF-AWARENESS

A		B	
5. ___		13. ___	
21. ___		29. ___	
45. ___		37. ___	
61. ___		53. ___	

___ + 40 − ___ = ___

SCORE #6: ADOPTING LIFELONG LEARNING

A		B	
14. ___		6. ___	
30. ___		22. ___	
38. ___		46. ___	
54. ___		62. ___	

___ + 40 − ___ = ___

SCORE #7: DEVELOPING EMOTIONAL INTELLIGENCE

A		B	
7. ___		15. ___	
23. ___		31. ___	
47. ___		39. ___	
55. ___		63. ___	

___ + 40 − ___ = ___

SCORE #8: BELIEVING IN MYSELF

A		B	
16. ___		8. ___	
32. ___		24. ___	
40. ___		48. ___	
56. ___		64. ___	

___ + 40 − ___ = ___

INTERPRETING YOUR SCORES

A score of . . .

0–39   Indicates an area where your choices will **seldom** keep you on course.

40–63   Indicates an area where your choices will **sometimes** keep you on course.

64–80   Indicates an area where your choices will **usually** keep you on course.

CHOICES OF SUCCESSFUL STUDENTS

SUCCESSFUL STUDENTS . . .	STRUGGLING STUDENTS . . .
accept personal responsibility, seeing themselves as the primary cause of their outcomes and experiences.	**see themselves as victims**, believing that what happens to them is determined primarily by external forces such as fate, luck, and powerful others.
discover self-motivation, finding purpose in their lives by discovering personally meaningful goals and dreams.	**have difficulty sustaining motivation**, often feeling depressed, frustrated, and/or resentful about a lack of direction in their lives.
master self-management, consistently planning and taking purposeful actions in pursuit of their goals and dreams.	**seldom identify specific actions needed to accomplish a desired outcome**, and when they do, they tend to procrastinate.
employ interdependence, building mutually supportive relationships that help them achieve their goals and dreams (while helping others do the same).	**are solitary**, seldom requesting, even rejecting, offers of assistance from those who could help.
gain self-awareness, consciously employing behaviors, beliefs, and attitudes that keep them on course.	**make important choices unconsciously**, being directed by self-sabotaging habits and outdated life scripts.
adopt lifelong learning, finding valuable lessons and wisdom in nearly every experience they have.	**resist learning new ideas and skills**, viewing learning as fearful or boring rather than as mental play.
develop emotional intelligence, effectively managing their emotions in support of their goals and dreams.	**live at the mercy of strong emotions**, such as anger, depression, anxiety, or a need for instant gratification.
believe in themselves, seeing themselves as capable, lovable, and unconditionally worthy human beings.	**doubt their competence and personal value**, feeling inadequate to create their desired outcomes and experiences.

FORKS IN THE ROAD

Why are these eight qualities so important? Because they shape many of the important choices we make. The road of life forks many times each day, and at every one we need to make a choice. Some of those choices are so significant they will literally change the outcomes of our lives. In college, students encounter opportunities such as work-study programs, majors, lunch with an instructor, study groups, social events, sports teams, new friends, study-abroad programs, romantic relationships, academic majors, all-night conversations, diverse cultures, challenging viewpoints, and field trips, among many others.

Other choices involve dealing with disappointing grades, homesickness, the death of a loved one, conflicts with friends, loneliness, health problems, endless homework, anxiety, broken romances, self-doubt, lousy class schedules, lost motivation, difficult instructors, academic probation, confusing tests, excessive drinking, frustrating rules, mystifying textbooks, conflicting work and school schedules, jealous friends, test anxiety, learning disabilities, and financial difficulties, to name a few.

In other words, college is just like life. There are always opportunities and obstacles, and the choices we make at each of these forks in the road determine whether we achieve our desired outcomes and experiences. It takes a lot more than potential to excel in college or in life. And you're about to find out how to succeed in both . . . despite inevitable challenges. You see, while life is generating a dizzying array of options, successful people are making one wise choice after another.

> I believe that choice—though it can be finicky, unwieldy, and demanding—is ultimately the most powerful determinant of where we go and how we get there.
>
> *Sheena Iyengar*

A FEW WORDS OF ENCOURAGEMENT

In this course, you'll be taking a personal journey designed to help you develop the empowering beliefs and behaviors that will help you maximize your potential and achieve the outcomes and experiences you desire. However, before we depart, let's see how you're feeling about this upcoming trip. Please choose the statement below that best describes how you feel right now:

1. I'm excited about developing the inner qualities, outer behaviors, and academic skills that have helped others achieve success in college and in life.

2. I'm feeling okay about this journey because I'll probably learn a few helpful things along the way.

3. I can't say I'm excited, but I'm willing to give it a try.

4. I'm unhappy, and I don't want to go!

In nearly every *On Course* group I've worked with, there have been some reluctant travelers. If that's you, I want to offer some personal words of encouragement. First, I can certainly understand why you might be hesitant. Frankly, I would have been a reluctant traveler on this journey when I was a first-year college student. I can tell you, though, I sure wish I'd known then what you're about to learn. Many students after completing the course have asked, "Why didn't they teach us this stuff in high school? It sure would have helped!" Even some of the most reluctant travelers have later said, "Every student should be required to take this course!"

I can't promise that you'll feel this way after finishing the course. But I can promise that if you do only the bare minimum or, worse yet, drop out, you'll never know if this course could have helped you improve your life. So, quite frankly, my goal here is to persuade you to give this course a fair chance.

Maybe you're thinking, *"I don't need this success stuff. Just give me the information and skills I need to get a good job."* If so, you're going to be pleased to discover that the skills you'll learn in this course are highly prized in the work world. In fact many companies pay corporate trainers huge fees to teach these same skills to their employees. Think of the advantage you'll have when you bring these skills with you to the job.

Or, perhaps you're thinking, *"I already know how to be successful. This is just a waste of my time."* I thought this, too, at one time. And I had three academic degrees from prestigious universities and a good job to back up my claim. Hadn't I already proven I could be a success? But when I opened myself to learning the skills that you'll discover in these pages, the quality of both my professional and personal life improved dramatically. I've also taught these skills to successful college educators (perhaps even your own instructor), and many of them have had the same experience I did. You see, there is success . . . and then there is SUCCESS!

Or, maybe you're thinking, *"I don't want to examine and write about myself. That's not what college should be about."* I understand this objection! When I was in college, self-examination was about the last thing on my to-do list (right after walking backwards to the North Pole in bare feet). Of course I had a "good" reason: Athletes like me didn't look inward. I labeled it "touchy feely" and dismissed self-exploration. I'm sure you have reasons for your reluctance: shyness, your cultural upbringing, or a host of other explanations that make you uncomfortable when looking within for the keys to your success. I urge you to overcome your resistance. You can learn now what it took me too many years to discover: Success occurs from inside out, not outside in. *You* are the key to your success. So, I hope you'll give this course your best effort. Most likely, it's the only one you'll ever take in college where the subject matter is YOU. And, believe me, if you don't master the content of this course, every other course you take (both in college and in the University of Life) will suffer. I wish you a great journey. Let the adventure begin!

> The battles that count aren't the ones for gold medals. The struggles within yourself—the invisible battles inside all of us—that's where it's at.
>
> *Jessie Owens, winner of four gold medals at the 1936 Olympics*

Journal Entry 1

In this activity, you will take an inventory of your personal strengths and weaknesses as revealed by your self-assessment questionnaire.

Remember: The five suggestions for creating a meaningful journal are printed on the inside back cover of *On Course*. Please review these suggestions before writing. Especially remember to copy the directions for each step (just the bold print) into your journal before writing.

1. **In your journal, write the eight areas of the self-assessment and record your scores for each, as follows:**

_____ 1. Accepting personal responsibility

_____ 2. Discovering self-motivation

_____ 3. Mastering self-management

_____ 4. Employing interdependence

_____ 5. Gaining self-awareness

_____ 6. Adopting lifelong learning

_____ 7. Developing emotional intelligence

_____ 8. Believing in myself

Transfer your scores from the self-assessment to the appropriate lines above.

2. **Write about the areas on the self-assessment in which you had your highest scores.** Explain why you think you scored higher in these areas than in others. Were there any surprises? Were there any high scores you disagreed with? If so, why? How do you feel about your higher scores? Your entry might begin, "By doing the self-assessment, I learned that I . . . ."

3. **Write about the areas on the self-assessment in which you had your lowest scores.** Explain why you think you scored lower in these areas than in others. Were there any surprises? Were there any low scores you disagreed with? If so, why? How do you feel about your lower scores? Remember the saying, "If you keep doing what you've been doing, you'll keep getting what you've been getting." With this thought in mind, write about any specific changes you'd like to make in yourself during this course. Your entry might begin, "By doing the self-assessment, I also learned that I . . . ."

All glory comes from daring to begin.

Eugene F. Ware

My journal from this course is the most valuable possession I own. I will cherish it always.

Joseph Haskins, student

One Student's Story

JALAYNA ONAGA
University of Hawaii-Hilo, Hawaii

It's amazing how fast someone can go from being excited about college to flunking out. A year and a half ago, I received a letter from the University of Hawaii at Hilo informing me that I was being dismissed due to my inability to maintain a GPA of at least 2.0. I wasn't surprised because I had spent the whole semester making one bad choice after another. I hardly ever attended classes. I didn't do much homework. I didn't study for tests. And I never asked anyone for help. Mostly I just hung out with friends who told me I didn't need to go to college. But, fast-forward to today and you'll see a woman who has clear goals for her future, the motivation to reach those goals, and a plan to carry her to her dreams. However, it took a lot of learning in order for me to make such a huge change in my life.

After taking courses for a while at a community college, I got permission to re-enroll at the university. I was so nervous! I worried that I'd get dismissed again and I'd never do anything with my life. A counselor suggested that I take the University 101 course, and I'm so thankful I did. While writing the *On Course* journals, I learned so much about myself and how I can succeed. I realized that when I first enrolled at the university, I was taking nursing courses because my parents wanted me to and I couldn't get motivated. This time I got inspired because my journals helped me look inside myself to figure out my own dreams for the future and to create a plan to reach them. For the first time, the plans I made were coming from my heart, not from someone telling me what I

should do. I realized that I really love kids and *my* dream is to teach second or third graders. That's when I made a personal commitment to attend every class and learn as much as I could. In later journals I learned that making a schedule and writing everything down helped me get the important things done. I even learned to ask for help, and when I was absent because my car broke down, I met with the teacher to find out what I had missed. Before tests, I found it inspiring to read over my journal because my own words reminded me of my dreams and why I should study hard to get them.

Best of all, my new choices really paid off. When the semester ended, I had three A's and a B+ and I made the dean's list. My University 101 course and the *On Course* textbook really changed me as a student and as a person. Not long ago, I was a student without a direction. Now I can envision myself in the near future teaching a class full of eager students, watching them learn and grow, just like I was able to do.

Understanding the Culture of Higher Education

 Focus Questions What is the culture of higher education? How does understanding that culture increase your chances of success in college?

In some ways, enrolling in college is like moving to a foreign country. That's because the culture of higher education is different from other cultures you have known, even that of high school. Like an immigrant to any new land, you'll be successful in college to the degree that you learn and adapt to its unique culture.

Geert Hofstede, a Danish psychologist and anthropologist, has studied cultures all over the world. According to Hofstede, culture is "the collective programming of the mind that distinguishes the members of one human group from another."

In other words, what makes people different isn't just the physical characteristics you can see. In fact, much more significant is their unique cultural programming: the sum of customs and beliefs they've learned from family, friends, schools, religions, and other groups to which they belong. Every culture on Earth is programmed to operate by its own unique software. And this is true of higher education as well.

Some aspects of a culture are obvious and visible, whereas others are subtle and invisible. To understand the distinction between visible and invisible culture, Brooks Peterson, author of *Cultural Intelligence*, suggests picturing an iceberg (see Figure 13.1). Above the waterline are the elements of culture we can perceive with our five senses. "Surface" culture includes such things as food, fashions, language, gestures, games, art, music, and holidays.

Below the waterline you'll find the more stable and significant features of "deep culture." Most of these features are invisible to tourists and recent immigrants. Deep culture consists of the shared beliefs, attitudes, norms, rules, opinions, expectations, and taboos of a group of people. For natives, these deep-culture features are usually taken for granted until someone disobeys them. Here's a simple example. When you arrive at a ticket line, what do you do? If you're from mainstream North American culture, you automatically go to the end of the line. No sign is needed because everyone knows that's what you're supposed to do. You probably don't even think about it unless someone cuts in front of you. When someone defies a cultural rule, others get upset. Cultural programs help a group or society run smoothly by keeping people in line (literally and figuratively).

Culture, then, is the collection of surface- and deep-level customs and beliefs that get passed on from generation to generation. Each culture provides "approved" choices at significant, and even insignificant, forks in the road. Culture tells us, "This choice is normal and that one is strange." Or, "This choice is right and that one is wrong." Or, "This choice is good and that choice

> What we call customs rest on top and are most apparent. Deepest and least apparent are the cultural values that give meaning and direction to life. Values influence people's perceptions of needs and their choice between perceived alternative courses of action.
>
> *Benjamin Paul, Anthropologist*

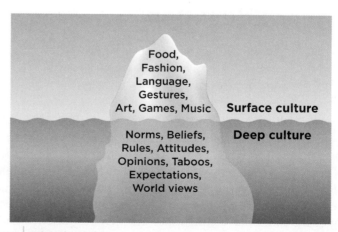

Figure 13.1 | Cultural Iceberg

398

is bad." At each fork in the road, our inner programs give us a nudge in the culturally approved direction.

To put it succinctly, "Culture is the way we do things around here."

CULTURE SHOCK

What happens, then, when *they* don't do things the way *we* do? Or, what happens when *we* don't do things the way *they* do? In other words, what happens when different cultures clash?

Here's an example of surface cultures clashing: You're traveling with a group of American students in China. In the province of Guangdong, students from a local university invite your group to join them for a meal. You've saved your appetite for a grand feast, and after many tasty appetizers, your hosts proudly present the main dish. *What the heck is that? Oh my god . . . they're serving a barbequed dog!* Chances are, you've just experienced a clash of surface cultures. Your mind races with judgments about what is appropriate, right, or good to serve for dinner. In North American culture, dogs are pets. We all know the unwritten rule: People don't eat their pets (let alone serve them to guests).

Now, consider a clash of deep cultures. At your college, you join a math study group that includes Tariq, a young man from Saudi Arabia. You're explaining how you solved homework problem number three when Tariq excitedly interrupts: "What you are saying can also work for numbers four and five!" Tariq takes over the conversation, and you wait quietly until he finishes. Then you've barely begun explaining your approach to problem six when Tariq, with great enthusiasm, cuts you off again. A few minutes later, he butts in once more, and now you're steaming. You've just experienced a clash of deep cultures: judgments about what is appropriate, right, or good to do in a conversation. The unwritten rule in some cultures (e.g., United States, English-speaking Canada, and England) is that speakers take turns speaking. In other cultures (e.g., Middle East, Southern France, and Spain), interruptions are expected. In fact, if someone doesn't interrupt, others may assume the person doesn't care about the subject under discussion.

Culture shock is the upset and stress we experience when confronted with behaviors and beliefs that differ significantly from our own. Because we are quite sure that our way is right, a typical response to culture shock is judgment: Tariq is self-centered, inconsiderate, and rude. As judgments fly and our discomfort increases, typical responses are fight (*I'm not putting up with this!*) or flight (*I'm outta here!*) Seldom is either choice helpful in achieving our desired outcomes and experiences.

Which brings us to the importance of understanding the culture and traditions of higher education in North America.

THE CULTURE OF HIGHER EDUCATION

Because college is a unique culture, expect some challenges as you adapt. Most differences in surface culture will be pretty obvious. For example, like all cultures, higher education has its own language, so you'll probably hear words that

> Culture shock can take its toll on us. It can make us feel anxious, disoriented, and depressed. . . . Minimizing culture shock requires new knowledge and insights as well as a certain degree of flexibility.
>
> *Richard Bucher,*
> **Building Cultural Intelligence**

sound foreign to you. Suppose an instructor tells your class, "The directions for your first paper are posted on Moodle. Be sure to do it in MLA format." These directions make little sense if you don't know the lingo. But it's not really that complicated. Here's what those familiar with college culture know:

Moodle is a computer software program that allows colleges to offer class content on the Internet. (A similar program is called BlackBoard.) If your instructor doesn't provide directions for accessing course information posted on the Internet, contact the folks in your campus computer lab for help.

MLA format is a set of guidelines provided by the Modern Language Association (MLA) for how writers in the humanities should identify research sources. By the way, writers in the sciences use a different format, one provided by the APA (American Psychological Association). For more information about these formats, you can ask a librarian or do an Internet search for help.

To learn additional surface features of college culture, see "Wise Choices in College: College Customs" (pages 34–38). Following the suggestions there will help you avoid a number of bumps and potholes in your journey through higher education.

Now for a few words about deep culture. As suggested earlier, these differences will be less obvious. In fact, you may find yourself off course and not even realize that the cause is a clash of deep cultures. That's why the sooner you learn the culture of higher education in general, and the culture of your college in particular, the better you'll be able to make wise choices and stay on course to academic success.

Throughout *On Course* we will be exploring the deep culture of higher education in North America, but let's take a look at one example here. Keep in mind that statements about any culture are generalizations. As with all generalizations, they will likely vary for individual campuses and certainly vary for individual instructors. However, you can use the following example (and those presented throughout the book) to gage where your college—or an instructor—stands in regard to each of these mindsets and make your choices accordingly.

One element of deep college culture that's almost sure to be important at your college is a high regard for intellectual curiosity. I've asked literally thousands of educators, "What inner qualities would you like your students to have?" *Intellectual curiosity* is a near unanimous choice. Your instructors want you to be as curious about their subject as they are. Or at least curious about something. They want you to think deeply about life. They want you to ask thoughtful questions and pursue the answers with enthusiasm. Questions like *Why? How do you know? Who else believes this? What's the cause? What's another explanation? When might this not be so? How can I use this?* Bottom line: Intellectual curiosity is greatly prized in the deep culture of higher education.

Toto, I have a feeling we're not in Kansas anymore.

Dorothy, in The Wizard of Oz

Schools, like ethnic groups, have their own cultures: languages, ways of doing things, values, attitudes toward time, standards of appropriate behavior, and so on. As participants in schools, students are expected to adopt, share, and exhibit these cultural patterns. If they do not or cannot, they are likely to be censured and made to feel uncomfortable in a variety of ways.

Jean Moule, Cultural Competence

A Dozen Differences Between High School and College Culture	
High School Culture—Assumes Immaturity	College Culture—Assumes Maturity
Students attend high school because they are required to by their parents or by law.	Students usually attend college because of a personal choice.
Teachers offer students many reminders to complete assignments.	Instructors give assignments and expect students to hand them in on time without reminders.
Teachers spend time disciplining students who create disruptions.	Instructors do not tolerate disruptive students and may bar them from the class.
Students typically spend 30 or more hours in class each week, and teachers cover the majority of course content during class.	Students typically spend 15 or fewer hours in class each week, and instructors expect students to learn the majority of course content outside of class.
Teachers and parents manage much of the students' time.	Students manage their own time.
Teachers are often pressured to "teach to the test" so that students can pass standardized assessments.	Instructors have more "academic freedom" in what and how they teach.
Academic standards are not always high, and savvy students often get good grades with little effort.	Academic standards are usually high, and all students need to figure out how to meet these challenging standards.
Family and friends provide students with advice or solutions for academic, social, and other problems.	Students solve their own problems or seek help at one of many support services provided by the college.
Students' choice of courses is relatively limited by graduation requirements.	Students have greater freedom to choose the courses they take and drop those they don't want to complete.
Teachers and parents minimize distractions that might otherwise hinder students' success.	Students must deal with distractions on their own, including parties, television, video games, Internet surfing, dating, sports, Facebook, drinking, road trips, and hanging out.
Educational costs are paid for by taxpayers, including text books.	Educational costs, including text books, are paid for by the student, the student's family, and/or by financial aid for which the student applies and, in some cases, must pay back.
Students have few choices.	Students have many choices.

So, how might a student clash with this aspect of deep college culture? Here's just one possibility. A student gets back a writing assignment, and the grade is lower than he expected. A *lot* lower. *Darn*, he thinks, *I spent hours writing that paper. What does the instructor expect anyway? This would have been at least a B in high school. Probably an A! What is she thinking!* For an answer, let's visit the instructor at home the night before where we catch her reading that very student's paper: *Darn, she thinks, this essay is so boring. It's as though the writer simply copied sentences from various Internet sites and strung them together as an essay. His main concern seems to be having enough words to fulfill the assignment. Where's the writer's curiosity, his passion, his quest for answers? What is he thinking!*

The student is discouraged, and the instructor is too. They both have good intentions yet neither may realize the problem: deep cultures clashing. He wants to get a good grade. She wants to see intellectual curiosity.

CHOICES AND CULTURE

The choices recommended in *On Course* exist as possibilities for every human being. However, here's a heads up: Sometimes an option presented in these pages may clash with your own cultural or individual programming. As such, you may judge them as inappropriate, wrong, or bad. For example, in Chapter 5 you'll read about the benefits of interdependence. This principle suggests that creating mutually supportive relationships can enhance your chances for success. However, if you've been raised in traditional North American culture, your default choice is likely to be independence. In fact, asking for help may feel so uncomfortable that pursuing your success alone may seem to be your only choice. There is certainly a time for *in*dependence, but what if choosing *inter*dependence at the right time can improve your chances for success?

Here's another example. As you've learned, *On Course* presents success principles and practices. Then it asks you to reflect on these strategies by writing guided journal entries. If you've been raised in a working-class culture, and especially if you are young and male, your programming probably favors action over reflection. Thus, writing reflective journals may feel uncomfortable. There is certainly a time for action, but what if choosing reflection at the right time can improve your chances for success?

Here's the point: Empowered people appreciate having choices . . . as many as possible. Having options usually increases anyone's likelihood for success, especially when seeking success in a new culture. At each fork in the road, empowered people decide which choice—from among many—will most likely help them create the outcomes and experiences they want.

In this course you will learn much about the surface- and deep-culture rules of higher education. In the process, you'll come to understand what natives of this unique culture judge to be appropriate, right, and good (and, conversely, what they believe is inappropriate, wrong, and bad). At some point early in the process, you may feel that you don't belong in this culture . . . you might even feel unwelcome. Just know that this is a natural part of figuring out and fitting

If all you have is a hammer, everything looks like a nail.

Carl Jung

into any new culture. If your culture is very different from the culture of higher education, at some point you may even ask yourself, "How much of my culture do I need to give up in order to succeed in college?"

It's up to each of us to decide when to follow a choice of our culture, when to follow a choice of another culture, or when to honor a choice born of our own wisdom. Whatever their source, the more options you have to choose from, the more empowered you will be to create the life you want.

Life is the sum of all your choices.

Albert Camus

Journal Entry 2

In this activity you will explore various aspects of surface and deep culture that you have experienced in school.

1. **Contrast the surface culture of the last school you attended with that of your present school.** From the following list, choose two or more surface-level features that are different for the two schools. Then, in a separate paragraph for each feature, explain how the two schools are different.

Number of students in a class	Age of students
Race or ethnicity of students	Economic class of students
Courses offered	Amount of homework
Popular out-of-school activities	Teachers' treatment of students
Alcohol	Academic preparation of educators
In-groups	Religions
Clothes	Food
Languages spoken	Dialects spoken
Sports	Amount of writing assigned
Amount of reading assigned	Drugs
Architecture of buildings	Favorite music
Holidays observed	Out-groups
Attendance policy	Methods of teaching
Involvement of parents	Classrooms

The heart and soul of school culture is what people believe, the assumptions they make about how school works.

Thomas Sergiovanni

Here's how your journal entry might begin if you chose "Age of students":

"The ages of students at my high school ranged from about 14 to 18 years old. Here in college the ages of students range from about 17 to 40 or even older. In my math class this semester, I have a mother and daughter who are taking the class together. Overall, students here in college seem to average about 10 years older than students in high school. A couple of the older students that I've talked with went to college before and dropped out. These students seem to take their schoolwork more seriously than the younger students. They hardly ever miss a class or fail to turn in homework."

During elementary and second education, teachers and parents primarily guide students, for the most part students take classes with the same peers, homework assignments are checked often, notes to parents are often sent about good academic progress, and children are to some extent protected from distractions and competing alternatives to education. In postsecondary education, however, students are expected to exercise control of their conduct, maintain motivation, develop plans for the future, exercise delay of gratification, and put into effect goals and learning strategies.

Hefer Bembenutty

2. **Describe the deep culture of the last school you attended.** From the following list, choose two or more deep-culture features. Then, in a separate paragraph for each, describe the school's invisible beliefs, attitudes, opinions, expectations, norms, and/or taboos toward . . .

Maturity

Academic integrity (cheating and plagiarism)

Motivation

Civility (common courtesy to others)

Time

College education

Study groups (student collaboration)

Grades

Speaking and writing in Standard English ("correct" grammar)

Intellectual curiosity

People who are different (ethnicity, religion, sexual orientation, etc.)

Self-awareness

Learning

Academic standards (difficult/easy)

Importance of a college education

Formality

Choices

Punctuality

Homework

Contributing to class discussions

Quality of teaching

Emotions

Academic freedom (teachers choose what/how to teach)

Self-confidence

Studying

For example, suppose you chose to describe your high school's deep-culture belief about "college." Your paragraph might say:

"My high school had students from seven small towns. Five of the towns were fairly well off economically. Two of the towns were pretty poor. Students from the five richer towns—I was one of them—pretty much expected we would enroll in college after graduation. A lot of us had parents and older brothers and sisters who had gone to college. Although we didn't talk about it much, it was a given we'd go to college, too. I never even considered another option, and I think that was true for my friends as well. In junior year, our guidance counselors started helping us go through college catalogues and fill out applications. In our senior year, word got around fast when someone got a letter of acceptance to a college. Now that I think about it, I feel bad for the kids from the other two towns. I'm not sure if any of them went to college or not. I saw one of them a couple of weeks ago working at a mini-mart. I wonder if he was as sure he would *not* go to college as I was sure that I *would*. I had a couple of classes with him in high school, and he was no dummy. I bet he could get a college degree if he wanted to. As far as I know, he didn't even apply. *On Course* talks about making wise choices at a fork in the road. Sometimes it seems like the choice is decided by your culture before you even get to the fork."

Becoming an Active Learner

 Focus Questions How does the human brain learn? How can you use this knowledge to develop a highly effective system for learning?

Successful athletes understand how to get the most out of their physical abilities. Likewise, to be a successful learner, you need to know how to get the most out of your mental abilities. Much has been discovered, especially in the last few decades, about how human beings learn. To benefit from these discoveries, let's take a quick peek into our brains.

HOW THE HUMAN BRAIN LEARNS

The human brain weighs about three pounds and is composed of trillions of cells. About 100 billion of them are neurons, and here's where much of our learning takes place. When a potential learning experience occurs (such as reading this sentence), some neurons send out spikes of electrical activity. This activity causes nearby neurons to do the same. When neurons fire together, they form what is called a "neural network." I like to picture a bunch of neurons joining hands in my brain, jumping up and down, and having a learning party. If this party happens only once, learning is weak (as when you see your instructor solve a math problem one day and can't recall how to do it the next). However, if you cause the same collection of neurons to fire repeatedly (as when you solve 10 similar math problems yourself), the result is likely a long-term memory. According to David Sousa, author of *How the Brain Learns*, "Eventually, repeated firing of the pattern binds the neurons together so that if one fires, they all fire, ultimately forming a new memory trace."

The human brain has the largest area of uncommitted cortex (no particular required function) of any species on earth. This gives humans extraordinary flexibility and capacity for learning.

Eric Jensen

Neurons before learning.

Neurons after learning.

In other words, if you want learning to stick, you need to create strong neural networks. In this way, learning literally changes the structure of your brain. Through autopsies, neuroscientist Robert Jacobs and his colleagues determined that graduate students actually had 40 percent more neural connections than those of high school dropouts. Jacobs's research joins many other brain studies to reveal an important fact: **To excel as a learner, you need to create as many neural connections in your brain as possible.**

THREE PRINCIPLES OF DEEP AND LASTING LEARNING

With this brief introduction to what goes on in our brains, let's explore how highly effective learners maximize their learning. Whether they know it or not, they have figured out how to create many strong neural connections in their brains. And you can, too.

How? The short answer is: **Become an active learner**. Learning isn't a spectator sport. You don't create deep and lasting learning by passively listening to a lecture, casually skimming a textbook, or having a tutor solve math problems for you. In order to create strong neural networks, you've got to participate actively in the learning process.

Now, here's the longer answer. Good learners, consciously or unconsciously, implement three principles for creating deep and lasting learning:

In a time of drastic change, it is the learners who inherit the future.

Eric Hoffer

1. **PRIOR LEARNING.** Brain research reveals that when you connect what you are learning now to previously stored information (i.e., already-formed neural networks), you learn the new information or skill faster and more deeply. For example, the first word-processing program I learned was Word Perfect. It took me a long time to learn because I had no prior knowledge about word processing; thus, my brain contained few, if any, neural networks relevant to what I was learning. First, I needed to learn what word processing can do (such as delete whole paragraphs) and then I needed to learn how to perform that function with Word Perfect. Later, when I was learning another word-processing program, Microsoft Word, I already knew what word processing can do, so I was able to learn this new program in a fraction of the time. Put another way, I already had neural networks in my brain related to word processing, and learning Microsoft Word got those neurons partying.

   The contribution of past learning to new learning helps explain why some learners have difficulty in college with academic skills such as math, reading, and writing. If their earlier learning was shaky, they're going to have difficulty with new learning. They don't have strong neural networks on which to attach the new learning. It's like trying to construct a house on a weak foundation. In such a situation, the best option is to go back and strengthen the foundation, which is exactly the purpose of developmental (basic skills) courses. However, there's no point trying to learn these foundational skills the same way you learned them before. After all, how you learned them before didn't make the information or skills stick. So this time you'll need to employ different, more effective learning strategies, ones that will create the needed neural networks. If that's your situation, this time you'll have the advantage of employing the more effective strategies described here in *On Course*. And if you're a learner with a strong foundation, you'll find strategies here that will increase your effectiveness as a learner even more.

2. **QUALITY OF PROCESSING.** How you exercise affects your physical strength. Likewise, how you study affects the strength of your neural networks and therefore the quality of your learning. Some information (such as math formulas or anatomy terms) must be recalled exactly as presented. For such learning tasks, effective memorization strategies are the types of processing that work best. However, much of what you'll be asked to learn in college is too complex for mere memorization (though many struggling students try). For mastering complex information and skills, you'll want to use what learning experts call **deep processing.** These are the very strategies that successful learners use to maximize their learning and make it stick. You'll learn both effective memorization and deep-processing strategies in the "Wise Choices in College" sections in later chapters.

> When information goes "in one ear and out the other," it's often because it doesn't have anything to stick to.
>
> *Joshua Foer*

> Mathematics teachers . . . see students using a certain formula to solve problems correctly one day, but they cannot remember how to do it the next day. If the process was not stored, the information is treated as brand new again!
>
> *David A. Sousa*

Don't use just one deep-processing strategy, however. Successful athletes know the value of cross training, so they use a variety of training strategies. Similarly, successful learners know the value of employing *varied* deep-processing strategies. That's because the more ways you deep-process new learning, the stronger your neural networks become.

When you actively study any information or skill using *numerous and varied deep-processing strategies,* you create and strengthen related neural networks and your learning soars.

3. **QUANTITY OF PROCESSING.** The quality of your learning is significantly affected by how often and how long you engage in varied deep processing. This factor is often called "time on task," and the most effective approach is *distributed practice.* The human brain learns best when learning efforts are distributed over time. No successful athlete waits until the night before a competition to begin training. Why, then, do struggling students think they can start studying the night before a test? An all-night cram session may make a deposit in their short-term memories, perhaps even allowing them to pass a test the next day. However, even students who got good grades have experienced the ineffectiveness of cramming when they encounter "summer amnesia"—the inability to remember in fall-term classes what they learned during the previous school year. That's the result of not creating strong neural networks that make learning last. To create strong neural networks, you need to process the target information or skill with numerous and varied deep-processing strategies and do it *frequently.*

In addition to how frequently you use deep-processing strategies, also important is the *amount of time* you spend learning. Obviously, deep processing for 60 minutes generates more learning than deep processing for 5 minutes. So, highly effective learners put in **sufficient time on task.** The traditional guideline for a week's studying is two hours for each hour of class time. Thus, if you have 15 hours of classes per week, the estimate for your "sufficient time on task" is about 30 hours per week. Many struggling students neither study very often nor very long. However, some fool themselves by putting in "sufficient time," but spend little of it engaged in effective learning activities. They skim complex information in their textbooks. They attempt to memorize information they don't understand. Their minds wander to a conversation they had at lunch. They rummage through their book bags and dresser drawers and closets looking

---

Three Principles of Deep and Lasting Learning

1. **Prior Learning.** Relate new information to previously learned information.
2. **Quality of Processing.** Use numerous and varied deep-processing strategies.
3. **Quantity of Processing.** Use frequent practice sessions of sufficient length distributed over time.

---

for their class notes. They play a video game or two. They phone a class-mate. They send a couple of text messages, and the next thing they know, it's time to go to bed. When they fail the test the next day, they complain, "But I studied *so long*!"

Some students have a chemical imbalance that prevents them from focusing for long periods of time and their learning suffers. If you think this may be true for you, make an appointment with your college's disability counselor to get help. But the reason most students struggle with learning is fully within their control. You don't need a genius IQ to be a good learner and do well in college. What you do need is a learning system that employs what we now know about how the human brain learns. Billions of neurons between your ears are ready to party. Let the festival of learning begin!

THE CORE LEARNING SYSTEM

Four general strategies are common to good learners. To remember these strate-gies, simply think of the word CORE (see Figure 13.2). CORE stands for **Collect, Organize, Rehearse,** and **Evaluate.** The CORE learning system is effective be-cause it automatically guides you to implement all three of the active learning prin-ciples discussed earlier. Thus, by applying what we know about how the human brain learns, the CORE learning system helps you create deep and lasting learning. Here's how it works:

Collect: In every waking moment, we're constantly collecting perceptions through our five senses. Without conscious effort, the brain takes in a mul-titude of sights, sounds, smells, tastes, and physical sensations. Most percep-tions disappear within moments. Some, such as our first language, stick for a lifetime. Thus, much of what we learn in life we do without intention. In col-lege, however, learning needs to be more conscious. That's because instructors expect you to learn specific information and skills. Then, of course, they want you to demonstrate that knowledge on quizzes, tests, exams, term papers, and other forms of evaluation. In college, two of the most important ways you'll collect information and skills are through reading textbooks and attending classes. You'll learn proven strategies for maximiz-ing the amount of high-quality information you coll-ect in these ways.

Organize: Once we collect information, we need to make sense of it. When learning in everyday life, we tend to organize collected information in uncon-scious ways. We don't even realize that we're doing it. However, in a college course, you need to organize information systematically so it makes sense to you. In fact, making meaning from collected information is one of the most important outcomes of studying.

Good learners, like everyone else, are living, squirming, questioning, perceiving, fearing, loving, and languaging nervous systems, but they are good learners precisely because they believe and do certain things that less effective learners do not believe and do. And therein lies the key.

Neil Postman
& Charles Weingartner

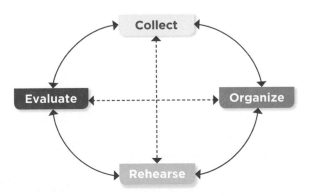

Figure 13.2 The CORE Learning System

Rehearse: Once we collect and organize our target knowledge, we need to remember it for future use. Rehearsing (also called "practicing") strengthens neural networks and makes learning stick. When you solve 10 challenging math problems, you're rehearsing. Over time, the process of solving becomes easier and more natural.

Evaluate: Life is great at giving us informal feedback about the quality of our learning. Maybe you tell a joke and forget the punch line. You know immediately you have more learning to do. Higher education, however, provides us with more formal feedback. Yup, those pesky tests, term papers, quizzes, lab reports, essays, classroom questions, and final exams. Evaluation, both informal and formal, is an essential component of all learning because without feedback, we can never be sure if our learning is accurate or complete.

Learning doesn't occur in a tidy, step-by-step fashion. At any moment while learning, you may need to jump to a different component in the CORE system. For example, while **Rehearsing,** you might realize that some information doesn't make sense to you, so you **Organize** it in a different way. At times you may engage two or more components simultaneously. For instance, when **Rehearsing** study materials, you're probably **Evaluating** your mastery of that knowledge at the same time. Thus, you can expect to use the four components of the CORE Learning System in any order and in any combination.

Although the CORE system is an effective blueprint for creating deep and lasting learning, not all learners prefer to **Collect, Organize, Rehearse,** and **Evaluate** in the same way. That's why you'll encounter many specific strategies in *On Course*. Your task is to experiment with and find the ones that work best for you. What you'll ultimately construct is a personalized learning system, one you can use for the rest of your life. In this way, you can be confident of your ability to learn anything you need to know on the path to achieving your goals and dreams in college and beyond.

Journal Entry 3

In this activity, you'll explore how you learned something (anything) using the approach of an active learner. Then you'll plan how you could use this same approach to improve your learning outcomes and experiences in college.

1. **Identify one thing you have learned simply because you enjoyed learning it.** It can be something you learned in school or anywhere else. If nothing comes immediately to mind, use the following questions to jog your memory. What do you know more about than most people (e.g., World War II or rare coins)? What are you good at (e.g., solving math problems or playing video games)? What skills have you mastered (e.g., using Excel spreadsheets or cooking)? What are your hobbies (e.g., vegetable gardening or reading mystery novels)? What have you spent a lot of time doing? (e.g., exercising or traveling)? To complete this step, simply write the completion of this sentence in your journal: "One thing I enjoyed learning is _____."

2. **With a focus on the information or skill identified in Step 1, write answers to each of the following questions. Use a separate sentence or paragraph for each answer.**

   A. How did you gather the information or skills you needed to learn this? (Collect)

   B. What did you do to learn the information or skills needed to learn this? (Organize)

   C. What else did you do to learn this? (Rehearse—Variety)

   D. How often did you engage in learning this? (Rehearse—Frequency)

   E. When you engaged in learning this, how long did you usually spend? (Rehearse—Duration)

   F. What feedback did you use to determine how well you had learned this? (Evaluate)

   G. How did you feel when you engaged in learning this? (Motivating Experiences)

   H. What were the rewards for learning this? (Motivating Outcomes)

3. **Write about the key points you have learned or relearned about learning and how you will use this knowledge to maximize your learning in college.** For example, your journal entry might begin, "By reading and writing about learning, I have learned/relearned that . . . . I will use this knowledge to maximize my learning in college by . . . ." Be specific!

   Be sure to use the five suggestions printed on the inside back cover of *On Course. Especially remember to dive deep!* Diving deep changes the neurons in your brain and leads to deep and lasting learning. As you may have already realized, writing an in-depth journal entry is a powerful way to deep-process your experiences!

I don't love studying. I hate studying. I like learning. Learning is beautiful.

Natalie Portman

Learning . . . should be a joy and full of excitement. It is life's greatest adventure; it is an illustrated excursion into the minds of noble and learned men, not a conducted tour through a jail.

Taylor Caldwell

One Student's Story

KASE CORMIER
Asheville-Buncombe Technical Community College,
North Carolina

At the beginning of my first semester in college, I was overwhelmed. I had been out of school for more than 10 years and wasn't sure how to make the adjustment to being back in school after all that time. In previous attempts at school I had felt dumb; I had an awful memory and a learning disability that made writing and spelling difficult. While looking over the syllabi for my five classes, I had no idea how I was going to fit all that knowledge into my brain. The information for Anatomy and Physiology was enough by itself; adding in essays, computer projects, and reading assignments from other classes made my head spin. On top of all that, I was required to take a study skills class. A friend who had taken the class before told me it was worth it. Skeptical, I responded, "Are you kidding me? There is no way I'll get anything out of that class, and I have no more time."

The week before classes began, I decided to get a head start on the dizzying amount of reading I had to do. I picked up the *On Course* textbook and opened to Chapter 1. I skimmed the pages lazily until I got to the section on "Becoming an Active Learner." The information on creating "neural networks" piqued my interest, and I read about the three principles of deep learning:

connect new information to things you already know, use a lot of different study techniques, and study often. Although it was interesting at the time, I had too much to do to let it sink in; yet as the semester progressed, those three principles began popping into my head. I could practically feel my neurons firing off faster and faster as I learned new material, trying to find ways to process and retain everything I was being taught. Every class moved quickly, and I found that I only had a short amount of time to learn something. I kept applying those techniques, and as long as I connected new information back to what I already knew, found new and creative ways to learn it, and repeated those activities often, I could fit so much more information into my head. Better than simply cramming for a test, those principles enabled me to do more than just learn new information. They helped me retain it as well.

These three learning principles were extremely important for Anatomy and Physiology because of how much information we were responsible for. Cramming for the next test wouldn't work; every section was laying groundwork for the future, and I needed to retain that information. To create varied learning experiences, I tried out several

different study groups, each with a different style of learning, until I finally found a group that I connected with; afterward, I supplemented my primary study group with other groups to have some variety. I worked hard with each group, even making up silly games to explore different ways of learning the material. One game was "flashcard races." We put the names of the cranial nerves on flashcards, shuffled them, and then raced to see who could put them in order first. The more different ways I studied the information, the stronger my neural connections became. I took every opportunity to study in open lab, and in class, I asked lots of questions. My classmates joked with me, saying that I asked "Why?" too much, but I explained that it helped me relate the information to things I already knew. After our final lecture exam (which happened to be on neurons), my study buddies all gave me a hug and thanked me for improving the study sessions with my silly games and constant questioning. We all got A's!

The *On Course* principles may seem worthless at first, but don't be fooled. They stay with you and change the way you learn. I am grateful that I took the initiative to read that first chapter before my classes started. In high school I was a C student, but this semester I earned a 4.0! Connecting information to what I already knew, using a variety of study techniques, and studying often definitely helped make my first semester back in college a success.

On Course Principles

AT WORK

I think we have to appreciate that we're alive for only a limited period of time, and we'll spend most of our lives working.

Victor Kiam,
Chairman,
Remington Products

Applying the strategies you're going to learn in *On Course* will not only improve your results in college, it will also boost your success at work. You're about to explore dozens of proven strategies that will help you achieve your goals both in college and in your career.

This is no small matter. Career success (or lack of it) affects nearly every part of your life: family, income, self-esteem, people with whom you associate, where you live, your level of happiness, what you learn, your energy level, your health, and maybe even the length of your life.

Some students think, "All I need for success at work is the special knowledge of my chosen career." All that nurses need, they believe, are good nursing skills. All that accountants need are good accounting skills. All that lawyers need are good legal skills. These skills are called hard skills, the knowledge needed to perform a particular job. Hard skills include knowing where to insert the needle for an intravenous feeding drip, how to write an effective business plan, and what the current inheritance laws are. These are the skills you'll be taught in courses in your major field of study. They are essential to qualify for a job. Without them you won't even get an interview.

But, most people who've been in the work world a while will tell you this: Hard skills are essential to get a job but they are often insufficient to keep it or advance. That's because nearly all employees have the hard skills necessary to do the job for which they're hired. True, some may perform these skills a little better or a little worse than others, but one estimate suggests that only 15 percent of workers lose their jobs because they can't do the work. That's why career success is often determined by soft skills, the same strategies you'll be learning in this book. As one career specialist put it, "Having hard skills gets you hired; lacking soft skills gets you fired."

A U.S. government report confirms that soft skills are essential to job success. The Secretary of Labor asked a blue-ribbon panel of employers to identify what it takes to be successful in the modern employment world. This panel published a report in 1992 called the Secretary's Commission on Achieving Necessary Skills (SCANS). The report presents a set of foundation skills and workplace competencies that employers consider essential for work-world success, and the report's timeless recommendations continue to be a valuable source of information for employers and employees alike. No one familiar with today's work world will find many surprises in the report, especially in the foundation skills. The report calls for employees to develop the same soft skills that employers include in job descriptions, look for in reference letters, probe for in job interviews, and assess in evaluations of their workforce.

The SCANS report identifies the following soft skills as necessary for work and career success: taking responsibility, making effective decisions, setting goals, managing time, prioritizing tasks, persevering, giving strong efforts, working well in teams, communicating effectively, having empathy, knowing how to learn, exhibiting self-control, and believing in one's own self-worth. The Conference Board of Canada published a similar report called the *Employability Skills Profile: The Critical Skills Required of the Canadian Work Force.* Both reports identify these necessary soft skills but don't suggest a method for developing them. *On Course* will show you how.

Learning these soft skills will help you succeed in your first career after college. And, because soft skills are portable (unlike many hard skills), you can take them with you in the likely event that you later change careers. Most career specialists say the average worker today can expect to change careers at least once during his or her lifetime. In fact, some 25 percent of workers in the United States today are in occupations that did not even exist a few decades ago. If a physical therapist decides to change careers and work for an Internet company, he needs to master a whole new set of hard skills. But the soft skills he's mastered are the same ones that will help him shine in his new career.

So, as you're learning these soft skills, keep asking yourself, "How can I use these skills to stay on course to achieving my greatest potential at work as well as in college?" Be assured that what you're about to explore can make all the difference between success and failure in your career.

Creators Wanted!

Candidates must demonstrate mastery of both the hard and soft skills necessary for career success.

Develop Self-Acceptance

 Focus Questions Why is high self-esteem so important to success? What can you do to raise your self-esteem?

Roland was in his 40's when he enrolled in my English 101 class. He made insightful contributions to class discussions, so I was perplexed when the first two writing assignments passed without an essay from Roland. Both times, he apologized profusely, promising to complete them soon. He didn't want to make excuses, he said, but he was stretched to his limit: He worked at night, and during the day he took care of his two young sons while his wife worked. "Don't worry, though," he assured me, "I'll have an essay to you by Monday. I'm going to be the first person in my family to get a college degree. Nothing's going to stop me."

But Monday came, and Roland was absent. On a hunch, I looked up his academic record and found that he had taken English 101 twice before. I contacted his previous instructors. Both of them said that Roland had made many promises but had never turned in an assignment.

I called Roland, and we made an appointment to talk. He didn't show up. During the next class, I invited Roland into the hall while the class was working on a writing assignment.

"Sorry I missed our conference," Roland said. "I meant to call, but things have been piling up."

"Roland, I talked to your other instructors, and I know you never wrote anything for them. I'd love to help you, but you need to take an action. You need to write an essay." Roland nodded silently. "I believe you can do it. But I don't know if *you* believe you can do it. It's decision time. What do you say?"

"I'll have an essay to you by Friday."

I looked him in the eye.

"Promise," he said.

I knew that what Roland actually did, not what he promised, would reveal his deepest core beliefs about himself.

> The foundation of anyone's ability to cope successfully is high self-esteem. If you don't already have it, you can always develop it.
>
> *Virginia Satir*

> Self-esteem is the reputation we have with ourselves.
>
> *Nathaniel Branden*

SELF-ESTEEM AND CORE BELIEFS

So it is with us all. Our core beliefs—true or false, real or imagined—form the inner compass that guides our choices.

At the heart of our core beliefs is the statement *I AM ___*. How we complete that sentence in the quiet of our souls has a profound effect on the quality of our lives.

High self-esteem is the fuel that can propel us into the cycle of success. Do we approve of ourselves as we are, accepting our personal weaknesses along with our strengths? Do we believe ourselves capable, admirable, lovable, and fully worthy of the best life has to offer? If so, our beliefs will make it possible for us to choose wisely and stay on course to a rich, full life.

For example, imagine two students: one with high self-esteem, the other with low self-esteem. Picture them just after they get very disappointing test scores. What do they do next? The student with low self-esteem will likely choose options that protect his fragile self-image, options such as dropping the course rather than chancing failure. The student with high self-esteem, on the other hand, will likely choose options that move her toward success, options such as persisting in the course and getting additional help to be successful. Two students, same situation. One focuses on weaknesses. One focuses on strengths. The result: two different choices and two very different outcomes.

The good news is that self-esteem is learned, so anyone can learn to raise his or her self-esteem. Much of this book is about how you can do just that.

KNOW AND ACCEPT YOURSELF

People with high self-esteem know that no one is perfect, and they accept themselves with both their strengths and weaknesses. To paraphrase philosopher Reinhold Niebuhr, successful people accept the things they cannot change, have the courage to change the things they can change, and possess the wisdom to know the difference.

Successful people have the courage to take an honest self-inventory, as you began doing in Journal Entry 1. They acknowledge their strengths without false humility, and they admit their weaknesses without stubborn denial. They tell the truth about themselves and take action to improve what they can.

Fortunately for Roland, he decided to do just that. On the Friday after our talk, he turned in his English 101 essay. His writing showed great promise, and I told him so. I also told him I appreciated that he had let go of the excuse that he was too busy to do his assignments. From then on, Roland handed in his essays on time. He met with me in conferences. He visited the writing lab, and he did grammar exercises to improve his editing skills. He easily passed the course.

A few years later, Roland called me. He had transferred to a four-year university and was graduating with a 3.8 average. He was continuing on to

> Self-esteem is more than merely recognizing one's positive qualities. It is an attitude of acceptance and non-judgment toward self and others.
>
> *Matthew McKay & Patrick Fanning*

AS SMART AS HE WAS, ALBERT EINSTEIN COULD NOT FIGURE OUT HOW TO HANDLE THOSE TRICKY BOUNCES AT THIRD BASE.

graduate school to study urban planning. What he most wanted me to know was that one of his instructors had asked permission to use one of his essays as a model of excellent writing. "You know," Roland said, "I'd still be avoiding writing if I hadn't accepted two things about myself: I was a little bit lazy and I was a whole lot scared. Once I admitted those things about myself, I started changing."

Each of us has a unique combination of strengths and weaknesses. When struggling people become aware of a weakness, they typically blame the problem on others or they beat themselves up for not being perfect. Successful people, however, usually make a different choice: They acknowledge the weakness, accept it without self-judgment, and, when possible, take action to create positive changes. As always, the choices we make determine both where we are headed and the quality of the journey. Developing self-acceptance helps us to make those choices wisely.

Journal Entry 4

In this activity, you will explore your strengths and weaknesses and the reputation you have with yourself. This exploration of your self-esteem will allow you to begin revising any limiting beliefs you may hold about yourself. By doing so, you will take a major step toward your success.

1. In your journal, write a list of 10 or more of your personal strengths. For example, mentally: *I'm good at math;* physically: *I'm very athletic;* emotionally: *I seldom let anger control me;* socially: *I'm a good friend;* and others: *I am almost always on time.*

2. Write a list of 10 or more of your personal weaknesses. For example, mentally: *I'm a slow reader;* physically: *I am out of shape;* emotionally: *I'm easily hurt by criticism;* socially: *I don't listen very well;* and others: *I'm a terrible procrastinator.*

3. Using the information in Steps 1 and 2 and score #8 on your self-assessment, write about the present state of your self-esteem. On a scale of 1 to 10 (with 10 high), how strong is your self-esteem? How do you think it got to be that way? How would you like it to be? What changes could you make to achieve your ideal self-esteem?

To create an outstanding journal, remember to use the five suggestions printed on the inside back cover of *On Course*. Especially remember to dive deep!

Wise Choices in College

COLLEGE CUSTOMS

Keep reminding yourself that entering college is like crossing the border into another country. Each has new customs to learn. If you learn and heed the following college customs, your stay in higher education will be not only more successful but more enjoyable as well.

1. Read your college catalogue. Catalogues are usually available in the registrar's or counseling office, and many colleges post a copy of the catalogue on their website. This resource contains most of the factual information you'll need to plot a great journey through higher education. It explains how your college applies many of the customs discussed in this section. Keep a college catalogue on hand and refer to it often. It's an essential guidebook for your journey through higher education.

2. See your advisor. Colleges provide an advisor who can help you make wise choices. Sometimes this person is a counselor, sometimes an instructor. Find out who your advisor is, make an appointment, and get advice on what courses to take and how to create your best schedule. Ask your advisor to help you create a long-term academic plan that charts your path all the way to graduation. Students who avoid advisors often enroll in unnecessary courses or miss taking courses that are required for graduation. Your tuition has paid for a guide through college; use this valuable resource wisely.

3. Understand prerequisites. A "prerequisite" is a course that must be completed before you can take another course. For example, colleges require the completion of calculus before enrollment in more advanced mathematics courses. Before you register, confirm with your advisor that you have met all of the prerequisites. Otherwise you may find yourself registered for a course you aren't prepared to pass. Prerequisites usually appear within each course description in your college catalogue.

4. Complete your general education requirements. Most colleges require students to complete a minimum number of general education credits. Typically, you need to take one or more courses from broad fields of study such as communication, natural science and technology, math, languages, humanities, and social and behavioral science. For example, to fulfill your requirement in science, you might need to complete 4 credits by taking any one of the following courses: biology, chemistry, astronomy, geology, or physics. Find a list of these required general education courses in your college catalogue, and check off each requirement as you complete it. Regardless of how many credits you earn, you can't graduate until you've completed the general education requirements. Depending on your college, general education requirements may be called core requirements, core curriculum, or general curriculum.

5. Choose a major wisely. You'll usually choose a major area of study in your first or second year. Examples of majors include nursing, early childhood education, biology, English, mechanical engineering, and art. You'll take the greatest number of courses in your major, supplemented by your general education courses and electives. Even if you've already picked a major, visit the career counseling center to see if other majors might interest you even more or be a better stepping stone to your chosen career. Your career counseling center can provide you with assessments to help you find a career that fits your interests and personality, and you can complete career inventories prior to choosing a major to help you narrow the best major for your intended career. For example, majoring in English is great preparation for a law degree. All majors and their required courses are available in your college catalogue. Until you've entered a major, you're wise to concentrate on completing your general education requirements.

6. Take a realistic course load. I once taught a student who worked full-time, was married with three small children, and had signed up for six courses in her first semester. After five weeks, she was exhausted and withdrew from college. There are only 168 hours in a week. Be realistic about the number of courses you can handle given your other responsibilities. Students often register for too many credits because of their mistaken belief that this choice will get them to graduation more quickly. Too often the actual result is dropped and failed classes, pushing graduation further into the future.

7. Attend the first day of class (on time). Of course it's wise to attend *every* day on time, but whatever you do, be present on the first day! On this day instructors usually provide the class assignments and rules for the entire semester. If you're absent, you may miss something that will come back to haunt you later. For example, find out each instructor's attendance policy and be sure you adhere to it. In some classes, it is possible to pass all tests and assignments and still fail a course because you didn't fulfill the attendance policy.

8. Sit in each classroom where you can focus on learning. Experiment. Try different places in the room. Many students focus best when sitting up front. Others prefer sitting on the side about halfway back, where they can see all of their classmates and the instructor during a discussion. Most students find that sitting in the back (especially in a large class) is the least desirable. Once you identify the place that best supports your learning, sit there permanently . . . unless you find that changing seats every day helps you learn better.

9. Study the syllabus. In the first class, instructors usually provide a syllabus (sometimes called a "first-day handout"). The syllabus is the single most important handout you will receive all semester. Typically, it contains the course objectives, the required books and supplies, all assignments and due dates, and the method for determining grades. This handout also presents any course rules you need to know. Essentially, the course syllabus is a contract between you and your instructor, who will assume that you've read and understood this contract; be sure to ask questions about any part you don't understand.

10. Buy required course books and supplies as soon as possible. College instructors cover a lot of ground quickly. If you don't have your study materials from the beginning of the course, you may fall too far behind to catch up. To get a head start on their classes, some wise students go to their college bookstore or an online bookstore weeks before the semester or quarter begins and purchase course materials. If money is tight, check with the financial aid office to see if your college provides temporary book loans. Or, as a last resort, ask your instructors if they will put copies of the course texts on reserve at your college library. As you will see later, having your own books for each course makes it much easier to gather and organize the knowledge you will need to learn.

11. Introduce yourself to one or more classmates and exchange phone numbers and email addresses. After an absence, contact a classmate to learn what you missed. Few experiences in college are worse than returning to class and facing a test that was announced in your absence.

12. Inform your instructor before a planned absence. Think of your class as your job and your instructor as your employer. Professional courtesy dictates notifying your employer of an absence you know about in advance. The same is true with instructors. Usually a quick email will do, and most likely you'll find your instructor's email address in the course syllabus.

13. If you arrive late, slip in quietly. Don't make excuses. Just come in and sit down. If you want to explain your lateness, see the instructor after class.

14. Ask questions. If the question you don't ask shows up on a test, you're going to be upset with yourself. Your classmates are equally nervous about asking questions. Go ahead, raise your hand and ask one on the first day; after that, it'll be easier. Additionally, asking good questions demonstrates to your instructor that you have intellectual curiosity, which is a great reputation to have in higher education. Later, I'll show you how to arrive at each class with nifty questions to ask.

15. To hold an extended conversation with your instructors, make an appointment during their office hours. Most college instructors have regular office hours; these times are usually included in the course syllabus and may also be posted on the instructor's office door. You can make an appointment in person before or after class, or you can call the instructor's office. Be sure to show up on time (or call beforehand to reschedule). Arrive with a clear goal, such as clarifying a comment the instructor wrote on your English composition, or learning how to correct a math problem that you got wrong on the homework, or discussing how you could better prepare for your next test in history. You'll find most instructors very receptive to meeting you during their office hours. At a minimum, plan to make one appointment with all of your instructors each semester.

16. Get involved in campus life. Most colleges offer numerous activities that can broaden your education, add pleasure to your life, and introduce you to new friends. Consider participating in the drama club, school newspaper, intercultural counsel, student government, athletic teams, band or orchestra, literary magazine, yearbook committee, science club, or one of the many other organizations on your campus. There's probably a list of options in your college's catalog, student handbook or on its website. Such options are usually referred to as "extracurricular activities." "Extracurricular" simply means that the activities are not part of an academic class.

17. Know the importance of your grade point average (GPA). Your GPA is the average grade for all of the courses you have taken in college. At most colleges, GPAs range from 0.0 ("F") to 4.0 ("A"). Your GPA affects your future in many ways. At most colleges a minimum GPA (often 2.0, a "C") is required to graduate, regardless of how many credits you have accumulated. Students who fall below the minimum GPA are usually ineligible for financial aid and cannot play intercollegiate sports, or, in some cases, are in danger of academic dismissal, particularly for students who are already on academic probation. Academic honors (such as the dean's list) and some scholarships are based on your GPA. Finally, potential employers often note GPAs to determine if prospective employees have achieved success in college.

18. Know how to compute your grade point average (GPA). At most colleges, GPAs are printed on a student's transcript, which is a list of courses completed (with the grades earned). You can get a copy of your transcript from the registrar's office. Transcripts are usually free or available for a nominal charge. You can compute your own grade point average by using the formula in the following box. Or you can do it online at http://www.back2college.com/gpa.htm. Figuring your GPA could be tricky if you're taking one or more developmental courses. At many colleges, grades in developmental courses do not offer credits toward graduation, so they may not be used for calculating a GPA. For example, if you were taking three courses and two were developmental, your GPA would be determined by the grade you received in just the one non-developmental course. To check your school's policy about this issue, read your college catalog or ask a counselor or advisor.

Formula for Computing Your Grade Point Average (GPA)

$$\frac{(G1 \times C1) + (G2 \times C2) + (G3 \times C3) + (G4 \times C4) + \cdots (Gn \times Cn)}{\text{Total \# of Credits Attempted}}$$

In this formula, G = the grade in a course and C = number of credits for a course. For example, suppose you had the following grades:

"A" in Math 110 (4 Credits)	G1 ("A") = 4.0
"B" in English 101 (3 Credits)	G2 ("B") = 3.0
"C" in Sociology 101 (3 Credits)	G3 ("C") = 2.0
"D" in Music 104 (2 Credits)	G4 ("D") = 1.0
"F" in Physical Education 109 (1 Credit)	G5 ("F") = 0.0

Here's how to figure the GPA from the grades above:

$$\frac{(4.0 \times 4) + (3.0 \times 3) + (2.0 \times 3) + (1.0 \times 2) + (0.0 \times 1)}{4 + 3 + 3 + 2 + 1} = \frac{16 + 9 + 6 + 2 + 0}{13} = 2.54$$

19. If you stop attending a class, withdraw officially. Students are enrolled in a course until they're *officially* withdrawn. A student who stops attending is still on the class roster at semester's end when grades are assigned, and the instructor will very likely give the nonattending student an "F." That failing grade is now a permanent part of the student's record, lowering the GPA and discouraging potential employers. If you decide (for whatever reason) to stop attending a class, go directly to the registrar's office and follow the official procedures for withdrawing from a class. Make certain that you withdraw before your college's deadline. This date is often about halfway through a semester or quarter.

20. Talk to your instructor before withdrawing. If you're going to fail a course, withdraw to protect your GPA. But don't withdraw without speaking to your instructor first. Sometimes students think they are doing far worse than they really are. Discuss with your instructor what you need to do to pass the course and make a step-by-step plan. Be sure to discuss your plans with your advisor as well. He or she might have insights about what will be best for your general education or major requirements and when courses are available for you to retake. If you discover that failing is inevitable, withdraw officially.

21. Keep a file of important documents. Forms get lost in large organizations such as colleges. Save everything that may affect your future: course syllabi, completed tests and assignments, approved registration forms, scholarship applications, transcripts, and paid bills. If you're exempted from a college requirement or course prerequisite, get it in writing and add the document to your files.

22. Finally, some college customs dictate what you should *not* do. Avoiding the following behaviors shows respect for your classmates and instructors.

- Don't pack up your books or put on your coat until the class is over.

- After an absence, don't ask your instructor, "Did I miss anything?" (Of course you did.)

- Don't wear headphones during class.

- Don't let a cell phone disturb the class.

- Don't side-talk with a classmate while the instructor or another student is talking to the class.

- Don't read or send text messages during class.

- Don't make distracting noises in class (e.g., clicking pen, popping gum, drumming fingers, and so on).

COLLEGE CUSTOMS EXERCISES

1. Find someone who has been at your college much longer than you have. Ask him or her, "What is one thing you learned about college customs that you wish you had known on your first day? How has knowing this college custom helped you?" Be prepared to report your findings.

2. Figure out a student's GPA who got the following grades:

"C" in Math 110 (4 Credits)

"D" in English 101 (3 Credits)

"C" in Sociology 101 (3 Credits)

"B" in Music 104 (2 Credits)

"A" in Physical Education 109 (1 Credit)

You may assume that all of these courses count toward the student's GPA.

3. For class discussion:

- Which college custom surprises you most?

- Which custom do you think will be most challenging for you?

- Which custom would you like to hear more about?

Accepting Personal Responsibility

I accept responsibility for creating my life as I want it.

SUCCESSFUL STUDENTS ...	STRUGGLING STUDENTS ...
adopt a Creator mindset, believing that their choices create the outcomes and experiences of their lives.	**accept a Victim mindset**, believing that external forces determine the outcomes and experiences of their lives.
master Creator language, accepting personal responsibility for their results.	**use Victim language**, rejecting personal responsibility by blaming, complaining, and excusing.
make wise decisions, consciously designing the future they want.	**make decisions carelessly**, letting the future happen by chance rather than by choice.

Case Study in Critical Thinking

THE LATE PAPER

Professor Freud announced in her syllabus for Psychology 101 that final term papers had to be in her hands by noon on December 18. No student, she emphasized, would pass the course without a completed term paper turned in on time. As the semester drew to a close, **Kim** had an "A" average in Professor Freud's psychology class, and she began researching her term paper with excitement.

Arnold, Kim's husband, felt threatened that he had only a high school diploma while his wife was getting close to her college degree. Arnold worked the evening shift at a bakery, and his coworker **Philip** began teasing that Kim would soon dump Arnold for a college guy. That's when Arnold started accusing Kim of having an affair and demanding she drop out of college. She told Arnold he was being ridiculous. In fact, she said, a young man in her history class had asked her out, but she had refused. Instead of feeling better, Arnold became even more angry. With Philip continuing to provoke him, Arnold became sure Kim was having an affair, and he began telling her every day that she was stupid and would never get a degree.

Despite the tension at home, Kim finished her psychology term paper the day before it was due. Since Arnold had hidden the car keys and Professor Freud refused to accept assignments sent by email, Kim decided to take the bus to the college and turn in her psychology paper a day early. While she was waiting for the bus, **Cindy**, one of Kim's psychology classmates, drove up and invited Kim to join her and some other students for an end-of-semester celebration. Kim told Cindy she was on her way to turn in her term paper, and Cindy promised she'd make sure Kim got it in on time. "I deserve some fun," Kim decided, and hopped into the car. The celebration went long into the night. Kim kept asking Cindy to take her home, but Cindy

always replied, "Don't be such a bore. Have another drink." When Cindy finally took Kim home, it was 4:30 in the morning. She sighed with relief when she found that Arnold had already fallen asleep.

When Kim woke up, it was 11:30 a.m., just 30 minutes before her term paper was due. She could make it to the college in time by car, so she shook Arnold and begged him to drive her. He just snapped, "Oh sure, you stay out all night with your college friends. Then, I'm supposed to get up on my day off and drive you all over town. Forget it." "At least give me the keys," she said, but Arnold merely rolled over and went back to sleep. Panicked, Kim called Professor Freud's office and told **Mary**, the administrative assistant, that she was having car trouble. "Don't worry," Mary assured Kim, "I'm sure Professor Freud won't care if your paper's a little late. Just be sure to have it here before she leaves at 1:00." Relieved, Kim decided not to wake Arnold again; instead, she took the bus.

At 12:15, Kim walked into Professor Freud's office with her term paper. Professor Freud said, "Sorry, Kim, you're 15 minutes late." She refused to accept Kim's term paper and gave Kim an "F" for the course.

Listed below are the characters in this story. Rank them in order of their *responsibility for Kim's failing grade in Psychology 101*. Give a different score to each character. Be prepared to explain your choices.

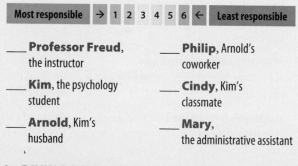

| Most responsible → 1 2 3 4 5 6 ← Least responsible |

____ **Professor Freud,** the instructor

____ **Kim**, the psychology student

____ **Arnold**, Kim's husband

____ **Philip**, Arnold's coworker

____ **Cindy**, Kim's classmate

____ **Mary,** the administrative assistant

▶ **DIVING DEEPER** Is there someone not mentioned in the story who may also bear responsibility for Kim's failing grade?

Adopting a Creator Mindset

 Focus Questions   What is self-responsibility? Why is it the key to creating the life you want?

When psychologist Richard Logan studied people who survived ordeals such as being imprisoned in concentration camps or lost in the frozen Arctic, he found they shared a common belief. They all saw themselves as personally responsible for creating the outcomes and experiences of their lives.

Ironically, responsibility has gotten a bad reputation. Some see it as a heavy burden they have to lug through life. Quite the contrary, personal responsibility is the foundation for creating success. Personal *response-ability* is the ability to respond wisely at each fork in the road, your choices moving you ever closer to your desired outcomes and experiences. The opposite is waiting passively for your fate to be determined by luck or powerful others. Whether your challenge is surviving an Arctic blizzard or excelling in college, accepting personal responsibility empowers you to make the most out of any situation.

I first met Deborah when she was a student in my English 101 class. Deborah wanted to be a nurse, but before she could qualify for the nursing program, she had to pass English 101. She was taking the course for the fourth time.

"Your writing shows fine potential," I told Deborah after I had read her first essay. "You'll pass English 101 as soon as you eliminate your grammar problems."

"I know," she said. "That's what my other three instructors said."

"Well, let's make this your last semester in English 101, then. After each essay, make an appointment with me to go over your grammar problems."

"Okay."

"And go to the Writing Lab as often as possible. Start by studying verb tense. Let's eliminate one problem at a time."

"I'll go this afternoon!"

But Deborah never found time: *No, really. . . . I'll go to the lab just as soon as I. . . .*

Deborah scheduled two appointments with me during the semester and missed them both: *I'm so sorry. . . . I'll come to see you just as soon as I. . . .*

To pass English 101 at our college, students had to pass one of two essays written at the end of the semester in an exam setting. Each essay, identified by social security number only, was graded by two other instructors. At semester's end, Deborah once again failed English 101. "It isn't fair!" Deborah protested. "Those exam graders expect us to be professional writers. They're keeping me from becoming a nurse!"

I suggested another possibility: "What if *you* are the one keeping you from becoming a nurse?"

The best years of your life are the ones in which you decide your problems are your own. You do not blame them on your mother, the ecology, or the president. You realize that you control your own destiny.

Albert Ellis

The more we practice the habit of acting from a position of responsibility, the more effective we become as human beings, and the more successful we become as managers of our lives.

Joyce Chapman

Deborah didn't like that idea. She wanted to believe that her problem was "out there." Her only obstacle was *those* exam graders. All her disappointments were *their* fault. *They* weren't fair. The *test* wasn't fair. *Life* wasn't fair! In the face of this injustice, she was helpless.

I reminded Deborah that it was *she* who had not studied her grammar. It was *she* who had not come to conferences. It was *she* who had not accepted personal responsibility for creating her life the way she wanted it.

"Yes, but …," she said.

VICTIM AND CREATOR MINDSETS

Deborah had a problem that was going to keep her from ever passing English 101. But the problem wasn't the exam graders. The problem was her mindset.

A mindset is a collection of beliefs and attitudes. Like a lens, it affects the way you see a situation and influences your resulting choices. A **Victim mindset** keeps people from seeing and acting on choices that could help them achieve the life they want. A **Creator mindset** causes people to see multiple options, choose wisely among them, and take effective actions to achieve the life they want.

When you accept personal responsibility, you believe that you create *everything* in your life. This idea doesn't sit well with some people. "Accidents and natural disasters happen," they say. "There are muggings, murders, and wars. People are marginalized, oppressed, and brutalized simply because they are different. Blaming the victims is unfair. To say these people created the terrible things that happened to them is outrageous."

These observations are, as far as they go, true. At times, we *are* all affected by forces beyond our control. If a hurricane destroys my house, I am a victim (with a small "v"). In this case I am victimized by a force *outside* of me. But if I allow that event to ruin my life, I am a Victim (with a capital "V"). In this case I am victimized by a force *inside* of me. Whether I am victimized from the outside or from the inside is a crucial distinction. When I have a Victim mindset, I become my own oppressor. When I have a Creator mindset, I refuse to be oppressed.

Civil rights activist Rosa Parks is a perfect example of this distinction. On the evening of December 1, 1955, Parks was returning home on a Montgomery, Alabama, bus. She had just completed a long day as a seamstress in a department store. When the driver ordered her to give up her seat to a white passenger, Parks refused and was arrested. A few days later, outraged at her arrest, African Americans began a boycott of Montgomery buses that ended 381 days later when the law requiring segregation on public buses was finally lifted. As a result of choosing defiance, Parks has been called the "mother of the modern day civil rights movement." In an interview years later, Parks was asked why she choose to defy the bus driver's order to move. "People always say that I didn't give up my seat because I was tired," she said, "but that isn't true. I was not tired physically, or no more tired than I usually was at the end of a working day. I was not old, although some people have an image of me as being old then.

426

I was forty-two. No, the only tired I was, was tired of giving in." In the face of an external oppression, Rosa Parks became an inspiring example of what one person with a Creator mindset can achieve.

So, is it outrageous to believe that you create everything in your life? Of course it is. But here's a better question: Would it improve your life to act *as if* you create all of the outcomes and experiences in your life? Answer "YES!" and watch a Creator mindset improve your life. After all, if you believe that someone or something out there causes all of your problems, then it's up to "them" to change. What a wait that can be! How long, for example, will Deborah have to wait for "those exam graders" to change?

The benefits to students of accepting personal responsibility have been demonstrated in various studies. Researchers Robert Vallerand and Robert Bissonette, for example, asked 1,000 first-year college students to complete a questionnaire about why they were attending school. They used the students' answers to assess whether the students were "Origin-like" or "Pawn-like." The researchers defined *Origin-like* students as seeing themselves as the originators of their own behaviors, in other words, Creators. By contrast, *Pawn-like* students see themselves as mere puppets controlled by others, in other words, Victims. A year later, the researchers returned to find out what had happened to the 1,000 students. They found that significantly more of the Creator-like students were still enrolled in college than the Victim-like students. If you want to succeed in college (and in life), having a Creator mindset gives you a big edge.

> I believe that we are solely responsible for our choices, and we have to accept the consequences of every deed, word, and thought throughout our lifetime.
>
> *Elisabeth Kübler-Ross*

RESPONSIBILITY AND CULTURE

In the 1950s, American psychologist Julian Rotter set out to study people's beliefs about who or what was responsible for the outcomes and experiences of their lives. He called it a study of "locus of control." *Locus* in Latin means "place" or "location." So, "locus of control" defines where people believe the power over their lives is located. Since Rotter's study, locus of control has been one of the

most examined aspects of human nature. What researchers discovered is that different cultures see locus of control differently.

People of some cultures believe they control their own destiny. Researchers call this mindset an *internal* locus of control. People with this mindset believe their outcomes and experiences depend on their own behaviors. This mindset is part of North American culture, where maturity is often defined as taking responsibility for one's own life. Not surprisingly, a strong part of the deep culture of North American higher education is a belief that college students are adults. As such, students are expected to make adult choices and be willing to accept responsibility for the consequences of those choices.

However, researchers found that people from some cultures assign responsibility for their fate to factors beyond their control. If you find that you are uncomfortable with the idea of personal responsibility, the cause may be found in your deep culture. For example, members of Latino culture, with roots in Catholicism, are likely to believe that a higher power is guiding their lives. The saying *Si Dios Quiere* ("If God Wants") reflects this belief. Muslims have a similar phrase in Arabic: *Insha'Allah* means "God willing" or "if God allows." Traditional Native Americans also value fate over self-determination. And members of working-class cultures—regardless of their ethnicity—may experience economic frustrations and doubt their ability to create the life of their dreams.

These differences in cultural mindsets highlight both the challenge and importance of deciding where our responsibilities begin and end. On the one hand, accepting too little responsibility is disempowering. We become little more than a feather floating on the breeze. On the other hand, accepting too much responsibility is disempowering as well. In some cases, we become like a pack mule crushed under the weight of problems not of our creation or in our control. The reality is that some choices truly are futile because of personal limitations or limitations imposed by fate or the will of others with more power. Like some kind of cosmic joke, one of our greatest responsibilities, then, is deciding what we are and are not responsible for, what we do and do not have control over. Worse, those decisions may change at the very next fork in the road. As a guideline to help you choose, in North American culture you'll usually be wise to adopt the philosophy of English poet William E. Henley, who in 1875 wrote: "I am the master of my fate; I am the captain of my soul." In fact, had Henley been a college student at the time, he might have added, "And I am the Creator of my GPA."

RESPONSIBILITY AND CHOICE

The key ingredient of personal responsibility is **choice.** Animals respond to a stimulus because of instinct or habit. For humans, however, there is a brief, critical moment of decision available between the stimulus and the response. In this moment, we make the choices—consciously or unconsciously—that influence the outcomes of our lives.

Numerous times each day, you come to a fork in the road and must make a choice. Even *not* making a choice is a choice. Some choices have a small impact: Shall I get my hair cut today or tomorrow? Some have a huge impact: Shall

---

Generally, European-American teachers believe in internal control and internal responsibility—that individuals are in control of their own fate, their actions affect outcomes, and success or failure in life is related to personal characteristics and abilities.

Jean Moule

By imposing too great a responsibility, or rather, all responsibility, on yourself, you crush yourself.

Franz Kafka

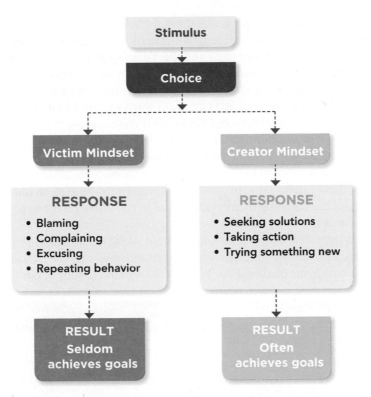

Figure 14.1 | Responsibility Model

I do think that the greatest lesson of life is that you are responsible for your own life.

Oprah Winfrey

When you make the shift to being the predominant creative force in your life, you move from reacting and responding to the external circumstances of your life to creating directly the life you truly want.

Robert Fritz

I stay in college or drop out? The sum of the choices you make from this day forward will create the eventual outcome of your life. The Responsibility Model in Figure 14.1 shows what the moment of choice looks like.

In that brief moment between stimulus and response, we can choose a Victim mindset or a Creator mindset. When we respond as a Victim, we typically complain, blame, make excuses, and then repeat ineffective behaviors. When we respond as a Creator, we pause at each decision point and ask, "What are my options, and which option will best help me create my desired outcomes and experiences?"

The difference between responding to life as a Victim or Creator is how we choose to use our energy. When I'm blaming, complaining, and excusing, my efforts cause little or no improvement. Sure, it may feel good in that moment to claim that I'm a poor Victim and "they" are evil persecutors, but my good feelings are fleeting because afterward my problem still exists. By contrast, when I'm seeking solutions and taking actions, my efforts often (though not always) lead to improvements. At critical forks in the road, Victims waste their energy and remain stuck, whereas Creators use their energy for improving their lives. There is only one situation I can think of where blaming and complaining can be helpful. That's when you use them to generate energy that motivates you to take positive actions. My personal guideline: Up to 10 minutes for griping . . . then on to being a Creator and finding a solution.

But, let's be honest. No one makes Creator choices all of the time. I've never met anyone who did, least of all me. Our inner lives feature a perpetual tug of war between the Creator part of us and the Victim part of us. My own experiences have taught me the following life lesson: The more choices I make as a Creator, the more I improve the quality of my life. That's why I urge you to join me in an effort to choose more often as a Creator. It won't be easy, but it's worth it. You may have to take my word for it right now, but if you experiment with the strategies in this book and continue using the ones that work for you, in a few months you'll see powerful proof in your own life of the value of making Creator choices.

"Oh, I get what you mean!" one of my students once exclaimed as we were exploring this complex issue of personal responsibility, "You're saying that living my life is like traveling in my car. If I want to get where I want to go, I better be the driver and not a passenger."

She was right. Personal responsibility is about taking hold of the steering wheel of our lives, about taking control of where we go and how we get there. Ultimately, each of us creates the quality of our life with the wisdom or folly of our choices.

Journal Entry 5

In this activity, you will experiment with the Creator role. By choosing to take responsibility for your life, you will immediately gain an increased power to achieve your greatest potential.

1. **Write and complete each of the five sentence stems below.** For example, someone might complete the first sentence stem as follows: If I take personal responsibility for my education, *I will focus on really learning and not just getting good grades.*

1. If I take personal responsibility for my education . . .
2. If I take personal responsibility for my career . . .
3. If I take personal responsibility for my relationships . . .
4. If I take personal responsibility for my health . . .
5. If I take personal responsibility for all that happens to me . . .

2. **Make a choice: Write about one of the following:**

A. **What have you learned or relearned in this journal about personal responsibility, and how you will use this knowledge to improve your outcomes and experiences in college . . . and beyond?** If you are aware that accepting personal responsibility conflicts with your own cultural or personal beliefs, explore how you will deal with that difference. You might begin, *By reading and writing about personal responsibility, I have learned . . .*

B. **Share the details of a personal experience in which you did or did not take personal responsibility and explain the effects of this choice on your life.**

I am a Shawnee. My forefathers were warriors. Their son is a warrior. . . . From my tribe I take nothing. I am the maker of my own fortune.

Tecumseh

Life is like a game of cards. The hand you are dealt is determinism; the way you play it is free will.

Jawaharlal Nehru

One Student's Story

BRIAN MOORE
Glendale Community College, Arizona

During my first semester in college, I was enrolled in a first-year English class. In high school I was usually able to pull off an A on my honors English papers without much work, and I thought I was a pretty good writer. So when I turned in my first college essay, I was expecting to get an A, or at worst a B. However, I was about to get a rude awakening. When we received our papers back a week later, I was shocked to see a C+ on my paper. I went to the instructor, and she said I just needed more practice and not to worry because I was in the class to learn. However, since I have high expectations for myself, those words weren't very comforting.

About that same time in my Strategies for College Success class, we were assigned to read a chapter in *On Course* about personal responsibility. The main idea is to adopt a "Creator" approach to problems, which I understood to mean basically seek solutions and not dwell on the negative. Then it clicked for me; I am responsible for my grades and I need to do whatever is necessary to get the ones I want. In high school, I could write one draft of an essay, turn it in, and I'd usually get an A, but that approach wasn't working in college. So, now I had to do something different. I started writing my papers before they were due and then meeting with my English teacher at least once a week to get her suggestions. Because I was a full-time student and also worked 17 to 20 hours a week in the cashier's office, sometimes I had to see her during times that were inconvenient. But I had to be flexible if I wanted her critique. During English class, we'd do peer editing, and I found that helpful, too. When I was in high school, I only spent about an hour or two writing an essay. Now I was spending at least three to five hours.

To my surprise, after some not-so-great increases in grades, I received what I had been waiting for: my first A on an essay. Although my final grade in English was a B, I learned a number of important lessons. It's really important to take your time with writing, to have your instructor or someone else read a rough draft and give you some suggestions, and then to write a final draft. I also learned that nobody can make the grade for you; you have to be responsible for yourself. I may not always get an A, but I learned to face a challenge, and no matter what grade I receive, knowing that I took responsibility as a "Creator" was the greatest lesson of all.

Mastering Creator Language

 Focus Question How can you create greater success by changing your vocabulary?

Have you ever noticed that there is almost always a conversation going on in your mind? Inner voices chatter away, offering commentary about you, other people, and the world. This self-talk is important because what you say to yourself determines the choices you make at each fork in the road. People with a Victim mindset typically listen to the voice of their Inner Critic or their Inner Defender.

The world of self-criticism on the one side and judgment toward others on the other side represents a major part of the dance of life.

Hal Stone & Sidra Stone

SELF-TALK

The Inner Critic

This is the internal voice that judges us as inadequate: *I'm so uncoordinated. I can't do math. I'm not someone she would want to date. I never say the right thing. My ears are too big. I'm a lousy writer.* The Inner Critic accepts too much responsibility and blames us for whatever goes wrong in our lives: *It's all my fault. I always screw up. I knew I couldn't pass biology. I ruined the project. I ought to be ashamed. I blew it again.* This judgmental inner voice can find fault with anything about us: our appearance, our intellect, our performance, our personality, our abilities, how others see us, and, in severe cases, even our value as a human being: *I'm not good enough. I'm worthless, I don't deserve to live.* (Although nearly everyone has a critical inner voice at times, if you often think toxic self-judgments like these last three, don't mess around. Get to your college's counseling office immediately and get help revising these noxious messages so you don't make self-destructive choices.)

Ironically, self-judgments have a positive intention. By criticizing ourselves, we hope to eliminate our flaws and win the approval of others, thus feeling more worthy. Occasionally when we bully ourselves to be perfect, we *do* create a positive outcome, though we make ourselves miserable in the effort. Often, though, self-judgments cause us to give up, as when I tell myself, *I can't pass math,* so I drop the course. What's positive about this? Well, at least I've escaped my problem. Freed from the pressures of passing math, my anxieties float away and I feel better than I have since the semester started. Of course, I still have to pass math to get my degree, so my relief is temporary. The Inner Critic is quite content to trade success in the future for comfort in the present.

Where does an Inner Critic come from? Here's one clue: Have you noticed that its self-criticisms often sound like judgmental adults we have known? It's as if our younger self recorded their judgments and, years later, our Inner Critic replays them over and over. Sometimes you can even trace a self-judgment back to a specific comment that someone made about you years ago. Regardless of its accuracy now, that judgment can affect the choices you make every day.

A loud, voluble critic is enormously toxic. He is more poisonous to your psychological health than almost any trauma or loss. That's because grief and pain wash away with time. But the critic is always with you—judging, blaming, finding fault.

*Matthew McKay
& Patrick Fanning*

During discussions about Inner Critic voices, I have had students say that in their culture, parents routinely criticize their children. The parents say they do it to help. A Japanese-American student said that if he brought home a test with a grade of 98 his parents would tell him that wasn't good enough. A Chinese-American woman said if she gained a pound her mother would tell her she was fat and no man would ever want to marry her. A Jewish-American student made a vase in her ceramics class and gave it to her mother as a present. Her mother proudly displayed the vase on the dining table. The next day, she asked, "What grade did you get for the vase?" My student replied that she had gotten a "C." Soon after, the vase disappeared, never to be seen again. I'm inclined to give these parents the benefit of the doubt. I'm willing to believe they thought they were helping their children, even showing love. Whatever their intentions, though, it was clear these parents had given great power to their children's Inner Critics.

The Inner Defender

The flip side of the Inner Critic is the Inner Defender. Instead of judging ourselves, the Inner Defender judges others: *What a boring teacher. My advisor screwed up my financial aid. Those people [referring to a minority group] are not as good as we are. My roommate made me late to class. No one knows what they're doing around here. It's all their fault!* Inner Defenders accept too little responsibility and, thus, their thoughts and conversations are full of blaming, complaining, accusing, judging, criticizing, and condemning others.

Like Inner Critics, Inner Defenders have a positive intention. They, too, want to protect us from discomfort and anxiety. They, too, want us to feel more worthy. One way they do so is by judging others as wrong or bad or "less than." By tearing others down, the Inner Defender tries to make us feel better about ourselves. In this light, you can perhaps see that prejudice and bias are important tools of the Inner Defender.

Another way Inner Defenders try to help us is by blaming our problems on forces that seem beyond our control, such as other people, bad luck, the government, lack of money, uncaring parents, not enough time, or even too much time. The Inner Defender of a college student might say, *I can't pass math because my instructor is terrible. She couldn't teach math to Einstein. Besides that, the textbook stinks and the tutors in the math lab are rude and unhelpful. It's obvious this college doesn't really care what happens to its students.* If I'm that student, I breathe a sigh of relief because now I'm covered. If I drop the course, hey, it's not my fault. If I stay in the course and fail, it's not my fault either. And, if I stay in the course and somehow get a passing grade (despite my terrible instructor, lousy textbook, worthless tutors, and uncaring college), well, then I have performed no less than a miracle! Regardless of how bad things may get, I can find comfort knowing that at least it's not my fault. It's *their* fault!

And where did this voice come from? Perhaps you've noticed that the Inner Defender's voice sounds like judgmental adults we have known: *You can't trust those people. They're not as good as we are. They're lazy. All they want*

What you're supposed to do when you don't like a thing is change it. If you can't change it, change the way you think about it. Don't complain.

Advice to Maya Angelou from her grandmother

433

is a handout. They are the reason for our problem! At other times, the Inner Defender sounds like our own voice when we were scared little kids trying to defend ourselves from criticism or punishment by powerful adults. Remember how we'd excuse ourselves from responsibility, shifting the blame for our poor choices onto someone or something else: *It's not my fault. He keeps poking me. My dog ate my homework. What else could I do? I didn't have any choice. My sister broke it. He made me do it. Why does everyone always pick on me? It's all their fault!*

Notice what the Inner Critic and Inner Defender have in common. They are both voices of *judgment*. With the Inner Critic, we point the finger of judgment inward at ourselves. With the Inner Defender, we point the finger of judgment outward at someone or something outside of us. We pay a high price for listening to either our Inner Critic or Inner Defender. By focusing on who's to blame, we waste our energy on judgments instead of positive actions. We spin in place instead of moving purposely toward our desired outcomes and experiences. To feel better in the moment, we sabotage creating a better future.

Fortunately, another voice exists within us all.

The Inner Guide

This is the wise inner voice that seeks to make the best of any situation. The Inner Guide knows that judgment doesn't improve difficult situations. So instead, the Inner Guide objectively observes each situation and asks, *Am I on course or off course? If I'm off course, what can I do to get back on course?* Inner Guides tell us the impartial truth (as best they know it at that time), allowing us to be more fully aware of the world around us, other people, and especially ourselves. With this knowledge, we can take actions that will get us back on course.

Some people say, "But my Inner Critic (or Inner Defender) is *right!*" Yes, it's true that the Inner Critic or Inner Defender can be just as "right" as the Inner Guide. Maybe you really *are* a lousy writer and the tutors in the math lab actually *are* rude and unhelpful. The difference is that Victims expend all their energy in judging themselves or others, whereas Creators use their energy to solve the problem. The voice we allow to occupy our thoughts determines our

> The object of teaching personal responsibility is to have the student substitute for the question "Who's to blame?" the question "What needs to be done?"
>
> *Nathaniel Branden*

choices, and our choices determine the outcomes and experiences of our lives. So choose your thoughts carefully. As mentioned earlier, I allow myself up to 10 minutes to complain, blame, and make excuses. Then I redirect that energy and look for what I can do about the situation.

THE LANGUAGE OF RESPONSIBILITY

Translating Victim statements into the responsible language of Creators moves you from stagnant judgments to dynamic actions. In the following chart, the left-hand column presents the Victim thoughts of a student who is taking a challenging college course. Thinking this way, the student's future in this course is easy to predict . . . and it isn't pretty.

But, if she changes her inner conversation, as shown in the right-hand column, she'll also change her behaviors. She can learn more in the course and increase her likelihood of passing. More important, she can learn to reclaim control of her life from the judgmental, self-sabotaging thoughts of her Inner Critic and Inner Defender.

As you read these translations, notice two qualities that characterize Creator language. First, Creators accept ownership of their situation. Second, they plan and take actions to improve their situation. So, when you hear **ownership** and a **plan**, you know you're talking to a Creator. At any moment, you can choose either mindset . . . and that choice will shape your destiny.

> You must change the way you talk to yourself about your life situations so that you no longer imply that anything outside of you is the immediate cause of your unhappiness. Instead of saying, "Joe makes me mad," say, "I make myself mad when I'm around Joe."
>
> *Ken Keyes*

VICTIMS FOCUS ON THEIR WEAKNESSES	CREATORS FOCUS ON HOW TO IMPROVE
I'm terrible in this subject.	I find this course challenging, so I'll start a study group and ask more questions in class.
VICTIMS MAKE EXCUSES	**CREATORS SEEK SOLUTIONS**
The instructor is so boring he puts me to sleep.	The instructor's teaching style makes it difficult for me to pay attention In this class, so I'll challenge myself to pay attention and take at least one page of notes each class period.
VICTIMS COMPLAIN	**CREATORS TURN COMPLAINTS INTO REQUESTS**
This course is a stupid requirement.	I don't understand why this course is required, so I'm going to ask my instructor to help me see how it will benefit me in the future.
VICTIMS COMPARE THEMSELVES UNFAVORABLY TO OTHERS	**CREATORS SEEK HELP FROM THOSE MORE SKILLED**
I'll never do as well as John; he's a genius.	I need help in this course, so I'm going to ask John if he'll help me study for the exams.
VICTIMS BLAME	**CREATORS ACCEPT RESPONSIBILITY**
The tests are ridiculous. The professor gave me an "F" on the first one.	I got an "F" on the first test because I didn't read the assignments thoroughly. From now on I'll take detailed notes on everything I read.

> Excuses rob you of power and induce apathy.
>
> *Agnes Whistling Elk*

(Continues)

(Continued)

VICTIMS SEE PROBLEMS AS PERMANENT	CREATORS TREAT PROBLEMS AS TEMPORARY
Posting comments on our class's Internet discussion board is impossible. I'll never understand how to do it.	I've been trying to post comments on our class's Internet discussion board without carefully reading the instructor's directions. I'll read the directions again and follow them one step at a time.
VICTIMS REPEAT INEFFECTIVE BEHAVIORS	**CREATORS DO SOMETHING NEW**
Going to the tutoring center is no help. There aren't enough tutors.	I've been going to the tutoring center right after lunch when it's really busy. I'll start going in the morning to see if more tutors are available then.
VICTIMS TRY	**CREATORS DO**
I'll try to do better.	To do better, I'll do the following: Attend class regularly, take good notes, ask questions in class, start a study group, and make an appointment with the teacher. If all that doesn't work, I'll think of something else.
VICTIMS PREDICT DEFEAT AND GIVE UP	**CREATORS THINK POSITIVELY AND LOOK FOR A BETTER CHOICE**
I'll probably fail. There's nothing I can do. I can't . . . I have to . . . I should . . . I quit . . .	I'll find a way. There's always something I can do. I can . . . I choose to . . . I will . . . I'll keep going . . .

I used to want the words "She tried" on my tombstone. Now I want, "She did it."

Katherine Dunham

When people choose a Victim mindset, they complain, blame, and make excuses, and they have little energy left over to solve their problems. As a result, they typically remain stuck where they are, telling their sad story over and over to any poor soul who will listen. (Ever hear of a "pity party"?) In this way, Victims exhaust not only their own energy but often drain the energy of the people around them.

Blaming . . . is a pastime for losers. There's no leverage in blaming. Power is rooted in self-responsibility.

Nathaniel Branden

By contrast, when people choose a Creator mindset, they use their words and thoughts to improve a bad situation. First, they accept responsibility for creating their present outcomes and experiences, and their words reflect that ownership. Next, they plan and take positive actions to improve their lives. *Ownership* and a *plan*. In this way, Creators energize themselves and the people around them.

Whenever you feel yourself slipping into Victim language, ask yourself: What do I want in my life—excuses or results? What could I think, say, and do right now that would get me moving toward the outcomes and experiences I want?

Journal Entry 6

In this activity you will practice the language of personal responsibility. By learning to translate Victim statements into Creator statements, you will master the language of successful people.

1. Draw a line down the middle of a journal page. On the left side of the line, copy the 10 Victim statements found on this page and the next page.

2. On the right side of the line, translate the Victim statements into the words of a Creator. The two keys to Creator language are taking ownership of a problem and taking positive actions to solve it. *Ownership* and a *plan*. When you respond as if you are responsible for a bad situation, then you are empowered to do something about it (unlike Victims, who must wait for someone else to solve their problems). Use the translations on previous pages as models.

3. Write what you have learned or relearned about how you use language: Is it your habit to speak as a Victim or as a Creator? Do you find yourself more inclined to blame yourself, blame others, or seek solutions? Be sure to give examples. What is your goal for language usage from now on? How, specifically, will you accomplish this goal? Your paragraph might begin, *While reading about and practicing Creator language, I learned that I . . .*

Remember to DIVE DEEP!

VICTIM LANGUAGE	CREATOR LANGUAGE
1. If they'd do something about the parking on campus, I wouldn't be late so often.	1.
2. I'm failing my online class because the site is impossible to navigate.	2.
3. I'm too shy to ask questions in class even when I'm confused.	3.
4. She's a lousy instructor. That's why I failed the first test.	4.
5. I hate group projects because people are lazy and I always end up doing most of the work.	5.

The way you use words has a tremendous impact on the quality of your life. Certain words are destructive; others are empowering.

Susan Jeffers

If you are in shackles, "I can't" has relevance; otherwise, it is usually a roundabout way of saying "I don't want to," "I won't," or, "I have not learned how to." If you really mean "I don't want to," it is important to come out and say so. Saying "I can't" disowns responsibility.

Gay Hendricks & Kathlyn Hendricks

437

VICTIM LANGUAGE	CREATOR LANGUAGE
6. I wish I could write better, but I just can't.	6.
7. My friend got me so angry that I can't even study for the exam.	7.
8. I'll try to do my best this semester.	8.
9. The financial aid form is too complicated to fill out.	9.
10. I work nights so I didn't have time to do the assignment.	10.

One Student's Story

ALEXSANDR KANEVSKIY
Oakland University, Michigan

When I began college, I was unmotivated and chose to blame others for my problems and my shortcomings. I was so much smarter than everyone that I didn't need to do all the work that everyone else did; at least that's what I thought. My favorite pastime was staring blankly at a television, rather than attending lecture or doing assigned homework. I figured everything would take care of itself without my interference. I had carried this uninhibited laziness with me through high school and it, unfortunately, translated into my college career. It was then that the gravitas of my situation hit me; at my current rate I was going to be dismissed from school. I was placed on academic probation my sophomore year and unless I improved, I was out.

This was when I first laid my eyes and hands on the *On Course* book. I didn't think much of it at first; just another guide for the misguided, full of backwards theories and advice that wouldn't help me, or anyone else. But from the first reading, I noticed that this book was different. It used different language, language that didn't bore me or induce disinterest. What's funniest, though, was that one of the first journals that I was assigned had the most profound impact on my changing as a student. Just as *On Course* used innovative and interesting language to teach, this journal was all about changing my own language. Rather than use language that blames others or is blatantly negative, that journal taught me to use positive Creator language.

I needed to think and speak in a language that searched for answers and solutions, not a language that kept me unmotivated and helpless. When I rephrased my thinking and speaking, the rest of life followed. All of a sudden, responsibility was in my own hands and the solutions that I needed, but was afraid to search out, became much clearer. Now that I knew there were, in fact, answers and solutions, I didn't look to blame those around me. I realized that it was up to me to find these solutions, that they would not magically appear before my eyes and that nobody else would find them for me. My faults and shortcomings became more apparent than ever, and my arrogance was startling. I saw that I was not smart enough to be exempt from school and from the work of my fellow students. They all searched for solutions and held themselves responsible for these solutions; I never realized this because I had never yearned for these solutions, and therefore never had responsibility.

(Continues)

I stopped expecting solutions to come to me naturally and started to work, rather than fall asleep at the television. Positive Creator language was only the first step, but what I took from this first lesson carried through to every other lesson in class and in life. I found that I was newly interested in my classes; homework became a pleasure because each assignment was yet another opportunity to learn. Rather than fall asleep at the television, I now fell asleep after studying. And probation? That became a thing of the past. Even in basketball (my sport of choice) I started to take more of an interest in passing, rather than scoring, and helping my teammates, instead of blaming them for mistakes. Amongst my friends I am now known as the "problem solver," which is just as surprising to me as it is to them. They've noticed a definite change, and I am glad to advise them to read my *On Course* book so that maybe they too will find a lesson that sparks their own improvement. *On Course* provided me with valuable steppingstones that have made me into a student and person who cares enough to take responsibility for his language and his actions, doing what needs to be done in order to succeed in school and in the outside world.

Making Wise Decisions

 Focus Questions How can you improve the quality of the decisions you make? How can you take personal responsibility for the outcomes and experiences in your life?

Life is a journey with many opportunities and obstacles, and each one requires a choice. Whatever you are experiencing in your life today is, to a great extent, the result of your past choices. More important, whatever you'll experience in the future will be fashioned greatly by the choices you make from this moment on.

This is an exciting thought. If we can make wiser choices, we can more likely create the future we want. On the road to a college degree, you will face important choices such as these:

Shall I . . .
- major in business, science, or creative writing?
- work full-time, part-time, or not at all?
- drop a course that bores me or stick it out?
- experiment with alcohol and drugs?
- study for my exam or go out with friends?

The sum of these choices, plus thousands of others, will determine your degree of success in college and in life. Doesn't it seem wise, then, to develop an effective strategy for choice management?

THE WISE CHOICE PROCESS

In the face of any challenge, you can make a responsible decision by answering the six questions of the Wise Choice Process. This process, you might be

> The end result of your life here on earth will always be the sum total of the choices you made while you were here.
>
> *Shad Helmstetter*

interested to know, is a variation of a decision-making model that is used in many career fields. For example, nurses learn a similar process for helping patients that is abbreviated ADPIE. These letters stand for Assess, Diagnose, Plan, Implement, and Evaluate. Counselors and therapists in training may learn a similar process for solving personal problems. This process was described in 1965 by William Glasser in his book *Reality Therapy*.

And the *NASA Systems Engineering Handbook* says, "Systems engineering [. . .] consists of identification and quantification of system goals, creation of alternative system design concepts, performance of design trades, selection and implementation of the best design, verification that the design is properly built and integrated, and post-implementation assessment of how well the system meets (or met) the goals." In layperson's terms, systems engineers use their version of the Wise Choice Process to achieve their goals.

You are about to learn a system that will empower you to take greater responsibility for creating your life as you want it to be despite the inevitable challenges that life presents.

1. **WHAT'S MY PRESENT SITUATION?** Begin by identifying your problem or challenge, being sure to define the situation as a Creator, not as a Victim. The important information here is "What exists?" (not "Whose fault is it?"). Quiet your Inner Critic, that self-criticizing voice in your head: *I am a total loser in my history class.* Likewise, ignore your Inner Defender, that judgmental voice that blames everyone else for your problems: *My history instructor is the worst teacher on the planet.* Instead, rely on your Inner Guide, your wise, impartial inner voice that tells the truth as best it can. Consider only the objective facts of your situation, including how you feel about them. For example:

   I stayed up all night studying for my first history test. When I finished taking the test, I hoped for an A. At worst, I expected a B. When I got the test back, my grade was a D. Five other students got A's. I feel depressed and angry.

   By the way, sometimes when we accurately define a troublesome situation, we immediately know what to do. The problem wasn't so much the situation as our muddy understanding of it.

2. **HOW WOULD I LIKE MY SITUATION TO BE?** You can't change the past, but if you could create your desired outcome in the future, what would it look like?

   I get A's on all of my future tests.

3. **WHAT ARE MY POSSIBLE CHOICES?** Create a list of possible choices that you *could* do, knowing you aren't obligated to do any of them. Compile your list without judgment. Don't say, "Oh, that would never work." Don't even say, "That's a great idea." Judgment during brainstorming stops the creative flow. Move from judgments to possibilities, discovering as many creative options as you can. Give yourself time to ponder, explore, consider, think, discover, conceive, invent, imagine. Then dive even deeper. If you get stuck, try one

of these options. First, take a different point of view. Think of someone you admire and ask, "What would that person do in my situation?" Or, pretend your problem belongs to someone else, and he asks you what you should do. What advice would you offer? Third, incubate. That is, set the problem aside and let your unconscious mind work on a solution while you do other things. Sometimes a great option will pop into your mind while you are brushing your hair, doing math homework, or even sleeping. Your patience will often pay off with a helpful option that would have remained invisible had you accepted the first idea that came to mind or, worse, given up.

- *I could complain to my history classmates and anyone else who will listen.*
- *I could drop the class and take it next semester with another instructor.*
- *I could complain to the department head that the instructor grades unfairly.*
- *I could ask my successful classmates for help.*
- *I could ask the instructor for suggestions about improving my grades.*
- *I could read about study skills and experiment with some new ways to study.*
- *I could request an opportunity to retake the test.*
- *I could take all of the online practice quizzes.*
- *I could get a tutor.*

4. WHAT'S THE LIKELY OUTCOME OF EACH POSSIBLE CHOICE?

Decide how you think each choice is likely to turn out. If you can't predict the outcome of one of your possible choices, stop this process and gather any additional information you need. For example, if you don't know the impact that dropping a course will have on your financial aid, find out before you take that action. Here are the possible choices from Step 3 and their likely outcomes:

- *Complain to history classmates: I'd have the immediate pleasure of criticizing the instructor and maybe getting others' sympathy.*
- *Drop the class: I'd lose three credits this semester and have to make them up later.*
- *Complain to the department head: Probably she'd ask if I've seen my instructor first, so I wouldn't get much satisfaction.*
- *Ask successful classmates for help: I might learn how to improve my study habits; I might also make new friends.*
- *Ask the instructor for suggestions: I might learn what to do next time to improve my grade; at least the instructor would learn that I want to do well in this course.*
- *Read about study skills: I would probably learn some strategies I don't know and maybe improve my test scores in all of my classes.*
- *Request an opportunity to retake the test: My request might get approved and give me an opportunity to raise my grade. At the very least, I'd demonstrate how much I want to do well.*

A person defines and redefines who they are by the choices they make, minute to minute.

Joyce Chapman

Destiny is not a matter of chance; it is a matter of choice. It is not a thing to be waited for; it is a thing to be achieved.

William Jennings Bryant

- *Take all of the online practice quizzes: This action wouldn't help my grade on this test, but it would probably improve my next test score.*
- *Get a tutor: A tutor would help, but it would probably take a lot of time.*

5. **WHICH CHOICE(S) WILL I COMMIT TO DOING?** Now create your plan. Decide which choice or choices will likely create your desired outcome; then commit to acting on them. If no favorable option exists, consider which choice leaves you no worse off than before. If no such option exists, then ask which choice creates the least unfavorable outcome. And remember that not making a choice is a choice.

I'll talk to my successful classmates, make an appointment with my instructor and ask him to explain what I can do to improve, and I'll request an opportunity to retake the test. I'll read the study skills sections of On Course *and implement at least three new study strategies. If these choices don't raise my next test score to at least a B, I'll get a tutor.*

Each situation will dictate the best options. In this example, if the student had previously failed four tests instead of one, the best choice might be to drop the class. Or, if everyone in the class were receiving D's and F's, and if the student had already met with the instructor, a responsible option might be to see the department head about the instructor's grading policies.

6. **WHEN AND HOW WILL I EVALUATE MY PLAN?** At some future time you will want to assess your results. To do so, compare your new situation to how you want it to be (as you described in Step 2). If the two situations are identical (or close enough), you can call your plan a success. If you find that you are still far from your desired outcome, you have some decisions to make. You might decide that you haven't implemented your new approach long enough, so you'll keep working your plan. Or you may decide that your plan just isn't working, in which case you'll return to Step 1 and work through Step 5 to design a plan that will work better. However, you're not starting completely over because this time you're smarter than you were when you began: Now you know what doesn't work.

After my next history test, I'll see if I have achieved my goal of getting an A. If not, I'll revise my plan.

Here's the bottom line: Our choices reveal what we *truly* believe and value, as opposed to what we *say* we believe and value. When I submissively wait for others to improve my life, I am being a Victim. When I passively wait for luck to go my way, I am being a Victim. When I make choices that take me off course from my future success just to increase my immediate pleasure (such as partying instead of studying for an important test), I am being a Victim. When I make choices that sacrifice my goals and dreams just to reduce my immediate discomfort (such as dropping a challenging course instead of spending extra hours working with a tutor), I am being a Victim.

However, when I design a plan to craft my life as I want it, I am being a Creator. When I carry out my plan even in the face of obstacles (such as when the campus bookstore runs out of a book that I need for class and I keep up with my assignments by reading a copy the instructor has placed on reserve in the library), I am being a Creator. When I take positive risks to advance my goals (such as asking a question in a large lecture class even though I am nervous), I am being a Creator. When I sacrifice immediate pleasure to stay on course toward my dreams (such as resisting the urge to buy a new cell phone so I can reduce my work hours to study more), I am being a Creator.

No matter what your final decision may be, the mere fact that you are defining and making your own choices is wonderfully empowering. By participating in the Wise Choice Process, you affirm your belief that you *can* change your life for the better. You reject the position that you are merely a Victim of outside forces, a pawn in the chess game of life. You insist on being the Creator of your own outcomes and experiences, shaping your destiny through the power of wise choices.

Journal Entry 7

In this activity you will apply the Wise Choice Process to improve a difficult situation in your life. Think about a current problem, one that you're comfortable sharing with your classmates and teacher. As a result of this problem, you may be angry, sad, frustrated, depressed, overwhelmed, or afraid. Perhaps this situation has to do with a grade you received, a teacher's comment, or a classmate's action. Maybe the problem relates to a job, a relationship, or money. The Wise Choice Process can help you make an empowering choice in any part of your life.

1. Write the six questions of the Wise Choice Process and answer each one as it relates to your situation.

The Wise Choice Process

1. What's my present situation? (Describe the problem objectively and completely.)
2. How would I like my situation to be? (What is your ideal future outcome?)
3. What are my possible choices? (Create a long list of specific choices that might create your preferred outcome.)
4. What's the likely outcome of each possible choice? (If you can't predict the likely outcome of an option, stop and gather more information.)
5. Which choice(s) will I commit to doing? (Pick from your list of choices in Step 3.)
6. When and how will I evaluate my plan? (Identify the specific date and criteria by which you will determine the success of your plan.)

2. Write what you learned or relearned by doing the Wise Choice Process. Be sure to Dive Deep. You might begin, *By doing the Wise Choice Process, I learned that I . . .*

Remember, you can enliven your journal by adding pictures cut from magazines, drawings of your own, clip art, or quotations that appeal to you.

One's philosophy is not best expressed in words; it is expressed in the choices one makes. In the long run, we shape our lives and we shape ourselves. The process never ends until we die. And, the choices we make are ultimately our own responsibility.

Eleanor Roosevelt

When I see all the choices I really have, it makes the world a whole lot brighter.

Debbie Scott, student

During my first semester of college I noticed a trend among my fellow students. Every time an assignment was due, many of them came to class with excuses instead of their completed work. I took this behavior personally because I had made time to complete all of my homework and prepare for class. I find it extremely disrespectful to the instructors and to those who come to class to learn whenever college students act like helpless children.

Also during my first semester, I happened to be taking "Strategies for Success," a class that introduced me to the *On Course* textbook. When I was invited to identify an important lesson worth sharing in a "One Page of Wisdom" assignment, I felt I needed to explain what I had learned throughout the semester the best way I knew how—through art. I looked back at The Wise Choice Process and the Responsibility Model for inspiration. As I did the preliminary sketches, I kept in mind the excuses I had heard students use over the last few months. I wanted my art to show that by making excuses, they were acting like Victims and were only hurting themselves.

I hope some of the students in my class saw themselves in the drawing; my goal was to make people think about their self-sabotaging habits and bad choices that stand in the way of their success. The road to success is filled with tough obstacles and tempting distractions, but by making wise choices at critical forks in the road, students on the journey will find success to be their ultimate destiny.

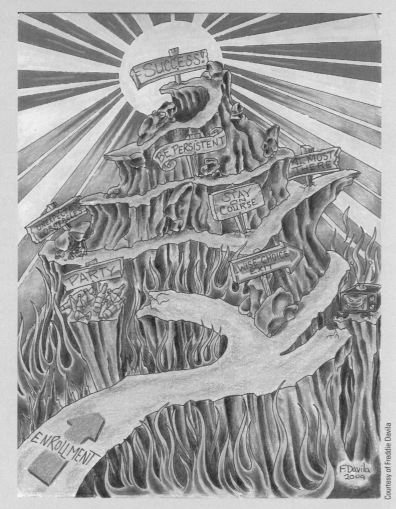

Courtesy of Freddie Davila

Photo: Courtesy of Freddie Davila

Personal Responsibility

AT WORK

A student once told me she'd had more than a dozen jobs in three years. "Why so many jobs?" I asked. "Bad luck," she replied. "I keep getting one lousy boss after another." Hmmmm, I wondered, 12 lousy bosses in a row? What are the odds of that?

Responsibility is about ownership. As long as I believe my career success belongs to someone else (like "lousy" bosses), I'm being a Victim, and my success is unlikely. Victims give little effort to choosing or preparing for a career. Instead, they allow influential others (such as parents and teachers) or circumstances to determine their choice of work. They complain about the jobs they have, make excuses for why they haven't gotten the jobs they want, and blame others or their own permanent flaws for their occupational woes. By contrast, Creators know that the foundation of success at work (as in college) is accepting this truth: *By our choices, we are each the primary creators of the outcomes and experiences of our lives.*

Accepting responsibility in the work world begins with consciously choosing your career path. You alone can decide what career is right for you. That's why Creators explore their career options thoroughly, match career requirements with their own talents and interests, consider the consequences of choosing each career (such as how much education the career requires or what the employment outlook is), and make informed choices. Choose your career wisely because few things in life are worse than spending 8 hours a day, 50 weeks a year, working at a job you hate.

Taking responsibility for your work life also means planning your career path to keep your options open and your progress unobstructed. For example, you could keep your career options open in college by taking only general education courses while investigating several possible fields of work. Or you could eliminate a financial obstacle by getting enough education—such as a dental hygiene degree—to support yourself while pursuing your dream career—such as going to dental school.

In short, Creators make use of the power of wise choices. They believe that there is always an option that will lead them toward the careers they want, and they take responsibility for creating the employment they want. Instead of passively waiting for a job to come to them, they actively go out and look. One of my students lost a job when the company where she worked closed. She could have spent hours in the cafeteria complaining about her bad fortune and how she could no longer afford to stay in school. Instead she created employment for herself by going from store to store in a mall asking every manager for a part-time job until one said, "Yes." In the time she could have wasted in the cafeteria complaining about her money problems, she solved them with positive actions.

When it comes to finding a full-time career position, Creators continue to be proactive. They don't wait for the perfect job opening to appear in their local paper or on an

445

Internet job site. They don't wait for a call from an employment agency. They know that employers prefer to hire people they know and like, so Creators do all they can to get known and liked by employers in their career field. They start by researching companies that need their talents and for which they might like to work. Then, they contact potential employers directly. They don't ask if the employer has a job opening. Instead, they seek an informational interview: "Hi, I've just gotten my degree in accounting, and I'd like to make an appointment to talk to you about your company. . . . What's that? You don't have any positions open at this time? No problem. I'm just gathering information at this point, looking for where my talents might make the most contributions. Would you have some time to meet with me this week? Or would next week be better?" Creators go to these information-gathering interviews prepared with knowledge about the company, good questions to ask, and a carefully prepared résumé. At the end of the meeting they ask if the interviewer knows employers who might need their skills. They call all of the leads they get and use the referral as an opening for a job interview: "I was speaking with John Smith at the Ajax Company, and he suggested that I give you a call about a position you have open." A friend of mine got an information-gathering interview and wowed the personnel manager with her professionally prepared résumé and interviewing skills; even though the company "had no openings" when she first called, two days after the interview, she was offered a position.

Accepting responsibility not only helps you *get* a great job, it makes it possible to *excel* on the job. Employers love responsible employees. Wouldn't you? Instead of complaining, blaming, making excuses, and thus creating an emotionally draining work environment, responsible employees create a positive workplace where absenteeism is low and work production is high. Instead of repeating ineffective solutions to problems, proactive employees seek solutions, take new actions, and try something new. They pursue alternative routes instead of complaining about dead ends. Creators show initiative instead of needing constant direction, and they do their best work even when the boss isn't looking. Creators are willing to go the extra mile, and this effort pays off handsomely. As someone once said, "There is no traffic jam on the extra mile." If you run into a challenge while preparing for a career, seeking a job, or working in your career, don't complain, blame, or make excuses. Instead, ask yourself a Creator's favorite question: "What's my plan?"

BELIEVING IN YOURSELF

Change Your Inner Conversation

 Focus Question How can you raise your self-esteem by changing your self-talk?

Imagine this: Three students schedule an appointment with their instructor to discuss a project they're working on together. They go to the instructor's office at the scheduled time, but he isn't there. They wait 45 minutes before leaving. As you learn what they do next, which student do you think has the strongest self-esteem?

Student 1, feeling discouraged and depressed, spends the evening watching television while neglecting assignments in other subjects. Student 2, feeling insulted and furious, spends the evening complaining to friends about the horrible instructor who stood them up. Student 3, feeling puzzled about the mix-up, emails the instructor to see what happened and to set up another meeting; while waiting for a response, this student spends the evening studying for a test in another class.

Which student has the strongest self-esteem?

It is the mind that maketh good or ill, That maketh wretch or happy, rich or poor.

Edmund Spencer

THE CURSE OF STINKIN' THINKIN'

How is it that three people can have the same experience and respond to it so differently? According to psychologists like Albert Ellis, the answer lies in what each person believes caused the event. Ellis suggested that different responses can be understood by realizing that the activating event (A) plus our beliefs (B) equal the consequences (C) (how we respond). In other words, A + B = C. For example:

Self-esteem can be defined as the state that exists when you are not arbitrarily haranguing and abusing yourself but choose to fight back against those automatic thoughts with meaningful rational responses.

Dr. Thomas Burns

Activating Event	+ Beliefs	= Consequence
Student #1: Instructor didn't show up for a scheduled conference.	My instructor thinks I'm dumb. I'll never get a college degree. I'm a failure in life.	Got depressed and watched television all evening.
Student #2: Same.	My instructor won't help me. Teachers don't care about students.	Got angry and spent the night telling friends how horrible the instructor is.
Student #3: Same.	I'm not sure what went wrong. Sometimes things just don't turn out the way you plan. There's always tomorrow.	Emailed the instructor to see what happened and to set up a new appointment; then studied for another class.

Ellis suggests that our upsets are caused not so much by our problems as by what we *think* about our problems. When our thinking is full of irrational beliefs—what Ellis calls "stinkin' thinkin'"—we feel awful even when the circumstances don't warrant it. So, how we *think* about the events in our lives is the key issue. Problems may come and go, but our "stinkin' thinkin'" stays with us. As the old saying goes, "Everywhere I go, there I am."

Stinkin' thinkin' isn't based on reality. Rather, these irrational thoughts are the automatic chatter of the Inner Critic (keeper of Negative Beliefs about the self) and the Inner Defender (keeper of Negative Beliefs about other people and the world).

So what about our three students and their self-esteem? It's not hard to see that student 1, who got depressed and wasted the evening watching television, has low self-esteem. This student is thrown far off course simply by the instructor's not showing up. A major cause of this self-defeating reaction is the Inner Critic's harsh self-judgments. Here are some common self-damning beliefs held by Inner Critics:

I'm dumb.	I'm unattractive.
I'm selfish.	I'm lazy.
I'm a failure.	I'm not college material
I'm incapable.	I'm weak.
I'm not as good as other people.	I'm a lousy parent.
I'm worthless.	I'm unlovable.

People dominated by their Inner Critic often misinterpret events, inventing criticisms that aren't there. A friend says, "Something came up, and I can't meet you tonight." The Inner Critic responds, "I screwed up again! I'll never have any friends!"

The activating event doesn't cause the consequence; rather, the judgmental chatter of the Inner Critic does. A strong Inner Critic is both a cause and an effect of low self-esteem.

What about student 2, the one who spent the evening telling friends how horrible the instructor was? Though perhaps less apparent, this student's judgmental response also demonstrates low self-esteem. The finger-pointing Inner Defender is merely the Inner Critic turned outward and is just as effective at getting the student off course. Here are some examples of destructive beliefs held by an Inner Defender:

People don't treat me right, so they're rotten.
People don't act the way I want them to, so they're awful.
People don't live up to my expectations, so they're the enemy.
People don't do what I want, so they're against me.
Life is full of problems, so it's terrible.
Life is unfair, so I can't stand it.
Life doesn't always go my way, so I can't be happy.
Life doesn't provide me with everything I want, so it's unbearable.

People dominated by their Inner Defender imagine personal insults and slights in neutral events. A classmate says, "Something came up, and I can't meet you tonight." The Inner Defender responds, "Who do you think you are, anyway? I can find someone a lot better to study with than you!"

The activating event doesn't cause the angry response; rather, the judgmental chatter of the judgmental Inner Defender does. A strong Inner Defender is both a cause and an effect of low self-esteem.

Only student 3 demonstrates high self-esteem. This student realizes he doesn't know why the instructor missed the meeting. He doesn't blame himself, the instructor, or a rotten world. He considers alternatives: Perhaps the instructor got sick or was involved in a traffic accident. Until he finds out what happened and decides what to do next, this student turns his attention to an action that will keep him on course to another goal. The Inner Guide is concerned with positive results, not judging self or others. A strong Inner Guide is both a cause and an effect of high self-esteem.

DISPUTING IRRATIONAL BELIEFS

How, then, can you avoid stinkin' thinkin'?

First, you can become aware of the chatter of your Inner Critic and Inner Defender. Be especially alert when events in your life go wrong, when your desired outcomes and experiences are thwarted. That's when we are most likely to complain, blame, and excuse. That's when we substitute judgments of ourselves or others for the positive actions that would get us back on course.

Once you become familiar with your inner voices, you can begin a process of separating yourself from your Inner Critic and Inner Defender. To do this, practice disputing your irrational and self-sabotaging beliefs. Here are four effective ways to dispute:

- **Offer evidence that your judgments are incorrect:** *My instructor emailed me last week to see if I needed help with my project, so there's no rational reason to believe he won't help me now.*

- **Offer a positive explanation of the problem:** *Sure my instructor didn't show up, but he may have missed the appointment because of a last-minute crisis.*

- **Question the importance of the problem:** *Even if my instructor won't help me, I can still do well on this project, and if I don't, it won't be the end of the world.*

- **If you find that your judgments are true, instead of continuing to criticize yourself or someone else, offer a plan to improve the situation:** *If I'm honest, I have to admit that I haven't done well in this class so far, but from now on I'm going to attend every class, take good notes, read my assignments two or three times, and work with a study group before every test.*

According to psychologist Ellis, a key to correcting irrational thinking is changing a "must" into a preference. When we think "must," what follows in our thoughts is typically awful, terrible, and dreadful. For example, my Inner Defender's belief that an instructor "must" meet me for an appointment or he is an awful, terrible, dreadful person is irrational; I'd certainly "prefer" him to meet me for an

Replacing a negative thought with a positive one changes more than just the passing thought—it changes the way you perceive and deal with the world.

Dr. Clair Douglas

Does it help to change what you say to yourself? It most certainly does.... Tell yourself often enough that you'll succeed and you dramatically improve your chances of succeeding and of feeling good.

Drs. Bernie Zilbergeld & Arnold A. Lazarus

appointment, but his not meeting me does not make him horrible—in fact, he may have a perfectly good reason for not meeting with me. As another example, my Inner Critic's belief that I "must" pass this course or I am an awful, terrible, dreadful person is irrational; I'd certainly "prefer" to pass this course, but not doing so does not make me worthless—in fact, not passing this course may lead me to something even better. Believing irrationally that I, another person, or the world "must" be a particular way, Ellis says, is a major cause of my distress and misery.

STEREOTYPE THREAT

Social psychologist Claude Steele of Stanford University has identified a kind of stinkin' thinkin' that afflicts cultural groups: *stereotype threat*. A stereotype is a generalization about members of a particular group. For example, African Americans are all excellent in sports but they aren't good students . . . or women are all terrific at taking care of children but they are poor at math and science. Stereotype threat is a fear that your behavior in a particular situation—such as taking a math test—might confirm a negative stereotype about a cultural group to which you belong. The resulting anxiety causes a self-fulfilling prophesy, and you do, indeed, perform down to the stereotype rather than up to your ability.

As an example of the effect of stereotype threat, Steele and his colleagues showed that when race was emphasized, African-American college students did less well than their white classmates on a standardized test. However, when race was not emphasized, African-American students' scores were equivalent to those of white students. Further studies have shown that the academic success of many cultural groups fall prey to stereotype threat, including Latinos, females in math, and students of working-class backgrounds.

Here's how stinkin' thinkin' seems to contribute to stereotype threat. Let's say a female student sits down to take a math test. That's the activating event. Next come her beliefs: She knows the stereotype—women aren't good at math. She doesn't want to be lumped into or reinforce that stereotype. She becomes anxious, distracted, and can't remember all she studied. The result is a self-fulfilling prophesy. She doesn't do as well on the test as she is capable of, and the culprit is her stinkin' thinkin'.

Besides causing immediate problems in test situations, stereotype threat may even cause people to avoid the threat area altogether. A woman may avoid majoring in math and science. A white man may reject playing basketball. A working-class student may lose motivation and drop out of college.

The strategies for disputing that were mentioned earlier can also be applied to stereotype threat. A woman may **offer evidence that the stereotype is wrong**: *I did pretty well in math and science in high school . . . and I just read that four women recently won Nobel Prizes in science and mathematics*. A white man may **question the importance of the stereotype**: *I may not be the best player on the basketball team, but so what . . . it's great fun*. A working-class student may **offer a plan to address the stereotype**: *My English teacher told us her parents were migrant farm workers; I'm going to talk to her about how she kept herself motivated to get a college degree*.

Another way to reduce the negative impact of stereotype threat has been suggested by psychologists Michael Johns, Toni Schmader, and Andy Martens in a

You mainly make yourself needlessly and neurotically miserable by strongly holding absolutist irrational beliefs, especially by rigidly believing unconditional shoulds, oughts, and musts.

Albert Ellis

Everyone experiences stereotype threat. We are all members of some group about which negative stereotypes exist, from white males and Methodists to women and the elderly.

Claude M. Steele

study at the University of Arizona. They gave a math test to one group of students and found that female students performed worse than the men. Before giving the math test to a second group, they told students briefly about how stereotype threat could negatively affect the performance of women. Specifically, they announced, "It's important to keep in mind that if you are feeling anxious while taking this test, this anxiety could be the result of these negative stereotypes that are widely known in society and have nothing to do with your actual ability to do well on the test." In this second round of tests, female students did as well as the men. It seems that simply knowing about stereotype threat can reduce its power.

The guiding principle in this section is simple: Choose wisely the thoughts you allow to occupy your mind. Avoid letting automatic, negative thoughts or negative stereotypes undermine your self-esteem or your results. Evict stinkin' thinkin' and replace it with thoughts that empower.

 Journal Entry 8

In this activity, you will practice disputing the judgments of your Inner Critic and your Inner Defender. As you become more skilled at seeing yourself, other people, and the world more objectively and without distracting judgments, your self-esteem will thrive.

1. Write a sentence expressing a recent problem or event that upset you. Think of something troubling that happened in school, at work, or in your personal life. For example, *I got a 62 on my math test.*

2. Write a list of three or more criticisms your Inner Critic (IC) might level against you as a result of this situation. Have your Inner Guide (IG) dispute each one immediately. Review the four methods of disputing described on page 65. You only need to use one of them for each criticism. For example,

IC: You failed that math test because you're terrible in math.

IG: It's true I failed the math test, but I'll study harder next time and do better. This was only the first test, and I now know what to expect next time.

3. Write a list of three or more criticisms your Inner Defender (ID) might level against someone else or life as a result of this situation. Have your Inner Guide (IG) dispute each one immediately. Again use one of the four methods for disputing. For example,

ID: You failed that math test because you've got the worst math instructor on campus.

IG: I have trouble understanding my math instructor, so I'm going to make an appointment to talk with him in private. John really liked him last semester, so I bet I'll like him, too, if I give him a chance.

4. **Make a choice: Write about one of the following:**

A. **Write what you have learned or relearned about changing your inner conversation.** Your journal entry might begin, *In reading and writing about my inner conversations, I have discovered that . . . .* Wherever possible, offer personal experiences or examples to explain what you learned.

B. One instructor said about this journal entry: "While I understand the importance of having students change their inner conversations, I don't think they ever actually apply what they write in their journals to the challenging situations in their lives. In other words, there's a big gap between what they learn and what they do." **Write a reply to this instructor expressing your opinion about her concern.**

One Student's Story

DOMINIC GRASSETH
Lane Community College, Oregon

Enrolling in college at the age of 28 was very intimidating to me. Having dropped out of high school at 15, I had a real problem with confidence. Even though I had a GED and was earning a decent living as a car salesman, I still doubted that I was smart enough to be successful in college. I finally took the leap and enrolled because I want a career where I don't have to work 12 hours a day, six days a week and never see my family. However, by the second week of the semester, I found myself falling back into old habits. I was sitting in the back of the classroom, asking what homework was due, and talking through most of the class. Negative thoughts constantly ran through my mind: *The teachers won't like me. I can't compete with the 18-year-olds right out of high school. I don't even remember what a "verb" is. I can't do this.*

Then in my College Success class, we read Chapter 2 of *On Course* about becoming a Creator and disputing "stinkin' thinkin'." I realized I had taken on the role of the Victim almost my whole life, and I was continuing to do it now. One day I was on my porch when I caught myself thinking my usual negative thoughts. It occurred to me that I was the only one holding me back, not the teachers, not the other students, not math, not English. If I wanted to be successful in college, I had to quit being scared.

I had to change my thinking. So I made a deal with myself that any time I caught myself thinking negatively, I would rephrase the statement in a way that was more positive. I started to truly pay attention to the thoughts in my head and question the negative things I was telling myself. After that I began sitting up front in my classes and participating more. I've always been kind of scattered, so I started using a calendar and a dry-erase board to keep track of what I had to do.

What amazes me is that I didn't really make that big of a change, yet I finished the semester with a 4.0 average! All I did was realize that what I was saying to myself was my underlying problem. I am responsible for my thoughts, and the choice about whether or not to succeed is mine. These days when I have a ridiculous thought going through my mind and I change it, I smile. It's very empowering.

Photo: Courtesy of Dominic Grasseth

Goal Setting

15

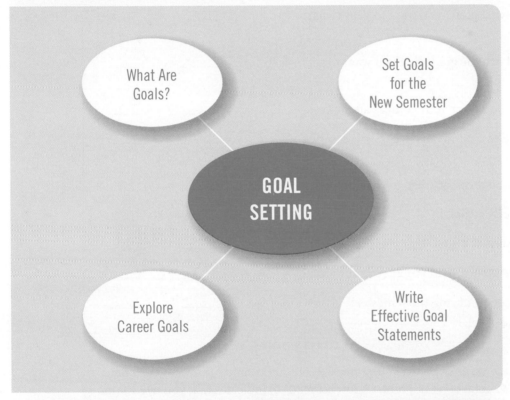

What Are Goals?

Set Goals for the New Semester

GOAL SETTING

Explore Career Goals

Write Effective Goal Statements

"Goal setting has helped me in a number of ways. I have found that setting goals for myself creates a sense of excitement. I know that if I set my mind to accomplish something, I can. This has been especially helpful in planning long-term goals. I have a sense of knowing that I will accomplish those goals no matter what obstacles may come into view."

Maria Mardis, Student

TERMS YOU SHOULD KNOW

Make a flash card for each term and/or use the flash cards on the Web site to learn the definitions.

Academic goals
Action plan
Action tasks
Career goals

Goals
Long-term goals
Personal goals
Proximal goals

Self-assessment
Short-term goals
Study goals

Where Are You Now?

Take a few minutes to answer *yes* or *no* to the following questions.

	YES	NO
1. Have you decided what grade point average (GPA) you want to achieve this semester?	_____	_____
2. Have you decided what grade you want to get in each of your courses?	_____	_____
3. Have you written down the grade that you want to get in each of your courses?	_____	_____
4. Are the goals that you set for your courses attainable?	_____	_____
5. Do you use words like *try* and *hope* when you describe your goals?	_____	_____
6. Have you thought about careers that you might want to pursue?	_____	_____
7. Do you set daily study goals?	_____	_____
8. Do you tend to achieve the goals that you set?	_____	_____
9. Do you tend to give up if you don't achieve your goals?	_____	_____
10. Do you revise your goals during the semester?	_____	_____
TOTAL POINTS	_____	

Give yourself 1 point for each *yes* answer to all questions except 5 and 9, and 1 point for each *no* answer to questions 5 and 9. Total up your points. A low score (0–4) indicates that you need some help in setting goals. A score of 5 to 7 indicates that you are effectively setting goals in some areas but not in others. A high score (8–10) indicates that you are using effective goal-setting strategies. What did you learn about yourself by completing this activity?

_____

_____

_____

WHAT ARE GOALS?

Goals are the ends toward which you direct your effort. In other words, goals are things you want to achieve, things you aim for as you pursue a certain course of action. Goals provide the motive for the effort that you expend when completing a task. Without goals there would be no effort. You can improve your academic performance in college by learning to set goals that motivate you to do well and that increase your chances for success.

Why Are Goals Important?

Goals are important in college because they help motivate you to attend classes, do your work, and study for exams. Without goals, you might not get out of bed to go to class; you might play video games all day instead of completing your assignments; or you might decide to go to a party rather than prepare for an exam. Of course, even in those cases, goals were driving your actions—just not toward any of your academic tasks. By setting goals, you can make decisions about how to spend your day. You can decide what to do, when to do it, how to do it, and even how hard to work on it.

Although you need motivation to achieve your goals, goals can also help you increase your level of motivation. How you set goals has an impact on whether they will motivate you. For example, research studies have shown that setting specific goals is more motivating than setting vague goals. When you know exactly what you want to accomplish, you'll be more motivated to complete the task. Short-term goals are also more motivating than long-term goals because they can be more easily achieved.

Goal Setting and Motivation

Achieving your goals also increases your motivation. Each time you achieve one of your goals, there are two important outcomes: You experience a sense of accomplishment and you increase your self-efficacy (your belief that you can successfully complete the task). As a result, you will have higher motivation to complete similar tasks in the future. Pintrich and Shunk, who conduct research studies on motivation, goals, and self-regulation, found that "when students attain their learning goals, goal attainment conveys to them that they possess the requisite capabilities for learning."[1] In other words, each time you achieve one of your learning goals, you reinforce in yourself the knowledge that you are capable of learning. These beliefs then motivate you to set new, challenging goals.[2]

---

[1] P. Pintrich and D. Shunk, *Motivation in Education: Theory, Research, and Applications* (Prentice Hall: Englewood Cliffs, NJ, 1996), p. 6.

[2] Ibid.

Goal Setting Improves Performance

You learned in Chapter 1 that setting goals increases your motivation and that being motivated improves your performance. You may be asking, how does that actually happen? According to Locke and Latham, who do research on goal setting, there are four main reasons to explain the process.[3]

- **Goals direct your attention to the task at hand.** Goals keep you working on an assignment and direct you back to it if you begin to think about something else or are distracted.
- **Goals mobilize effort.** Goals motivate you to work hard (to increase your effort) in order to complete the task.
- **Goals increase persistence.** Goals help you continue to work on the task (persevere) even when the task becomes difficult.
- **Goals promote the development of new strategies when old strategies fall short.** Goals help you monitor (keep track of and evaluate) the effectiveness of the strategy or strategies that you are using to complete the task. Goals can help you determine whether the strategy is working, and, if it isn't, goals can motivate you to select another strategy to use.

Characteristics of Goals

To be both useful and motivating, the goals you set must have some important characteristics. Your goals should be self-chosen, moderately challenging, realistic, measurable, specific, finite, and positive (see Figure 15.1).

FIGURE 15.1

Characteristics of Goals

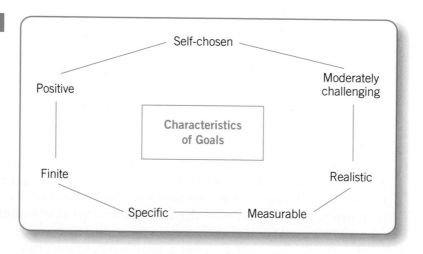

---

[3]E. A. Locke and G. P. Latham, *A Theory of Goal Setting and Task Performance* (Englewood Cliffs, NJ: Prentice Hall, 1990).

1. **Goals should be self-chosen.** Goals that are set by your parents, teachers, or friends may not always work for you. You need to determine or choose your own goals; you need to decide what you want to accomplish. If you set your own goals, you will be more motivated to achieve them.

2. **Goals should be moderately challenging.** You probably were told to set high or even exceptionally high goals for yourself in college; you may have been told to "shoot for the stars" or "go for straight As." In fact, this may not be the best advice. If your goal is to achieve all As during your first semester in college, you may be disappointed. As soon as you "lose your A" in one class, you may feel that you failed to achieve your goal and be tempted to give up.

   One way to set moderately challenging goals is to consider what you have done in the past. Of course, everyone is different, but high school grades are fairly good predictors of college success. Why were you successful in some classes yet unsuccessful in others? You may have been more motivated, so you may have worked harder. Of course, if you didn't work very hard in high school, you can do better in college if you choose to apply yourself; increased effort can make a difference. Even so, you should set moderately challenging goals that will require you to achieve more than you did before but will not place undue pressure on you.

3. **Goals should be realistic.** Think about whether your goals are attainable. It would be unrealistic to expect to get a B or better in Calculus if your math background is very weak and your high school grades in math were never higher than a C. To set realistic goals, you must carefully evaluate your chances of achieving each goal. Using the Five-Step Approach to setting goals (discussed later in this chapter) can help you make this decision.

4. **Goals should be measurable.** A goal is measurable if you can determine whether you reached it. It would be difficult to determine whether you achieved your goal if you just wanted to "do well in a course." How can you measure that? What does "well" really mean? It undoubtedly means different things to different people. It would be much easier to measure your success if you had aimed for an A or a B. At the end of the semester, you should be able to look at your final grade in a course and at the grade you set as your goal and evaluate your effort.

   Goals for specific study sessions need to be measurable, too. Studying chemistry is not a measurable goal. "I will read pages 12 to 22 in my chemistry text and work all the sample problems" is a good example of a measurable goal statement. At the end of your study session, you'll be able to determine whether you did what you planned to do.

5. **Goals should be specific.** The more specific your goals are, the more motivated you'll be to achieve them. Getting a B+ in College Algebra is a specific goal; getting a "good grade" in College Algebra is not. Study goals should be specific, too. The goal "I'll do my homework at 7:00" is rather vague. It's

important to think of your homework as a series of individual assignments. You need to write separate goals for each of your assignments. A more specific goal statement is, "I'll do problems 1 to 20 in my chemistry text (page 54) at 7:00 on Tuesday."

6. **Goals should be finite.** Goals need to have a limited time frame. You just learned that you need to set a specific time to start a study goal. You need to set a specific time to complete your goals, too. Setting deadlines to complete your study goals seems rather obvious. If a paper is due by Friday, you need to have it done by Friday. However, you might decide to have the paper done by Wednesday so that you can prepare for your big biology exam on Friday. You might also want to set intermediate deadlines to complete different parts of a task. Without a deadline, many students tend to put off starting, working on, and completing their tasks. As you'll see in the next chapter, setting deadlines is also an important time management tool.

7. **Goals should be positive.** Negative goal statements tend to make you feel that you can't really succeed; they aren't motivating. "I don't want to get any lower than a C in any of my classes," "I won't go to dinner until I get this Calculus work done," and "I'm not going to fail this test" are all examples of negative goal statements. You'll always do better if you are working toward something— when you have a positive attitude.

Also avoid using words like *try, think, hope,* and *should* when you describe your goals. What's wrong with including those kinds of words? You're right if you said that they offer "a way out." If you state your goal this way: "I'm going to *try* to write my sociology essay tonight," and later push your paper away unfinished, you may say to yourself, "Well, I did *try.*" Positive goals that emphasize success help motivate you to get your work done.

Long- and Short-Term Goals

Most students have long-term goals in mind when they enter college. Even if you don't know exactly what major you want to pursue, you have probably thought about getting a degree and getting a job. You may even know what field interests you most. Long-term goals are helpful to your success in college because they give you direction. *Long-term goals* are the objectives you set for yourself for the end of the year, for four or five years from now, or even for a lifetime. However, there are times when long-term goals can seem awfully far in the future. That's where short-term goals can help. *Short-term goals,* also known as *proximal goals,* can be set for an hour from now, for the end of the day, week, month, or semester. Completing a reading assignment, writing an essay, getting a B in a course, getting off probation, or making the Dean's List are all examples of short-term goals. Think of your short-term goals as steps toward achieving the long-term goals you've set for yourself. By accomplishing daily, weekly, and semester goals, you move closer to your long-range academic, personal, and career goals.

Academic, Personal, and Career Goals

In college it's important to balance your academic, personal, and career goals. *Academic goals* relate to your course work. They include things like going to class, completing assignments, and preparing for exams. Your academic goals should be your highest priority in college. To achieve your academic goals, you need to learn to set study goals, too. *Study goals* can be defined as the objectives you want to achieve during a particular study session. During a study session, you might complete a reading assignment, begin work on a term paper, or prepare for an exam.

Personal goals, like making new friends, participating in clubs or sporting events, exercising, or even doing your laundry, are important, too. However, if you allow yourself to focus only on your personal goals, you may find that you have little time left for study.

Career goals are long-term goals that guide you toward the type of work you want to pursue after graduation. Doing well in college now can help you achieve those goals. Think about what you want to do five years from now, or even ten years after that. What are your aspirations for the future? Later in this chapter, you'll have an opportunity to explore your career goals. For now, though, remember that career goals can motivate you to achieve both your academic and your personal goals.

SET GOALS FOR THE NEW SEMESTER

The most important time to set your goals and start using specific strategies for achieving them is during the first three weeks of the semester. Setting new goals often involves making changes. You need to be willing to change the way you do some things to achieve your goals. If you make academics your first priority and get off to a good start in each of your classes, you'll find you'll continue to do well throughout the semester. Some of the strategies that will help you achieve the academic goals you set include: being open to change, setting priorities, planning for early success, learning to calculate your GPA, and revising your goals periodically.

Be Open to Change

Throughout this text you'll be introduced to a wide variety of new learning and study strategies. Although it's important for you to learn how and when to use these strategies, you also need to apply the strategies to your own course work both in and out of class. Some students welcome the opportunity to learn new study strategies, but others find the idea of changing the way they study and learn to be somewhat threatening.

Reasons Students Are Reluctant to Make Changes

Some students are reluctant to make changes. Are you? Prochaska and Prochaska suggest four reasons that people have difficulty changing their behavior: (1)They believe they can't change, (2) they don't want to change, (3) they don't know what to change, and (4) they don't know how to change.[4] I've also discovered from my own students that there are other reasons that students are reluctant to make changes, especially academic changes. These reasons are: (1) they don't think the change will help, (2) they don't use the strategies correctly, and (3) they don't achieve success immediately. Let's take a closer look at each of these reasons.

They Believe they Can't Change. Some students actually believe that they cannot change the way they do things. Some of them say things like, "I've always been a C student," or "I can't do it any other way; that's the way I am." In many cases that belief actually makes students more reluctant to try new strategies, perhaps because they don't believe that anything will make a difference in their performance.

They Don't Want to Change. Some students have a hard time changing the way they do things—they like keeping things the same. A few years ago I had a student named Jeff in my class. He told me that he had failed his first Psychology exam and was upset about his grade. He asked me for some specific suggestions for how he should study for the exam. I spent some time talking with him and suggested that he start studying by making flash cards for all of the terms, predicting test questions, and self-testing with both. A few weeks later, Jeff came to class and told me that he had failed his second exam. I was surprised that he had done so poorly and asked him how many of his word cards and questions had appeared on the exam. He replied that he hadn't made any cards and hadn't predicted any questions. When I asked him why he hadn't used those strategies, he responded that he felt comfortable studying his way. I tried one more time to explain why he needed to change the way he studied but he seemed unwilling to do anything other than read over the material three more times. He kept saying that he liked doing it his way. I finally said (rather loudly), "But your way isn't working, is it?" Finally, I promised him that if he would just try this new way to study one time, I'd never bug him again. He probably saw that as a way to get me off his back, so he did agree to try the strategies. Several weeks later, Jeff came to class very proud to report that he had gotten

[4] J. O. Prochaska and J. M. Prochaska, "Why Don't Continents Move? Why Don't People Change?" *Journal of Psychotherapy Integration*, 9 (1) (1999): 83–102.

an A on his third Psychology exam. With a sheepish grin, he admitted that my suggestions did help. From that point on, Jeff was willing to try new strategies.

When your old ways of doing things aren't working, even though they are familiar and comfortable, you need to be willing to try something else.

They Don't Know What to Change. Many students start college studying the same way they did in high school. They use methods that worked just fine at that time, only to find that they don't work for their college exams. These students are often very frustrated because they don't know what to do differently. They don't know what they are doing that is working and what they are doing that isn't working.

They Don't Know How to Change. Many students know that their study methods aren't working. They may even realize that reading over their notes three times, or reading the chapter six times, didn't help them answer the exam questions. They don't know, though, how to do it differently, so they don't make any changes. They haven't been taught or haven't discovered on their own other more effective ways to learn the material.

They Don't Think the Change Will Help. Some students are reluctant to try new strategies because they don't think they will work. They may be feeling that it's not worth their time or their effort to use a different strategy, because the outcome won't be any different. When students know that something will work, they are more willing to try it. Are you? When you aren't sure a strategy will work, you may not be motivated enough to spend the time and effort to use it.

They Don't Use the Strategies Correctly. Some students are willing to try a new study strategy once to see if it will work. Whether they ever use it again seems to depend on many factors. One of them is whether the strategy worked. Perhaps you've had this same experience. Susan decided to make up question cards to prepare for one of her exams. She came to my office to tell me that the strategy just didn't work and she didn't plan to use it again. When I asked her why she felt that way, she told me that she had failed her exam. I asked her how many question cards she had prepared, and was shocked when she told me she had made 200 question cards. That certainly seemed like a sufficient number of cards to prepare for a test on four chapters. I then asked Susan how many times she had practiced answering her questions. She responded that she didn't have time to practice them; it had taken her right up to the test time to make them out. I tried to explain to Susan that she had only used the first part of the strategy, and that she also had to practice answering the questions until she knew them all.

They Don't Achieve Success Immediately. Some students are reluctant to continue using a new strategy when they don't achieve their goals on the first try. A student,

Leroy, had earned an F on his first exam in History and decided to use the Five-Day Study Plan to prepare for his next exam. He decided that using that strategy should help him earn a B on the exam, and he worked hard to get that B. When he got his exam back, he was disappointed with his grade and told me that the strategy didn't work and he wouldn't use it again. When I asked why he felt that way, he told me he had only gotten a 79 percent on the test—a C. I asked him what grade he needed to earn a B, and he said an 80 percent. He didn't seem to realize that he had earned a high C instead of an F, or that he was only 1 point from a B.

Change Takes Time

Learning new strategies will help you achieve your goals, but change does take time. Not all of the strategies presented in this text or in your class are going to work for you. That's why you need to try each one and find the ones that work for you. As you experiment with the various strategies, keep track of your progress. If you don't reach your goal the first time you try a new strategy, don't give up on it. You may need to practice using the strategy a few times until you master it; or you may need to check with your professor to make sure that you're using it correctly. You may find that making even a small change in the way you're using a strategy will help you be more successful. When you see how the changes you make (over a period of weeks) improve your performance, you'll be more open to make other changes.

Set Priorities for the First Three Weeks

If you make academic goals your top priority for the first three weeks, you'll practically ensure success. Many students think that the first few weeks of a new semester are a breeze; typically, there are no exams, and often there are few papers, projects, or presentations. What you do during those first few weeks, though, often affects your performance during the rest of the semester. If you start doing your reading and other assignments right from the beginning, getting your work done will become a habit. In the same way, attending classes and meeting with study groups and tutors will also become part of your daily routine. Another real advantage of working hard right from the start is not falling behind in your work. If you don't keep up with your assignments, you may never catch up before your first round of exams and you won't be properly prepared for them. On the other hand, if you work hard during the first three weeks, you'll be able to find out early if your strategies are working. If they aren't, you can make changes before your exams. By working especially hard at the beginning of the semester, you also learn to make your academic goals your top priority.

Plan for Early Success

Another way to get off to the right start is to plan for early success. Earning an A or a B on the first quiz or first homework assignment should be one of your short-term goals. Once you get an A or B on one of your quizzes or assignments, you won't want to lose it. That first A or B lets you know you can do the work—thus increasing your self-efficacy. Your early success lets you know that by attending all your classes and working hard, you can succeed. That motivates you to keep working hard in all your classes. Early success leads to more success because:

- Success increases motivation.
- Success builds self-efficacy.
- Success lets you know that your strategies are working.

The Tip Block on next page lists ten tips that should help you get off to the right start this semester. Read through the list now and put a check mark (✓) in the box next to the tips that you use already. Put a star (*) in the box next to the tips that you want to use.

Plan Rewards

When you think about achieving your goals, a ten- or fifteen-week semester can seem like a long time to wait. Unfortunately, there aren't many "warm fuzzies" or immediate rewards in college. You may not get a grade on an assignment until the fourth or even the seventh week of the semester. You also may find that you miss that pat on the back or verbal recognition that you got in high school. It can be hard to stay motivated when no one is "telling you" that all your hard work is paying off, so you need to begin to reward yourself. Establish a method for rewarding yourself for knowing the answers to the questions that the professor asks in class, for being able to explain the solution to a problem, or even for being up to date on your reading assignments. If no one else is there to give you that pat on the back, give it to yourself.

Consider Consequences

If using rewards isn't helping you achieve your short-term goals, you may need to consider seriously the consequences of your actions. Think about how not achieving one or two of your short-term goals might affect the successful completion of your long-term goals. You learned earlier in the chapter that each of your goals is made up of a series of steps or smaller short-term goals. If you leave out one or two of those steps, you may not be able to complete the larger task. Consider the steps to achieving your goal as rungs of a ladder. If you eliminate too many or even one at a critical location, you may never get to the top: Each step is crucial for achieving success.

Ten Tips to Get Off to the Right Start This Semester

☐ **Be selective in choosing classes.** Choose courses your first semester that will help you build the skills you need to succeed in college or entry-level courses in your major. Taking a class you find interesting is another good way to start out. Your advisor will help you select appropriate courses.

☐ **Go to all classes and take notes.** Your goal is to write down as much information as you can. Four weeks from now, you won't remember much of what you heard today. Edit your notes within twenty-four hours to organize and expand on the information.

☐ **Keep up with your reading assignments.** Break down long reading assignments into more manageable units of about seven to ten pages. Read ten pages, then switch to another subject. Take a short break; then go back and read ten more pages. Remember to carefully highlight your text or take notes as you read.

☐ **Learn to say no.** While you're attending college, you don't have time for many outside activities. You may find that working, taking care of yourself and your family, and going to school is all you can handle. When you do say no, explain that when you complete your education, you'll be happy to help out.

☐ **Create a good study environment.** Find a quiet place to study. If studying in your dorm room or at the kitchen table is too distracting, find another place to do your work.

☐ **Set realistic grade goals.** Although many students are very successful in college, they don't get all As their first semester. Earning a B or a C your first semester (or any semester) is fine. Consider what you can accomplish in each of your courses.

☐ **Study for exams by writing and reciting out loud.** You won't learn the information by just reading it over and over. Writing and reciting are active strategies that help you learn the information.

☐ **Learn to predict exam questions.** This is important for all exams, but it is critical for essay exams. After you predict five to ten possible questions, plan the answers, and learn the main points before the exam.

☐ **When taking exams, relax, and be sure to read the directions.** Answer the easiest questions first, skipping the ones that you don't immediately know. Then go back and complete the ones that you skipped.

☐ **Go to your college learning center when you need help.** Don't wait until it's too late. Stop in to talk about any classes in which you're having difficulty. Getting suggestions on how to study or signing up for tutoring can improve your grades dramatically.

Learn How to Calculate Your GPA

To achieve your grade goals this semester, you need to consider how the grade you earn in each course contributes to your overall grade point average (GPA). Learning how to calculate your GPA will help you set better goals for the new semester. Decide on the overall GPA that you want for the semester and then work backward

FIGURE 15.2

John's GPA
Calculation Chart

John's Grades

Course	Grade	Numerical Value	Credits	Grade Points
Sociology	B	3.0	3	9.0
English	C	2.0	3	6.0
Algebra	A	4.0	3	12.0
Chemistry	B	3.0	4	12.0
Phys. Ed.	A	4.0	1	4.0
			14	43.0 = 3.07 GPA

in order to set your individual course goals. For example, let's say you decided to aim for a 2.75 for the semester. You could achieve that average in a number of ways. You could have one A (4.0), one B (3.0), and two Cs (2.0) and get a 2.75. You could also earn a 2.75 for the semester by getting three Bs and one C.

In order to calculate your GPA, you need to calculate the grade points that you earn in each of your courses. Grade points are determined by multiplying the grade's numerical value by the number of credits assigned to the course. An A in a one-credit class is worth 4 grade points, whereas a C in a four-credit course is worth 8 grade points. It appears here that the C is worth more, but it's not—you have to divide your total grade points by your total credits in order to determine your GPA. (If your college doesn't use the same numerical values for grades, adjust the table accordingly.) Look at the example in Figure 15.2.

In order to determine his GPA, John listed each of his courses, the grades he earned, and their numerical values. He then listed the credit value for each course and multiplied that by the numerical value of the grade to determine the grade points for each course. After calculating the grade points for each course, he added up his total credits and his total grade points. The final step is to divide the total grade points (43) by the total credits (14). John earned a 3.07 for the semester. If John had used this method at the beginning of the semester to predict his grades, he would have had the opportunity to decide whether a 3.07 was a satisfactory goal for the semester. If he had decided that he wanted to earn a higher GPA, he could have gone back and recalculated his GPA by changing one or more of the grades in order to reach his goal. If John's goal had been a GPA of 3.25, he might have decided that he had to earn a B instead of a C in English. This would have improved his grade point total to 46 points, while his credit total would have stayed the same at 14. His new GPA would have been 3.285.

Revise Your Goals Periodically

It's important to rethink your goals at some point during the semester. Some students tend to play it safe and set unrealistically low goals for themselves at the beginning of the semester. It may seem like a good idea to set safe goals; that way you always are successful at what you set out to do. However, safe goals can also hold you back because they don't challenge you to achieve all that you might be able to achieve. Some students have the opposite tendency; they set goals that may be completely unattainable. By doing this, they are setting themselves up for failure and disappointment.

Remember, goals should be moderately challenging; they should be just a little out of reach so that you can work toward them. How can you find just the right level of challenge? You can't, at first. Once you gain some experience in college, however, you'll become much better at knowing what you can achieve. Until then, you need to revise your goals as you gather more information about your skills and your performance. Of course, you could change your goals, raise them or lower them, at almost any time during the semester. However, the best time to review your grade goals is after the first exam. If you decided to work for a B in College Algebra but got a high A on the first exam, you should revise your goal upward. Your first exam demonstrated that you're capable of doing A work and consequently capable of getting an A in Algebra.

Many students continue to improve in courses after the first exam, so you need to review your goals again after the second, third, or even fourth exam. In general, you should sit down and really think about where you are and where you want to be after the first round of exams, after midterms, and about two weeks before final exams.

WRITE EFFECTIVE GOAL STATEMENTS

By putting your goals in writing, you increase the probability that you will actually accomplish them. However, another factor that affects your success is how you formulate your goal statements. You can write down the first thing that comes to mind, or you can spend some time and explore each of your goals by using the Five-Step Approach to goal setting. Developing and implementing an action plan for each of your goals can also help you achieve them.

Use the Five-Step Approach

Writing effective goal statements isn't as easy as it sounds. You need to consider what you want to accomplish, any obstacles that could prevent you from achieving your

FIGURE 15.3

Tomi's Five-Step
Approach to
Setting Goals

COURSE: _____ Biology _____

STEP 1: Tentative Goal Statement

I want at least a B in Biology.

STEP 2: List of Obstacles

1. There is a ton of reading, and I usually put it off.

2. I have trouble following the lecture, and I struggle to take notes.

3. Class would be easy to skip because it's in the auditorium and attendance isn't taken.

4. The book is very hard to read and understand.

5. The class is so big that I am easily distracted.

6. The subject matter is very difficult for me.

STEP 3: List of Resources

1. I will set up a schedule to read 15 pages each night.

2. I'll read the chapter before the lecture. I'll rewrite my notes afterward.

3. I can't afford to miss class. I'll go from my 8:00 class directly to Biology at 9:00.

4. I'll highlight and take notes as I read.

5. I'll read Chapter 6 on Concentration early and sit up front.

6. I'll get a tutor in the learning assistance center.

STEP 4: List Your Motivation

Biology is my major and I need to do well.

STEP 5: Revised Goal Statement

I will achieve a B in Biology this semester.

goal, and the resources available to you. You then need to think about your motivation and revise your goal statement as necessary. Because each of your courses has different requirements, you must consider each course separately. If you're taking five courses, you must go through this process five times. See Figure 15.3 for an example of the Five-Step Approach to setting goals.

STEP 1: Write Down What You Want to Accomplish

This initial description can be thought of as a tentative goal statement. The easiest way to begin your tentative goal statement is with the words "I want to." Think about what you want to accomplish.

STEP 2: Write Down Any Obstacles

Think about whether there are any course requirements, assignments, tests, or other factors that could jeopardize your success. Make a list of the difficulties you may encounter. Some students, for example, panic when they find out that their exams are going to be essay exams. You might consider this an obstacle if you know that you ordinarily don't do well on essay exams. Others may be concerned about attendance policies or oral presentations.

STEP 3: Write Down Any Resources Available to You

First, consider your general resources. You have successfully completed twelve years of school, so you have acquired some of the skills that can help you become a successful student. You have also acquired a background in quite a few subject areas. In addition, you probably earned some As and Bs, so you know that you can be successful in your academic pursuits. If you're a returning adult student, you also have developed skills in meeting deadlines, setting priorities, and managing multiple tasks—all necessary skills for college success. All of these things are general resources that will help you achieve your goals.

Next, consider each of the obstacles you listed individually. Think about how you might use your resources to overcome each obstacle. Write down specific resources you could use to achieve each goal. Specific resources include your friends and family, the faculty and staff members at your college, and you yourself. For instance, if you have difficulty with essay exams, you could go to your professor or to your college learning center to get some help before the exam.

STEP 4: List Your Motivation

Setting a goal is easy, but achieving it takes time, effort, and perseverance. Take a few minutes to think about why you want to achieve that goal. What's your motivation? Getting in touch with your motivation can help you decide how hard you want to work and why it's worth the effort.

STEP 5: Review and Revise Your Goal Statement

Now you're ready to write your final goal statement. In some cases you may find that you don't change your tentative goal statement at all; in other cases you may revise it. Check to be sure that your final goal statement is well written and takes into consideration the seven characteristics of effective goals.[5]

Develop an Action Plan

To achieve your long- and short-term goals, you need to develop an action plan. An *action plan* is a carefully thought-out method of implementing a strategy to achieve

---

[5]Based on ideas from Walter Pauk, *How to Study in College*, 4th ed. (Boston: Houghton Mifflin, 1989).

your goal—one that will help you get from where you are to where you want to be. Writing an action plan for a long-term assignment (such as a term paper, semester project, or portfolio) can help motivate you to work on the task throughout the semester because you have to identify each step of the process in advance. DaShawn's action plan for writing a history paper is shown in Figure 15.4. You can develop an action plan on notebook paper, on an index card, or by using the form shown in Figure 15.4, which can be found on the *Orientation to College Learning* Web site.

FIGURE 15.4   DeShawn's Action Plan

Goal: **Prepare my history paper on family heritage**

Target Date	Action Tasks	Materials Needed	"To Do" Date	Evaluation
January 17	Prepare outline	Directions for assignment	January 14	✓
January 17	Prepare interview questions	List of possible questions	January 14	✓
January 17	Call my grandmother to schedule a time to visit and talk to her about my family	Planning calendar, phone #	January 15	✓
January 20	Ask my grandmother specific questions and jot down her responses below each of my questions	Typed questions, clipboard	January 16	✓
January 20	Tape record the interview just in case I miss something important	Tape recorder, extra batteries, extra tape	January 16	✓
January 24	Write the rough draft	Notes, questions, tape, assignment directions	January 19	✓
January 25	Have my grandmother review the paper to check to be sure my facts are correct	Questions and responses, rough draft	January 22	✓
January 26	Type my paper on the computer. Do the cover sheet and introduction, too	Rough draft, directions for cover sheet and introduction	January 23	✓
January 27	Proofread and make any necessary corrections	Handbook, rough draft	January 25	✓
January 28	Turn in the paper	Paper and question sheet with answers	January 28	✓

Outcome: I completed my paper on family heritage ahead of schedule.

Set Action Tasks. *Action tasks* are the specific tasks that you need to complete to achieve your original goal. To write a term paper, you might include action tasks such as choosing a topic, writing a tentative thesis statement, using an online database to identify three to six good sources of information, taking notes on the source materials, developing an outline, and so on.

List the Materials You Need. Think about any materials you may need to complete your action tasks and list them on your plan next to each task. For example, to take notes on your sources, you would need to have your laptop or index cards, copies of your articles or books (or if you can't check them out, a list of where each is located in the reference area of the library), and a pen or pencil.

Set Time Frames. You need to set a target date for the completion of each of your action tasks. Giving yourself one week to complete each step in the plan is a good guide for completing a term paper, for example. Then set up a "To Do" date—a specific date and time to work on each of the tasks. Set the "To Do" date for the next action task when you complete the previous one. Checking off each task as it is completed can help you see the progress you're making and motivate you to keep working until you achieve your goal.

Evaluate Your Plan. Finally, after completing your plan (and your goal), conclude your action plan with an outcome statement describing how well the plan helped you achieve your goal. You could list, for example, the date that you actually finished your term paper, any problems that you encountered using the plan, and the grade that you received.

EXPLORE CAREER GOALS

You may find that setting career goals helps you put your academic and personal goals into perspective. When you know what you want to accomplish during your college career, it's easier to be motivated to work hard toward those goals. Many students enter college knowing what they want to do when they graduate—they've already decided on a future career. Taking classes that you find both interesting and relevant can help you get motivated right from the start.

What happens, though, if you enter college undecided about a career choice? Does that impact your motivation? In some instances, it can result in a lack of motivation to work hard. If you feel that your courses are irrelevant, uninteresting, or unimportant, you could be less motivated to excel. However, some colleges encourage students to explore a wide variety of courses before choosing a major. By taking entry-level courses in a number of areas, you might find courses that suddenly become relevant, interesting, and important to you. In this section, you'll have an opportunity to explore a number of strategies that will help you do a self-assessment, explore career goals, choose an appropriate major, and evaluate your choices. So, if you haven't decided on a career goal—or even if you have—learning more about setting career goals can help you make a more informed and accurate decision.

Do a Self-Assessment

The first step in setting career goals is to do a self-assessment. A *self-assessment* is a systematic review of the factors that can affect your career path. Before you can choose a career path, you need to gather information about yourself. Gaining a better understanding of who you are will make it easier to select an appropriate career. You need to find out more about your skills, your interests, your values, and your motivation to make a good decision.

What Are Your Skills?

Think about your strengths and your weaknesses. What courses were you good at in high school? Which gave you the most difficulty? If you're good at math, for example, you may want to think about careers that require those skills, such as accounting, chemistry, physics, computer science, or engineering. If you said that math was your weakest subject, you may want to think about professions that don't require those skills, such as communication, history, social work, or some areas of education. Of course, just because you weren't good at math doesn't mean that you can't become good at math. Some students do very well in college math courses and move on to complete their degrees in spite of poor performance in high school math.

What Are Your Interests?

Even if you are great at math, you may not find math and math-related courses very interesting. Instead, you may be more interested in literature, history, or communication. As you explore a career, remember that you will have to do that job each day for many years. You want to select a career that will allow you to get up in the morning for work that you find interesting and rewarding.

What Are Your Values?

Before choosing a career, you need to think about what type of career fits well with your personal and professional value system. Do you want to help others, or are you interested in a career that provides you with security and status? Do you want a career that may put you into situations that involve practices that conflict with your beliefs? How you respond to these questions is important in considering the role that values play in choosing a career.

How Motivated Are You?

Your level of motivation also plays a part in choosing a career. For some career choices, you would need to go on to earn a graduate or professional degree. Are you motivated enough to continue your schooling for three or more years after you complete your college degree? To become a dentist, doctor, psychologist, college professor, or lawyer, you would need to complete several additional years of training.

Let's say that you decided to pursue a career in business instead. You could graduate and get a good job working in a variety of businesses. Would you like to be your own boss, or do you want to work for someone else? It would take a great deal of motivation on your part to start your own business. Many small business owners work more than a typical forty-hour work week. Other professions require a high level of motivation on a daily basis. Becoming a teacher, member of the clergy, social worker, doctor, or nurse, for example, may require you to be even more motivated to do the job because other people are depending on you every single day. Putting others' needs before your own requires extra motivation on your part.

Explore Career Choices

Once you complete your self-assessment, your next step is to explore some possible career choices. You can gather a lot of information on campus through your career center, from your professors and advisor, and from other students. You'll also find that you can learn about various career opportunities from family members and friends, through volunteer work and internships, or by job shadowing. Finally, there are many online resources for career exploration.

Campus Resources

If you have no idea what you want to do after graduation, go to your career center, where you can complete inventories that will give you ideas about careers that match your interests, skills, values, and motivation. Your professors can provide you with a wealth of information about possible careers in your major. If you're taking a class that you really like, talk with your professor about the types of careers that are available in that field. Your advisor is another excellent resource. He or she can help you match your skills and interests to various majors on campus. Other students are a great resource because they are also going through or may have already gone through part of this process. Getting others' opinions about various career choices can provide you with a lot of good information. Occasionally, though, you might get misinformation, so do some research yourself.

Community Resources

There are also many resources outside of your college community. Attending job fairs, doing volunteer work, participating in job shadowing, and completing internships can give you some real-life experiences that may tell you whether you want to pursue a particular career.

Online Resources

There are many Web sites devoted to career exploration. Search online for any career you are considering and you'll find hundreds of links. You can find career tests to take online (be careful, though, as some of these are not free, and others are tied to various job-training schools), information on degree requirements, salaries, job opportunities, and even locations where there are openings in various careers. Be sure to explore a number of sites before making a tentative decision about your career path.

Choose Your Major

Once you have an idea of the type of job you want to pursue, you need to check with your advisor or advising center to find out which major on your campus will provide you with the educational requirements you need. Making a preliminary decision about a career path early in your college career can help you select the appropriate major during your freshman or sophomore year. The advantage of an early decision is that you'll be able to complete all of your degree requirements in a shorter time frame than the student who waits until his or her junior or senior year.

If you enter college having already selected a major, you can explore various careers that match your major. In this case, your professors and advisor can be very helpful by sharing information on various jobs that would be open to you. However, many students change their major at least once during their college career (I did). This has its advantages, in that students who change their major tend to persist in college and graduate. Furthermore, students who change their major are actually more likely to graduate with a degree that allows them to enter a field that is a better fit for them. However, unless you make the switch fairly early, it may take you longer to complete your degree requirements.

Evaluate Your Decision

As you move through your college career, stop and reassess your career choice at the end of each semester. The courses you complete (or withdraw from) can provide you with valuable information about the choice you made. Think about your skills: Are you earning high grades in your major classes? Think about your interests: Is this something you want to do for the rest of your life? Think about your values: Will you feel comfortable with the decisions you will have to make in the career you chose? Think about your motivation: Will this career require you to work harder or put in more hours than you want? You should also know that many people change careers during their lifetime. As you select your major and enroll in your general education courses, you need to prepare yourself not only for this career but also for other possible future careers. Building a strong skill set can prepare you for any career you may choose in the future.

SUMMARY

Setting goals helps motivate you to attend class regularly, keep up with your day-to-day assignments, and complete long-term projects on time. Writing goal statements that are self-chosen, moderately challenging, realistic, measurable, specific, finite, and positive will help you accomplish the goals that you set this semester and can increase your motivation. Setting priorities is also important to your success because you'll need to find the right balance between your academic and personal goals. To achieve your goals this semester, you must be open to change—you must be willing to try new strategies. Using the Five-Step Approach to setting goals can help you realistically set grade goals for each of your courses. Making academics your top priority, especially for the first three weeks of the semester, will get you off to a good start. Setting career goals can also help you choose the right major and increase your motivation and performance in college. The important thing to remember is that career goals help motivate you to set and achieve your academic goals, which, in turn, help motivate you to set and achieve your study goals. Why are you in college? Think about it.

ACTIVITIES

1. Make a list of ten goals that you would like to accomplish this semester. Then list ten goals that you would like to accomplish tomorrow. Label each of the goals as an academic (A) or personal (P) goal. Do you have an overabundance of personal goals? Were your first three goals on each list academic or personal goals? How would you change your lists so that your academic goals have top priority?

2. During the first five minutes of the class, make a list of five to ten goals that you plan to accomplish for the week. Then share your list with a group of your classmates. As each student's list of goals is reviewed, identify the type of goal (work, personal, or study) and decide how well it's formulated according to the seven characteristics of good goal statements. Make suggestions for changing some of the goal statements to make them more positive, realistic, measurable, and specific.

3. In a paragraph or two, describe your long-term goals. Where do you see yourself in five years? In ten years? Be specific as you describe the kind of lifestyle that you hope to have. What's your motivation? Make a list of the reasons that you want to achieve those goals.

4. Justin is a new college student who works occasionally on weekends. He wasn't scheduled to work next weekend, so he signed up for the bus trip to the away football game. However, after making his plans, he found that he had an exam in psychology and an English paper due the following Monday. To complicate matters, he was called in to work for eight hours on Sunday. Should he go to the game on Saturday? What are his alternatives? How would his decision affect his academic or personal goals? What would you do?

5. Make a list of five changes that you've made so far this semester. List five changes that you want to make this semester but haven't made yet. Why did you make the changes on your first list? What's stopping you from making the changes that you haven't made? Jot down

your answers to each of these questions on notebook paper and then get together with your group to discuss your responses.

6. Create a chart to keep track of the changes that you make in the next couple of weeks. List up to ten changes that you make in your study techniques, time management, or class participation (or any other change you make). Be sure to record the outcomes of these changes as you learn them.

7. Go to the *Orientation to College Learning* Web site and download one copy of Activity 2-2 from the Activities Packet for each of your classes. Use the Five-Step Approach to set goals for all your courses.

8. Use the Action Plan form on the *Orientation to College Learning* Web site to create an action plan for one of your long-term assignments. Divide the assignment into a series of action tasks and include both Target Dates and "To Do" dates for each step. Then share your plan with a group of your classmates. What suggestions did they have for improving your plan?

9. To begin your career self-assessment, jot down your responses to each of the following questions. What are your strengths and weaknesses in school? What are your interests? What majors or careers are not at all interesting to you? What values are important to you that may affect your career choice? How motivated are you? How hard (and long) are you willing to work after college to prepare for your career? After completing your self-assessment, describe the career choice(s) you are considering.

10. Now that you've completed Chapter 2, take a few minutes to repeat the "Where Are You Now?" activity, which is also located on the *Orientation to College Learning* Web site. What changes did you make as a result of reading this chapter? How are you planning to apply what you've learned in this chapter?

CHAPTER REVIEW

Terms You Should Know: Take the matching test located on the *Orientation to College Learning* Web site (www.cengagebrain.com) for practice.

Completion: Fill in the blank to complete each of the following statements. Then check your answers on the Web site.

1. Goals should be_____ challenging.

2. You should avoid words like _____ and _____ in your goal statements.

3. The third step in setting goals is to list your _____.

4. _____ _____ help students break long-term goals down into individual steps.

5. Doing a career self-assessment involves a review of your skills, interests, _____, and _____.

Multiple Choice: Circle the letter of the best answer for each of the following questions. Be sure to underline key words and eliminate wrong answers. Then check your answers on the Web site.

6. The goal statement, "I will earn an A or B in Biology" should be revised because it is not
   A. specific.
   B. measurable.
   C. realistic.
   D. positive.

7. Why should you revise your goals?
   A. You may have set your goals too low.
   B. You may have set your goals too high.
   C. After the first exam, you'll have a more accurate picture of your performance.
   D. All of the above are good reasons.

Short Answer/Essay: On a separate sheet, answer the following questions:

8. What are four main reasons that setting goals improves performance?

9. Why should students make academics their top priority for the first three weeks of the semester?

10. Why is it important to balance academic, personal, and career goals in college?

 Tutorial Quiz: Take the tutorial quiz located on the *Orientation to College Learning* Web site for additional practice.

Improving Concentration

16

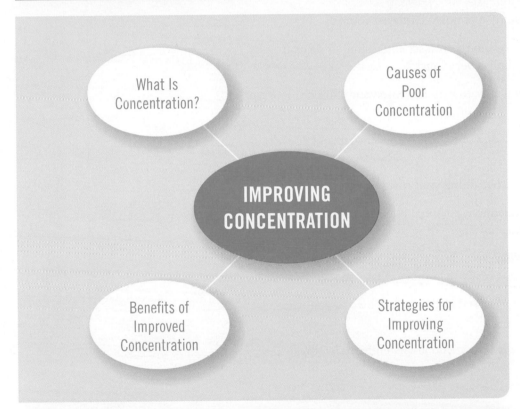

What Is Concentration?

Causes of Poor Concentration

IMPROVING CONCENTRATION

Benefits of Improved Concentration

Strategies for Improving Concentration

"I think I have the ability to concentrate better now than I used to. Before, I used to always drift off while studying, but now when I start to, I catch myself I can stay focused, and I am able to maintain my concentration much better. I have learned many new techniques for improving concentration, which I have put to use. I believe that when I am able to concentrate on my work, I also study much better."

Martin Ng, Student

TERMS YOU SHOULD KNOW

Make a flash card for each term and/or use the flash cards on the Web site to learn the definitions.

Concentration
Deep concentration
Distraction
External distractions

Focusing at will
Internal distractions
Light concentration
Limiting your focus

Moderate concentration
Multitasking
Sustaining your focus

477

Where Are You Now?

Take a few minutes to answer *yes* or *no* to the following questions.

	YES	NO
1. Do you have trouble getting back into your work after you've been interrupted?	_____	_____
2. Do you read and study in a noisy, cluttered room?	_____	_____
3. Do you find that even though you schedule study time, you don't actually accomplish very much?	_____	_____
4. Do you use any strategies to help increase your ability to concentrate?	_____	_____
5. Can you concentrate on your work even if the subject doesn't interest you?	_____	_____
6. Do you text when you're doing your assignments?	_____	_____
7. Do you tend to think about personal plans or problems when you are reading and studying?	_____	_____
8. Do you find that when you finish reading your textbook assignment, you don't really remember what you read?	_____	_____
9. Do you get totally engrossed in the material when you read and study?	_____	_____
10. Do you daydream a lot when you are listening to lectures?	_____	_____

TOTAL POINTS _____

Give yourself 1 point for each *yes* answer to questions 4, 5, and 9, and 1 point for each *no* answer to questions 1, 2, 3, 6, 7, 8, and 10. Total up your points. A low score (0–4) indicates that you need some help improving your concentration. A score of 5 to 7 indicates that you are using some good strategies but not others. A high score (8–10) indicates that you are already using many good concentration strategies. What did you learn about yourself by completing this activity?

_____

_____

_____

WHAT IS CONCENTRATION?

Concentration is focusing your attention on what you're doing. Concentration is important in just about anything you do, but in this chapter we'll focus on improving concentration during reading, listening, and studying. It's hard to describe what concentration is, but it's easy to explain what it isn't. Consider the following example. If you're reading a chapter in your Introductory Sociology text, you're concentrating on it only as long as you're thinking of nothing else. As soon as you think about how many pages you have left to read, what time you're going to eat dinner, or what the professor will discuss in class, you're experiencing a lack of concentration. If you stop to think about the fact that you should be concentrating on the assignment, you've lost your concentration. Let's look at another example. If, during a lecture class, you get a text message and read it, you've lost your concentration. You may even find that you've missed several new points that your professor just introduced.

Being distracted interferes with your ability to attend to or focus on the task at hand. In each of the above examples, you were actually concentrating on something. The problem is that you were concentrating on something other than the lecture or the reading material—you were concentrating on the distractions.

The Three Levels of Concentration

As you read one of your text assignments, ask someone to time you for about twenty minutes. Each time you think of something else, or even look up from your reading, put a check mark in the margin of your book. At some points during the twenty-minute period, you may have noticed that you were more focused on the material than at other times. Look back at the check marks you made in your book. Did you find that you weren't always concentrating at the same level? Where were most of your check marks located? Were more of them located in the early pages of the assignment? Were there fewer toward the end? Why does this happen?

To understand why students are less distracted toward the end of a twenty-minute reading period, let's take a closer look at how concentration works. Anne Bradley has divided concentration into three levels: light, moderate, and deep[1] (see Figure 16.1).

Light Concentration

When you first sit down to read or study, you're in a state of *light concentration*. This stage of concentration continues for about the first five minutes of study. At

---

[1]Adapted from Anne Bradley, *Take Note of College Study Skills* (Glenview, IL: Scott, Foresman, 1983), pp. 41–42.

FIGURE 16.1

The Concentration Cycle

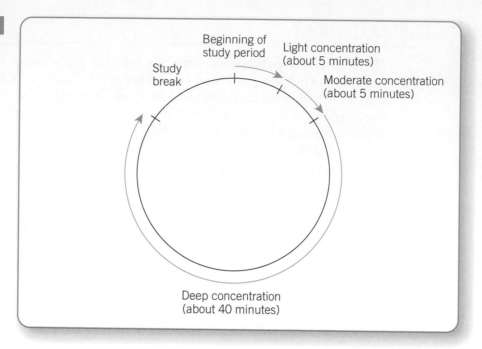

this point, you're just getting settled into your reading, listening, or studying. Students in light concentration can be seen wiggling around in their chairs, checking messages, or pulling out study supplies. When you're in light concentration, you're easily distracted. You may hear people talking down the hall, notice other students walking into the room, be annoyed by any noise occurring around you, or find yourself thinking about other things. You don't accomplish much during this stage, and very little, if any, learning actually occurs.

Moderate Concentration

During the next five minutes or so, if you aren't interrupted, you'll move into *moderate concentration*. At this point you begin to pay attention to the material that you're reading, hearing, or studying. You may find that you're actually getting interested in the lecture or text material. In this stage you'll probably find that you're not as easily distracted. Although you may lose your concentration if someone talks directly to you, you may not notice the voices of people talking down the hall or even someone walking into the room. Some learning occurs in this stage.

Deep Concentration

When you're in *deep concentration*, you are totally engrossed in your work—you aren't thinking about anything except what you are hearing, writing, or reading. During a fifty-minute study session, you should spend forty minutes in deep concentration. Of course, if you're really working well on a task, you don't need to stop after forty minutes. It's at this stage in the concentration cycle that you're working most effectively and have the highest level of comprehension. You learn the most and can complete more work in less time when you're in deep concentration.

Some students indicate that they aren't sure whether they've ever been in deep concentration. Have you? The two best indicators are being startled out of it and losing track of time. Have you ever jumped when someone came up behind you and touched your arm? Because you were in deep concentration, you may not have even noticed that person enter the room or call your name. When you're in deep concentration, you're not aware of the clock ticking, the door opening, or things that you normally would find rather distracting. Have you ever been surprised by how long you actually worked on a particular task? Were you ever late for a class or appointment because you lost track of time? You can easily lose track of time when you're in deep concentration, so be sure to set an alarm if you need to be somewhere at a particular time.

The Concentration Cycle

You may be thinking it would be easy to reach a high level of concentration—that after an initial ten minutes or so, you will be in deep concentration. Unfortunately, this isn't the way it really works for many students. Instead, they move in and out of the three stages of concentration.

Look at the diagram of the ideal study session in Figure 16.2A. In this situation, you would be able to work in deep concentration for forty minutes during a

FIGURE 16.2

Study Sessions and Levels of Concentration

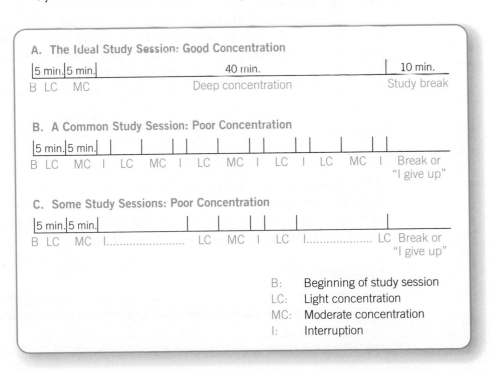

A. The Ideal Study Session: Good Concentration

| 5 min. | 5 min. | 40 min. | 10 min. |

B LC   MC   Deep concentration   Study break

B. A Common Study Session: Poor Concentration

| 5 min. | 5 min. |

B LC   MC   I   LC   MC   I   LC   MC   I   LC   I   LC   MC   I   Break or "I give up"

C. Some Study Sessions: Poor Concentration

| 5 min. | 5 min. |

B LC   MC   I........................   LC   MC   I   LC   I...................   LC Break or "I give up"

B: Beginning of study session
LC: Light concentration
MC: Moderate concentration
I: Interruption

481

fifty-minute study session. Unfortunately, some students never get into deep concentration. They move back and forth between light and moderate concentration because they are distracted constantly (Figure 16.2B). Every time you're distracted, you move back to the stage of light concentration. If you get a text message and stop to read it, you've been distracted. If you stop to check how many more pages you still have to read, you've been distracted. If you look up when someone walks past you in the library, you've been distracted. If a family member asks you a question, you've been distracted. If you check your e-mail or your phone, you've been distracted. Each time you're interrupted while you're listening to a lecture, working on a homework assignment, or studying for a test, you move out of deep concentration.

If you can minimize distractions, you may find it doesn't take you quite as long to get interested in the material on your second or third try. However, you will still have to move through the "warming up" stages again before you can reach a state of deep concentration. Some students, however, have interruptions that aren't quite as brief. They don't just look to see who called or sent an e-mail or text message; they respond to them. A number of students admitted that they spend ten to twenty minutes or more networking, texting, or talking on the phone during a typical study session (Figure 16.2C). These long distractions use up a lot of study time and require more time to move back through light and moderate concentration. If you tend to study in places where you're often interrupted, your study session may more closely resemble the concentration cycle in Figure 16.2B. Although you may think you're spending a lot of time studying, you may actually accomplish very little.

You may also find that your ability to concentrate varies from text to text (what you study), place to place (where you study), and time to time (when you study). You may have to use more active strategies or different strategies in order to increase your ability to concentrate when you're working on material that doesn't interest you, in noisy or distracting study areas, or even at different times of the day.

Three Types of Concentration Problems

Most students have concentration problems, but not all students actually have the same problems concentrating. There are three types of concentration problems: difficulty focusing at will, difficulty sustaining your focus over a period of time, and difficulty limiting your focus to one task at a time.[2]

Focusing at Will

Have you ever noticed that you have difficulty concentrating when your professor begins to lecture? You may find yourself looking around the room, pulling out your

---

[2]Becky Patterson, *Concentration: Strategies for Attaining Focus* (Dubuque, IA: Kendall Hunt, 1993).

notebook and pen, or even thinking about whether you'll get out of class early. If you have trouble focusing your attention at the beginning of the lecture, you may have difficulty *focusing at will*—being able to turn your attention to the task the instant you begin working.

Why can some students concentrate immediately while others find it difficult to focus their attention? Many students have developed techniques to focus at will. If you've ever competed in sports, picture yourself at that critical moment when you're about to "make your move." Do you go through a ritual designed to calm yourself, to focus your attention, to remove all other distractions? Ball players, bowlers, tennis players, and runners (just to name a few) all have strategies for focusing their attention just as they shoot a foul shot, attempt a difficult split, serve, or begin a race. Of course, listening to a lecture, writing a paper, and reading a text chapter aren't exactly the same as sporting events, but you can use the same techniques to focus your attention.

Some students use self-talk to focus at will, saying to themselves things like: "Pay attention; Okay, I need to do this; Let's get going now!" However, creating a verbal prompt is only one way to help you focus at will. Other students find that creating physical prompts are just as effective. Taking your seat and pulling out your notebook and pen (or opening your laptop) may be enough to focus your attention in a lecture class. Some students can instantly begin to concentrate when they sit down at a table or desk, open a textbook, or begin to work on the computer. Anything that you associate with concentrating on your work can help you learn to focus at will.

Sustaining Your Focus

Although learning to focus your concentration immediately is important, *sustaining your focus*—maintaining your concentration over a period of time—is also important. As you learned in the previous section on the concentration cycle, this isn't as easy as it sounds. Some students have difficulty maintaining their concentration no matter what the task. Other students, however, can concentrate for long periods of time when reading their text assignments but are constantly distracted when doing their math, and vice versa. What makes the difference? Obviously, distractions that occur when you're working will interfere with sustaining your focus. However, the difficulty level of the task, your interest in the material, and your level of motivation all could be factors. In the next two sections, you'll learn more about the causes of poor concentration and some suggestions for improving concentration. Many of the strategies described will help you sustain your concentration for a longer period of time.

Limiting Your Focus

The final concentration problem involves *limiting your focus*—being able to focus on only one task at a time. You may find this to be especially difficult during high-pressure weeks. You need to learn to focus your attention on one page in your text (without looking over at the English paper you must do for tomorrow), one math problem (without thinking about how many others are on the page), or studying for one exam (without thinking about the other two you have this week). Strategies that involve creating a good study environment can help you avoid distractions. The strategies that you learned for setting goals, managing your time, and establishing priorities will also help you focus on one task at a time.

CAUSES OF POOR CONCENTRATION

Have you ever found that you're sitting in a lecture class thinking about what you want to do after class, rather than focusing on the lecture? If you're like most students, you have. Many students daydream, think about other things they need to do, or look out the window at some point during class. When that happens, they are concentrating on something else—they are distracted. A *distraction* is anything that diverts your focus (attention) from the task at hand. There are two main types of distractions that interfere with concentration. *External distractions* come from outside of you and include noises such as the ping of a text message, your phone ringing, the beep of an e-mail message, other people talking, the television show you're watching, or the music playing in the background. *Internal distractions* are things that come from inside of you. They are things you think or worry about. Some common internal distractions are anxiety caused by a certain course, the feeling that study won't help, worry over personal problems, feelings of boredom, dislike for a course or assignment, and indecision about what to do next. Many students even worry about the fact that they can't concentrate, and that worry interferes further with their ability to concentrate on their work.

Although internal and external distractions appear to be the causes of concentration problems, they actually stem from other problems. The real causes of most concentration problems are lack of attention, lack of interest, and lack of motivation.[3] By identifying the real reason for your concentration problems, you'll be able to select the appropriate strategy to overcome each of them.

Lack of Attention

One of the most common causes of concentration problems is lack of attention. Many students have difficulty focusing on their work. Do you? If you said yes, you may have concentration problems because you are constantly surrounded by

---

[3]Based on ideas from "AIM to Listen," from *The Secretary* magazine, reprinted in *Communication Briefings*, 1991.

distractions. In order to move into deep concentration, you need to reduce those distractions. Turning off the television, muting your phone, and establishing a good study environment will help you move into deep concentration. Then you won't even notice many of the external and internal distractions that would have interrupted your concentration.

Lack of Interest

You've probably already found that it's easy to concentrate when you're interested in what you're doing. Do you find that you can concentrate well in some lecture classes but not in others? Is it easier to stay involved in your reading in some of your texts but not in others? If you answered yes to either of these questions, your level of interest in the course or in the material may be the reason for your concentration success in one course and difficulty in the other. Without a high level of interest, it's easy to lose concentration, especially when you're surrounded by distractions.

Lack of Motivation

Lack of motivation is another cause of poor concentration. If you aren't motivated to earn a college degree, it's hard to go to class, read your text assignments, take lecture notes, and prepare for exams. If you ever find yourself asking, "Why am I doing this assignment?" "Why am I sitting in this class?" or "Why am I in college?" you may have a motivation problem. If you don't see the relevance of the course or the assignment, it's hard to stay focused on the task. If you aren't motivated to earn high grades, it's going to be very difficult to exert the level of effort you need to do well. To improve your ability to concentrate, you need to be motivated to succeed. As you know, motivation affects what you do and how you do it. When you're motivated to learn something, you're more likely to create an atmosphere that is more favorable to learning, push yourself to focus on the task, and use active strategies to increase your concentration.

Concentration Problems During Lecture Classes

Many students experience problems with concentration when they're trying to listen and learn in class. Do you ever have trouble concentrating on the lecture your professor is presenting? What gets in your way? One of the more common problems is distractions caused by other students. It's hard to concentrate on what your professor is saying when the person sitting next to you is constantly talking to you or to someone near you. Even a conversation two or three rows behind you can interfere with your ability to stay focused on the lecture.

Internal distractions also lead to concentration problems during lecture classes. Worrying about personal problems and thinking about what you have to do after class are common internal distractions. Feeling ill, hungry, or tired are all common internal distractions.

Do you have more trouble concentrating when you're not interested in the lecture topic? It's more difficult to pay attention to the lecture when the topic is uninteresting or hard to understand. Some students have problems when they're not actively involved in the class; they have difficulty playing the role of a passive observer. Other students complain that it's impossible to stay involved and focused on a lecture when the professor always mumbles or speaks in a quiet voice. Still others have problems when the professor doesn't ask questions or interact with them during the lecture.

Finally, some students have concentration problems during lecture classes because of their attitude toward the class or the material. Do you have more trouble concentrating when you place a low value on the course? It's hard to sustain your focus when you aren't motivated to listen and take notes. In situations like this, many students begin to daydream, think about more interesting things, or even doze off.

Concentration Problems When You Read Your Text

Do you have trouble concentrating when you read some or all of your text assignments? Many students indicate that they have more trouble concentrating when they read than at any other time. Unlike lecture classes, where your professor may help keep you focused by varying his or her tone of voice or by asking questions, you alone are responsible for concentrating on your reading assignments.

External distractions such as a cluttered or uncomfortable study environment, noise, and other people, are common causes of poor concentration when reading. How many times this week were you interrupted as you tried to read a text assignment? Do you need complete silence in order to concentrate on your reading assignments? If you live in a dormitory, finding a quiet study place can be quite a problem. However, students who live at home find that a family can be just as distracting.

The time of day that you tackle your reading assignments also can affect your ability to concentrate. If you try to do your reading late at night, you may experience more difficulty staying focused because you're tired. Concentration requires effort, and it's harder to make that effort when you're tired. Have you noticed that it's more difficult to concentrate on the road when you're driving late at night and feel tired? For the same reason, many students have more difficulty maintaining their concentration when they try to read late at night or for long periods of time without a break.

Concentration Problems When You Study for Exams

Some students have a lot of trouble concentrating when they're preparing for exams. Aside from the usual external distractions, they often experience other types of problems. Some students are not as motivated to focus on the task of test preparation early in the semester because they don't put as much value on the first exam. Other students get distracted when they study because the material is difficult or uninteresting. Some students have concentration problems because studying is not a specific assignment like "read pages 186 to 201." Any time your goals are vague or you're not sure what to do, it's more difficult to stay focused.

A common complaint from students is that they get tired of studying and begin to think of other things. Some think about things they would rather be doing or things that their friends, who don't have exams, are doing. Worrying about what the test will be like, what questions will be on it, and how well you will do are all common internal distractions.

Using passive study strategies also leads to poor concentration when preparing for exams. Many students still study for college exams by simply reading over the text and lecture material. If you use passive strategies, you'll be more susceptible to both internal and external distractions.

STRATEGIES FOR IMPROVING CONCENTRATION

By now you probably realize that problems with concentration are fairly common for college students. Although it may make you feel better to know you aren't the only person in the world who can't concentrate, it doesn't help you correct the problem. Many students indicate that they have a problem concentrating, but they don't know how to correct it. You can improve your ability to concentrate by using motivational and organizational strategies, by creating a good learning environment, by dealing promptly with internal distractions, by using active learning strategies, and by monitoring your concentration.

Use Motivational and Organizational Strategies

You can improve your concentration by using many of the motivational and organizational strategies. Several of the most helpful strategies are having a positive attitude, creating interest in the task, setting goals, and using time-management strategies.

Develop a Positive Attitude Toward Your Work

Having a positive attitude toward your assignments is critical to focusing at will. First, you must want to do the assignment. You need to see the relevance, value, and importance of the task. Before beginning the task, think of how it will benefit you. Second, you must believe that you can do the assignment. Tell yourself you can successfully complete the task. Self-doubt, or feelings of anger or frustration about the task, will interfere with your concentration. A positive attitude will help you focus as you begin to study and help sustain your focus until you complete the task.

Create Interest in the Task

Have you found that when you're interested in the material, it's easier to concentrate? If you're getting ready to read a chapter for your Western Civilization class, for example, and you really aren't very interested in what happened in Egypt 5,000 years ago, you might have difficulty sustaining your focus. You need to find ways to generate interest in the task. One way to do so is to preview a chapter before reading it. As you look through the chapter (see Chapter 7 for how to do a preview), you may notice topics that are interesting to you. I've always been fascinated by the great pyramids, have you? If you find even one section in the chapter that sounds interesting, you'll increase your motivation to read and may find that you can concentrate more on the chapter.

Another method of generating interest in the task is to change the task to make it more interesting. If you find reading chapters to be boring, don't just read them. Do something interesting while you read. If you like taking notes, take notes as you read. If you like writing questions in the margin of your lecture notes, write questions in the margin of your text as you read the chapter. If you like using a particular study strategy—if you find it interesting, challenging, or fun—you'll like completing the original task more.

Breaking the task down into smaller segments will also help you maintain your concentration. You can stay more focused on the material when you read ten pages of the chapter at a time instead of trying to read the entire chapter. If you aren't particularly interested in your math assignment, you may find that doing one-third of your math homework is less boring than trying to do it all at one time. Switch to a different subject for a while and come back later and do some more.

Use Goal-Setting Strategies

Setting clear, specific goals can also help you achieve better concentration. If you know exactly what you want to accomplish when you begin an assignment, you'll be able to limit your focus to the task at hand. Setting learning goals can help you determine what you need to learn or accomplish during a specific study session. It's equally important to know exactly what you need to do to complete the assignment—you need to understand what the professor expects from you and what the grading criteria will be. If you aren't sure about how to do the assignment, check with a classmate or your professor. If you don't, you may find that you'll have problems concentrating on the task because you'll be worrying about whether you're doing it correctly. Having a clear purpose in mind can help you limit distractions as you complete your work.

Use Time-Management Strategies

Almost any of the time-management strategies that you learned will help you improve your concentration. Using "To Do" lists and planning calendars are critical to good concentration. One of the most common internal distractions among college students is the worry that they won't get their work done. Many students report that they're constantly thinking of other assignments when they try to concentrate on their work. Do you? If you develop a study schedule each day and assign each of your study tasks to a specific time block, you won't have to worry about getting your work done. You'll be able to focus completely on each task as you work on it, knowing that you have already scheduled all of the others. By organizing your study time, you can better focus your attention on one task at a time.

Create a Positive Learning Environment

You can dramatically improve your ability to concentrate by creating a positive learning environment. The first step is to control external distractions, and the best way to do so is simply to eliminate them. If you can't eliminate them, then you need to reduce the amount of time you spend on the distractions. Some specific strategies are listed in the Tip Block. You'll find that where you choose to do your work, though, is a major factor in contributing to or reducing problems in concentration.

Find a Better Location

In lecture classes, you can avoid most external distractions by moving to the front of the room. Fortunately, most students who chat during class tend to sit in the back. However, you still occasionally may find yourself sitting near some noisy students. If the students sitting near you keep you from concentrating on the lecture, get up and move. You also can be distracted by things going on around you. If you find yourself looking out the window or watching what goes on in the hall, find a seat where you can't see out the window or the door. Instead, make the professor the center of your line of vision.

Although it's fairly easy to find a new seat during lecture classes, it's not as easy to find a new place to study when you can't concentrate. Whether you live in a dormitory or at home, you're surrounded by noise. Some students stay in their rooms or work at the kitchen table even when they can't concentrate, almost out of stubbornness. "It's my room and I should be able to work there" is a commonly heard

Ten Tips for Setting Up a Good Study Environment

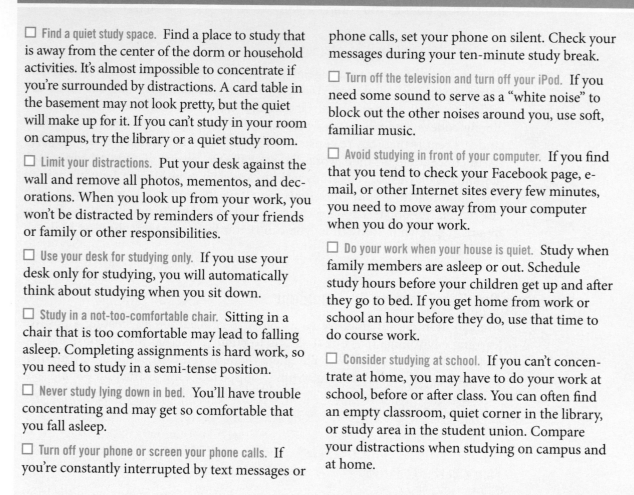

☐ **Find a quiet study space.** Find a place to study that is away from the center of the dorm or household activities. It's almost impossible to concentrate if you're surrounded by distractions. A card table in the basement may not look pretty, but the quiet will make up for it. If you can't study in your room on campus, try the library or a quiet study room.

☐ **Limit your distractions.** Put your desk against the wall and remove all photos, mementos, and decorations. When you look up from your work, you won't be distracted by reminders of your friends or family or other responsibilities.

☐ **Use your desk for studying only.** If you use your desk only for studying, you will automatically think about studying when you sit down.

☐ **Study in a not-too-comfortable chair.** Sitting in a chair that is too comfortable may lead to falling asleep. Completing assignments is hard work, so you need to study in a semi-tense position.

☐ **Never study lying down in bed.** You'll have trouble concentrating and may get so comfortable that you fall asleep.

☐ **Turn off your phone or screen your phone calls.** If you're constantly interrupted by text messages or phone calls, set your phone on silent. Check your messages during your ten-minute study break.

☐ **Turn off the television and turn off your iPod.** If you need some sound to serve as a "white noise" to block out the other noises around you, use soft, familiar music.

☐ **Avoid studying in front of your computer.** If you find that you tend to check your Facebook page, e-mail, or other Internet sites every few minutes, you need to move away from your computer when you do your work.

☐ **Do your work when your house is quiet.** Study when family members are asleep or out. Schedule study hours before your children get up and after they go to bed. If you get home from work or school an hour before they do, use that time to do course work.

☐ **Consider studying at school.** If you can't concentrate at home, you may have to do your work at school, before or after class. You can often find an empty classroom, quiet corner in the library, or study area in the student union. Compare your distractions when studying on campus and at home.

statement. But if you've tried unsuccessfully to eliminate the distractions in your study area and you still can't concentrate on your work, you have only one other option. You need to find somewhere else to study. It may not seem fair that you have to gather up all your materials and go somewhere else, but if you can't change your study environment, you have to find a new one. Finding a good place to read and study may require some experimentation. Try working in different places at different times of the day to see which study area works best for you. The library, study rooms, and empty classrooms are usually good study areas. If you're living at home, you may find that setting up a table or desk in the basement or the attic is the only way you can avoid constant interruptions. Once you find a good place to work, establish a regular routine. Studying in the same place at the same time each day helps you get down to work and can improve your concentration.

Reduce Multitasking

Multitasking originally was a term used to refer to the performance of more than one task at a time by a computer. Today, *multitasking* is often used to describe the performance of multiple tasks at one time by people. What do we mean by multitasking? If you're reading a chapter in one of your texts and stop for a few seconds to check the text message that just popped up on your phone, you're multitasking. If you're typing a paper and talking on your cell phone at the same time, you're multitasking. If you're doing your math while watching the game on TV, you're multitasking. You may be thinking that everyone does such things. You're probably right. You are surrounded by technology; in fact, you are surrounded by technology that is always on, because you don't like being out of touch. In class, most professors expect their students to turn off their cell phones. Some do; some turn them to mute. Some students can't resist the vibrating cell and quickly check to see who called or check a text message. Do you? Students in large classes (especially if they sit near the back) admit to texting throughout the class.

Does multitasking interfere with performance? More and more people are researching that topic, especially as it relates to talking on cell phones while driving and to surfing the Net while working. The answer so far is that there is definitely a problem. Most studies indicate that neither task is performed as well as it could have been if it had been done exclusively. One reason for this problem is that you are constantly shifting your attention from one task to the other. Obviously, this interferes with concentration. If you're texting while listening—or watching television while studying—you're interrupting your concentration every time you shift from one task to the other. If you're trying to send a text message while listening to a lecture, you can't focus on what your professor is saying (or write down the information) and, at the same moment, type the message.

Minimize Distractions

If you can't eliminate all of your distractions, it's important to minimize them as much as possible—to reduce the length of each distraction to the smallest possible time frame. For example, if your phone rings and you answer it, you'll probably spend a few minutes (or many minutes) responding to the caller. If, on the other hand, you set your answering machine or voice mail to pick up your call, you'll spend a much shorter time frame dealing with the call. When you hear the phone ring, you might say to yourself, "I'll get that later," go right back to work and return the call when you complete that particular task. To avoid being interrupted by text messages or e-mail, mute your computer and phone. Check your mail during your ten-minute study break. If you must peek to see who's sending a text, tell yourself you'll respond as soon as you finish your work. If you only spend a few seconds on a distraction, you should be able to move back into deep concentration very quickly. If you spend five or ten minutes (or longer) away from your work, you'll find it takes a lot longer to get back into deep concentration.

Deal with Internal Distractions

Once you set up a quiet study environment, you should see a big difference in your ability to concentrate. However, just eliminating external distractions doesn't guarantee that you'll be able to focus on your work. Many students find that after they eliminate the external noises around them, they notice the internal "noises" even more. Although you can't really eliminate internal distractions, you can take steps to keep them from interfering with your work.

Deal with Competing Activities

No matter how focused you are when studying, it's not unusual to think about other things. If you think of something that you want or need to do, or if you come up with an idea for another assignment, jot it down; then continue with your work. The key is to minimize the distraction—to keep it as short as possible. Then you can move back to deep concentration more quickly. If you don't write it down, you'll probably continue thinking about it or even begin to worry that you may forget it. In either case, you'll be concentrating more on the internal distraction than on your assignment.

Deal with Academic Problems

Worrying about academic problems is another common internal distraction. Instead of worrying, do something! Go see your professor and share your concerns about the course. Get a tutor or have a talk with yourself about what you need to do to meet your goals. Remind yourself that getting down to work and doing your best are steps in the right direction. Then, if you still don't understand the material or can't do the problems, ask for help. Remember, it's easier to block out internal distractions when you have confidence in yourself as a student. You'll gain this confidence by learning that you can be successful in college, not by worrying about it.

Deal with Personal Problems

Personal worries and concerns are common internal distractions. Many students allow an argument with a boyfriend or girlfriend or family problems to interfere with their concentration. Make a decision to do something about your problem as soon as you complete your work. Write down exactly what you plan to do and return immediately to your study tasks. Call a friend and talk honestly about your problem or schedule an appointment at your campus counseling center. Some students find that writing about whatever is bothering them in a journal or talking it out with friends helps them experience a feeling of closure about the problem.

Use Active Learning Strategies

One of the best ways to keep external and internal distractions from interfering with your concentration is to become more involved in the lecture, the text, or your test preparation. You can generate this high level of involvement by using active learning strategies. Many students allow internal and external distractions to interrupt their study because they use passive learning strategies that just don't work.

You may have noticed that you concentrate better when you do math problems and grammar exercises or complete a study guide for one of your textbooks. Why does this happen? One possible reason is that you like those classes or assignments more than some of your other classes. However, another reason may be that you need to use active learning strategies to complete those tasks. Solving problems, correcting grammatical errors in sentences, and looking for answers to study guide questions are all active strategies that get you involved in and help you focus your attention on the material. Because you're actively involved when working on the material, you can concentrate more effectively on your assignments.

Strategies for Lecture Classes

Taking notes during the lecture helps you focus on what your professor is saying. If you know that you're going to have to write something, you'll be more motivated to pay attention. You may actually find that lecture classes become more interesting and go much faster when you take notes.

Many students have trouble concentrating during lecture classes simply because they're not actively involved in what's going on in the class. Asking and answering questions, predicting what the professor will say next, and taking notes are all ways of becoming more involved during lecture classes. Actively participating in class is one way to eliminate internal and external distractions and increase concentration.

You may also find that you can increase your concentration in lecture classes by sitting directly in your professor's line of vision. You're more likely to pay attention if you feel as if you're on the spot. It's pretty hard to fall asleep or look out the window when your professor is standing right in front of you. If you focus your attention on the lecture and take notes, you'll be able to block out distractions more easily.

Strategies for Reading Text Assignments

Being an active reader significantly improves your ability to concentrate on your textbook assignments. Have you ever read a paragraph—or even an entire page of text—and then realized that you had no idea what you had just read? Even though your eyes did "look at the words," your mind was elsewhere. Using a reading/study system, previewing, highlighting, and taking notes are active strategies that can improve your concentration. You can also increase your concentration by creating word cards as you read your assignment. Becoming familiar with the technical terminology can help you understand your reading assignment more easily. Writing questions in the margin also helps you focus on the important information in the text.

Strategies for Test Preparation

How can you maintain your concentration as you prepare for exams? Jennifer sums it up well: "When studying for a test, I'm active. I don't just reread my notes and the chapter. I write down what I need to know from the text and then I rewrite my notes." Just reading over the textbook and your lecture notes isn't a very effective way to improve your concentration when you study. You need to increase your involvement with the material. When you prepare for an exam, dig through the material, looking for the important information. You can't take notes, create study sheets, or write questions in the margin without thinking critically about the material. Reciting key information out loud and self-testing are just two of the many rehearsal strategies that also can help you learn the material. Remember: The more actively involved you are in studying the material, the easier it is to maintain your concentration.

You can also increase your concentration by using motivational strategies. Maria motivates herself to study by thinking about getting a good grade, saying: "You just need to make the decision that you want to succeed." Taking breaks, switching subjects, and planning rewards help increase your motivation, and they also can help increase your concentration. It's much harder to stay focused on your work when you become tired or bored. When you just can't concentrate anymore, stop and take a break. Then switch to a different subject to eliminate feelings of boredom and fatigue. Setting deadlines and limiting the amount of time that you allow for each of your study tasks also can motivate you to concentrate more effectively. Deadlines make you feel rushed, so you actually force yourself to concentrate better (unless you've left yourself too little time—in that case, your level of anxiety and the number of your internal distractions may increase).

Monitor Your Concentration

Monitoring how often you lose your concentration can be very helpful in learning how to improve your concentration. Put a check mark in the margin of your book or your lecture notes every time you're distracted. At the end of your class or study session, count the number of interruptions. Make a commitment to reduce that number the next time you read or go to your lecture. In a few weeks, you may find that your ability to concentrate improves dramatically.

When you notice that you're daydreaming or thinking about other things, try to figure out what actually triggered your loss in concentration. If you can pinpoint the cause of your distraction, you're only one step away from the solution. Hold yourself accountable for your lapses in concentration—find a way to overcome them. Remember, you can improve your ability to concentrate, but it is you who must take the responsibility for doing so.

BENEFITS OF IMPROVED CONCENTRATION

There are many benefits to improved concentration. One of the most obvious is that you'll be able to make better use of your time. You'll find that when you spend the majority of your time in deep concentration, you get more done during a study session. In addition, because you're operating in deep concentration for a longer period of time, you'll gain a better understanding of the material. It stands to reason that if you spend most of your time focused on the course material, you'll learn and remember more of it than if you're constantly distracted.

Improved concentration during lecture classes can help you take better lecture notes. If you're focused on the information your professor is presenting rather than on other people, negative thoughts about the course, or personal plans, you'll take better notes. In addition, you may find that you become more involved in the lecture and gain a better understanding of the material. You'll be able to form connections between the material being presented and the material you already know. This helps you learn and understand what you're hearing.

You may also notice that once you set up a better study environment, you're better able to prepare for quizzes and exams. Working in a quiet, nondistracting study area can have a positive effect on what you study and learn. Setting goals and using active study strategies will not only improve your concentration but also your mastery of the material. After concentrating on your studies for one or two hours, you'll be pleased by what you were able to accomplish. Knowing that you are well prepared increases your self-confidence and leads to higher self-esteem.

SUMMARY

Most college students have problems with concentration (focusing their attention). If you're focusing on the conversations around you or those going on out in the hall, instead of on your professor's lecture, you're concentrating on the wrong thing. If you find that you're putting a lot of time into your studies but not getting much accomplished, you probably have a concentration problem. During an ideal study session, students move from light to moderate to deep concentration—the level where most learning occurs. During a typical study session, however, students move in and out of these stages of concentration because of interruptions or distractions.

The most common indicators of concentration problems are external and internal distractions. It's easy to blame all concentration problems on a noisy room or a cluttered desk, but the real culprits are lack of attention, lack of interest, and lack of motivation. By monitoring your distractions, you can pinpoint why you're having concentration problems and select the appropriate strategies to gain more focus. Avoiding common distractions and using active study strategies can help you increase your concentration. Creating a positive learning environment is critical to good concentration. If you set goals, focus your attention, increase your interest, and improve your motivation, your ability to concentrate will improve.

ACTIVITIES

1. Draw a time line to evaluate your last fifty-minute study session. Plot the interruptions that you experienced and how much time you spent in each of the three levels of concentration. What did you discover?

 2. Once you've identified the causes of your concentration problems, you need to think about why you want to improve your concentration. What's your motivation? List five reasons that you believe improving your concentration will benefit you this semester and/or in the future.

3. Review Emily's list of distractions from a one-hour study session, available on the Web site. Label each distraction as external or internal and personal or academic. Then jot down a suggestion for how Emily should have dealt with the distraction. Discuss your responses with the other members of your group. What would you have done if this were your study session? Note: Emily read four pages of her Biology text in one hour during this study session.

4. Choose a section of a text that you haven't already read. After you finish reading, make a list of the distractions you experienced. Repeat the task using another text or at a different time of day. What differences did you notice in your ability to concentrate on the two reading assignments? Share your results with your group. What were the most common problems?

5. Make a list of the problems or difficulties that you experience in at least two of your lecture classes. What differences did you notice in your ability to concentrate in each class? What were the causes of your concentration problems? Share your results with your group. What were the most common problems?

6. Create a chart to monitor the types of concentration problems you experience in each of your classes. List the names of your classes down the left column. Then write the following headings across the top: Focusing at Will, Sustaining Your Focus, and Limiting Your Focus. In each box of your chart, indicate whether you have problems in lecture classes (L), when reading your text assignments (R), or when studying for exams (S).

7. From the Web site, download one copy of Activity 6-3, 6-4, or 6-5 from the Activities Packet. What advice would you give to each of the students? Compare your responses with those of others in your group.

8. Use the Monitor Your Concentration Chart on the Web site. Record up to ten concentration problems you encounter over a one-week period. Include one or more strategies that you used to improve your concentration. What changes did you make to improve your concentration during the week? How well did your strategies work? What motivated you to make those changes?

 9. Write three concentration problems that you experienced during the past week on each of three index cards. Put the last four digits of your student number at the top right corner of the back of the card (do not use your name). After the cards are shuffled and distributed to various groups within the class, discuss each of the problems assigned to your group. Discuss possible solutions to the problem and write several of the best on the back of the card. Select one or two of the most common (or most interesting) to describe to the class. At the end of the class period, each student can claim his or her card (by student number) and make use of the suggestions that were offered.

 10. Now that you've completed Chapter 16, take a few minutes to repeat the "Where Are You Now?" activity, which is also located on the *Orientation to College Learning* Web site. What changes did you make as a result of reading this chapter? How are you planning to apply what you've learned in this chapter?

CHAPTER REVIEW

 Terms You Should Know: Take the matching test on the *Orientation to College Learning* Web site (www.cengagebrain.com) for practice.

Completion: Fill in the blank to complete each of the following statements. Then check your answers on the Web site.

1. _____ college freshmen experience concentration problems.

2. Some students never get into _____ concentration.

3. Use _____ study strategies to improve your concentration when studying for exams.

4. Both _____ and _____ distractions affect your ability to concentrate during lectures.

5. Having difficulty concentrating at the beginning of a task is referred to as a problem focusing at _____.

Multiple Choice: Circle the letter of the best answer for each of the following questions. Be sure to underline key words and eliminate wrong answers. Then check your answers on the Web site.

6. Which of the following is *not* one of the real causes of poor concentration?
   A. Lack of interest
   B. Lack of attention

C. Lack of motivation

D. Lack of self-efficacy

7. You can reduce your distractions by

   A. studying in an empty classroom.

   B. using your desk only for study.

   C. screening your phone calls.

   D. doing all of the above.

Short Answer/Essay: On a separate sheet, answer the following questions.

8. Describe the characteristics of each of the three stages of the concentration cycle.

9. How should students overcome problems with internal and external distractions?

10. How will improving your concentration benefit you in college?

Tutorial Quiz: Take the tutorial quiz located on the *Orientation to College Learning* Web site for additional practice.